D1242344

ALSO BY DAVID STAHEL

Joining Hitler's Crusade
Mass Violence in Nazi-Occupied Europe (with Alex J. Kay)
The Battle for Moscow
Operation Typhoon
Nazi Policy on the Eastern Front, 1941 (with Alex J. Kay and Jeff Rutherford)
Kiev 1941
Operation Barbarossa and Germany's Defeat in the East

RETREAT FROM MOSCOW

RETREAT
FROM MOSCOW

A NEW HISTORY OF GERMANY'S
WINTER CAMPAIGN, 1941–1942

DAVID STAHEL

Farrar, Straus and Giroux   l   New York

Farrar, Straus and Giroux
120 Broadway, New York 10271

Grateful acknowledgment is made for permission to reprint fourteen maps
from The Australian National University, College of Asia and the Pacific,
CartoGIS Services.

Library of Congress Cataloging-in-Publication Data
Names: Stahel, David, 1975– author.
Title: Retreat from Moscow : a new history of Germany's winter campaign, 1941–1942 /
    David Stahel.
Other titles: Reconceiving Germany's winter campaign, 1941–1942
Description: First edition. | New York : Farrar, Straus and Giroux, 2019 | Includes
    bibliographical references and index.
Identifiers: LCCN 2019019746 | ISBN 9780374249526 (hardcover)
Subjects: LCSH: Moscow, Battle of, Moscow, Russia, 1941–1942. | World War,
    1939–1945—Campaigns—Russia (Federation)—Moscow. | Germany. Heer.
    Heeresgruppe Mitte—History. | Germany. Heer—History—World War, 1939–1945.
Classification: LCC D764.3.M6 S83 2019 | DDC 940.54/21731—dc23
LC record available at https://lccn.loc.gov/2019019746

Designed by Richard Oriolo

Our books may be purchased in bulk for promotional, educational, or business
use. Please contact your local bookseller or the Macmillan Corporate and
Premium Sales Department at 1-800-221-7945, extension 5442, or by e-mail at
MacmillanSpecialMarkets@macmillan.com.

www.fsgbooks.com
www.twitter.com/fsgbooks • www.facebook.com/fsgbooks

10 9 8 7 6 5 4 3 2 1

Lovingly dedicated to
Priscilla, Gerard, Samuel, and David

CONTENTS

RETREAT FROM MOSCOW

INTRODUCTION

Germany's winter campaign of 1941–1942 has commonly been seen as the "first defeat" of the Wehrmacht in the Second World War. Indeed, two of the most recent books about the fighting near Moscow by Robert Forczyk (2006) and Michael Jones (2009) both share the subtitle *Hitler's First Defeat*.[1] The most thorough and comprehensive study of the period is actually an earlier work by Klaus Reinhardt, whose pioneering study has remained the standard work in spite of being first published in 1972.[2] Rejecting the accepted view, which saw Stalingrad or Kursk as the classic turning points of Germany's war, Reinhardt was among the first to argue that the battle of Moscow, especially in the winter of 1941–1942, constituted the decisive event of the war, which represented, as his subtitle claimed, "the failure of Hitler's strategy."

For those not familiar with my former studies of German operations in the east, the fighting at Moscow will not be portrayed in this book as Hitler's "first defeat," nor even the turning point of the war, because I argue that both already took place in the summer of 1941. Such a proposition may strike some as counterintuitive given that, at the most basic level, the story of Germany's summer campaign is typically characterized by fast-moving panzer groups, calamitous cauldron battles, and staggering sums of Red Army losses. Perhaps even more conclusive is the fact that, at the end of it all, Hitler's armies stood deep inside the Soviet Union, ultimately threatening Leningrad, Moscow, and Sevastopol. The logic here appears simple: Germany's first defeat, whenever that might have been, certainly could not have come before the first winter of the war.

The problem with this logic is that it separates German operations from their strategic context. Battles do not exist in a vacuum, and they should not be seen as ends in themselves. The sheer accumulation of battlefield "victories" in 1941 clearly did not suffice to knock the Soviet Union out of the war, and it was this failure that ultimately proved so ruinous to Germany's prospects. Heavily restricted access to raw materials, critical production bottlenecks, and bitter policy debates governing the allocation of resources to the armed forces were fundamental to the outcome of a large-scale industrialized war. Indeed, it was Germany's grim long-term economic prospects that first directed Hitler's attention toward an eastern campaign, but embarking on it came with huge risks.[3] Either Hitler would secure his long-prophesied *Lebensraum* (living space) in the east and ensure limitless access to almost any resource Germany might require in its war against Great Britain, or the Wehrmacht's air and sea war in the west would be disastrously undercut by a parallel, high-intensity land war in the east. Thus, it was absolutely essential for Germany to end any prospective war against the Soviet Union as quickly and as decisively as possible—there was simply no economic or military contingency for anything else.[4] Under these circumstances, some authors have attempted to argue Germany's dominance by pointing to the far greater problems in the Red Army during the summer campaign. Yet the contexts for the two forces were entirely different; the Wehrmacht had to win outright at all costs, while the Red Army had only to survive as a force in being.

What made German operations in the course of 1941 so important to the war's ultimate outcome was not just their failure to secure Hitler's all-important victory, but the cost of so many battles to the Wehrmacht's panzer groups. In its ruthless pursuit of victory, the German *Ostheer* (eastern army) became a very blunt instrument, and there was simply no way of reconstituting this offensive power without a very long period of inactivity that the unrelenting warfare in the east would never permit. As the chief of the Army General Staff, Colonel-General Franz Halder, acknowledged in his diary on November 23: "An army, like that of June 1941, will henceforth no longer be available to us."[5] Accordingly, the summer and fall of 1941 saw the Wehrmacht achieve stunning successes, but from a strategic point of view it failed to do the one thing that really mattered—defeat the Soviet Union before its vital panzer groups were blunted. Once Operation Barbarossa (the code name for the German invasion of the Soviet Union) passed from being a blitzkrieg to a slogging war of matériel, which was already the case by the end of the summer, large-scale economic deficiencies spelled eventual doom for the Nazi state.

If Germany suffered its first and most significant setback in the summer of 1941, what then is the relevance of studying the 1941–1942 winter campaign? Is it simply one of the many stepping-stones in the long decline of Nazi Germany or is there something unique about this period? Indeed, if we no longer consider it Germany's first defeat, then what kind of defeat was it? If battles need to be placed in a larger context to ascertain their significance, we should not assume that Germany's winter retreat, any more than its summer advance, is the only indicator of "success," or in this case "defeat." If the war in the east was, since the end of the first summer, a battle of attrition, then the relative cost of German and Soviet operations determined their worth, and the outcome of any single encounter cannot be decided simply by asking who held the field at the end of the day. In the vast expanses of the east, ground mattered far less than resources, but both the Nazi and Soviet regimes struggled to understand this. Moreover, because of their shared obsession with prestige as well as their grandiloquent ideological worldviews, surrendering ground, even for a tactical/operational advantage, was consistently viewed as defeatist and cowardly. By the same token, offensive operations were consistently pursued by both sides to the detriment of the attacking forces, which were routinely overextended, lacked adequate supply, and became exposed to enemy counterattack.

By the beginning of December 1941 conditions at the front saw both armies suffering frightful shortages and living in desperate conditions across most of the line. Inevitably therefore the strategic calculus for the success of any operation was how much damage it could inflict upon the enemy and, by the same token, what the corresponding cost of that operation would necessitate. With armies stretched, resources typically inadequate, and mobility for most units limited, avoiding wasteful operations was more significant than the alternative of doing nothing at all. Yet for both the German and Soviet high commands there was little appreciation of this. Time and again positions were to be seized or defended "at any cost," while success was measured by the acquisition of a set objective and not the sacrifices it entailed.[6] While this remains a by-product of the inexorably ideological nature of the Nazi/Soviet view of war, it should not be accepted as our own standard for determining the value of events. Clearly, the ends did not always justify the means, so we should not simply assume that the most basic indicator of military success—seizing ground from the enemy—was in every instance vindicated.

In 1941 one of the central problems for the Red Army and the Wehrmacht was the lack of alignment between operational planning and strategic reality. Both sides were attempting far too much and expecting more of their forces than they could ever hope to deliver. During Operation Barbarossa, the *Ostheer* leadership pursued its advance with an almost obsessive determination, oblivious to the exhaustion of their men and the debilitating matériel losses within their mobile formations. This led directly to the dangerous position the Germans found themselves in near Moscow on December 5 when the first Soviet counterattacks began. Initially the Red Army's offensive capitalized on the overextension of the central part of the German front, where multiple armies, under the direction of Army Group Center, were left dangerously exposed. Soviet success was also aided by the Wehrmacht's unpreparedness for the cold, but each new Soviet advance encouraged ever more ambitious thinking until soon Stalin and the *Stavka* (the Soviet high command) were themselves undermining their own potential to strike a major blow.

Making matters worse, the Red Army on the offensive was in no way comparable to the Wehrmacht in 1941. Its hard-won professionalism, training, and experience enabled the German army to cope much better with excessive expectations than could the fledgling Red Army, whose ill-prepared officer corps was barely able to handle the more passive demands of defensive warfare, much less the skills required for a major offensive. Little experience in conducting forward operations and far too few qualified staff officers made functional command and control haphazard at best, leading in many instances to the infantry attacking in isolation without the support of heavy weapons or coordinated movements. A remarkable number of Soviet officers did not even attempt to "soften up" German positions and simply charged the enemy lines in senseless massed attacks. The German records are replete with such examples, and not surprisingly, soon after the offensive began, Soviet orders appeared expressly forbidding these kinds of wasteful charges.

On the other side, December 5 represented the exhaustion of Army Group Center's own offensive and, at long last, the concentration of remaining resources on the much-neglected defense. While this counted for little in the immediate situation, over time remaining on the defensive wherever possible acted to conserve strength, while fieldworks such as bunkers or fortified villages acted as important force multipliers,[7] which in a resource-poor environment greatly aided German forces. Where the front could no longer be held, retreat bought the German armies precious time and allowed them to fall back on their supply lines. This functioned remarkably well for the first two weeks of the offensive until Hitler's halt order, which forbade any withdrawal unless approved by himself, came into effect. Hitler's grasp of military principles was heavily colored by ideological precepts that undercut Germany's defensive war just as Soviet forces were themselves being driven to excess. In this instance, the halt order was Hitler's blanket solution that immensely complicated Army Group Center's response.

Far from being the critical element that stiffened the backbone of the German army, Hitler's halt order was a military disaster, which took no account of local circumstances and proved deeply unpopular among Army

Group Center's hard-pressed commanders. It assumed that the only require-ment for holding a position was the requisite "will" to resist, which immedi-ately cast doubt on any commander's request for a retreat. Just how deeply the generals at the front resented the imposition of Hitler's new order is one of the revelations of this study, which will demonstrate an orchestrated pat-tern of coordinated defiance that goes well beyond anything previously un-derstood about the period. The oft-cited postwar claim, even by some former German officers, that the halt order somehow constituted "an immoveable barrier preventing . . . [the army] from pouring back in wild retreat" could not be further from the truth.[8] From the commander of Army Group Cen-ter down, the halt order was typically viewed, like the Red Army, as some-thing to be staunchly opposed and carefully outmaneuvered. Occasionally, this opposition was openly flaunted to the detriment of the protagonist, but more often than not it was carefully "managed" behind the scenes, so that the army high command and Hitler could not oppose what they did not know about—and there was a lot they did not know about.

Such bold "initiative" at the front reflects the fact that the German army's hallmark system of "mission-oriented tactics" (Auftragstaktik), which historians have previously determined ended, or at the very least was seriously curtailed, from the first winter of the war in the east, was in fact alive and well.[9] Commanders operated on their own terms to preserve their forces (and sometimes their own lives) by taking steps that purposely defied Hitler. This was not an act of resistance toward Hitler or his regime; it was motivated by self-preservation and professional instinct, which acted in the service of Nazi Germany, not in opposition to it. The army's unadulterated support for Hitler and his war aims in the east was never in question, even when the dictator openly spoke of the coming war requiring a ruthless "war of annihilation."[10]

The real crisis period of the German winter campaign extended from mid-December to mid-January, when Hitler finally relaxed his halt order and allowed three German armies a last-minute withdrawal. Yet even in this period of strategic crisis, the Red Army operated as an unwieldy, blunt in-strument smashing itself relentlessly against the German lines. In places this saw German positions being overrun and tactical breakthroughs of the line, but these were the exceptions, not the rule, and the cost to the Red Army was staggering.

This study will consider all six of Army Group Center's constituent armies (Ninth, Third Panzer, Fourth Panzer, Fourth, Second Panzer, and Second) to present a complete picture of events, rather than one that simply follows the crisis points in the line and offers no comparative context across hundreds of kilometers of front.[11] The idea of a crisis in Army Group Center was more often than not a localized phenomenon: every army experienced one, but at different times and to different degrees, and never all of them at the same time. Ninth and Fourth Armies, for example, were relatively quiet sectors with few retreats for the first two weeks of the Soviet offensive, while later the situation reversed with the panzer armies, especially the Second and Third, generally considered secure.

One method of assessing the winter fighting is to consider its raw cost, and the most basic indicator here is casualties. Grigorii Fedotovich Krivosheev's landmark study of Soviet casualties estimated that the Red Army's aggregate daily losses for the initial period of the Moscow counteroffensive (December 5, 1941, to January 7, 1942) were more costly than the Moscow defensive operations (September 30 to December 5, 1941). The former cost 10,910 men (dead and wounded) each day, while the latter exacted a daily average of 9,823 casualties. Even if we compare the Moscow counteroffensive to the Kiev defensive operation (July 7 to September 26, 1941), the average daily losses of the latter came to 8,543, substantially fewer again.[12] This does not mean that the total losses for the Moscow counteroffensive were higher overall because its operational period was shorter, but that the casualties were more concentrated between December 5 and January 7, 1942. More recently, Lev Lopukhovsky and Boris Kavalerchik have persuasively argued that Krivosheev's figures, which were made up of reports submitted to the Soviet high command, excluded large numbers of losses resulting from German encirclements or other wartime circumstances where no reports could be made. This demonstrates that earlier periods of the war were in fact much more costly to the Red Army, but the evidence provided by Lopukhovsky and Kavalerchik also revises upward the Soviet winter losses. Their detailed analysis of the wartime records reveals as many as 552,000 casualties for the month of December, 558,000 for January and a further 528,000 in February, equaling a winter total of 1,638,000 Soviet losses.[13] This is a figure that surely questions the extent of Stalin's "victorious" winter campaign, especially when one considers that total German casualties for a slightly longer period (November 26, 1941, to February 28, 1942) came to just 262,524.[14] Soviet losses were more than six times those of the Germans in the winter of 1941–1942, making the argument for Germany's "defeat" much more relative.[15] The result vindicates John Erickson's characterization of Soviet infantry in this period as little more than a "mob of riflemen," which he argued was "thus inviting heavy casualties" until they were supported by more heavy weaponry.[16]

For all the dramatic depictions of Army Group Center's frozen soldiers and the often-exaggerated parallels with Napoleon's disastrous retreat, the actual number of German dead compares favorably to the earlier periods of the war. In fact, there were fewer German deaths in December 1941 (40,198) than in the preceding months of July (63,099), August (46,066), September (51,033), and October (41,099). Only in the months of June (25,000 in just nine days of combat) and November (36,000) were fewer German deaths recorded. January (48,164) and February (44,099) 1942 were somewhat higher, but nothing like the death toll resulting from real German disasters, such as that seen in January and February 1943 following the loss of Stalingrad and the German Sixth Army. Here the German death toll for the same two months reached a staggering 248,640.[17]

Finally, the winter of 1941–1942 is unique because it is one of the only times in the war that Germany successfully matched its strategy to its operations. When Hitler issued War Directive 39 on December 8, ordering the Ostheer to "abandon immediately all major offensive operations and go over to the defensive," the gap between Army Group Center's means and ends closed to something barely achievable, which was more than could be said of preceding war directives that overestimated Germany's offensive capabilities and confidently predicted "military mastery of the European continent after the overthrow of Russia."[18] Such hubris, however, was much less evident by early December as Hitler's new war directive explained: "The way in which these defensive operations are to be carried out will be decided in accordance with the purpose which they are intended to serve, viz.: To hold areas which are of great operational or economic importance to the enemy."[19]

Army Group Center held a string of important Russian cities, which facilitated supply, offered shelter, assisted rear area organization, and functioned as valuable transportation nodes. They could also be counted upon as rough indicators of where local Soviet offensives would be directed and thus channeling their forces on the approaches and, if reached, forcing them to assault German strongpoints. These included Kursk, Orel, Briansk, Kaluga, Viaz'ma, Rzhev, Kalinin, and behind them all Smolensk, where Army Group Center had its headquarters. By January 1942 the *Stavka*'s general offensive sought to execute two major envelopments, a smaller one to close at Viaz'ma and a larger one at Smolensk.[20] Yet neither of these two cities would fall to the Red Army, just as neither of the two encirclements would succeed. German defensive operations, while sometimes desperate, successfully defended all of their major strategic locations except for Kalinin (which was on the front line when the Soviet offensive began) and Kaluga.

The Soviet plan was not just looking to capture population centers, but to encircle and destroy major sections of Army Group Center.[21] In fact, the destruction of the whole army group was sometimes called for in Soviet plans. Yet Germany not only successfully maintained its chain of strategic locations, the army group also endured intact without losing an army, a corps, or even a single division. Of course, some of these formations became so worn down by the fighting that they hardly functioned as corps or divisions, but in spite of being occasionally cut off and subjected to all manner of punishment, no major German formations were lost. The same cannot be said of the Red Army, which became so overextended that, at its worst, one and a half Soviet armies—some 60,000 Soviet troops—became cut off and were mostly destroyed.

German operations, therefore, not only sufficed to preserve their formations and defend their strategic objectives, but also, by doing so, frustrated the Soviet offensive plan and exacted a tremendous toll on the Red Army.[22] It was something of a role reversal from the summer and autumn, when the Red Army had successfully foiled Germany's strategic intentions, but as already observed, both regimes habitually pursued wildly overblown plans.

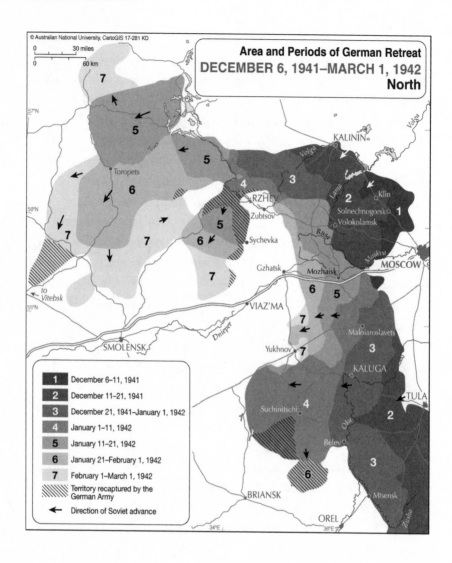

© Australian National University, CartoGIS 17-281 KD

Area and Periods of German Retreat
DECEMBER 6, 1941–MARCH 1, 1942
North

	December 6–11, 1941
1	December 6–11, 1941
2	December 11–21, 1941
3	December 21, 1941–January 1, 1942
4	January 1–11, 1942
5	January 11–21, 1942
6	January 21–February 1, 1942
7	February 1–March 1, 1942
	Territory recaptured by the German Army
←	Direction of Soviet advance

In the winter, however, Germany proved dominant tactically, operationally, and even strategically. Army Group Center, while terribly battered by the winter fighting, was not destroyed by it, and would go on to maintain a remarkably strong position in the center of the Eastern Front for another two and a half years.

If the present study seeks to reassess one aspect of the winter period, it is to question who benefited the most—or lost the least—from the 1941–1942

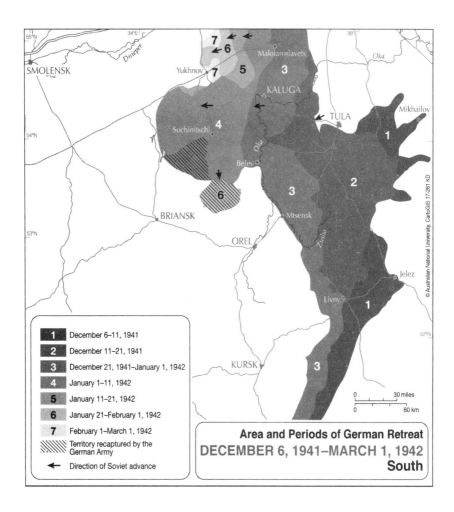

Legend:

1 December 6–11, 1941
2 December 11–21, 1941
3 December 21, 1941–January 1, 1942
4 January 1–11, 1942
5 January 11–21, 1942
6 January 21–February 1, 1942
7 February 1–March 1, 1942
▨ Territory recaptured by the German Army
← Direction of Soviet advance

Area and Periods of German Retreat
DECEMBER 6, 1941–MARCH 1, 1942
South

0   30 miles
0   60 km

winter campaign. Marshal Georgi Zhukov, who commanded the Soviet Western Front during the winter fighting, wrote in a draft of his memoirs (which only came to light much later):

> The History of the Great Fatherland War still comes to a generally positive conclusion about the [first] winter offensive of our forces, despite the lack of success. I do not agree with this evaluation. The

embellishment of history, one could say, is a sad attempt to paint over failure. If you consider our losses and what results were achieved, it will be clear that it was a Pyrrhic victory.[23]

Identifying the winter period as a Soviet Pyrrhic victory does not ameliorate Germany's own dire circumstances or exonerate the decisions of Hitler and the Army High Command (*Oberkommando des Heeres*—OKH) in precipitating the circumstances that led to Army Group Center's winter crisis. Even many of the leading commanders in the field contributed significantly to the awful state of affairs Germany confronted by early December, although in their subsequent writings they would choose to pin all of their woes on higher authorities. Most important, whatever measure of success Germany's winter campaign had, it did not change the fundamental point that Field Marshal Ewald von Kleist made after the war: "Everything was based on the hope of a decisive result by the autumn of 1941."[24] That was not changed by the winter campaign, nor could it ever have been. But Germany certainly lost far fewer men in the fighting, frustrated the Soviet strategic plan, and emerged in the spring unbroken and best placed to recapture the initiative for another major summer offensive. Investigating how Army Group Center achieved this is the central purpose of this study.

The need to understand the centrality of the Nazi-Soviet conflict to the outcome of the Second World War cannot be overstated. It was not just one more front in the war against Hitler's Germany, it was *the* front. The Wehrmacht invaded the Soviet Union with almost 150 divisions (over 3 million men), while in North Africa the Western allies engaged Rommel's famous *Afrikakorps* with just three German divisions (45,000 men). Even after D-Day, almost three years from the launch of Operation Barbarossa, the Western allies would never face more than 25 percent of the German army in their campaigns across Western Europe. The German army was battered to death in one campaign after another on the Eastern Front. Yet the Wehrmacht's path to destruction was by no means devoid of major reversals, while Soviet "successes" were often won at a staggering cost, which sometimes hindered rather than helped the Red Army's final victory. The winter of 1941–1942 is a case in point and a caution against oversimplified conclusions based on a superficial analysis of what was achieved. Stalin's counteroffensive constitutes one of the clearest examples of Soviet strategic overreach, which underestimated Germany's enduring tactical and operational dominance and led to horrendous losses. In the final analysis Army Group Center was far from defeated in the winter fighting, *Auftragstaktik* did not disappear as a result of Hitler's halt order, and the Wehrmacht's response was much more offensive than has previously been understood. Moreover, the prevailing historical narrative dominated by Germany's "crisis and retreat," while not always incorrect, ignores the fact that Army Group Center's withdrawals were often operationally successful and strategically necessary. The new line Army Group Center occupied defended valuable Russian cities in highly favorable battles of attrition. As one summative report from the 7th Infantry Division stated two weeks into the Soviet offensive: "In this struggle, there is no armistice, there is only victory or defeat. The task of the German Eastern Army is to force a German victory with all means and under all circumstances."[25] This task was almost universally understood, and whatever the cost to the German troops and the occupied Russian population, it was Hitler—not Stalin—who achieved his strategic goals for the winter.

1

HUNGRY AS A BEAR

The Soviet Counteroffensive Begins

T hough there were localized attacks on December 5, the Soviet winter campaign began in earnest on December 6. It was far from the Red Army's first offensive operation of the war. In fact, there had been some two dozen major counterstrokes over the preceding five and a half months.[1] None had met with much success, although collectively they played a role in harrying the *Ostheer*, forcing it to defend bitterly as well as attack persistently. The difference with the Soviet offensive in early December was less the Red Army than the state of the German forces they were encountering. On paper Army Group Center was 1,708,000 men strong as of December 1, but it was a shadow of its former strength in real terms. The front extended for some 850 kilometers in linear distance, the men were

poorly provisioned given the winter conditions, and they were utterly exhausted after months of constant operations. At the focal point of the Soviet
offensive, on the right wing of the Western Front, attacks north of Moscow
proceeded with a 2.5 to 1 superiority over the Germans in manpower.[2] Many
of the Soviet formations committed to battle had not taken part in the grueling fighting that had defended Moscow throughout October and November. In fact, German intelligence did not even know that Stalin had multiple
reserve armies with which to attack, which is part of the reason that Army
Group Center was pushed as hard and as far as it was.[3]

The role of gathering German intelligence on the Red Army belonged
to Foreign Armies East, which operated as part of the Army High Command
(OKH). The unit was headed by Colonel Eberhard Kinzel, a Prussian staff officer whose record of intelligence failures throughout his tenure in command
(1939–1942), and especially in Operation Barbarossa, was extraordinary. He
had no specialist intelligence training, did not speak Russian, and had no
previous familiarity with the Soviet Union.[4] Yet it was only toward the end of
1941 that Halder, as the chief of the Army General Staff, noted "symptoms of
decline in the Ic [intelligence] service."[5] As recently as November 22 Kinzel's
Foreign Armies East had dismissed the prospect of a major Soviet winter offensive, concluding that the movement of Soviet forces from quiet sectors to
endangered ones indicated that the Western Front "probably had no more
reserves available aside from those that had already been brought from the
Far East."[6] Such a conclusion is in part explained by the removal of countless intelligence officers throughout the *Ostheer* to compensate for the loss
of officers on the front line. This, Halder noted, resulted in the absence of
intelligence functions on the Eastern Front especially at the divisional level
and below.[7]

In the last week of November, the *Stavka* had begun transporting five of
the newly raised reserve armies, formed behind the Volga River, to the front
lines.[8] Three of these, the Twenty-Fourth, Twenty-Sixth, and Sixtieth, took
up positions east of Moscow, while the remaining two were sent south. The
Tenth Army was deployed west of the Oka River, downstream from Kashira,
while the last Soviet army, the Sixty-First, was committed behind the right
flank of the Southwestern Front.[9] The existence of these armies remained

unknown to the German high command, but even without them, Halder predicted in a presentation to Hitler on November 19 that the Red Army would number some 150 divisions along with 20 to 30 tank brigades by 1942. At the same time, the Army High Command projected a parallel decline in the *Ostheer* to a total of only about 122 divisions (infantry, motorized, panzer, SS, mountain, and security).[10]

By December 5 German intelligence was receiving disturbing new evidence of massive Soviet concentrations behind the lines at Riazhsk and Dankovo (some 2,000 newly discovered troop wagons and locomotives). Besides the fact that it was then too late to reorganize the forward positions substantively, the reports were not analyzed properly, meaning that there was almost no sense of urgency or concern. Foreign Armies East seemed incapable of concluding that the Red Army might pose a substantive threat to Army Group Center in spite of the fact that serious Soviet offensives had recently begun against Tikhvin and Rostov in the sectors of Army Groups North and South.[11] It is evidence of the striking institutional decline within the OKH that frequent, enormous failures by Foreign Armies East continued to pass while Kinzel remained at his post. Only in March 1942 did Halder finally have him replaced, stating simply that he "does not satisfy my demands."[12] Yet while the German high command seemed baffled by Soviet strength, more junior officers with far less access to intelligence predicted the Red Army's growth with far greater accuracy. Hans Meier-Welcker, a General Staff officer in the 251st Infantry Division, wrote home on December 1, "the military strength of the Soviets is far from exhausted; it will even gain new strength in the course of the winter. Yes it is astounding what is to be taken out of this country."[13]

While Soviet strength around Moscow remained formidable, in spite of the losses the Western Front had sustained since early October (in the battles of Viaz'ma and Briansk), the Red Army did not have inexhaustible reserves of manpower, with just 1.1 million men as of December 6. Moreover, across the central part of the front the Soviets possessed only 774 tanks. And while that many may have existed on paper, serviceability rates meant that operational strengths were lower again.[14] Clearly, the Red Army's offensive could not sustain wildly disproportionate casualties for long. The initial success of the

Soviet counteroffensive owed more to German overextension, exhaustion, and lack of mobility than the operational proficiency of the attacking Red Army units. Illustrative of the depths to which Army Group Center had sunk were the comments of the commander of the XXXXIII Army Corps, General of Infantry Gotthard Heinrici, who wrote home in a letter on December 6:

> The army has not been able to reach the desired success. And it did
> not help that the strength of the remaining units had dwindled to
> such a ridiculous level and that the men were mentally and physically
> extremely exhausted after five months of offensive warfare, while
> the Russian was sending more and more troops against us . . . We
> have nothing like that. Our victories have brought us to the end of
> our tether.[15]

On the same day, the commander of Army Group Center, Field Marshal Fedor von Bock, alluded to the deprivations of his men when he wrote rather understatedly in his diary that winter clothing was "far from satisfactory." He then continued: "First it was too late in coming, so that even today not all units have their winter things, and now it is inadequate in quantity as well as quality." Bock also noted that the temperature had sunk to thirty-eight degrees below zero Celsius and that vehicle motors were frequently failing in the freezing conditions.[16] Such problems were far less common in the better prepared and equipped Soviet reserve armies, who were also fresh and for the most part combat ready.

By the evening of December 5 Army Group Center's overextended front spanned from the western edge of Lake Volgo, where Colonel-General Adolf Strauss's Ninth Army held a long section of horizontal line all the way to the east of Kalinin at the Volga Reservoir.[17] Here General of Panzer Troops Georg-Hans Reinhardt's Panzer Group 3 was dangerously stretched in a diagonal position from the northwest to the southeast near Solnechnogorsk (on the map it ends with the 23rd Infantry Division). Reinhardt's position protected the northern flank of Colonel-General Erich Hoepner's Panzer Group 4, which was at the forefront of the abortive drive on Moscow. South of Hoepner was Field Marshal Günther von Kluge's Fourth Army, to which

Hoepner's panzer group was subordinate. Kluge's army was made up mostly of infantry divisions in static defensive positions running vertically down to the Oka River (ending on the map with the 52nd Infantry Division). Here Army Group Center's front bulged to the east in confused and scarcely held positions resulting from Colonel-General Heinz Guderian's unsuccessful attempt to encircle Tula with his Second Panzer Army. To the south of Guderian, General of Panzer Troops Rudolf Schmidt's Second Army had just captured the town of Jelez, some 185 kilometers from Tula. Yet Schmidt's front extended another 150 kilometers farther south to the junction with Army Group South at the small town of Tim (70 kilometers east of Kursk).

Many of these positions, especially those of the panzer commanders Reinhardt, Hoepner, and Guderian, were dangerously overextended, but nothing had been spared in Bock's relentless drive for Moscow and Tula. Already on December 5, just as Operation Typhoon, the code name for Germany's Moscow offensive, was finally called off, Soviet attacks were registered by two of Reinhardt's divisions (7th Panzer Division and 14th Motorized Infantry Division). A single reserve battalion was all Reinhardt could provide as initial support, but no one at the highest levels suspected just how profound the danger was.[18] At the front, however, local intelligence told a very different story. Heinz Otto Fausten recalled from December 5: "The Moscow-Volga canal lay before us, and on the other side, masses of Russians were suddenly appearing. The sheer number of them left us speechless. There were endless marching columns, soldiers on skis, in white coats. And then there were tanks, artillery units and countless motor vehicles. Where had they all come from?"[19] As Fausten and his comrades nervously observed the vanguard of Zhukov's counteroffensive, out of sight, well behind Soviet lines, tens of thousands more troops were moving up. The night of December 5 was the eye of the storm. Germany's autumn Typhoon had finally abated just as the Soviet winter storm was about to break.

Anton Günder, a medical orderly, recalled: "I had woken up at about 6:00 a.m. on December 6 and was just getting something to eat when all hell broke loose outside."[20] Even before dawn, Soviet attacks had severed the connection between Major-General Franz Landgraf's 6th Panzer Division[21] and Major-General Hans Freiherr von Funck's 7th Panzer Division. By early

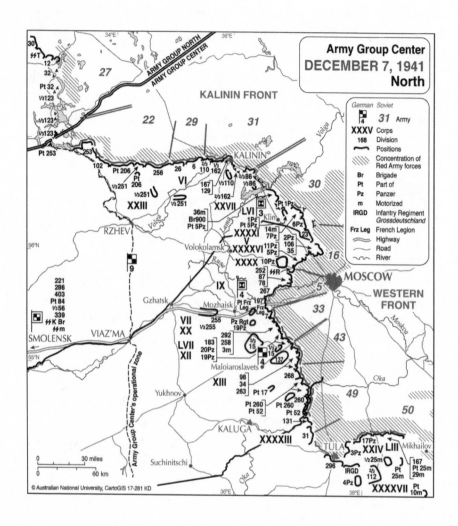

morning Reinhardt's panzer group was under attack across the whole of its line with the only available army group reserve, Colonel Walther Krause's Motorized Infantry Regiment *Lehrbrigade* 900, being dispatched to bolster his front. Reinhardt even ordered the company that guarded his panzer group's headquarters to the front, leaving his command post entirely unprotected. As the day developed, the center and right wing of Major-General Hans Gollnick's 36th Motorized Infantry Division suffered multiple break-

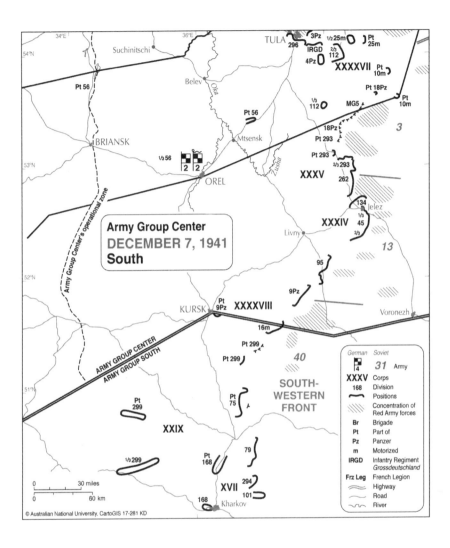

Army Group Center
DECEMBER 7, 1941
South

throughs between one and four kilometers in length.[22] As one officer from the division noted: "Salvoes of enemy artillery fire rolled along our lines, growing in intensity. And the Russian infantry attacked *en masse*. They quickly penetrated our positions."[23] Already on the first day of the Soviet offensive Gollnick employed successful counterattacks to eliminate most of these early breakthroughs, but these required the commitment of the division's last reserves, and much worse was still to come.[24] Such offensive countermeasures played a key role in Germany's winter campaign, which existing operational accounts have largely neglected.

Army Group Center's winter campaign was not an exclusively defensive battle. There were constant local German counteroffensives directed not to seize new ground but to expel enemy breakthroughs, restore the continuity of the line, or savage exposed and unsupported Soviet spearheads. Without the protection of prepared positions, and often having advanced beyond the support of their own heavy weaponry, these frequently unexpected German counterattacks, conducted typically by motorized formations, could be remarkably effective. The war diary of Panzer Group 3 noted that even in the midst of the developing Soviet offensive some enemy breakthroughs were extinguished by panzer counterattacks with "heavy losses for the enemy."[25] The problem was so acute that Zhukov included a warning in his directive of December 9: "Protect forces' operations with antitank defenses, reconnaissance and constant security, bearing in mind that, when withdrawing, the enemy will search for opportunities to counterattack."[26]

Even the initial assaults on German lines were too often poorly led and executed, dependent for success more on men and matériel than on skill and expertise. Soviet forces were, after all, hurriedly assembled reserve armies without the experience or officer training that a major offensive required. This did not mean ground could not be won against the weaker German positions, but holding it against German counterattacks was often harder than the initial breakthrough. Moreover, when Soviet forces did attempt to break through a strong German position without adequate resources, the cost was heavy, and the rigidity of the Soviet command system, which did not accept failure, led to repeated futile attacks. On December 6 Lieutenant Hans Reinert of the 296th Infantry Division wrote: "We keep asking ourselves why the Russians make these pointless attacks, repeatedly at the same positions which we have now closed up around, so that nothing can escape us anymore. What are they trying to achieve? Yes, maybe they'll get some settlements [but] so what?" It was estimated by the divisional staff that this single engagement had cost the Soviets at least 2,000 men.[27] Another German account from December 6 noted simply: "We mowed down many of the attackers, either by shooting them or forcing them to the ground by the effect of our fire."[28] Pavel Ossipov, an artilleryman in the Red Army, recalled from the first days of the offensive: "Especially the young people saw for the first time a lot of blood and learned the horrors of war . . . It was bad."[29] Of course Soviet propaganda preferred to emphasize their successes, which men like Dmitry Vonlyarsky proudly provided: "The force of our artillery barrage knocked out many of their firing points, and then we charged forward in a massed infantry attack. The men around me were screaming and howling as we jumped into the enemy's trenches. We finished off the remaining defenders with grenades, bayonets and knives."[30]

With the Soviet offensive gaining in momentum over the day and every available unit committed, Reinhardt resolved to begin his retreat that night. There were immediate implications, not least of which being the necessity to coordinate the withdrawal with the left wing of Kluge's Fourth Army (which consisted of Hoepner's subordinate panzer group). Kluge, however, wanted to delay the withdrawal as long as possible both to prepare for the evacuation and to "demonstrate to the enemy that the withdrawal was not as a result of his pressure."[31] Such an idea would soon prove illusionary, but it confirms just how far removed the German command was from understanding the enormity of the unfolding events. Not only was the Red Army forcing the retreat of a German panzer group, but there were already signs that German morale and discipline were breaking down as a consequence. Anton Günder recalled of December 6: "Everyone was pulling out. There were no orders any more. Seeing some fleeing others panicked . . . We succeeded in getting most of our medical equipment out, and tried to keep up with the remnants of our company—but whoever fell behind was lost."[32] On the same day Gerhardt Linke noted in his diary the confusion and disorder in the rear: "Everywhere terrible traffic jams. A welter of carts and wagons of absolutely different units congested the roads."[33]

As Panzer Group 3 struggled to organize its retreat under intense enemy pressure, Hoepner too was preparing to withdraw his forces up to sixty kilometers to maintain the cohesion of the German front.[34] Yet the prospect of an immediate retreat entailed, according to Hoepner, "great loss of equipment." Most of the artillery batteries had only a single tractor to tow them, meaning any withdrawal would have to be completed in stages, one gun at a time. "Even so," Hoepner concluded, "the destruction of captured goods (panzers, guns), which we are forced to leave behind, cannot be completed in such a short time."[35] Whatever the difficulties, Halder at the OKH agreed that a withdrawal, to what he called the "Klin Line," was necessary.[36] The new front was proposed to run from the Volga Reservoir in the north down to the town of Klin and then south to link up with the Fourth Army's current positions. Essentially it removed much of the bulge in the German line north of Moscow, which Reinhardt's troops had fought so hard to win in late November.

Farther south Guderian had finally accepted the futility of his plans to encircle Tula and had called off the attack. There had already been some serious local attacks on Second Panzer Army's eastern flank, and with the Tula operation abandoned, Guderian ordered a withdrawal from its advanced positions on the night of December 5–6. Reacting to this order on December 6, General of Panzer Troops Leo Freiherr Geyr von Schweppenberg's XXIV Army Corps reported that "a great number of our trucks and other equipment will be left behind and must be destroyed."[37] As Guderian observed in his memoir: "All the sacrifices and endurance of our brave troops had been in vain."[38] Yet Guderian accepted none of the responsibility for this dire circumstance, preferring instead to blame the high command in spite of having advocated for the offensive at every stage. Thus, a completely unplanned and improvised retreat was set in motion, which found no favor among the weary men. Erich Hager, who fought in the 17th Panzer Division, was digusted by the fifty kilometers ceded on December 6 alone.[39] Likewise, Fritz Köhler, who was fighting north of Tula, despaired at the news and pleaded in his diary: "How far will the captured land be given up?"[40]

Contrary to some popular representations of the winter fighting, the Soviet counteroffensive did not begin everywhere along Army Group Center's front on December 6. It developed in staggered fashion, which reflected the difficult conditions of subzero warfare as well as the complex task of coordinating such a large and relatively inexperienced force over so many kilometers of front. While Reinhardt's panzer group was retreating under great duress, Guderian's withdrawal was not yet the subject of sustained enemy pressure. Hoepner was resigned to his panzer group's withdrawal but, unaware of what was coming, believed he could determine its pace and timing. Strauss's Ninth Army was also being heavily assaulted on its right wing north of the Volga Reservoir and around Kalinin, but while there were some enemy penetrations, no one in the army's command was yet contemplating a withdrawal.[41] The front along Kluge's Fourth Army remained quiet; however, in the extreme south, Schmidt's Second Army brazenly defied orders and continued to attack eastward. Already on December 6 Bock noted in his diary that Schmidt's army was "once again" warned not to advance beyond positions necessary to safeguard the existing line. Yet again on December 7 the attacks continued, resulting in "costly fighting with strong enemy forces" as well as excessive losses from frostbite, with one regiment alone reporting 318 cases.[42]

The best-known aspect of the *Ostheer*'s winter campaign in 1941–1942 is the fact that it was unprepared for the freezing climate and suffered greatly as a result, but how greatly? In December alone some 90,000 noncombat German casualties were reported. Most were cases of frostbite, from which men recovered more quickly than from typical battle wounds. About 70 percent were back serving with their units within six months, while the figure for battle-induced wounds saw 60 percent of men returned in the same period. The greatest difference between the two was the much lower mortality rate in frostbite cases, which stood at around 1.5 percent. A key problem in assessing the impact of exposure to the freezing conditions is that German statistical surveys only collected data on casualties resulting from enemy action (killed and wounded) and missing (MIAs and POWs). Figures therefore tended to significantly underestimate the number of men listed as "sick" and given a ten-day recovery certificate. No less than 228,000 such certificates were authorized in the winter period, although given the desperate conditions this is unlikely to be an accurate tally, either because officers refused to release sick men or overworked medical staff did not have time to assess and provide paperwork for every man. In consequence, the number of Germans recorded as "sick," especially in Army Group Center, needs to be seen as a conservative estimate.[43]

Not surprisingly, the German high command sought to deflect criticism of their total lack of preparedness for what they called Generals "Mud" and

"Winter," the seasonal Russian allies. Yet there was nothing surprising about mud, frost, and snow in western Russia in October and November. As one former officer in the OKH noted after the war: "That it is cold in Russia at this time belongs to the ABC of an eastern campaign."[44] Similarly, Churchill mocked the German command in a May 1942 speech, stating: "There is a winter, you know, in Russia. For a good many months the temperature is apt to fall very low. There is snow, there is frost, and all that. Hitler forgot about this Russian winter. He must have been very loosely educated."[45] In fact, the German high command had gambled everything on victory at Moscow before the onset of the most serious winter weather, and the men of Army Group Center were left to face the consequences.

Erich Hager claimed in his diary on December 6 that the thermometer had reached minus forty-six degrees Celsius in his area of operations near Tula.[46] Franz Frisch observed that, in addition to the cold, visibility was reduced to practically zero as a result of the easterly winds blowing snow.[47] Siegfried Knappe wrote of how his fingers became so cold in spite of his gloves that it became impossible to perform any precise function, including firing a rifle. His account alluded to the impact this was having upon his morale: "I could not help wondering if our superiors in Berlin had any idea of what they had sent us into. Such thoughts constituted defeatism, I knew, but that threat seemed of little consequence at the moment."[48] Knappe may have kept such "defeatist" thoughts to himself, but he was far from alone. Max Kuhnert recalled after the war: "Wading through the high snow, slipping and stumbling, one minute freezing because of the icy winds and the next minute getting sweaty because of the fatigue, pushed our morale very low."[49] Essentially, the soldiers were unable to see a way out of their suffering and feared that worse was still to come. As Helmut Günther observed the despair around him he recalled: "Only those who experienced it can understand [there were] men with inadequate clothing and who were short of sleep, hungry and with no hope for any improvement in the situation."[50] The freezing conditions were torment enough in themselves. And with German morale already low, the Soviet counteroffensive was about to plunge Army Group Center into a realm of chaos, danger, and despair that few could imagine.

If the Soviet winter offensive caught the German high command by surprise, the events of December 7 were to prove positively astounding. Joseph Goebbels, Hitler's propaganda minister, noted in his diary: "Suddenly like a bolt from the blue, the news breaks that Japan has attacked the United States. The war has arrived."[51] Clearly, the war had arrived for the people of the United States, but why Hitler took the decision to expand his own list of enemies, especially given his lack of success in the east, has been less clear. Hitler had some idea of American industrial potential, but grossly underestimated its quality and quantity. He had often expressed the view that time was not on Germany's side and that America had to be defeated, or at least held in check, before it could intervene decisively, as in the First World War. Thus, in Hitler's view, war with America was inevitable. Indulging wild overestimations of Japanese military strength as well as his exhilaration at the news that the U.S. Pacific Fleet had been sunk at anchor, Hitler foresaw no better time to explain a new war to the German people and expand the conflict on his terms.[52]

After the war some of Hitler's commanders claimed to have felt incredulity at such a rash decision,[53] but in fact the Japanese entry into the war was greeted, according to Major-General Walter Warlimont, by "an ecstasy of rejoicing" throughout the high command.[54] The audacity of Japan's undeclared strike appealed to Hitler's brashness and helped shift attention away from the drudgery of dealing with the Eastern Front.[55] According to Heinz Linge, Hitler's personal assistant and valet, on December 11, the same day Hitler declared war on the United States, discussion at lunch revolved around American military potential. "Halder was scornful, drawing from his experiences in the First World War. American officers could stand no comparison to Prussian—they were businessmen in uniforms who shivered for their lives. In the art of war they had a long way to go."[56] It was the same kind of dismissive thinking that had fed the underestimation of the Soviet Union six months before. The chief of the operations department in the Army General Staff, Colonel Adolf Heusinger, commented: "We help the yellow race in battle against the white, the English help the Mongol-Russian against us, and the yellow race will soon help us against the Mongolian."[57] As for Hitler, Linge recalled a long speech seething with scorn. "Hitler leaned right back and poured out his contempt for the Americans. He pointed out that an American car had never won an international tournament; that American aircraft looked fine, but their motors were worthless. This was proof for him that the much-lauded industries of America were terribly overestimated."[58]

The regular digest of German public opinion, complied by the Security Service (Sicherheitsdienst, SD), revealed a stalwart resignation among the population. The report for December 15 claimed "the declaration of war on the United States did not come as any surprise and was widely interpreted as official confirmation of what already existed in reality."[59] This related to U.S. military support for Britain and the Soviet Union under the so-called Lend-Lease Act, in which everything from raw materials to weapons were shipped to the European allies fighting Germany. It was President Roosevelt's method of fighting the war without being formally engaged, yet very few Germans realized the scale and sophistication of American industrial potential or how quickly that could be mobilized. Siegfried Knappe's later admission was typical: "I did not realize what it would mean for Germany . . . I just felt that the United States had been helping England and Russia with material aid all along and that now we would finally be able to strike back at them."[60] Such confidence born of ignorance was widespread, but on the Eastern Front the tone of enthusiasm among the troops tended to change between the initial news of Japan's attack and Hitler's declaration of war four days later. In the immediate aftermath, letters from soldiers spoke excitedly of a reprieve for Germany. Lieutenant Georg Kreuter wrote in a letter on December 8: "Japan has declared war on America! That helps shorten the war, especially when the hitherto successes continue."[61] Willi Lindenbach concurred, describing the advent of war in the Pacific as "a gift of heaven."[62] Heinrici, the commander of the XXXXIII Army Corps, also welcomed the news, although he correctly doubted that Japan would opt to engage the Soviet Union directly. The real benefit to the Eastern Front, Heinrici reasoned, was that "it stops—or rather hampers—supply transports from America and England to Russia. And this helps a lot."[63] Yet the advent of war in the Pacific became a false promise for the soldiers of the Eastern Front because rather than alleviating their burden, Hitler's decision to declare war on the United States only added to it. After huddling around radios to hear his impassioned speech justifying yet another war, the soldiers' moods turned somber. Ludwig Bumke wrote home in a letter on December 12, "hopefully that is the last surprise. The Japanese have won some big victories, which pleases us. Hopefully they will continue to do so and that it will not become a thirty years' war."[64] Gottlob Bidermann also sounded a note of trepidation, claiming that he and many of his comrades "now believed that only the greatest of skill and luck could bring us total victory."[65] It was a forlorn hope, but even if the soldiers did not yet know victory was beyond them they could at least infer it would now be a longer and harder war. As Konrad Jarausch wrote, "now there certainly won't be an end to it all."[66] Such a realization produced a fatalistic indifference, in part because war with the United States seemed too far away from their everyday reality, but also because few wished to dwell on the implications. As Josef Perau wrote: "Today came the news of war with America. But that goes so far beyond our immediate experience that I do not want to speculate much about the consequences. The situation forces us to 'a necessity.'"[67]

Those unencumbered by the drudgery and toil of life at the front, and indeed with an infinitely better strategic view of the war, knew immediately what Hitler's declaration meant. Winston Churchill was unequivocal in his memoirs: "We had won the war . . . How long the war would last or in what fashion it would end no man could tell, nor did I at this moment care. Once again in our long island history we would emerge, however mauled or mutilated, safe and victorious . . . Hitler's fate was sealed."[68] Likewise, Charles de Gaulle remarked at the time: "Well then, this war is over . . . In this industrial war, nothing can resist the power of American industry."[69] Given that American Lend-Lease aid was already flowing across the Atlantic to Britain and, albeit much more slowly, to the Soviet Union, the decisive economic imbalance had already been a factor for some time.[70] Since June 1941, some fifty-seven ships, carrying 342,680 tons of supplies, had departed American ports for the Soviet Union. This was not a great deal given the scale of the conflict in Eastern Europe, but American war production was only in its early stages, and plans were afoot for a truly remarkable expansion. In fact, on the very day of Japan's attack, and well before Hitler's declaration of war, Roosevelt's cabinet assured its European allies that "the outbreak of the war should not interfere with the flow of supplies to Britain and Russia."[71]

While there was political will to maintain Lend-Lease aid, that did not mean that industrial production was able to meet the demands of a war in Europe and Asia. This, however, was resolved at the Arcadia Conference in Washington between December 22, 1941, and January 14, 1942, at which Churchill and Roosevelt approved the "Europe First" strategy to prioritize the defeat of Nazi Germany over Japan. The hopes expressed by German soldiers on the Eastern Front—that Pearl Harbor would deny the Soviets vital war equipment—had been thoroughly dashed. This should have been cause for some celebration in Moscow, but the bottleneck in Allied shipping meant supplies going from American factories to the Soviet front were well behind the agreed-upon monthly totals stipulated by the First Protocol (signed October 7, 1941). By mid-January 1942 the Soviet government vehemently protested the shortfall, claiming only 16 of the promised 705 American tanks and 85 of an agreed 600 planes had been delivered. Roosevelt instructed the navy that more had to be done. The conditions of the First Protocol were clear, he said; "we simply cannot go back on it."[72]

While the United States struggled to meet its obligations, Britain's proximity to Soviet ports and advanced mobilization of war industries meant it was by far the more important source of Lend-Lease aid during the period of the First Protocol (October 1941 to June 1942). In fact, recent research suggests that by the end of 1941 some 32 percent of all Soviet medium and heavy tanks were British in origin. Numerous Soviet tank battalions attacking Army Group Center in early December as part of Zhukov's counteroffensive included British-supplied Matildas and Valentines. The drawback of these British tanks was their unsuitability to the extreme cold. They tended to remain functional only until they reached the hazardous conditions at the front. One Soviet report even recommended that the Matildas be held back until March, as they were "apparently African vehicles."[73] In fact, after their arrival British tanks underwent modifications for winter service in the Soviet Union with a new transmission for the Matildas and spurs for the Valentines' track plates. Despite the problems Britain was much closer to meeting its obligations under the First Protocol, with 466 tanks delivered out of a promised 750.[74]

What had changed in Britain by the end of 1941 was the clamor of some newspapers as well as the labor unions and the Communist Party for an immediate "second front" in Western Europe, either in the form of tactical coastal raids or a full-scale invasion.[75] The agitation was never militarily sound, but it benefited from a groundswell of sympathy, especially among the working class, for the perilous plight of the Soviet cause. Compounding the problem was the perceived inadequacy of Britain's own war effort in North Africa, which had stalled since the failure of the Battleaxe offensive in June 1941. The new British commander, General Claude Auchinleck, was rebuilding his forces and was wary of being coerced into premature action, but the consequent stalemate was politically intolerable for Churchill given the scale of fighting in the east. Insisting upon action in North Africa, Churchill told Auchinleck: "It is impossible to explain to Parliament and the nation how it is our Middle East armies had to stand for four and a half months without engaging the enemy while all the time Russia is being battered to pieces."[76] It was not until the second half of November that Auchinleck's Crusader offensive gave the British government something tangible to counter the claims that "the Battle of Britain is being fought on the eastern front."[77] Pearl Harbor and the Japanese attacks in the Far East ended calls for a second front, which caused Churchill to ask rhetorically where the nation would have been had an invasion of France been attempted.[78]

While the United States and Britain were doing all in their power to aid the Soviet Union, German diplomats lamented that their new Japanese ally was not being pressured to play any role against the Soviet Union.[79] Hitler's declaration of war upon the United States, in full support of Japanese war aims, demanded nothing of Japan in return. Then on December 15 the Japanese presented their Axis allies with a draft agreement for a military convention that divided the world into spheres of military operations along the seventieth degree of east longitude (some 2,000 kilometers east of Moscow or almost 4,000 kilometers from the Pacific Ocean), with Germany and Italy responsible for the territory to the west of that line and the Japanese for lands to the east. The treaty offered no Japanese aid in the war against the Soviet Union, in spite of placing the eastern half of Siberia within their sphere of operation. Hitler thought it better to encourage Japan to seek the maximum possible conquest at the expense of the British Empire and opted to accept the plan. There was not even an attempt to have Japan halt American

Lend-Lease supplies reaching Soviet ports at Vladivostok. The new treaty designating fields of operations was signed by the Axis powers on January 18, 1942. Only at this point, more than a month after Hitler's declaration of war against the Americans, did the German government make belated requests to the Japanese leadership imploring them to halt American shipments to Vladivostok as well as do everything possible to tie down the maximum number of Soviet troops along their shared border. Such requests were to be met with disappointment for the Germans; this was the consequence of Hitler's disastrous foreign policy decisions in the wake of Pearl Harbor.[80]

For Army Group Center any prospect of relief from Japan's attack on Pearl Harbor was wholly misplaced. The expansion of the conflict into the Pacific and Southeast Asia only confirmed that Japan had opted against opening a front against the Red Army. Moreover, thanks to Hitler's declaration of war against the United States, Roosevelt was able not only to engage Nazi Germany directly, but also to establish a "Europe first" policy. Yet whatever the strategic realities of Germany's position by December 1941, German soldiers could scarcely conceive of such matters and were in any case entirely preoccupied by their own circumstances, especially at the flashpoints of Army Group Center. As one study by Sönke Neitzel and Harald Welzer observed, "the issue of whether the war was still winnable was sometimes irrelevant to soldiers trying to carry out a specific task, be it holding their position, avoiding capture by the enemy, or saving the lives of subordinates. Knowledge of the larger context does not automatically rule out actions independent of that knowledge. As a general rule, interpretations and decisions in concrete situations are usually made without references to the 'big picture.'"[81]

The unexpected Soviet offensive was causing local crisis, and the scope of the Red Army's attack was expanding along Army Group Center's front. Far from the winter pause German troops had hoped for, the fighting was resuming with a frightening intensity. The strain this caused, after months of tireless action, left many soldiers on the brink of physical and mental exhaustion. As one man recalled: "Most of us had walked perilously along this border line between sanity and madness . . . Laughter was never far from tears; optimism rubbed shoulders with black despair; and death marched side by side in our ranks with life. Nothing normal remained."[82] Hans Rehfeldt wrote on December 15: "I close my eyes and try and lift myself into a more beautiful and bright world, without this damned war!"[83] Yet for many there was no escaping the conflict, as another soldier wrote: "All human beauty seems to be taken from us. We no longer have any enthusiasm, no ideals, no dreams, not even illusions."[84] Part of the problem was that fighting on the defensive meant the initiative had shifted, forcing the Germans to react and fight battles on Soviet terms rather than their own. This, coupled with the uneven encounters they were forced to fight, became a source of immense nervous anticipation, especially as rumors spread of the first German retreats. As one soldier recalled: "Somehow we had an inkling that this would be the last evening that we would spend in our old, trusted circle. We were not blind, and the general situation at the front was making itself depressingly obvious."[85] Egon Schmitt, a Catholic priest who was transferred east toward the end of 1941, remarked on the degree to which the men embraced religious services to sustain what he called their "spiritual energy." When Schmitt conducted Mass, he claimed to have had 90 to 100 percent attendance, "and their attitude was unquestionably good and serious, better than I had expected given the conditions."[86] For some, however, the pressure was simply too much. Writing about his friend Max Limberger, Erich Kern noted: "One day I found him unshaven and uncombed at the table in his bunker, writing letters. He seemed dismayed. 'What's the matter?' I asked him. 'Tomorrow I'll die!' was his answer. 'When you see Lina [his fiancée], bring her my greeting. I am writing to all my relatives.' I tried to talk him out of this idea, but it was useless . . . At noon the following day, one shot was fired: Limberger was dead, shot in the head by a Russian sniper."[87]

In the face of growing desperation, the commander-in-chief of the army, Field Marshal Walter von Brauchitsch, responded on December 8 with an instruction to officers throughout the army emphasizing that the "inner mental attitude of every individual" had to be made aware of the "decisive struggle for an ideology." Soviet numerical superiority had to be countered by faith in Germany's leadership and troops. The message linked the "inner resistance" of the men to ideological precepts as well as "welfare in all spheres and constant spiritual guidance."[88] The irony, however, was that Brauchitsch himself had become deeply pessimistic about Army Group Center's situation and by December 15 was noted to be "very despondent" and saw "no way" of enduring the winter.[89] For the men at the front, resistance was less about instructions from the high command than simple survival. As Helmut Günther described it: "Were we brave? What a hopelessly stupid word: Brave! . . . When we were in the midst of a tight spot, there was no time to think about it. When it was done, one started to contemplate what could have happened, but soon swept that away. You were happy to have come through it again alive. Nobody wanted to die!"[90] Franz Frisch expressed a similar sentiment when he wrote: "When the retreat from Moscow began, I felt it was the end. Yet, the motto of our service in Russia was: 'You have to have a positive attitude.'"[91] Perhaps being positive was too much to expect for many of the men, but fighting for their lives was an almost universal motivation. Helmut Pabst explained his mental state in letters home as: "someone who wants to create a vacuum round himself because he's grown almost indifferent to everything. I feel fine like that. I find pleasure in hardening myself against all these miseries, setting my strength and peace of mind against this dog's life, so that in the end I may profit by it."[92] It was clear that men coped in different ways, but as Bernhard Kroener observed, German morale during the winter was sustained, at least in part, by the fact that the men were not forced to defend in one position. Retreat was an option. Unlike the horrors of trench warfare between 1914 and 1918 when individuals felt they could not "escape," in December 1941 German soldiers had, according to Kroener, "at least a subjective belief that they could evade the enemy and remain, in part, masters of their own destiny."[93] Such a sense of empowerment, however illusionary at times, was fundamental to German morale because the Soviet offensive was actually still in a nascent phase. The Soviet reserve armies were still moving to the front, adding momentum by the day, but even more to the point—no one in Army Group Center's command fully comprehended just how many men were coming their way.

2

DODGING THE
SOVIET BULLET

Army Group Center Holds

By the second day of the Soviet offensive (December 7), the Soviet Thirtieth Army had narrowly maintained its breach in Reinhardt's Panzer Group 3 north of Klin. As Halder at the OKH noted, "great tension" surrounded the situation.[1] Reinhardt wrote in his diary that the panzer group was desperately trying to restore the breaches in the line by sending radio operators, engineers, antiaircraft gunners, truck drivers, staff officers, and even a group of musicians to the front.[2] In a letter to his wife Reinhardt confided that, while he always maintained his composure before his men, "inside one fights with one's self and suffers." On tours of the front he wrote that he felt helpless being only able to offer "thanks and recognition" before departing with further demands that the men continue to hold and do their duty.[3] Bock at Army Group Center was doing all in his power to find reserves, pleading "for even the last bicyclist."[4] The best he could get was a single regiment from the 255th Infantry Division and a battalion of engineers from Reinhardt's neighbor Panzer Group 4. Such a pitiful result from an army group of more than 1.5 million men speaks to the exhaustion of its many formations after more than five months on the offensive. It also highlights the weaknesses local German commanders across the front identified in their own defensive positions and their profound reluctance to release any units. Only the day before, Halder had written in his diary about freeing young German workers for the front by replacing them with Soviet prisoners of war. Similarly, on December 9 Halder ordered that preparations begin for sending units of the relatively poorly equipped security divisions, acting in the army groups' rear areas, to the front. Finally, on December 10 four German infantry divisions stationed in France (the 88th, 208th, 216th, and 246th) were also ordered to prepare for transportation to the east.[5]

With reinforcements so limited, on December 8 Bock agreed to place Reinhardt's panzer group under the command of Hoepner's Panzer Group 4 to coordinate the situation better, but also, as Bock noted in his diary, "for now Hoepner will be more interested in helping Panzer Group 3."[6] Such assistance was needed more than ever. The Soviet advance had almost cut the rail line connecting Kalinin and Klin. Reinhardt had however resolved to redeploy Major-General Walter Krüger's 1st Panzer Division to try to stem the deepening penetration of Gollnick's 36th Motorized Infantry Division. Attacking from the south, Krüger's vanguard encountered Soviet forces late on December 8 and in a minor action exacted "heavy losses" on the advanced Soviet forces, while taking 120 POWs and seizing some artillery and mortars.[7] Such a local reversal had no immediate impact on the general Soviet advance toward Klin, but it was a clear warning of what the German "offensive defense" could do. Meanwhile, with Gollnick's right flank broken, Soviet forces concentrated on his left. They sought to overrun the division completely, but in desperate fighting the division held firm, and the only two villages lost were quickly recaptured in determined counterattacks.[8] Indeed the Germans were discovering that the vanguard of Soviet forces were extremely vulnerable because they often advanced beyond the support of heavy weapons or lacked the ability to coordinate artillery fire rapidly. On December 9 Lieutenant Ludwig Freiherr von Heyl, belonging to Gollnick's 36th Motorized Infantry Division, successfully counterattacked a sizable Soviet force threatening to overrun a small German detachment defending the village of Arkhangel'skoe. After the action, Heyl wrote: "11:45 a.m.—crisis passed. About 150 Russians lie in heaps. Our soldiers immediately pull the boots and fur coats off the dead bodies."[9]

Maintaining the cohesion of his front was purely a stopgap measure for Reinhardt. His panzer group urgently attempted to retreat to the new Klin Line with whatever could be carted or carried westward. The immediate problem, however, was organizing transportation to the rear for all articles of war that had been brought forward during the offensive. As Heinrich Engel noted in his diary: "Everywhere there were 'dead' vehicles and tanks that simply could not function any longer." The remedy was to have each of the functioning vehicles tow one, and sometimes two, of the disabled vehicles.[10] Despite such expediencies not everything could be transported, and with strict orders that nothing be left for the advancing Red Army, German engineers set to work destroying any weapons and vehicles that could not be evacuated to the rear. "It is unbelievable what we have destroyed," Fritz Hübner wrote home on December 7 before detailing the methods of destruction his unit employed. Artillery pieces had hand grenades dropped down their tubes, tanks had a three-kilogram explosive charge placed inside and detonated, and trucks either had their motor blocks drilled or hand grenades placed in their engines. "It was dangerous and very depressing work," Hübner concluded.[11] The quantity of equipment destroyed in the first days of the retreat was remarkable. Major-General Heinrich Wosch's 14th Motorized Infantry Division reported that between December 6 and 8 his division had eliminated 2 tanks, 6 antitank guns, 8 armored scout cars, 17 tractors, 73 automobiles, 99 motorcycles, and 123 trucks. Funck's 7th Panzer Division provided less precise information for the same period but recorded 10 artillery pieces and "a great number of trucks" had been destroyed. Its panzer regiment had only 15 operational tanks remaining, while the report ended: "Further matériel losses must be expected."[12]

In spite of high numbers of destroyed and abandoned vehicles, there was still terrible traffic congestion on the roads leading to Klin, indicating that Reinhardt's panzer group was far from immobile. Heinrich Engel wrote on December 8 that his road was "continuously jammed" and that although it was only fifteen kilometers to the town his tank required nineteen hours to cover the distance.[13] By December 9 the Soviet advance continued unchecked, and the capture of Klin appeared imminent. The consequences for Panzer Group 3, as Klin was its forward communication, supply, and transportation hub, would have been catastrophic. Reinhardt was doing everything in his limited power to hold off the Red Army, but privately he was nearing despair, confiding in his diary: "Everything failing, troops at the end of their tether. Is everything lost? No, this cannot be!"[14] The following day, as the gravity of his situation weighed on him, Reinhardt wrote to his wife that none of the help promised to him had arrived and that he was "anxious with worry and doubt." He then continued: "I doubt if I can continue in command, whether another should take my place. On the other hand, that would be desertion."[15] Such dark thoughts mirror comments in the war diary of the panzer group, which, owing to the congested roads, was struggling to get supplies and munitions to the rear-guard units covering the retreat.[16] The situation was extremely precarious. The Red Army was at the gates of Klin, bombing and shelling directly into the town, while the retreat proceeded at a snail's pace and the panzer group's defensive front threatened to collapse for lack of supply.

It was at this low point that Krüger's 1st Panzer Division launched itself into the vanguard of the Soviet advance with devastating results. The consolidated strength of the panzer division drove headlong into the unsuspecting enemy with what the divisional war diary described as the "highest losses in blood." The Soviet front was completely overrun, with over 1,800 killed and 950 POWs. But the Germans recorded capturing only three enemy tanks, two antitank guns, and ten mortars—a factor that was both disproportionately small for the number of infantry and no doubt an element of Krüger's success.[17] Reinhardt was overcome with relief and wrote that in Klin there was "great joy" at the successful attack.[18] The Soviets had suffered a serious setback, but it was still only a local reversal, even if it had bought Reinhardt's panzer group some much needed time.

The Soviet breakthrough north of Klin may have been the most serious threat to Army Group Center north of Moscow, but it was by no means the only breach of the front. Strauss's Ninth Army was also struggling to contain a Soviet penetration to the east of Kalinin. But with reinforcements lacking, Bock was unequivocal: "9th Army will and must help itself."[19] Strauss did just that, and by December 10 he reported success, claiming that the Soviet onslaught had "passed its culmination." Werner Beermann wrote home in a letter on December 9 that his regiment alone counted some 600 Soviet dead before its lines with just 3 Germans killed and 20 wounded.[20] In fact, however, the Red Army's Kalinin Front had only briefly suspended its attack to reorganize its offensive. On December 11 a renewed Soviet offensive, with orders to capture Kalinin, began, and Strauss was again scrambling to contain it.[21]

While the fighting near Kalinin and Klin naturally assumed the focus of German attempts to counter the Soviet offensive, the reality was that further attacks—often unable to penetrate the German line—were taking place in dozens of positions across Army Group Center's front. Soviet failures reflect the cumulative cost of the Red Army's offensive. For example, the 2nd SS Division *Das Reich*, serving as part of Hoepner's Panzer Group 4 northeast of Moscow, reported beating back an enemy assault that left 1,500 dead before its front lines.[22] One soldier from the division noted: "Aim, squeeze, work the bolt and aim again. This time the attackers were met with such intense rifle and machine-gun fire that it was only a question of how stubborn they would be in continuing their attempt . . . the battle was decided. The dead Russians lay scattered across the countryside, in many places in heaps."[23] The SS division also sustained losses, albeit far less.

If the die-hard offensive mentality of the German high command had ruined its panzer forces during the preceding months, at least now there was an understanding, even by Hitler, that operations must come to an end and everything be devoted to the defense. On December 8 Hitler issued War Directive 39, which in its opening sentence unambiguously set out the new strategic approach to the war in the east, requiring the *Ostheer* to "abandon immediately all major offensive operations and to go over to the defensive."[24] The next day Bock ordered the preparation of a line running (from south to north) through Kursk–Orel–Medyn–Gzhatsk–Rzhev–Lake Volgo.[25] It was a far more radical withdrawal than the localized Klin Line north of Moscow and a timely recognition, even before the full force of the Soviet offensive was known, of the need to shorten the Eastern Front both to economize on forces and to reduce the distance of moving supplies.

The Soviet command was anxious to hasten its offensive and exploit the vulnerabilities of the depleted German armies around Moscow. Yet they were exasperated at the poor, even disastrous, operational methods frequently employed by frontline commanders. Marshal Boris Shaposhnikov, the Red Army's chief of the General Staff, issued a directive on December 8 offering the most rudimentary instruction on engaging German forces: "Upon encountering enemy strongpoints, leave small screening detachments to contain them, and resolutely develop the offensive in force against flank boundaries and gaps in the enemy line." These strongpoints were to be destroyed by "the operations of second and following echelons," which often did not exist. But even more to the point, Shaposhnikov's directive failed to account for the difficulty of the winter conditions as well as the inability of his many green officers to coordinate flanking attacks.[26] Lieutenant-General K. K. Rokossovsky, whose Sixteenth Army was on the offensive just north of Moscow, noted in his postwar memoir that the deep snow and severe frost "prevented us from engaging in enveloping movements away from the roads to cut off the enemy routes of withdrawal." Rokossovsky's account also took issue with the German generals who "instead of blaming the Russian winter for their defeat, should perhaps be grateful for the harsh weather that enabled them to retreat with less losses than they would otherwise have suffered."[27]

The issue of inexperienced and sometimes downright incompetent Soviet officers was addressed by Marshal Zhukov, the commander of the Western Front. He became so incensed by the massed assaults that he issued a special order on December 9, which opened: "I order: 1. Categorically forbid you to conduct frontal combat with enemy covering units and to conduct frontal combat against fortified positions."[28] That such elementary orders were necessary to prevent wasteful frontal assaults reflects the tactical disparity between the opposing forces, which helped to compensate for Army Group Center's overextension. Larry LeSueur, an American war correspondent stationed in Moscow, wrote of a meeting with General Leonid Govorov and being assured that the Russian soldier was "traditionally skillful with a bayonet," while the German Wehrmacht "did not place much dependence on it." The encounter ended with the general informing LeSueur that "he could recall no instance where the German soldiers had ever stood up to a bayonet charge, with the Russians yelling their age-old 'Oorah!'"[29] Even with no experience at the front, LeSueur was rightly skeptical.

By comparison the German adaptation to defensive warfare was rapid and, as we have seen, combined whenever possible a potent offensive element. One of the most proficient proponents of this new offensive defense style of warfare was General of Panzer Troops Walter Model, the commander of the XXXXI Army Corps, who made excellent use of mobile battle groups (Kampfgruppen—an ad hoc formation made up of small units) and earned a reputation for imposing ruthless discipline during moments of crisis. Model, who had already accrued a good degree of defensive experience against a numerically superior Red Army during the final stages of the September fighting at Kiev, was then tested to the limit.[30] His method, which was by no means unique to XXXXI Army Corps even in December 1941, entailed leaving infantry divisions to hold or "fix" the enemy in place (owing to their limited mobility), while anything that could be mobilized was assembled into a battle group. The battle group was the key to German defenses because it acted as a mobile reserve to plug gaps or reinforce endangered sectors, and served as a counterstriking option at any point of vulnerability.

Equally important to the German defense was the maintenance of order in a typically confused and dangerous situation, something that the Wehrmacht, with its reputation for harsh discipline, was well disposed to do. Indeed, during the winter retreat the death penalty was used frequently to ensure obedience. Armin Böttger remembered hearing at his morning parade that a death sentence had been passed on a comrade who deserted his post: "Though horrified we made no criticism of the sentence . . . Inwardly we accepted what had been hammered into us in training: 'This is what happens to a deserter.'"[31] Model could be extremely callous and unforgiving toward both his staff officers and his own troops, but no one could dispute his determination to salvage critical situations. In one instance at a congested crossroads he reprimanded the responsible officer with his pistol drawn. Not for nothing Model earned himself the nickname *Frontschwein*—"the Frontline Pig." As Model's biographer concluded: "Even the staff officers who had smarted under his verbal lash now admitted that Model's direct relationship with the men and barely harnessed brutality paid great dividends during the retreat."[32]

Such a diverging assessment of Soviet offensive and German defensive proficiency in early December cannot disguise the worrying predicament confronting Army Group Center. Lieutenant-Colonel Hellmuth Stieff, the operations officer at Kluge's Fourth Army, wrote home to his wife on December 7 that the war was *"utterly different to how it is portrayed to you by that preposterous propaganda. We are standing on a knife's edge every day here."*[33] The sense of foreboding was even greater among the troops. Gerhardt Linke wrote home on the same day: "The men are all worn out. They just collapse. What is going to happen? Not a single fresh soldier to take the place of those who dropped out."[34] Similarly, after enduring so much in the preceding months, Fritz Sigel lamented the menacing uncertainty that even worse could await him: "My God, I've never experienced anything like this . . . My God, what has Russia in store for us?"[35] Werner Adamczyk, whose unit seems to have held out hope that they would not be remaining in the east over the winter, was then informed that every man was needed at the front and that there would be no transfers home. "This news had a devastating effect on our morale. Hopelessness emerged in every one of us. My imagination exaggerated my already established fears a hundredfold."[36] Clearly, the psychological burden of facing a major retreat as well as a resurgent and aggressive Red Army took a huge toll on the men. Yet unlike previous German offensives, in which the army command ordered operation after operation with little to no concern for the ability of the men to sustain them, physical and mental endurance was now at least a feature of the conversation at the highest levels.

On December 8, 1941, Bock and Halder discussed Army Group Center's fraught situation. The chief of the Army General Staff compared the unfolding crisis to the western front in 1918. Bock then summarized the situation in the blackest of terms: "No section of the army group's front is in a position to hold off a serious Russian attack." Halder was surprised by this and questioned: "On no section? Not even by Fourth Army?" Bock's response was unequivocal: "No!" He then elaborated on the conditions of the troops at the front. When Halder spoke again he was almost pensive: "Operationally there is nothing to expect from the Russian, but again and again he brings together such a mass of manpower at individual positions."[37] Of course Halder's dismissal of Soviet operations was characteristic of his derisive attitude toward the Red Army, which had contributed so much toward the *Ostheer's* precarious overextension. Yet at least now there was some recognition of the consequences. Bock's final comment to Halder was a plea for reinforcements, set together with a warning about the consequences of inaction. "Everyone should be clear that if I don't get reserves the danger is enormous."[38]

The following day (December 9) another revealing exchange between the two men took place. Halder expressed hope that Bock's forces would withstand the Soviet offensive and predicted the offensive would last until the middle of the month or even until the end of the year. "Then our army will be *kaputt* [broken]," Bock interjected. "The German soldier does not go *kaputt!*" Halder retorted. But Bock refused to be sidetracked: "I don't want to whine and complain, but I want to have reserves."[39] Halder promised to do what little he could. Such a lack of understanding for the plight of the average soldier was symptomatic of Halder's pervasive National Socialist thinking, which emphasized the primacy of individual "will" over any circumstance. Bock was not immune to this brand of thinking either, but he also could not ignore the reality of his army group's situation.

With preliminary planning for a retreat between 100 and 145 kilometers under way, Bock instructed the individual army commands to make their own preparations. Kluge at Fourth Army, however, expressed serious doubts, preferring instead to try to muddle through with local adjustments and improvised defenses.[40] Kluge emphasized the practicalities, pointing out that the equipment losses so far entailed would be multiplied many times over, while the Red Army would be battering the new line within three days.[41] Yet his opposition also reflected Fourth Army's stronger position relative to the other armies. Kluge's forward defenses were somewhat better prepared and, for the time being, much less threatened. Bock, however, was mindful that a major retreat would be far safer if conducted on German terms rather than forced by Soviet pressure. It was a delicate balance between preserving the weakened army group by not pushing it too far, too fast, and, at the same time, gaining a much-needed buffer away from an aggressive enemy whose plans and resources were unknown. Army Group Center's winter campaign had hardly begun, but a sense of fear was already palpable.

Hoepner, now in command of Panzer Groups 3 and 4, wrote to his wife on December 8: "Everyone is screaming for help."[42] Likewise, in its war diary Panzer Group 4 commented on the weakness of the German infantry against the greater numbers they were encountering and was grateful for the scarcity—so far—of Soviet heavy weaponry. Accordingly, the Soviet offensive impetus was "not so highly rated, but its mass was demoralizing."[43] The German retreat manifest as a very public display that the Wehrmacht's fortunes in the east had turned for the worse, which fed the cynicism of some soldiers who questioned the competence of their commanders. Willi Lindenbach wrote home on December 8 that he was observing Fourth Army's withdrawal, before adding: "Everyone drives back, no one knows where . . . It is terrible, an army in retreat. But it was predictable. One cannot just advance forever."[44] Even more important, the retreat confirmed Germany's stunning reversal at Moscow, which Goebbels's propaganda had unwisely done so much to disseminate in October and November. Suddenly, the Allied world had a much-needed counterpoint to fill newspaper columns awash with stories about Japan's victories in the Far East. Arvid Fredborg, a Swedish journalist based in Berlin, noted as early as December 8: "That the situation was critical became at once obvious . . . The powerful Russian attack was a genuine surprise to the German Government."[45] Mihail Sebastian, a Romanian Jewish writer who kept a journal throughout the war, noted on the same day that the evening's German communiqué opened with a new and unexpected message: "The continuation of operations and the form of battle in the east hinge upon the arrival of the Russian winter. Over great stretches of the eastern front, only local operations are now being reported." Even without knowledge of the Soviet offensive against Army Group Center, Sebastian perceptively observed, "The Germans are talking of a winter lull as if it were an established fact."[46]

If the situation north of Moscow was not sufficient to refute the idea of a winter lull then Army Group Center's even longer southern flank provided ample evidence. Colonel-General Heinz Guderian and General of Panzer Troops Rudolf Schmidt served as the respective commanders of Second Panzer Army and Second Army in early December 1941.[47] They were both panzer commanders who were exponents of mobile warfare, in which success depended upon headstrong and aggressive commanders pushing forward at all costs. This practice, however, often drove the panzer units well beyond their operational limits, and by early December both Guderian's and Schmidt's armies were overextended and extremely vulnerable. That neither man recognized the danger of his actions is illustrated by the fact that Schmidt defied orders and continued the attack even after Bock ordered a complete halt on December 5.[48] In Guderian's case he accepted none of the responsibility for his own army's exposed position in early December and in fact credited himself in his memoir with having saved the situation because he ordered his panzer army to halt on December 5 hours before Bock's general order. "I decided on my own responsibility," Guderian wrote after the war, "to break off the attack on the 5th of December; had I not done so a catastrophe could not have been avoided."[49] In fact, Guderian was far too late.

Ninety kilometers east of Tula the town of Mikhailov was held by elements of Lieutenant-General Friedrich-Wilhelm von Loeper's 10th Motorized Infantry Division, which was one of the first German units south of Moscow to be hit by the Soviet offensive. The attack took place at night. As the war diary of the XXXXVII Panzer Corps recorded on December 7, in "some units panic developed," and after sometimes "only weak resistance," the men fled to the south and west, "leaving numerous machines, above all trucks."[50] Fortunately for Guderian, the heavy losses at Mikhailov were so far an isolated instance and confirmed for the panzer general that an immediate withdrawal of his far-flung divisions was absolutely necessary. The retreat proceeded under increasing pressure on December 7, 8, and 9, but progress was made.

As in the north, the beginning of the German retreat should not suggest that serious combat was suspended. As Guderian noted in a letter to his wife on December 8: "The Russians are vigorously pressing forwards and we still have to be on our guard . . . We're able to hold out only in a makeshift way."[51]

Bruno Trappmann recalled the dread one such Soviet attack instilled within him: "I saw something strange coming towards us. I strained my eyes trying to identify it. Against the lightening sky it looked like a line of dark trees that had the strange ability to move towards us. As it came closer to us, I saw it was a dense line of Russian soldiers advancing steadily, elbow to elbow. I was afraid; my heart was pounding. I thought for certain it was the end for all of us. There were so many coming at us."[52]

Combat casualties for the Germans were heavy, but overwhelmingly so for the Red Army. Lieutenant-General Wilhelm Stemmermann's 296th Infantry Division was holding the line west of Tula when elements of the Soviet Fiftieth Army attacked, breaking into its line in several places. Rapid counterattacks eliminated the penetrations and restored the line, while the frontal nature of the Soviet attacks came at a devastating cost. In front of just one of Stemmermann's regiments, 700 dead were counted and no ground had been made.[53] Similarly, Major-General Heinrich Clössner's 25th Motorized Infantry Division repulsed a series of attacks and reported over 1,000 dead before its lines, while 471 POWs had been captured by means of a rapid counterattack. The same process repeated itself on December 10 when Loeper's 10th Motorized Infantry Division cut off and captured another 500 POWs after counterattacking following a failed Soviet assault.[54] The German aptitude for offensive defense was exacting a heavy toll on the often poorly coordinated Soviet attacks.

Naturally, the demands of the retreat, punctuated by periods of intense combat at subzero temperatures, severely taxed the strength of Guderian's troops. Major-General Gerhard Berthold's 31st Infantry Division reported that all its combat companies together totaled just 650 fighting men.[55] The war diary of Major-General Hermann Breith's 3rd Panzer Division spoke of the "inhuman strain," with some companies in constant combat for ten days, "including nights," their combat strength "almost sunk to zero." In one company of sixty men, thirty-five were running high fevers.[56] In extreme cases units became so apathetic they no longer fought, even to save their own lives. In one such case from December 9 a report from General of Infantry Walther Fischer von Weikersthal's LIII Army Corps stated: "The soldiers are no longer able to offer up resistance. They don't fight anymore."[57] Such soldiers, in the pit of desolation and despair, were simply beyond the reach of their officers. As one soldier recalled: "There was nothing left that could give me hope and there was no future in sight other than suffering."[58]

While the fatigue and anguish of these men is entirely understandable, what is perhaps more remarkable are the many stories of human endurance, which ultimately kept Guderian's feeble panzer army alive. In a letter home on December 11 General Heinrici, commanding the XXXXIII Army Corps, marveled at some of the sights he had witnessed:

> Look at the guys who have been facing the enemy for weeks in this freezing weather. With thirty others they share a lice-ridden panje shed, without soap, unwashed and unshaven for days, with infected wounds all over the body due to constant scratching because of the lice, in ragged uniforms, filthy and covered in bugs. Look at them and hear what they are saying when they were, according to the doctor, unfit for duty due to ulcerous legs. They all declared on 26 November: "We are not going into the field hospital; we are not leaving our comrades alone right before the attack." And they came with us the next day in minus 10°C with dressed feet and without socks. And this young lieutenant H. whom I visited with his company, who showed me his men and was found unconscious the next morning. He was wounded three days ago and did not say a word, because he did not want to leave his company, which had almost lost all its NCOs [non-commissioned officers]![59]

Thomas Kühne's research into the social world of the German soldier sheds light on the profound bonds between men that acted to reinforce notions of unit cohesion and group loyalty, beyond any reference to duty or patriotism. According to Kühne, the nature of German comradeship at the front incorporated certain "homoerotic" feelings, which must be firmly dissociated from what contemporaries saw as the reviled act of manifest homosexuality. In the language of "comradeship," an asexual love among men could be openly discussed, facilitating male bonding, emotional support, and even close physical contact without violating cardinal military virtues or established images of masculinity.[60] It was precisely because the rejection of homosexuality was so complete that men felt at liberty to express affection without any sense of stigma or shame. Comrades became a surrogate form of family, which provided a powerful mechanism for coping with the brutalizing effects of warfare.[61] As Gottlob Bidermann wrote: "We had become old together and had developed a brotherhood between us, a closeness of spirit and trust that those who live in safety throughout their lives cannot know."[62] Likewise, Helmut Günther observed: "Only through such comradeship was it possible to survive all the madness around us."[63]

The sense of the unit as "home" and men as "family" was also evident in soldiers' writings. Martin Pöppel wrote in his diary: "Here a man looks at other Germans and sees his brother, his home."[64] Such tight bonds were also linked with Germany's fighting prowess, as Karl Fuchs wrote home in a letter: "A great friendship binds us German soldiers together out here . . . This loyalty is the essence of the German fighting spirit. We can depend on each other unconditionally. Each one of us sets the example for the other and that makes us strong."[65] It was this intimate form of comradeship, forged through months of fighting in the Soviet Union, that acted as a central prop holding up Army Group Center in its hour of greatest need. The lengths to which soldiers expressed their profound devotion to one another all too often reflected the tragedy of war. Henning Kardell forbade his men from venturing out into no-man's-land to rescue a wounded man, but his closest comrade refused to obey. "He went out to bring his friend back and was killed when he trod on a mine. We mourned that man, for his courage and his self-sacrifice. What he had done was the most one man could do for another."[66]

While the emotional bonds of comradeship were intangible and provided a physical and mental endurance that could not be quantified in military reports or plans, the mechanical durability of the Second Panzer Army was concrete and far more calculable. As with the panzer and motorized divisions north of Moscow, the problem was maintaining mobility. By only the second day of Guderian's withdrawal, Major-General Willibald Freiherr von Langermann-Erlancamp's 4th Panzer Division was reporting 10 percent losses in matériel. Breith's 3rd Panzer Division, by contrast, had not yet had to leave behind anything.[67] That changed the next day (December 9) when Breith's division, under pressure from Soviet attacks, abandoned a sizeable number of inoperative vehicles. Others were destroyed, and there was hardly a truck left in the division that was not towing something.[68] Overall, Guderian acknowledged that the losses of vehicles and guns "exceed all our fears."[69] He did, however, claim a positive note, when he wrote: "Fortunately we have so far been able to keep our fine tanks in running order."[70] That was, however, untrue. The tank regiments of the panzer divisions had long since been reduced to a tiny fraction of their establishment size, so the 4th Panzer Division, for example, which started the war with 169 tanks, was reduced to just 16 on December 12. On the same day, Major-General Wilhelm Ritter von Thoma's 20th Panzer Division, which started the war in the east with 245 tanks, reported that just 30 remained operational.[71] Thus, by virtue of their smaller numbers, keeping a handful of tanks in running order was obviously an easier task than the many hundreds of other vehicles. Yet individual accounts contradict Guderian's claim and confirm that the panzer army's tanks were in fact breaking down and being destroyed by the crews. Erich Hager, who served as a tanker in Colonel Rudolf-Eduard Licht's 17th Panzer Division, noted in his diary on December 9: "Everything which is left is being blown up so that nothing falls into Russian hands. Three tanks from our regiment blown up. There are eight of us now."[72]

With so many vehicles having to be destroyed, some of the men quickly became specialists at demolition. Hans Rehfeldt, who served in the elite infantry regiment *Großdeutschland*, wrote that the process went "quite fast." His preferred method was a hand grenade behind the radiator.[73] Of course just getting vehicles to move was not the only impediment to the withdrawal. On December 9 the weather was warmer and a downpour of sleet led to icy conditions, which "greatly hindered all movement."[74] On some routes there were also reports of "undisciplined driving," leading to congestion and delays.[75] More worryingly, fuel was so scarce for Guderian's army, and especially General of Panzer Troops Joachim Lemelsen's XXXXVII Panzer Corps, that doubts were being expressed about the ability to continue the withdrawal. As the Panzer Army's war diary noted on December 10, "by any immediate forced withdrawal great confusion and heavy losses are expected." The next day the diary framed the lack of fuel supplies in even more direct terms: "in the current situation this must lead to a manifestly serious crisis."[76]

Given all the problems of movement, Guderian, like Kluge, was reluctant to effect a further withdrawal of the front. As Guderian told Bock, there was "no advantage, because the retreat weakened the troops more than holding."[77] The problem with Kluge and Guderian was that they still underestimated the magnitude of what was in motion. Neither had suffered greatly yet, and intelligence about Soviet resources and plans was poor. Lemelsen's XXXXVII Panzer Corps even noted that intelligence gathering was so degraded that the responsible officers were left roving the front "almost always on foot" and that "constant local surprises occur."[78] Accordingly, the panzer army really only knew what it was up against when it hit their front lines. In his wartime letters Guderian accepted that the Soviets had been underestimated on many levels, although he did not attribute any blame to himself. As he wrote his wife on December 10: "The enemy, the size of the county and the foulness of the weather were all grossly underestimated, and we are suffering for that now."[79] The panzer general also failed to consider that more surprises might be in store for Germany and that, given the *Ostheer*'s lack of preparation for the winter, the worst was yet to come.

The signs were already apparent. Just as Kluge only had to look north to where Reinhardt's panzer group was reeling backward, Schmidt's weak Second Army on Guderian's southern flank was imploding. After Schmidt brashly continued his attack in the face of Bock's halt order, his army was hit on December 8 by an unexpected Soviet offensive. The seven depleted divisions of the Second Army were estimated to have a combat strength of just four divisions, and Schmidt beseeched Army Group Center for at least four additional divisions, which Bock could not provide.[80] The total length of the Second Army's line extended for some 260 kilometers, giving each division a front of roughly forty kilometers to defend.[81] Bock managed to have a motorized SS brigade redirected to support Schmidt, but it would take some days to arrive and was in no way adequate to deal with the speed of the collapsing front. On December 9 Guderian was asked to send whatever he could spare south, but he rejected the appeal and on the following day suggested to Bock that Kluge's (more northerly) Fourth Army should find the reserves necessary to support Schmidt.[82] Bock, who was used to dealing with Guderian's obstinate behavior, especially when it came to giving up units to neighboring commands, instructed the panzer general to help with whatever could be spared. In the meantime, Bock had scraped together a security division from the rear area and a single infantry regiment. The situation, however, was rapidly spiraling out of control.

The Soviet attack on Schmidt's army struck between the 45th and 95th Infantry Divisions with a section of the latter overrun and destroyed. There was at least a 26-kilometer-wide hole in the German front, and with no reserves, Schmidt was worried his army would be cut in two and driven back on Orel and Kursk, leaving an enormous 140-kilometer gap in the German front. The Soviet forces opposing Second Army were not especially large or well equipped; in fact, the breakthrough was made by a half-dozen Soviet tanks subordinated to a cavalry division.[83] As Bock observed in his diary on December 11, "The breakthrough against Second Army is due less to the employment of powerful forces by the Russians than it is to a breakdown by our totally exhausted troops."[84] Schmidt must also be held to account for his army's overextension and exhaustion, especially when his front was already so long. Heinz Postenrieder's diary recorded the sense of confusion and alarm caused by the Soviet attack on Second Army: "The Russians are pushing us closer and closer together. The division gives way, more and more masses of troops come into the small village. A snowstorm rages . . . At 2:30 the radio connection breaks. Shatilovo has been overrun."[85]

By December 12 Army Group Center had endured the first week of the Soviet offensive in reasonably good order. With the exception of Second Army, the long front was either holding or withdrawing largely according to a German agenda. Matériel losses were being incurred, but one should not overstate the value of what was being lost. Many of the broken-down vehicles were in appalling condition, and for the most part, little more could have been expected of them in the prevailing conditions and on the poor eastern roads. More to the point, Soviet attacks were making slow headway and proving particularly costly. Furthermore, in places where they were successful, the advance risked becoming exposed to forceful and, in places like Klin, devastatingly effective German counterattacks. The situation for Bock was serious, but the crisis was a local phenomenon, and in the absence of better intelligence, Army Group Center hoped in vain that the Soviet attacks would soon dissipate.

3

BETWEEN THE HAMMER AND THE ANVIL

Army Group Center Between Hitler and Stalin

T he destructiveness of the German withdrawal was only to some extent directed toward military equipment that could not be evacuated. For the most part, it was felt by the Soviet people themselves. Indeed, while many people associate the devastating German scorched-earth policies with their retreats of 1943–1944, they in fact began in 1941 in the first days of the Soviet winter offensive. It was at this time that the term *Wüstenzone* came into common military usage within the Wehrmacht. *Wüstenzone* can be translated literally as "desert zone" and referred to the level of destruction that was to be carried out. On December 7 Guderian's Second Panzer Army issued an order to all its subordinate corps instructing them that the ground before the new front line must be "so completely destroyed that the enemy will not find any housing or defenses for at least a distance of five kilometers." Two days later Guderian repeated this order, making special mention of the need to "burn villages," a practice that was already evident in some of the divisional war diaries.[1] Major-General Walter Nehring's 18th Panzer Division reported on December 7 that the construction of a "desert zone" had begun "through the burning of all localities" close to its front line. Nehring, however, went much further. Blaming an attack on Red Army men who had infiltrated his lines in civilian clothes, he ordered all military-age men arrested and all women and children marched east across Soviet lines. In one place the women and children were fired upon and forced back to German lines.[2]

Similar activities were occurring north of Moscow. Lieutenant-General Rudolf Veiel's 2nd Panzer Division noted in its war diary on December 6 that before leaving any locality the houses were to be searched and certain items appropriated. These included any textiles, winter clothing, furs, felt boots, white linen for camouflage, domestic appliances, windowpanes, oven pipes, livestock, food of any kind, horse carriages, and above all sleds. On the following day (December 7) a corps order arrived at Veiel's division with instructions on how to conduct the evacuation of the civilian population. All men between fifteen and sixty years of age were to be arrested and transferred to POW camps. The remaining population was to be placed in schools, barns, or churches while their homes were burned down, and then marched to the rear—the Soviets should encounter no buildings or people.[3] General of Panzer Troops Georg Stumme's XXXX Panzer Corps was even preparing for future withdrawals by mining the rear areas, detonating any structures that offered a viewing platform and burning all population centers east of the Istra River.[4] All signage and identifying insignias were to be removed from the roads, with only German graves left intact and unmolested. The locations of these were registered by a responsible officer.[5]

Although the German scorched-earth policy was targeted at the Red Army, the burning of homes and appropriation of valued possessions no doubt condemned countless civilians as temperatures dropped to minus forty degrees Celsius in December.[6] Wilhelm Prüller observed these forced evictions and felt a degree of regret for the fate of the civilians but quickly dismissed it. Writing in his diary on December 7 he noted: "The villages lying in front of us are burned down now, so that the Russians can't use them against us. Behind us on the hills bunkers will be constructed as a winter defense line. Probably we shall move back from here too, and burn down all these villages behind us . . . The population really isn't to be envied. But all softer emotions must be sacrificed for tactical necessity."[7] Some German soldiers felt no remorse whatsoever and even enjoyed burning villages. One letter from a Private Meyer stated: "Every day and every night there is skirmishing between us and the Russians. The burning of villages provides delightful relaxation."[8] Likewise, Gerhard Bopp wrote on December 10: "It's going quickly forwards, or more accurately backwards . . . Unfortunately, we are not allowed to do the 'igniting,' which is left to special detachments."[9] Yet not all German accounts expressed malicious joy. Josef Deck was retreating through the small town of Bogoroditsk (southeast of Tula), which was already going up in flames, when he encountered a woman with her baby who fearfully asked if her home would be burned. Deck soon found out that it would be, but he and his comrades remained behind long enough to ensure that her home was spared.[10] Yet such acts of kindness were the exception, and the sheer scale of these operations was immense. Gerhardt Linke observed so many fires burning around him that they were able to "light up the nocturnal sky."[11]

As Army Group Center struggled to accept its worrisome new predicament, the question of blame was never far from the surface. For months the German high command had relentlessly ordered offensives, always assuming that Soviet reserves were more depleted than their own and that each new attack brought the *Ostheer* one step closer to deciding the war. By December 5 the result was that the panzer forces were devastated, the German armies were operating well in advance of their logistical support, and the men were utterly worn out. At the same time, the Red Army remained a coherent fighting force all along the Eastern Front and was forcing Germany to surrender its most recent gains as well as threatening to demolish the whole mystique of the invincible Wehrmacht. Recriminations for such a state of affairs were not long in coming, and Hitler took the lead. Showing no sympathy, or even comprehension, for Army Group Center's position, he instead attacked the army commanders. As his army adjutant, Major Gerhard Engel, noted from December 8:

> [Hitler] does not believe in fresh Russian forces, considered it all a bluff, assumed it likely that these were the last reserves from Moscow. The OKH enemy reports were exaggerated and deliberately presented in a negative tone. It would not be the first time that Germans had lost their nerve at the fateful hour. He did not want to hear the expression "pull back" again. On and on he continued, but one sees from it all how unsettled and uncertain he is.[12]

While Hitler had his doubts about the information he was receiving, he was not yet seeking to take over command of the army, although he showed almost no regard for Brauchitsch, the commander-in-chief of the army. On December 7 Halder wrote in his diary: "The commander-in-chief is hardly even a messenger boy anymore. The Führer goes over his head to the army group commanders. The worst however is that the supreme command does not understand the condition of the troops and indulges in half measures when only big decisions could help."[13] Halder did not elaborate on what kinds of "big decisions" might have helped the *Ostheer*, but it was clear that Hitler failed to understand, or accept, the turn of events in the east.

On December 9, the day after Hitler had complained about the OKH's supposedly exaggerated reports, Guderian directed his own frustrations at Bock. After setting out the difficulties of his panzer army, he carefully suggested that "among the troops and the non-commissioned officers a crisis of confidence has broken out." Bock inquired in whom they were lacking confidence and, before awaiting an answer, suggested Guderian fly directly to the high command to inform them of this. Guderian did not answer the first question and rejected the second. Bock then strenuously defended himself, telling Guderian that he had made repeated reports on the army group's situation to both the OKH and OKW (*Oberkommando der Wehrmacht*—High Command of the Armed Forces).[14] With nothing else to offer, Bock concluded with a damning repudiation of Guderian's concerns. As Bock recorded in his diary: "The conversation ended with me telling him that complaints were useless here, I could not give him reinforcements, either one held out or let himself be killed. There were no other choices."[15] On one level Guderian's thinly disguised criticism of the German command was justified—certainly from the perspective of the troops and non-commissioned officers—but presenting this to Bock in an accusatory tone, as if Guderian shared none of the blame, reflects the panzer general's audacity and self-deception. While Guderian took aim at Bock, the substance of his message, given Hitler's ardent rejection of the latest OKH reports, was wholly justified.[16] A crisis of confidence in the German leadership on the Eastern Front was entirely understandable and even long overdue. The generals at the front had of course been complicit in bringing about this dire state of affairs, but at least since December 6, once confronted with the implications of their decisions, they were seeking action as well as sometimes scapegoats.

On the evening of December 9, Kluge, who was unaware of the earlier exchange between Bock and Guderian, reported the complaints of Heinrici, commanding the XXXXIII Army Corps, to Army Group Center. Kluge ended his report by quoting Heinrici directly: "The army command seems to have no idea." Bock immediately responded with the same strenuous defense he had offered to Guderian, insisting daily reports had been provided to the OKH and concluding: "I cannot do more. All that I have left is to resign." Kluge responded that Brauchitsch or Halder had to come to the front to see the conditions for themselves.[17] That same evening Bock's chief of staff at Army Group Center, Major-General Hans von Greiffenberg, spoke with Halder about the crisis of confidence in leadership, and they agreed that Brauchitsch should write to the army and panzer group commanders assuring them that he was fully informed of their situation at the front.[18] Brauchitsch's letter of assurance, attempting to convince the generals that he understood all their varied concerns, was a total of just four sentences long.[19] Such a lackluster effort may have done more to confirm, rather than calm, the fears at the front, but more to the point, it was not Brauchitsch anyone needed to convince.

As Halder had written days earlier, the commander-in-chief of the army was relegated to delivering messages, the most important of which he was neither writing nor authorizing. Halder was effectively running the OKH, and while he certainly lacked a credible understanding of what was possible, the real problem was Hitler. In fact, there is no record that any of the discussions about a crisis of confidence in the German leadership ever reached the dictator's ears, which in itself confirmed the extent of the problem. Certainly, Brauchitsch was too cowed and docile to confront Hitler with such an explosive topic, and Halder probably dismissed it for political reasons, suspecting it would only draw the dictator's ire, while harming the OKH's standing even further. Thus, the OKH merely resolved to continue passing on its own daily reports, while Hitler, for the time being, continued to reject their veracity and question their conclusions. The results could be seen in a conversation with Goebbels on December 13 when Hitler confidently told his propaganda minister that the *Ostheer* would push "at least to the Ural [Mountains]" in the course of the coming year.[20] Such statements only confirmed the crisis of confidence among Bock's generals.

While the field commanders were clearly worried about mismanagement and complacency at the highest levels, what the German soldiers themselves thought seems to have varied greatly. There is certainly evidence from their writings that blame was directed at the high command, and while this might be normal in any army, especially one in the predicament of Army Group Center, Hitler was seldom singled out for this kind of criticism. It was the officers who were accused of being the "hero of the rear" and having "definitely never sat in a foxhole."[21] Yet the negative tone and wry barbs are contrasted by the surprising extent to which the men sought to defend their officers, and especially Hitler, from blame. In most instances this seems to have taken the form of supplanting German failure with an overemphasis on Soviet power, allowing the writer to incorporate themes of Nazi propaganda about "hordes from the east." According to this narrative, the smaller German army had performed remarkably well given the huge mismatch in men and resources.

Even after the Soviet winter offensive had begun, faith in the army leadership, and particularly Hitler, was embraced by some of the men as a source of hope. Helmut Günther records an exchange with his fellow soldiers about the strategic situation:

[OBERMAIER:] Stop, you armchair strategists . . . Turn in and go to sleep. If someone heard you talk like that they'd think that those in the rear, who ought to know, are stupid.

[WERNER:] Ivan is already far behind us, closing up the shop and, if we don't watch out, we'll be caught sitting inside!

[GÜNTHER:] You old pessimist. The guys with the red stripes on their pants [general staff officers] will certainly know when it is time for us to worry. Maybe Ivan simply has run out of people.[22]

In another exchange one man told his comrade how bad the general situation looked, to which he received the reply: "That's just your imagination. It's no longer a question of gaining territory but who wins the war of morale. If the Russians imagine we're weak, then they've made a mistake. Don't forget what a marvelous head Adolf has on his shoulders."[23] According to one doctor in Army Group Center it was only after weeks of retreat and crisis upon crisis that in February 1942 he finally concluded that the "hitherto unbounded trust of the troops in the leadership" was lost.[24] Moreover, after a tour of inspection at Army Group Center, Colonel Hermann Ochsner, a representative of the OKH, reported to Halder on December 13 that the mood of the troops was "good."[25]

If the high command still enjoyed a basic perception of competence among the troops it begs the question where any crisis of confidence was rooted. The division and corps files clearly illustrate the acute shortages and problems, and while these were discussed throughout the armies, army group, and OKH, concrete "action" is harder to determine. It seems that taking decisive steps, especially with regard to Hitler, was avoided at the army level and above—those with the only access to Hitler. Why did Brauchitsch, Halder, and Bock not adopt a more forceful tone? Why did Guderian not seize Bock's offer to fly to East Prussia and make his case directly to Hitler? Much of the explanation has to do with the Wehrmacht's pervasive command culture. Their central values of bravery, obedience, devotion to duty, and emotional "hardness" were key in determining how behavior was perceived and evaluated.[26] Complaints, doubts, and vulnerabilities were signs of weakness and reflected more upon the man than the circumstances. Thus, the military culture, especially in Hitler's presence, almost precluded critical assessments. As one former visitor to Hitler's headquarters observed:

> [Field Marshal Wilhelm] Keitel controls the Führer's headquarters. Before his "Generals" or anyone get to Adolf to make a report they are given detailed instructions by Keitel [as to] *what* they are to say, *how* they are to say it, and only then are they allowed into Adolf's presence. For example, if a "General" had to report that a withdrawal was necessary, at the time when the first withdrawals occurred, when people weren't yet accustomed to the idea of Germans withdrawing, they had to say the following: "My Führer, I consider it better not to hold that position but to move here. That is to say, not that we are withdrawing, but because the positions there are more favorable." Whereas that was entirely untrue, they had been flung out.[27]

Keitel certainly served in this role, but the quotation overemphasizes his importance. The predominance of National Socialist military thinking was the real culprit in distorting the messages Hitler received. In Hitler's presence generals typically self-censored their own reports and, in some instances, buckled completely and simply agreed with Hitler. Yet even when the messages came through unfiltered, as could be the case when reports were read aloud, Hitler would often angrily reject the conclusions and launch into a monologue of denunciation as if this invalidated and corrected the problem. The generals of the OKW and OKH typically did not seek to "represent the front," and not because they lacked courage, although some were spineless men; they simply agreed with Hitler. Far from possessing the "steadfastness and impelling energy"[28] that saved the German army in the winter of 1941–1942, Hitler was avoiding the issues but was supported in this by his senior commanders.

A further and more tangible explanation for the compliant attitude of the generals was sheer greed. From 1940 onward, field marshals and colonel-generals, the two highest ranks, received secret monthly tax-exempt supplements to their already generous salaries, which more than doubled their income. On top of this, in 1941 and 1942 select officers also received "birth-day presents" of up to 250,000 RM (reichsmarks), and later in 1944 a small number of generals were also given huge landed estates. The payments were in no way official and were not to be made public under any circumstances. Each recipient was made aware that the money came personally from Hitler and would continue entirely at his discretion. As Norman Goda's research revealed, such payments came with an explicit "quasi-contractual relation-ship in which huge amounts of money would be exchanged for obedience."[29] Thus, Field Marshals Brauchitsch, Bock, and Kluge were earning an illegiti-mate 4,000 RM a month, while Colonel-Generals Halder, Guderian, Hoepner, and Strauss were receiving an extra 2,000 RM a month. Kluge, who enjoyed one of the best relationships with Hitler in 1941, was one of the select few to receive what members of the German resistance would later refer to as a "birthday bond." In October 1942, he received 250,000 RM, a sum also paid to Field Marshals Keitel, Wilhelm Ritter von Leeb (commanding Army Group North), and Gerd von Rundstedt (former commander of Army Group South). After the war the generals made no reference to these payments in account-ing for their actions or inactions during the war.[30] Their wartime devotion to Hitler was often problematic enough without the suggestion that their highly valued honor was in any way influenced by bribery. Obviously, it is impos-sible to know the exact motivation such money played for each man, but the inducement of such large sums can only have won Hitler favor, and the war-time record shows that many of the recipients were not inclined toward confrontation with the dictator.

If the German troops retained a general measure of faith in their com-manders, this is not to say it came without qualifications. The most common complaint was the absence of winter clothing, which by early December 1941 was a criticism that had been dragging on for two months. The extent of the problem justified, in the starkest of terms, a questioning of faith in the Ger-man leadership. More than a month earlier, on November 1, the army's senior quartermaster-general, Major-General Eduard Wagner, gave absolute assur-ances that the *Ostheer* would be adequately supplied for the winter. Goeb-bels was thrilled and wrote in his diary: "Everything has been thought of and nothing forgotten. If the enemy places his hopes in General Winter and believes that our troops in the east will freeze or go hungry he is completely mistaken."[31] However, Wagner's assessment went beyond the wildly optimistic; it was simply impossible. According to Colonel Wilhelm von Rücker, attached to the planning staff of the quartermaster-general's office, "a few hundred additional trains would have had to be sent" to meet the needs of the troops for the coming winter.[32] Not only was there not the transport capacity for winter equipment, but also other high-priority matériel, such as fuel and ammunition, were already failing to arrive in the required quantities, and the quartermaster-general had to have known this.[33]

By November 13 Wagner had had a complete change of heart and acknowledged there were nowhere near enough trains reaching Army Group Center, meaning the urgently requested winter clothing could only be transported to the front at the expense of other supplies and in any case would not arrive until February 1942.[34] As General Schmidt observed in a letter to Lieutenant-General Friedrich Paulus, the senior quartermaster I at the OKH: "As far as winter clothing is concerned, the quartermaster-general deserves every curse that can be hurled at him . . . This total lack of foresight and care makes even these splendid fellows of ours dispirited and rebellious . . . Then in the newspapers they read wonderful speeches—'come what may, this winter our brave soldiers need not fear the cold.'"[35] Clearly, the credibility gap between the Eastern Front and the home front was enormous, and the consequences for morale were immensely damaging.

It was the absence of winter clothing that the troops at the front most squarely associated with incompetence and ineptitude within their own army. As Werner Adamczyk wrote: "I hated the supply troops (they were sitting way back in the rear in warm houses while their support became weaker and weaker)."[36] Some officers did not help perceptions by taking priority on the trickle of winter clothing that was reaching the front. "Some lovely gear has arrived from the homeland," Otto H. observed. "The officers of course get the best stuff, and the ordinary soldiers get the leftovers."[37] Temperatures varied greatly in early December, from minus twenty-nine degrees Celsius on December 7 to minus twelve degrees three days later. On December 13 the temperature fell again to minus twenty.[38] Lacking the appropriate clothing for such freezing temperatures, Lieutenant-General Kurt von

Tippelskirch, who commanded the 30th Infantry Division, asserted after the war: "The weather was a more damaging and dangerous factor than the Russian offensive operations. Besides lowering morale, the weather accounted for the greater part of the German casualties."[39] Even in those sections where weather casualties exceeded battle casualties, one cannot discount the consequences of the fighting as the reason that so many German troops were caught out in the freezing conditions. Nevertheless, there is evidence for Tippelskirch's claim. On the first day of the Soviet offensive, a regiment of Lieutenant-General Justin von Obernitz's 293rd Infantry Division reported 12 dead and 57 wounded in combat, while on the same day 318 cases of frostbite were recorded, with 103 of these requiring amputations. Some of the wounded also froze to death on sleds while being transported to the rear.[40]

With their summer uniforms so inadequate for the freezing conditions, soldiers were wearing anything they could get their hands on. Franz Frisch wrote: "So we covered ourselves up with anything . . . We used bed covers, tablecloths, curtains, anything at all to provide a layer of warmth."[41] Under any normal circumstances wearing nonregulation clothing while in uniform was a serious infraction, but by then everyone was doing so including the officers.[42] Edmund Blandford described his unit as being "wrapped up like mummies" with scarves covering everything but their eyes. The absurdity of their appearance was not lost on the men, but it was no laughing matter. "Outside we were covered in frost and ice and had to keep on the move to prevent freezing up."[43] Similarly, Helmut Günther noted: "Even the wildman picture that we presented in these clothes failed to draw a smile. No longer was there anything to be seen of a military uniform."[44]

With so few winter uniforms available, the civilian population became the obvious target for trying to make good the shortfall. Not only did this pillaging take place, as we have seen, in areas destined to be evacuated, but it also occurred well behind Army Group Center's front. Lieutenant-General Otto von Knobelsdorff, commanding the 19th Panzer Division, ordered searches of the houses in Maloiaroslavets, some forty kilometers behind the front, looking for felt boots, furs, and snowshoes.[45] Josef Eberz wrote how the shortage of gloves in his unit was to be remedied by the local population.

Civilians were told they could receive fifty pfennigs (half a reichsmark) for a pair, but if anyone refused the gloves would simply be seized.[46] Yet there were also pockets of support for the Germans within the occupied population, which owed less to anything the Wehrmacht offered than the past terrors of Soviet rule, especially in rural areas with devout Orthodox beliefs. Wilhelm Hebestreit wrote that the local population would say, "Nix Bolshevism," and that they "could almost never be moved to accept money" for the wares the German soldiers so urgently sought to acquire.[47]

The radical transformation in the appearance of the German army quickly became a potent symbol of decline as well as a convenient tool of Soviet propaganda. The "Winter Fritz" became a stock character of Soviet satire, depicting stereotypical Prussian officers clothed in the outlandish drawers of a babushka.[48] At the same time, the prominent Soviet writer Vasily Grossman published a scathing article in *Krasnaya Zvezda* about the new-look German army: "When marching into European capitals, they tried to look impressive . . . And it was the same men who entered this Russian village one morning. There were shawls over these soldiers' heads. Some were wearing women's bonnets under their black helmets and women's knitted pantaloons."[49] Likewise, the famous Soviet writer Ilya Ehrenburg observed during a tour of the front in January 1942: "One [captured German] sergeant I saw was wearing a woman's knit waist. Many soldiers wrap their heads in women's kerchiefs. Now the Germans do not look very soldierly."[50]

While accounts of the first period of winter fighting on the Eastern Front typically concentrate exclusively on areas where there was combat, it must be understood that long sections of Army Group Center were not actively engaged during the first half of December. When Army Group Center's offensive toward Moscow was finally called off on December 5, only a handful of Bock's divisions were still attacking, the rest having already adopted winter positions. Even after December 6, most of the Ninth and Fourth Armies were left in relative peace until at least the middle of the month. Whenever possible the German soldiers occupied themselves in their bunkers or peasant huts where they not only found shelter from the cold but also engaged in leisure activities.

One of the key problems for soldiers in dugouts, bunkers, or peasant huts was a lack of lighting. This was less a security measure than a simple dearth of candles, lamps, and fuels. As Alexander Cohrs wrote on December 11: "Unfortunately we had absolutely no light. Even during the day, it was so dark that only by straining the eyes could one read something."[51] With short winter days, it was not uncommon for men to sit together for hours on end conversing in the darkness. Yet their conversations built camaraderie as well as providing a more immediate outlet for problems and concerns. As Willy Peter Reese noted: "Our conversations revolved around relief—the perpetual delusion—and around home and flight. Bitterly we complained about hunger, cold, need, and our disappearing position."[52] Rumors about relief, resupply, or reinforcement were a constant source of speculation for the men, and because nobody could typically identify the origins of such hearsay it was usually impossible to confirm or deny what was being said. The fact that everybody was suddenly telling the same story, however, gave it a guise of veracity. Gossip often spread like wildfire because the rumors were generally positive pieces of information that the men wanted to hear and believe. As Wilhelm Prüller noted hopefully in his diary in late December: "Everyone is talking of the rumour that we'll be relieved in January."[53] Yet almost always such enticing rumors proved unfounded, and by the winter months most men had become bitterly resistant to any gossip that only resulted in disappointment. As Max Kuhnert wrote: "Rumours came to our ears that we were to find winter quarters and stay there till spring, when Hitler would resume the offensive and finish the war. If only we could have believed it, it would have been nice, but at the moment we didn't believe anything and more because, since October, we had been hearing similar stories."[54] Indeed, commanders at times tried (unsuccessfully) to stamp out what amounted to disinformation. As one order from Model's XXXXI Army Corps instructed: "All rumour-mongering must be energetically countered immediately. If such cases are found, immediate court-martial-like action must be taken against the guilty."[55] Rumors aside, the shared time conversing among the men was the single most important act in forging camaraderie, allowing fears and joys to find expression and bonds to be made. As Helmut Pabst observed: "In the evening we talk about serious matters; about our situation, our impressions and experiences; about changes in character, about our jobs before the war and those we'll do afterwards; about what is to become of us, of Russia, and of Germany. Then there are jokes."[56]

Humor was one of the most important coping mechanisms for the soldiers at the front even though to the outsider a lot of it would be considered a ghoulish and macabre "gallows humour."[57] As one soldier remarked: "If we made jokes before some mission that were not entirely *kosher*, it was to cover our fear."[58] Similarly, Willy Peter Reese observed: "Our humour was born out of sadism, gallows humour, satire, obscenity, spite, rage, and pranks with corpses, squirted brains, lice, pus, and shit, the spiritual zero."[59] Such black humor often involved irony, which provided an insightful view into the war from the average soldier's perspective. During the winter retreat a cynical expression circulated among the soldiers, often preceded by a reversing of the helmet or field cap: "Forward, comrades, we've got to pull back!"[60] Similarly, the German military abbreviation "Mot," denoting motorized divisions, was sardonically changed by the men to "Hot," reflecting the extent to which their previously mobile divisions had devolved to horse-drawn draft power.[61] Another joke foretold that in 1962 a disheveled band of German soldiers would be found wandering in China who were no longer even able to speak German. They would still wear their medals but would have been forgotten by the high command.[62] When the German high command later issued a special medal for those who had served in the east during the first winter of the war (*Medaille Winterschlacht im Osten 1941/42*) it was mockingly dubbed by the men the "order of the frozen flesh" (*Gefrierfleischorden*).[63]

Helmut Pabst's letters recount in some detail the humor he shared with his comrades, which even in the worst of times he noted, "always gets the better of us." Pretending to be serious, one of his friends would pick up a map of Russia and announce, "Now, once we get to Kazan . . ." (Kazan being over 700 kilometers east of Moscow). Another would follow: "Does anyone know where Asia is?" When one of the men spoke longingly about being home for Christmas, one of his comrades replied: "He didn't say which year." There were also jokes about how one might speak to officers, especially those conducting training exercises who had not served in the east. One man would take on the role of the officer: "200 yards beyond village, Russian infantry! What's your action?" To which another answered: "You tell them you're going to the village to catch a few chickens for the frying pan . . . What else?"[64] Even in the strictly hierarchical Wehrmacht, the relationship between the men and the officers was sometimes familiar enough to allow for humor. When Colonel Heinrich Eberbach was promoted to divisional command after his predecessor was wounded, the "grim wit" of his men wished him *Hals und Bauchschuß*. This was a play on words from *Hals und Beinbruch*, for which the equivalent English expression would be "Break a leg!," but instead Eberbach was essentially being told, "Get shot in the neck and stomach."[65]

After 1941 the Nazi newspaper *Der Völkische Beobachter* published several collections of jokes under the title *Privates Are Laughing: Humor from the Front*. The humor it recorded was often defined by its "bitter" tone, and for men who had to endure the "Russian swamps," supposedly without "wine, women and songs," laughter was the only recourse. According to one submission by Werner Lass and Hans-Adolf Weber, it was only through the hard experiences of the front that soldiers' humor acquired its amusement and joviality. Depictions of German superiority are conspicuously absent, and instead the curious self-directed irony reemerges, including some unlikely (because they were published in the Nazi press) depictions playing upon the German failings of the winter.[66] Yet many of the most "bitter" jokes could never have been published in Nazi newspapers. Hermann Göring was the most obvious target, especially for soldiers, given his extravagant military uniforms covered in what seemed to many excessive decorations. As one joke ran: "Göring recently added an arrow to the many medals on his chest. It's there as a direction sign. 'To be continued on my back.'"[67] "Whispered jokes" about Hitler were also made. "What is the difference between Christ and Hitler? With Christ one died for all."[68] "What is the difference between the sun and Hitler? The sun 'rises' in the East, while Hitler 'sinks' in the East."[69]

German humor was also fed from abroad, with BBC broadcasting providing an endless stream of satirical caricatures of Hitler and his Nazi government. An exiled Austrian actor, Johan Müller, who used the pseudonym Martin Müller, could imitate Hitler speeches so well that people could often only tell it was not the Nazi dictator by what was said. After Hitler had promised "final victory" in 1941, Müller couldn't resist the opportunity to revisit this statement as Hitler at the end of 1941:

My message today coincides with the conclusion of a year in which I guaranteed final victory. But the year has only concluded according to the calendar, the same Gregorian calendar that was forced upon the Germanic world by international Jewry and a Roman pope named Gregor who had been bribed by Freemasons. Do we National Socialists, who have given the world a new order, want to be told by shadowy foreign forces when a year begins and when it ends? No, my radical comrades, I alone am entitled to decide when a year commences and when it concludes.[70]

While joking and laughter helped alleviate the everyday stresses of duty on the Eastern Front, the mortal dangers the men faced could not so easily be brushed aside, and led many to seek protection in seemingly irrational superstitions and charms.[71] There developed concepts of "soldier's fortune," which varied from unit to unit and sometimes from man to man, but typically involved a carefully prescribed ritual or habit of what must, or must not, be done to remain safe. As absurd as some of these were, they were often deadly serious for the men involved. As Henry Metelmann related in one such story:

"My father brought home an old musical box he found in a junk shop," recounted a *Schütze* [infantryman] as we played. "He spent months in secret, taking it apart to clean it until every piece of the mechanism gleamed like new—a Christmas present for Mama. Two ballerinas twirled to the music. Between them were three bells—each chimed a different note. Little bluebirds on wires pecked at two of the bells to make them ring but the third bird was missing. Papa handed her the present as we ate on Christmas Eve. When Mama saw the box, she burst into tears. 'What is it?' Papa asked. Poor Mama couldn't speak. Dabbing her eyes with her napkin she left the table and came back with her purse. She opened it and to our astonishment took out the third bluebird. 'My father brought that very same musical box from France in 1918, when he was a soldier,' said Mama. "I used to play with it for hours on end when I was a little girl but we had to sell it to buy food. I cried my eyes out when I learned it was going so he took off the bluebird and gave it to me to keep. He said it sang a song that only its companions could hear and that one day it would call them back.'" The *Schütze* reached into his tunic pocket and took out a small oilskin bag. "Look," he said, taking the third bluebird from the bag. "Mama said it will take me home safely when it returns to its companions."

"Huh—superstitious nonsense," snorted another member of the machine-gun crew. "If a shell has your name on it, you've had it just like any of us," he said, trumping one superstition with another.

Metelmann concluded the story by explaining that the man with the bluebird was later shot by a sniper but survived. He wrote his mother: "Have been shot through both cheeks but can still talk. The bluebird is coming home. See you soon."[72] While objects or rituals were often the focus of such superstitions, sometimes the veneration of hardened veterans turned to fabled status among younger men, who maintained all manner of myths that typically rendered the idol impervious to harm or a trusted barometer for danger. As Hans Roth wrote in his diary in late December: "There we sit and stare into the open fire. Each of us is occupied in his own thoughts. There is great unrest inside me; I feel that some sort of enormous atrocity is brewing against us. As my comrades all of a sudden cling blindly to my predictions, good or bad, I must not show my feelings."[73] Other forms of superstition could be entirely personal and were less concerned with survival than death. Some men were even said to have "predicted" their own deaths, which was "proven" by farewell letters to relatives or confiding in comrades that they could "feel" their days were numbered. Bernard Häring, a Roman Catholic priest, wrote of one such instance: "As soon as we were unloaded from the lorries, this young man joined me and said, 'I want to make my confession right now. I have a feeling that I am close to my last hour.' So while we walked, he made his confession with striking humility and trust. I still remember the sincerity and purity of this wonderful person. A couple of days later, I heard from his friends that he had been killed while trying to save a wounded comrade."[74]

Although soldiers were typically restricted to the immediate area of the front, there were recreational opportunities even in the east for those fortunate enough to earn passes. One of the most important services offered by the German Red Cross to soldiers of the *Ostheer* was the establishment of so-called "soldier's homes" (*Soldatenheimen*), otherwise referred to as "recovery homes" or "comradeship homes." Nazi propaganda considered them to be "islands of home" behind the front. In April 1941 there were already some 290 soldier's homes mainly in France, Belgium, and Norway, but in 1942 this number had risen to some 600 across Nazi-occupied Europe, including many in Ukraine and Russia. Some of these attracted thousands of soldiers each day, while others accommodated only a few dozen visitors. They provided German meals and were staffed mainly by female relief workers and members of the German Red Cross. All the homes had rooms allocated for reading, writing, music, and discussion.[75] They operated as holiday retreats for the soldiers without enough leave to travel all the way back to Germany. Annette Schücking, a former law student who worked in one such soldier's home in Novograd-Volynskii, noted that the men "hadn't been around women for a long time." There were of course local women, but as Schücking noted, "they couldn't talk to them—and they all had an intense need to talk."[76] On December 7, 1941, she noted that the men "don't complain, never speak about the war, never from operations, they are thankful for a match, a smile, a small remark."[77] Martin Pöppel described his visit to a soldier's home:

As we have a few hours to kill we go to the German soldier's home, once a Russian hotel. It looks grandiose from the outside, but not from within. Very basic furniture, no decoration at all in the rooms. However, we enjoy the excellent goose served up by the Red Cross, by the attractive nurses in their flattering uniform and red Cossack boots. It can't be easy for these young girls, in enemy territory so far from home.[78]

Even as the Soviet winter offensive was gathering momentum in the first half of December, there was as yet no sense of impending crisis across all of the Eastern Front or even within Army Group Center. Soldiers were at last able to read and write Christmas letters, wash their uniforms or clean weapons, and improve what many expected to be their winter quarters. There was even enough free time for boredom to set in. As Werner Adamczyk recalled: "For the time being, the war had come to a standstill. There was no action on either side. All was quiet, except for the howling wind."[79] Instances of "bunker tantrums" stemmed from the stress of large numbers of men having to live together in close proximity.[80] Albert Neuhaus referred to a form of "Russian cabin fever" by which the men in his bunker were constantly snapping at each other and making the atmosphere hard to bear.[81] Willy Peter Reese depicted even more fractious relationships: "We were all sick and irritable. Outbursts of rage and hate, envy, fistfights, sarcasm and mockery stood in for whatever might have remained of comradeship."[82]

Most of the men, however, just appreciated the break. The diary of H. C. von Wiedebach-Nostitz recounted how he and his comrades enjoyed their free time in and around Kaluga behind Kluge's Fourth Army. On December 13 Wiedebach-Nostitz wrote: "The following days are thoroughly comfortable. We have got ourselves a stove and we also have electric light. We have time for reading and writing. We go to the town, take a bath and go to the cinema which is close by." Over the next few days they explored Kaluga, visiting its few shops as well as a Russian tea house with the powerful odor of *makhorka*, the Russian tobacco. It was only on December 19, as they set out in search of a Christmas tree, that they came across a German roadblock and heard that Soviet troops had broken through the front lines twenty kilometers away.[83]

4.

KEEPING THE WOLF FROM THE DOOR

The Panzer Groups Retreat from Moscow

When the Soviet winter offensive began in earnest on December 6, it did not include wide-ranging objectives. The initial plans submitted to the *Stavka* by Zhukov called for only limited counterattacks, aimed at repelling the German pincers threatening Moscow.[1] It was not until this had clearly been achieved that on December 13 the Soviet press triumphantly lauded their success. There had also been success in recapturing the town of Tikhvin from Leeb's Army Group North, but it was the gains before Moscow, against the Wehrmacht's concentrated panzer groups, that became the source of so much pride and joy.[2] Of course the Soviet press could not speak of the cost of these operations, nor the frustrations of Soviet generals at the tactical ineptitude of their lower- and middle-echelon commanders.

On the other hand, in the context of a year like 1941, which had seen the Red Army endure so much incompetence, waste, and loss, the Soviet advance in early December was a dramatic turnaround. As one of Vasily Grossman's friends wrote to him: "I have seen a lot. Everything is very different to how it was in the summer. There are a lot of broken German vehicles on the roads and in the steppe, lots of abandoned guns, hundreds of German corpses, helmets and weapons are lying everywhere. We are advancing!"[3]

The problem with the Red Army's apparent success was that it fired Stalin's imagination for far greater gains, just as Hitler's summer victories had led him to grossly overestimate the strength of the *Ostheer*. From mid-December, Stalin was suddenly speaking about the destruction of Army Groups North and Center as well as a great lunge into the Ukraine.[4] He even told the British foreign secretary, Anthony Eden: "The Russians have already been to Berlin twice [in 1760 and 1813] and will be a third time."[5] In pursuing such outlandish objectives Stalin threatened to squander the Red Army's limited potential. Soviet operations had thus far been modestly successful. On a limited number of fronts, the Germans were being pushed back, not destroyed, while the requisite cost to Soviet forces was sometimes staggering. The situation argued for greater concentration, especially of heavy weaponry and armored forces, but Stalin was captivated by notions of a sweeping general offensive, exploiting the *Ostheer*'s weaknesses all along the front.

Measuring the cost of operations to each side is complicated by many factors, not least because the fighting was so uneven across Army Group Center's vast front. In places, Soviet forces overran German positions, creating havoc and spreading fear, but in other instances, whole Red Army units were annihilated within minutes of beginning their attack. Soviet figures for German losses, even in classified wartime reports, were typically inflated, but if we accepted them as a high-end estimate then between December 6 and 13, the Thirtieth Army, advancing on Klin, captured 186 guns; 1,200 automatic rifles; and just over 1,000 motor vehicles.[6] When one considers that many of those vehicles were either no longer serviceable or provisionally so, the loss to Panzer Group 3 in real terms was less than it appeared on paper. Of course, other Soviet armies would have added to this total, but for the opening week of a major offensive that had achieved almost complete surprise, Soviet war booty was not remarkably high. Naturally, the Soviet press lauded its achievement, and Moscow-based Western war correspondents, like Philip Jordan, filed news stories that noted: "Hour by hour the almost legendary tale of booty grows greater—dead, wounded, captured tanks, guns, rifles."[7] Yet what the Soviet propaganda, trumpeting the spoils of victory, conspicuously failed to address was the cost of these operations to the Soviet units involved—an oversight that made absolute sense at the time but should not color our view of the December fighting.

The early period of Germany's retreat is perhaps best characterized as a forced fighting withdrawal with localized instances of crisis, confusion, and disorder, but it was not true that the German army "collapse[d] with a crash" under "the blows of the Red Army," as excited Soviet newspapers of the time liked to suggest.[8] Indeed, a snapshot of Army Group Center from Bock's diary on December 12 suggests the situation, while serious, was still very much under control. The breakthrough at Schmidt's Second Army was the most pressing concern, but Bock noted that it was "only cavalry" in the gap and had not ruled out "bringing the remnants of the exhausted 45th and 134th divisions back to a covering position," which, within days, would in fact eventuate. The retreat of Guderian's Second Panzer Army, Bock noted, was "going according to plan," although another breach northwest of Tula was "a source of worry." The withdrawal of Hoepner's panzer group was "apparently successful," while "the sparse reports" from Reinhardt's panzer group "sound somewhat more favourable." Strauss's Ninth Army was still threatened around Kalinin, but Bock noted that "on the whole" the latest Russian attacks had been repulsed.[9]

With difficulty and at considerable cost, Army Group Center was so far weathering the Soviet offensive, but many more Red Army units were moving up to the front, and no one knew how much more Army Group Center could take. Cyrus Sulzberger, an American war correspondent who arrived in Moscow on December 13, recalled seeing a constant stream of "Red Army trucks, staff cars and motorcycles on their way to the front."[10] On Army Group Center's northern wing, Strauss's Ninth Army was bitterly contesting every meter of ground around Kalinin and even launched a modestly successful counterattack with the 251st Infantry Division.[11] Hans Meier-Welcker, a staff officer in the division, noted in a letter on December 14 that the attack yielded fifteen captured guns and ten destroyed enemy tanks with more damaged.[12] Yet Strauss possessed almost no mobile reserves, and Reinhardt's neighboring Panzer Group 3 was in no position to afford him support should his situation worsen. Accordingly, Bock issued instructions that "the most thorough possible preparations" for the evacuation of Kalinin begin. The following day (December 14), Soviet pressure forced Strauss to surrender more ground, which further endangered his hold on Kalinin, leading the commander of the Ninth Army to seek and receive permission from Bock to abandon the city "if it becomes necessary." On the evening of December 15, Strauss determined that the moment had come and ordered evacuation as well as the blowing up of bridges on the Volga, Tvertsa, and T'maka Rivers, which all ran through the city.[13]

At Reinhardt's Panzer Group 3, the reprieve granted by the 1st Panzer Division's devastating counterattack on December 11 did not last long, and by December 13 Klin was again seriously threatened, with Reinhardt jotting quickly in his diary: "Terrible evening, emergencies everywhere."[14] Desperate rear-guard actions bought critical time, allowing countless units from the panzer group to pass through Klin and escape the advancing Red Army closing from the northwest, east, and south. The bottleneck was on the road heading west, which was terribly congested and repeatedly blocked by small units from the Soviet Thirtieth Army infiltrating through the porous German lines to the north.[15] Ultimately, Reinhardt's retreat proved too slow, and his line broke west of Klin before Krüger's 1st Panzer Division could escape the town, which was cut off, along with 800 to 1,000 German wounded still awaiting evacuation. A plan to break out was immediately ordered, to be preceded by a feint to divert Soviet forces from the main attack. The operation was launched within hours and achieved complete success. Soviet resistance was swept aside, and the division, with most of the wounded, pushed its way back to German lines. As Major Oldwig von Natzmer wrote: "Substantially intact, the division emerged from the pocket of Klin, taking along its casualties and nearly all of its equipment."[16]

Such an action emphasizes the flexibility of the German panzer division, even in such a reduced state, to adapt, plan, resource, and execute a major operation within just a few hours. It was one of the few instances since December 6 in which Soviet forces had managed to carry out Zhukov's order, not only to get around the flank of a major German formation, but to encircle it. The failure to destroy Krüger's division was masked by the success of liberating Klin, but the event posed a fundamental problem for Zhukov's insufficiently trained and underequipped forces. How were they supposed to destroy German formations without greater support and concentration?

With the battle for Klin over, Model's XXXXI Army Corps asked the panzer group for a clear objective "to strengthen the morale of the troops."[17] The fact that no one seemed to yet know where the retreat was taking them or how much farther they would have to go was understandably a cause for concern, not least for the officers, who were trying to manage meager resources while planning local operations outside of a strategic concept. Willi Lindenbach was a doctor trying to manage the evacuation of his many patients; on December 12 he wrote in a letter home: "The situation is still completely unclear, no soldier, no officer, knows what will actually happen."[18] Reinhardt knew about Bock's proposed line running through Kursk–Orel–Medyn–Gzhatsk–Rzhev–Lake Volgo, but that was some 140 kilometers to the rear, and he asked in his diary, "Why so far?"[19]

The demands of the retreat were punishing for the men and the staff. Landgraf's 6th Panzer Division reported on December 12 that the last tank in the division had been lost, while on the following day it reported that only 300 men remained combat ready and that "the division is no longer operational." Furthermore, it was noted that "one commander and a further four officers collapsed because of exhaustion and strain." The conditions for the divisional staff were barely manageable; thirty officers worked out of one eighteen-square-meter room. The war diary sat on a twenty-liter jerrican, while a door on props was used for the general's map.[20] Even at the panzer group headquarters, the desperate conditions allowed for no indulgence, even for Reinhardt. In a letter to his wife on December 15 the general wrote:

> Myself and my ten general staff officers live in one dirty, completely soot filled room (because of the oven), with a few candle stubs. We are hungry and thirsty (because our food vehicle has got lost) and

worry from hour to hour without news or with changing information good and serious. We sleep—as much as we can sleep with the coming and going, the telephone, the traffic before the window and the nerve-racking tension—until the next morning, when without washing and no breakfast etc. we move to the next headquarters.[21]

If conditions were hard for the staff officers, the men of the panzer group were exposed to far worse. Heinrich Engel told how even in the extreme cold some men preferred to walk because there was a risk of developing frostbite while sitting on vehicles. At night, the limited number of houses meant that men "lay practically on top of each other," while the dysfunction in supply meant that a system of barter developed. Engel recorded the questions on the road: "'Comrades, don't you have a half a can of gasoline for my vehicle? For two cigarettes? Five cigarettes?' We could not help him. We had no reserves of gasoline for ourselves."[22] More worrying were the scenes of destitution and aimlessness among some of the men, which was implicit in the break-down of command and control. Gerhardt Linke wrote during a break from the retreat on December 17: "The sights we saw are unbelievable. Soldiers in a state of utter neglect roam about like real tramps."[23] General of Panzer Troops Ferdinand Schaal, commanding Reinhardt's LVI Panzer Corps, be-lieved that control over the situation was slipping away: "Discipline began to crack. There were more and more soldiers making their way back to the west, without any weapons, leading a calf on a rope, drawing a sledge with potatoes behind them—just trudging westward with no one in command . . . It was the most difficult time the panzer corps ever had."[24] While the order and discipline of the German retreat were clearly in danger, Albert Neuhaus at least provided one weighty explanation for why the men endured and kept going. As he wrote in a letter to his wife on December 15, while the men may not have known where exactly they were going, "they are all happy about coming closer to the homeland."[25]

Reinhardt's flagging discipline was as much a response to Army Group Center's predicament as it was one of its causes. The worse discipline be-came, the more it fed disorder and in rare instances panic. Given that the retreat was always racing the Soviet advance, the withdrawing German columns were only protected by whatever units were deployed to form a rear guard, but in the often confused circumstances, this was no guarantee of security. The mere suggestion of Soviet tanks was sometimes enough to set off a panic, which often ended whatever order prevailed in traffic control. When a Soviet attack was snapping at the heels of Heinrich Engel's unit, he noted later in his diary: "When we wanted to join the column on the road there was frantic activity. Everyone tried to get back fast, but the column only moved slowly. Often two or three vehicles were next to one another. That caused the notorious jams."[26] Hans von Luck recalled desperate scenes in which wounded men, left on the side of the road, would plead: "Take us with you or else shoot us."[27] Gerhardt Linke lamented the waste of such frantic flights to the rear as all manner of equipment and munitions were dumped for the sake of speed. Writing in his diary on December 16 he noted: "Everywhere smashed up vehicles were lying upside down, the goods they were carrying scattered all over the place. Frequently they had been abandoned in too great haste. Morale and discipline have been among the chief sufferers during the retreat. How much valuable ammunition that could have been saved was jettisoned here!"[28]

Cohesive and disciplined formations became the backbone of the German defense. The war diary of Krüger's 1st Panzer Division noted on December 15 that despite the "complete exhaustion and terrible tension" of the past days, "the troops never lost their sense of security in the face of the enemy."[29] The best commanders fostered this sense of security, even when they had nothing tangible to offer their distressed men. As Reinhardt wrote to his wife on December 15: "I was with my men daily, not to enforce regulations, that was not necessary, but so that everyone knew it was do or die. Through my presence I showed that, even when I couldn't help them, at least I was prepared to live, feel and suffer with them."[30] Such gestures from the highest officers in the field did wonders for inspiring devotion, while squeezing every last drop of vitality from the men.

Yet all the goodwill in the world was no substitute for matériel factors when the Soviet advance became too threatening. It was in these circumstances that Panzer Group 3 flashed its teeth by launching short and sharp counterstrokes. These obviously had a tangible effect on Soviet forces, but more important they had an intangible effect, far beyond their frequency, in making Soviet commanders uneasy about exploiting too far too fast. As Timothy Wary's study of German defensive doctrine observed of the winter fighting, "When breakthroughs were achieved, follow-up thrusts minced timidly forward as Soviet commanders looked fearfully to their flanks for non-existent German ripostes."[31] Yet often enough German counterattacks were very real, such as one Funck's 7th Panzer Division launched on December 12 with some tanks and about 100 men. Soviet casualties were not recorded, but their forward positions were overrun, and Funck's men captured mortars and five antitank guns.[32] Not surprisingly, Hans von Luck, who served in Funck's division, noted of the winter retreat: "Except for intense reconnaissance activity, the enemy made no very strong direct pursuit of us."[33]

With Klin now behind Reinhardt's panzer group and Bock's proposed winter line still a long way to the rear, an interim line was adopted that was much closer to Panzer Group 3's current position. This new line followed the Lama River south from the Volga Reservoir through Volokolamsk. A frozen river typically offers little of a defensive asset, but the Lama had already been fortified on both banks by the Red Army to oppose Bock's November offensive. The positions were rudimentary, but with the ground frozen to a depth of one meter, they offered an enormous advantage to Reinhardt's men in the coming battles.[34] The Lama Line was occupied from December 16 onward, but a dispute soon arose over how best to deploy its limited formations. A telling entry from the war diary of Veiel's 2nd Panzer Division reflects the changing conception of warfare against a numerically superior foe. Dating from December 11, the entry read: "The division is of the opinion that it could contribute much more to the great defensive battle if it were concentrated instead of being loaned out to positions, where the infantry cannot hold and panic when attacked by small reconnaissance patrols."[35] Yet Colonel Hans Röttiger, who was Model's chief of staff at XXXXI Army Corps, later wrote of the corps' positions along the Lama: "The Russian usually noticed very soon the gaps which thus formed along this line, consisting solely of strong points. Taking advantage of this condition, they carried out thrusts into the depth and rear of the position. Rigorous training was necessary to convince the troops of the necessity of occupying as uninterrupted a front line as possible."[36] In practice strongpoints were more and more the preference of the men—whatever their orders demanded—both because of the added sense of security, but also because strongpoints were typically centered on systems of bunkers, a hamlet or a village where there was the promise of warmth.[37]

Reinhardt's line along the Lama River was soon under heavy Soviet attack. Before noon on December 18, Krüger's 1st Panzer Division was attacked three times in battalion strength at one position and four times in regimental strength at another. Yet as the panzer group's war diary noted: "All attacks were repelled with heavy losses in blood for the enemy."[38] Major-General Erhard Raus, at the 6th Panzer Division, wrote after the war that enemy tactics tended to be both predictable and crude. Attacks usually proceeded along existing roads or paths beaten into the snow by vehicles. They built "snow tunnels" toward the German positions, which channeled Soviet attacks and resulted in heavy losses. Worst of all, Soviet commanders insisted upon using infantry charges to break through the German positions, which could succeed against isolated foxholes but not against suitably fortified positions. It was not only the futility of these attacks, but their staggering repetition that astonished German soldiers. As Raus noted: "Mowed down by machine guns, the first wave would be followed by a second attack, which moved forward a short distance over the bodies of the dead before coming to a standstill. This was repeated by as many as ten waves, until the Russians bogged down from heavy losses and exhaustion."[39]

While Panzer Group 3's static defense clearly exacted a high toll on Soviet attacks, Röttiger, at XXXXI Army Corps, noted that a more "active" approach to holding the Lama Line was the most effective form of defense. "Most of the time," Röttiger wrote after the war, "we carried out an offensive defensive and, inflicting heavy losses on the enemy, repelled all attacks which the Russians launched against the Lama position." Not only did the Lama Line grant the panzer group a strong position from which to defend and launch counterattacks, but also, according to Röttiger, it allowed his corps a general reprieve to rebuild some of its combat strength.

[XXXXI] Corps used this lull at the front to rehabilitate and organize its units, which had been heavily mauled and partly intermingled in

the course of the proceeding engagements . . . By replenishing our
deleted ranks with newly arrived reinforcements and by repairing
our weapons, we were able to increase slowly our combat strength
and combat effectiveness. All elements of the divisions which
were not needed for the operation were moved to "rehabilitation
centers" in the rear . . . As a result, command and troops viewed the
approaching winter warfare with increasing confidence.[40]

If Röttiger took solace from occupying the position on the Lama, it was
in many ways a reflection of the hard days that proceeded it. Panzer Group
3's retreat from Klin was paralleled to the south by Hoepner's Panzer Group
4, which likewise endured grueling days during its retreat west to the Lama
and more southerly Rusa Rivers. Hoepner wrote to his wife on December 12
about the immense strain under which he and his panzer group labored:

One only gets bad news. It is frightening to hear the telephone ring
and it is never quiet . . . The mass of Russians is crushing us. Their
fighting spirit is low, but our people are overtired, they fall asleep
standing up and are so lethargic that they no longer throw themselves
to the ground when shot at. Losses from frostbite are almost as
numerous as those from battle. Our situation has despairing
similarities with Napoleon in 1812 . . . It is incredibly hard to keep
one's nerve. The commanding generals scream for help. Almost every
day [General of Infantry Hermann] Geyer [commanding the IX Army
Corps] sends a written jeremiad. In addition, Kluge and Bock call
from the rear; question, question, give advice and orders that are
not possible to implement. Even [Colonel Walter Chales de] Beaulieu
[the chief of staff at Panzer Group 4] has become thick-skinned and
abrasive on the telephone. Incidentally, he is so nervous that he can
no longer sleep at night.[41]

The war diaries from Panzer Group 4's formations certainly justify
Hoepner's harrowing sense of foreboding at what he was hearing, and this
was compounded by his inability to offer any substantive relief to his hard-

pressed commanders. Each local crisis had to be handled with whatever resources were to hand because typically nothing and no one was available
to come to their aid. As a case in point, Major-General Walter Scheller's
11th Panzer Division sustained a heavy Soviet attack in the early morning
of December 18 that broke through its lines and led to the capture of an important town behind its front. With no prospect of external reinforcement,
Scheller ordered the last divisional reserves and every one of his few remaining tanks to gather for an immediate counterattack. By midday the Soviet
offensive had been halted, ten Soviet tanks were destroyed, and the town
recaptured.[42]

Certainly not every division had the resources to react with such success,
yet higher-level commanders had to be careful to separate what was real from
the confusion, fear, and fatigue that sometimes blackened the reports of desperate commanders. Many of the reports about local breakthroughs quickly
lurched toward dire predictions, which sometimes reflected more the strain
on the officers than the actual events on the ground. Even the highest-level
commanders sometimes reflected this mind-set. On December 13, when one
sector of General of Infantry Richard Ruoff's V Army Corps was broken by
twenty Soviet tanks, he insisted that the whole front of his corps was about
to collapse.[43] This did not happen, and the crisis soon passed, which is not to
suggest the peril was not real, but fear was clearly becoming a factor even
at the high levels. One might even suggest that the phenomenon identified
as "panzer fright," when men fled their positions for fear of Soviet tanks—
sometimes even before attacks were launched—was creeping its way up the
chain of command. As Hoepner indicated in his letter home, the struggle was
as much about holding one's nerve as commanding his forces. With a chorus
of frantic voices screaming for help, and 1812 in the back of many minds,
the needs of the front required a ruthless triage of priorities. The frightened
men were no longer simply those at the front, and Hoepner moved quickly to
address the thinly disguised panic emanating through the telephones at his
headquarters.

On December 14 Hoepner sent out an order to all his corps commanders,
including those in Panzer Group 3. His message was clear: "Firm leadership
of all units is required, including rearward services." Hoepner then listed

what this meant in practice: "Ruthless action against panic mongers, stimulate troops through making them aware the battle is about life and death, use each weapon to the last cartridge, attack tanks that break through, take with you all heavy weapons." As for the civilian population, the panzer groups were to take no chances: "Any hostile attitude by the population is to be immediately, severely punished."[44] Looking to stimulate the troops and arrest fraying nerves, some of Hoepner's corps commanders had already issued orders to similar effect. Stumme, who commanded XXXX Panzer Corps, evoked National Socialist rhetoric when he told his men: "The final victory is assured for us, if we remain hard on ourselves, willing for battle and, with the certainty of our superiority to the enemy, each does his duty."[45] For those, however, who did not do their duty, the penalty was to be severe.

For some time, commanders across the Eastern Front had complained that the extraordinary demands on their men, as well as the loss of so many officers, was responsible for a rise in indiscipline. In late November, an incident involving eight soldiers found guilty of neglecting their duty while on guard led to prison sentences of at least three years (and some much longer). The problem was that these men committed, according to German army regulations, a serious offense, but in consequence were being granted the opportunity to escape the privations and relentless hardships of the Eastern Front. This seemed insufficient punishment to many officers, and so Nehring, the commander of the 18th Panzer Division, made it known to his troops on November 29, 1941: "As all instructions and warnings, as well as the publication of previous sentences by court-martial to long prison terms have hitherto had no instructive and deterring effect, the court-martial is compelled to threaten with making use in the future of the heaviest punishment—the death sentence."[46]

It seems that Nehring's order did not, however, take immediate effect. Two weeks later, in mid-December, an NCO withdrew his men from the front without orders because he feared a Soviet tank attack was imminent. He was charged with cowardice and sentenced to ten years in prison. By the end of December, however, a new order was issued to the men of the division: "Corporal Franz Aigner, staff company II/Panzer Regiment 18, was sentenced to death by court-martial on the charge of cowardice . . . Every case of cowardice will be severely atoned for with death. The troops are thoroughly to be instructed on this by the company commanders personally."[47] Indeed, throughout 1942, the death penalty for soldiers in the Wehrmacht increased tenfold over 1941, from 102 sentences to 1,192.[48]

While penalties were certainly becoming much harsher, many soldiers in fact avoided any sentence at all, especially for desertion, because in the chaos of the retreat men easily became separated from their units and could take days to find them again. It was therefore very difficult to separate the many lost from the few deserters. One solution was the establishment of rearward collection centers, which prevented anyone, aside from logistics personnel, from passing through. All others were formed into scratch combat formations and sent back up to the front.[49] The "rehabilitation centers" that Röttiger wrote about were a more formal variation on this model, taking in shattered formations and offering them short periods of rest, while their depleted units were reorganized into a smaller number of new formations.[50]

Beyond the encroaching Red Army, the problem that most threatened Hoepner's withdrawal was the lack of fuel for his vehicles. Already on December 9, the panzer group's war diary had warned that "a supply crisis must result" given the high consumption rates and very limited deliveries of fuel.[51] Six days later, the war diary reported that the situation had become "catastrophic," with operational tanks and trucks being destroyed simply because they lacked the fuel to continue the retreat. The panzer group therefore requested urgent supplies of fuel be flown to forward airfields.[52] On December 16 Stumme's XXXX Panzer Corps suggested prohibiting any further retreat until fuel supplies could be brought forward because the alternative entailed "countless losses in vehicles."[53] Major-General Gustav Fehn's 5th Panzer Division projected 500 to 600 of its vehicles would have to be left behind if more supplies of fuel did not arrive soon. On December 17 the panzer division reported fuel supplies for 50 percent of its vehicles sufficed only for another ten kilometers.[54] Nor was it simply the retreat that suffered; the protection afforded by local counterattacks depended equally upon fuel supplies and Major-General Walter Scheller's 11th Panzer Division had used so much in one recent attack that on December 14 it reported the possibility of having to destroy its own vehicles and even some tanks.[55]

Part of the problem was the lack of traction on the icy roads, which kept fuel consumption rates high and forced vehicles to drive long distances in the low gear. As one soldier noted on December 14: "The icy ground caused us much trouble. It took tremendous effort to drag the machines up the steep inclines."[56] Helmut Günther encountered the same problem, describing one hill as "a sheet of ice" with vehicles again and again sliding down or off to one side. Men attempted to place rags on the road, while others pushed. Some succeeded to the top, but the congestion was so great that impatient drivers attempted to find a new overland route through the snow-filled fields; most were soon stuck fast.[57] Walter Tilemann recounted the chaos caused by an antitank trench, which was some fifty meters deep and slowed all movement to a crawl, even with the greatest of effort. As Tilemann recalled: "All the soldiers were very agitated. I heard hectic orders. 'Damned rat trap,' growled one soldier. 'God have mercy if Ivan attacks now.'"[58] That was exactly what happened, and chaos ensued. "Flashes, deafening thunder, fire, gun smoke, cracked metal and screaming men . . . It was a matter of chance whether one survived or was torn apart."[59]

The winter conditions introduced countless complications that German commanders had simply never anticipated. Writing to his wife on December 17, Hoepner conceded: "I'm going through terrible days. At night I am tormented by the memories of 1918. But here, in war against the winter, one is even more powerless than against the enemy."[60] The shortage of fuel and vehicles meant that increasing amounts of matériel also had to be left behind. Major-General Wolfgang Fischer's 10th Panzer Division reported on December 17 that it had to abandon, and therefore destroy, 120 tons of munitions, 300 rifles, and 10 trucks.[61]

Yet the Germans' destructiveness was never more complete than when they took on Russian homes and infrastructure. As Gustav Schrodek observed: "'Scorched earth'—a terrible phrase! Even worse was the reality."[62] Other German soldiers also felt uneasy about such wanton destruction, which as one observed was not "commensurate with our perception of ourselves as a civilized people."[63] Sometimes, however, their aversion was motivated by self-interest: "I would not like to be taken prisoner in the next Russian offensive, because I can more or less imagine what they will do to

German prisoners after they have come through the areas we have emptied and the burnt-out villages and find the [Soviet] soldiers executed by the side of the road."[64] One order on December 15 from General of Panzer Troops Heinrich Freiherr von Vietinghoff's XXXXVI Panzer Corps called for limiting the burning of Russian towns "for propaganda reasons." Later on the same day, however, a corrective was issued: "On the order of the panzer group, all towns are to be burned, because prisoners of war inform us that among the Russians considerable instances of frostbite have occurred."[65] Sometimes the destruction was limited, such as in Solnechnogorsk, where only a small number of the town's buildings were destroyed because they were made of stone and there were not enough explosives available.[66] On the whole, however, Panzer Group 4's scorched-earth policy was as systematic as it was destructive. As Josef Deck wrote on December 14: "The burning villages on the road were completely devoid of life. People and animals had been collected and driven away."[67]

The human cost was simply accepted by the German command, although the implications for the civilian population were plainly apparent to both officers and men. Fritz Farnbacher agreed that the burning of civilian houses "has to be done," but he then added: "We also aren't allowed to ask if the civilian population starves, freezes or dies in some other way."[68] During the retreat the new command post for Panzer Group 4 was relocated to a house in the town of Gzhatsk on the Smolensk-Moscow highway; however, in the war diary a point was made of commenting on how difficult it was for the responsible officer to remove the people living there, as they had simply refused to go.[69] Witnessing another eviction, Henry Metelmann noted how the process was handled:

> Our orders were to occupy one cottage per crew, and to throw the peasants out. When we entered "ours," a woman and her three young children were sitting around the table by the window, obviously having just finished a meal. She was clearly frightened of us, and I could see that her hands were shaking, while the kids stayed in their seats and looked at us with large, non-understanding eyes. Our Sergeant came straight to the point: "*Raus!* [Out!]" and pointed to

the door. When the mother started to remonstrate and her children to cry, he repeated *"Raus!,"* opened the door and waved his hand towards the outside in a manner which could not be mistaken anywhere . . . Outside it was bitterly cold . . . I watched them through the small window standing by their bundles in the snow, looking helplessly in all directions, not knowing what to do . . . When I looked back a little later, they were gone; I did not want to think about it anymore.[70]

German soldiers who did choose to think about such actions justified them in a variety of ways. Hans Rehfeldt accused the Russians of having done the same things when they were on the retreat.[71] Walter Böttger claimed that no consideration needed to be shown for the civilian population because in Russia "the law of war governs."[72] After the war, Hans Sturm went so far as to portray Germany's scorched-earth policy as a Soviet-concocted fiction: "Russian assault troops torched their own villages to make the German retreat more difficult. Later, many of these crimes would be blamed on the Germans, and many POWs condemned for it in show trials in 1949."[73] Whatever the consequences, German occupation policies ruthlessly served their military objectives and helped sustain the retreat.

Despite his losses in matériel and some local points of crisis, Hoepner's panzer group managed to fall back in reasonably good order to the Lama and Rusa Rivers. This was a source of huge relief to the men of the panzer group, who knew all too well from their own offensive operations that the Soviets needed only to get ahead of the slow-moving German retreat in order to turn an organized withdrawal into a calamitous rout. As Gustav Schrodek from the 11th Panzer Division wrote: "Given the circumstances, everything went relatively well as far as Volokolamsk [on the southern reaches of the Lama River]. In and of itself—amazing. We had grown accustomed to quite other scenes during the Russian retreats."[74] Likewise, Helmut Günther recalled: "If the Russians had pursued immediately with all their available forces, chaos would have been the inevitable result. Incomprehensibly, they only followed hesitantly, at least here in the sector between Istra and the Rusa [River]."[75] Of course, the Red Army had its own problems with mobility in the freezing conditions, but command and control also hindered the speed of the Soviet advance. Hoepner's retreat was largely complete by December 18, although at this point Soviet forces, following close behind, began to heavily assault the new line.

Scheller's 11th Panzer Division was attacked by Soviet tanks, and its line was broken, causing some measure of consternation. However, Hoepner's order from December 14 required immediate counterattacks at points of enemy penetration. A hastily assembled battalion threw back the Soviet force, destroying ten enemy tanks in the assault, but German casualties were such that the unit was deemed no longer fit for combat.[76] In other areas of the front, Soviet assaults were beaten back, even when supported by tanks. On December 18 Thoma's 20th Panzer Division reported destroying six enemy tanks and damaging two more, while on the same day the nearby 255th Infantry Division eliminated nine Soviet tanks.[77] As Benedikt Sieb recalled: "The Russians were everywhere with tanks, they could drive because the ground was frozen hard. They attacked left, right and centre. We had to lay mines quickly so that the tanks couldn't break through."[78] German troops were typically impressed by the bravery and resolve displayed by Soviet troops, but having taken part in so many attacks themselves, they often observed elementary mistakes which were exploited to full advantage. As one German soldier wrote home on December 14: "The Russian is a very good, hard soldier. None of us thought the Russian would be as good as he is. He is as strong as us in weaponry, only the leadership is missing."[79]

With Reinhardt's and Hoepner's panzer groups withdrawn up to 100 kilometers westward, Army Group Center's front was now much straighter and, consequently, considerably shorter than it had been two weeks previously. The retreat north of Moscow had proven costly but was by no means a calamity. Indeed, the Red Army's gains had come at a much greater cost in lives. But to observers on either side of the front, soldiers and civilians alike, Germany's retreat from Moscow was what mattered. For the first time on a large scale, Germany's much-vaunted Wehrmacht was seen to be recoiling in the face of the enemy. Philip Jordan in Moscow listed some of the liberated Soviet villages and towns and then remarked that these were "small victories, which when added together make a formidable total."[80] At the same time, in

Germany, Helmuth James von Moltke, an aristocrat and avowed opponent of the Nazi regime, wrote in a letter on December 12: "There is constant bad news from Russia. Not only that we are retiring along the whole front, but also that there are signs of disintegration among the troops, which bode ill. There are reports that north of Moscow tank units blew up their armored vehicles . . . The whole eastern front may offer a very surprising picture in a few days."[81]

5

DIGGING IN HIS HEELS

Hitler Orders a Halt

A s Army Group Center fought for its survival, of critical importance was the fact that every soldier, whatever his field of specialization, had received the infantry's rigorous combat training. Thus, in any emergency, rear-areas service personnel could be expected to function competently and follow basic tactical commands.[1] In fact, many had seen some measure of action during the preceding months in the Soviet Union, and some men even maintained that fighting in the infantry, while physically demanding, was not technically difficult. Heinz Frauendorf stated: "When it comes to actual warfare, it may sound cynical, but you just get used to it. You get into a routine and develop an almost animalistic instinct about it."[2] The Soviet attacks they were called to repel often proceeded in such predictable and unimaginative forms that in at least one instance the troops questioned if the Soviet tactic was to first exhaust German ammunition before launching a serious attempt to break through their lines.[3] It all underscored the delicate balance between Soviet numerical superiority and tactical ineptitude versus German professionalism and overextension.

At Kluge's Fourth Army the pressure from the Soviet offensive varied from slight to moderate. Up to December 18 Lieutenant-General Friedrich Kirchner's LVII Panzer Corps and General of Infantry Friedrich Materna's XX Army Corps troops were still in the same positions they had occupied since late October. The same was true at Strauss's Ninth Army for General of Infantry Albrecht Schubert's XXIII Army Corps and General of Engineers Otto-Wilhelm Förster's VI Army Corps. This is not to suggest these formations did not experience combat—there had been large-scale Soviet attacks since December 5—but they were not being forced to cede ground, engage in a retreat, or confront a situation that might be considered critical. Clearly, the focal points of retreat did not tell the whole story of Army Group Center.

By the same token, Kluge had his own very real concerns. In addition to the fact that Hoepner's and Reinhardt's panzer groups came under the umbrella of Fourth Army's command, and were therefore Kluge's responsibility, the army had an unresolved emergency on its southern flank. As Bock noted in his diary on December 18: "The several day-old threat of new pressure on the right wing of the Fourth Army is uncomfortable. The enemy has crossed the Oka [River] and forced back the very weak forces there. The Russians also attacked the Fourth Army's other fronts, largely without result."[4] Hellmuth Stieff, Kluge's operations officer, nervously observed on December 13 that the army possessed no reserves, while new Soviet forces were constantly being deployed. Yet much of Fourth Army's front was fortified, and importantly, it had not completely exhausted itself during the November offensive on Moscow, allowing Stieff to conclude: "in our current condition it's enough for now."[5] Over the following days Fourth Army's position did not change much at all, but Kluge's staff were anxiously reading the reports of retreats to the north and south, knowing that if these were to continue they would also have to pull back in order to maintain contact on the flanks. The alarm at what was taking place and the fear about where it all would end caused Stieff to write in a letter on December 17: "It is the worst situation so far that a German army has found itself in, including the World War. But somehow we will and *must* be the master of the situation, because all our lives depend upon it."[6]

Kluge's concern about his southern flank resulted from Guderian's negligence. The Soviet breakthrough west of Tula split Heinrici's XXXXIII Army Corps and Geyr von Schweppenberg's XXIV Army Corps, both of which belonged to Second Panzer Army. Yet Guderian refused to take any responsibility, ignoring the gap and expecting Kluge to find the resources to deal with it, which elements of the 137th Infantry Division were sent south to do. In fact, in a letter to his wife, Guderian disingenuously complained, "my northern neighbour ruptured again," and then suggested he could offer no help "because I cannot overturn the entire eastern front on my own."[7] Bock was again very frustrated with Guderian, who had earlier opposed sending any reinforcements to Schmidt's embattled army but was now demanding Kluge deal with the twenty-kilometer gap in his own lines. Colonel Gustav Harteneck, Schmidt's chief of staff at Second Army, proposed a solution to Bock on December 12 that won his army the support it so badly needed. He suggested that a single command should be created from Tula down to Kursk to better direct resources, which effectively meant subordinating Second Army to Guderian's Second Panzer Army. Bock immediately liked the idea because he knew Guderian's opposition to sending help south was based largely upon his resentment toward losing "his" formations to another army. Schmidt appears not to have liked the idea, but Bock made the decision anyway.[8]

Guderian then commanded two armies, which the Second Panzer Army's war diary proudly referred to as "Army Group Guderian."[9] Not surprisingly, Guderian was suddenly much more amenable toward sending aid to Second Army, which immediately followed in the form of Licht's 17th Panzer Division. Yet he was still stubbornly refusing to address the gap west of Tula, which admittedly was difficult given Soviet pressure on other areas of his long front. But his stubbornness with authority often paid off. Indeed, it was not the first time that Bock had perhaps granted Guderian too much autonomy in his command. Kluge was certainly of the opinion that Guderian needed to be kept on a much tighter rein and would shortly seek to do so.

In the meantime, Bock attempted to convince Guderian that the Tula gap had to be addressed. On December 15, after what he described as a "difficult conversation," Bock wrote in his diary that Guderian "refuses to acknowledge any possibility of closing it [the Tula gap] from the south."[10] In his memoir Guderian simply blamed Kluge, claiming that the four battalions of the 137th Infantry Division sent to his aid were "totally inadequate" and that, as a result, the "vital gap could not be closed."[11] It was to become a wound in the side of Army Group Center, and the longer it went unattended the more it would fester, but neither at the time nor afterward would Guderian accept any responsibility for what was to transpire.

The danger of such gaps was illustrated in Schmidt's Second Army, where the breach in the front was growing. As the army's war diary noted on December 13: "From a tactical breakthrough it has become an operational [offensive] because no reserves are available behind the front."[12] Both Lieutenant-General Conrad von Cochenhausen's 134th and Lieutenant-General Fritz Schlieper's 45th Infantry Divisions were caught behind the Soviet advance and ordered to fight their way back.[13] Heinz Postenrieder served in Cochenhausen's division and wrote in his diary on December 14: "It is barely light and all hell breaks loose . . . I partake in an infantry counterattack, MG whistles, bullets whiz by like bumble bees, low-flying Russian airplanes attack the fleeing columns, mow down horses, cars burn. I lie pressed to the ground, shoot and have given up hope of seeing home or my Christl again."[14] Cochenhausen's division took until December 15 to reach German lines but arrived in surprisingly good order, although Cochenhausen himself suffered a nervous breakdown on the night of December 13 and shot himself in his car. Schlieper's division was not so fortunate, being broken up with heavy losses, while scattered formations made their way back to German lines on December 16.[15] One surviving soldier from the 45th Infantry Division later wrote of his "horror" at learning that his unit had been surrounded and claimed to have remained behind enemy lines for up to two weeks, "constantly attacked by the Russians. Many nights we had sacrifices, I will not forget what we were doing during this time. This no one at home can imagine."[16]

The problem with closing the gap was that Schmidt's remaining five divisions were all dangerously overstretched, including his sole panzer division, Lieutenant-General Alfred Ritter von Hubicki's 9th Panzer Division. Indeed Hubicki's division provides a telling example of the brazen overextension within Schmidt's army. On December 12 the panzer regiment retained just ten operational tanks, while the division had only 25 percent of its nominal matériel. Its combat strength amounted to five understrength battalions with which Hubicki had to hold a front forty-five kilometers in length. As the divisional war diary complained: "A well-led Russian attack must tear the thin, overstretched forward line wide open."[17]

The collapse of Schmidt's front forced the general retirement of his whole line, which was conducted immediately. Willy Peter Reese, from the 95th Infantry Division, wrote in his journal of the extremely taxing physical demands caused by conducting the retreat entirely on foot:

> The moonlight shone down on the silent column of fugitives slowly making their way through the snow, reeling, slithering, stumbling westward. Ahead of us was uncertainty, perhaps no-man's-land, perhaps the enemy; behind us, certainly, the pursuing Russians. We were dog-tired on this third night without sleep . . . We staggered on. Even as we marched, we were overmanned by sleep. Our eyes closed, our legs went mechanically on; then our knees went, and we keeled over, awakened by pain, by the fall, pulled ourselves together, knelt, someone helped us to our feet, and with the last strength lent us by the fear of death, we trotted on. Any rest spelled death, we were told. The Russians are coming! That call worked like the crack of the whip: On![18]

Another soldier from the 262nd Infantry Division wrote home in a letter on December 18: "The retreat totally exhausted us, the constantly overstrained nerves sometimes wanted to give up. We just hope that we can celebrate Christmas in peace."[19]

By December 17 reinforcements were arriving to help patch the breach in Schmidt's line, and the retreat in the south was ordered to a halt at the town of Livny (120 kilometers southeast of Orel). Here the Soviets directed

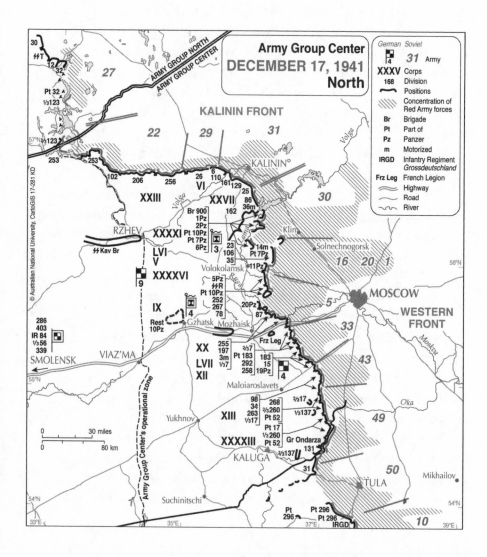

a renewed attack, but given the town's strategic importance this had been anticipated, and the available German forces were concentrated and dug in. As the war diary of the XXXXVII Panzer Corps noted on December 16, the watchword for the defending German battle group was "Be strong where the enemy comes, the rest of the area just monitor with reconnaissance patrols." Once again, the tactical result was unambiguously one-sided. The six enemy

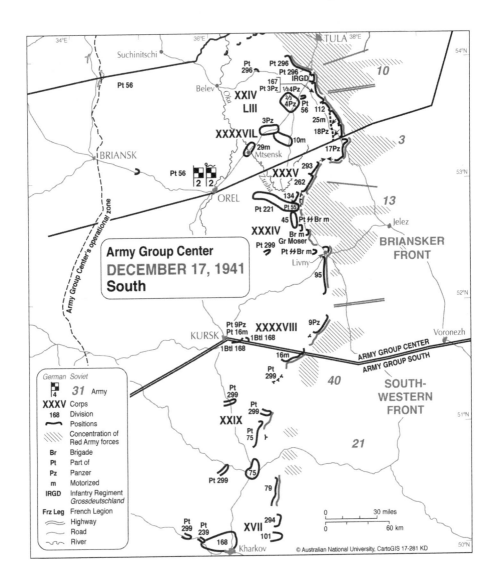

Army Group Center
DECEMBER 17, 1941
South

© Australian National University, CartoGIS 17-281 KD

attacks, from numerous directions, were blunted with heavy losses. As the war diary continued: "A great number of dead were counted, prisoners and booty were captured."[20] Clearly, German experience and tactical superiority, identifying where the Red Army was likely to attack and positioning itself for maximum advantage, ensured victory despite the corps' tired and deprived troops. Even Hubicki's ramshackle 9th Panzer Division proved itself to be a potent force when on December 17 it identified a large gathering of Soviet forces and launched a preemptive attack with its small number of tanks. It forced the enemy to retreat in chaos and recorded some five hundred enemy dead.[21] Schmidt was buoyed by such victories but lamented the weakness of his forces, and on December 18 reported to Army Group Center: "If only we had more strength! The Russian is so bad; achieves everything only with numbers. If one could offensively defend all attacks would be stopped. But we have no reserves and no forces for this."[22]

While such successes underscored the professionalism of the Wehrmacht, meeting the daily demands of forced marches, heavy fighting, and constant stress depended upon much more than just German training and know-how; they emphasized Schmidt's ruthless insistence on discipline. An order he issued on December 12 read: "Individuals who make defeatist remarks to be singled out and shot as an example."[23] Willy Peter Reese's journal appeared to vouch for Schmidt's reputation as one of the toughest army commanders on the Eastern Front. "One sentry who collapsed in a haystack and carried on sleeping was court-martialled and shot. Another was unable to find the unit to which he was taking a message in the darkness and was sentenced to death for cowardice in the face of the enemy. Whoever stole food, even a piece of bread, was executed for looting. It was a tense time."[24] Guderian's approach was very different. In contrast to his often tense and even belligerent behavior toward his superiors, he was much closer to his men and seemed genuinely concerned for their well-being. In a letter to his wife on December 16, he told how he frequently could not sleep at night: "my brain goes around and around while I try to think what more I can do to help my poor soldiers who are out there without shelter in the abominable cold."[25] Guderian was certainly not about to have them shot for matters of indiscipline, but he also did not interfere with Schmidt's cold-blooded methods, just as in his later career, as chief of the Army General Staff in 1944–1945, he did not oppose the countless executions of German soldiers for desertion by his brutal army commanders.

The need for discipline was paramount given the incredibly complex task of completely repositioning the panzer army without prior planning, under constant enemy pressure, and in the midst of a Russian winter. Commanders had to maintain contact with one another, share roads, divide meager supplies, and trust that neighboring formations would stand their ground and cover each stage of the retreat. When a formation buckled under pressure, the consequence was immediate, requiring either the instant injection of reserves or a general retirement of the line. When Lieutenant-General Friedrich Mieth's 112th Infantry Division failed to hold on December 12, Guderian's plan to settle on the Stalinogorsk-Shat-Upa Line became impossible, and another retreat ensued.[26] This in turn prevented even the most basic planning, stockpiling, and reorganization, to say nothing of rest for the men. The implications were seen in the problems recorded by the 18th Panzer Division, which pointed to fatigue and the progressive break-down in command and control. On December 15 the war diary noted: "The irresponsibility of drivers and those responsible for trucks, as well as their exaggerated nervousness, increase the loss of trucks. At the same time, it must be admitted that officers and non-commissioned officers have lacked responsibility and avoided action at difficult points." Four days later the same diary recorded panicked reports about one of its battalions being sur-rounded, which caused some consternation, until it emerged that none of it was true. As the war diary explained: "It emerged that the reports were ex-aggerated, which resulted from the general nervousness that in individuals rose to panic levels."[27]

Soviet pressure and occasional infiltrations of the German line were also having a tangible effect, albeit at considerable cost to the Red Army. Wilhelm Prüller's unit made up part of the rear guard for Clössner's 25th Mo-torized Infantry Division and described the harrowing conditions of combat on December 17:

At 4.00 alarm is sounded . . . Without waiting for orders, I place the platoon between the houses and spread out the carbines. Meanwhile the enemy artillery has stopped, for the Russians are already quite near us. It's still pitch dark, and there isn't any point in firing yet since you can't see your targets clearly. After a moment's thought, . . . I have a white Verey light shot up, and in that moment we shall aim and shoot with all our various weapons . . . For nine seconds it's like broad daylight, you can see the whole ground in front of us. The Russians have advanced to within 100 metres. But my boys are already shooting like mad so as to use every bit of the light. Then it's dark again . . . In the light of the many Verey lights, you can see clearly that some of the Russians have already disappeared towards the rear; but there are plenty of them left in front of us. We're all praying for it to get light: the Verey lights are getting short.[28]

On the following day (December 18) Second Panzer Army's war diary recorded the intense fighting at Clössner's division with "heavy losses for the enemy" and one German battalion counting 600 dead in front of its lines. Unlike some Soviet attacks, however, this battle inflicted considerable German casualties, though no figure was recorded.[29] Prüller's diary entry eschewed any sense of triumphalism and instead adopted a tone of dejected fatalism. "The Russians are bringing up reserves all the time; they unload them right in front of our noses . . . they attack us in droves—and probably not only in this region; and we can't do anything against them. If it goes on like this, they'll crush us with their numerical superiority alone."[30]

The same dilemma confronted the German high command. To stand and fight risked being overwhelmed, yet buying time by retreating risked losing so much precious equipment and vehicles that the front could not be held anywhere. In his discussion with Brauchitsch on December 13, Bock steadfastly refused to make any decision and insisted that Hitler take ultimate responsibility. Yet Bock appears to have deemed holding the front as the lesser of the two evils, claiming it was "doubtful whether sufficient forces will reach the rear to hold a new, unprepared and significantly shorter position."[31] Kluge, who had earlier favored holding the line, now tended toward retreat, but that was probably influenced by the fait accompli on his northern and southern flanks, which threatened to force his hand. Brauchitsch, typically, remained a bystander. Overawed by the turn of events and the crushing weight of responsibility, the commander-in-chief of the army was more than willing for Bock to demand that Hitler—not the OKH—decide the best course of action.

The following day Brauchitsch went from Bock's headquarters in Smolensk to the Russian city of Roslavl to meet with Guderian and Kluge to gain a firsthand account of the situation. Brauchitsch was trying to counter fears that the high command ignored the problems at the front, but in the past he had also used such meetings to tell Hitler things in the name of his generals that he feared saying himself. In this way he hoped to avoid any potential backlash from the dictator. Guderian pressed the point that reserves were desperately needed to restore combat strength and that "without the sending of replacements it is questionable whether the panzer army can carry out its orders." Unbeknownst to Guderian, Hitler had that day redirected three trainloads of new tanks away from Army Group South to his Second Panzer Army.[32] This amounted to seventy-eight Mark IIIs and twenty-five StuG IIIs (assault guns). Given that as of December 16 Guderian's Second Panzer Army reported a total of "about forty" operational tanks, this constituted a more than 200 percent increase in his tank numbers, but they still had to get from Kremenchug in Ukraine to Orel.[33] Guderian's goal, though, was to secure permission for a continued retreat, if necessary all the way to the Oka River, which ran from Kaluga down to Orel. For the bulk of Second Panzer Army's forces, this constituted a further ninety kilometers to the rear.[34] Guderian argued that the Oka River had served as part of the German front in October and was therefore partly fortified, but he also hoped to hold the line farther east depending upon the situation.[35]

Given his willingness to take direction, it was not surprising that after his meeting with Guderian, Brauchitsch returned to see Bock in Smolensk and suggested "that the gradual withdrawal into a rearward position, as charted on the map by the army group, is unavoidable."[36] Also present at Bock's headquarters was Colonel Rudolf Schmundt, Hitler's chief military adjutant and a trusted member of his inner circle, who was probably sent to ensure an independent report of the options at hand.[37] That evening Schmundt called General of Artillery Alfred Jodl, head of the Wehrmacht's operations department, to seek the approval of Hitler, which was immediately forthcoming. As Bock recorded in his diary, "[Hitler] had nothing against a straightening of the projecting salients at Klin and Kalinin, also that a withdrawal by Army Group Guderian was inevitable." Hitler then added, however, that no further retreats would be allowed, but prefaced this with the ambiguous condition "as long as the most necessary preparations had not been made in the rear-ward lines."[38] This Bock interpreted as permission for further withdrawals so long as some kind of rearward position was prepared, and he immediately issued orders for work on the Rzhev-Gzhatsk-Orel-Kursk Line.[39]

To satisfy Hitler's requirement, Bock prepared to use whatever was at hand—"construction units, residents and police units"[40]—but in practice this meant press-ganging civilians into forced labor. An order from Strauss's Ninth Army, circulated to Panzer Groups 3 and 4, spoke of mustering labor by means of a "special order," which not only utilized the local population, but also envisaged transporting them from "greater distances" and accommodating them in the nearby villages. Their task was not only to prepare the German positions, but to "create an absolute 'desert' at least twenty or possibly thirty kilometers deep. In this zone the Russians should not find a house, a barn, a bunch of straw, a specimen of livestock or a potato."[41] Reinhardt's panzer group also drew attention to the difficulty of acquiring labor, estimating that the area under its occupation contained just 10 percent men and the remainder women and children. Beyond the sheer lack of manpower, for anyone not already working for the occupation authorities, the official ration was seventy grams of fat per week, one and a half kilograms of bread, and two kilograms of potatoes. Even this was by no means guaranteed; in some areas the German authorities considered anyone unable to work for them to be simply "useless eaters." As a result, many Soviet civilians worked for the Germans simply to survive.[42]

On the afternoon of December 15 Brauchitsch arrived back in East Prussia and that evening met with Halder. Brauchitsch cast the situation in the blackest of terms, as Halder wrote in his diary: "He [Brauchitsch] is very despondent and sees no way of rescuing the army from its difficult situation."[43] There is much evidence to suggest that the commander-in-chief was clinically depressed and simply unable to cope with the demands of his post—and especially with Hitler, who openly jeered at him in conferences and blamed him for all of the army's problems in the east. Brauchitsch's fragility made him reluctant to report anything that might incur Hitler's wrath; but he was relentlessly ridiculed anyway. His helplessness in the face of Hitler, and utter victimization, meant the commander-in-chief also shrank away from resignation, and so, not knowing what else to do, he carried on. When Colonel Hermann Balck reported to Brauchitsch on November 30 following a tour of the Eastern Front, he recalled encountering a "sick, broken man" who, after hearing Balck's bleak news, broke down. "Why don't you go and tell him [Hitler] yourself?" Brauchitsch despaired. "We are finished."[44]

Not only was Brauchitsch psychologically frail; he was also an ambulatory cardiac patient, having suffered a severe heart attack only five weeks before in early November.[45] On December 6 Hitler's army adjutant, Major Gerhard Engel, noted the tense atmosphere after another punishing browbeating by Hitler. "Trust between F. [Führer] and OB [Brauchitsch] is no longer apparent. Every situation is uncomfortable. OB is attacked and remonstrated by F." Engel then provided the first indication of the major change that was about to sweep the German high command. In conversation with Brauchitsch that evening, the beleaguered field marshal told Engel that he could no longer continue for professional as well as health reasons. He suggested that he be replaced by either Kluge or General of Infantry Erich von Manstein, commanding the Eleventh Army in Army Group South. Brauchitsch was no doubt signaling his desire to resign in the hope that Engel would act as a surrogate to Hitler. Engel told Schmundt, who approached Hitler with the news. According to Engel's later conversation with Schmundt, Hitler seems to have rejected Brauchitsch's suggested alternatives, probably because Hitler had never wanted a strong, independent-minded army commander, which was why he opted for Brauchitsch in the first place. Hitler also told Schmundt that he could think of no alternatives, which suggests that Brauchitsch, for all Hitler's scorn and loathing, served the dictator's purposes, both as an unquestioning instrument of his will and as a passive source of blame for any frustrations. Apart from the fact that Kluge and Manstein were much more assertive, Hitler, who valued the abilities of both men, wanted them in the field. Schmundt then suggested that Hitler himself take over command of the army. Hitler's reaction to this was not recorded, but clearly the idea would have appealed to him since it would formalize the current relationship with the army and give him a direct role in the war on the Eastern Front, which had become his main preoccupation. When Engel expressed shock at the thought of Hitler taking over command, Schmundt insisted that Hitler was the best option to restore trust in the army.[46]

On December 16, only two days after a consensus in strategy for Army Group Center had seemingly been achieved, Hitler appeared to renege on the agreement for a general withdrawal of Army Group Center, although he continued to sanction some of those already in motion to straighten the front. A scapegoat yet again, the commander-in-chief of the army was ordered to leave Hitler's afternoon military briefing, and Schmundt was instructed to maintain direct contact with Army Group Center, suggesting that Hitler felt somehow misinformed about the events of December 14. Hitler forbade Kluge's Fourth Army from withdrawing "one step further" and ordered that the current gaps in the line be closed by reserves. When all of this was communicated to Bock, the exasperated commander of Army Group Center could only respond that he had no reserves.[47] Yet Bock generally supported Hitler's decision since he was aware there was not the fuel for the vehicles or the draft power for the artillery (owing to crippling losses among horses) to ensure their arrival at the new line. Nonetheless, such was the threat on some sectors of the front that Bock feared acts of open defiance, in which "units will possibly pull back without orders." Schmundt countered by elaborating on Hitler's own reasoning, pointing to Army Groups North and South being able to hold their own fronts, which had led the dictator to conclude: "I can't send everything into the winter because Army Group Centre has had its line breached in several places."[48]

At the conclusion of their meeting, Bock delivered another bombshell announcement for Hitler. Having already informed Brauchitsch on December 14, which unsurprisingly did not seem to have been passed on, Bock told Schmundt that his own health was "hanging by a silk thread" and that, with Hitler's agreement, "a fresh force belongs here." After midnight Hitler telephoned Bock, and although there was no record of Bock's request to stand down, Hitler had been fully advised by Schmundt of Bock's position, quoting "almost word for word, the pros and cons of staying or retreating." Bock at last felt assured that his message, with all its inherent warnings, had been fully conveyed and understood. He was also left in no doubt about Hitler's emphatic determination "not to take a single step back," but to hold the line where it stood.[49] Bock was grateful for the clarity from above, but one senses he feared the worst. Whether this precipitated his desire for replacement is impossible to say, but he did have a history of serious stomach problems and had been largely bedridden from September 1940 until February 1941. In any case, radical change was afoot. The short period of the authorized retreat had reached its end, and a new era of fanatical resistance, led by Hitler himself, was about to begin.

At midnight on December 16–17, Hitler ordered Brauchitsch, Halder, and Heusinger to his headquarters, where he instructed them on the new approach to the war in the east. Hitler was unequivocal: there would be no further talk of a general withdrawal. "Building rearward lines is a fantasy. The front suffers in only one respect: The enemy is more plentiful in soldiers. He does not have more artillery. He is much worse than us." The remainder of the meeting was dedicated to mustering more men and matériel for the front. A division from Denmark was to be sent by ship to Tallinn; 2,000 SS men were to be flown from Kraków; 200 transport planes were to be made available with more to be provided by Army Group South, and more fighter squadrons were to be sent east.[50] This was all in addition to a previously agreed release of four and a half divisions from Colonel-General Friedrich Fromm's Replacement Army as well as five divisions from France (three of which were earmarked for Army Group Center).[51]

While Schmundt was dealing with Bock on December 16, he also found time for a flight to Orel airfield to answer Guderian's "urgent request" for a meeting. He hoped to gain a direct line to Hitler, pleading his case for more reserves and suggesting that the survival of his army depended upon it.[52] Of course, neither Brauchitsch nor Schmundt could make any such promises because, beyond the fact that there was simply nothing more to be had, neither man possessed the authority to do more than convey Guderian's request. Disgruntled and fed up, that evening Guderian poured out his frustrations in a letter to his wife: "The people from the OKH and OKW, who have never seen the front, have no idea of these conditions; they merely wire impossible orders and reject all our requests and suggestions."[53] Yet Guderian was greatly heartened by having achieved a direct line to Hitler through Schmundt. Guderian ascribed to Hitler an almost breathtaking degree of influence over Army Group Center's desperate situation. As the panzer general wrote: "I am only happy that the Führer is now at least in the picture and will hopefully intervene with his usual vigour in the bureaucratized gears of the army, the railways and other machinery."[54] Guderian's letters show he was feeling the strain of events and was suffering both physically and emotionally. His long-standing sciatica was again causing him discomfort. Most of all, Guderian saw no way out of his predicament and confided to his wife: "I cannot recall having ever been so anxious for professional reasons as I am now, and I only hope that I can endure it."[55]

As he had with Bock, Schmundt dutifully reported Guderian's concerns back to Hitler, and in the early hours of December 17 the dictator telephoned the panzer general to assure him everything would be done to rush aid to the front. Hitler made three points: first, that transport squadrons would be assembled with one reserved for Guderian's army; second, that two groups of destroyers (Messerschmitt Bf 110 fighter-bombers), already active, would receive replacements to bring them up to full strength, while a new group would be dispatched to the front; third, that replacements and fresh divisions would be sent from France. In the meantime, Guderian was instructed to maneuver his army into a position "which can be strengthened," but Guderian countered that in the deeply frozen ground digging was not possible.[56] Hitler, however, remained resolute; the retreat must come to an end.[57]

Later that morning Bock sent an order insisting that any future withdrawal of a division or larger formation required his personal approval. Guderian immediately protested and requested that he be granted "complete autonomy" as the situation was changing from hour to hour. He met with three of his corps commanders—Geyr von Schweppenberg (XXIV), Weikersthal (LIII), and Lemelsen (XXXXVII)—and all agreed that the panzer army could not hold a position in front of the Oka River.[58] As one of his commanders told him: "If only we were mobile and had our old combat strength, then it would be child's play."[59] That of course was wishful thinking, but it suggests German commanders were more concerned about the erosion of their ability to strike and maneuver than about the Red Army's numerical superiority. After all, the folly of poorly coordinated Soviet attacks was a daily occurrence. On December 14, for example, a regiment of Breith's

3rd Panzer Division reported an attack by 250 Soviet troops, which resulted in all but six being killed. The same regiment had launched an attack of its own the day before and, without noting its own casualties, listed 114 POWs and 123 dead Soviets along with some captured matériel.[60]

Guderian was determined to direct his armies on his own terms and therefore sought permission from Army Group Center to fly to Hitler's headquarters and, as he wrote after the war, "to describe to Hitler what position my army was in."[61] It is unclear what more Guderian expected; it is more likely that the panzer general sought to regain freedom of movement for his armies by pleading their "special case." Certainly, over the course of Operations Barbarossa and Typhoon, Guderian had never reacted well to any "interference" in his panzer group and army, and now, with every movement westward having to be approved from above, the panzer general seized the opportunity to plead for his autonomy. Another major consideration must have been Bock's impending replacement by Kluge—with whom Guderian had had a very quarrelsome past. On December 17 Kluge told Guderian that Hitler's forthcoming order must be adhered to, "in such a way that as much as possible is preserved of the army. No area is to be given up unnecessarily but neither is it to be held if troops are to be wiped out as a result." Kluge's interpretation allowed for a surprising degree of flexibility. This may be because the precise wording of the order had not yet been released, but it may also suggest a variance between the acknowledgment of the order and its practical application in local instances. For the time being however, Guderian resented Kluge's instruction, and in his reply ten hours later he invoked Hitler's name as a means of trumping Kluge's superior rank and position. As Guderian wrote: "I know the Führer's mind. I will do everything I can . . . I need freedom of action and cannot ask whenever I want to move a division."[62] The panzer general was even less inclined to relinquish his "freedom of action" to Kluge than he would have been to Bock, although the new commander of Army Group Center, having already experienced Guderian's flagrant insubordination, was determined to ensure obedience. Confrontation was just a matter of time, but, unlike Bock, Kluge had no compunction about using his own direct line to Hitler to enforce his authority.

On December 18 Hitler's famous "halt order" (*Haltbefehl*) came over the teletype at Army Group Center and read:

> The Führer has ordered: Larger evasive movements cannot be made. They will lead to a total loss of heavy weapons and equipment. Commanding generals, commanders, and officers are to intervene in person to compel the troops to fanatical resistance in their positions without regard to enemy broken through on the flanks or in the rear. This is the only way to gain the time necessary to bring up the reinforcements from Germany and the west that I have ordered. Only if reserves have moved into rearward positions can thought be given to withdrawing to those positions.[63]

This was the order that for many has come to define Army Group Center's response to the Soviet winter campaign and that, one might argue, continued to exert an influence over Hitler's thinking throughout the remainder of the war. Analysis of the order is at the heart of any study in this period, with historians expressing divergent opinions. At the superficial level the order can be seen as a product of Hitler's iron determination, which saved Army Group Center and staved off a Napoleonic-style disaster in the east.[64] In the early postwar era, this viewpoint was touted by men such as the former Reich's press chief, Otto Dietrich, as evidence of the dictator's resolve and energy, which he claimed were "Hitler's great traits as a military leader."[65] Even some of the generals, who typically after the war liked to blame every possible oversight or blunder on Hitler's interference, exempted the halt order. The chief of staff of the Fourth Army during the December battles, Colonel Günther Blumentritt, wrote: "Hitler believed that he personally could ward off the catastrophe which was impending before Moscow. And it must be stated quite frankly that he did in fact succeed in doing so. His fanatical order that the troops must hold fast regardless in every position, and in the most impossible circumstances, was undoubtedly correct."[66]

In fact, Hitler's halt order had many more implications, and its consequences should by no means be accepted as universally beneficial to Army Group Center. Hitler's order was a blanket solution to a highly nuanced problem. Above all, the order was an act of desperation, resulting from the lack of a credible alternative rather than the virtue of the one at hand. Yet this did not prevent some of Hitler's generals from identifying him as Army Group Center's savior, almost by default.[67] For Lieutenant-General Kurt von Tippelskirch, the fact that there was no panicked flight in the face of Soviet attacks qualified as Hitler's "one great achievement."[68] Similarly, Blumentritt added: "Hitler realized instinctively that any retreat across the snow and ice must, within a few days, lead to the dissolution of the front."[69] Yet there was nothing "instinctive" about it; the avalanche of reports from Army Group Center hammered home the message of shortages in fuel, horses, trains, trucks, spare parts, as well as the general exhaustion of the men. Understanding the potential losses inherent in a headlong retreat to a distant and undefended line was hardly the mark of genius, and it is therefore not surprising that the OKH, Bock, and Kluge initially supported it. It was Guderian who was in the process of rebelling against the order, and Kluge would soon make an example out of him.

Yet Guderian was not necessarily wrong. While a general retreat entailing the loss of Army Group Center's heavy equipment would clearly have been destructive, it was not an either-or scenario. Retreats could be managed to ensure the front was withdrawn without undue loss or the exposure of a neighboring formation's flank. Under such conditions there was no downside to a withdrawal, while on the plus side, German supply lines shortened and the Red Army's extended. Alternatively, the risk of holding stubbornly everywhere often did much more harm than good. Hitler did, of course, allow some retreats after December 18, but these should not be interpreted as examples of flexibility.[70] They were typically achieved after days of unrelenting argument and mounting crisis, in which the interim costs in blood made a farce out of Hitler's objections and complicated the withdrawal process. They also covered only the most prominent flashpoints on the front; Hitler simply could not deal with every crisis in need of review or even a fraction of them, but his order did not allow for independence at the divisional, regimental, battalion, or company level. As the commander of the 253rd Infantry Division, Lieutenant-General Otto Schellert bluntly concluded after the war: "The Hitler [halt] order was to have disastrous consequences."[71]

The wording of the order itself reflected Hitler's retreat into the National Socialist conception of "will," in which "fanatical resistance" could seemingly trump an enemy "broken through on the flanks or in the rear." It was an entirely ideological response without attention to mitigating circumstances or local conditions. Even Blumentritt's endorsement, maintaining that troops had to hold even "in the most impossible circumstances," reflected his own acceptance of the order's National Socialist precepts.[72] While Hitler was given the credit for saving Army Group Center, it could just as easily be argued that many soldiers were left no choice. Sometimes they clung to their fortified villages for no other reason than a lack of transport upon which to escape. Others feared the deadly cold more than Soviet counterattacks, and still others remained where they were out of sheer exhaustion or to care for wounded comrades who could not be evacuated. Thus, pragmatic and very human considerations also played a role in holding Army Group Center in place.

Far from knowing the limits of his army, it was precisely Hitler's baleful decisions, in conjunction with the OKH, that left Army Group Center in such a dreadful position at the beginning of the winter. Hitler understood nothing of the local conditions to which he insisted his orders apply, and he would subsequently refuse withdrawals even when commanders on the spot insisted they would benefit tactically. The idea, therefore, that Army Group Center owed its survival simply to Hitler is at best ill-conceived and at worst acceptance of Nazi propaganda.

What Hitler's halt order did do though was provide strategic clarity in an increasingly confused and tense situation, but this too should not be overstated. Past studies have emphasized Hitler's imposition of rigid discipline, but the German army did not lack obedience. As we have seen, commanders across the front were already vigorously reacting to ensure orders were followed and any wayward situations were brought under control. There has also been a common conclusion that the halt order stymied individual initiative and stripped field commanders of their flexibility to respond to threats.[73] This has been interpreted as the end of the German army's use of *Auftragstaktik* (a command method stressing decentralized initiative within an overall strategic framework).[74] Recent research from Miguel Lopez has rejected this notion and even suggested that at the corps and divisional level command-ers were knowingly complicit in subverting Hitler's halt order.[75] According to Lopez, it was the insistence on flexibility and the endurance of *Auftragstak-tik* that allowed a fluid response to the Soviet attacks—in defiance of Hitler's order—and prevented German positions from being needlessly overrun. At the same time, this method called for timely German counterattacks to re-store positions and thereby cover unauthorized withdrawals. It was a local form of elastic defense, which allowed German forces to pull out where the enemy was strongest and hit back when they were overextended. Divisional and corps commanders more and more observed these "illegal" maneuvers without sanction or reprimand and often even actively advised and sup-ported them. These counterattacks constituted successful and largely un-known aspects of the winter fighting. Thus, while some German units were annihilated by their rigid adherence to Hitler's halt order, others adopted a more flexible approach, causing inconsistency among units between the ac-knowledgment of the order and its practical application in local instances.

Such a dichotomy between order and execution may appear somewhat at odds with the Wehrmacht's reputation for rigid discipline, but even Blu-mentritt, who certainly approved of Hitler's order, suggested that during the retreat from Moscow inconsistencies were noted. As he told Basil Liddell Hart after the war: "Moreover, those tussles [within the German command] are not reflected in the operation orders. Documents are no safe guide for history—the men who sign orders often think quite differently from what they put on paper. It would be foolish to take documents that historians find in the archives as reliable indications of what particular officers really thought."[76] The famous cases of Guderian and Hoepner authorizing re-treats are known because they were too senior to hide their misdeeds, but they were hardly the outstanding exceptions. Lopez's research using case studies from three of Army Group Center's infantry divisions indicates that unauthorized withdrawals took place in each of the formations studied, sug-gesting that many more junior commanders acted against Hitler's order but managed to do so covertly.[77] The present study, conducted on a much larger set of primary material, confirms and develops these findings. It suggests Army Group Center's survival rested not on Hitler's order, but on the unwillingness of many commanders to surrender their freedom of action, while exploiting the ambiguities of *Auftragstaktik* to, as much as possible, direct their defensive operations as they saw fit.

Marco Sigg has conducted the most comprehensive study of *Auftrag-staktik* and has shown that regulations and training papers in fact allowed a subordinate officer to act against his orders in one clearly defined set of circumstances. If the mission (the intention of the order) was endangered or an unanticipated opportunity arose, but authorization from higher command was impossible owing to time pressure or communication difficulties, then the officer on the spot was empowered to act—even against his orders—to achieve the mission.[78] Such independent action was very much the exception rather than the rule, highlighting both the exceptionalism of Army Group Center's response and the widespread rejection of Hitler's halt order. Given that exemptions to the halt order required gaining Hitler's personal authorization, the sheer number of requests and the associated communication difficulties meant the conditions for officers acting contrary to instructions were always apparent. Moreover, if the objective was broadly interpreted to preserve the army's strength, prevent enemy breakthroughs, or avoid a collapse, withdrawals might be seen as serving the intention of stabilizing the German front, even if not holding it rigidly. The uncertainties in the practice of *Auftragstaktik*, whether a question of legitimate interpretation or, more likely, entirely contrived to subvert Hitler's baneful interference, provided a small measure of freedom to counter the Red Army's winter offensive. In time, such defiance would take its own toll on the commanders within Army Group Center, but even before this began, the German army itself was to be subjected to Hitler's new leadership.

6

PUT TO THE SWORD

The End of Brauchitsch

A s the German high command grappled with changes in personnel and policy, the available record reflects little discussion of how the regime should explain the army's retreat or the replacement of high-profile generals. Given the desperate situation unfolding in Army Group Center, which was becoming increasingly well known in Germany as a result of soldiers' letters, maintaining the credibility of the German press and its ability to control the Nazi message had to have been paramount. Yet the same ideological delusions that undercut Germany's military campaign were also undermining their propaganda war. On December 20 Goebbels announced that between December 27 and January 4 (later extended to January 11), a gigantic collection of winter equipment for the Wehrmacht would be carried out. He called it "a Christmas present from the German people to the Eastern Front," and the response was huge, with over 67 million items donated.[1] Yet while many historians have interpreted this response as evidence of the great success of Goebbels's winter relief campaign, the public opinion reports compiled by the SD reveal it was in fact received by many Germans as confirmation of a crisis in the east, which also explains their willingness to give generously.[2] Arvid Fredborg, the Swedish journalist in Berlin, observed that Goebbels's speech "fell like a bombshell among the public," and noted that people were questioning why this was happening now. After all, "was it not reasonable to expect winter at the beginning of December."[3] The Polish underground fed such concerns with posters of a freezing German soldier huddled in a woman's fox-fur collar.[4]

At the front the soldiers were also hearing of Goebbels's campaign, which they openly mocked as a public relations whitewash, having already seen far too many cases of frostbite and knowing that few of the garments being donated were likely to appear anytime soon. Gerhardt Linke wrote in his diary on January 2 of having seen a cinema newsreel showing soldiers receiving fur coats, while the announcer stated that the men of the Eastern Front were "splendidly equipped." As Linke dismissively concluded, "it is sure to be Easter before these things get here."[5] Albin Gagel was even more scathing, calling into question the basic practicalities of Goebbels's campaign. "Trainloads of fur coats were supposedly sent east. That enterprise was surely grandstanding on the part of our leaders. How could a few fur coats make any difference to the poor bastards in the middle of a snowstorm in Russia? And how would a small woman's coat be made to fit a man, especially over his uniform and gear? I wondered what really happened to those fur coats."[6] Yet Goebbels was less interested in practicalities than in what he believed was an enthusiastic public response. Accordingly, some absurd items were indeed shipped east, including a bright blue jacket with gold buttons and fastenings. Wilhelm Moldenhauer cynically observed that the troops could "put on the finest masquerade."[7]

If collecting ladies' scarves was not evidence enough of the *Ostheer*'s decline in fortunes, Hitler's parallel decision to replace the commander-in-chief of the German army as well as approve the release of Field Marshal Bock could hardly have done more to signal discord and division. Brauchitsch's replacement finally came on December 19 after a final stormy meeting with Hitler from which the sixty-year-old field marshal emerged shattered and beaten. He told Keitel before leaving: "I am going home—he has sacked me. I can't go on any longer."[8] With those words Brauchitsch's thankless tenure as commander-in-chief of the German army ended. Upon his return to the army headquarters at Mauerwald (some twenty kilometers northeast of Hitler's "Wolf's Lair" headquarters), the field marshal was greeted by a somber atmosphere. Colonel Balck was present and recalled the occasion in his memoir: "The mood was gloomy. Halder spoke warmly to us about Brauchitsch's accomplishments . . . Brauchitsch had aged and looked tired . . . He said his heart could not take the stress any longer . . . It was touching. The end of a man whose only mistake was that he could not deal with Hitler."[9] It was hardly Brauchitsch's only mistake, and from Hitler's point of view, it was what made him perfect for the job in the first place. Yet what mattered now was explaining his conspicuous departure amid Germany's most pressing crisis of the war so far.

Extraordinarily, Hitler's only action was to issue a general instruction to the troops offering no acknowledgment of Brauchitsch's service or explanation for his departure. He simply informed them that he was now in command of the army, which could only stoke speculation of the rift in the high command. The instruction read:

> Soldiers of the army and the Waffen-SS! Our struggle for national liberation is approaching its climax! Decisions of world importance stand before us! The army bears the primary responsibility for the battle! I have therefore, as of this day, taken command of the army. As a soldier who fought in many [First] World War battles I am closely tied to you in the will to victory.[10]

It was therefore left to Brauchitsch to issue his own farewell to the troops and explain his departure:

> Soldiers!
> In a time of imminent great decisions, the Führer has today personally taken command of the army, which bears primary

responsibility for the struggle. At the same time, he granted me my request, which had been decided some time ago, to release me from the leadership of the army on account of my heart condition.

Soldiers!

For almost four years, I have been your commander-in-chief and led the best army in the world. For Germany, these years comprise a wealth of great historical events and for the army the greatest military successes. I look back on this time with pride and gratitude, proud of your achievements, thankful for your loyalty. Great tasks have been achieved, while greater and more difficult ones are still to come. I am convinced that you are up to the task.

The Führer will lead us to victory.

Make the will steel hard, eyes front!

Everything for Germany![11]

Brauchitsch's heart condition was real enough and sufficient in its own right to justify his departure, but because his November heart attack had not been made public, it appeared to be an all-too-coincidental cover story, especially since Hitler's own public statement noticeably avoided paying any tribute to his most senior army commander.

If Brauchitsch's departure was not already a public relations debacle, the regime compounded the situation by ignoring the issue domestically. There was no immediate announcement by the Nazi press, which would have allowed them to "spin" the story in the most beneficial manner possible. Arvid Fredborg first found out about the story from a fellow journalist in London and noted that none of his informants in Berlin knew anything about it.[12] On December 21 the American press broke the story and naturally linked it to a serious crisis in the east, which prompted Goebbels to press Hitler urgently for permission to make a public statement.[13] An announcement was made that evening, and German newspapers first reported the story on December 22, three days after the event, suggesting the regime was somehow hoping to avoid the issue altogether. The story proved explosive, and Fredborg noted, "a wave of rumours concerning the von Brauchitsch incident swept Berlin," but again the regime stubbornly refused to deal with the fallout and rejected making any further statement. As Fredborg commented, "when questions were asked the only reply was that the matter was closed."[14]

The foreign press had a field day with the news, while Germans secretly listening to foreign radio broadcasts received no corrective counterpoints from their own press, implying the story was every bit as toxic to the Nazi regime as foreign propaganda suggested it was. The Italian foreign minister, Galeazzo Ciano, noted in his diary on December 22: "The liquidation of Brauchitsch is the topic of the day. British and American radios talk of nothing else. The German embassy is staggered by the news."[15] The British media went so far as to suggest Brauchitsch was an amalgam of Field Marshal Helmuth Moltke the Elder and General Erich Ludendorff, implying he had been the linchpin of Germany's past successes. As Goebbels observed with incredulity in his diary: "One must know Brauchitsch to really appreciate the comedy of such a claim."[16] For once Goebbels was absolutely correct, but as he above all should have known, propaganda was not about truth but about the perception of truth, and on this issue Allied propaganda appeared far more believable. Larry LeSueur, the American war correspondent in Moscow, noted that the Soviet press was reporting Brauchitsch was fired "for his colossal failure to take Moscow."[17] Around the same time, Ilya Ehrenburg published an article in which he declared: "Hitler cannot conceal this defeat from his people. He puts all the blame on Field Marshal Brauchitsch, the commander-in-chief of yesterday."[18] Even in Axis member countries like Romania, the population was able to read between the lines of what was being reported. As Mihail Sebastian wrote in his diary on December 22: "Brauchitsch has been removed . . . The simple fact of the change in command is a recognition of failure on the Russian front."[19]

By December 23 Goebbels was well aware of the humiliation Brauchitsch's dismissal had become with foreign media, even in neutral countries, speculating about a crisis of the highest order. As Goebbels wrote in his diary, "abroad the resignation of Brauchitsch is building to an ever-greater sensation." Turkey, he noted, was being swept up by the "spell of these rumours and alarmist reports." Even in unofficially Allied Spain, which had a whole division of volunteers serving on the Eastern Front, Goebbels noted signs of "wavering" support and that "the German chances are no longer as highly rated as a few weeks before." Yet he obstinately refused to engage with the issue and contented himself that it would all blow over in a few days.[20]

Nowhere did the implications of Hitler's momentous decision to assume control of the army matter more than in Germany. While Goebbels probably could not have done much to contain the fallout from the international story, the fact that he also abandoned the issue on the home front proved disastrous. Brauchitsch may have been a weak and ineffectual commander-in-chief, and the change in command may only have formalized what had already been the case for months, but none of this was popularly known. To the average German, Brauchitsch was synonymous with some of Germany's greatest military victories. It was inconceivable to most Germans that a man in his position might be indecisive and inept, racked by pessimism and doubt, fearful of his encounters with Hitler and medically unfit for the job either physically or mentally. To the German command, he was no loss at all, but to the German public he was a symbol of their past success, and his departure was an incontestable watershed. In such circumstances the absence of information fired the rumor mill, drove people to foreign broadcasts, and ultimately resulted in scarcely anyone believing the official line that he stepped down of his own volition on health grounds.

The first Germans to hear the news were of course the soldiers on the Eastern Front. Even before any form of foreign propaganda had the chance to pervert the message, the official proclamations were mistrusted. As one soldier wrote home on December 21: "We were absolutely thunderstruck when we heard this morning of the change in command of the armed forces. The Führer himself has taken charge. This was announced in a laconic order. I suspect there is a connection between this change and our retreat."[21] A German lieutenant claimed that upon hearing the news of Brauchitsch's departure one of his fellow officers announced: "Let us have a drink—I have a bottle of rum. Now everything is clear—we shall perish anyway."[22]

All manner of rumors suddenly began to spread, and the news immediately became the hottest topic of speculation. Adolf B. eagerly wrote home to his family: "Did you hear about Brauchitsch's resignation? What do you think about it?"[23] In his letter home, Martin Steglich referred to the conjecture circulating as to the cause of Brauchitsch's demise: "Miscalculation? Rostov-on-

Don? Klin? Tikhvin? Who knows!"[24] Ernst Gerber also wondered as to the cause of Brauchitsch's departure but had no answers.[25] Wolfgang Buff just referred to it as "the incomprehensible news of Brauchitsch's resignation."[26]

The same gossip and thirst for knowledge then spread throughout Germany, with one mother writing her son in the east: "The changes in command have also given rise to much guesswork. Of course, we'll never know the truth."[27] Another woman in Stuttgart suggested: "Perhaps Brauchitsch should have the Italian command, or in East Asia, or something where he is more important than with us. I do not like to condemn what I cannot know."[28] Ulrich von Hassell noted in his diary on December 23: "The more one ponders the removal of Brauschitsch the stronger grows the impression that a crisis of the first magnitude is near at hand."[29] The same day Victor Klemperer made a similar observation about Germany's position: "A few weeks ago the Russians were officially 'annihilated.' Now they are to be annihilated in spring. They only need to hold on 'fanatically' to what has already been conquered."[30] The French intellectual Jean Guéhenno questioned what Hitler hoped to offer by taking over command of his stricken German armies. "Will it make the snow melt in Russia? Will it unfreeze his planes and tanks? Will it give clothes to his soldiers?"[31]

The best evidence for German popular opinion in the immediate period after Brauchitsch's removal remains the secretly compiled reports of the SD, which revealed that the news was greeted with "astonishment in large sections of the population." Furthermore, Brauchitsch's heart condition "was generally identified as not believable," but the real reason for the change remained a source of "great guesswork." The most popular theory linked Brauchitsch's removal to Goebbels's collection of winter clothing and equipment, suggesting the commander-in-chief was somehow responsible for the shortages for the soldiers in the east.[32] Such a theory was also advanced after the war by Otto Dietrich, the former Reich's press chief, who claimed: "The lack of proper winter equipment for the soldiers in the east had deeply shocked the German people. Brauchitsch was the scapegoat."[33] Alternative theories identified by the SD reports attributed the underestimation of the Soviet armament potential and military power to Brauchitsch's leadership, while another segment of the population simply assumed that the move had little to do with the commander-in-chief of the army but instead reflected Hitler's need to direct events personally in "the current threatening situation."[34] Even Goebbels had to concede on December 25 that the situation surrounding Brauchitsch's replacement "is more discussed among the population than had been assumed."[35]

The most important issue raised by Brauchitsch's departure was what the army itself thought about being under Hitler's direct command. The evidence suggests it was a polarizing issue. Friedebald Kruse wrote home in a letter on December 23 that the news of the change "depresses me," and then went on to conclude: "It is the first time that the confidence in the troops has had to suffer. Among the great changes even our general must go."[36] Clearly, many of the men associated Brauchitsch's departure with the failure of the campaign, which affected some men very personally. Wilhelm Streit told a Soviet interrogator after his capture in January: "What sort of morale can there be? When Brauchitsch was dismissed, we knew that things were bad. Brauchitsch had been victorious everywhere. Two of our officers committed suicide."[37] Lieutenant Otto Bente expressed indignation about both the rationale for Brauchitsch's departure and the qualifications of Hitler to replace him: "Von Rundstedt was sacrificed because of the retreat from Rostov and now another von Brauchitsch—another well-educated general—is to go because of the failure to capture Moscow. Adolf Hitler—who has no military qualifications at all—is to take over as supreme commander. What sort of effect is this supposed to have on our officer corps?"[38] Philipp von Boeselager agreed and commented: "Hitler needed a scapegoat for this winter disaster, and so deliberately dismissed the commander-in-chief, as if to say: 'If I'd been in charge, it would have been different.'"[39] It was after Hitler assumed command of the army that the men began to exchange a joke that parodied the Nazi slogan "The Führer leads and we follow," which soldiers now derisively modified to "The Führer takes the lead and we take what follows."[40]

While there was certainly no shortage of ill feeling, and even open hostility, toward Hitler's leading the German army, many men also appear to have supported the move. Heusinger, the chief of the operations department at the OKH, noted in a letter that Hitler's new role was welcomed by the army "en masse."[41] At the front, Hans Rehfeldt recalled being thrilled by the news and spoke of "the unlimited confidence in our 'greatest warlord'—Adolf Hitler."[42] Another soldier wrote excitedly on December 25 that Hitler was "the boldest and greatest of all," the one who would "find a path to victory."[43] For these men, Hitler's reputation was as yet unblemished, and Brauchitsch's departure acted as a lightning rod for grievances with the army command. Rejoicing at the news, Albert Neuhaus suggested in a letter home that blunders had been made in the deployment of the army: "And the Führer will place his soldiers where it is correct."[44] Likewise, Kurt Grumann wrote in his diary on December 21: "The Führer himself has taken command into his own hands. I assume that this change is connected with our withdrawal, which might have been avoided if matters had been organized with more foresight and if deliveries had been made on time."[45] Others simply welcomed a change at the top and were less discriminating about who was to now lead them so long as it was not Brauchitsch. Without mentioning Hitler, Lieutenant Ludwig von Heyl wrote: "I am hardly surprised by the dismissal of Brauchitsch. He badly mismanaged the push on Moscow in mid-November, left the provision of supplies and ammunition in utter chaos and of all those who 'talked up' the chances of this last assault, he was without doubt the worst offender."[46] Similarly, after suggesting that Brauchitsch was not up to the demands of the war, Hans Jürgen Hartmann concluded: "Perhaps Hitler—in the very highest position—can make a better estimate of what can or cannot be undertaken on a daily basis."[47] Some weeks later the report of a Major Oehmichen, one of the OKH's front-line observers for the operations department, concluded after a visit to Fourth Army: "The fact that in the ordinary soldier's mind the change in the high command is linked with the conviction of a fundamental turn for the better, is a gain for which no personal sacrifice is too high."[48]

Even within the senior army command there was an outpouring of enthusiastic support for Hitler, possibly in the naïve assumption that Hitler would act as an advocate for the army and solve many of their outstanding administrative battles in the tangle of overlapping agencies used to run the war. The army commanders also knew just how weak and indecisive Brauchitsch had been and perhaps would have warmly welcomed any replacement. One cannot ignore the fact that National Socialist sentiment was rife among the army command and that Hitler was for many an infallible choice. Hermann Balck told of a rejuvenation within the OKH as a result of the change. "The reaction to Hitler taking command was having a surprising effect. 'Everything will be good, now that the Führer has taken over,' could be heard over and over again. Even [Colonel Hans] Krebs [chief of staff at VII Army Corps] commented, 'I would have never thought that even today this could have such an influence.'"[49] Indeed the only prominent commander at the time to register his clear opposition was Hoepner, who on December 20 wrote to his wife: "Brauchitsch has been excused. A. H. has taken over command of the OKH. [Field Marshal Walter von] Reichenau installed for Rundstedt, Kluge for Bock. Those are sad signs."[50]

The man closest to Brauchitsch in the OKH was Halder. Though publicly he showed concern for his former chief following his departure, privately he despised him and may even have held ambitions of replacing him. On December 25 Halder wrote an open letter to the commanders of the army groups, armies, and panzer armies/groups on the Eastern Front; ostensibly his aim was to "prevent rumours" by insisting that Brauchitsch had been replaced on account of his ailing health. Yet Halder also suggested that he had requested that Hitler relieve him of his duties.[51] In his postwar memoir, written shortly before he was hanged at Nuremberg, Keitel alluded to Halder's keen interest in Brauchitsch's fragile health and appeared well aware that an end to his tenure was near. Keitel then added: "It was evident that Hitler also recognised that a crisis was looming, but he stubbornly resisted all the War Office [OKH] schemes outlined by Halder."[52] It is unclear exactly what Keitel meant by "schemes," but conceivably Halder was angling to be Brauchitsch's successor.[53] Another possibility, advanced by Jürgen Förster, is that Halder felt the position of an army commander-in-chief could be scrapped altogether, which by implication would have elevated the status and responsibility of Halder's own post.[54]

Whatever Halder was pushing for, his request that Hitler relieve Brauchitsch of his duties was motivated less by concerns for Brauchitsch's health than by the security, and possible advancement, of his own position. The suggestion that Brauchitsch was simply inadequate in such a role was undoubtedly true, but that had been known for months, if not years, and no one had acted to remove him on that basis, probably because he could be success-fully manipulated by both Hitler and Halder. What prompted Halder to oust Brauchitsch may well have been the general hostility directed toward the OKH and its "desk generals" by Hitler, which since the launch of the Soviet counteroffensive had markedly intensified. Halder was desperate to deflect any blame for the current state of affairs, and Brauchitsch was the perfect punching bag. At a military conference in late January 1942, Halder blamed every possible shortcoming on Brauchitsch's past tenure as commander-in-chief. According to Gerhard Engel's notes: "[Lieutenant-Colonel Heinz] von Gyldenfeldt and I were furious that he [Halder] seized every opportunity to cleverly denigrate the absent former C-in-C and attribute to him all previ-ous decisions and recommendations which were opposed to F.'s [Hitler's] thinking. Today he said: 'Mein Führer, if the field marshal had listened to you and me occasionally, today we would be in this position or that position.'"[55]A month earlier, when Halder addressed his open letter to the commanders of the Eastern Front, he projected a false tone of benevolent concern for the reputation of his former chief, but his duplicity did not end there. He concluded the letter with a ringing endorsement of Hitler as Brauchitsch's replacement, telling the generals: "We can and should be proud that the Führer himself is now at the head of our army."[56] Having schemed against Brauchitsch, it should come as no surprise that Halder's sincerity toward his new commander-in-chief was equally calculated and conditional.

Since the invasion of Poland, Halder had attended just fifty-four confer-ences with Hitler, which equated to fewer than two a month, but from this time on he was required to attend daily, which he managed to do while pro-jecting a positive relationship with Hitler. Halder wholeheartedly supported Hitler's halt order on the Eastern Front, while patiently enduring his tedious monologues and at times pointed questions.[57] His loyalty, however, was a facade motivated by self-interest, which Heusinger described as the hope of becoming Hitler's "supreme advisor."[58] Yet Halder's self-interest extended much further. In December 1941 both he and Brauchitsch were hedging their bets on Germany's future under the Nazis and were testing the water with the German resistance to see what future options might be on the table. Halder had earlier been involved in the resistance movement but had largely turned his back on it after the 1938 Munich agreement. The former diplomat and anti-Hitler conspirator Ulrich von Hassell noted in his diary on December 21, 1941:

> For several weeks now Brauchitsch and Halder have felt that their position has weakened. They are justifiably indignant that they have been made scapegoats for the reverses in Russia . . . Now they begin to see the light . . . A little later [sometime after December 2] Brauchitsch himself confessed to his nephew that it was necessary to take action and he wanted to confer with me. Halder expressed similar statements to Thomas. Still later, however, Halder withdrew his statement in conversation elsewhere. My informant maintains that he had said we must wait now for spring and final triumph over Russia.[59]

Clearly, both men were disillusioned with Hitler. Brauchitsch's career was ending on a sour note, and he viewed Germany's war effort, perhaps in part because of his depression, in the blackest of terms. Halder, on the other hand, was much more of an opportunist. He had no intention of being dragged down with Brauchitsch and so adopted the fraudulent roles of a protective collaborator and loyal subordinate publicly, but was a blame-shifting backstabber in his private conversations with Hitler. Halder also viewed the war effort in far more optimistic terms and certainly believed there was still a path to a German victory. His engagement with the resistance was therefore a clear sign of his ambition, keeping his options open and positioning himself to exploit whatever opportunities might be presented. Yet it also confirms that his devotion to Hitler, like that of Brauchitsch, was dubious at best and subject to his own self-serving interests. There was still much about the authoritarian Nazi state that Halder found appealing, and he experienced no moral quandary about the methods and policies being pursued, especially in the east, but he did have a view on how best to run the army and the war, and he was uncompromising about defending it.

It is doubtful that much of the fallout from Brauchitsch's departure reached Hitler, but the implications of taking over as commander-in-chief of the army only increased his already impossible workload as head of state, head of the Nazi Party, and now commander-in-chief of the German army. According to Halder's postwar account, Hitler announced the change in command to him with the words: "This little affair of operational command is something that anybody can do. The task of the [army] commander-in-chief is to educate the army in the idea of National Socialism. I know of no general who could do this in the way I want it done. So I have decided to take over command of the army myself."[60] It was a conceited claim, if it was ever made, although Hitler did have a predilection toward ideological education, which to his mind underwrote a soldier's "iron will" and formed the basis of his new halt order.

Hitler made no attempt to counter the obvious implication that Brauchitsch was being punished for the turn of events in the east. Indeed, that view was openly encouraged within the top ranks of the Nazi Party as well as in Hitler's inner circle.[61] Above all, Hitler had grown to detest Brauchitsch and, no doubt encouraged by men like Halder, subsequently spoke of him with the utmost loathing, having convinced himself that he had in fact somehow ruined the eastern campaign. As Goebbels wrote on March 20, 1942: "The Führer spoke of him [Brauchitsch] only in terms of contempt. A vain cowardly wretch who could not even appraise the situation, much less master it. By his constant interference and consistent disobedience, he completely spoiled the plan for the eastern campaign as it was designed with crystal clarity by the Führer."[62]

For high-ranking commanders in the army, Brauchitsch's legacy was more mixed. Some wrongly believed that he was punished for confronting Hitler with the truth of what was happening in the war,[63] while others held precisely the opposite view. General of Infantry Dietrich von Choltitz, for example, singled out Brauchitsch and the high command for the army's complicity to Hitler: "trouble is that we participated without a murmur; Brauchitsch and those fellows."[64] Others condemned him for accepting the secret monthly tax-exempt supplements paid to field marshals, but his fellow officers, not surprisingly, hardly considered his role in the army's criminal activity, and when it was raised, his culpability was either downplayed or rejected.[65]

Administratively, Hitler made Halder's office directly responsible to him and transferred all other duties and offices to Keitel as head of the OKW.[66] Thus, offices like Fromm's Replacement Army and Army Armament Department, and Major-General Bodwin Keitel's (younger brother to Wilhelm Keitel at the OKW) Army Personnel Department suddenly found themselves working through a whole new chain of command.[67] In his day-to-day administration Hitler continued to rely heavily, as he had done in the past, upon his adjutants for both special tasks and the coordination of policy within the new "Army High Command Staff"; this was a body that aimed to oversee and administer the army's interests within the overall framework of Keitel's office.[68] The response to this new arrangement was largely positive, with praise even coming from the *Gruppenleiter II* in the army's organization department—one Major Claus Schenk Graf von Stauffenberg, who would go on to deliver the bomb to Hitler's briefing room in July 1944. The "new solution," Stauffenberg concluded, was working better than before to serve Germany in the "decisive struggle."[69] Likewise, Fromm told his military district commanders: "The Führer's taking command is an honour for the army. The army's work will become easier not more difficult."[70]

Brauchitsch's role in the Second World War is often understated. Yes, he was completely overawed by Hitler, manipulated by Halder, and ineffectual in many aspects of his office, but his departure from the army is usually given short shrift, with the conclusion being that he had been bypassed by the real decision makers in the German high command. Yet this, while true, much more reflects the final months of his command. In almost four years of service, Brauchitsch's mark on the German army was unquestioningly significant in both policy matters as well as command decisions. In shaping an officer corps second to none in the purity and strength of its National Socialist thinking, as his general order of December 18, 1938, stipulated, he was surely successful.[71] Moreover, his administrative role in expanding and preparing the army for its early operational success cannot be discounted any more than his willingness to accommodate and advance Hitler's war of annihilation in Eastern Europe. Brauchitsch never again met with Hitler following his dismissal, but he did make one more contribution to public life following the failed assassination of Hitler in 1944. He published an article in the Nazi *Völkischer Beobachter* in which he condemned the attempted putsch and welcomed "as a National Socialist and former commander-in-chief of the army" Heinrich Himmler as the new commander-in-chief of the Replacement Army.[72] It was a spineless final act of submission, possibly undertaken to cover his own tangential involvement with the conspirators, but it forms one final stain on his prominent, if regrettable, role in the Second World War.

With all the interest garnered by Brauchitsch's replacement, Bock's departure was a much more modest affair. The disparity in the treatment of the two is somewhat ironic, given that Bock commanded by far the largest and most important army group in the east, which was at the center of both the failure to take Moscow and its subsequent retreat, while Brauchitsch was scarcely able to command much beyond his own staff. Since Bock's departure came at the same time as Brauchitsch's and was also explained on health grounds, Bock became worried that his reputation might be tainted by association.[73] On December 17, even before Bock knew of Brauchitsch's impending replacement, the field marshal became concerned that his own request to be relieved looked too much like he was deserting his post. He discussed the matter with Brauchitsch, who emphatically assured him that was not the case, but Bock then contacted Schmundt to ask how Hitler viewed the matter. As Bock declared: "I would very much rather collapse at my post than bear the consequences of the accusation of 'desertion.'" Schmundt gave the same unequivocal answer, but Bock then wondered if a more sinister motive was at work and if he was being reprimanded in some way for Army Group Center's difficulties. Bock recorded Schmundt's answer in full:

> No, on the contrary, in yesterday's discussion about this very topic he [Hitler] emphasized your great services and said: after the serious illness of last year, combined with the demands of this campaign, he could completely understand your sick report. I can assure you unequivocally that you can set your mind at rest about this.[74]

There is no reason to doubt that Schmundt's assurance was accurate, given that Hitler treated Bock very cordially when they met on December 22 and was even prepared to acknowledge that another command would be found for him once he had recovered. This was not long in coming; on January 17, 1942, Reichenau, commanding Army Group South in Ukraine, died of a stroke, and Bock was appointed his successor.

Kluge arrived at Army Group Center on December 18 in order to be briefed by Bock before assuming command the following day. Bock was uncertain if Kluge was a transitory stand-in or his permanent replacement, but Kluge evinced confidence that he was here to stay.[75] Indeed it was Kluge's self-assurance that endeared him to many of the men who knew him best. Blumentritt, his dutiful chief of staff at Fourth Army, described him as "that man of iron,"[76] while Greiffenberg, his new chief of staff at Army Group Center, would later note the field marshal's "dynamic" and "optimistic spirit" as well as his "determination to hold out to the end."[77] Equally, Hermann Balck from the OKH suggested: "Kluge made a very energetic and clear impression."[78] But Kluge was not just moving into the headquarters of Army Group Center; he was also entering the bourgeoning epicenter of the army's resistance movement to the Nazi regime.

Headed by Army Group Center's operations officer (Ia), Lieutenant-Colonel Henning von Tresckow, the movement had unsuccessfully tried to recruit Bock after subtly trying to persuade him for months. His two aides, Major Carl-Hans Graf von Hardenberg and Lieutenant Heinrich Graf von Lehndorff, were members of the conspiracy and did all in their power to influence Bock. When that failed, Tresckow adopted a more direct approach and openly attacked Hitler for the emerging winter crisis, but when Bock became aware of what Tresckow was suggesting, the field marshal became furious. Bock wanted nothing to do with the conspiracy, and he stormed out of the room shouting: "I will not tolerate any attack on the Führer. I shall stand before the Führer and defend him against anyone who dares attack him."[79] As Tresckow's adjutant, Lieutenant Fabian von Schlabrendorff, observed, the efforts to win over Bock were "a total failure," but fortunately Kluge soon offered a whole new prospect for success.

Kluge proved more amenable to the conspiracy than Bock, but it was an uphill battle. Time and again throughout 1942, Tresckow thought he had Kluge on board, only to be met with equivocation and indecisiveness. Kluge was also swayed by Hitler's charm and rewards, being the recipient of one of the infamous "birthday bonds"—a cash gift on his sixtieth birthday (October 30, 1942) of 250,000 RM. Additionally, Kluge was granted permission to conduct building works on his estate (permission which was otherwise almost impossible to get during the war). Kluge gratefully accepted the money and also took advantage of the building authorization, but when the conspirators learned of the payment they used it as leverage against him. Kluge was told that in the judgment of history he could only justify acceptance of the money if he did so in order to maintain a facade of loyalty while working for the overthrow of Hitler's regime.[80] Ultimately, Kluge would conditionally join the plot to assassinate Hitler in 1944, but his long-running vacillation, maintained even after the war had decisively turned against Germany, reflected his conflicted National Socialist sympathies as well as his reasonable fear of the plot's failure. In either case, the new commander of Army Group Center was something less than Blumentritt's vaunted "man of iron."[81]

At 11:00 A.M. on December 19, the same day that Brauchitsch was relieved of command, Bock appeared for the last time before his staff at Army Group Center. "I asked them to remain firm and confident," Bock subsequently wrote in his diary, "because I believe that the end of the present 'dirty period' is in sight. The Russians can scarcely have all that many forces left."[82] Consistent with so many of his previous estimations regarding Soviet strength during his six-month tenure in the east, Bock was again dead wrong. Army Group Center's winter crisis was only just beginning, and Kluge would have to deal with it.

7

THE BEAR WITHOUT ANY CLAWS

The Inadequate Red Army

By the time of Hitler's halt order, the Soviet attacks by Zhukov's Western Front, in cooperation with the Kalinin Front and the right wing of the Southwestern Front, had succeeded in eliminating the threatening German bulges to the north and south of Moscow. Already by December 12, the Red Army had liberated some four hundred villages, including Strelkovka, where Zhukov had grown up and his mother and sister had lived until the advancing Germans forced their evacuation in November.[1] They were the fortunate ones. The soldiers of the Red Army were discovering that the reality of German occupation validated Soviet propaganda. There were, indeed, "wholesale robbery, despoliation of the population, and monstrous atrocities."[2] One report suggested that some 2,500 civilians and

Soviet POWs had so far been discovered shot or hanged.[3] It was therefore clear to the advancing Red Army that German cruelty had not been overstated, and subsequent research into the scope of the war of annihilation in the Soviet Union has borne out this conclusion.[4] To cite just one example from Orel, which in December 1941 was the headquarters for Guderian's and Schmidt's armies, a German soldier later told the following story without knowing that his conversation was being secretly recorded: "An MG 42 was set up in the main aisle of a church. Then the Russian men, women and children were made to shovel snow; then they were taken into the church, without knowing at all what was happening. They were shot immediately with the MG 42 and petrol was poured on them and the whole place was set on fire."[5]

Not surprisingly, such actions emboldened the Soviet cause. By the same token, the average Red Army soldier, enduring brutal discipline under the harshest of conditions, was suddenly confronted with the alternative to any thoughts of surrender. As one German intelligence officer reported in February 1942: "It is no longer because of the lectures from the *politruks* [political commissars] but out of his own personal convictions that the Soviet soldier has come to expect an agonizing life or death if he falls captive."[6] Working in Fourth Army's headquarters, Hellmuth Stieff knew enough about German occupation methods to write in a letter on December 13 that the danger his army was confronting was "necessary and is the just divine punishment" for what he called a "non-German system of vengeance and lust for murder."[7] Such measures were also playing right into the hands of Soviet propaganda, as a Soviet colonel told Alexander Werth, a British war correspondent in Moscow: "It's a horrible thing to say, but by ill-treating and starving our prisoners to death, the Germans are *helping* us."[8] Indeed, from December 1941 to January 1943, the Leningrad journal *Propaganda and Agitation* included more articles on German atrocities than any other topic aside from the heroic exploits of the Red Army.[9] Meanwhile Philip Jordan, one of Werth's colleagues in Moscow, gauged the popular sentiment and highlighted "the frightful bitterness and hatred that the Germans have sown."[10]

While demonizing the German enemy was simple, Soviet propaganda found it much harder to build a positive view of its own army among the rank and file. Organization, equipment, and training for the new forces taking part in the winter offensive typically ranged from rudimentary to non-existent, while their treatment by officers was often shocking. The most famous examples were the penal units and blocking detachments—troops placed behind the front lines during a battle in order to shoot soldiers attempting to retreat. These formations formally became part of the Red Army in July 1942, but they existed in ad hoc forms from the first months of the war.[11] Yet even more sinister examples of the ruthlessness of the Red Army existed from the winter of 1941.[12] Georg Kreuter wrote home in a letter on December 16 that the Soviet enemy "wants to appear quite strong . . . The Russian bluffs, he attacks in part with civilians."[13] Dragooning civilians into joining attacks was not just done to increase the sheer size of the attacking force; it was at times deliberately organized to absorb German bullets in the hope of preserving the soldiers behind. After observing a massed Soviet attack that was shot to pieces by German infantry, Heinrich Haape, a German doctor from the 6th Infantry Division, wrote:

> And then something even more grotesque came to our notice. Two old women were cowering against the wall—in their muffled state we had taken them for men. They and about fifty more old men and women, civilians from the Russian-held villages, had been forced to run in front of the Red troops when they charged our positions. All but the two old women of this human shield had been shot down by us and trampled underfoot by the troops behind . . . Three were wounded but still alive.[14]

Soviet soldiers did not even have to participate in such disastrously one-sided battles to witness their horror. As their men marched to the front, the carnage was evident for all to see. One senior Soviet commissar became concerned by such sights, as well as by the implications for the men. "Not rarely," he reported, "the corpses of soldiers . . . go uncollected from the battlefield . . . although it would be entirely possible to bury our comrades with full military honours."[15] In fact, with the ground frozen solid, burial was a problem for both sides, and bodies were sometimes "stored," awaiting the spring thaw.[16] The commissar continued: "Corpses on the field have a political resonance that affects the political-moral condition of the soldiers and the authority of the commissars and commanders." If seeing so many bodies was not horrific enough, another commissar's report stated that the soldiers were sent into the fields to strip the dead of their weapons and equipment "so that we could use them the next morning."[17]

By 1942 the shortage of officers for the Red Army meant the only requirements for receiving a commission were six years of education and no criminal record; consequently a lot of new officers were commanding with no formal military education or professional skills. Compounding the problem, many were killed or wounded before they gained the necessary experience to command effectively.[18] Lieutenant-General Filipp Ivanovich Golikov, who commanded the Soviet Tenth Army until February 1942, wrote after the war that his headquarters staff were "poorly selected and of low competence." Moreover, "the poor tactical capabilities of forces led to many mistakes in combat: to frontal assaults, sluggish action, inadequate provision of fire-support when advancing, to inadequacies in co-operation and also to unnecessary losses. The army operated without a fully prepared rear, without regular deliveries of munitions, fuel and provisions. Divisional and army-level horse-drawn transports fell behind."[19]

The dearth of leadership in the Red Army led Soviet propaganda to focus on the highest ranks, where the perception of competence and proven success were easier to sell. Accordingly, although Stalin remained the ultimate harbinger of the Red Army's wisdom and success, on December 13 *Pravda*, the Soviet daily newspaper, introduced many of the front commanders to the Soviet public. Zhukov and eight other commanders were pictured on its front page—only the second time Zhukov had been pictured in the Soviet press since the war began.[20] It was the beginning of the wartime Zhukov myth, his name associated only with unqualified successes. As his biographer concluded: "This was not true . . . But belief in the myth inspired confidence in him at every level of the Red Army, not least among the lower ranks to whom he became a legendary figure."[21] There was some irony in this given that Zhukov's well-earned reputation for cruelty and draconian measures was felt by his soldiers most of all, but from December 1941 there was an attempt to counter the richly deserved perception of poor leadership within the Red Army.

The real triumph of Soviet propaganda was the ability to transform a war effort replete with unparalleled disasters and colossal miscalculations into a narrative of ultimate success. On December 22 Ilya Ehrenburg published an ambitious article commemorating the six-month anniversary of the war in which he addressed the perception of German success by framing the war through the eyes of the German soldiers:

> Six months ago, they snorted joyfully: the war seemed then like light entertainment. With much delight, they looted the first Belorussian villages. They argued as to which bacon was better, Serbian or Ukrainian. They thought that they were invincible. Have they not been in Paris? Did not they sail all the way to Narvik? Did they not cross the mountains of Epirus? They came to us whistling a tune. Where are they? In the ground . . .
>
> Germans still send their tanks against us. But they are no longer the same Germans. Water eats away a stone. Our resistance has eaten away the German spirit. Where is their former cockiness? They do not dream of Moscow restaurants, but of a village hut, of a roof over them, even of a pigsty . . . They freeze to death in December.[22]

Certainty there could be no denying the scale of German losses in the east or the comparative reversal of fortunes between June and December 1941, but Soviet propaganda could never honestly address the disparity in losses without revealing the true scope of the Soviet debacle.[23] Still, as in the sensation generated by Brauchitsch's dismissal, successful propaganda is about the perception of truth, not truth itself. Accordingly, the beginning of the German retreat became evidence enough for a major Soviet victory. However, the cost in blood for the Red Army made December 1941 scarcely discernible from earlier months of the war. It was not the Germans who were now sustaining massive casualties on the defensive—they continued to suffer a disproportionately small number of losses—the only change was that the Red Army's bloodletting continued, yet now it was driven by their own offensive operations rather than those of the Wehrmacht. As outlined in the introduction, G. F. Krivosheev's study of Soviet casualties set daily losses in the first period of the Moscow counteroffensive at a higher rate than for the preceding periods, when the Red Army was on the defensive.[24] More recent work by Lev Lopukhovsky and Boris Kavalerchik revised upward the Soviet winter total, arriving at more than 1.6 million Soviet losses, which tells its own story when set against the German total of just 262,524 casualties for a slightly longer period (November 26, 1941, to February 28, 1942).[25]

With the German-Soviet war now a battle of attrition, the notion that the winter constituted a German "defeat" cannot be argued from casualties inflicted or sustained. Indeed, assessing these alone would suggest an extremely one-sided contest. More helpful is the strategic context, which intriguingly shows both sides achieving their stated goals by December 19. The Stavka had successfully eliminated the bulges to the north and south of Moscow, which even Hitler had not attempted to oppose.[26] The German withdrawals caused a number of local crises but had thus far avoided major troop encirclements and the much-feared Napoleonic collapse. After discussing the military situation with Hitler on December 18, Goebbels summed up in his diary: "Nowhere is it dangerous."[27] The following day, Goebbels dismissed the trumpeting of Soviet successes, commenting, "In reality they are not victories, rather just thrusts in empty space."[28] Of course, while Soviet propaganda certainly overstated their successes, Goebbels's representation went too far in playing them down. The Soviet offensive was hitting much more than simply "empty space," but it was a very long way from categorically defeating Army Group Center.

December 1941 was the first time in the war that Germany was able to adapt its operational success to a (barely) realizable strategic goal; in doing so it was also winning the war of attrition in blood, although almost certainly not in matériel. If winning territory is assumed to be the only worthwhile goal in warfare, as some seem to reason, then December 1941 was of course a Soviet success. Yet after winning vastly more land over the proceeding five months, Germany had not managed to end the war, and one might well argue they would have been far stronger in December 1941 had they opted to gain somewhat less. In any case, for Soviet propaganda the German retreat was the "proof" of a Soviet victory. To help sell this message, Pravda wanted an actual picture of Germans retreating through a snowy landscape, and to get it they photographed recently captured POWs with wind and blowing snow created by an airplane propeller.[29] The representation of the event seemed perfectly plausible, but it was built upon a distortion.

The verdict of Soviet propaganda should not be uncritically accepted as the judgment of history; we need to be discriminating in how we identify and corroborate the conditions of "victory" as well as "defeat." While the Soviet soldier often appears in German accounts as the consummate winter fighter, provisioned and equipped for the freezing conditions, this was by no means always the case. The Western Front's initial request for 340,000 sets of winter clothing was met in full, but a subsequent request on October 29 for a further 558,000 sets fell woefully short and meant that even elite guards units were sometimes inadequately clothed. Field kitchens were also in very short supply, limiting access to hot food, while the necessary balance of combined arms weaponry, essential to support a major offensive, was often grossly deficient. This lack helped the German defense as well as enabling its weak counterattacks, giving the Wehrmacht a sometimes exaggerated effectiveness. As an example, much is often written about the effectiveness of the Soviet T-34 and KV series tanks, which could traverse sixty to seventy centimeters of snow, but the ST-2 tractor that might tow supporting artillery or antitank guns could only cope with fifteen to twenty centimeters of snow. By the same token, the workhorse of the Red Army, the GAZ-AA truck, could only cope with up to twenty centimeters of snow even with chains.[30] The absence of support vehicles meant Soviet tanks, even when technically superior, were soon a liability without fuel, munitions, mechanical assistance, or accompanying arms like artillery.

Ammunition was also severely rationed for the Soviet offensive owing to production shortfalls, while tank production by the end of 1941 had fallen to less than 20 percent of prewar figures.[31] As a result, the winter offensive was tank-light, which was no doubt another factor in the survival of many German units. On December 1, the combined strength of tanks for the Kalinin, Western, and right wing of the Southwestern Front came to just 667 units, and only 205 of these were T-34s or KVs. The great bulk of these tanks (over 600) were concentrated in Zuhkov's Western Front, but they were seldom employed in concentrated numbers and tended to be parceled out in battalion- and brigade-sized units in support of infantry.[32] Indeed, at this stage of the war, Soviet tanks were estimated by Walter Dunn to last for just fourteen hours of combat.[33] During the course of December, the Western Front would receive three more Independent Tank Battalions made up mainly of the light (six-ton) T-60s. The 133rd Independent Tank Battalion, for example, had twenty T-60s, one T-34, and ten KV tanks. In spite of continuing reinforcement, by February 15, 1942, the Western Front reported that just 153 of its tanks remained operational, reflecting the short life span of its armored forces on the offensive.[34]

By December 16, what would later be identified as the first phase of the Soviet winter offensive to win back a buffer zone before Moscow had largely been achieved. From December 13 onward, Zhukov was planning a follow-up second phase, in which he envisaged another advance with "an average distance of 130 to 160 kilometers west and northwest of Moscow."[35] Operationally his plan was unambitious, and on paper it even looked crude, consisting of largely frontal attacks against the German line, but Zhukov believed his ill-trained armies and substandard officers would struggle to cope with anything more. His intention was to create mobile groups within each of his armies (consisting typically of a cavalry division, tank brigade, and rifle brigade) and have them exploit weaknesses in the German front, opening the way for the main forces. Ultimately, the final objective was a line just east of Smolensk, which Zhukov wanted to reach before the end of the winter. However, to obtain this he estimated that his second phase would require the injection of four fresh armies from the *Stavka* reserve.[36]

Stalin was in agreement with the plan and gave it his assent, but he refused to authorize any of the new armies for Zhukov's front and instead allocated them to attacks on the flanks, reinforcing the Kalinin Front and reconstituting the former Briansk Front to the south of the Western Front. It was a clear sign of Stalin's hubris. Not only was he, backed by the *Stavka*, again assuming responsibility for major operational decisions, which he had stepped back from in the aftermath of the disastrous battle of Kiev, but it appears Stalin's goal was nothing less than the complete encirclement of Army Group Center. Colonel-General Ivan Konev's Kalinin Front was to strike south and southwest to Rzhev and then press on to Viaz'ma, while Colonel-General Yakov Cherevichenko's Briansk Front was to attack northwest toward Briansk and then north to close the trap at Viaz'ma.[37] The distances were huge; the necessary logistical apparatus was absent; the climate could not have been less favorable; and the Red Army had proven itself too unsophisticated even to encircle weak German divisions, let alone the bulk of Army Group Center. If there was one thing that Stalin should have learned from Germany's failure in 1941, it was the virtue of restraint, but instead the dubious second phase of the Soviet winter offensive was set in motion—only this time it was destined to meet a far less malleable opponent.

Soviet success was of course always relative to the German response, and the fact that Army Group Center had thus far opted for withdrawal in critical sectors of the front gave the *Stavka* a misleading sense of confidence. Hitler's halt order changed this, but the retreats did not end as unconditionally as the order intended. German commanders reserved for themselves a degree of autonomy that Soviet officers could not have imagined, and this acted to allieviate the worst implications of Hitler's new order. It meant that German units attempted to repel Soviet attack, but when the pressure became too great they typically opted for withdrawal over annihilation. The Red Army, on the other hand, had no such culture of independent appraisal or questioning of orders, and the strictly hierarchical structure meant that even the most foolhardy orders were faithfully carried out.

One must be careful not to oversimplify the German response to Soviet attacks. Army Group Center was by no means operating with a free hand, and many commanders felt unreasonably constrained by Hitler's new order. Among the senior commanders there was near universal condemnation. Before he left his post, Bock talked tough about a strict implementation of the order, but he was not the one having to live with the consequences. Kluge immediately found himself caught between the pleas for flexibility from his subordinate officers and Hitler's pigheadedness. Kluge rejected every appeal he felt he could risk, but clearly identified grave threats that justified withdrawals and from the beginning was seeking local exceptions from Hitler. On December 17 Hoepner wrote to his wife that the proposed order was a "death sentence" for his panzer group.[38] On the same day, Reinhardt noted in his diary: "Order from above: 'Annihilation or hold'! What with?!"[39] Strauss at Ninth Army believed a slow withdrawal to be the "one correct solution" but offered no resistance and issued a "clear order to the army."[40] Schmidt bitterly rejected Hitler's new order and complained to the army group that "rigidly imposed . . . the order leads to very great danger. We have the thinnest front, reserves are absent." He then warned that if forced to accept the order, his Second Army faced "annihilation."[41] Guderian was the most outspoken of all, defiantly refusing even to pass on the order. On December 19 he informed the army group:

> The situation is more serious than one could imagine. If something is not done soon, things will happen that the German armed forces have never before experienced. I am prepared to take these orders and file them. I will not pass them on even under threat of court-martial. I want at least to give my career a respectable ending. I would rather die first.[42]

The unanimity of opinion among Army Group Center's commanders illustrates the ingrained command culture from which they all stemmed. Becoming a General Staff officer was an exceptionally demanding process, designed to induct only the best and the brightest. Accordingly, candidates were tested and retested across a broad range of subjects both military and nonmilitary. Scholastic excellence was as highly valued as proficiency in leadership and military drill. The aim was to produce well-rounded, freethinking officers able to solve problems and innovate without recourse to higher authority. There can be no question such qualities gave German officers a marked advantage over their opponents, and that counted as much in defensive warfare as it did on the offensive. The idea of removing an officer's independence of command went against the very heart of the general staff's flexible command culture. Under such circumstances, it is perhaps surprising that more commanders did not voice their disapproval with the same vigor as Guderian, especially if they equated the new orders with the "annihilation" of their force. On the other hand, as the evidence below might suggest, official compliance with Hitler's order, while granting subordinate officers local autonomy, was a more pragmatic solution than Guderian's ultimately self-defeating objections.

Given the Wehrmacht's well-known reputation for offensive warfare, some authors have expressed surprise at the army's equivalent proficiency in defensive fighting. The supposition seems to be that attack and defense are wholly distinct forms of warfare, which in practice is false. Given that Germany's conception of future warfare during the interwar period was dominated by defensive thinking, rather than offensive, we should hardly be surprised by the German army's adaptability.[43] There was also much more defensive fighting between June and December 1941 than a cursory view of the German operations might suggest. For aspiring General Staff officers, both the attack and defense were emphasized, and as Jörg Muth's study of command culture concludes: "The [German General Staff] examination was clearly designed to find out if the applicant had only been lucky in the former parts or if he really was made of the right stuff and if his mind worked as flexibly in attack as it did in defense or retreat."[44]

On December 18, 1941, the second phase of the Soviet winter offensive opened, and by the following morning Halder opened his situation report for Army Group Center with the words "Attacks everywhere."[45] Hoepner and Reinhardt had already made it clear that their current positions on the Lama and Rusa Rivers were temporary and that they did not believe these could be held for long.[46] In light of Hitler's halt order, they had repeated this warning to Army Group Center, with Reinhardt even suggesting that it was questionable "whether his divisions could be brought to a standstill."[47] Reinhardt offered no explanation for the comment but was clearly suggesting his forces might not respond to orders, which might be understood two ways. First, Reinhardt was genuinely concerned about junior commanders not obeying his orders and that, faced with overwhelming Soviet strength, units might simply retreat to save their own skins. A second possibility, however, is that Reinhardt was exploiting the confusion at the front and the decline in discipline to provide cover for unauthorized withdrawals. We have already seen that German commanders at the very top disagreed in the strongest of terms with Hitler's halt order, so what did they do about it, if anything at all? The reply to Reinhardt's comment came from Bock, who at that point had yet to give up command of Army Group Center; he told his panzer commanders: "Hold your fist in the back of your people!"[48]

Bock's uncompromising stance sounds somewhat hypocritical given his own request to depart the front. Clearly, talk of stiffening backbones was cheap, especially when those demanding it had nothing more to offer the men than their own example, which in Bock's case was worthless. Meanwhile, on the Lama-Rusa front the reestablishment of the German line revealed for the first time just how much equipment had been lost during the retreat. Ruoff's V Army Corps, for example, reported on December 20 that it had lost some 300 machine guns and fifty 3.7-centimeter and ten 5-centimeter antitank guns, as well as more than seventy pieces of artillery. At the same time, Geyer's IX Army Corps had lost eighty artillery pieces of various calibers.[49] Two days earlier, on December 18, Hoepner reported to Army Group Center that his panzer group retained just 25 to 30 percent of its weaponry.[50] Under such circumstances the prospect of holding the new front, while being strictly forbidden to retreat, was understandably a daunting one. There were some limited reinforcements for the combat units, either through combing out the rear echelons and sending idle specialists (artillery crews without guns, truck drivers without trucks) to the infantry or from the return to service of men on convalescence or canceled leave. Gerhardt Linke's unit received some 200 reinforcements, but in his diary he noted derisively: "Many of them cannot even handle their own rifles properly."[51] Five days later, on December 21, Linke noted that another 70 men, including two officers, reached his section of the front, but on the same day about the same number were lost to sickness, frostbite, or wounds. Summing up the nervousness at the front, Linke concluded his entry: "What will these conditions bring to us? . . . The men walk around as if they were doomed. Are they really going to let us go to the dogs?"[52]

If there was tension among the men it was also felt by their commanders. Reinhardt's panzer group was nominally under Hoepner's command, but Reinhardt conducted his own affairs and did not accept any direction from Panzer Group 4. Hoepner complained to Kluge and even asked that Reinhardt's panzer group instead be placed under Strauss's command, which Kluge immediately rejected. The problem, according to Hoepner, was that Reinhardt was completely self-focused and took no account of the wider front. In his position on the Lama, Reinhardt was refusing, under all possible pretexts, to cover a broader section of the front in spite of occupying just twenty-five kilometers of the line with six divisions, while Ruoff's V Army Corps and Vietinghoff's XXXXVI Panzer Corps (both also belonging to Panzer Group 4) alone covered twenty-four kilometers of front each "with a great deal less strength." Moreover, Hoepner protested that the staff at Panzer Group 3 observed no chain of command and freely sent reports to the OKH, Army Group Center, and Fourth Army, as well as Hoepner's own group. Perhaps most telling of all was Hoepner's charge that Panzer Group 3 misrepresented events at the front in order to justify its withdrawals. The accusation stemmed from an overheard telephone conversation with the OKH in which someone from the panzer group claimed "that the retreat of its neighbour is the reason for its own retreat," which Hoepner insisted was not true.[53] Assuming this was not an honest mistake, it suggests that the panzer group's command staff was not opposed to blatant fabrication if it served its purposes. Desperate times called for desperate measures, and even flagrant insubordination in defiance of authority was not beyond General Staff officers.

Two days later, on December 21, Hoepner again locked horns with Reinhardt after he refused an order to release Veiel's 2nd Panzer Division to stem a growing crisis for Ruoff's V Army Corps at Volokolamsk. As Panzer Group 4's war diary noted: "In a sharp tone general Reinhardt reported that giving up further forces is out of the question because the order to do so gives a false assessment of the situation." Hoepner's written reply was equally blunt. He informed Reinhardt that he alone could best judge the situation because only he, not Panzer Group 3, had an overview of the situation.[54] Reinhardt simply refused to give up Veiel's panzer division, but that evening he instead agreed to dispatch a single battalion from Landgraf's 6th Panzer Division. Even this meager concession was opposed by Colonel Walther von Hünersdorff, the chief of staff at Panzer Group 3, but as Reinhardt reasoned, "what is the point of us holding if the right [flank] breaks."[55] Clearly, Panzer Group 3's motivation was entirely self-interested, while orders from above were purposefully disregarded.

Hoepner by this point had had enough and, almost certainly after discussion with Kluge, sought radical change. The replacement commander for Fourth Army, General of Mountain Troops Ludwig Kübler, had still not yet arrived from Army Group South to assume his new post, and consequently Kluge was giving commands over the telephone to his overwhelmed former chief of staff, Blumentritt.[56] Fourth Army was therefore in desperate need of a commanding officer, and Kübler was still days away from arriving. Although no record of a conversation between Hoepner and Kluge confirms their collusion, the sequence of subsequent events suggests this was an opportunity to deal with the recalcitrant Reinhardt. On December 22, Panzer Groups 3 and 4 were detached from Fourth Army's nominal command,[57] and the next day Kluge ordered Reinhardt to depart Panzer Group 3 immediately and stand in as the commander of Fourth Army.[58] At the same time, Hoepner informed Panzer Group 3 that it would fall under the command of General Ruoff, forming his V Army Corps and Panzer Group 3 into "Group Ruoff."[59] The intention was clearly to remove Reinhardt and allow Ruoff to access whatever he needed from Panzer Group 3 to fend off the Soviet attacks at Volokolamsk.

Reinhardt was incredulous at what was being proposed, seething in his diary: "such nonsense, to give a panzer group to an infantry corps commander." He was also furious that Ruoff was already trying to remove Veiel's panzer division, and it is not beyond the realm of possibility that Reinhardt's proclivity for deceitfulness may once again have led him to disobey Kluge's order. Reinhardt's new orders arrived at midday on December 23, and two hours later he replied that the weather situation did not allow him to fly or drive to Fourth Army's command post at Maloiaroslavets (some 140 kilometers away). Admittedly, at this time there were very heavy snowfalls, which complicated movement, but they probably did not mean it was impossible for Reinhardt to leave his headquarters. When Kluge telephoned at 5:00 P.M., Reinhardt had still not departed and simply insisted it was impractical to do so; the two argued, and Kluge demanded he depart for Maloiaroslavets even if only on a sled. The next morning Reinhardt was still at Panzer Group 3's headquarters awaiting a *Storch* aircraft to take him to Maloiaroslavets. "Insanity," Reinhardt protested in his diary, "when Kübler is already on the way to Fourth Army."[60] Conveniently for Reinhardt, the aircraft developed a technical problem, and by midday Kluge could wait no longer and instead appointed Stumme, the commander of XXXX Panzer Corps, to stand in at

Fourth Army.[61] Reinhardt was overjoyed. "12 o'clock, decision that I can stay. Thank God."[62] The result also appears to have torpedoed Hoepner's plan for Ruoff to direct Panzer Group 3, which reflects not only the seeming impotence of higher commanders to rein in rebellious subordinates, but also that undesirable orders were to some extent "subject to approval" by manipulating local circumstances. Rather than subordinate commanders losing their independence to command in the wake of the supposed end of *Auftragstaktik*, clearly in some quarters that independence was fiercely defended.

Further proof of that independence came as Soviet attacks continued to hit Panzer Groups 3 and 4 up and down the line, leading to local withdrawals for which there is no evidence of authorization from the high command. On the morning of December 21, the war diary of Vietinghoff's XXXXVI Panzer Corps recorded that Fehn's 5th Panzer Division evacuated the villages of Lyzlovo and Kuz'minskoe in the face of "reinforced enemy pressure." There was no suggestion of demanding a fight to the last man, but later that same afternoon a counterattack was organized in which the enemy suffered considerable losses in men and equipment. Two Soviet companies were captured as well as a German radio van and an antitank gun. As the report concluded: "In spite of days of retreat, the local success shows that the morale of the troops is still intact and, with determined leadership, are still capable of great achievements."[63] Although precise figures do not exist for every panzer division in Army Group Center, Fehn's division was almost certainly the strongest in tank numbers and therefore among the best placed to deliver counterblows. On December 21, his panzer regiment retained an impressive eighty-seven operational tanks (twenty-six Panzer IIs, forty-eight Panzer IIIs, and thirteen Panzer IVs), with another thirty tanks awaiting maintenance. The problem was fuel. On December 17, Fehn's division reported that it could provide just half of its vehicles with fuel and even then only for short distances. This was the trade-off for retaining so many vehicles, which of course was much less of a problem in the panzer divisions with the highest fallout rates from the retreat.[64]

The real worry was that the *Grosstransportraum*, the truck-based transport fleets bridging the railheads with the armies, would not have the fuel to continue bringing large stocks of munitions forward to sustain the defensive battles.[65] It was a circumstance that exacerbated the already nervous situation at the front as limited stocks of munitions diminished. This was the most pressing problem at Ruoff's V Army Corps, where Volokolamsk had already been given up in sustained fighting and, on December 24, the town of Ivanovskoe was surrendered on account of "no munitions." Once again, German troops were not standing and fighting to the last man; they were withdrawing even when that meant losing large towns like Volokolamsk. Ruoff's communiqué to Panzer Group 4, informing them of his retreat, did not seek their permission, while Hoepner offered no rebuke in reply.[66]

Ruoff's report also made clear that without immediate aid from Panzer Group 3 the situation would soon become "catastrophic" and that Major-General Ernst Dehner's 106th Infantry Division would be "annihilated."[67] Hoepner immediately contacted Reinhardt, as the commander of Panzer Group 3 recorded in his diary: "Cry for help from Hoepner, we should help V.A.K." Yet Reinhardt was still reluctant to dispatch his own forces and only agreed to another battalion (which he would not release until the following day) as well as 5,000 artillery shells. Ruoff pleaded for tanks, but Reinhardt scoffed at the idea. "Impossible," he wrote in his diary. "6th Pz. Div. has none." This was essentially true of Landgraf's 6th Panzer Division, but Reinhardt offered nothing from Veiel's 2nd Panzer Division, which on December 24 possessed thirty operational tanks, or from Krüger's 1st Panzer Division, which on December 21 commanded twenty-three.[68]

The German defense depended on three possible responses to Soviet attacks. Firstly, a conventional static defense in which the quantity of defensive fire was judged to be greater than the forward momentum of the attacking force. This was by far the most conventional response, making it the easiest to prepare and conduct, but it also had a strong record of success. Soviet attacks were so frequent that the men hardly needed orders to know what to do, especially if they occupied familiar positions and more so again if these positions were well prepared with dugouts and clear fields of fire. Local intelligence was crucial, but seldom could a defending commander ever be entirely sure in advance if his defensive fire was in fact superior to the attacking momentum of the enemy, and countless positions were overrun, especially after the halt order was issued. In his first meeting with

Stalin, William Standley, the new United States ambassador to the Soviet Union, promised to offer whatever aid he could, to which the Soviet dictator's response was unequivocal: "He [Stalin] replied that the Russians were killing many, many Germans at the front, that the poor Germans had received orders that they must not retreat or give way an inch and the result was that they were killing them like pigs."[69] Clearly, Stalin wanted to impress his ally and may not have known (or cared) just how costly assaults on German positions could be, even if successful. The Red Army did kill many Germans in static positions, but their own losses were completely disproportionate.

The reality was that the static defense was still effective against the predictably ill-conceived and unimaginative Soviet attacks. In one of many after-action reports, Veiel's 2nd Panzer Division recorded an attack on December 23 in which 11 Germans were killed, 9 were wounded, and 11 were missing, but before their lines 300 Soviets lay dead and only 100 rifles and 11 machine guns were found.[70] As Nikolai Ranzen, a Russian émigré who worked as a translator in Dehner's 106th Infantry Division, noted after a series of failed Soviet attacks near Volokolamsk on December 22: "The Soviets are having high losses. Seeing that, our soldiers' spirit and self-confidence are rising."[71]

On December 18 Colonel-General Wolfram von Richthofen, commanding the VIII Air Corps, which provided aerial support for Army Group Center, reported optimistically to Goebbels that Soviet attacks were "without any strategic significance" and sought only "to somehow gain territory." This the Red Army had succeeded in doing "here and there; but in most instances, when they push further than we would desire, they are pushed back and must pay a very heavy toll in blood."[72] Even when large groups of enemy armor were employed, as on December 24, when an estimated thirty to forty Soviet tanks attacked south of Volokolamsk, the fragile German front was able to hold through concentrated artillery fire and Luftwaffe support, which on this occasion left ten Soviet tanks destroyed.[73] Of course, this was not always the case, and "panzer fright" among the German troops was by no means always an overreaction, but the overwhelming majority of Soviet attacks on static German positions in December 1941 failed, often with appalling results.

If the conventional static defense was the first German option against Soviet attack, the second option was counterattack. This had to be employed either preemptively, before the Soviet defenders could anticipate such an action and consolidate their strength, or from an unexpected direction. If the enemy force was numerically stronger in men and equipment, as was frequently the case, counterattacking was a treacherous undertaking, but for that reason often an unanticipated one. Such a response typically required some kind of mobile reserve, reliable intelligence from aerial or POW reports, and experienced leadership. If all of these could be brought to bear, the results were often positive. On December 21, the war diary of Vietinghoff's XXXXVI Panzer Corps advocated this form of "offensive defense" as the best approach to German security. "The conduct of battle is no longer simply positional warfare, but must, through frequent counterattacks, become a war of movement. The Russian must be caught before the positions at an early stage. He now believes he is in the pursuit, so that he will not expect an energetic defense. This will soon stop the attacks."[74] Such a solution was no doubt correct in theory but depended upon resources that weakened and overstretched infantry divisions typically did not possess. Consequently, after Hitler's halt order a static defense was, at least officially, the only option available.

As we have already begun to see, however, some German commanders were reluctant to give up their independence of command and were withdrawing even after the halt order was issued. Typically, such actions could be explained by "force of circumstances," events beyond the control of the responsible officers, and therefore they could not be accused of insubordination. Reinhardt's exploitation of "gray areas" to justify his defiance of Hoepner and Kluge was one of the more brazen examples of what could be done to camouflage disobedience. As Lieutenant-Colonel Rudolf-Christoph von Gersdorff, Army Group Center's chief intelligence officer (Ic), observed after the war: "In those weeks and months [after the halt order was issued] the troops at the front learned to 'get around' militarily senseless decisions. 'Attacks by numerically superior enemy forces and the effect of extraordinarily heavy artillery fire' would be blamed for the limited withdrawals of the front."[75] Clearly, officers (not "the troops," as Gersdorff suggested) looked upon retreat as a third option, albeit as a last resort, in dealing with Soviet attacks. On December 24 Hoepner reflected upon the implications of the halt order and made clear his opposition to surrendering his authority. As the panzer general wrote: "Finally, I must have some freedom in the leadership. It is often necessary to act quickly to counteract a small setback or prevent a larger one. I manage the available means and the possibility of its employment better than an authority, which sits 1,000 km behind the front."[76]

Indeed, in the week after Hitler's halt order was issued, German records show that withdrawals were constantly being considered, even if not always carried out. On December 22, Panzer Group 3's war diary noted that the heavy snowfalls and the limited network of roads meant that "a suddenly ordered and quickly executed retreat is no longer possible."[77] Theoretically, the weather conditions should have been irrelevant; a retreat by Reinhardt's forces had not been possible since December 18. Yet clearly, and understandably, German officers were more interested in preserving their forces, as well as their own lives, and wanted the assurance of knowing that, if counterattacks and static defenses could not hold the enemy, an escape plan of last resort was open to them. Accordingly, retreat remained an unauthorized and unofficial—but no less real—option on the Eastern Front in late December 1941.

8

THE BATTLE OF NERVES

Army Group Center on the Brink

A s Reinhardt and Hoepner defended their positions on the Lama and Rusa Rivers, to their north Strauss's Ninth Army was conducting an authorized withdrawal, having begun its retreat from Kalinin on December 15. Hitler's intention was that the Ninth Army would halt on a line running through Staritsa (some seventy-two kilometers southwest of Kalinin) and there cover the north flank of Army Group Center. Strauss, however, was skeptical. So far he had conducted a successful withdrawal, carefully maintaining the cohesion of his long front, while moving it a few kilometers each day. Staritsa was a rough midway point between Kalinin and Rzhev, but it was really only a geographic spot on the map with extremely limited natural defenses. The Volga River ran through Staritsa, but on a parallel course to Ninth Army's retreat, affording it no protection. Strauss was worried that without any prepared positions an enduring defense would not be possible; on December 21 he flew to Kluge's headquarters to request that he be allowed to continue the withdrawal all the way to Rzhev, where the Volga River turned northwest and would thus offer him at least some protection. Rzhev, however, was the northern anchor of Bock's Rzhev-Gzhatsk-Orel-Kursk Line, now known as the Königsberg Line, which Hitler had argued was no better prepared than the more forward line he had selected. Hitler had also cited the unavoidable loss of equipment entailed in any attempt to reach the Königsberg Line. Thus, Kluge was not about to challenge the halt order for the Ninth Army, which appeared to be one of the most secure areas of Army Group Center's front. Accordingly, Strauss's request was rejected, and he was ordered to make a stand at Staritsa.[1]

Given Stalin's reinforcement of the Kalinin Front to bolster attacks on Army Group Center's wing, as well as the critical lack of mobile forces to plug any holes in Strauss's front, the difficulty of seeking to hold a line running through Staritsa was not to be underestimated. Even with the relief created by their continued withdrawal, Halder repeatedly noted the "heavy attacks" on Ninth Army's front leading up to Christmas.[2] Yet, just as the army chief of staff had time and again underestimated the strength of the Red Army, Halder remained stubbornly convinced that the enemy offensive could not last much longer and attempted to assure Kluge on December 21 that if the army group could just hold its positions the Soviet offensive "would be all over in fourteen days." Moreover, Halder reasoned that the Soviets "cannot continuously maintain these frontal attacks" and that, as a result, any further retreats by the army group would "possibly yield too early and for nothing."[3] It was an extraordinary set of statements, which again highlighted just how differently the high command understood the events at Army Group Center.

Understanding these two opposing interpretations might best be done by identifying how each side conceived of its solution. At the front, it was all about pragmatic, tangible outcomes—quantities of fuel, numbers of men, length of the front, strength of the enemy—all of which were quantifiable. Yet National Socialist military thinking allowed another engagement with this reality. It introduced an intangible dimension which, because it could not be measured, could be demanded in whatever quantities were required to balance out the deficiencies at the front. As Halder noted from his meeting with Hitler on December 20: "The front needs to have the will to hold."[4] The concept of "will" was Hitler's solution to the crisis, which even his National Socialist officer corps struggled to comprehend. As Hoepner wrote on December 24: "The fanatical will alone achieves nothing. The will is there. The strength is not. The strength is numerically small for the space."[5] General of Infantry Erich von Manstein, who in December 1941 was commanding an army in the Crimea, wrote after the war:

> This brings me to the factor which probably did more than anything else to determine the character of Hitler's leadership—his overestimation of the *power of the will*. This *will*, as he saw it, had only to be translated into *faith* down to the youngest private soldier for the correctness of his decisions to be confirmed and the success of his orders ensured . . . Such a belief inevitably makes a man impervious to reason and leads him to think that his own will can operate even beyond the limits of hard reality—whether these consist in the presence of far superior enemy forces, in the conditions of space and time, or merely in the fact that the enemy also happens to have a will of his own.[6]

Hitler's concept of "will" made him infallible. Success at the front proved the virtue of his "iron determination," while failure reflected only upon the inadequacies of the men and officers involved. As one indoctrinated soldier attempted to explain in his postwar memoir: "The struggle is not lost on the physical plane first, but on higher planes, which is to say first spiritually and then mentally, and only when the struggle in these two areas has been lost, does defeat occur on the physical battlefield."[7] Of course morale is fundamental to combat, but the fallacy inherent in National Socialist military thinking was that it allowed Hitler, or any of his commanders, to treat tangible factors as secondary, no matter how dire the shortage.

Although Strauss's request for a continued retreat to Rzhev was rejected by Kluge, this did not stop elements of Ninth Army from continuing with local withdrawals, for which there was no apparent authorization. Förster's hard-pressed VI Army Corps continued to fall back on the night of December 21, but not fast enough for Lieutenant-General Helge Auleb, who commanded the subordinate 6th Infantry Division. Auleb rejected the constant halts to conduct "rearward resistance," which he claimed was a long-since outdated concept as well as being a "forbidden tactic." Auleb also clashed with Förster over the burning of enemy villages during his retreats, but not for any moral reasoning. The commander of the 6th Infantry Division claimed the huge fires acted "better than a letter to the enemy commander" in alerting the Soviets of German intentions and thereby provoking attacks that endangered the retreat. Auleb even claimed in his unpublished postwar memoir not to have always carried them out, which if he did so, could only have added to the friction with Förster. On December 25 he was relieved of his command.[8] Auleb was dismissed because of his reluctance to conduct the retreat according to the wishes of his higher command, which suggests that the discussion within the higher echelons was less about *whether* to retreat, but rather how best to conduct it. Indeed, Auleb would not be the last general with differing views on how best to manage the retreat to be forced to relinquish his command.

Once Strauss's Ninth Army had begun its retreat in the middle of December, the Fourth Army remained Army Group Center's only major formation not to have undertaken a significant withdrawal of its front, but plans to do so were well advanced when Hitler's halt order was issued. Two weeks earlier Fourth Army's flanking formations protruded eastward on both ends of its front, but by December 18 the reverse was true with a slight bulge in the German line, consisting of Kluge's former army. Fourth Army's front was just sixty-eight kilometers from Red Square along the main east-west highway, meaning that, in spite of having thus far avoided serious Soviet attention, one could hardly expect it to remain a quiet sector for long. Indeed, the new phase of Zhukov's offensive, which began on December 18, targeted Fourth Army specifically. Thus, when Blumentritt received Hitler's order from Greiffenberg at Army Group Center instructing him "not to retreat a single yard," he experienced a sense of dread: "Fourth Army prepared to fight its final battles. Only a miracle could save it now."[9] The effect this had on Blumentritt was observed by Fourth Army's operations officer, Hellmuth Stieff, who wrote in a letter on December 22 that the army's chief of staff was visiting the front in the hope of being killed: "he cannot be held back, because his nerves are completely finished, that is at least my impression."[10]

Fourth Army's front was established along the line of the Nara River with a good system of trenches and bunkers built in many cases before the ground had begun to freeze. Accordingly, initial Soviet attacks against the north and center of the army's front were quickly blunted; however, the south faced an immediate crisis.[11] Since Guderian had repeatedly abrogated any responsibility for closing the gap between his XXXXIII and XXIV Army Corps, the former corps was eventually subordinated to Fourth Army, leaving it with an open southern flank. The new Soviet offensive therefore was aimed at exploiting the breech and advancing, virtually unopposed, to envelop Heinrici's XXXXIII Army Corps and strike toward Kaluga, the main communications, supply, and administrative center for the southern section of Fourth Army's front. Writing home on December 19, Heinrici despaired at his situation and at what Hitler's new order demanded:

> Yesterday, after sometimes very heavy combat, we succeeded in holding up the pressing enemy. Yet that does not change the overall situation, which is still more than serious. Now even the supreme leadership realizes that the fate of the entire campaign is at risk. Before that no one wanted to listen to our warnings. Both on the large and the small scale there have been enough reports about the condition and the weakness of our troops. Irrespective of our lack of winter clothing, insufficient provisions, poor supplies and depleted strength, the army high command wanted to advance on Moscow, Guderian on Tula. All precautionary measures were put aside. Now they tell us to sacrifice ourselves to get it right again.[12]

At the front, Gerhard Bopp was confronting the same frightening reality. On December 21, he wrote in his diary: "Front must be held to the last man!"[13] What this meant in practice was soon evident to those units that attempted to stand their ground against overwhelming odds. Hans Pietzcker wrote to his mother five days after Hitler's order was issued: "Dear Mother, it was sad, it was bitterly difficult—of my thirty-six men only six are still with me . . . we held out, loyal to our duty and responsibility . . . we were undefeated, we knew our tasks and our orders."[14] Pietzcker's account plainly illustrates the error of Hitler's thinking. What the depleted German front desperately needed was not more dead heroes, but thinking soldiers, men who evaded Soviet attacks when they had to and stood their ground when they could. The dubious honor of fighting to the last six men was a very narrow view of "victory," orders or not. Moreover, such "heroic" examples might well have galvanized others to seek alternatives, to spare the lives of their men and serve the army in a more sensible and professional capacity. Willi Lindenbach summed up in a letter on December 20: "Hopefully the front will hold, that is what we all wish."[15] "Hoping" the front would hold was as intangible as "willing" the front to hold, but with little control over their environment soldiers were left with no alternatives. Their officers, on the other hand, were trained not to blindly follow orders, but to always seek better solutions by identifying and pursuing initiatives, especially when their survival was at stake.

The Soviet drive on Kaluga was a rare instance of impressive speed and skillful maneuver. Indeed, Army Group Center's staff map for December 21 shows no sign of Soviet forces anywhere near Kaluga, but events on the ground were moving faster than they could be reported. The Soviet strike force consisted of cavalry, some tanks, and infantry on skis. They had already penetrated into the German rear on December 19, with additional forces continuing to mount attacks against Heinrici's XXXXIII Army Corps, pinning down his forces.[16] In Kaluga, the arrival of enemy troops caused consternation, as H. C. von Wiedebach-Nostitz recorded in his diary on December 21:

We hear a long spell of 8.8 gunfire and a lot of noise on the roads.
There is almost an atmosphere of panic in the town. Early on
the Russians have reached the edge of the town where a severe
engagement is under way. Many vehicles are trying to leave the town.
Machine guns and anti-tank guns are set up on the most important
streets . . . The Russians are slowly forced out of the town.[17]

Max Kuhnert was also in Kaluga when the Soviet attack came and was ordered to destroy two trains that had just arrived full of desperately needed supplies as well as Christmas packages for the men. Not surprisingly, before carrying out their orders, Kuhnert and his group first wanted to save as much as possible by loading up their horses and some baggage carts:

> But the next order we got was to blow up the train and run. The Russians had reached the outskirts of Kaluga and were in armored strength . . . First the explosions and crackling of the train wagon with all our dream goodies in it—and we had to leave most of the things we had loaded behind. Our skin was more important than the biscuits, the Christmas parcels, the winter clothing, the cognac and the cigarettes. We kept going nearly crazy with exhaustion . . . I held on to the tail of the horse in front to be pulled along at times . . . I started to sweat because of the effort and fatigue, but stopping to rest was too dangerous, not only because of frost, but also because of the Russians. They had still not been checked and seemed to move faster than us; we could hear shooting and shouting behind us.[18]

Such accounts provide insight into the waste, fear, and chaos that had, until then, not threatened major German supply centers. The situation at Kaluga was the focal point of frantic discussions within the high command, with Halder referring to it on December 21 as "the great crisis point." Kluge and Greiffenberg spoke with Hitler and Halder several times a day seeking permission for withdrawals, but these were repeatedly refused. After detailing the extent of the crisis in his diary Halder concluded: "Order to hold is given." Summing up a later telephone conversation with Kluge on December 21, Halder disdainfully wrote: "Under the demands of his subordinate troops he [Kluge] is increasingly weak. One must make him hard."[19] Kluge was hard; unlike Halder, he was not shying away from the difficult decisions or the consequences of inaction. In fact, after Hitler and the OKH dismissed his fears, Kluge defied his orders and, on his own authority, granted Heinrici limited freedom of movement to maneuver his corps away from the encroaching Soviet forces. As Heinrici wrote on December 22: "I am again standing at the high point of Russian pressure. Basically, we are already fully encircled. Yesterday the situation was hopeless. We were anticipating our end in the encirclement. At the very last minute, Kluge gave permission to withdraw again. That prolonged our existence a little bit longer."[20] Clearly, even Kluge was at times prepared to secretly undermine Hitler's halt order. Given that the only record of this stems from a private letter by Heinrici to his wife, one may well wonder if there were other violations he privately authorized without leaving a record.

Kluge's subsequent adjutant, Captain Philipp Freiherr von Boeselager, later maintained that Kluge was a "highly intelligent and brave" man who possessed a "clear strategic view and always grasped the interrelationship between the economy, geopolitics and military planning." If true, this would suggest an uncommon aptitude among his contemporaries at the top of the army to conceive of operations within a somewhat broader context and plan accordingly. Kluge's skillful management of scant resources, forceful personalities, and the extremely delicate matter of managing Hitler would seem to support Boeselager's observation. Yet in achieving all of this, the field marshal's adjutant also noted, Kluge could be at times "more than difficult" to serve.[21] Kluge may have taken liberties with Hitler's halt order, but, as we shall see, that did not mean he would brook any insubordination among his own commanders, which is all the more reason to conclude that the persistent defiance of the halt order within his army group was part of his response.

Whatever Kluge's skills he was no longer in command of Fourth Army, which desperately needed good leadership, having inherited from Guderian Heinrici's XXXXIII Army Corps with a dangerously open southern flank. To make matters worse, on December 22, a new Soviet attack broke through Heinrici's northern flank, leaving the XXXXIII Army Corps exposed on both flanks, cut off from the rest of Fourth Army, and in imminent danger of encirclement.[22] Still, the high command remained unmoved. Halder, while acknowledging "an exceptionally difficult situation," nevertheless continued, "a solution is not foreseeable."[23] Under such circumstances, it was easy to understand the exasperation at Fourth Army's command. Hellmuth Stieff wrote to his wife on December 22:

Everywhere alarm bells are ringing, and today I had to report to the
Field Marshal three times in great haste that the army will cease
to exist in eight days if the Führer does not rescind this crazy order
to hold everything where it is without consideration for enemy
breakthroughs! . . . Our troops are so worn-out in these inhuman
circumstances that I cry when I think of them. My nerves are
completely gone . . . But I must be strong, not for myself, but for my
poor, poor men.[24]

Not only was Heinrici's XXXXIII Army Corps in grave danger, but General of Infantry Hans Felber's XIII Army Corps also had an open southern
flank, and Fourth Army, with no reserves, confronted being "rolled-up"
from the south.[25] Heinrici was in total despair, writing: "Sleeping, eating,
drinking—everything is over. Only our whipped-up nerves keep us awake.
But soon this will go beyond our strength, to run for our lives day after day
without seeing any change, no change for improvement."[26]

On December 23 Kluge was again desperately trying to gain approval for
a substantial withdrawal of Fourth Army's southern flank, but he was countered by Halder's absurd reasoning. "Kluge judges this situation as operationally very serious," Halder wrote in his diary. "I see it less operationally and
more tactically very uncomfortable."[27] One wonders on what basis Halder felt
entitled to contradict the information Kluge was supplying from the front, but
perhaps this was his method of showing up his army group commander for his
apparent weakness. Nevertheless, Kluge's unrelenting attitude as well as the
hour-by-hour deterioration of the situation eventually won a concession from
Hitler. As Kluge told Hitler: "I must now confront the question, whether we are
to stand and let ourselves be killed or withdraw the front and sacrifice a certain
amount of matériel, but get away with the rest." Hitler dithered somewhat, but
eventually agreed: "If there is no other way, I give you freedom of maneuver
to issue the order to withdraw." Kluge promised only to give the order "if [he
saw] no other way out of the dilemma."[28] In reality of course the order was as
good as given. Kluge and his corps commanders in Fourth Army must have felt
an enormous sense of relief, but also bitter incredulity at the wasted time and
the absurdity of having to seek permission to save their own men.

Felber's XIII Army Corps retreated to the northwest, while Heinrici's XXXXIII Army Corps fell back on Kaluga. Fourth Army's only mobile division in the southern half of its front was Knobelsdorff's 19th Panzer Division, which had been tied up in heavy defensive fighting as part of Kirchner's LVII Panzer Corps. Kluge knew his only chance of stemming the Soviet breakthrough was to free Knobelsdorff's division and hit back at the surging Soviet advance. At considerable risk, Knobelsdorff's division was eased out of the line, reinforced by over 1,000 replacements, and sent south to counter the Soviet attempt to roll up the German flank.[29] The crisis on Fourth Army's southern flank was far from resolved, but at least the destruction of major formations had been avoided for now. Having barely survived intact, and perhaps knowing of Kluge's courageous act of insubordination, Heinrici was hardly consoled and foresaw the dangers inherent in the army's new commander-in-chief. Writing home on December 24, he perceptively observed: "Who the gods wish to destroy they first make blind . . . And in complete blindness they are keeling over into the abyss. And they will end in four weeks by losing their army before Moscow and later on by losing the whole war."[30]

What must not be overlooked in the attention devoted to the southern flank of the Fourth Army is the success of its center and north against very heavy enemy pressure. The sustained Soviet attacks were in places disastrous for the Red Army. Knobelsdorff's division alone sent reports claiming hundreds of enemy dead along narrow sections of its front.[31] At the same time, Fourth Army's intelligence intercepted evidence that suggested they were not the only ones dealing with an obstinate and irresponsible command. One message from a Soviet regimental commander stated: "Temporarily impossible to carry out attack as ordered. Twelve-hour postponement necessary." The reply from his senior officer was as pitiless as it was unequivocal: "You will attack at once. If not, I'm afraid your health will suffer."[32] The war diary of Kirchner's LVII Panzer Corps noted on December 22 that the quality of Soviet troops was generally poor, but their ability to refresh their units posed a constant danger:

> Illustrative of the enemy, it is worth noting that under multiple
> uniform coats of the fallen, civilian clothing was found. Apart from

a few good Russian formations, which have suffered considerable losses in the last few days, the units are thrown together and quickly transported, so the Russian can constantly replenish his formation. In this way, he is continuously allotted rested men who, in their numerical superiority, are a considerable fighting force against our battle-weary troops.[33]

Colonel Hermann Balck from the OKH was dispatched to the front by Halder on December 21, along with four other officers, ostensibly to instill "self-confidence and restore order."[34] This gave Balck an opportunity to gain insight into the defensive fighting at the front, and he later recalled: "The Russians attacked with everything they had. They had little artillery and fewer tanks, but they had people, whoever they could muster, without re-gard for their ability to regenerate their army."[35]

Even with Germany's crisis points along Army Group Center's long front, the overall "success" of the Red Army's grinding advance cannot be separated from its losses. The Soviet mood was publicly one of jubilation and triumph, spurred by what, on the surface, appeared to be Germany's great disaster in the east, but 1941 was not 1812, and the propaganda war was not the real war. The Soviets could celebrate their first "victory," but there was little recognition that in a war of attrition there would have to be many more campaigns to follow, and squandering countless men in irresponsible attacks was actually making the road to Berlin longer, not shorter. Still, Ilya Ehrenburg took his best shot at exploiting the Soviet advance, and on De-cember 22—the six-month anniversary of the war—he extolled the Soviet people with his famous analogy of the attacking bear. "The Germans have been campaigning in the east for six months . . . They had already divided up the skin of the Russian bear. But there seems to have been a slight hitch somewhere: 'Before you can say "knife" the bear is on top of you.'"[36]

The bear certainly was on top at Volokolamsk and around Kaluga, but—to extend Ehrenburg's analogy—bear traps and hunters remained on guard along much of the rest of the front. Farther south, the Second Panzer Army and Second Army were struggling to deal with their own emergent cri-ses both at the front and within their own command. Guderian had a well-deserved reputation as a headstrong, independent commander whose success reflected his innovation and boldness, but he also had a predisposition for disloyal, egocentric, and intransigent behavior. Hitler's halt order evoked all of these emotions in Guderian, and with the demands of his men uppermost in his mind, the panzer general was in no mood to take orders he did not agree with. For the first time in the war there is also evidence that Guderian was struggling emotionally, no doubt compounded by his months of unrelenting activity—including a number of near-death experiences while visiting the front. His formerly towering self-confidence had become a facade. When Richthofen visited Guderian at the beginning of the Soviet offensive, he alluded afterward in his diary to the shattered man he encountered: "To Guderian. Very open discussion. He is only externally hard, otherwise made of jelly. I actually wanted to be consoled by him and instead had to do it myself for him! Bitter and difficult."[37] Likewise, Schmidt, who had daily contact with Guderian, observed on December 19 that the once "great optimist" had reached "the end of his hopes."[38] In Guderian's letters to his wife the intractable situation at the front seemed to gnaw at him, and the ever-present feeling of helplessness was compounded by the genuine affection he felt for his men. On December 16, Guderian wrote despairingly: "How we are supposed to come out of this, I don't yet know myself."[39] It all acted to reinforce a kind of siege mentality, in which Guderian cared only about his panzer army and how best to preserve it.

While Bock was still in command of Army Group Center he had agreed to Guderian's request for him to meet with Hitler personally. Guderian had justified this by claiming that he wanted to "explain" the position of his army, but it became clear that Guderian had an agenda of his own, and freeing himself from any operational control was central to it. Guderian departed for Hitler's Wolf's Lair headquarters in East Prussia on the morning of December 20 and spent most of the day in transit. Schmidt held temporary command of the combined armies and was kept busy with a new Soviet breakthrough on the southern wing of Second Army between Hubicki's 9th Panzer Division and Lieutenant-General Sigfrid Henrici's 16th Motorized Infantry Division. Reports suggested that the front had been broken in two places, with medium and heavy Soviet tanks having penetrated the front and advanced to the Tim River.[40] Kluge was already lobbying Hitler to allow Lieutenant-General Werner Kempf's XXXXVIII Panzer Corps (to which Hubicki's and Henrici's divisions belonged) to withdraw behind the Tim. Kluge also sought to give up the indefensible town of Livny, but in return he wanted Hubicki's panzer division to launch a counterattack on December 21 aimed at eliminating the Soviet breach. Kluge was clearly at pains to exploit any Soviet overextension as well as to demonstrate to Hitler that he was not just interested in withdrawals. Yet the field marshal also warned Hitler that, even if Hubicki's attack was successful, this was only a temporary solution and that holding the current line was "impossible." He also requested "freedom of action to make local withdrawals, where the situation and the avoidance of unnecessary losses demands it."[41]

On the afternoon of December 20 Hitler's answer came through, rejecting any withdrawal or freedom of movement. As the dictator told Halder, "Every man must defend himself where he is. No withdrawals to rear positions that are not prepared."[42] In response Kluge's headquarters replied that "the danger exists that the army group will eventually be frontally overrun."[43] The planned counterattack of Hubicki's panzer division became a series of actions running from December 20 to December 22 in which a total of over 1,000 Soviets were killed and four artillery pieces captured.[44] It was not enough to eliminate the danger, but it stunned Soviet forces and bought some time for Kempf's forces to continue holding, albeit with losses, east of the Tim.

In spite of Hitler's declaration, Kluge did not stop badgering the high command with reports from the front and appeals to allow withdrawals. Halder called Army Group Center and made it clear that Hitler would only allow a withdrawal to the Tim when Kluge could personally assure him "that the rearward line is so prepared that a successful infantry defense can be guaranteed." Kluge could not, and did not, make any such promise, but his patience was wearing thin. He even called into question the underlying logic of the halt order. "It may happen," he told Halder, "that the events are stronger than the will which opposes them."[45] Such a statement may seem rather obvious and uncontroversial, but the aura of the "will" was strongly associated with military notions of *Kampfgeist* (fighting spirit) and *Siegeswille* (desire for victory); anyone who questioned them was almost by definition a defeatist. New in his post, Kluge had to tread carefully, but as with the situation at Kaluga, the field marshal was discovering that the line between observing Hitler's order and preventing the annihilation of his units in the field left no room for maneuver. Guderian, on the other hand, had already come to this conclusion and had taken matters into his own hands.

Guderian's plane landed at Rastenburg airfield at 3:30 P.M. on December 20, but it was 6:00 P.M. before he was taken in to see Hitler. According to Guderian's postwar account, he was greeted by Hitler with "a hard, unfriendly expression in his eyes";[46] however, another attendee singled out Guderian, claiming that "his psychological state was terrible, and this was not lost on F."[47] One may infer that neither man was in the mood for compromise. It would appear Guderian's intention was to win from Hitler whatever concessions he could, but, either way, the panzer general was determined to continue leading his combined armies as he saw fit, which meant continuing to fall back regardless of Hitler's new order. The evidence for this was pieced together by Kluge and his staff during the course of the day as they feverishly tried to account for all of Guderian's units to gain the most accurate picture possible of the situation. What slowly became apparent was that Guderian had covertly moved one regiment from each of Second Panzer Army's forward divisions all the way back to the Oka River, where he was establishing a new position.[48] At its shortest point on the existing front line this involved a retreat of some seventy kilometers, and at other points considerably farther. It was an unmistakable prelude to the wholesale retreat of the Second Panzer Army all the way back to the southern reaches of Bock's old Königsberg Line. The audacity of what Guderian was attempting was measured not just by the degree of his defiance, bordering on open rebellion against the high command, but by the implications for Army Group Center's ability to maintain a cohesive line. Presumably, Guderian had simply given up on this since Heinrici's XXXXIII Army Corps, on his north flank, had become separated from his panzer army. In any case Kluge was outraged. He was doing all in his power to win more space as well as freedom of action for Guderian's forces, while the panzer general was conspiring to utterly undermine his authority, while at the same time forsaking the rest of the Army Group Center.

Kluge immediately placed a call to Halder and laid out for him the extent of Guderian's insubordination. Halder insisted that Guderian "absolutely must stop," but Kluge suspected the panzer general was beyond simple orders and told Halder: "Guderian's conception is so pessimistic, one must assume that he has lost his nerve."[49] Under the circumstances one would have thought Guderian's dismissal was assured, either for his flagrant disobedience or, if Kluge was correct, on health grounds. Yet neither general suggested this course of action, although Kluge may have suspected that his next suggestion would lead to the same outcome. Given that Guderian had just arrived at Hitler's headquarters, Kluge told Halder to inform Hitler of everything Guderian had done, "so that he can discuss the further conduct of the Second Panzer Army with him." Halder agreed to make the call and later reported back to Kluge that it resulted in a "dramatic" encounter.[50]

Guderian's postwar memoir offers a rather different account of the events leading up to his confrontation with Hitler. In his own rendition it was Guderian himself who boldly told Hitler of his intention to withdraw both armies to the new Oka position, and this is what precipitated Hitler's dramatic outburst. When confronted with the evidence of his retreat, Guderian attempted to explain that his withdrawal to the Oka had already been approved by Brauchitsch during his visit to Roslavl on December 14. This was a weak argument given that Hitler's halt order clearly superseded anything that predated it. Guderian then claimed to have opposed holding Hitler's current line by suggesting "that the withdrawal was already in progress and that there was no intermediate line at which it could be halted for any length of time before the rivers [Oka and Zusha] were reached."[51] Expecting he could present Hitler with a fait accompli that went expressly against his own order was surely wishful thinking, and this was soon made clear to Guderian. Frustrated and upset, Guderian had an exchange with Hitler that gives a plausible insight into Hitler's National Socialist conception of warfare as well as the naivete of men like Guderian who went on serving Hitler until the final weeks of the war.

> [GUDERIAN:] Then this means taking up positional warfare in an unsuitable terrain . . . If such tactics are adopted we shall during the course of this coming winter, sacrifice the lives of our officers, our non-commissioned officers and of the men suitable to replace

them, and this sacrifice will have been not only useless but also irreparable.

[HITLER:] Do you think Frederick the Great's grenadiers were anxious to die? . . .

[GUDERIAN:] The intentions I have heard expressed will lead to losses that are utterly disproportionate to the results that will be achieved . . .

[HITLER:] But you are seeing events at too close a range. You have been too deeply impressed by the suffering of the soldiers. You feel too much pity for them.[52]

The meeting ended where it had begun, in disagreement. Halder assured Kluge that Hitler had "straightened out"[53] Guderian, but the panzer general claimed that as he was leaving he had overheard Hitler telling Keitel: "I haven't convinced that man!"[54] This last statement was undoubtedly true, but to the high command Guderian's compliance, if not his agreement, was all that mattered, and the panzer general returned to the front with his plans to force a retreat in tatters. Kluge was left in the awkward position of still trying to convince Hitler and the OKH of the need for retreats, but he had to distinguish his more moderate plan for a "stage-by-stage" withdrawal from Guderian's rash flight to the Oka and Zusha Rivers.[55] In private Kluge agreed that the Oka Line was an acceptable end goal, but it was politically impossible to sell. Meanwhile, Guderian's high-handed, devil-may-care attitude had worn the field marshal's patience to the bone.

When Guderian arrived back at his headquarters in Orel on December 21 he set to work ensuring Hitler's orders were understood by his subordinate formations, but the war diary of his Second Panzer Army warned that without additional forces, a rigid defense would lead to "the collapse of the front in a matter of days." Among the most threatened sectors was Weikersthal's LIII Army Corps, for which an enduring defense of its long front was deemed "more than questionable."[56] The Second Army fell under the same strict orders not to surrender any more ground. While Schmidt knew he had no choice but to obey, he issued another warning about the implications of Hitler's order:

Rigidly conducted, however, the order leads to very great dangers. We have the thinnest front, reserves are absent. The Russian is superior. He is close to his good railway network. He can move operationally and tactically and thus form points of concentration. These circumstances must lead to break-ins and breakthroughs. Breakthroughs can only be rectified by counterattack . . . [If] one has no forces to counterattack, then local relocation mixed with counterthrusts must be used to restore the situation.[57]

While the respective army commands feared the strategic implications of Hitler's stubbornness, at the front the dangers of attempting to hold weak positions against superior enemy forces were even more apparent. Adolf B. wrote home on December 21: "We were only recently in such a tight spot that we thought everything, and I mean everything, had to be given up! For who from us would want to fall into the hands of these Soviet beasts? 'Before us the enemy, on the left no connection, on the right no connection and behind us the Russian,' so now and then you have to imagine our situation!" The next day (December 22) he wrote claiming that "the situation was often so precarious" that he and his comrades just wanted to escape "the Soviet hell."[58] When Gottfried Becker was informed by his lieutenant that no more retreats would be allowed and that the current position, with half-dug foxholes, would form the new winter line, he was outraged. "He got to be kidding!" Becker thought; "those at the 'top' had to be nuts."[59]

Survival became a day-to-day achievement, and with strict orders not to fall back, the men were effectively fighting with their backs to an invisible wall. Every soldier knew that failure to hold the line meant death or capture, and it added enormously to the stress of combat. One soldier noted that "one hour on guard against the enemy costs more nerves than an attack in a tank."[60] Erich Hager from the 17th Panzer Division wrote in his diary on December 21: "The infantry have suffered the most in this retreat. I don't want to write any more details about it . . . Heavy artillery fire over our heads. The Russians will be coming."[61] Wilhelm Prüller alluded to the frightening sight of the enemy moving up to attack: "The whole horizon is now black with Russians, . . . wave after wave follows one another."[62] An unnamed soldier from Schmidt's Second Army left a diary in which he noted on December 23: "If the Soviets attack with heart and seriousness, we are lost."[63]

Given the sometimes fearsome odds against holding exposed and weakly defended positions, it is not hard to see why local commanders acted on their own initiative and defied Hitler's order by engaging in unauthorized retreats. Of course, those same odds ensured that spontaneous retreats also took place, in which the men simply fled the field in terror, often at great cost and under fire. Willy Peter Reese, who served with the 95th Infantry Division, recalled one Soviet attack on Dubrovka: "They came at night. We put up no resistance, because fighting, sacrifice, and war, none of it mattered anymore. A remnant of us fled across the plain to Belaya."[64] Likewise, Hans Roth described opposing a Soviet attack on December 22 supported by tanks and troops on skis, which swept over his unit "like a tornado." He and his comrades attempted to resist, but as he wrote in his journal after the battle, it was hopeless:

> An icy eastern wind forces snow into our faces; our eyes are swollen shut, our weapons refuse to operate. We have visibility of no more than ten meters away. The muffled roars of hand grenades, wild screams, horrific hand-to-hand combat is happening all around us. Two cannons are overrun.
>
> There is no more holding on—everyone for himself!
>
> In Kolchos, two kilometers behind the front line, our group gathers back together. We wait and wait, for half of our unit is still missing—no one else appears.[65]

While individual accounts confirm that such panicked flights took place, they can offer no insight into how often they occurred. The army's files are also largely inconclusive on the subject, in part because officers may have felt the need to cover up any unauthorized withdrawals, but also because of the difficulty of verifying at what point in a battle retreats took place. Did the men defend their positions to the point at which their lines were being overrun and then attempt to flee (as in Roth's account) or did they make the decisions they knew their officers could not and retreat before it was too late (as in Reese's account)? A conclusive answer requires more targeted re-search, but one may hypothesize that the results depended upon a host of factors, including the position of the unit, its recent casualties, the morale of the men, the number of officers and their access to ammunition, supporting fire, reinforcement, etc.

One notable report from Nehring's 18th Panzer Division suggested that the most serious problems stemmed from the lack of supplies, general fa-tigue, and ever-present cold, but not Soviet attacks, which seemed to enjoy no success. Included in the division's war diary on December 20, the report read:

> There is no thought of rest. Despite all the necessary measures food is irregular. Against the unusual cold—nights down to −40° C— adequate winter clothing is missing. In addition, there is the great psychological strain that this retreat, which almost looks like an exodus, provokes. Nevertheless, the enemy succeeds in no place, neither by day nor by night, to achieve success against our tired and exhausted men. On the contrary, by defenses and counterattacks, he sustains heavy losses.[66]

Clearly, Nehring's example could not speak for all of Guderian's divi-sions, but it suggests the resilience of major German formations even in the face of so much hardship. At least on this section of the front, the Red Army appeared to be the lesser concern. Moreover, in the following days, the divi-sional war diary noted the repeated failure of enemy assaults, culminating on December 23 with Nehring launching an armored counterstrike, which forced a local Soviet retreat and resulted in an estimated 300 enemy dead, 75 POWs, and the capture of twenty machine guns, hundreds of rifles, and one antitank gun.[67]

In the aftermath of Guderian's meeting with Hitler the panzer general claimed to have faithfully observed the halt orders, but the evidence sug-gests that this was not strictly true.[68] Guderian spent much of December 22 at the front with Weikersthal's LIII Army Corps, which on that day had sus-tained multiple breakthroughs of Stemmermann's 296th Infantry Division.

That night Guderian called Kluge and told him that following Hitler's order would mean the destruction of Stemmermann's division, but he was still not granted freedom of action. Yet an individual account left by Hans Reinert, a lieutenant in the 296th Infantry Division, confirms that an order was given on December 22 to retreat: "Well the order: Back! We are completely morally done in. I can't describe what we feel in these minutes. It's too enormous. We could howl aloud."[69] As Stemmermann's division fell back on Belev, which was on the Oka River, Guderian must have known he could not hide what was happening from Army Group Center. On December 23, he admitted that he had authorized the retreat and that the remainder of the Second Panzer Army would likewise have to fall back to the Oka and Zusha Rivers within the next two to three days. The response from Army Group Center was immediate and unequivocal; Guderian was warned that his order to Stemmermann did not have Hitler's approval, while the withdrawal of his panzer army was deemed unacceptable "under any circumstances."[70]

On the morning of December 24, Guderian again reported the deployments of his Second Panzer Army, and it quickly became evident to Kluge that the panzer general was still withdrawing his forces. Kluge placed a call to Halder and told him that Lemelsen's XXXXVII Panzer Corps as well as elements of Weikersthal's LIII Army Corps were both on the move westward and that Guderian had been dishonestly reporting their positions. Halder was irate and flatly declared that Guderian should be court-martialed.[71] Kluge seemingly had his opportunity to rid himself of Guderian, but at the critical moment he did not go through with it, probably because he was also aware that what the panzer general was doing made more sense than a hopeless last stand on frozen fields with no natural defenses. The commander of Army Group Center therefore argued that Guderian's withdrawals were made "under the compulsion of circumstances."[72] Certainly, soldiers' letters from December 24 make clear that this was also true on some sections of the front. Hans Pietzcker wrote at length of the growing Russian pressure and the difficulty of their fighting withdrawal toward Orel. He even noted after beginning another march to the rear: "Only afterwards came the order for us to continue the fighting retreat." Not only was Pietzcker's unit being issued orders that defied the German high command, his local commander had clearly reached the same conclusion and was prepared to act on his own initiative. The virtue of these decisions was reflected in the conclusion of Pietzcker's letter, where in spite of their withdrawals, a Soviet attack suddenly caught them in the flank. "We were pushed aside, had to run for our lives, a hundred yards behind us the Russians. Comrade fell next to comrade. Then we threw everything off, in order to be able to run better."[73]

As Kluge was grudgingly covering for Guderian, the bad news continued to pour in. Schmidt reported on the afternoon of December 24 that he had given up Livny and was threatening to do the same at Novosil.[74] Kempf's XXXXVIII Panzer Corps was in full retreat toward the Tim all along its extended front in spite of there being no authorization from the OKH or Hitler.[75] Whatever the halt order stated on paper, it was abundantly clear that the army commanders were calling the shots at the front and allowing withdrawals, rather than demanding resistance to the last man. Kluge may not have been prepared to enforce Hitler's authority, but his own was a different matter; having protected Guderian from dismissal, he perhaps foolishly expected some loyalty in return. On the evening of December 24, Army Group Center's war diary tells of how Kluge shared with Guderian "his thoughts" about closing the gap between Belev and Kaluga as well as strengthening Second Panzer Army's left flank on the Oka-Zusha Line. Guderian's hostile reply reflects both his despair at the strategic situation as well as his contempt for any higher authority's ability to deal with the situation. As Army Group Center's war diary recorded: "Colonel-Gen. Guderian replies that he does not have the slightest hope that anything will be changed due to the unending interference and the intended measures in the overall situation . . . He then asks for removal from his post because, according to him, the measures which were ordered would not change the overall situation. He had no objection if one was to bring him before a military tribunal."[76]

How much of this was bravado is hard to tell. It is not even clear if Guderian was railing against Kluge, Hitler, or just the whole high command. Guderian was emotionally exhausted. His self-destructive behavior may have been a symptom, conscious or not, of his need to escape the grinding pressures of command without the guilt of deserting his long-suffering men. Unable to accept any responsibility for his own role in the slow destruction of his panzer army, Guderian preferred to blame his superiors for everything that was wrong. Such thoughts reinforced his rebellious attitude, while the absurdity of Hitler's halt order fed his conviction that he was protecting his men from a nonsensical high command. Yet by December 24 the halt order was only six days old, and Guderian had hardly observed it anyway. In his final days of command, the panzer general's allegiance had switched from the high command to his men. He no longer cared for orders or the chain of command. He openly challenged Kluge to dismiss him and, by freely declaring himself ready to face a military tribunal, was flaunting his insubordination. Indeed, while Guderian remained in command he might just as well be considered a rogue general fighting an independent war. Moreover, the longer Guderian was permitted to operate outside the chain of command, the more his example would embolden generals who likewise disagreed with their orders.

Major elements of Guderian's army had already reached the Oka-Zusha Line by the evening of December 24. Kluge ended his conversation with the panzer general by issuing a stern warning that no further movements westward were to be undertaken without Hitler's prior approval.[77] Even to Kluge, these must have felt like empty words. The only real choice was to accept Guderian's insolent independence or replace him. There could be no middle ground.

9

THE MORE THE MERRIER

Christmas 1941 and the Supply Crisis

T he evening of December 24 is *Heiliger Abend*, the last day of Advent on the Christian calendar, when Christmas is celebrated in Germany. Irrespective of the conditions, which varied widely along the Eastern Front, there were plans everywhere to mark the event with some form of celebration, and Army Group Center, for all its difficulties, was no different. In some cases plans for the festivities had been in motion for weeks with food, alcohol, and presents for the men being stockpiled. Soldiers took to decorating their bunkers or village huts with candles, door wreaths, and Christmas trees. "Everyone was busy and overly busy," wrote Franz Leiprecht, "be it with cleaning the bunker and decorating or crafting adornments for the Christmas tree."[1] Men created improvised tree ornaments out of the packaging of gun cleaning kits, strips of tinfoil cut from chocolate wrappers, and cotton to represent snow, and sometimes soldiers wrapped the trees in shiny wire. Candles or wax-filled tin cans with a wick, known as Hindenburg lights, were placed on larger trees, while paper stars were affixed to the highest points.[2] The results were often modest but enough to remind the men of the world that they had left behind.

While the celebrations granted many a welcome evening of distraction, for others it only led to thoughts of home and family. Gerhard Bopp wrote in his diary on December 24: "This year I am experiencing absolutely no Christmas atmosphere; rather I am embittered and it is cold and empty inside me. The saddest Christmas Eve I have ever taken part in."[3] Hermann Vogel noted in his diary: "Of course, the mood was terrible."[4] Leopold Schober wrote that he and his comrades were in no mood for a celebration and spent the evening quietly writing letters and thinking about their relations.[5] For Helmut Günther's group there was also no Christmas spirit. The melancholy mood simply overwhelmed everyone. As he lay down to sleep that night, Günther sarcastically commented to a comrade about their "great Christmas Eve," to which the man mockingly added, "And peace on earth!"[6] Helmut Fuchs wrote of himself on Christmas Eve being, "unwashed, unshaven, dirty and hungry," while his lice were "rebellious."[7] For Wilhelm Prüller the stark contrast between a Christmas celebration and his life on the Eastern Front led to some profound reflection. Writing in his diary, Prüller mused: "as we stand between death, destruction, night and darkness here and life, happiness, light and joy at home; perhaps it is we, more than all the others, who can comprehend the meaning of this divine rebirth."[8]

Such thoughts were an obvious indication of how *Heiliger Abend* provided a powerful reminder for Christians to reflect upon their faith and attempt to draw strength from it. Engelber Aringer wrote of the Christmas celebrations as something akin to "experiencing the great holy hour at Bethlehem: Christ is born for us."[9] Ernst Tewes, a newly arrived Catholic priest, celebrated Mass on Christmas Eve at a hospital with many wounded, some clearly still in pain. He noted that many received Holy Communion "like men, who after a long hunger, saw bread again and reached for it." Inspired, Tewes concluded: "At the moment, I would not rather be anywhere else than here in dark Russia."[10]

Another Catholic priest, Josef Perau, wrote of celebrating his Christmas Mass with 300 to 400 soldiers: "No bells called them, no festive church full of glamour and sweet music lured them. They came into a cold, dark barn and surrounded a humble altar, where a priest celebrated Mass. That was all. But they had understood, that that really was *everything*."[11] The spiritual comfort of reengaging with a Christian message of faith, hope, and love, in the context of a savage war with no end in sight, inspired many a prayer for peace.[12] Yet some commanders did not miss the opportunity to leverage heightened Christian sensibilities to promote the righteousness of Germany's war against the atheist communists.[13] Henry Metelmann wrote of the speech his commanding officer gave in which he reminded his men "of the meaning of Jesus and Christmas, that our task in Russia was a holy one and that we had God on our side." He then concluded with "a prayer about God and the Führer."[14]

The Germans were not the only ones who sought to use Christmas as an engine for propaganda; it was also ruthlessly exploited by the Soviets to attack German morale. On December 24, Soviet planes flew over the German lines dropping thousands of "Christmas cards," offering seasonal greetings from the Soviet Union. A picture of a snowy landscape with a field of crosses topped by German helmets was captioned: "Living space in the east."[15] Ilya Ehrenburg contributed another of his blistering articles to *Izvestia*, this one entitled "German Christmas," in which he wrote:

> Under a snow-swept fir tree lay a German soldier. His dead white eyes looked westward. In his pocket, we found a letter from Wernigerode:
> "Dear Willy: Our German Christmas comes soon. We shall celebrate it without you. Martha and I hope that you will not forget us and will send us some presents for our Christmas tree."
> Here is their German Christmas . . . Martha and Anna are standing in front of an empty Christmas tree. It is adorned with three burned-down candles and a tarnished star from last year. And here's Father Christmas with the presents. He has a postman's cap on his head. What is he taking out of his bag? A fur cap, a Russian ham, some stockings for Anna? No, it is an envelope: "Your husband died the death of a hero on the eastern front."

Hang this official notification on the Christmas tree right under the dim star of your Führer . . . The postman is carrying many such notices. He knocks at each door. This Santa Claus will not miss anyone, he will forget neither Hilde, nor Emma, nor Frieda.

Such is your German Christmas![16]

The attempt to appropriate Christmas found some resonance with the troops, but most simply wanted to forget the war and looked forward to an apolitical celebration marked by a rare feast shared with close comrades. Food was at the center of preparations, and its procurement, in spite of the Christian ethos, took no account of the widespread hunger reported among the civilian population in places like Kaluga, Briansk, and Orel.[17] Indeed to some extent the hunger resulted from Germans' pilfering the local population, although individual soldiers took the Christmas spirit seriously enough to share their food, especially with the children. The best treats arrived in packages from Germany, the flood of which over the preceding weeks only added to the strain of the already overburdened logistics system. Indeed, many soldiers would not receive their Christmas packages until January, and some even as late as March 1942, but at least, as one account noted, "Nothing had gone bad in the Russian cold; everything was perfectly preserved."[18]

What did arrive in time for Christmas 1941 was all manner of treats— cake, biscuits, ham, sausages, chocolate, prunes, nuts, cocoa, cigars, cigarettes, tobacco, puddings, preserves, coffee, and tea. Men who had received nothing typically shared in the packages of their comrades or in some instances were given parcels addressed to deceased men or those who had been wounded and evacuated to the rear.[19] As Kurt Meissner recalled: "Christmas came and a little bit of good cheer, for we received parcels, not only from our own folk, but from strangers who donated something for the brave lads on the eastern front, and it made our lives a little easier. But it also made us rather homesick."[20] The same sentiment was expressed by Gottlob Bidermann: "A feeling of homesickness swept over me as I eagerly tore open the crumpled wrapping, and the sweet smell of gingerbread filled our surroundings, contrasting sharply with the acrid smell of unwashed woollen uniforms, heavy leather equipment, grease and oil . . . The contents of the

Christmas packages were equally divided; the wine from the canteens sent warmth through our cramped limbs."[21]

In some areas there was also a special Christmas ration for the men, which varied in size from place to place, with the most generous received by the men undertaking the siege of Leningrad in the quieter region of Army Group North. Here, Wolfgang Buff listed an almost astounding bounty, which for every man in his unit included one bottle of red wine, one bottle of cognac, one bottle of sparkling wine for every three men, one tin of canned fruit, two apples, sixty cigarettes, tobacco, cigars, a pack of razor blades, twenty-seven blocks of chocolate, a packet of biscuits, four bags of sweets, and almost a pound of Christmas biscuits.[22] Such a windfall was unheard of in Army Group Center, although Josef Krauss was certainly among the luckiest when he wrote home that every man in his unit had received a ration of one packet of biscuits, one bottle of wine, six cigars, thirty cigarettes, and for every two men a bottle of schnapps.[23] As Albert Neuhaus wrote home in a letter: "The Christmas packet of the Wehrmacht arrives and the mood is good."[24]

If the treats from the Christmas packages whet the appetites of the men, the feasts being prepared all along the front soon provided what many would consider their best meal since crossing into Russian territory. Paul Wortmann wrote to his parents on December 25 of "a princely meal," with masses of meat and a bean salad.[25] Hans-Joachim S. wrote to his wife of preparing for his comrades a Christmas dinner of goose, green cabbage, cream sauce, and a poultry salad for which he was roundly praised.[26] Erich Hager noted how he and ten of his closest comrades crammed themselves into a single vehicle to share a pot roast and reminisce of home.[27] Albert Neuhaus noted that his Christmas roast marked only the fourth time since the beginning of the campaign that he had eaten a roasted, and not boiled, meal.[28] Yet not everyone was so lucky. Max Kuhnert noted that his unit had hardly any food and between twenty-six men shared a meal of two tins of sardines, a packet of synthetic honey, two loaves of bread, and several potatoes.[29] Helmut Günther was even less fortunate, recalling: "On this day, of all days, we were left without rations. Who knew where the supply vehicles were stuck?"[30]

In the absence of family, camaraderie was the essential ingredient to keeping homesickness at bay, allowing the men to indulge in shared family rituals at the front. Heinz Postenrieder wrote in his diary of how he and his comrades sang heartfelt German Christmas songs as local Russians marveled in curiosity.[31] Josef Deck wrote how the singing allowed him to forget all the commotion of the preceding days.[32] Paul Wortmann took part in an eight-man choir, formed specially to entertain his company for the occasion, and they performed to "great applause."[33] Other performances were more contrived, with one unit commander forcing his men to sing and casting a "mistrusting eye to ensure everyone sang along."[34] Harmonicas were often the only available musical accompaniment, to which one soldier noted, "[in] voices hoarse with cold, we sang softly to the music."[35] Yet the Christmas carols themselves brought back memories and stirred up emotions, so that many of the accounts end on a sober note, especially when it came to singing the tranquil lyrics of "Stille Nacht" ("Silent Night"). Henry Metelmann noted that this song in particular was "emotionally laden,"[36] while Walter Tilemann observed that "some soldiers had moist eyes."[37] Another soldier claimed that after their rendition of the song, "it could hardly have been more solemn in a church than in the company of these men."[38] Erwin Wagner was more to the point: "no one was ashamed of the tears he wiped from his eyes."[39]

Perhaps the most profound experience was that of Werner Adamczyk, who became so struck by the reverence of the occasion that he was able to transcend all of the hatred that surrounded him:

> One fellow got out his accordion and intoned with a soft touch the beloved Christmas carols. He then started to sing along, he had a most wonderful voice and it did not take long for all of us to join in. I was touched with feelings of calmness and the thought occurred to me that one is supposed to love his enemy. While all kept singing, I became quiet, with my thoughts turning inward. I tried to visualize the enemy soldiers. They must be just like us, with the same hope of surviving this slaughter. The only difference was the language and the doctrines of the respective governments. They were doing their duties, just as we were doing ours. In my meditation and prayer, I became able to feel love for the common Russian soldier.[40]

While Adamczyk opened his heart to the shared humanity of Germany's most demonized enemy, other German soldiers equated such sentimentality with weakness. Hans Roth tried hard to banish even the tender thoughts of his own family. "Just don't think," he told himself in his diary on December 24; "don't become soft, wipe away the ice from under your eyes!"[41] Far from embracing any thoughts of a shared humanity, Wilhelm Prüller saw Christmas as a rallying cry to arms. "If the Russians attack today," Prüller fumed in his diary entry, "not one of them will come out of it alive. A cold fury is in us now. And, if we think a little deeper and more carefully, a certain pride; for it is because of us millions of others can celebrate this, the most German of all holidays, in peace and security."[42]

Prüller's insistence that any Russian attack on December 24 would be decisively repulsed was disproven up and down Army Group Center's line. Russian Orthodox Christians also celebrated Christmas, and could do so somewhat more openly since the German invasion had relaxed a number of Stalin's restrictions on the church.[43] Yet Orthodox Christians followed the older Julian calendar, which meant that they celebrated Christmas on January 7, 1942 (in spite of the fact that the Julian calendar had been officially replaced in Soviet Russia by the Gregorian calendar in 1918). Thus, December 24 and 25 hold no special significance for Orthodox Christians, other than a perfect opportunity to disrupt the most cherished German celebration. As Erwin Bartmann noted: "The odd burst of Russian shells soon turned into a continual thunderous drum roll—*Trommelfeuer*—a Christmas Day present. The Russians always made a point of mounting an attack on days the German calendar showed a celebration. We of course reciprocated these compliments on days important to the Russians."[44] Accordingly, local German commanders knew to expect a major Soviet push. As one major in the 134th Infantry Divisions warned his men on December 24, "Boys, I am as fed up as you, but we have to hold out. If our front breaks none of us will get home again."[45] On December 25 Ernst Guicking wrote his wife that his unit had expected a "surprise" Soviet attack, but remarked proudly: "He was cut off as never before. Our artillery had those boys in direct fire."[46] Heinrich Haape recalled that his unit received its own special attention on Christmas Eve when the enemy mounted their first night attack. Yet Haape's account also alludes to an almost routine procedure that had developed in combat, which underlines both the assumed failure of the Soviet attack and the regularity of German counterattacks. As Haape wrote at the outset of the Soviet attack: "I knew that Kageneck [Haape's comrade] would remain in the village until the Russian attack had been beaten back and until the counterattack had been made."[47]

Willi Thomas wrote sarcastically that 1941 was the best Christmas that he had ever experienced. "The enemy attacked all day long. Overwhelming strength. We had no defense against their tanks. The entire position had been reduced to soot and ashes . . . As it seems, overnight we have been encircled. So we have to defend ourselves on all sides."[48] Thomas survived the encirclement, which was not uncommon in the first winter of the war, as German counterattacks were often able to relieve such positions. Helmut von Harnack told of how he commanded one such relief operation:

> On Christmas Eve enemy attacks reached a new level of ferocity, as Russians recklessly charged forward, heedless of losses. I took command of an amalgamated company of infantry, tanks and self-propelled guns and we were always in the thick of the action. There was one unforgettable moment. We smashed through enemy forces and rescued an encircled German battalion. The relieved commander looked over at me, and then shouted across the hubbub of battle: "My best Christmas present ever!"[49]

Max Kuhnert's Christmas celebrations were also cut short by an overwhelming Soviet attack, which swept over his unit's front lines. There was no thought of defending to the last man, but instead a hastily mounted retreat was set in motion: "We just had enough time to get away. The Russians had broken through—there [were] just too many of them, and in the pitch darkness, with drifting snow and biting wind, it had been too difficult to hold them with the limited weapons we had."[50] Another Soviet attack on December 25 threatened to encircle Werner Adamczyk's unit, and again there was no thought of defending the positions to the end. Instead, the order for immediate retreat was issued, as Adamczyk wrote:

We jumped up like lightning had struck us. For the moment there was chaos, the command had come so unexpectedly. No one wanted to be left behind . . . "Have your rifles ready, Ivan is almost here!" was the next advice . . . Two of our trucks could not be started in time and were blown up with demolition charges. With feelings of panic we were on the go. Would we get out of here in time? That was everyone's anxious concern.[51]

Such Soviet successes in breaking through the German front were undeniable tactical successes, but they rarely translated into any kind of operational success. Major German formations, regiments or above, were seldom encircled, much less destroyed, and when the German front re-formed, the dangerous and costly Soviet attempts to penetrate it began again. Indeed, for all their local successes, the Soviet attacks on December 24 repeated many of their earlier disasters. As Hans Roth noted in his journal on December 24: "Our shells tear into the rows of storming Reds, shredding large holes in the Asian pack. These guys fear shells like the plague, since there are no tanks to back them up as they retreat shortly thereafter. Oh holy night! Twice they return tonight, and twice we herd them back with their heads bloodied. Oh holy night!"[52] Ivan Sawenko was a lieutenant in the Red Army who led a raid on the German lines intending to seize food and alcohol supplies, which had been observed being unloaded by the Germans for their Christmas celebration. Sawenko's unit was not deterred by the almost complete lack of men guarding the front and assumed they were overly occupied with the festivities. In fact, it was a ruse, the Germans having anticipated that the Soviets would seek to exploit the occasion. Once Sawenko's men had reached the German stores and started seizing their plunder, machine guns opened up on the rooftops of the houses and "mercilessly shot us down."[53]

For the German high command, Christmas was a mixed affair. Reinhardt at Panzer Group 3 noted that the afternoon was spent repelling several Soviet attacks before finding time for a Christmas celebration with his staff.[54] At Fourth Army's headquarters in Yukhnov the atmosphere was much tenser. The Soviet breakthrough between Felber's XIII and Heinrici's XXXXIII Army Corps was threatening the collapse of the army's entire right wing. As Hellmuth Stieff noted in a letter from December 25, his staff knew what was at stake and "this did not allow for much Christmas spirit."[55] Indeed, Blumentritt, who had been visiting the front, was still in Maloiaroslavets, which was now threatened by the Soviet breakthrough to the south. As he told the British historian Liddell Hart after the war, "I and my staff spent Christmas day in a small hut . . . with tommy guns on the table and sounds of shooting all around us."[56] Always conscientious when it came to his men, Guderian spent Christmas Eve visiting a number of field hospitals. His presence brought "a little good cheer to many a brave soldier," but, especially given his own fragile state, Guderian noted, "it was a heart-rending business."[57]

At the army's headquarters in Mauerwald, Halder depicted a far more festive, even carefree atmosphere. First there was an outdoor Christmas celebration held for all the staff of the headquarters, which Halder enjoyed for almost two hours and described as "Very full of atmosphere." At 7:00 P.M. he moved inside for a second celebration around his dinner table with his closest associates in the high command.[58] It was very different from the doleful atmosphere at the front, where homesickness and melancholy were never far from the surface even at the best Christmas celebrations. For those men who "celebrated" on an empty stomach or even spent the evening fighting for their lives, the relative indulgences at Mauerwald perfectly illustrated the dichotomy between the army high command and the men of Army Group Center. Those same divisions, which had in fact been growing for months, contributed to a tangible breakdown in trust as well as an increasing willingness of commanders to direct their forces on their own terms.

The issue that contributed most to the feeling of abandonment at the front was supply. The resources Army Group Center received had never been sufficient, but while in past months the shortfalls acted only to constrain each new offensive, now the shortages threatened the very survival of the front. The problem was already acute in November when just 16 trains a day were reaching Army Group Center instead of the minimum 31 required for basic subsistence.[59] Figures for December are even harder to determine. A high percentage of trains dispatched to the front never arrived on account of the extreme cold damaging the rail infrastructure or the locomotives themselves. Across the whole of the Eastern Front some 1,643 supply trains arrived at the front in December, 58 fewer than in the previous month of November. This theoretically meant an average of 53 trains a day were reaching the front, but that was for all three army groups.[60] Not only were fewer trains arriving at the front, but the demands of the winter required vastly more rail transportation than before. Bulky winter clothing, replacement equipment, and troop trains attempting to bring more men to the front all required extra capacity.[61] On December 10 Heusinger informed Army Group Center that the transportation of two to three new divisions from Western Europe would be en route as of December 16, but that these would then require a full four weeks to reach the front.[62]

Lieutenant-General Rudolf Gercke, the chief of Wehrmacht transport responsible for running the trains, reported to Halder on December 15 that the supply of the Eastern Front required some 300 trains a day, but that this had not been possible given shortages in coal, personnel, iron, water pumps, siding track, and provisions for the men. Two days later, on December 17, Gercke reported to Hitler the inflated figure of 122 trains a day departing for the Eastern Front. It is unclear where this figure came from, but it may reflect the difference between the number of trains dispatched to the front and the number of those arriving.[63] It is therefore very possible that many trains were not progressing all the way to the front before unloading their stock and turning back. This artificially suggested more trains were servicing the *Ostheer* than in fact was the case. Gercke's planning schedules, therefore, functioned far more effectively on paper than in practice, which meant he was reporting bogus figures and was almost certainly aware of this fact. Indeed, Gercke confidently told Hitler that by January 1, 1942, the number of trains reaching the front every day would increase to 140 trains a day, and by March 1 some 180 trains a day.[64] It was an astonishing claim given that the opposite trend was taking place. Not only were there fewer trains arriving in December than in November, but January saw a steep decline in train arrivals at the front, from a total of 1,643 supply trains in December to 1,420 trains in January. This resulted in a reduction from 53 trains a day to just 45.[65]

Administrative difficulties also impacted the operation of the logistical system. Wagner's position as the army quartermaster-general gave him authority over the stockpiles of supplies, the depots at which these were stored, and the haulage vehicles, but not the railways themselves, which fell under Gercke's auspices. Gercke worked within the OKW's timetables and constraints, while Wagner served the OKH, and the interests of the two command organizations did not always coincide. Thus, while Wagner was responsible for the organization and distribution of supplies at each end of the railways, he held little power over what quantities could be shipped or when these would arrive.[66] By the end of December Hitler had become aware of the gap between what Gercke promised and what was being delivered to the front. As his Luftwaffe adjutant Nicolaus von Below noted, the Eastern Front had "no winter clothing, no protection against the cold and no means for sufficient supply. Hitler was very agitated."[67] Acting against the wishes of the army, Hitler took radical action. He transferred responsibility for almost all rail operations in the east to the Reich Ministry for Transportation, essentially handing responsibility for the rail network in the occupied eastern territories to civilian authorities.[68] It would only be in the summer of 1942 that the army groups in the east would at last be given direct command over their supply apparatus.[69]

While it had taken six months for the gross inefficiency in the supply system to prompt action at the top, there was far less room for illusion at the front. Hoepner was among the more clear-eyed commanders, writing in a letter on December 21: "The miscalculation in the German plans can in no way be explained by the conditions of the winter campaign. Winter is not to blame here, but an organic mistake in the work of the OKW during the planning of the war."[70] These two sentences Hoepner underlined with a thick red pencil. Even Goebbels acknowledged that Barbarossa had been fundamentally corrupted by its neglect of logistics, writing in his diary on December 10: "The supply problem is without question the decisive one in the east. We did not recognize this before the outbreak of the eastern campaign, and must now gradually learn."[71]

The unforgiving problem of distance, combined with a wanton lack of investment in the *Ostheer*'s logistical apparatus, singlehandedly doomed Operations Barbarossa and Typhoon, but what stands out most is the singular failure of the German high command to learn the lesson of overextension.[72]

National Socialist military thinking set strategic and operational goals without reference to detailed staff work. In the Nazi conception of warfare success depended first and foremost upon resolute, positive leadership, which was seen as inseparable from the Wehrmacht's success. The problem was that this led men like Gercke, Wagner, and Halder to dismiss the myriad of difficulties undercutting the complex delivery of supplies to the front. The solution was simple: the greater the problems, the greater the man required to surmount them. The language of success, of resolute "can-do," became an almost axiomatic response, especially in administrative jobs where engaging in self-delusion was less likely to get you killed than at the front.

During the German advance, very few Russian locomotives had been captured in a serviceable condition, which was important as the process of converting the wider Soviet rail gauge to the narrower European standard progressed far too slowly to keep pace with the advance. The hope had been that Soviet rolling stock would continue to operate on captured sections of the network, allowing Germany to move supplies by rail ahead of the gauge conversion process. By the winter the lack of Soviet locomotives led to a new problem: German trains had their cooling pipes fixed to the outside of their boilers, and in the freezing conditions some 70 to 80 percent burst.[73] Yet problems extended well beyond the winter conditions.[74] Rail traffic control was chaotic, not only leading to inefficiency, but becoming so bad that whole trains disappeared, while others were "hijacked" by local authorities. There were not enough people working at the railheads, meaning that loading and unloading trains took longer than necessary, at least until Soviet POWs were press-ganged into service. There were also administrative and communication problems in dealing with the local people employed by the German authorities, and some of these civilian appointments operated as spies for nascent partisan groups.[75] Sabotage was still relatively minor and infrequent in 1941, but when it did occur, it only further compounded an already crisis-ridden system and demanded ever more resources be devoted to protect stations, depots, rail yards, and bridges.[76]

Blumentritt, at Fourth Army, summed up the extent of the supply problem: "The lines of communication with Germany, fantastically long and extremely tenuous, were scarcely adequate to keep the armies fed with ammunition and essential supplies."[77] This was reflected throughout the war diaries of Army Group Center, with Panzer Group 4 remarking that the situation was becoming more strained by the day. It concluded: "The future development of supply depends solely on the repair of the locomotives damaged by the heavy frost. The urgently requested engineering equipment, ammunition, etc., can unfortunately only be obtained after the current crisis is surpassed."[78] Such was the importance of the rail lines that the German defense prioritized defending the towns with railheads in order to maintain the vital flow of resources.[79] As Schmidt noted of his army: "Second Army's fate hangs on holding the railroad . . . If the railroad cannot be held then what happens to Second Army will undermine the entire eastern front."[80]

While the railways were the crucial artery delivering supplies to the front, the other arm of the logistical apparatus was the truck-based transport fleets (*Grosstransportraum*) bridging the railheads with the front. These motorized transport columns were already in grave difficulties even before the Soviet winter offensive. Just 15 percent of truck depots across the Eastern Front were operational in November 1941.[81] As an indication of what that meant, each army would on average need to transport between 2,500 and 3,000 tons of supplies a day, but Second Panzer Army could manage just 360 tons, and the other armies were no better.[82] The declining fleet of trucks was further reduced by a critical lack of antifreeze oil and "cold breaks" in the leaf springs. In fact, Halder reported on December 13 that one-third of the remaining vehicles in Army Group Center were no longer serviceable.[83]

The reduction in daily deliveries to the armies was not simply a result of lost transport capacity. Heavy snows and icy conditions quickly rendered the roads impassable and, in the case of the former, required hundreds, if not thousands, of workers to clear. Otto Will, who served in the 5th Panzer Division, wrote in his diary on December 23: "Yesterday we have already begun to free a road that is impassable for vehicles . . . The snow is almost one meter high and is completely untouched." The following day he continued: "We cannot tell how far we will have to remove the snow. As far as the eye can see, the road is under an untouched, closed cover of snow. Nowhere is there a village to be seen or a road to which we could connect."[84] Another problem in transporting supplies to the front was that, until Hitler's halt order came into effect, supply columns attempting to reach the front had to go against the tide of retreating men and vehicles, leading to further delays.[85] As Hans von Luck, who was fighting at the front with the 7th Panzer Division, noted: "Supplies got through to us only with difficulty, sometimes not at all. The truck drivers had to make their way against the stream of units flowing back. If they failed, there was suddenly no fuel. The best we could do then was to fill up our most important vehicles; the others we had to destroy and leave behind."[86]

The loss of vital equipment on account of fuel shortages and the inability to prepare properly for the retreat proved more costly to Army Group Center than the running battles with the Red Army. The use of tanks was determined by the availability of fuel. Thus, Veiel's 2nd Panzer Division reported to its corps command that twelve tanks could be made available for the following day "with thirty km range."[87] One soldier recalled being instructed to find fuel for his unit by any means possible, noting in his diary: "How and where, that is irrelevant. That is up to us."[88] Of course, when fuel stocks were exhausted, the culling of vehicles was the inevitable consequence, and as the aggregate number of vehicles shrank in the course of the retreat, fresh supplies of fuel suddenly proved sufficient for what remained. Accordingly, reports of "adequate" fuel stocks were not usually a reflection of the volumes being delivered, but rather the absolute decline in vehicle numbers.[89] Already at the beginning of the Soviet offensive, Hellmuth Stieff noted that 75 percent of Fourth Army's trucks were no longer operational, with no spare parts arriving to repair them.[90] Searching two motor pools for parts to repair the vehicles in his own unit, Heinrich Engel wrote of encountering "hundreds of disabled vehicles."[91] Units competed for whatever spare parts did arrive, and the supply depots were increasingly staked out by representatives from tank companies waiting for the next delivery. This led to what one officer described as "fierce struggles for priority items."[92] Nor was it just trains that on occasion disappeared from army manifests; trucks too were privately dispatched all the way to Germany to bring back urgently needed supplies and sometimes specialist goods. In one such case, a truck was sent from Knobelsdorff's 19th Panzer Division all the way back to Spandau in Berlin to bring back sausage production machinery.[93]

As vehicle numbers sharply declined, so too did the number of German tanks. In December, 519 German tanks were lost, which is considerably more than the monthly tallies for the preceding months of November (385), October (325), and September (241). The heavy December losses also exceeded new production, ending a trend that the autumn months had been able to avoid. January continued the steep losses, with another 426 tanks lost and only 387 new models produced.[94] As tanks were often prioritized for fuel, such high losses were not simply an indication of fallout rates on the retreat. Rather, the figures point to the heavy fighting in Army Group Center over the winter period, with panzer regiments rushed to plug gaps and deliver sharp counterblows. The high German tank losses in the summer period often counted a large share of the obsolete Mark I and II tanks or the similarly inferior Czech T-35 and T-38 (incorporated into the German army after the occupation of Czechoslovakia). By December, however, these older tanks were largely gone, meaning the high losses included a far larger share of the best German Mark III and IV tanks. Accordingly, some 461 Mark IIIs were lost in December and January, whereas only 218 were lost in September and October.[95]

With the *Ostheer*'s logistics so clearly inadequate, German units were typically forced to fend for themselves. And the best source of replacement vehicles was the Red Army. According to Franz Frisch, even during the period of the winter retreat, the Germans could replenish some of the lost transport capacity by capturing enemy vehicles. In fact, this might be one reason for the prevalence of local counterattacks. As Frisch wrote: "if a unit was able to capture somewhere on the way a Russian truck, those bastards were so simple you could fix the carburetor and make a fire under the engine. Then we cranked the truck, and as soon as the Russian truck was running, we started to pull the German truck . . . We tried to capture Russian trucks as much as we could. It saved our lives."[96] German records also indicate success in seizing Soviet tractors. Officially the figure was only 2,000 during the course of the war, but as with every vehicle type, many more were seized from the battlefield by the passing units and pressed into service without any formal accounting.[97] These so-called black supplies remained unofficial so that units would not lose priority in claiming what little was on offer through regular army channels of supply.

Captured Soviet tanks were another source of replenishment, although to a far lesser extent. In the course of 1941 the Red Army lost over 20,000 tanks, most of which were total losses, but even those that were salvageable rarely found their way into German service.[98] From July 1941 a special staff was authorized to gather together captured Soviet tanks, but from the beginning major difficulties arose. Capturing fully functional Soviet tanks was extraordinarily uncommon; typically they had sustained some form of battle damage or sabotage by their former crews. Where this was not the case, German frontline units had often raided the tanks for anything salvageable. Thus, when the requisition staffs finally took possession of them they were almost always immobile. Repairs could only be effected if the tanks could somehow be transported to the German workshops, but as the panzer and motorized divisions moved east, so too did their mobile workstations. Recovering tanks from the field, not surprisingly, prioritized the German models. Even if a disabled Soviet tank could be recovered, the overburdened repair crews could not keep pace with the breakdowns and damage to German vehicles without worrying about isolated Soviet models, for which they had no spare parts. Understandably, therefore, very few Soviet tanks could be salvaged, although by the end of October about 100 were put into German service, mostly from the BT series, T-26s, and a few T-60s. The relative absence of the best Soviets tanks (T-34s and KV-1s and 2s) in the German inventories almost certainly suggests that such prized tanks were not abandoned by the panzer divisions but, wherever possible, were taken along as valuable spoils of war and included within their "black" (unofficial) inventory.[99] In the war diary of Model's XXXXI Army Corps there was even an instruction diagram on how best to dig in a captured Soviet BT tank to function as a fixed defensive field fortification (see illustration in insert).[100] Indeed, Soviet tanks could sometimes be captured in surprising numbers even as late as December, with Veiel's 2nd Panzer Division seizing 25 Soviet tanks between December 3 and January 2, including two of the enormous fifty-two-ton KV-2s.[101]

German units had a remarkable ability to improvise solutions to their logistical problems, but in doing so they could be utterly callous toward the local population. In order for German units to retain as much maneuverability as possible, as well as aid in the flow of supplies, Knobelsdorff's 19th Panzer Division issued an instruction to its troops on December 22 that sledges and horses were to be seized "without concern for the civilian population."[102] Gerhard Bopp wrote of taking one man's horse and sledges for the trivial compensation of four cigarettes.[103] Others were determined to provide for themselves without the slightest concern for the locals. Kurt Neuman wrote home in a letter: "I'm just frozen, mainly my feet. But the first chance I get I'll plant the business end of my carbine against some Russian's throat and make him take off his warm felt boots. That'll help a bit."[104] Sometimes German soldiers showed utter disregard for the fate of the civilians even in the face of Russian generosity and kindness. Willy Peter Reese noted in his journal:

> We were oblivious to the way we were often given food when we set foot in a hut, to the peasants giving us their *makhorka* [strong Russian tobacco] to smoke, a woman freely offering us a couple of eggs, or a girl sharing her milk with us. We still dug around in every corner, even if we let what we had taken just go bad later . . . Our commanders kept telling us that we were the lords of the universe in a conquered country.[105]

At the end of December Gerhardt Linke wrote in his diary about villagers attempting to retrieve foodstuffs from their homes after they had been expelled by German soldiers. "But we must be stern and inflexible on this point: the scanty food supplies they left are ours. We chased away all claimants with an unequivocal warning not to show their faces again. Let starvation finish the job begun by our arms."[106] Such ruthlessness has been identified by Jeff Rutherford as a key concept in the Wehrmacht's "military necessity" ethos. This demanded the use of any and all means, regardless of their ethical or moral costs, to ensure success on the battlefield, resulting in typically impressive combat effectiveness, but also frequent recourse to extreme acts of violence, especially toward Soviet civilians.[107]

The demands of Army Group Center in December, however, simply could not be met within the impoverished area of Russian occupation. Requisitions and improvisations only went so far in bridging the huge deficit in supplies reaching the front. As one senior officer recalled after the war: "Improvisations could never be expected to compensate for the lack of vision and the fundamental blunders of the German leadership."[108] Yet this only became the predominant view after the war. In December 1941, a Nationalist Socialist perspective demanded solutions be found and accepted no "excuses" for circumstances beyond a general's control. As Goebbels, who received daily military briefings and was well informed of the situation at the front, fumed in his diary on December 31:

> Unfortunately, the military transport system fails in every respect. Our desk generals do not have the necessary conceptual abilities for suddenly emerging new situations. They are always only able to act successfully when they have all the resources. But war, with a great superiority, requires no talent. One must also try to win at war, when one is at a material and manpower disadvantage. Then it depends on the genius of improvisation. The ingenious improvisation, however, is not learned from general staff work, but must spring from a creative imagination. Our desk generals, however, are not creative and imaginative, they are pure systematists.[109]

Characterizing the transportation crisis at the end of 1941 as a "suddenly emerging new situation" was just as wrong as assuming that creative and imaginative solutions were not already at work. Moreover, lambasting the generals for not improvising a solution conspicuously ignored Hitler's own failure to understand the military geography of the Soviet space and its impact on German operations and logistics. Army Group Center survived the winter of 1941–1942 despite its logistical apparatus, not because of it.

10

PLAYING WITH FIRE

Guderian Gets Burned

O n December 25 the chief of the operations department of the Luftwaffe, Major-General Hoffman von Waldau, commented in his diary that if the events of the coming eight days did not fundamentally change, then the *Ostheer* would have overcome "the first mountain of the winter campaign." Waldau claimed to see evidence that the army had "overcome the shock" of the Soviet offensive and that "the defensive will of the front is—again—there."[1] Yet his hopes were disappointed. Between Christmas and the New Year the situation rapidly deteriorated. What Waldau labeled "the defensive will" had never been absent—the vast majority of German men had fought tenaciously. The Soviet breakthrough that threatened to engulf the right wing of the Fourth Army deteriorated, but even more worryingly for Kluge, it would soon be matched by a new crisis at Strauss's Ninth Army. More than ever, the German command was at war with itself. There were three separate responses to the crisis, each staunchly advocated by Hitler, Kluge, and Guderian, respectively, and all fundamentally at odds with one another. In the end, none of them predominated, and German strategy became an amalgam of fanatical defense tempered by periodic and typically unauthorized withdrawal. The lack of a single, coherent response wasted precious time, divided scant resources, and led to interminable debates within the high command.

Although such a strategic divergence was evident throughout Army Group Center, it was nowhere more pronounced than in Second Panzer Army, where Guderian was openly defying the high command. Kluge had thus far tolerated Guderian's insubordination, and on December 24 even interceded to shield him from the fallout that his headlong retreat to the Oka-Zusha Line might have caused, but still the panzer general showed no gratitude or willingness to curtail his rogue activities. The final act came on December 25 when Kluge discovered that Guderian had authorized Lemelsen's XXXXVII Panzer Corps to abandon the small settlement of Chern, which, not for the first time, went expressly against his own orders. Incensed by yet another example of Guderian's flagrant contempt for his authority, the field marshal telephoned Guderian and sternly took him to task. Guderian made no attempt to dispute his insubordination and only justified his actions by replying: "In these unusual circumstances I lead my army in a manner I can justify to my conscience."[2] It was the end for Kluge. He telephoned Halder and told him he could no longer work with Guderian, and presented the army chief of staff with an ultimatum: "Either he or I." Kluge justified his demand with what turned out to be a final salute to Guderian's achievements. "I have the greatest respect for Colonel-General Guderian and he is a fantastic commander, but he does not obey. In this situation, I can only transmit and execute the Führer's orders if I can rely on my army commanders." Kluge was at pains to point out to Halder that Guderian's blatant defiance was the issue, not his strategic assessment. "I am basically entirely on Guderian's side," Kluge told Halder; "one cannot simply let himself be slaughtered, but he must obey and keep me oriented."[3]

Halder then spoke with Hitler, who quickly authorized Guderian's dismissal.[4] According to Gerhard Engel, Hitler's army adjutant, for days it had been clear to Hitler that Guderian was no longer able to lead.[5] Likewise, his Luftwaffe adjutant, Nicolaus von Below, remarked that Hitler saw Guderian as "fully '*durchgedreht*,'" which may be translated as "out of control" or colloquially used to describe someone as "crazy."[6] Perhaps more to the point, Russell Hart has noted that throughout his career Guderian often reacted with despondency and gloom when confronted by failure, and December 1941 was his nadir.[7]

Guderian's post was to be taken over by Schmidt, who would jointly command both Second and Second Panzer Armies. As a fellow General of Panzer Troops and the only other army commander in "Army Group Guderian," Schmidt was, on the one hand, the logical choice. Given the circumstances of Guderian's dismissal, however, Schmidt was a curious selection. As recently as December 24 Schmidt had without any higher authorization ordered Kempf's XXXXVIII Panzer Corps to abandon the town of Livny and to proceed in full retreat toward the Tim River.[8] Kluge reminded him "that as a result of the Führer's order, for the time being, everything must be done to hold"; however, Schmidt employed Guderian's tactic of presenting his superior with a fait accompli, claiming Kluge's order "came too late."[9] The following day—the same day Guderian was being replaced for his insubordination—Greiffenberg (Kluge's chief of staff at Army Group Center) reiterated that any withdrawal must first gain Hitler's authorization, to which Schmidt replied that his order had been given "under the force of circumstances" and that he had had "no other choice."[10] Schmidt's actions were simply another indication that the army's response to Hitler's halt order was in no way as unequivocal as intended.

The dismissal of Guderian was difficult for his men to accept, especially since they believed he had only acted in their best interests. An unsubstantiated rumor circulated among the men at the front that Guderian cried when he found out that he was being relieved of his command.[11] Herman Balck noted that the news "hit everybody very hard,"[12] while Colonel Heinrich Eberbach described Guderian as a commander "with whom everyone had felt a kinship."[13] Joachim von Lehsten wrote: "All our commanders—at divisional, regimental and battalion level—were talking about it. It was an absolute disaster—our soldiers found Hitler's action incomprehensible. Everyone respected and admired this man; a remarkable leader of outstanding ability."[14] Lemelsen, at XXXXVII Panzer Corps, went so far as to send a request to Field Marshal Keitel asking him to reinstate Guderian, but it did no good.[15]

At 1:00 P.M. on December 26, Guderian bid his final goodbye.[16] The panzer commander did not hold back when he addressed his staff, and his speech reportedly included harsh criticism of Hitler's order.[17] Bernd von Lorringhoven, who was a staff officer at Second Panzer Army, noted "a deep bitterness over the measures that Hitler ordered."[18] Likewise, Colonel August Schmidt of the 10th Motorized Infantry Division recalled: "Guderian was dismissed because he had the courage to stand up to Hitler and challenge his misguided halt order, an order which threatened to destroy our entire army."[19] The prevalence of such views suggests that the undermining of the halt order was not simply the result of one or two recalcitrant generals. For this reason the practice was not ended by making an example of Guderian as the egregious offender.

This should have come as no surprise to Hitler. He had already relieved Rundstedt of command of Army Group South in November for defiantly ordering Kleist's First Panzer Army to begin a retreat from Rostov.[20] Evidence of large-scale unauthorized withdrawals is also evident at the highest levels of Army Group North. On December 15 Leeb desperately sought Hitler's permission to pull back his endangered forces to the east of the Volkhov River, but when no decision was forthcoming, Leeb took the decision himself without informing anyone in the high command.[21] By the end of 1941 the OKH was sufficiently aware of the disconnect between orders and outcomes that Halder felt it necessary to draft a new directive, which he circulated throughout the OKH, army groups, and armies. Halder's language left no doubt that *Auftragstaktik*, the ability of lower-level commanders to implement orders on their own terms but supposedly within a broader strategic framework, was being exploited to undercut the halt order. Of course, *Auftragstaktik* worked on the assumption that subordinates understood the intent of the orders, introducing a potential ambiguity that Halder sought to clamp down on. The fact that *Auftragstaktik* had been a cornerstone of the German army's military success since the reforms of the nineteenth century was lost on Halder, whose devotion to National Socialist military thinking was blinding. Accordingly, Halder instructed:

> The soldier's duty to obey leaves no room for the sensibilities of subordinate commanders; rather it requires the most rapid and best possible execution of orders as desired by the authority issuing them. We shall master it if we firmly seize the reins of command without consideration of inappropriate sensibilities, if the commanders are entirely frank and truthful in their reports, and if a single will, the will of the Führer, prevails from the highest levels down to the soldier at the front.[22]

Such a directive was not the end of *Auftragstaktik*, as many historians have concluded, but a clear sign that Hitler's halt order had failed to overturn generations of successful German military culture, tradition, and practice. Guderian's dismissal, while leading his army to safety, might convince some that he was a martyr to the independence of command, even if Guderian's degree of independence, as Kluge discovered, took the concept much too far.

Kluge was painfully aware of the discrepancy between the demands of Hitler's order and the survival of his army group. To make matters worse, Guderian's obstinacy only weakened Kluge's ability to negotiate flexibility. The field marshal was forced to argue for what he called "a middle standpoint," which rejected both Guderian's penchant for immediate withdrawals as well as the OKH's determination to hold out to the last man. Instead, Kluge argued that in the case of operational Soviet breakthroughs, as opposed to local tactical penetrations, German forces had to be granted permission to retreat. In making his case Kluge did not mince words: "In the cases of a Russian operational breakthrough it depends on nothing less than the life or death of the army." Halder, however, remained unconvinced and replied that he saw "no possibility" for a "middle solution."[23]

The weight of events on the southern flank of Army Group Center was squarely on Schmidt's shoulders, and further withdrawal, for the time being at least, was no longer an option. As Schmidt wrote his wife, the new command of two armies "was not simple and weighs on the nerves."[24] Nevertheless, Schmidt's two armies had now reached the Oka-Zusha Line, which was identified as the "final winter line," and everywhere preparations were under way to develop and strengthen the new positions. Nehring's 18th Panzer Division reported that its engineers had managed to prepare only the most rudimentary fieldworks, typically by blasting foxholes and bunkers for the men. Further building materials were having to be transported to the front over icy roads, and there was not enough local housing to accommodate all of the men.[25] Yet by December 28 Lemelsen's XXXXVII Panzer Corps reported that the conclusion of the retreat, the repair of weapons, and the arrival of replacements had "slightly improved" the strength of Nehring's division and Major-General Max Fremerey's 29th Motorized Infantry Division.[26] On the same day sixty-three new armored fighting vehicles arrived at Orel for Schmidt's combined armies.[27] At Kursk, major new formations were also arriving, including elements of the 442nd Infantry Regiment and the first units of Lieutenant-General Friedrich Gollwitzer's 88th Infantry Division, which had been hurriedly transported from France.[28] There was also the formation of the first German ski companies in Lemelsen's XXXXVII Panzer Corps and Weikersthal's LIII Army Corps. Colonel Heinrich Eberbach, who commanded the panzer regiment of the 4th Panzer Division, even suggested that they could raise a battalion of Russians, armed with captured Soviet matériel, and each company commanded by a German non-commissioned officer.[29] In the fight for survival on the southern flank of Army Group Center, everything was being done for the defense of the Oka-Zusha Line, and while Schmidt's prospects of standing his ground were still far from certain, his armies, thanks in no small part to Guderian's long and skillfully executed retreat, were better placed than at any time previously to withstand the Soviet offensive.

Another crucial element in Schmidt's defensive arsenal was the newly developed hollow-charge warhead, known in German as "red-head" (*Rotkopf*) munitions, which for the first time gave antitank gunners a powerful defensive weapon against the Soviet T-34s and even (at shorter ranges) the giant KV-1 tanks. The hollow-charge shell was not an entirely new weapon, but Hitler had repeatedly refused to allow them to be used at the front for fear that if one was captured by the Soviets and they quickly produced their own variant, the shells could be just as devastating to German tanks. As recently as December 20 Kluge had pleaded for the release of the shells. When Halder once again turned down his request, Kluge informed him that owing to the shortage of antitank weaponry his infantry would simply have to run away from Soviet armored attacks.[30] Almost certainly because of Army Group Center's desperate situation, Hitler finally changed his mind, and on December 22 hollow-charge shells were released for use on the front lines.[31] The advantage of such shells should not be overstated, as they were really only effective against the extremely thick armor of the KV-1. Moreover, at a maximum range of about 130 meters, they had poor flight characteristics, rendering them not very accurate. Nevertheless, KV-1s were rarely employed that winter, and when they did appear it was mostly against Army Group North.[32] Whatever the limitations of the new hollow-charge shells, the opportunity to knock out T-34s with a single round was almost too good to be true, and the results soon proved their worth.

On December 28, a German Mark IV tank from Hubicki's 9th Panzer Division engaged two T-34s at a distance of 1,000 meters. The Mark IV fired the new hollow-charge munitions and destroyed each with a single round.[33] Kempf's XXXXVIII Panzer Corps, to which Hubicki's division belonged, celebrated the achievement in its war diary by noting, "the excellent effect of the red-head shell, which has now been proved, gives the troops an enormous boost."[34]

In the final week of 1941 Schmidt's armies continued their harrowing defensive struggle against unrelenting Soviet pressure. The results, however, continued to produce disproportionate outcomes in favor of the Germans. Willy Peter Reese, serving in the 95th Infantry Division, wrote of an utterly senseless night attack by Soviet cavalry that ended in disaster: "The expanse of the plain lay open in front of us, in the ghostly light of the moon, and across it charged the Cossacks with their wild 'URRAH,' like a band of ghosts toward our group. In the fire of our rifles and our one gun, an attack of some four hundred Russians faltered."[35] Hans Roth wrote only of the tedium of battle in his journal on December 26: "All day long, the rattling of machine guns does not stop; all day long, the squad huddles

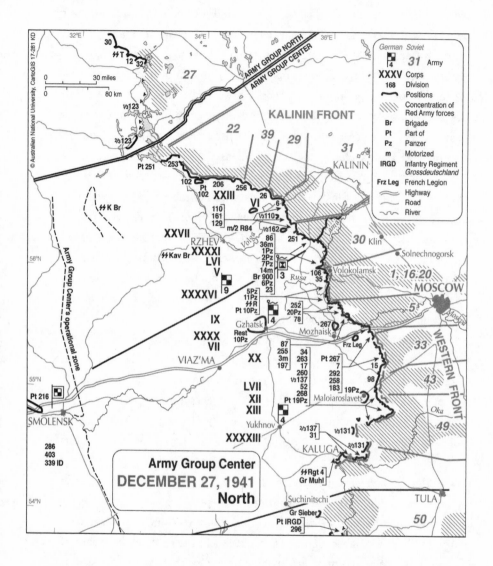

Army Group Center
DECEMBER 27, 1941
North

in their holes and defends themselves against the enemy."[36] After days of enemy attacks, Henrici's 16th Motorized Infantry Division reported 800 Soviet dead before just one position, "evidence," the war diary told, "of the high, bloody losses the enemy has sustained."[37] German counterattacks and small-scale offensives were also a continued feature of the winter fighting and a vital element in Schmidt's defense. On December 30, for example,

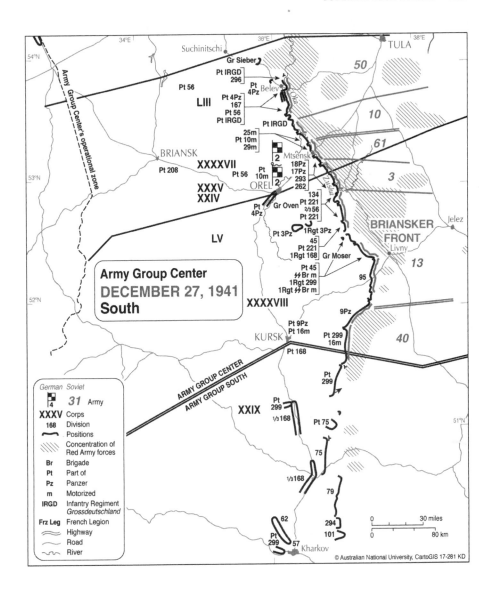

Langermann-Erlancamp's 4th Panzer Division attacked Soviet lines near the village of Krivtsovo, breaking through the front lines and driving a number of kilometers into their rear. In the course of an afternoon the panzer troops wreaked havoc, killing an estimated 600 enemy troops and emerging with over 100 POWs.[38]

While Schmidt's front was holding, the bloodletting, although often grossly disproportionate, was by no means entirely one-sided. In the summer and fall offensives, Guderian had pushed his men to their physical and psychological limit, so that now, after weeks of retreating in freezing temperatures, punctuated by desperately hard fighting, the survivors who took stock found their units shattered. As Gerhard von Bruch noted: "If the Russians attack in strength, they will overwhelm us." Bruch's prediction proved correct. On Christmas Eve his unit numbered 170 men, and a day later, after a major engagement, only 20 remained with the unit. Bruch was unequivocal: "Things look bad—in fact catastrophic."[39] Observing the war effort from Berlin, Goebbels acknowledged that while the Eastern Front was missing men, they were also in short supply on the home front. His conclusion, however, was to blame the German people, "who have brought too few children into the world and now must pay dearly."[40] From Moscow Ilya Ehrenburg celebrated German losses in the fighting around Moscow and claimed that the Soviet capital had proved "the Verdun of this war for the Germans."[41]

While Schmidt was the new commander on Army Group Center's southern flank, after a week of desperate deficiency Kluge's former position at Fourth Army was at last filled by the December 26 arrival of General of Mountain Troops Ludwig Kübler.[42] Kübler had previously served as a corps commander in Army Group South, but he had won favor with Hitler by writing a battle report on the Uman encirclement (July/August 1941) that heavily emphasized his own role. Kübler then sent the report directly to Hitler's headquarters, as well as a number of other, higher offices, without informing his own Seventeenth Army command. The self-aggrandizing ploy paid off when Hitler, not the OKH, selected Kübler as Kluge's replacement.[43] Not only did Fourth Army have a new commander, but Blumentritt, the army's chief of staff, received a new appointment at the OKH and was replaced by Colonel Julius von Bernuth on December 27.[44]

According to Blumentritt, Kübler arrived with the reputation of being "a tough soldier," exactly the kind of man Hitler wanted in command of the dangerously exposed Fourth Army.[45] Hitler told Kübler that he was "to hold and not give up a step of ground except under compulsion."[46] Coming from the relative calm of the XXXXIX Mountain Corps, which occupied a secure position on the Mius River in Army Group South, Kübler was an inexperienced army commander who was suddenly thrust into the most vulnerable sector of the Eastern Front. His promotion was the quintessential poisoned chalice, but even so Kübler never inspired much confidence, lasting less than a month in the job. Initially, at least, he attempted to doggedly maintain Fourth Army's position against tremendous odds and in the absence of adequate manpower and supply.

Whatever his own failings, there can be no denying that Kübler inherited a calamity on his southern flank. Heinrici's XXXXIII Army Corps confronted a long and dangerously open southern flank as well as a new Soviet break-through to the north, effectively cutting the corps off on both flanks and posing an immediate danger of encirclement. Only Kluge's unauthorized approval to fall back toward Kaluga prevented a disaster. Likewise, Felber's XIII Army Corps, to the north of Heinrici, now confronted an exposed south-ern flank, for which Knobelsdorff's 19th Panzer Division was pulled out of the line farther north to attempt to close. In attempting to solve one problem, however, Fourth Army was seriously weakening the defensive front of Kirch-ner's LVII Panzer Corps, where Knobelsdorff had previously been deployed. It was a domino effect, grounded in the fact that Fourth Army simply did not have the forces necessary to defend its long front.

As Kübler assumed command, the inevitable next domino fell. On December 27 Lieutenant-General Erich Schroeck's 98th Infantry Division, part of Kirchner's overstretched LVII Panzer Corps, reported enemy break-throughs, which spread chaos and fear, threatening a breakdown of com-mand and control. As reports reaching Kirchner's corps noted: "The division reports that the individual leaders and the troops lost their nerves, even the word 'panic' is used."[47] One non-commissioned officer in Schroeck's division recalled: "The enemy was suddenly superior to us . . . And how small, how small our group had become!"[48] There were no reserves to plug the gaps, and only through a fighting withdrawal could they hope to maintain the line before another significant breech of Fourth Army's front resulted.

At Army Group Center, Kluge was fighting his own lost battle to gain the necessary freedom of action. On December 26 he presented the case for a major withdrawal of Fourth Army's southern and central line to close the gap be-tween Felber and Heinrici as well as to offset the risk of further operational breakthroughs. His plan involved withdrawing five corps (XXXXIII, XIII, XII, LVII, and XX), although Kluge also suggested that it was time to consider pulling back Army Group Center's entire front. Halder, however, did not even want to suggest the idea to Hitler, claiming he would only reject it and insist that, once begun, there would be "no more holding out." The conversation, recorded verbatim in Army Group Center's war diary, continued:

> [HALDER:] I dare not tell the Führer that I have received reports that eighty percent of a battalion froze to death during the retreat. The Führer would reply that these casualties would not have occurred if positions had been held.
>
> [KLUGE:] The men are not freezing to death because they are on the march, but because they are standing outside and fighting outside and have no positions. Is the army command staff hiding the fact that we are dealing with an operational breakthrough here? Has the army command any other ideas?
>
> [HALDER:] The right wing of the Fourth Army should be withdrawn and mobile elements pitted against the enemy.
>
> [KLUGE:] I have no more mobile forces! . . . An operational breakthrough must be expected . . . Whether the Führer likes it or not he will have to order a retreat. If supplies cannot be delivered, things will soon collapse.[49]

While Halder seemed amenable to the idea of pulling back Fourth Army's right wing, it remains unclear if this pertained to just Heinrici's gravely endangered XXXXIII Corps or a more comprehensive solution. In any case, it was all a moot point until Hitler agreed, a fact that a deeply frustrated Kluge addressed in his final statement on the matter: "The Führer will have to come down from cloud-cuckoo-land and have his feet set firmly on the ground."[50] Yet there was no further word from the OKH, and that evening in his own diary Halder made no mention of a conversation with Hitler.[51] If Halder did raise Kluge's concerns with Hitler, then there is no record of it, and if he did not, then Kluge was correct—the OKH was indeed hiding Army Group Center's fears that they were confronting an operational breakthrough.

Whatever role Halder played in supplying information to Hitler, there is no record of Hitler authorizing a major withdrawal for December 27 and 28. And yet that is exactly what began to happen. Where the order for this movement originated is not exactly clear, but a coordinated movement of the 15th, 98th, 34th, and 263rd Infantry Divisions began. Erwin Wagner, who served in the 263rd Infantry Division, wrote after the war that he and his men were aware that their retreat took place in direct defiance of the halt order, but he portrayed this as stemming from a local decision. As Wagner wrote: "We were, of course, bound by such instructions [not to abandon positions] and the unit commander too. But in our precarious situation we had to act on our own authority, and our unit commander did so with an energy I had not yet seen in him. We repeated our last message three times in succession: 'We are clearing out—end!'"[52]

Even on Fourth Army's more secure left flank there is again clear evidence of a limited withdrawal, but without a clear paper trail for who ultimately authorized it. On December 27 Thoma's 20th Panzer Division was confronting its own heavy Soviet attacks, which were inducing panicked responses from the front lines. The division initially responded that "panic-like attitudes or panic-like instances must be countered with the severest means, if necessary with the weapon . . . It is now about life and death." Yet shortly afterward an order arrived from the corps ordering a withdrawal of ten to twelve kilometers, emphasizing the need to enforce the scorched-earth policy.[53] Such an order could not wait to transition through the chain of command to gain Hitler's authorization (even if it was forthcoming). Commanders may also have reasoned that following local actions where the front moved, a few kilometers would not have been so evident to the OKH and Hitler on the 1-to-1-million-scale maps that they used to follow the war.

Lieutenant-General Wilhelm Wetzel's 255th Infantry Division was located close to Thoma's position, and although the leadership agreed in principle with Hitler's halt order, a sentence in the war diary indicates that because of the uncertainty of the surrounding units, a withdrawal could never be completely dismissed. Accordingly, the war diary noted: "The division must therefore always count on this possibility and therefore cannot leave everything to the defence."[54]

While sectors of Fourth Army's front were unmistakably moving west-ward, the pressure of Soviet attacks continued to mount, and by December 30 Kübler frantically telephoned Kluge to tell him that a breakthrough would shortly overwhelm the front east of Borovsk. This was the sector of Materna's XX Army Corps and northern wing of Kirchner's LVII Panzer Corps. As Kübler told Kluge, "the divisions can no longer hold. I have never had such an urgent report from the troops." If Kluge was behind the previous authorizations for withdrawal, which seems likely, he could only succeed if they continued stage by stage, "under pressure from the enemy." In accordance with his "middle solution," the line also had to hold for periods, not least because a constant retreat would only result in a fate like Guderian's. Accordingly, Kluge informed Kübler he would have to hold for the time being: "In these positions we cannot capitulate so quickly."[55] Yet Kluge immediately contacted the high command and began requesting authorization to withdraw.

Responding to Kluge's requests, Hitler insisted that he saw no end to such withdrawals and even suggested that they could "go right back to the Polish border." He then insisted that, contrary to the perceptions of the front, he had to command with "cold reason." Hitler then argued that the strength gained by a shortened front line, which Kluge maintained would result from the withdrawal, would only be offset by the consequent loss of matériel during any retreat. Hitler took such logic to the extreme: "Every retreat requires loss. If this withdrawal only ends at our border, we will have no more matériel and without matériel everything is lost." Hitler then told Kluge that in the First World War he had often endured ten-day-long artillery barrages and that the troops had continued to hold their position even with only 10 percent of their strength. Dumbfounded by Hitler's ignorance of the situation, Kluge pointed out that it was not minus twenty to thirty degrees Celsius in France during the First World War. Perhaps out of frustration, Kluge then repeated a comment from Lieutenant-General Ernst-Eberhard Hell, commanding the 15th Infantry Division: "The commanding general has insisted that if one ordered the 15th Div. to hold, the troops would cease to do so as a result of excessive exhaustion." Given what Kluge and other commanders at the front had been allowing, this was almost a direct challenge to Hitler's authority; either he could allow the requested withdrawal or "the troops" would undertake one anyway. Ending the discussion, Hitler emphatically declared: "If that is the case, then it means the end of the German army."[56]

The historical literature has tended to cast Kluge as an overly cautious man who shied away from the bold action of the panzer commanders, notably Guderian, with whom he came into sharp conflict even before December 1941. Yet it was precisely Kluge's more measured approach that allowed him to achieve what he could behind the scenes, picking his battles with the high command in order to win what he felt he must. Caught between Stalin's hammer and Hitler's anvil, he desperately struggled for any room in which to maneuver, all the while maintaining a remarkable degree of composure amid the unrelenting pleas for help from the front. His attempt to advocate a "middle solution" between all-out retreat and fanatical resistance may be explained by the fact that he was the first army commander with wartime experience on the Eastern Front to take over an army group command. He therefore understood the plight of the army commander and was able to command with a "give and take" attitude that demanded obedience where necessary but offered relief where possible. Instead of Hitler's obstinate and entirely impractical insistence on holding every meter of ground, it was Kluge's shrewd military and political acumen as well as his dogged determination that was holding Army Group Center together.

An hour after Hitler had indignantly cut off their conversation, the dictator called Kluge again and another long conversation ensued, which eventually returned to the question of Hell's 15th Infantry Division, whereupon Hitler declared: "The 15th Division must stand. Under no circumstances is it possible to determine the retreat of an entire army by the independent action of a division." Yet Kluge would have none of it. He would have Kübler send whatever forces he could to support Hell's division, but he bluntly informed Hitler that the division would not remain where it was. "The condition of the 15th Division is such that one can order whatever one wishes, it will no longer hold."[57] Kluge made his case with every argument at his disposal, but they were lost on Hitler. The following day the dictator reached his decision to refuse any withdrawal. As Hellmuth Stieff, the operations officer at Fourth Army, wrote to his wife: "It's absolutely sickening and always the same. A permanent 'too late,' because the high command directs every division itself; we can do nothing without their consent and have become completely superfluous letter carriers."[58]

The level of disdain no doubt fed disobedience, but this was also something that Kluge had to control if the duplicity in response to the halt order was not to become overt. Accordingly, on December 31 Schroeck, the commander of the 98th Infantry Division, was relieved of his position by Kluge because he refused the orders of Materna (his corps commander), Bernuth (Fourth Army's chief of staff), and Kübler to halt his withdrawal.[59] As with Guderian, there were limits to Kluge's tolerance. Taking a hard line against men like Schroeck signaled that the "middle solution" was not just a counterpoint to Hitler's position. It sent an unambiguous message to subordinate commanders that there were limits and consequences to unauthorized withdrawals, while at the same time allowing Kluge to demonstrate obedience to the halt order.

While Kluge spent the final days of December unsuccessfully seeking preemptive solutions to the serious threats along Fourth Army's front (and the army group more generally), Kübler's southern wing was the only area he had permission to withdraw. Heinrici's XXXXIII Army Corps was falling back on Kaluga, while Felber's XIII Army Corps was retreating toward the northwest. Meanwhile, Knobelsdorff's 19th Panzer Division was sent down from the north to catch the Soviets in the flank and restore contact between Heinrici and Felber. By December 28 Fourth Army could report on the success of Knobelsdorff's attack and the closure of the gap, although small groups of Soviet troops still remained to be cleared.[60] The insoluble problem for Fourth Army was its wide-open southern flank. The gap extended from Kaluga right down to the northern formations of Second Panzer Army at Belev, a distance of some eighty kilometers. Kübler had nothing with which to close it, and while Guderian had been in command he had shown no interest in the problem. This left Heinrici's corps desperately exposed, and his withdrawal to Kaluga was only a temporary solution. Soviet forces, with nothing to stop them, were driving west and northwest. The envelopment of Kaluga was only a matter of time.

The threat to Heinrici's corps was not entirely conventional. The Soviets were exploiting their breakthrough largely through a cavalry division of the Red Army. The division was nominally supported by formations of infantry, tanks, and artillery, but it was the cavalry that could maintain movement in the deep snow and therefore thrust well in advance of the heavy weaponry or logistical network required to support them.[61] Such flexibility threatened German supply lines, but the largely independent cavalry lacked the strength to challenge well-defended locations. Attempts to do so ended in disaster. Benno Zieser wrote of one Soviet cavalry attack:

> Cavalry. Unbelievable. Dozens of mounted Russians suddenly appeared and made a frontal charge. That opened the Russian attack. Rank suicide. The next instant our heavy automatic began barking away. There was the hell of a row and the attackers were showered with metal. Those horses were jolly good targets, and how they pranced and shied and galloped, with their riders shot out of the saddle, some of them dangling by one foot in the stirrups and the maddened animals dragging them in furrows through the snow. That effort collapsed as suddenly as it had begun; it was hopeless.[62]

According to the intelligence Henrici gleaned from captured Soviet cavalrymen, every Russian male adult in the newly won territories was pressed into service. They fought without uniforms and shared a rifle between four or five men. To further support the extended Soviet advance, airborne units (the first of many more to come) were dropped deep behind German lines (to the southeast of Yukhnov) on December 29. In this instance only about ninety men were dropped with light weapons and food for three days.[63]

As Heinrici closely observed the enemy movements, it was all too apparent to him that either his corps had to be permitted to continue with its retreat or it would become entombed at Kaluga. Preparations were already under way. On December 26 Gustav Vetter observed how the 3,000 Soviet POWs held at Kaluga began their march toward Roslavl over two hundred kilometers away. These men were already weak, and those who fell were shot by their guards. As Vetter noted in his diary: "When they are gone, you can see countless dead lying on the street. There are a few of the prisoners who carry parts of human bodies (arm, foot, etc.) in their pockets (for eating). When somebody falls, some of them fall upon him to take off his clothes and food. All look emaciated and bad, have a direct animal look."[64] Observing such scenes, the German soldiers, who were fully aware that Soviet forces were pushing past them to the west, must have contemplated with horror the prospect of becoming POWs themselves. H. C. von Wiedebach-Nostitz noted in his diary: "The whole thing looks somewhat tricky, since nobody knows, indeed, what the Russians will get up to, possibly cutting off the retreat. We are already waiting impatiently to get going."[65]

Kluge was likewise impatient, but there was no way he could abandon a major center like Kaluga without Hitler's authorization. On December 29 he made his case to the dictator, informing him that even Yukhnov, seventy kilometers northwest of Kaluga and the new command post for Fourth Army, was now under threat from fast-moving Soviet forces. Yukhnov and Suchinitschi (eighty kilometers to the southwest of Kaluga) were also transportation hubs and, Kluge argued, vital to the supply of Kübler's army.[66] Kluge therefore insisted these had to be defended, but at the cost of giving up Kaluga. Hitler responded with the usual questions about how much matériel and supplies would be lost, but ultimately even he could see that Heinrici would lose everything if he remained at Kaluga. The order for withdrawal was given that same day.[67]

Unlike earlier retreats Heinrici's men were then retreating into contested territory, a symptom of Hitler's ad hoc approach to command, which prevented timely decisions. As Heinrici lamented in a letter: "Supporting measures are so meagre and everything is always too little too late."[68] Lieutenant Erich Mende described the harrowing retreat from Kaluga in his diary: "So we moved from village to village, from forest to forest, to have some protection from sight and cold, while the Russians pushed kilometers past us into the hinterland." Villages, Mende noted, were defended against Soviet attacks and became islands of semi-reprieve in a treacherous fighting retreat. Yet those same German-occupied localities were sometimes surrounded and cut off, leading Mende to observe, "the time of the encirclement of German units began."[69] Max Kuhnert's account alluded to the turmoil of the retreat, reflecting its highly improvised and chaotic origins: "In those

days it seemed to be utter confusion most of the time, and it was very difficult to know who was who, who was where, and indeed where was where."[70]
Likewise, Gustav Vetter's diary for December 30 captured the desperation
and fatigue of the retreat: "Seen terrible images on route of retreat. Many vehicles lost. Walked 35 kilometers on foot. Everything lost, have only what I
have on my body."[71]

While Heinrici's men confronted a perilous march to the northwest, they
had at least narrowly avoided being trapped in Kaluga by both the Red Army
and Hitler. Heinrici could take some comfort in the fact that his northern
flank was again secure and that he was no longer cut off from the remainder
of Fourth Army. His XXXXIII Army Corps, however, was a shattered wreck.
As Heinrici observed in a letter to his wife on January 2: "Our troops are in a
pitiful state. On top of our heavy losses is the frostbite. How long the men can
survive nobody knows."[72]

11

TURNING THE SCREWS

Ninth Army's Near Collapse

I f Kluge didn't already have enough on his plate managing the crisis on his right wing, in the days following Christmas the left wing threatened its own collapse. In many respects, Strauss's Ninth Army had been a model of grit and skill in its long but carefully executed withdrawal from Kalinin. Since early December Strauss had fended off repeated attacks by Konev's Kalinin Front as he made his way to the "Staritsa Line," where he was ordered to halt and go into winter positions. The immediate problem for Strauss was that there were no "positions," nor any significant natural defenses to anchor his line on, and with Konev's numerically superior forces constantly pressuring the Ninth Army, Strauss had unsuccessfully sought permission for a further withdrawal to Rzhev, on the so-called

Königsberg Line. With no other option, Strauss dutifully marshaled his resources for a fighting defense of the Staritsa Line. Yet he kept Kluge fully
apprised of Ninth Army's situation and continually pushed for freedom of
action to fall back on the Königsberg Line.[1]

The daily battles soon took a toll, which Strauss's already depleted divisions could scarcely afford, and units added desperate requests for reinforcements alongside their regular reports of losses. On December 27
Major-General Stephan Rittau's 129th Infantry Division reported 438 losses
over three days of hard fighting.[2] The Ninth Army viewed the ensuing contest as an existential question, with the war diary noting: "there is no longer
any illusion . . . the next two weeks will decide if the army is to be or not to
be."[3] Even at the OKH Halder observed on December 25: "Ninth Army begins
to crumble."[4] This, however, did not make him any more agreeable to a withdrawal, and as the situation worsened in the coming days, it was again left to
Kluge to plead for Hitler's permission to allow a retreat.

In the meantime, Strauss could only hope that the heavy defensive fighting would exhaust Soviet strength and momentum faster than his own army's powers of resistance. Such fragile hopes however depended upon the
notoriously inaccurate estimates of Foreign Armies East, the army's intelligence service, but also, thanks to Hitler's order, the absence of a real alternative. If Ninth Army was clutching at straws, the local reports of its own
intelligence service at least provided some substantiation. On December 26,
Strauss reported to Army Group Center that a defecting Soviet officer had
claimed the Red Army was "at the end of its strength," with many cases of
frostbite and shortages of food.[5] Soviet POWs and intercepted radio reports
also pointed to there being little fuel for vehicles and some Red Army units
going days without eating.[6]

Whatever the Red Army's problems, Konev's orders to attack were as
inflexible as Strauss's to defend.[7] Accordingly, all along Ninth Army's front
on December 26, reports came in of heavy fighting, with the army's war
diary noting that "enemy attacks number in the dozens."[8] Although these
were pushing Strauss's Staritsa Line to the very point of collapse, they were
also inflicting staggering losses on the attacking forces. Mikhail Gubanov,
who worked as a translator in Rittau's 129th Infantry Division, wrote that

in his sector alone the Germans took 90 POWs, counted 200 dead, and estimated enemy wounded at between 700 and 900. As a Russian émigré who volunteered for service in the east, Mikhail Gubanov's observations of the fighting reflect less a sense of desperation for the Germans and more one of monotonous routine. He even recalled an episode when a German gun commander calmly approached him during the battle: "'Please, move away, I'm opening fire now, and the enemy will answer by concentrating all their fire on me.'" As Gubanov's account continued: "He makes the request as politely as if he were asking someone to step aside in a tramcar. Ten minutes earlier this officer had released his gun detachment to go and warm themselves in the neighboring huts, and in another minute, [they] would be sweeping the attackers with rapid fire." It all reflected a sense of the mundane, of habitual routine in which repeated Soviet attacks were sometimes more tedious than frightening. As Gubanov's account concluded, "It is clear that the infantry is doing what they had already done many times in battle, and had been taught to do earlier, in peace-time. A good machine is operating."[9] Another witness to the fighting was Heinrich Haape, a doctor in the 6th Infantry Division. Haape recalled one attack in which almost 1,000 Soviet troops charged the German lines, which were defended by just 200 men.

> In the bright moonlight, and with the additional help of flares, the German fire was deadly and the Russians wavered and retreated . . . Again and again the Russians regrouped their forces and attacked, and each time they were halted by the deadly rifle and machine-gun fire of our men . . . For five and a half hours the slaughter continued until the Russians had had enough and withdrew, trying to carry back some of their wounded. But they left more than a hundred dead, immediately in front of the houses we had defended. Our casualties amounted to four dead and six wounded.[10]

While such examples suggest a one-sided contest, which a significant number of the Soviet attacks appear to have been, this was certainly not always the case. In places, the Soviet pressure on Ninth Army raised grave fears of a breakthrough. On December 26, Förster, commanding the VI Army

Corps, having committed his last reserve, requested permission from Ninth Army to pull back his line. Strauss refused, citing Hitler's order, but Kluge, while endorsing Strauss's decision, then added "only when the VI A.C. threatens to be smashed, is withdrawal (but not to a great degree) in order."[11] It was precisely this kind of caveat that undermined Hitler's order and made clear that "fanatical resistance" was not to be continued past the point of making strategic sense. While Kluge's intervention alleviated the most immediate strain, it was no solution to the scope and scale of Konev's late December offensive, and the very next day Förster was again pleading for permission to withdraw along with Schubert's XXIII Army Corps. Strauss contacted Army Group Center, and again permission was granted "for tomorrow evening," but not just for local movements. Kluge was proposing withdrawal to a new, yet to be determined, line. As Ninth Army's war diary noted:

> For the first time, under the power of events beyond human control, the difficult decision was taken to withdraw the Staritsa Line at certain points, which was to have been held under all circumstances according to the Führer's order. Without this, the front, in view of the ever-growing enemy pressure, would rupture. Then the connection would be broken, leadership and influence on the individual units would be eliminated, and a rapid dissolution of the army would be the inevitable consequence. However, in these fateful hours the [Ninth] army command feels the great responsibility of saving the army from its otherwise certain destruction.[12]

Such an order was a direct challenge to the authority of Hitler and the OKH, but Kluge was no doubt hoping to secure permission beforehand. In the meantime, the Ninth Army would have to hold tight, to which Strauss stated: "I will resume the battle tomorrow, but if this mode of fighting is continued, the army will bleed to death."[13] The defense of Ninth Army's long front was already something of a sham, since the extreme nighttime temperatures (falling to minus thirty degrees Celsius and below) were forcing the troops into nearby villages and houses. This left kilometer-wide gaps in the line, which were under only the most rudimentary observation from reconnaissance troops. As Ninth Army's war diary noted: "The defensive front is, therefore, practically a more or less connected series of houses."[14] Moreover, the relentless combat was taking a toll on the men. A report noted that while many were still motivated by a "good spirit and will to hold out," increasingly they were "becoming more and more apathetic."[15] In what may be the most extreme case, a company commander threatened his men with a pistol.[16] The demands of the war were sometimes just too much. As Helmut von Harnack wrote home in a letter on December 27:

> Again and again one thinks that the war cannot get any harder, and always it does. Since 21 December, we have been in a fierce defensive battle, which reached a climax on Christmas Eve and on the first and second days of Christmas. With unimaginable recklessness the Russian attacked, completely unaffected by everything, even the great losses . . . The strength of nerves, which the German soldier showed here, is probably the greatest demanded of him by this campaign.[17]

There was no decision from Hitler on December 28 as to whether a withdrawal would be permitted. Strauss had warned Army Group Center that every hour threatened an operational breakthrough by the Soviets, which only a retirement to the Königsberg Line could offset.[18] Kluge presented this danger to Hitler on December 29 and suggested a "slow withdrawal" to the Königsberg Line, but this was rejected: Reinhardt's and Hoepner's panzer groups did not have enough fuel to withdraw their lines in accordance with Ninth Army's right flank. Even more damning, Hitler cited an explosive report from Richthofen (commanding the VIII Air Corps), who claimed on the basis of his aerial intelligence that the Ninth Army was presenting misleading reports. According to what Richthofen told Hitler, several towns reported as enemy occupied were still in German hands. In places, the enemy had been "forced by counterattacks to flee back to their own troops," and there was no trace of the Soviet cavalry movement that was supposed to have trickled through to the southeast. Richthofen concluded his disparaging report by suggesting that the command of the VI Army Corps (headed by Förster) appeared to be "very nervous."[19] Hitler, of course, seized on the report, as it reaffirmed his belief that the real problem was one of "will" and that the situation was not always as bad as the army made out.

Kluge was incredulous. He pointed out to Hitler that the situation looked different from the air and that Förster and his divisional commanders were reliable men. Yet Hitler would not hear of it. Mere hours later he ordered that Förster be relieved of his command.[20] The question of appointing an interim successor was met by the unorthodox suggestion that the best man for the job was Richthofen himself, who had proven so critical of Förster. Remarkably, Hitler accepted this proposal, leading to what Halder described as a "dramatic discussion" when Hitler informed Richthofen of his new command.[21] In fact, Richthofen only remained in command of VI Army Corps for three days before General of Infantry Bruno Bieler took over on January 2.[22] Nevertheless, it was an absurd situation. The commander of Army Group Center's only air corps was being tasked with a corps command in Ninth Army. This new assignment certainly dissuaded Richthofen from further interfering in army matters, but it could not reverse the damage he had done.

Meanwhile, Strauss was left to contemplate the impending collapse of his army. As he told Greiffenberg at Army Group Center, "a reasonable relocation" was the only solution, because plugging the breakthroughs "no longer works." Resigned to his fate, Strauss concluded: "we will fight to the last, but I am convinced it is senseless."[23] His subordinate commanders, however, were not prepared to fight to the last. The commander of the 86th Infantry Division, Lieutenant-General Joachim Witthöft, ordered his men on December 29: "Do not stubbornly hold. Prepare Kalitsino for evacuation and destruction." On the same day, Rittau, commander of the 129th Infantry Division, ordered his men: "Fight with maneuver! Inflict losses on the enemy, if necessary, abandon a few strongly attacked villages. Avoid costly counterattacks which are not absolutely necessary! Allow enemy to accumulate! Enemy also lacks sufficient reserves."[24] Schellert's 253rd Infantry Division, acting on orders it received from XXIII Army Corps, continued to prepare for "retrograde movements" until December 31.[25] Evidently, major formations in Ninth Army planned to defend themselves against not only the Red Army but also Hitler's pointless fanaticism. Yet while divisional and corps commanders insisted upon local freedom of maneuver, this was no solution to countering major operational breakthroughs. The scale of the Soviet offensive had to be met by a coordinated strategic response at the army and army group level.

On December 30 Halder acknowledged in his diary the "very difficult crisis at Ninth Army," condescendingly adding, "where apparently the leadership temporarily lost their nerve."[26] That Halder was part of the reason such men, not only in Ninth Army but throughout Army Group Center, were so anxious and agitated seemed entirely lost on him. As the army's nominal point of contact with Hitler, Halder shamelessly abrogated all responsibility for his commanders in the field and left Kluge to fight every battle on their behalf. Halder had never commanded an army in the field, nor had he ever shown the slightest interest in visiting the Eastern Front. Nevertheless, he considered his merely theoretical understanding of events sufficient to determine what was, and was not, possible. Accordingly, his strong support for Hitler's emphasis on "fanatical resistance" and the importance of "willpower" had a hollow ring.

On December 30 and 31 Kluge repeatedly pressed the high command to allow Ninth Army's withdrawal. Kluge unsuccessfully debated the issue for two hours on the telephone with Hitler on December 30 and then, undeterred by his past failures, tried again on the morning of December 31.[27] Speaking first to Halder, Kluge outlined Ninth Army's now frantic case for withdrawal. Yet when Kluge called back that evening to receive Hitler's decision, Halder informed him that he had not even passed on the information. At first Halder claimed that he had not had the opportunity to prepare a proposal for Hitler but soon arrived at the real reason for his inaction: "the Führer will never agree to a withdrawal to a predetermined line." Kluge had waited all day for nothing, and Ninth Army's latest reports were not even reaching Hitler. His patience was at an end, and in a bout of frustration, he gave Halder a piece of his mind: "I must demand, that Colonel-General Strauss relocate, so that a catastrophe does not result on the Staritsa front . . . You cannot see how the people look! . . . If, as I have proposed for a long time, we had relocated earlier, this would have been planned and done in full order. Now this cannot be guaranteed with stricken divisions that are incessantly attacked. We are falling back, whether we want to or not!"[28]

Kluge was not exaggerating; the Ninth Army's front was at last collapsing under the weight of Soviet attacks. Even Strauss, who had been one of the few senior commanders in Army Group Center who appeared ready to hold to Hitler's order even against his better judgment, authorized Richthofen's shattered VI Army Corps to retreat. It was unauthorized by the high command, but the corps was disintegrating, and not surprisingly, Richthofen was unable to do anything about it. Lieutenant Paulheinz Quack, who was serving in Richthofen's corps, wrote on December 31: "The retreat in places is turning into a rout . . . The whole front in our area is dissolving. Nowhere is there still a system and clear plan."[29]

Ninth Army was breaking apart, and Halder was not even passing on Kluge's reports. Halder not only had little real comprehension of what was happening at the front, but he was also supported in his views by a particularly insular culture at the OKH, which since Brauchitsch's departure and the now daily contact with Hitler was becoming more and more a mouthpiece for the dictator's viewpoint, much as the OKW was. Heusinger, Halder's chief of operations, wrote in a letter on December 31 that the situation on the Eastern Front could only be mastered "with extreme effort" and that one could not allow retreats, "because that way things will only get worse."[30] Likewise, Hermann Balck, who worked in the OKH's Inspectorate of Armored Forces, wrote in his memoir of a discussion with Hitler at the end of December: "I pleaded with Hitler not to withdraw under any circumstances . . . This was a crisis that could not be solved operationally . . . The demand to hold under such conditions might sound brutal, but in reality it was the greatest clemency."[31] With this tide of supporting opinion, Halder found it easy to dismiss Kluge's repeated badgering, and every day that formations like Strauss's held out provided its own validation of the "hold fast" mentality, over the more "emotional" reactions of generals at the front.

Just before midnight on December 31 Kluge was at last able to speak with Hitler, and he did not mince words. He flatly told Hitler that Strauss had authorized VI Army Corps to retreat. Kluge then explained to Hitler the virtue of his "middle solution," which rejected wholesale retreats of the kind Guderian had sought but emphasized "elastic warfare," which necessitated the flexibility to pull back on occasions. Kluge concluded: "I ask for freedom of maneuver. You must trust me that what I do is right. Otherwise I cannot function. We do not only want what is the best for Germany, but also for you." Hitler posed some questions and agreed to Strauss's withdrawal of VI Army Corps, but before allowing anything else he wanted to speak "with his gentlemen." At 1:30 A.M. Hitler called Kluge and informed him that having spoken with everyone, "especially Colonel-General Halder," there could be "no great rearward movement, even at the risk of a breakthrough."[32] Kluge was then subjected to a long rambling justification, which Otto Dietrich claimed "shattered Kluge's arguments."[33]

Kluge, however, was not to be defeated. After enduring such a nonsensical diatribe, the commander of Army Group Center lashed out with a surprise of his own. He informed Hitler that Strauss had already ordered the retreat.[34] It may have been that Kluge's frustration simply got the better of him, for there is no evidence in Army Group Center's comprehensive war diary that Strauss had in fact taken his defiance so far. On the other hand, Kluge may have decided that he had nothing more to lose. Having appealed to both reason and personal loyalty, he now attempted to present Hitler with a fait accompli. The result was one of Hitler's furious outbursts, in which, according to Dietrich, the dictator "raged and shouted, kept at it and at it, insisted and commanded."[35] Army Group Center's war diary recorded Hitler as bellowing: "It is impossible to initiate an operational movement without the approval of the high command. The troops will have to stop right where they are."[36] Kluge had no more cards to play and conceded. There would be no strategic withdrawal of Ninth Army; the same order was dutifully passed on to Strauss. Ninth Army had to remain in place, but Kluge was soon vindicated by the Red Army—Ninth Army would be falling back with or without orders.

While Strauss and Kübler's armies confronted the prospect of major formations becoming encircled, between them Hoepner's and Reinhardt's panzer groups were experiencing a very different winter war. The most dangerous sector for the two panzer commanders was that of Ruoff's V Army Corps, which lay just to the west of Volokolamsk in the area of Hoepner's Panzer Group 4. Here the fighting took the form of a back-and-forth slogging match, which proved costly to both sides but much more so to the less experienced Soviet formations. On December 25 an attack by two Soviet regiments against the center of the corps ended in a bloody defeat, but the following day another attack against Dehner's 106th Infantry Division broke through his lines.[37] Hoepner asked Reinhardt if the nearby 6th Panzer Division could quickly dispatch a relief force, and ten tanks were sent to restore the situation.[38] On December 28 Ruoff's corps counterattacked and, in costly fighting, retook the heights west of Ivanovskoe and Mikhailovka. In the course of the fighting, a number of Red Army units were encircled, and a Soviet relief force, sent to free them, lost nine tanks in the attempt.[39] It was gritty fighting, and while V Army Corps certainly confronted a serious situation, unlike corps commanders in the Fourth and Ninth Armies Ruoff did not have to worry about his flanks; there was just one direction from which his enemy always came, and mobile support formations were much closer to hand.

Observing some of the costs of this fighting, one man from Dehner's 106th Infantry Division wrote in a letter on December 29:

> If one stands in Timonion or Pashkovo on a high hill and looks around, one can see a strange rampant, of dark color. Looking through binoculars, one sees—these are all corpses of Soviet soldiers. They are piled around our two villages. These are all consequences of endless Soviet attacks inflicted upon us. Three to four times a day, sometimes even more than that they are charging us, advancing with companies and battalions, frequently from two or three sides—and all are mowed down by machine guns . . . One can say that we are not in a war here, but in a slaughterhouse . . . How our boys are holding on despite all this is beyond comprehension.[40]

Such depictions make clear at what price Soviet ground was being retaken, which must also be seen in the context of Germany's own winter crisis. All of the worry, anguish, and debate within Army Group Center was precisely to avoid the reckless loss of life, which all too many Soviet commanders invited with their headlong attacks into prepared German defenses. This is not to ameliorate Army Group Center's dangerous predicament or excuse the German high command's own disastrous understanding of the war, but the results of bad decision making were not the same on both sides. Even Strauss's and Kübler's armies were typically not suffering comparable rates of losses as their attackers. Regardless of the Soviet Union's favorable strategic situation, local Red Army commanders were often unable to capitalize on account of their poor training and lack of experience, while their opponents compensated for their numerical inferiority by the fact that they were skilled veterans who were frequently well led. This did not preclude Soviet tactical successes, but it certainly made them much more costly.

Even against the German panzer troops, like Fehn's 5th Panzer Division, against which Soviet tactical breakthroughs occurred on December 25 and 26, the results were negligible because achieving the breakthrough was only the first step.[41] Penetration of the front line had to be rapidly followed up and supported with reserves to exploit the confusion and drive into the German rear. This was often where Soviet forces failed to capitalize on their achievement, meaning German reserves could react to the danger before a crisis ensued. Certainly, the Soviet breakthroughs caused German casualties, but even in these instances they were seldom proportionate to their own losses.

For all that German tactical proficiency achieved, the contrast with Soviet units should not be seen as an affirmation of strength. The shortfall in men for Hoepner and Reinhardt was, as everywhere, a serious concern. The active strength of Dehner's 106th Infantry Division on December 27 was reported as a mere three hundred troops, and while a transport of replacements arrived on the same day, these men had no winter clothing. Only 20 percent had rifles, the remainder just pistols.[42] For Reinhardt's panzer group, the absence of reserves meant that the men at the front could not be rotated into the rear and, owing to the cold, were "completely exhausted."[43] Alois S. wrote home on December 26 that his unit had been on the front lines for six weeks, "living in holes in the ground they call bunkers, and often without absolute necessities." Since the beginning of the war in the east his company had suffered 90 percent casualties, counting dead, wounded, and missing. "So I am one of the few who is still here, and there is not one of my old comrades around anymore."[44] Another soldier lamenting the endless hours of duty wrote: "Our people are kaput. You've got to say it and see why: one hour outside, one

hour in the hut, watch, alarm, sentry duty, listening duty, observer duty, occupy the MG post—one thing after another. This has been going on since
November 28."[45]

Hoepner was skeptical that Germany would simply outlast the Soviet offensive, and he certainly did not think this could be a matter of two weeks, as
Halder had recently suggested.[46] Writing on December 24, Hoepner noted:
"It is very questionable, according to the experiences so far, whether the opponent will bleed to death. Regarding his last available forces, the experience of the last four weeks has made us very skeptical."[47] Indeed, the whole
campaign in the east justified this opinion, with countless Soviet armies
destroyed and a remarkable, even unprecedented, level of force generation.
The Red Army was, in fact, numerically stronger on paper at the end of 1941
than it had been on June 22 when Operation Barbarossa was launched, although the overall quality of these formations was markedly lower.[48]

To a lesser extent the same was true of the *Ostheer*. Hitler's minister for
armaments and munitions, Fritz Todt, was shocked by what he encountered
during an inspection tour of the east. According to what Todt reportedly told
Albert Speer upon his return on December 27, there were hospital trains in
which the wounded had frozen to death and widespread despair among the
soldiers. As Speer wrote of Todt: "Deeply depressed himself, he concluded
that we were both physically incapable of ending such hardships and psychologically doomed to destruction in Russia."[49] Goebbels, on the other hand,
with no experience of the Eastern Front, took the contrasting opinion and insisted that heavy losses simply had to be accepted as part of warfare. Writing
in his diary on December 28 the propaganda minister argued: "We now have
to prove that we can not only give, but also take. A war does not just consist
of victories, but also defeats or setbacks. Whoever cannot do this, should not
undertake war."[50]

The problem for Reinhardt and Hoepner was not just inadequate manpower, but insufficient supplies of every description. Hoepner wrote to his
wife on January 1: "The troops are screaming for replacements, munitions
and fuel."[51] Above all, food supplies presented the greatest concern. Given
the freezing temperatures Reinhardt's panzer group complained that the
men needed an increase in the fat ration to seventy-five grams a day as well

as two warm meals and half a loaf of bread each.[52] Such a diet was entirely appropriate, but completely impractical, given the severe limitations of the German transportation network. Heavy snowfalls around the Christmas period, reported in places to be two to three meters, closed roads and cut off villages. Hoepner's panzer group reported having no reserves of food, and by December 28 Vietinghoff's XXXXVI Panzer Corps reported that 80 percent of its troops at the front were without any food at all. For the first time, requests were being made for the Luftwaffe to drop food to the front, while every available man was being detailed to shovel snow to clear the roads.[53] Otto Will, from Fehn's 5th Panzer Division, wrote in his diary on December 27: "We can shovel as much as we want; the road cannot be cleared. We work like crazy and still progress only gradually. Throughout the whole day, we are working without break in this weather."[54]

While the panzer groups certainly had their own problems, they were spared from the upheaval erupting on their northern and southern flanks. In fact, Reinhardt's panzer group was even enjoying a degree of relative quiet, though in something akin to the eye of a storm. On December 30 Reinhardt traveled to Model's headquarters at XXXXI Army Corps and then toured the front of Veiel's 2nd Panzer Division and Gollnick's 36th Motorized Infantry Division. Writing to his wife on December 31, Reinhardt noted the turmoil in other parts of Army Group Center before continuing: "This is not the situation with us; on the contrary, I spent all of yesterday at the front and could only be pleased at how firm and positively our troops have held out, despite all the difficulties that lay behind us."[55] Of course, the writings of the soldiers themselves suggest that not all the men in Reinhardt's panzer group felt so upbeat, but clearly there was a much greater sense of security in the area of Panzer Group 3. Röttiger, the chief of staff at XXXXI Army Corps, noted that the position on the Lama River, which was already well suited to defense, had been developed since mid-December so that "the defensive strength of the Lama position was increasing continuously." This, Röttiger noted, included "dug-outs that could be heated and thus provide some sort of protection to the troops against the inclement weather conditions."[56]

Even more important, on December 29 the war diary of Model's XXXXI Army Corps included a report compiled from enemy defectors, which stated that the Red Army was "tired of attacking" after sustaining "heavy losses."[57] It was not hard to see why. Krüger's 1st Panzer Division reported another attack on December 31 in which the Soviets attempted to rush their lines over a frozen lake with no cover. The attack was easily stopped, but only after an estimated 200 men were killed on the ice.[58] The war diary of Reinhardt's panzer group reported that a "majority" of Red Army men were issued alcohol before such attacks, which, although impossible to substantiate, might suggest why the men attempted tactically disastrous assaults.[59] Certainly alcohol was sometimes a factor. Ivan Sawenko, a lieutenant in the Red Army, wrote home in a letter on December 21: "Before each attack, our soldiers were given a full glass of undiluted alcohol; the impetus for this was the capture of the enemy positions. So was the saying: 'Drunk? Excellent! When seizing height X you also get something to eat! If the enemy leaves something behind.'"[60] Not surprisingly, Model's XXXXI Army Corps reported on December 29: "The troops feel themselves superior to the enemy in the defensive. Battle morale is good."[61]

Whatever degree of security Reinhardt and, to a lesser extent, Hoepner enjoyed, they both remained adamant that preserving their strength was as much about defending themselves from the Red Army as it was about preventing Kluge's attempts to snatch their tiny reserves to restore the situations in Fourth and Ninth Armies. Their obstructionism stemmed from their own perceptions of weakness as well as the firsthand knowledge, and even trauma, of themselves having been forced into treacherous retreats by a numerically and materially superior enemy. In any case, neither man wanted to give anything up to Kluge and steadfastly refused to consider the situation from any vantage beyond their own sectors. This was in spite of the fact that the collapse of their respective neighbors would, at the very least, entail a dangerously open flank and further threaten their already precarious supply lines and routes of retreat.

Reinhardt's support for Dehner's 106th Infantry Division on December 26 was strictly conditional on having those tanks returned to his panzer group, and already on December 28 he was agitating to have them back. Hoepner agreed to this in principle but told Reinhardt on December 30 that he could not release them until January 5.[62] Such protectionism was almost certainly driven by fear and made commanders even more reluctant to give up their reserves, no matter how dire the situation of their neighbors. In his letter on January 1, Hoepner thanked his wife for her best wishes regarding his frayed nerves, before continuing: "They are often so tense, that it would not take much for them to tear. Yesterday, I became so coarse to Kluge, that I said: 'I will not tolerate.'"[63] The issue at stake was Kluge's demand that Hoepner provide mobile reserves for Kübler's Fourth Army, which Hoepner bitterly resented. "When, with all manner of chicanery, I have made a reserve, the army group takes it away to fill a hole of the neighbors. They can or must always withdraw, while I am supposed to hold."[64] The fact that Hoepner was himself a recipient of his neighbor's goodwill did not appear to influence this judgment. Nor did Hoepner seem to have any sympathy for the fact that Kübler was attempting to hold a far greater stretch of front, while commanding far fewer mobile divisions.

Reinhardt was also reluctant to send any support to the flanks. Referring to Strauss and Hoepner in a letter to his wife on December 31 as his "bad neighbors," Reinhardt elaborated:

> Both sides cause us worry. We are always standing between two fires, whether we should take the last shirt off our back to help, whether it really is so bad at our neighbors, or whether we should remain hard, so that we ourselves are not placed in danger. In addition, we are pressed from above, we should obviously help because apparently there is unexpected confidence in the panzer troops. You can just imagine how stressful this game of nerves is. We can always only tell our commanders that <u>we</u> are not guilty of this disquiet and have to hope that, with the help of God, everything will be well.[65]

Reinhardt may have hoped that all would be well, but beyond his own section of the front, he was not prepared to do much to ensure it.

Even more important than sending whatever small detachments of reserves might have been available, the best way for Reinhardt and Hoepner to support their neighbors would have been to agree to a withdrawal of their own front. As Ninth Army pleaded for permission to retreat to the

Königsberg Line and Kluge pressed the case with all his energy to the high command, Reinhardt and Hoepner acted to scuttle the attempt. With reasonably developed positions on the Lama and Rusa Rivers and considerably narrower fronts for their divisions, the panzer group commanders wanted to avoid falling back at all costs. Having heard on December 29 that Strauss was clamoring for retreat, Reinhardt protested to Kluge and insisted, with a degree of merit, that he did not have the fuel supplies to undertake another withdrawal.[66] Reinhardt even claimed: "If Panzer Group 3 should have to withdraw, I'll only come with the carbines on the shoulder."[67] Ultimately it was Kluge's choice, or at least it should have been, but Reinhardt did not let it come to that. In his diary, Reinhardt dismissed Kluge's support for Strauss as "soft," and he reported speaking with Hoepner where it was decided that they would take their case directly to the OKH, going over Kluge's head.[68] Their advocacy for holding tight and forbidding any withdrawals was just the kind of stalwart resolution that the OKH and Hitler were looking for. They certainly suffered no sanction for going outside the chain of command; in fact Reinhardt was promoted to the rank of colonel-general on January 1, 1942, while on the same day both panzer groups were redesignated Third Panzer Army and Fourth Panzer Army. The fact that both panzer commanders had been able to undertake their own desperately necessary retreats in the two-week period before the halt order was introduced somehow failed to evoke the slightest consideration in either man. They simply viewed the war from their own short-term best interests, even though, from Kluge's point of view, commitment to these narrow interests risked undermining Army Group Center's strategic position as a whole.

On December 31, as Ninth Army's position on the Staritsa Line was collapsing, Reinhardt still maintained that he had nothing to spare. Kluge had to point out the obvious: "that help is in your own interest [and] absolutely necessary, even if only a battalion with a few tanks."[69] Reinhardt eventually gave in, agreeing to precisely these numbers—one battalion and a few tanks, "until afternoon 1.1, latest morning 2.1."[70] The fact that Kluge—a field marshal commanding six armies, on paper some 1.7 million men—was haggling back and forth over a depleted battalion and a handful of tanks speaks volumes about the state of Army Group Center as well as its dire lack of reserves.

It also contradicts the supposition that *Auftragstaktik* ended with Hitler's halt order. Reinhardt was at liberty to authorize, or not, the dispatch of these forces to Ninth Army, while Kluge preferred to convince his subordinate of the mission rather than order it arbitrarily. It was Hitler, supported by the acquiescent OKH, who unwisely chose to ignore local initiative, expertise, and freedom of execution, while ensnaring the high command in senseless tactical details. As Hoepner wrote contemptuously to his wife on January 1: "A. H. [Adolf Hitler] now commands over corps."[71]

What Hitler and the OKH could not understand was that there was no blanket solution to Army Group Center's problems because there was no generic experience of the Soviet winter offensive. At the beginning of December, it was the panzer forces of Guderian, Reinhardt, and Hoepner who were overextended and dangerously exposed, while Fourth and Ninth Armies held their lines against modest Soviet attacks. By the end of the month, the situation was reversed. The panzer forces were breathing a sigh of relief, having reached the Oka and Zusha Rivers in the south and the Lama and Rusa Rivers in the north, while Ninth and Fourth Armies then were subjected to the weight of major Soviet offensives, but without the freedom to maneuver when and where local commanders deemed best. Of course, many commanders took matters into their own hands, but often only when no other option was available and time had been squandered in futile attempts to get higher commands to understand and accept their situation.

If the December fighting was not equal between the various armies and panzer groups, the same was also true even within each of these formations. Given the different starting strengths, access to supplies, and attention from the Red Army, one cannot speak of a generic winter experience for the divisions, and therefore a standing order on their employment made no sense. In the winter months, Army Group Center was not wholly in crisis, as is commonly assumed even today. Rather, the crisis manifested more as a relative, local phenomenon, at certain sectors over specific periods. The ability of the Soviet forces to encircle major German forces was small to begin with but was greatly enhanced by Hitler's halt order. With the order in place, only last-minute authorizations to withdraw or open defiance by the German officers themselves managed to avoid formations being cut off. Indeed, one may well ask how much more effective German resistance would have been had Kluge been granted the freedom to make timely withdrawals when and where he and his local commanders deemed best. This would also have freed officers to concentrate on the urgent tasks at hand in the field, and not on seeking to reverse the stubborn refusals of the high command. Whatever the result might have been, even with the halt order Army Group Center came through December functional and intact, proving itself still capable of decimating any Soviet formation that was ineptly thrown against its lines. At the same time, the sum of the army group's December retreats equaled just 3 percent of the total ground won in the Soviet Union since the start of Operation Barbarossa.[72] The inability of the Red Army to capitalize on its breakthroughs, encircle major German formations, or even win ground at anything less than an exorbitant cost, meant that Army Group Center, for all the faults of its command and however messy on the ground, had so far frustrated the Soviet winter offensive. In fact, Germany's strategic aim to "hold areas which are of great operational or economic importance to the enemy" had so far been achieved.[73] Kursk, Orel, Briansk, Viaz'ma, Rzhev, and above all Smolensk remained firmly in Army Group Center's hands throughout December. The question was if this could be maintained into 1942.

12

RANK AND FILE

Soldiering in Army Group Center

T he year 1941 came to an end in circumstances few German soldiers could ever have imagined. When they crossed into the Soviet Union most expected another rapid Blitzkrieg victory, and well into the autumn the majority of German troops still anticipated an end to the fighting that would allow their units to return home for Christmas. Even at the start of December, as prospects of Christmas in Germany looked forlorn, there was still no sense that a major Soviet offensive was about to be launched. Thus, reflecting back on the year proved a sobering exercise for many of the men in Army Group Center. Some were still in shock. Willi Lindenbach wrote on December 31: "The last part of this year 1941 was the most terrible part of life that I have so far experienced. I will remember it forever."[1] Heinrich Haape wrote that he and his comrades drank a toast to 1942 in demure silence, while their efforts to be festive "were not very successful. We were sadly mindful of the missing faces, and 1942 did not strike us as having entered on a particularly well-omened note."[2] Indeed many of the men were more concerned by what the New Year would bring than the disappointments of the year that had passed. A private by the name of Hänseler wrote home in a letter on December 31: "We celebrated the New Year without any special festivities or formalities. The one question uppermost in our minds is: Will 1942 bring us peace?"[3] Likewise, Erich Kern recalled in his memoir: "And the New Year? What would it bring? How many of us would survive? Would we see our homeland again in 1942?"[4] Franz Leiprecht's letter noted simply: "A hard year lay behind us—what will the new bring?"[5]

While uncertainty about the future abounded, there was also no shortage of men determined to celebrate the New Year. Perhaps precisely because of the many threats to Army Group Center, they preferred not to think about what had been or what was to come. Martin Pöppel's unit was in the army group's rear area when someone noticed the date. The men seized upon the opportunity to start "drinking determinedly." A short time later Pöppel observed others doing the same: "like ourselves, they're all paralytically drunk."[6] Indeed, in spite of the army group's supply problems, liberal quantities of alcohol appeared to have been available at most New Year celebrations. H. C. von Wiedebach-Nostitz's diary noted wine and cognac,[7] while Ernst Gerber's group celebrated with sparkling wine.[8] A group of thirty men from Landgraf's 6th Panzer Division captured a small hut only fifty meters from Soviet positions and then proceeded to drink wine to see in the New Year.[9] Otto Allers's group of eleven men shared three bottles of sparkling wine, one bottle of cognac, and several liters of schnapps.[10] Anton Böhrer wrote how his unit drank rum, cognac, and sparkling wine, "almost all French product."[11] Even Erich Mende, whose group was cut off near Kaluga, wrote of "a resourceful spirit" discovering a small bottle of vodka with which his commander toasted the New Year "and wished us all to get out of the pocket."[12]

For men without access to bottled alcohol the solution was bootleg spirits, which Fritz Hübner noted was prepared by their company cook to be a specially "drinkable warm beverage," because "pure it tasted like rat poison." Hübner's men could not be given too much of this "devil's brew," in case there was an enemy attack.[13] Another soldier conspicuously referred to his group drinking what he referred to as "vodka," which produced a "good mood" and kept the men from sleeping before the New Year arrived.[14] A study of alcohol-related problems in the Wehrmacht showed, not surprisingly, that consumption rates rose sharply in the second half of 1941 and that this caused serious health problems, not least of which were from bootleg distilleries that sometimes produced deadly concoctions. In fact, from the autumn of 1939 to the summer of 1944 (when records became fragmented), nearly three-quarters of the 1,800 autopsy reports of German soldiers who died of alcohol or drugs attributed the death to denatured alcohol poisoning. In the cases of methanol poisoning, the vast majority of cases (95.9 percent) occurred after the invasion of the Soviet Union.[15]

Indeed, the abuse of alcohol was hardly unique to special occasions like Christmas and New Year's; men in the Wehrmacht and SS drank profuse amounts, and its association with criminal convictions proved it was a serious concern for discipline.[16] Yet drinking was one of the few ways to "escape" the Eastern Front—dull the winter cold, ease the melancholy of homesickness, or drown out the brutal reality of warfare. It was a remedy from which few abstained, especially on the Eastern Front, and the army's culture encouraged heavy drinking even in spite of hefty punishments for infractions related to alcohol abuse.

If alcohol was the essential ingredient in New Year's celebrations, it was not the only means by which German soldiers marked the end of 1941. Wolfgang Buff wrote of how he and his comrades relit their Christmas tree candles and sang carols once again.[17] Otto Will's group also sang together but opted for "soldier's songs." The remainder of the night they spent playing cards and telling stories of their experiences, and when the clock struck twelve, they toasted 1942 and wished one another well for the coming year.[18] More dramatic celebrations were typically taking place outside the bunkers and huts, as German artillery and antiaircraft guns unleashed firework shows across many sections of the Eastern Front. Ernst Gerber wrote in his diary that ten minutes before midnight a gun sounded, and "then followed a banging without comparison in all the surroundings." The men huddled at the windows to observe "the beautiful fireworks, with every fifth round in the magazine being a tracer. Signal rockets were also fired." Gerber and his comrades then left their shelter and started firing off their own munitions.[19] Another soldier wrote to his sister that at 11:30 P.M. a "fantastic shooting from all posts" erupted, so that "one could think he was in a great battle."[20] Heinz Postenrieder simply wrote that at midnight, "the front trembles."[21] Franz Leiprecht noted that when the clock struck twelve: "The whole section of front began a hellish shooting. Flares of all colors brightened the sky. Yes, our guns even sent a few New Year's greetings to the enemy."[22] There were no fireworks or flares in Fritz Hübner's region of the front, just a heavy midnight bombardment of the Soviet lines to mark the occasion.[23] Hans Rehfeldt had the opposite experience as Soviet Katyusha rockets, nicknamed "Stalin's organ" by German troops, fired a midnight salvo at his village.[24]

At 8:00 P.M. German time, Goebbels was on the radio to read Hitler's New Year's greetings to the troops, which the propaganda minister later described in his diary as "the song of praise for German courage and valor." Hitler's tribute was directed especially to those on the Eastern Front, and it concluded with a pledge "that the year 1942 would lead to the smashing of Bolshevism and the Soviet system."[25] It was an outlandish promise, especially after all the misplaced hopes of 1941. Indeed, only two days later Goebbels, who never dared criticize Hitler's choice of words, referred to the famous speech of Otto Dietrich given in October 1941 in which he informed the German and international press that the war in the east had been "decided."[26] In Goebbels's judgment there had seldom been a statement that had "caused such severe damage as this," and yet Hitler had now drawn another line in the sand for 1942.[27] Not surprisingly, after reading Hitler's speech on New Year's Eve, Goebbels was uncharacteristically downcast. "No one is interested in celebrating. Everywhere it is attempted to read the future. I do not get involved in such attempts. The future is so dark that no one is able to somehow shed light on it."[28]

Even at the OKH, where Hitler's military illusions typically found favor, a private letter from Heusinger to his wife set out his own doubts for 1942. The chief of the army's operations department foresaw the coming year as "mostly being on the defensive," which "cannot yet bring about a deci-sion."[29] Hoepner and his command staff celebrated the evening together, but the panzer group's war diary sounded a downcast note: "There is a heavy shadow over the end of the year. December saw a great hope [of victory] un-done." Then the diarist attempted to conclude on an upbeat note by insisting: "The Will must overcome this crisis!"[30] If the German command sounded a dejected note, Larry LeSueur, the American correspondent, claimed that the celebration in Moscow was "the gayest Russian New Year's Eve in years. Con-fidence is everywhere. The army newspaper *Red Star* said editorially today that the Germans can and must be beaten in 1942."[31] Clearly, delusions about what would be achieved in the coming year were not unique to Hitler.

While small groups of men in dugouts and huts entertained themselves independently on New Year's Eve, there were some attempts at the company or battalion levels to provide organized amusement for the men, often musical performances or comedy routines. Anton Böhrer had a professional come-dian in his unit who took to the stage for three hours with his assistant, and "one could not avoid laughing." Yet Böhrer described another show with Rus-sian performers that was "very miserable."[32] Judging by soldiers' writings, frontline theater was not a common form of entertainment in 1941, and most of it was organized locally or by soldiers themselves. While the standard may not have been high, many of the most successful performances were those that played to the soldiers' own brand of humor and sentimentality, which did not always conform to the wishes of the officers. Without explain-ing why, Paul Wortmann wrote that his role in a theater piece had "greatly angered the gentlemen officers." Yet this it seems had been the whole point, as Wortmann concluded: "It was therefore a resounding success."[33] Hans Meier-Welcker wrote of attending a "village cultural event" in a disused cin-ema performed by Russian farmers, mainly girls and old men. "The Russians sang many old songs. When one hears Russian music one starts to love the country. The country has an extraordinary capacity to endure suffering."[34]

As the war continued, frontline theater became its own industry financed and organized by a multitude of groupings that both cooperated and com-peted. These included the Wehrmacht, the German Red Cross, the Strength Through Joy movement, and Goebbels's propaganda ministry. Some programs were made up of regular theater companies who conducted special tours of the front, while others were permanent frontline entertainers who had been conscripted to perform for the Wehrmacht. In addition, there were commercial touring companies and independent operations run by volunteers. The acts were as varied as civilian theater, but the content was often designed to give soldiers a link to the homeland. Overall, the standard was not high, and there were continual complaints about the poor level of performances.[35]

Cinema for the soldiers was a rarity in 1941 and typically only available in the bigger population centers near the front like Orel, although there were a small number of mobile projector vans that toured the front. The chances, however, of a German soldier seeing one of these films was extremely small. Adequate organization for front cinema was lacking, and there were serious technical deficiencies in projectors, generators, and technical personnel. Beyond these constraints, film stock was also in very short supply, and for the 7,043 German cinemas in 1941, the Wehrmacht only received about fifty copies of any of the forty new films produced each year between 1939 and 1944.[36] As a result, there were precious few resources available for the Eastern Front. Reinhardt's Panzer Group 3, for example, had one mobile projector van in 1941 and noted that even if every day 1,000 men could see a film it would still take between four and six months before each man had attended a single movie. Yet even this single van was so badly damaged by the Soviet roads that it had to be sent back to Germany for repairs, and months passed before a replacement arrived.[37]

Cinema was a cherished pastime, and its scarcity at the front made it all the more beloved. A cinema in Orel became extremely popular with the men of the Second Panzer Army.[38] At least early in the war, films were not viewed as an engine for propaganda, although a visit to the cinema included much more than just the main feature. Advertisements were followed by the weekly Wochenschau, or newsreel, and then there was the Kulturfilme—a short film of popular education. After 1939, the Wochenschau was concentrated on the war and was pure propaganda, which proved effective for civilians, while German soldiers viewed it with far greater skepticism and even outright disgust. The tone was triumphant and heroic, less with a goal of communicating real information concerning the war than with impressing the audience with German military superiority.[39] In the winter of 1941–1942 the irony of such a message would not have been lost on those German soldiers who had the privilege of attending a cinema, and it only deepened their suspicions about what the home front understood of the conflict in the east.

The paucity of organized recreational entertainment meant much of the soldiers' free time was spent in the warm confines of their dugouts or shelters, which also determined many of their activities. What was different by the end of 1941, and in stark contrast to the opening weeks and months of the war, was how everyday recreational activities began to parallel the demands of the war. No longer did military events dominate soldiers' letters and diaries; the war had become a tedium of suffering and repetition from which the men sought diversion and distraction at every opportunity. Erich Hager's diary for December 28 provides an example of how the war had become just one more thing among much more banal and routine events. Hager wrote:

> Awake and the cards in my hands already. Now 17.00, then *Skat* [a German card game]. There are canteen goods. Cigarettes, up to 20 packets. Next to us in position, firing all morning, the house shakes. They are firing 3 km at the Russians, who attack brazenly. They have heavy losses. Battle group was bombed. Sergeant Burger slightly wounded with shrapnel in the head. Roast beef. Got 3 letters. News from Arthur. What will it be, a boy or a girl? In the evening played *Skat*. Lots of noise because of Artillery. G [illegible] caught again, is already in the field hospital.[40]

With the war now an unremarkable event and much of military duty just a gloomy routine, the question for the men was "What should we do now?"[41] Indeed the question was entirely dependent upon Soviet activity, but even in Army Group Center there were relatively quiet sectors like Lieutenant-General Hermann Meyer-Rabingen's 197th Infantry Division, which ironically was guarding the main east-west highway between Smolensk and Moscow. Meyer-Rabingen's division had seen some action in December, but by the end of the year was still occupying the same positions it had at the end of November.

To keep the men occupied with wholesome diversions, the authorities in one region strongly emphasized board games, and on December 30 about a thousand games, including nine men's morris, draughts, and dominoes, were requisitioned from a Russian factory and distributed to the men. The soldiers, however, were far from impressed and rejected them in favor of "real" games such as cards, chess, and dice cup. "Everything else," the report noted, "is regarded as childish."[42] The favorite card games were *Skat* and *Doppelkopf*, which—much more than just a pastime—were also serious business, given that they facilitated another beloved source of soldiers' amusement—gambling. Hans Sturm won 300 RM in a game of *Skat*, making the loser furious, but as Sturm recalled: "The men laughed with delight at his misfortune."[43] Erich Hager's group were compulsive card players, and the stakes were also high, as he wrote in his journal on December 26: "Another snowstorm and bitter cold again. We're used to it. What do we do? Play cards, won 17 to 4, won 230 RM, great!"[44] William Lubbeck considered gambling foolish but nevertheless partook in games of *Skat*, which he referred to as "a 'thinking' card game." He even believed that such games had a military utility: "Our games helped keep me mentally alert in case of a Red Army attack. Like smoking, drinking, gambling, or other forms of relaxation, they also simply provided a temporary means of escape from the tension and tedium of war."[45]

While gambling was commonplace, it is difficult to characterize the extent to which it was a problem. Helmut Günther noted after the war: "What were we supposed to do with all that money anyway? Wooden matches, twine, sparkplugs and field-stove heating candles were far more important! There were neither taverns nor shops here where we could spend our money. For us money served as game tokens, that's all!"[46] Willy Peter Reese agreed: "Money had become meaningless. We used paper money for rolling cigarettes or gambled it away indifferently. Several got so far into debt that they couldn't pay with a year of their soldiers' wages, and that wouldn't be called in either."[47] Yet money was not entirely worthless on the Eastern Front. Hans-Albert Giese wrote to his mother in December and asked her to draw money from his bank account and buy and send him a list of requested items.[48] A month later, however, Giese wrote that "at the moment" he was able to buy "very many" items from his local military canteen.[49] There were also goods for sale at the market in Smolensk, such as cigarettes, alcohol, and specialty foods, but the prices were very high and well beyond the wages of local Russians, meaning it was mostly the Germans doing the buying.[50]

While cards and gambling were popular social activities, reading and letter writing were the most common individual pursuits. Recalling the first winter in the east, Franz Frisch wrote: "When I was inside there was little to do except read and improve my chess playing and try not to think about being cold, until it was my turn to stand guard outside."[51] The problem for men who liked to read was twofold. First, there was a dearth of reading material available on the Eastern Front, and second, the short winter days meant that it was already too dark to read inside by 3:30 P.M., and not every dugout or bunker offered sufficient lighting for reading. As one soldier noted, gasoline was burned in a tin can, "so we could at least see something when the cold food was shared out."[52] Even if light sufficed, as Erich Kern complained, reading material was "extremely scarce in Russia."[53]

Among the most requested were German newspapers, but they were in very short supply due to the shortage of paper and the lack of transport capacity to the east. Books were less affected by the paper shortage since public collections throughout the war yielded over 43 million titles. The most popular titles were light reads in genres such as adventure, romance, crime, and almost anything from Karl May (who was best known for novels set in the American Wild West).[54] Hans Olte, for example, wrote that he wanted "cock-and-bull stories and other such trashy novels. Something that will distract one from the everyday."[55] Another soldier noted that the demand was greatest for cheap twenty-pfennig novels, which he stated could "refresh" one's spirit.[56] Yet the delivery of books was affected by the transportation difficulties to the Eastern Front, which in the winter of 1941–1942 proved insurmountable.[57] Some did arrive in packages sent from home, but for the authorities there were obviously far more important priorities.[58] Hans Kröhl, who was stationed at Istra in early December, discovered many German books in a house owned by a Jewish professor. The professor, who was hiding in the house, said Kröhl could take some of the books with him, observing: "In the next few days retreating German soldiers will burn down our house anyway."[59]

While reading was extremely popular, there was no more common individual activity than writing letters home. Some homesick men wrote letters as often as possible, while others only seldom put their thoughts to paper, but almost no one wrote nothing. Field post was the one link to Germany, to loved ones and to all that was familiar to the men. On a daily basis some 15 million letters were having to be transported between Germany and the front, which, given the transportation problems, meant only a fraction were getting through.[60] As an illustration of the volume, a transport section of the 2nd Panzer Division noted that between October 2, 1941, and January 31, 1942, it had transported 530 tons of essential war matériel and eighty tons of field post.[61] Such a figure is all the more remarkable when one considers just how few letters were actually arriving at the front during the winter months. Otto Hilger wrote to his family on January 20 that "We are all hoping for our Christmas post." He then added: "Our slogan: Nearer to field post!"[62] Likewise, Albert Neuhaus complained to his wife: "I also think that more has to be done to help because post from home is ultimately the only source of joy we have here."[63] The 19th Panzer Division reported in early January that it was at last receiving a large delivery of post dating from the middle of October.[64] The only consolation for the overburdened logistical system was that Army Group Center's winter retreat somewhat reduced the distances of transportation, while the constant fighting left less time for writing. As Werner Beermann explained in a letter on January 25, between mid-December and the first half of January, "none of us had time to write," because "many important things stood in the way."[65]

After going weeks without post, one soldier commented, "you notice that field post is just as important as rations and ammunition, because it has to sustain and nourish our spirits, our emotions. And to sustain the soldier as a human being, to prevent him from becoming a raw brutalized instrument of war, that is the higher task of the letter writer back home."[66] Similarly, William Lubbeck noted that:

> When a soldier is fighting a thousand miles away from his native soil, mail from home provides a tremendous boost to morale. Because of military censorship, we could not write about our units, where we

were or our battles at the front. At the same time, letters to those back home provided us a momentary release from war's miseries and gave loved ones relief from their constant anxiety over the soldier's fate . . . Like most soldiers, I read and reread these messages from home and devoted a large portion of my free time to writing letters in reply. In my experience, news from home was one of the most significant factors shaping a soldier's capacity in combat because it determined his state of mind and morale. Throughout the war, these letters were as important to sustaining our souls as food was to sustaining our bodies.[67]

Yet it was this same vital exchange of information between the Eastern Front and the home front that Goebbels worried constituted an ominous threat to the German war effort. Much more than writing about their units or battles, Goebbels was concerned that soldiers were writing at length about their frightful hardships, the lack of supplies, and the falsehoods in German propaganda.[68] Since mid-October he was apprehensive about a decline in morale on the home front after his own propaganda had raised impossible expectations of victory in the east. The failure of German operations and the onset of a major Soviet offensive only served to confirm the negativity emanating from the field post, which was seriously undermining the Nazi regime's credibility. Goebbels's solution was to issue an instruction through the OKW on the "art of writing letters," which called for an emphasis on "manly, hard and clear letters . . . differentiating between impressions best locked deeply in the heart because they only concern soldiers at the front and those which can be, and should be, related at home to keep them informed about the war." In line with National Socialist conceptions of soldiering, the instruction then asserted that anyone who complained was "no true soldier."[69] Goebbels's instruction, however, seems to have had little discernible impact on the tone in which letters were written, which is not surprising given that letter writing was one of the few private spaces available to men in the east and for many an essential emotional outlet.

In addition to field post, packages from home (usually accompanied by a letter) gave the soldiers a tangible link to the homeland. With the army struggling to provide even things essential for the army group's survival, packages were often the only opportunity for "luxury" items. One soldier listed the contents of his package, which included a notebook, small envelopes, skin cream, mineral pastilles, vitamin tablets, razor blades, cigarettes, and biscuits.[70] The fact that far fewer packages were arriving on the Eastern Front in the winter months meant their contents were even more valuable, which sometimes led to stealing. Alexander Cohrs grumbled in a letter on December 19 that "The stealing is very bad again." He then told how a man bringing the post to his unit was discovered to have opened one of the packages, eaten its contents, and then claimed to have "lost" it on the way.[71] The increase in stealing appears to have been just one symptom of the high casualties and a general breakdown in unit cohesion. In early January Gerhardt Linke complained: "With regard to the morale and discipline of the soldiers, facts may be observed today which formerly had no existence in our regiment . . . It begins with the careless way in which the men handle arms and equipment and throw their rifles around, and ends with the downright stealing from one another. In general, with very many of them the word 'comradeship' does not evoke much respect."[72] The rejection of replacements, who were seen as not belonging to the core group, created a division between old and new members, which directly impacted cohesion as more and more of the original group disappeared. Heinrich Haape wrote: "But we had been lucky in the 3rd Battalion; the spirit of comradeship had been something out of the ordinary. The spirit was still there, but the battalion as we had originally known it had virtually ceased to exist." He then made clear his determination to remain a part of his veteran group within the battalion: "If I happened to be still alive when the small remnant of the 3rd Battalion was wiped out, it would be the end of any desire for comradeship on my part."[73]

A famous study from Edward Shils and Morris Janowitz asserted that German soldiers formed "primary groups" around which the cohesion of their units was sustained.[74] This thesis was later disputed by Omar Bartov, who claimed that by the end of 1941 these primary groups had largely been destroyed and that group cohesion was therefore maintained by ideological factors.[75] On the surface Haape's testimony might suggest Bartov was correct, but what Bartov failed to account for was the formation of new primary groups among replacements. The longer these survived the more the barriers broke down between themselves and the surviving cadre of the oldest veterans.[76] Indeed, Thomas Kühne's research might dispute whether men like Haape would really have opted for solitude over forging bonds with new men. As Kühne's study of comradeship made clear, the need for companionship on the Eastern Front was an extremely powerful motivation. Companionship provided a sense of "power, security and a safe haven" against "the impotence, insecurity and loneliness of soldiers trapped in the workings of the military obedience and subjugation machine."[77]

Soldiers' accounts do give some insight into the loneliness of those who found themselves on the outside of the primary groups or those whose unit functioned as a collection of individuals rather than a cohesive company. In the first instance Hans Frenzel's diary for January 5 noted: "I continue to live in isolation. I cannot become intimate with anyone. Solitude. I am surrounded all the time by men who lack any refinement, who are completely egotistical and seeking their own advancement, forever licking boots. Narrow-minded fools. Impossible to converse with them freely; so I keep quiet . . . A pitiful life."[78] Willy Peter Reese referred to a similar phenomenon, only in his case there appeared to be no group dynamic to join and instead every man fended for himself.

> The extent of my life and thoughts never got beyond tiredness, fantasies of desertion, need for sleep, hunger and cold . . . I had no comrades. Everyone fended for himself, hated anyone who found better booty than himself, wouldn't share, would only trade, and tried to get the better of the other. There was no conversation beyond the day to day. The weaker was exploited, the helpless left in misery. I was deeply disappointed, but then I too had become hard.[79]

Compared to the incalculable benefits of group acceptance and support, competing for survival even with one's comrades was a wretched existence, especially on the Eastern Front. Comradeship was for most men akin to family at the front. As Gottlob Bidermann wrote, "it was only in the company of landsers that we now felt truly at ease."[80]

Such familiarity among the men gave many bunkers a homey feeling where the degree of intimacy allowed for shared sorrows and joys, which sometimes found expression through music. Henry Metelmann recalled fondly: "I always liked the peace and warm comradely atmosphere of the evenings when we sat together around the table and played cards or chess, with candles as our only source of light. We had two mouth-organs in our crew and after having bedded down on our blankets we played and quietly sang."[81] Helmut Günther wrote how one man in his unit had traveled through the Soviet Union with his guitar and regaled his comrades with heartfelt serenades about the loneliness of soldiering. Yet music at the front was not all about solemn contemplation; Günther also wrote of upbeat bunker parties: "Things really took off when he stood up and started to dance. Werner strummed the strings, Loisl beat on the table with the frying pan and I drummed on a cooking pot with my bayonet. Boy, we really got going!"[82]

While some groups made their own music, others listened on a radio or, in rare instances, a gramophone. As Erich Hager noted in his diary toward the end of January: "We don't do much today. Play the gramophone. Great dance music, also Viennese waltzes."[83] In the winter of 1941–1942 Goebbels formed a new orchestra called the "Reich Light Music Orchestra." Its main task was to perform on the radio for members of the armed forces by providing music "with a swing to it." This was in response to a stark increase in soldiers tuning in to British radio stations out of dissatisfaction with the musical content on German stations. It was a rare instance of thinly disguised ideological compromise. Anything swing or jazz had previously been denounced by Goebbels and his propaganda as "black" or "Jewish" music. Now such concessions to soldiers' preferences were being sold as examples of "German Jazz" or "lively rhythms." Such rebranding was not lost on the listeners, and while soldiers may have enjoyed the music, the issue provoked heated debate within the Nazi Party.[84]

Another example of Goebbels's willingness for musical compromise was the 1941 hit "Lili Marleen," which in 1938 he had rejected for radio play because of its melancholy lyrics and somber melody. Consigned to obscurity, it was found in a crate of old records by an employee at the Wehrmacht radio station in Belgrade in August 1941 and played every evening at the same time—9:57.[85] As elsewhere, it became a sensation among soldiers in the east, and Goebbels dared not deny the troops a song that enjoyed such a tremendous resonance.[86] As Albert Neuhaus wrote home on January 1: "The soldiers listen and sing each evening to the song 'Lili Marleen' on the radio."[87] Yet Goebbels was perhaps correct in judging the song's depressing tone, which forced many men to reflect on a world from which they were cut off. As Max Kuhnert recalled: "How strange, I thought, as the ten o'clock news from Germany came through, introduced as always, first by a bugler and then the very popular tune of 'Lili Marleen', here I am sitting literally in the middle of nowhere, in snowed-in Russia, listening to this. I could not help feeling rather sorry for myself then, and also very homesick."[88]

If free time at the front was mainly used for recreational activities, it was also important to maintain personal hygiene, which in the freezing temperatures men were sometimes reluctant or unable to do. The consequences of inaction could be dire. Gerhardt Linke described visiting men at a battalion aid station, writing in his diary on January 6: "They had no chance to change for months. So far no laundry facilities have been provided. For that you need not only soap and water but also some assurance that you will have time to dry your wash. One soldier had his whole lower hip covered with suppurating sores the size of 10-pfenning pieces. His pants had constantly irritated him. Nowadays things have reached a point where the doctors will pass a man in condition like that."[89] Sometimes the soldiers could find Soviet women who were willing to do laundry for the men in exchange for food or some form of payment, but even then, soldiers did not typically possess a second uniform, or even soap.[90]

Proper bathing facilities were even harder to come by, and often soldiers were reduced to a sponge bath with a bucket of water and little privacy. Anything more elaborate was a sheer matter of luck, determined by a unit's proximity to a town with functional public baths or to a peasant hut with a rare *Banya* (sauna or bathhouse). After two months of winter, Heinrich Engel had the good fortune to be quartered in a house with a *Banya* and explained the effect of his first bath: "I took my first Russian bath in the sauna. The Russian with whom we were quartered made all the preparations and scrubbed us. That hot cleaning was too much for me. For the first time in my life, I passed out but came too [sic] after a short period."[91] Another soldier wrote in his diary after a bath: "This is always a great recuperation for mind and body."[92] The joy associated with cleanliness was a reflection of just how unhygienic the men really were. Hendrik Verton described his unit's *Banya* as "a civilised 'island' of only a few square yards, but in another world. We felt that we were in paradise."[93] Yet the baths could not rid the men of one of their single greatest torments—lice. As Hans Sturm recalled: "It was not the fighting which was the most terrible thing about this country. It was the filth, the temperature, the vermin."[94]

Without proper treatment lice proved almost impossible to expel and were potentially life threatening. The human body louse is the only vector of *Rickettsia prowazekii*, a bacterium that causes epidemic typhus. While epidemic typhus was the most common of louse-borne diseases on the Eastern Front, it was not the only disease transmitted by the lice. *Rickettsia quintana* caused trench fever, and *Borrelia recurrentis* relapsing fever. There was also spotted fever, but this was spread by mites, ticks, and fleas, not lice.[95] The men were therefore instructed to keep themselves free of lice, but this proved almost impossible without mobile delousing stations, which did not appear on the Eastern Front until the end of 1942.[96] As one doctor noted: "Every single man in the battalion was infested with lice, but in the face of the greater demands made on the medical unit by the constant fighting and deadly cold, this was no longer of much consequence."[97]

The only solution to keep the lice infestation at bay was a protracted nightly louse hunt. As Benno Zieser wrote: "Every evening we sat bent over the oil lamp hunting out the unwanted little visitors . . . But in the feeble light it was not so easy to see the brutes, they knew how to hide, too."[98] Helmut Pabst suggested these delousing sessions were a routine way of spending one's free time: "When the majority have gone to sleep I start writing, and sometimes we play a game of chess while others take off their shirts for the nightly louse hunt."[99] The implications of not keeping the lice in check could be maddening, as Alexander Cohrs explained in a letter home: "My nerves were completely at the end. If a Russian attack had come, I believe I would have set myself as a target to be freed from torment. One day, I captured 130 in my shirt, until I gave up counting."[100]

Lice were not the only problem. The general filth of living in earthen bunkers and overcrowded peasant huts meant the men were sharing their warm abodes with every manner of vermin and insect. As one soldier wrote: "Bedbugs bothered us at night, fleas broke our rest, and lice multiplied in our uniforms. Spiders, flies, wood lice, and cockroaches scuttled over the tables and over our faces and hands."[101]

While hygiene was a constant challenge at the front, the health of the men in confined spaces was not helped by the high numbers of heavy smokers. One soldier estimated that three-quarters of the men in his unit smoked and that he himself had only started because of the "stressful environment."[102] Paul Schwering wrote to his mother of the importance of smoking: "When I smoke, I forget everything, that is so good because the soldier's life is not so easy."[103] By the end of 1941, however, Germany's stocks of tobacco had declined to such a degree that production of cigarettes in the coming weeks and months would have to be reduced by half.[104] Already in 1941, Arvid Fredborg observed in Berlin "enormous queues gathered outside all the tobacco shops."[105] Not surprisingly, the shortages in Germany were even more apparent on the Eastern Front, causing complaints among the men that there was "almost nothing to smoke."[106] As William Lubbeck recalled: "Because the supply of tobacco in our rations was inadequate to meet the demand, cigarettes became a currency when trading or gambling."[107] Hans Olte even wrote his parents begging for them to send him cigarettes, writing in block letters: "And WANT TO SAVE YOUR SON, THEN JUST SEND HIM CIGARETTES."[108] In desperation, some men turned to the pungent Russian *makhorka*, a coarse and very strong tobacco grown in Ukraine and Russia.[109] This, however, was not a favored option among many of the men. One called it "awful stuff,"[110] while Karl Fuchs dismissively declared: "Russian cigarettes are for the birds."[111] Gottlob Bidermann told how he and his comrades would cut the tobacco for their pipes, but they discussed at length how to obtain the best aroma. One claimed that it is best after soaked in fig juice, while another firmly asserted that corn schnapps was the answer.[112] Since neither was available, none of these theories could be tested.

The men of Army Group Center did not live in perpetual combat, and their ability to balance the demands of the front with some form of distraction, and even at times enjoyment, was essential to their continued success and endurance. The winter temperatures and restriction of movement led to a considerable amount of time spent in bunkers and fortified villages, which offered not only protection from the enemy and the cold, but also, in most instances, vital spiritual sustenance that preserved their resistance.

13.

REINFORCING FAILURE

Stalin's January Offensive

While the soldiers of Army Group Center rang in the New Year in dimly lit dugouts and overcrowded peasant huts, celebrations were much more enthusiastic in Moscow, due in no small part to the apparent success of the Red Army.[1] Stalin himself was full of good cheer. He was convinced the war had turned irrevocably against the Germans, and that if 1941 had been the year of defeats, 1942 would be the year of "complete" victory. Yet while the Soviet Union had recaptured a small fraction of the ground it had lost, the Red Army was still reeling from the staggering casualties it had sustained—and was continuing to sustain—at the front. As countless poorly prepared Soviet officers were discovering, raw manpower was no substitute for professionalism, which was why smaller German units were still able to decimate much larger Soviet formations. Since the start of the war in 1941, an almost inconceivable total of some 200 divisions had been destroyed and wiped off the Soviet order of battle.[2] In pure manpower terms, the Red Army had lost 2,993,803 killed in action and some 3.3 million POWs, to which must be added untold millions of sick and wounded casualties, not to mention civilian losses.[3] By comparison the German *Ostheer* had sustained a total of 830,903 casualties in 1941, 302,595 killed.[4] Under such circumstances there appeared little cause for Stalin's end-of-year celebration, although perhaps it just underlines the extent of his indifference to the lives of his own people.

What fed Stalin's optimism was not just the apparent success of pushing back Army Group Center, but the recapture of Tikhvin and Rostov in the north and south. It allowed him to indulge the profound misconception that the whole German *Ostheer* was on the brink of total defeat and that the issue could be decided by one more all-out effort. Such thinking was not unlike Hitler's enduring delusion that every new offensive until December 5 would achieve the elusive "decisive" victory. Moreover, Stalin experienced the war as did the German high command: through the movement of lines on a map; he possessed no real understanding of, or interest in, the extraordinary difficulties under which his troops labored. In fact, Stalin was in many respects even more insulated from the problems of the front than Hitler was because of the pronounced fear his generals had of him, which pervaded many of their reports and forestalled the expression of any opposition in his presence.

At the front, the reality of the Red Army's December offensive looked markedly different from the perspective of men who assaulted the German defenses. Mikhail Geykham, a lieutenant in a Siberian division, volunteered for service at age seventeen after graduating early from high school and was made an officer after only a three-week training course. Even many years after the war, Geykham had not absorbed the popular sentiment of a winter victory. Instead he was bitterly indignant: "We hadn't been prepared to fight a war with fewer losses . . . We didn't have enough supplies or anything . . . Our officers weren't ready for this war."[5] Likewise, Geotgi Osadchinsky's account eschewed any triumphalism, testifying to the punishing demands of the advance: "It was exhausting for our troops to be marching fifteen kilometers every day. We entrenched ourselves, fired at the enemy, waited for our infantry to catch up, moved forward, took up fresh positions, and fired again. We never had time to celebrate anything."[6] Cyrus Sulzberger, an American journalist, was granted a rare visit to the front near Volokolamsk, where General Andrey Vlasov's Twentieth Army was fighting. His December war dispatches were aimed at an American public hungry for any good news to counter the surging Japanese advance, and yet his tone is positively flat. Sulzberger alludes to both the shortages and suffering of the Red Army, writing:

> I have noticed in the Soviet arsenal everything from brand-new
> self-propelled guns to old howitzers, stamped with the Czar's double
> eagle and the dates 1914, 1915. Vast quantities of ammunition
> and tank fuel are hauled up on horse-drawn sleighs . . . Columns
> and columns of infantry—tired, tough veterans with hard-bitten
> faces—slog along at post-haste march, bending under the weight of
> automatic rifles and dragging metal ammunition cases in the snow;
> fatigued, strong, weather-beaten men.[7]

When Sulzberger reached a battlefield, his dispatch described the extent of Germany's scorched-earth policy: "This desolate landscape evinces the usual tragic scars of war—burned houses, ruined churches."[8] Not surprisingly, exhausted Soviet troops had little cause for rejoicing at their gains.

The Red Army's leadership was also taking a long, hard look at German defensive tactics with a major study that was commissioned by the General Staff's military-historical section to systematize and glean lessons from the ongoing experience of the war. It was only completed in 1943 and not declassified in Russia until 2006. Under the subject heading "The overall character of the enemy's defense," the study noted:

> The enemy's defensive system during this period was built
> according to the principle of organizing strong points and centres of
> resistance . . . covered by a system of flanking and enfilading fire from
> machine guns, mortar batteries, and automatic riflemen . . .

The enemy widely employed the practice of cold-proofing dugouts located along the main communications arteries. The Germans, with machine guns and automatic rifles, would sit it out until the moment of our attack; with the start of the attack they would run out and occupy their positions in the nearby trenches and firing points.

The enemy's company strong points were often located on raised areas; the terrain in front of the front line was well scanned, which made it possible to organise fire . . . The enemy widely employed several reserve positions for his weapons; machine gunners, automatic riflemen, and certain guns, moving from one position to another, created the impression of a large force at the defender's disposal . . .

He sought, by the concentrated rifle and machine gun fire, and fire from artillery, mortars, and automatic rifles, to destroy the attacking units before they could reach the front line. In case of a breakthrough of the forward position and our units' rupture into the depth of the defensive position, the Germans counterattacked with regimental and divisional reserves along the flanks of the tactical breakthrough, aiming their blow at the centre of the breakthrough. Under favorable conditions, when the attacking [Soviet] troops were weakened and disrupted, counterattacks were launched in front of the forward defensive line.[9]

While Army Group Center's strategic position was marked by withdrawals, inadequate supply, and a complete lack of preparation for the winter conditions, at the tactical and even operational level, combat typically favored the Germans. Rokossovsky, whose Sixteenth Army was pressing its advance to the north of Moscow, recalled the costs of the late 1941 period with surprising candor for a Soviet-era memoir. After detailing his successes Rokossovsky continued:

But it was hard going for us too. The Sixteenth Army had suffered great casualties in the course of the protracted defensive fighting and subsequent counteroffensive. The divisions numbered no more than 1,200 to 1,500 men each, artillery and mortar men, engineers, signalers and staffs included. The number of infantry effectives was small indeed, and our command and political personnel had also suffered serious losses in the fighting. The situation in the neighboring armies was no better.[10]

It was an ominous starting point for a renewed offensive in 1942, but even more to the point, Soviet strategic aims even in December had proven too ambitious for the resources at hand, and that shortfall was about to get much worse.

On December 13 Zhukov had argued for another advance of his Western Front with "an average distance of advance from 130 to 160 kilometers west and northwest of Moscow."[11] Stalin readily accepted the plan but refused to authorize any of the new armies Zhukov had requested and instead allocated these troops to strengthening attacks on the flanks (at Kalinin Front and Briansk Front). Stalin had in mind nothing less than the complete encirclement of Army Group Center.[12] It was a colossal undertaking for which the Red Army was manifestly unprepared, unsupported, and grossly deficient in the necessary command and control skills. The second half of December had already illustrated the dangers of failing to exploit costly tactical breakthroughs, which stemmed, in no small part, from spreading available reserves too widely, diluting the strength of subsequent attacks. Even in the best-case scenario, penetrations of the German front could not be followed up in good time, and the Soviets were forced to repeat the process against a re-formed line, while in the worst-case scenario, the depleted attackers were themselves exposed to counterattacks. As a result, Soviet attacks across the breadth of Army Group Center's long front were in effect only sharing the pain more evenly. The attacks confronted all of Kluge's major formations with a degree of crisis, but nowhere decisively. By avoiding one or two armies bearing the full brunt of Soviet strength, as Zhukov had intended, Army Group Center had a much better chance of surviving. As General Nikolai Khlebnikov noted in his memoir, the result of the December fighting was typically a failure to do anything more than push the German front back:

Theoretically, in principle, everyone agreed that what would provide for the success of the offensive was decisive superiority over the enemy on the decisive sector of the front. However, in practice . . . this axiom of military theory was certainly not adhered to in all instances. It hence often happened, that a well thought out deep thrust turned into a series of frontal attacks which only "expelled" the enemy, rather than resulting in his encirclement and destruction.[13]

Ilya Ehrenburg published a propaganda piece on December 30 that offered a useful characterization the Red Army's advance: "This is not a rout, but neither is it a strategic retreat; this is a retreat under pressure from our forces."[14]

If the Soviet generals thought the encirclement of Army Group Center was too much for the Kalinin, Western, and Briansk Fronts, Stalin drew the opposite conclusion. In the first days of 1942 he directed new plans to be drawn up for an expanded offensive, which he then introduced on January 5 by informing his most senior officers: "The Germans seem bewildered by their setback at Moscow and are poorly prepared for the winter. Now is the time to go over to a general offensive."[15] As if destroying Kluge's army group was not in itself a colossal undertaking, Stalin was now proposing to launch simultaneous offensives against Army Groups North and South. According to Zhukov's account, Stalin was looking to "defeat Army Group North and lift the blockade of Leningrad," while at the same time in the south the new plan was "to defeat Army Group South and liberate the Donets Basin." Stalin also stipulated that additional forces "were expected to free the Crimea." These tasks were, of course, in addition to the stated aims in the center to "trap the main forces of the enemy around Rzhev, Viaz'ma and Smolensk." Orel and Kursk were also to be captured.[16] It was a breathtaking example of hubris and, coming from Stalin himself, not one that could be openly disputed.

When Stalin invited comment, Zhukov took the opportunity and again pressed for a concentrated effort focused on his own Western Front. Zhukov argued:

There conditions are the most favorable and the enemy has
not had time to restore the fighting capacity of his forces. But a
successful continuation of the offensive will require reinforcements
in manpower and equipment, especially tanks, without which
we cannot expect to make much progress. As for offensives near
Leningrad and in the southwest, forces there face formidable enemy
defenses. Without powerful artillery support our troops would be
unable to break through, they would be worn down and suffer heavy
and completely unjustified losses. I would favour reinforcing our
troops on the Western Front and waging a stronger offensive there.[17]

Zhukov's opposition was endorsed by Nikolai Voznesensky, the chair-
man of the State Planning Commission, who argued that there were not the
material means to sustain simultaneous offensives on all fronts.[18] Indeed, by
January 1942 the Red Army had a total of just 600 heavy tanks and 800 medium tanks.[19] Even these were only as useful as their tactical employment
allowed, and a damning report by the *Stavka*, issued on January 22, highlighted "a range of failings in the battlefield use of tank forces, as a result of
which our units lose large numbers of tanks and personnel." The report then
cited three broad areas of concern in the employment of tanks:

1. Up to now co-operation between infantry and tank formations
   and units is poorly organized with infantry commanders failing
   to establish concrete objectives and hastily doing so; the infantry lagging behind in the attack and not reinforcing advance positions captured by the tanks; in defense infantry not covering
   tanks in defensive positions; and in retreat even failing to warn
   commanders of tank units of the changed situation and throwing
   tanks into the arms of fate.
2. Tank attacks are not supported by our artillery, and artillery
   does not accompany the tanks, as a result of which fighting vehicles are lost to enemy anti-tank artillery.
3. Field commanders are extremely hasty in the development of
   tank units, throwing them into action in packets as they arrive,

not setting aside time for the conduct of even the most elementary reconnaissance of the area and enemy positions.[20]

The employment and support of armored forces pointed to the Red Army's deficiency in combined-arms warfare, which the high levels of attrition in tanks, and especially their crews, reflected. Another report from Zhukov's Western Front stated: "Tank crews themselves, having been given objectives, attempt to reach them without the appropriate skills, in a straightforward manner, and most frequently attacking frontally. Tankers do not study the terrain for concealed approaches to enemy positions and dead ground, as a result of this irresponsibility they suffer high casualties."[21]

As the example of tanks demonstrates, the Red Army's lack of matériel was greatly compounded by human factors, underscoring Voznesensky's opposition to an expanded "general offensive." Stalin, however, was not interested in dissenting opinions and curtly dismissed Zhukov and Voznesensky's objections with the words "We must quickly smash the Germans so that they cannot attack when the spring comes." In fact, Stalin had already issued directives to most of the Front commands. The generals were merely being informed of a decision already taken. When Zhukov inquired of Shaposhnikov why Stalin had even bothered to invite comment, the army's chief of staff replied: "I just don't know, old fellow, I just don't know."[22]

The ineptitude of the Red Army was not unknown to Stalin, and he even complained about officers launching wasteful attacks, but this did not deter him from setting in motion the most ambitious Soviet offensive since the first week of the war. In Stalin's mind the Germans were vulnerable. Given the enormous overestimation of German losses, said to be 300,000 killed between December 6 and January 15 (which in reality was almost a third more than in the entire war), it is perhaps less surprising that he viewed the Red Army's own casualties as acceptable.[23] Stalin, like Hitler, could not foresee a long war, and just as the German dictator predicted victory in 1942, so too Stalin believed that the coming year would bring triumph. On January 10 Stalin sent a directive to all of his front and army commands, declaring: "Our task is to deny the Germans this breathing space, to drive them to the west without a halt, to force them to expend their reserves before spring, when we will have new and large reserves, and the Germans will have no large reserves, and to thus secure complete defeat of the Hitlerite forces in the year 1942."[24]

The Red Army may have been materially weak, but its manpower reserves were reasonably large. While this offered an illusion of strength, it did not itself translate into offensive success. The poor state of the Red Army was, in the first instance, a result of the horrendous losses of 1941, but in the second instance, it was also a result of Stalin's purges, which left a legacy of doctrine and training programs that were completely inadequate to compete with the Wehrmacht.[25] When reports of the results of disastrous Soviet attacks against German lines did reach Stalin's ears, he contented himself with harsh words for the perpetrators but consistently failed to understand the depth of the problem, which required a sweeping institutional response. In one instance, Stalin presented the problem as simply a failure to coordinate artillery support:

> Often we send the infantry into an attack against the enemy's defense line without artillery, without any artillery support whatsoever, and after that we complain that the infantry won't go against an enemy who has dug in and is defending himself. It is clear, however, that such an "offensive" cannot yield the desired effect. It is not an offensive but a crime—a crime against the Motherland and against the troops which are forced to suffer senseless losses.[26]

The extent of the problem was only fully addressed in an extraordinary order issued by Zhukov in March 1942 toward the end of the rolling Soviet offensives. The order highlighted "the criminally negligent attitude of commanders of all levels to the preservation of Red Army men of the infantry."[27] It was a problem Zhukov had already highlighted in the opening days of the offensive, when on December 9 he categorically forbade "frontal combat against fortified positions."[28] The failure to heed this order again speaks to the systemic nature of the problem and the need for root-and-branch reforms in the training and appointment of officers. For the winter of 1941–1942 the Red Army needed tasks equal to its abilities, and what Stalin had imposed was greatly in excess of what was possible. Zhukov's March order to his

Western Front made this damningly clear: "In letters and discussions hundreds of instances are provided where commanders of units and formations wipe out hundreds and thousands of people in attacks on intact defenses and intact machine guns, on unsuppressed fire-points during poorly prepared attacks."[29] As the war diaries from all of Army Group Center's armies and panzer groups have confirmed, Zhukov's Western Front was by no means unique in this kind of self-inflicted slaughter. Nor were the higher echelons of the Front command as faultless as Zhukov's order might suggest. Commanders on the front lines were sometimes placed under extreme pressure to achieve objectives, even threatened with harmful consequences, forcing them into actions that sometimes contravened their better judgment. The results belie the myth of a resurgent Red Army exercising a powerful superiority to inflict on the German army its "first defeat" of the war. In a war of attrition, Germany was doing a far greater share of the killing, while achieving its winter objectives, which Stalin had all but ensured the Soviet Union would not. Finally, if the loss or gain of ground is what denotes success then clearly the Red Army had won something, but only if those gains are divorced from the question of cost, which they should not be. Indeed, one may well hypothesize that the same gains (or more) could have been achieved, and at less cost, if more modest objectives had been set with a far greater concentration of effort.[30]

The dogmatic nature of Soviet officer training was all too often based on draconian treatment, which drilled into the men rote responses to supposedly standard actions. The treatment of trainee officers was scarcely better than that of rank-and-file recruits, with many menial, but physically demanding, tasks. The fostering of independent action or any kind of unorthodox technique was viewed as dangerous, and the emphasis was on rigid discipline and carrying out orders. David Samoilov viewed his instructor at a training camp for infantry officers as a "bestial and innate scoundrel" whose idea of education was instilling a fear of failing to obey.[31] In a somewhat more lighthearted illustration of just how dogmatic Soviet officers could be, Cyrus Sulzberger recounts attempting to take a photo of Red Army soldiers marching past when a young lieutenant confronted him. "Who are you?" the officer demanded, pointing his rifle at him. Sulzberger explained in poor

Russian that he was a journalist, to which the lieutenant instinctively replied: "'Oh!' he says. 'American. We will take Berlin.'"[32] Of course, innovation and originality were not completely absent from a minority of Soviet officers; in part because creativity was so exceptional, it had the potential for real success. The liberation of Naro-Fominsk, for example, was aided by an operation involving some one hundred Soviet troops who managed to approach and assault enemy lines dressed as German soldiers.[33] Yet in the winter fighting such instances of innovation remained the exception rather than the rule.

The Soviet Union's aggregate losses from June 1941 to the end of the winter offensive were without precedent in warfare. Already there was scarcely a Soviet family without loss, and the final tally would clearly demand far greater sacrifice. Larry LeSueur, the American war correspondent, offered a moving glimpse of a crowd of peasant women bidding farewell to three young Red Army men leaving for the front. Emotions were high, but it was only as the train began to pull away that one of the mothers began to weep and wail as she broke from the crowd and followed the departing carriage. LeSueur writes, "her cries started a wave of hysteria among all the older peasants on the platform. They who had seen war ravish this bloodstained land only twenty years ago knew what war meant."[34] Indeed, a soldier joining the Red Army in the winter of 1941–1942 had very long odds of surviving the war without being wounded or killed, and if the older peasants already knew what to expect, the young men of the Red Army quickly learned just how cheaply their lives could be sold. This was also reinforced by German propaganda efforts toward Red Army soldiers during the winter, which emphasized the massive Soviet losses against the so-called "German wall of blood" with pictures of battlefields strewn with their own dead dropped on Soviet lines.[35]

The costs of war were learned not just from futile Soviet attacks, but from the advance itself. As soldiers approached newly liberated villages, they received a devastating introduction to the reality of German captivity and occupation. Georgi Osadchinsky wrote of entering a village to see what remained: "All that was left were the Russian stoves with their crumbled pipes, the ruins of the church and the frames of the brick buildings. In the last one we found more than a hundred corpses of Red Army prisoners and civilians. All had been shot."[36] Likewise, Vladimir Goncharov wrote: "In the small village we have just taken the Germans shot all its male inhabitants. And yesterday we found some Russian POWs, who had managed to escape from a nearby camp—they are telling us horrifying stories about conditions there."[37] Nikolai Verzbitski's unit was in the region east of Maloiaroslavets, and he wrote of encountering "ragged" and "wild-eyed" civilians moving back through their lines in single file. Verzbitski stopped a woman and asked her about her experiences under German occupation, to which she replied:

> They slaughtered all the cattle and chickens. They ate every two hours. They didn't let us into our cottages. We had to sleep in the open and cook on bonfires. They did allow some of the mothers with small children to sleep under the beds or in the porches . . . They burned the village as they left. They left two houses at the request of the women, so that there would be somewhere to shelter the children. But three *versts* [a Russian measure of length, about 1.1 kilometers] away the Germans were hanging and beating people.[38]

While some areas of German occupation were better than others, the general experience appeared to range between those who allowed the most basic provision for survival and those who did not. In the larger population centers a telling feature of German rule was the gallows, which were erected on town squares in Volokolamsk, Kalinin, and Livny. As one observer noted: "On the public squares in their German cities Germans put up trees for Christmas; in our towns they put up gallows."[39]

On occasion, there was an opportunity for retribution, as one Soviet officer described in his diary on December 24, when three "Fritzes," who were "probably arsonists," were captured before they could flee the Soviet vanguard. As the diary continued: "Two of them we shoot without interrogation, one we send under escort to Division HQ . . . on the way . . . the local population reckoned with him for everything."[40] In another instance the women of a collective farm noted how a bottle of inflammable liquid held by a German soldier and intended to burn down a peasant house had exploded in his hand. As the observer noted: "Now he lies like a lump of charred meat, an example of crime and punishment."[41] While Soviet abuses were often cast as some form of retribution or punishment, there were also instances of outright murder. The British communist Charlotte Haldane, who visited the Soviet Union during the war, spoke with one Soviet soldier about the taking of German POWs, to which she was told: "'Prisoners?' He gave a short laugh. 'What would we want with prisoners? We'd have to feed them, wouldn't we? We need our food for our own people.'"[42]

While the killing and the mistreatment of German prisoners was not uncommon in many units of the Red Army, there was universal satisfaction taken from the masses of captured war matériel that Army Group Center had been unable to evacuate. During his tour of the front, Larry LeSueur observed how "the work of salvaging German war equipment was going on hurriedly." The soldiers searched houses, barns, and attics for anything of value, depositing everything into piles of machine guns, submachine guns, rifles, bayonets, etc. Beyond weapons, engines were removed from trucks, while wrecked staff cars were searched for papers of value and everything was meticulously recorded in inventories. LeSueur concluded: "Mounds of captured war equipment were growing on the snow."[43]

While liberation by the Red Army ended one ordeal for the people of the former occupied zones, some dangers remained. The Germans often left booby traps on items of interest, and mines and unexploded ordinance littered the fields. Vladimir Goncharov observed: "We were witnessing such terrible things. Outside one house we found the body of a two-year-old child, killed by a mine."[44] There was also very little food in the newly liberated areas, and larger towns like Kaluga faced crisis, as General Rokossovsky commented: "The townspeople were in a terrible plight and we had to take urgent measures to save many from starvation."[45] In theory, the Red Army was the people's salvation, and yet they often added to the ordeal of the peasants. They were often accused of commandeering what little food and draft animals remained. In fact, one liberated town had by the spring experienced a threefold increase in its mortality rate.[46] Malnutrition may have not been the root source, but the weakening it caused was a major factor in the epidemics of typhoid fever, scarlet fever, and measles, which ravaged the occupied zones in the early months of 1942.[47] Perhaps even more terrifying, the

NKVD (*Narodnyi Komissariat Vnutrennykh Del*—People's Commissariat for Internal Affairs) soon arrived in the villages, tasked with identifying those who had collaborated with the Germans, and by the end of January, sometimes on the flimsiest of evidence, they had arrested nearly 1,400 people.[48] As one NKVD instruction read: "When moving into the area, liberated from the enemy forces, it is essential to establish and fix the political mood of all layers of the population in relation to the restoration of Soviet power."[49]

While the NKVD tended to overestimate pro-German sympathies in the liberated Russian territories, which after all had only been occupied for a matter of weeks, there were elements of the wider Soviet population that did collaborate. Some 55 to 65 million Soviet citizens experienced German occupation, most of them from 1941 onward. As the Germans advanced, Soviet authorities managed to evacuate between 7.5 million and 10 million people before the Wehrmacht arrived, while another group of between 6 and 9 million people fled by their own means. Those least equipped to flee German occupation were often those most at risk from it—the desperately poor, the old, and the very young. Those able-bodied men who had not been drafted by the Red Army and did not flee the German advance soon found themselves the preferred targets of German work details as well as any reprisals for actions perceived to be anti-German. As news spread of German occupation methods, men everywhere sought to hide in the forests, sometimes joining partisan groups, while others undertook the perilous journey to the east in order to cross the front line back into Soviet territory. As a result, women were often the core of Soviet households in the occupied territories. Panzer Group 3 reported that the population in its area of occupation was 30 percent women and 50 percent children.[50] This makes sense; the Soviet Union had a very high proportion of young people, with 45 percent under the age of twenty in 1941.[51]

Officially Hitler had forbidden the recruitment of Soviet citizens for any kind of service within the *Ostheer*, but serious manpower shortages led many commanders to turn a blind eye to the increasingly common practice. Throughout the territories occupied by Army Group Center, Belarussians, Ukrainians, and Russians worked as so-called *Hiwis* (*Hilfswillige*, or auxiliary volunteers), serving as translators, drivers, medics, horse grooms, cooks, servants, and guards.[52] The number of *Hiwis* working for the Germans is almost impossible to estimate because the official prohibition meant they were seldom recorded in army manifests, yet their work helped ease the great strain on the troops, which made them a generally popular addition.[53] According to Alexander Dallin, there was no political significance in taking on such jobs; men simply accepted the food and relative security that service to the Germans offered.[54] Sometimes *Hiwis* were recruited from the civilian population, but it was not uncommon for officers or units to "adopt" a captured Soviet soldier and "allow" him to work for them.[55] Of course there were also anti-communists among the *Hiwis* as well as many with a strong desire to avoid further service in the Red Army. Some may simply have been motivated by fear of the alternative—a German POW camp.

The *Hiwis* were not just a source of labor; they also brought valuable local knowledge. As Max Kuhnert noted: "Peter, the prisoner I had taken a few weeks earlier, proved very helpful indeed . . . He looked after our horses quite well, proved handy if we needed things explained to us, and if we needed food he would come into farmhouses with us and in most cases got what we wanted or needed."[56] Not surprisingly, the extent of a prisoner's usefulness was often the measure of his value. The *Hiwi* in Helmut Günther's group was praised for his versatility: "He was a very capable fellow and developed into a jack-of-all-trades. He got our rations in Borodino with a horse-drawn sleigh, provided firewood, and was happy if he could sit among us after finishing his work. We did not treat him in any way as an enemy, and that was probably what bonded him so much to us."[57] Indeed, sometimes *Hiwis* became the closest of comrades. While working at a German field hospital, Josef Perau described his relationship with four former Red Army men and a Russian nurse as the "absolute best of comradeship."[58] Indeed, much of the Nazi rhetoric surrounding "inferior people" (*Untermenschen*) was forgotten in these relationships, although this did not preclude other Slavs from being viewed with contempt by the same German soldiers.

On occasion the *Hiwis* were a source of contention within their own units, as some German soldiers were not prepared to tolerate them. One non-commissioned officer remarked that it was "grotesque, how intimately" many German soldiers "behaved with the Russians—contrary to all slogans—and how both sides derive an advantage from it."[59] Max Kuhnert wrote that "quite often, some of our chaps didn't treat [Peter] very nicely and I had to step in to make it quite clear to them that Peter was one of us and should be treated with compassion."[60] Similarly, Helmut Günther, who served in an SS division, noted early troubles. "Initially, there were some difficulties with the higher-ups, but our 'diplomatic skill' worked it out so that Gregor, as we called him, could stay with us."[61]

While the employment of *Hiwis* was a clear expedient, the benefits of the practice did not change Hitler's prohibition, and therefore it remained an ad hoc policy without official sanction or encouragement. Given the *Ostheer*'s insatiable demand for labor, to say nothing of the possibility of arming Soviet citizens to fight the Red Army, there was increasing pressure for a pragmatic change. In January 1942 Otto Bräutigam, an advisor to Alfred Rosenberg, who headed the Ministry of the Eastern Territories, argued for the setting up of a "Russian counter-government" led by a "de Gaulle" figure, who could be chosen from among the captured Red Army generals. The idea, however, went nowhere on account of Rosenberg's timidity and Hitler's ardent objections, but Bräutigam was not the only one to push the idea.[62] Professor Theodor Oberländer, who was affiliated with a group known as the "Ukrainian Nightingale Battalion Group," approached Hitler to advocate for the Ukrainian national cause and to argue against the mistreatment of its people. He was, however, rebuffed by the dictator, who told him: "You don't know what you are talking about. Russia is our Africa, and the Russians are our niggers."[63] Whatever Hitler may have wanted, in the east the demands of "military necessity" consistently trumped ideology.[64] Indeed, both Bräutigam and Oberländer went on to help direct German involvement in the Caucasus in 1942, and their efforts to win over the Islamic population received the support of army commanders.[65]

While Soviet peoples serving as *Hiwis* in noncombatant roles were by far the most common form of support for Army Group Center, there were in fact a small number of Russian fighting formations in existence by the winter of 1941–1942. The first such formations appeared in July, when Army Group Rear Area commanders were authorized to use demobilized Soviet POWs to create an auxiliary police force (*landeseigene Hilfspolizei*).[66] In the same month, Cochenhausen's 134th Infantry Division reportedly offered POWs enlistment on equal footing with German troops.[67] Yet the most consistent and energetic advocate for the use of Soviet manpower was Strauss's Ninth Army, which had its proposals for recruiting *Hiwis* conveyed to all of Army Group Center's armies and panzer groups.[68] In addition, Strauss employed more than 100 White Russian émigrés as translators, in spite of their being specifically forbidden to serve in the German army by Hitler. In fact, Strauss's personal translator, Boris von Kartsov, was himself a White émigré who helped coordinate widespread recruitment throughout Europe for the Ninth Army.[69] In August 1941 Strauss's army fielded the first company-size Russian military formation made up of volunteers and Soviet POWs, commanded by the émigré Aleksandr Zaustinskiĭ. By November the formation had grown to 330 enlisted men (six companies) and 15 Russian commanders. Zaustinskiĭ's main responsibility had been to combat partisans, but during the winter fighting at Rzhev the unit was deployed against the Red Army and acquitted itself well in battle, in spite of sustaining over 100 casualties.[70] Hitler relented somewhat in December 1941, allowing non-Slavic populations to form legions, which opened the door for Turkestanis, Armenians, Azerbaijanis, Georgians, north Caucasusians, Volgans, and Crimean Tatars to arm.[71] Such tentative steps toward raising an indigenous eastern force were, however, too little too late, because National Socialism brooked no compromise in the arming of Slavs and would continue to resist doing so until it made no difference.

In the winter of 1941–1942 Soviet manpower was making a tiny contribution to Germany's fighting forces but played a far more significant role in the form of noncombatant *Hiwis*. The largest Soviet contribution to the German war effort, however, was in agricultural or industrial labor. From September 1941 to the end of the year some 308,000 Soviet POWs were put to work inside Germany,[72] while many more served the army's economic needs in the east. Civilian workers from the Baltic states and the Ukraine were also recruited for work in Germany, although their numbers in 1941 were still relatively small. Such arrivals, along with foreign workers from Czechoslovakia, Poland, Holland, Italy, France, Belgium, and Yugoslavia, who had been arriving since 1939, added some 3.5 million people to Germany's labor force by the end of 1941.[73] One disgruntled party official complained in the winter:

"The racial-political situation today is such that we no sooner get rid of 500 Jews from the area of the Reich than we immediately bring in ten times the number of racially undesired foreign races."[74] Yet even with millions of foreign workers Germany was in no way keeping pace with the economic demands of the war, leading to a ruthless new recruitment drive in the east directed by the new head of the General Plenipotentiary for Labor Deployment, Fritz Sauckel. "Eastern workers" (*Ostarbeiter*) were to be brought to Germany, with initial targets set in February 1942 for another 380,000 agricultural and 247,000 industrial workers.[75]

Eastern laborers were the only group of civilian workers, other than the Polish, who were subjected to compulsory identity marking. They were being forced to wear, in a clearly visible position, a square piece of material bearing the designation "OST" in white letters on a blue background (the Poles wore a "P").[76] Their treatment and living conditions were typically appalling, especially in mines, factories, and construction jobs. One French prisoner of war compared his camp to one of the many "Russian camps," which he said were "horribly overfilled, men, women and children herded together . . . the provisions usually inedible."[77] Fourteen-year-old Olga Selezniova wrote in a letter home in May 1942: "It would be better to die than to be here . . . We were sold . . . as if we were slaves."[78] Eastern workers were kept in barrack compounds enclosed by barbed wire, and the guards were entitled to use corporal punishment to maintain order.[79] Even worse conditions confronted Soviet POW laborers, who before Sauckel's appointment saw many dying of malnutrition soon after arrival. This caused the OKW's military-economic office and the Reich group for industry to complain that it was pointless importing hundreds of thousands of workers only for them to be starved to death upon arrival. The issue was especially important in the case of skilled workers from the east, as one industrial contractor callously observed: "If in the case of road building in the East we employ 2,000 Russians, and as a result of inadequate food supplies we lose a few hundred Russians per quarter, the missing laborers can simply be replaced by new Russians." On the other hand, the report continued: "In the manufacturing processes of an armaments plant it is simply not possible suddenly to exchange a man, who has been operating a special piece of machinery, with another worker."[80] As so often in Hitler's Germany, even a fundamental problem like manpower could not escape the inherent contradiction between murderous racial ideology and the practical imperatives of production. Yet, even in spite of such losses, by the end of 1942 Sauckel's brutal recruitment of eastern workers had raised the number of foreign workers in Germany to 5.6 million.[81]

14

HANGING IN THE BALANCE

Fourth Army's Impending Encirclement

A s the New Year began, Schmidt's Second Army, with its three corps (Kempf's XXXXVIII Panzer Corps, General of Infantry Erwin Vierow's LV Army Corps, and Rudolf Kaempfe's XXXV Army Corps), was holding a long line from the east of Kursk to the east of Orel. This constituted about 160 kilometers as the crow flies, but the contours of the front made it closer to 200. The only consolation for such a long front was that at each end the army had a major center of transportation and supply, at least when supplies were available. With Guderian gone, there was a determination to hold the current line, and Soviet attacks, while rumbling all along the front, were nowhere more intense than in the extreme south. It was here that Henrici's 16th Motorized Infantry Division was attempting to guard the approaches to Kursk as well as maintain contact with Lieutenant-General Willi Moser's 299th Infantry Division, which formed the vital connection between Kluge's army group and Reichenau's Army Group South. Attacks had been continuous since late December, and on January 1 a new Soviet offensive headed by twenty-five to thirty tanks caused Kempf (Henrici's corps commander) to authorize a limited withdrawal. Kempf sought reinforcements from Hubicki's 9th Panzer Division to the north, but there were only four serviceable tanks in the whole division.[1] With units stretched and often lacking firm contact with their neighboring formations, the combat was typically confused, and as one soldier fighting east of Kursk later noted: "Due to the lack of a contiguous front line, it is possible for the enemy to circumvent individual positions and attack us from the rear or from our flanks."[2]

On January 2 Schmidt was sufficiently worried about his army's southern flank to transfer the motorized elements of Breith's 3rd Panzer Division from Vierow's corps to help bolster Henrici's division.[3] Breith's division had become the fire brigade of Second Army and had even been used in highly effective offensive actions to clear threatening enemy positions along the front. In one series of actions to clear a section of the front known as the "Trudy curve," it reported killing five hundred enemy troops for the loss of thirty-nine men. Breith's division also captured a good deal of equipment, including numerous German items that the Red Army had acquired during its advance. Of thirteen captured antitank guns, three were German; of twelve mortars, five were German; of twenty-one machine guns, five were German; and of sixteen trucks, three were German. The regimental staff was also partly outfitted with German telephones and radios.[4] Clearly, the German scorched-earth campaign had not always been as effective as the orders demanded.

By January 3 the fighting in the south was desperate. Henrici's division struggled to hold the line, despite having destroyed ten Soviet tanks and heavily damaging four more.[5] The constant action in new positions, without time to prepare bunkers or any other form of protection from the elements, led to an estimated 40 to 50 percent of those in the front line suffering various degrees of frostbite. In one regiment the figure reached 80 percent.[6] Yet the Germans were not the only ones suffering from the cold; Leonid Rabichev, a Red Army officer who took part in the January fighting toward Kursk, recalled:

> I saw a horrifying sight. An enormous space stretching to the horizon was filled with our tanks and German tanks. In between them there were thousands of sitting, standing or crawling Russians and Germans frozen solid. Some of them were leaning against each other, others hugging each other. Some propping themselves with a rifle, others holding a sub-machine gun . . . It was terrible to think of the wounded, both ours and Germans, freezing to death. The front had advanced and they had forgotten to bury these men.[7]

At the front, the Red Army continued to attack relentlessly as losses on both sides mounted. Hans Roth wrote in desperation on January 4:

> I follow my orders feverishly, do reconnaissance, operate the machine guns, the artillery, throw hand grenades.
> Every single man fights unimaginably. Twenty-five times the Russians attacked today with tank support.
> Many times tonight the pig has infiltrated the city for a short time, in our counterattacks we threw him back each time. We men are standing like iron in the defense despite terrible losses and terrible temperatures (–42°C), for a large part with frozen hands and feet. Being sick is not an option, we are fighting for our bare life.[8]

The fighting raged for the first full week of January as Henrici's and Moser's divisions became entangled in their attempts to stem the Soviet breaches both north and south of the army group boundary. In fact, when Breith's 3rd Panzer Division arrived to join the fray, it technically did so a few kilometers into Reichenau's Army Group South. By January 8 Soviet attacks in the south, as along all of Second Army's front, had largely ceased, and German intelligence indicated that Soviet reserves were being redirected north to exploit the gap between Schmidt's and Kübler's armies.[9]

The withdrawal of Soviet forces soon exposed sections of the front to German counterattack. On January 8 Hans Roth took part in one such raid on Soviet lines, which he estimated resulted in some 360 enemy soldiers being killed. After the Soviet offensive had ended, Roth wrote how a German probe found their lines to be weakly guarded and completely unprepared to meet an attack. As Roth then noted: "The surprise of the sleeping Russians is one hundred percent successful. Most of them do not even get the chance to get up. Without mercy everything and everybody is gunned down or clubbed to death on their sleeping cots. The whole nightmare lasts about a half hour. Strelekaja [the village] burns down to the ground, in every hut there are twenty to thirty dead Russians; the houses become places of cremation."[10]

While Schmidt's Second Army struggled to parry the attack on its southern flank, to the north his Second Panzer Army had the much more intractable problem of closing the gap to Fourth Army. While Guderian had been in command, there had been no attempt to deal with the breach because his Second Panzer Army was retreating faster than Soviet forces could outflank it. Kübler, however, had no such luxury. Pressure from his open southern flank had already led to the loss of Kaluga and the near encirclement of Heinrici's XXXXIII Army Corps. With Schmidt ordered to hold the Oka-Zusha Line and Soviet forces pressing deep into the gap, the danger to the north could no longer be overlooked. Accordingly, Second Panzer Army was scratching together whatever it could spare to protect the northern flank and eventually contribute to sealing the breach. Kübler was even more active and, with Kluge's support, had secured the transfer of Stumme's XXXX Panzer Corps from Hoepner's panzer group in order to deal with the crisis on the southern flank. Stumme's new task was to proceed with elements of Knobelsdorff's 19th Panzer Division, Fischer's 10th Panzer Division, Loeper's 10th Motorized Infantry Division, and an assortment of supply troops and military police. Stumme was also given command of one of the first German divisions to arrive on the Eastern Front from France, Major-General Werner-Albrecht Freiherr von und zu Gilsa's 216th Infantry Division.[11] Its arrival was staggered, with the first 4,000 men, including Gilsa, directed to hold the town of Suchinitschi. This was an extremely dangerous, even foolhardy, assignment, given that Suchinitschi was in the middle of the ninety-kilometer gap, and Gilsa was a long way from the support of either Stumme's still scattered forces to the north or Schmidt's ramshackle assembly to the south. No sooner had Gilsa reached the town when on January 4 the surging enemy tide swept around his flanks, trapping 4,000 German troops in the town and subjecting them to immediate attacks from the north, south, east, and southwest. Gilsa's men repelled all attempts to penetrate their perimeter but radioed that they were now completely encircled and cut off from all supply.[12]

Hitler characteristically demanded that Suchinitschi be defended to the last, "like the Alcázar" had been held during the Spanish Civil War.[13] On January 6, however, Stumme told Kübler that limited supplies of ammunition and food would mean that Suchinitschi could be defended for "only another few days." Thus, he argued against the demand for fanatical resistance to the bitter end and instead recommended that "before a necessary capitulation, a fighting withdrawal with all forces along the railroad be ordered."[14] Stumme knew that his remaining forces were much too weak to have any hope of reaching Suchinitschi; in fact his units were struggling to hold Soviet attacks against Yukhnov, where Kübler's command post was in the process of being evacuated to the southwest. Gilsa's detachment had only a single day's supply of artillery shells remaining, and more could not be airdropped because they would likely explode on impact. Significantly, though, there was not yet any shortage of infantry ammunition.[15]

Even before it was apparent that Stumme was incapable of providing relief from the north, Schmidt instructed his Cuno battle group to attempt to reach Suchinitschi. Yet before this attack got under way, the arrival of even more Soviet units rendered any attempt pointless.[16] On January 7 Schmidt proposed a powerful new allocation of forces for the drive on Suchinitschi. He directed Langermann-Erlancamp's XXIV Army Corps (the previous commander, Geyr von Schweppenberg, was forced to return to Germany owing to serious illness) to lead the 4th and 18th Panzer Divisions in a major new relief operation.[17] Joining Langermann-Erlancamp's corps were elements of another newly arrived division from France, Major-General Hans-Karl von Scheele's 208th Infantry Division.[18] Even with some of Schmidt's strongest divisions, the undertaking remained a formidable one. German intelligence

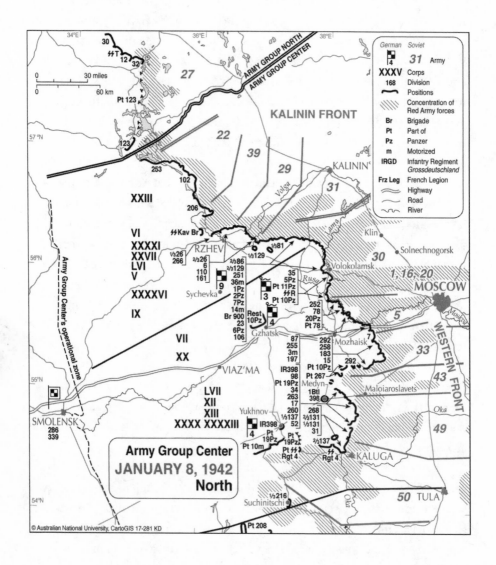

estimated some five Soviet cavalry divisions and another five to seven rifle divisions were occupying the bulge.[19]

While the encirclement at Suchinitschi as well as the unopposed Soviet presence in the north dominated Second Panzer Army's attention, the situation along the Oka and Zusha Rivers, which occupied the vast majority of its forces, was anything but quiet. Yet there was no sense of crisis there. In spite

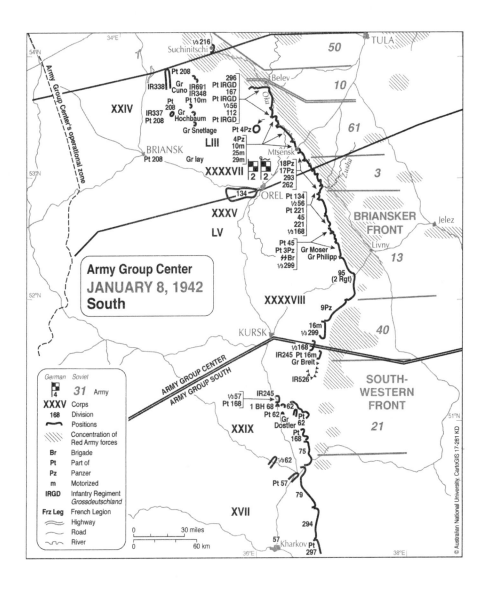

of numerous attacks by the opposing Briansk Front, German defenses were solid. It was this favorable circumstance that ultimately allowed Schmidt to redeploy divisions toward the north. Indeed, Soviet attempts to penetrate Second Panzer Army's line in early January were often hopelessly inadequate and openly mocked by the German soldiers. Wilhelm Prüller noted in his diary on January 1: "During the past days—quite often in the nights too—the Russians attacked, but were beaten back. They advanced in such a silly way that the whole thing looked more like a demonstration than an attack. They would stop on the incline, apparently to rest, and made a wonderful target for our artillery. And after a few shots they would disappear over the brow of the hill again, running like stuck pigs."[20] Likewise, Ferdinand Melzner from the 167th Infantry Division wrote in a letter on January 2: "The Russians constantly assault our lines, no matter how bloody their losses were. People still do not seem to matter a great deal to these Siberian brothers, otherwise the sight of their comrades, who lie around cold and lifeless in their hundreds, would discourage them somewhat."[21] On January 8 Adolf B. wrote of "wave after wave" of Soviet attacks launched against his position, with each one simply "mowed down by our brave troops." What astonished him most was that each new disaster was followed by precisely the same pointless form of attack; "the Bolsheviks nevertheless hope to be able to break through with the last wave."[22]

Even more illustrative of the disparity in professionalism between the veteran troops of the Second Panzer Army and the green Soviet reserves thrown into the offensive was the proficiency of the Germans in alternating so effectively between attack and defense. Anywhere that Soviet pressure had proved dangerous the German front was withdrawn a short distance, even when at times this granted the Red Army a foothold on the western bank of the river. The flexibility of German arms and the confidence of its commanders meant that before Soviet positions could be consolidated or substantially reinforced, a counterstroke would follow to retake the former positions. There is no indication of authorization for these withdrawals from the high command; in fact they were not discussed beyond Second Panzer Army, which suggests that Schmidt had granted his forces their own measure of independence, perhaps under the condition that any withdrawals on the west banks of the Oka or Zusha Rivers always be followed by counterattacks. In any case, on January 1 Major-General Dietrich von Saucken's 4th Panzer Division attacked into Soviet positions with devastating effect, killing, according to the divisional war diary, over 1,000 enemy troops and capturing 139 POWs. German dead amounted to less than one-tenth of this number, at seventy-four men.[23] Colonel Heinrich Eberbach, who took part in the attack, recalled: "The Russian

Field Marshal Günther von Kluge commanded Fourth Army until he took over Army Group Center from Field Marshal Fedor von Bock on December 19, 1941. He led Army Group Center through the worst of the winter crisis.

(*Bundesarchiv*, Bild 146-1973-139-14)

A German assault gun (*Sturmgeschütz*) tows a Mark III German tank in the retreat from Moscow in December 1941.

(*Bundesarchiv*, Bild 183-84001-0011, photographer: Hans Lachmann)

Hitler at the Reichstag on December 11, 1941, declaring war upon the United States of America. (*Bundesarchiv*, Bild 183-B06275, photographer: Heinrich Hoffmann)

Bodies of Soviet soldiers killed by German fire are stacked to form a makeshift defensive wall in early 1942.

(*Bundesarchiv*, Bild 101I-004-3633-30A, photographer: Richard Muck)

Colonel-General Erich Hoepner commanded Panzer Group 4 until early January 1942, when it was renamed Fourth Panzer Army.

General of Panzer Troops Georg-Hans Reinhardt commanded Panzer Group 3 until early January 1942, when it was renamed Third Panzer Army.

An improvised German defensive position belonging to Second Panzer Army near Orel. The snow walls offered a degree of camouflage, as well as protection from the freezing winds. The stovepipe suggests some kind of bunker was dug in below.
(*Bundesarchiv*, Bild 101I-287-0872-06, photographer: Koll)

The commander of XXXXIII Army Corps and, later, Fourth Army General of Infantry Gotthard Heinrici (right), with Field Marshal Günther von Kluge
(*Bundesarchiv*, Bild 146-1977-120-09, photographer: Johannes Bergmann)

Adaptation to the harsh Russian winter was an essential aspect of Army Group Center's response to the December–January crisis in the East. Here, a Ju-87 has been fitted with snow runners. (*Bundesarchiv*, Bild 101I-392-1334-04, photographer: W. Wanderer)

A German soldier in a dug-in defensive position with improvised protection against the wind. (*Bundesarchiv*, Bild 146-1992-055-33, photographer: Mährlen)

General of Panzer Troops Rudolf Schmidt commanded Second Army and, after Colonel-General Heinz Guderian's dismissal, Second Panzer Army.

(*Bundesarchiv*, Bild 183-2005-1017-520, photographer: Mossdorf)

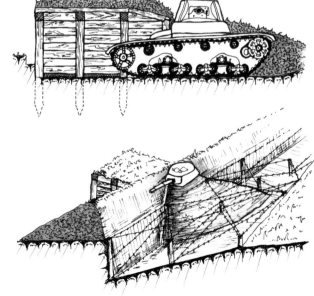

Captured Soviet tanks were sometimes dug into the ground to serve as fixed defenses. The drawings here provided instructions for how best to achieve this.

(Copy of German original by Chrisie Rotter)

General of Panzer Troops Walter Model (left) met with Hitler upon taking over command of Ninth Army from Colonel-General Adolf Strauss.

(*Bundesarchiv*, Bild 183-2012-1210-500, photographer: Hoffmann)

division was delivered a devastating blow. A second Russian division suffered the same fate. The remnants were tossed back across the Oka . . . The spoils of war obtained from the Russian were considerable . . . As a result, the division was able to reduce its losses in weaponry considerably."[24] Such decisive examples of offensive defense, repeated in countless places along Army Group Center's front, play almost no role in the standard analysis of the winter campaign, which is dominated by a "retreat and defeat" narrative. In fact, even through the worst period of the Soviet winter offensive the German army never stopped being a potentially deadly adversary on the offensive, which contributed not only to the wide disparity in losses, but also to the Germans' feeling of superiority even in the midst of Army Group Center's withdrawal.

While Saucken's success on January 1 was of a particularly large scale, many attacks were more modest in their achievements, but no less decisive. On January 6, Fremerey's 29th Motorized Infantry Division launched two spoiling attacks, first against a Soviet-held village named Butyrki, which resulted in 100 enemy dead for the loss of 4 Germans—a kill ratio of twenty-five to one. After seizing the village, Fremerey's assault group had instructions to take whatever equipment might be of use, while destroying whatever makeshift shelters as well as any fieldworks the Soviets had managed to erect. There was to be no attempt to hold Butyrki; the assault party was to return to German lines before launching a second raid against the village of Shalamovo. This too was successful, with the enemy fleeing in disorder to the east and northeast, while the Germans again took their spoils, enacted scorched-earth tactics, and withdrew before a battalion-size Soviet counterattack was organized.[25] Keeping the enemy weak, nervous, and off-balance, as well as supplementing Second Panzer Army's precarious lifeline of "hand-to-mouth" logistics, was the purpose of such raids.[26] As one soldier wrote on January 2: "In front of us, in the direction of the enemy, is a desert zone many kilometers deep, all the villages are burnt down, the inhabitants are driven eastwards, we have taken those fit for military service as prisoners!—Unspeakably great misery all round!"[27] Such textbook offensive operations gave local German commanders the initiative, even sometimes when they were outnumbered and nominally on the defensive. Their tactical success should not obscure the points of real crisis confronting Army Group

Center, but even when it was forced into retreat, the "cost-to-gain" ratio for the Red Army was seldom advantageous.

By January 8 the situation for Schmidt's two armies was generally favorable, the new defensive line had been established since Christmas, contact was maintained with Army Group South, and forces were able to be released from the line to deal with the situation in the north. Importantly, the Soviet Briansk Front troops had shown themselves to be in no condition to launch another major attack, and efforts were now directed, in accordance with Stalin's plan for a January offensive, to concentrate on exploiting the breach between Schmidt and Kübler. If the turn of events meant Schmidt could breathe a sigh of relief, Kübler's troubles were only just beginning.

The situation at Fourth Army was still fraught; the gaping hole on Kübler's southern flank was only one of his headaches. Farther north, numerous divisions were having difficulty holding against Soviet attacks, and in the area east of Maloiaroslavets, Kirchner's LVII Panzer Corps and Materna's XX Army Corps were on the brink of buckling. Once again Hitler categorically refused permission for a withdrawal. On January 2, the front finally split between Kirchner and Materna, creating a new hole in Kübler's front, which made even Halder concede in his diary, "there is no way of seeing at the moment how it can be closed again."[28]

Hitler's interference was not limited to a stubborn refusal to allow timely withdrawals. In addition, he wasted critical time with meaningless details, even down to the tactical level. As Gersdorff, Army Group Center's chief intelligence officer, recalled:

> Hitler got on the phone many times each day with Field Marshal
> von Kluge. We General Staff officers invariably needed to listen in
> on these discussions, so that if necessary we could chase down the
> information for questions from Hitler that the field marshal could
> not answer immediately. It was in this fashion that I personally
> experienced the following conversation:

> HITLER: *Herr Feldmarschall*, how many machine guns are currently
> in action at the cemetery in Maloiaroslavets?

KLUGE: I'll have someone find out right away.

After some time, the answer was obtained by an inquiry going through the responsible army and then by way of the corps, division, regiment, and battalion.

KLUGE: *Mein Führer*, there are four machine guns in action at the Maloiaroslavets cemetery.
HITLER: *Herr Feldmarschall*, see to it that there are at least six machine guns assigned there.[29]

The fact that Hitler could seriously concern himself with such irrelevant details without recognizing how ludicrous it must have appeared to the senior officers at Army Group Center only confirms his illusion of control over the situation. Indeed, Maloiaroslavets fell that same day (January 2) with or without extra machine guns in the cemetery.

The situation at Fourth Army was desperate, and dealing with Hitler had become impossible. At Fourth Army command, Hellmuth Stieff fumed at the costs of such mismanagement, lamenting the difference between a timely withdrawal and a Soviet breakthrough that would entail "immense difficulties and losses." Venting to his wife, Stieff bitterly condemned Fourth Army's orders as "a crime of the high command," which reflected a "complete misunderstanding of the circumstances." Stieff's final comment alluded to the utter helplessness he felt: "Sometimes it is a complete mystery to me how we should get out of this mess at all."[30] Kluge was also becoming worn down. He was in constant contact with Hitler and thus bore the brunt of the dictator's fanciful notions about the power of "will," which he reinforced with tales of all he had supposedly endured during the First World War. On January 2 Halder noted in his diary: "Repeated discussion with Kluge, who no longer knows what to do and speaks of a crisis of confidence."[31] At the very least, Kübler and Kluge wanted a withdrawal of Kirchner's and Materna's corps, so that there might be some chance of reestablishing a front, but Halder would not depart from Hitler's instructions and insisted that before any withdrawal could be contemplated the hole first had to be closed.[32] Not surprisingly, Halder remarked on the "great commotion" caused by Kübler and Kluge, which led to another showdown with Hitler that produced a "dramatic scene." Hitler even called into question the generals' courage "to make hard decisions."[33] It was an intolerable situation, and when the generals complained there were not the reserves to seal the breach, Hitler insisted they would have to come from neighboring formations. The dictator then radically redrew the boundary between Fourth Panzer Army and Fourth Army in a manner that immediately gave Hoepner responsibility for the area of the new Soviet breakthrough as well as the northern section of what had been Kübler's army.[34] It was Hitler's way of both penalizing Kübler's inability to deal with the situation as well as rewarding the apparent stabilization Hoepner had achieved along the Lama and Rusa Rivers.

What was left of Fourth Army consisted of five corps (LVII, XII, XIII, XXXXIII, and XXXX) threatened by open flanks to the north and south. Heinrici's XXXXIII Army Corps, which had endured the threat of encirclement for almost three weeks, was once again seeking permission to withdraw in order to ensure its survival. Beyond the danger of encroaching Soviet formations on the elongated southern flank stretching to the west, ammunition supplies were also growing desperately short. Every man not already serving at the front was ordered to give up all but his last rifle clip.[35] On January 1, Heinrici told Kübler that the front could only hold a few more days, but the commander of the Fourth Army replied that everyone had to stay where he was. As Heinrici complained in a letter to his wife, "He [Kübler] has been sent here as a strong man, now he should impress upon the high command *our* opinion, in consideration of all the circumstances, or declare he would rather take over a corps again."[36] Four days later (on January 5), Heinrici again confronted Kübler and asked him despondently if he was to instruct his commanders to fight like the Soviets had done throughout the 1941 campaign, "the Russian, who never learned, until he was surrounded."[37] Kübler was in fact sympathetic, but his hands were tied.

On January 5 when Kübler was able to meet in Roslavl with Kluge and Schmundt (Hitler's chief military adjutant), the commander of Fourth Army railed against the lack of operational freedom, insisting: "If one voluntarily goes back a few kilometers, one takes everything with him; if the enemy breaks through and one must hurry back, everything remains."[38]

While Kübler wanted operational freedom, he rejected any major withdrawal of the front on the grounds that he lacked the fuel to take all of his equipment with him. He was therefore very much in agreement with Kluge's "middle solution" of shorter, step-by-step withdrawals. Revealingly, even in the midst of such a crisis, the commander of Fourth Army still maintained that he could achieve anything if only he had replacements and the ability to move supplies. The enemy, Kübler insisted, was "substandard" and, according to the day's report from the front, "was completely drunk" in the attack. Schmundt interjected that nine thousand trucks were en route to the east, but such optimistic assertions from members of Hitler's inner circle were viewed with deserved skepticism at the front.[39] Even the welcome arrival of new divisions from France was viewed with some dismay when it emerged that a good portion of these troops had no winter equipment or uniforms.[40]

Later that evening Kübler pressed Kluge about the precarious situation for Heinrici's XXXXIII Army Corps. Regimental commanders were demanding to know if they were to be sacrificed. Kluge insisted that was not the case and expressed the hope that Hoepner could deal with the situation in the north. Then he made a startling admission to Kübler. Fourth Army's war diary recorded Kluge's words: "As the former commander of the Fourth Army, I will see how they can be helped. If this is not possible, a big decision will have to be taken. I have now, by my own decision, withdrawn the left wing of the Fourth Army and it will be difficult to justify this to the high command."[41] Clearly, Kluge was undermining the halt order and taking independent action to authorize withdrawals without going through Hitler and the OKH. He was even declaring that "a big decision" would be taken if "help" was not forthcoming. Kluge was once again operating in the extremely narrow space between what he believed he could justify up the chain of command that would relieve his hard-pressed formations and what he judged those same formations could stand under enemy pressure. As Lieutenant-General Moritz von Faber du Faur observed of Kluge: "He knows what is possible and what is impossible, but he keeps this knowledge to himself. He is a very courageous man of a high intellectual military level. If he were given a free hand, he would find the right solution, but he is not given a free hand."[42] Kluge may not have been granted a free hand, but part of the knowledge he kept to himself was that he sometimes took it anyway.

As for Kübler's concerns for Heinrici's XXXXIII Army Corps, Kluge was not yet willing to grant permission for a withdrawal, believing that the corps could hold its positions a while longer. Kluge was perhaps also unwilling to tempt fate after having just authorized a forbidden withdrawal on Fourth Army's northern flank. Kübler insisted that soon there would be no more troops to man the defenses, which Kluge acknowledged, but the field marshal expressed the hope that Hitler's promised reinforcements, numbering 220,000 men, would begin arriving at the army group from mid-January onward. In the meantime, Kluge offered nothing but praise for Heinrici's fortitude, while reaffirming to Kübler: "I will not leave Fourth Army in the lurch."[43] It was likely that Kluge offered such an assurance with a good measure of sincerity, but it must have come as cold comfort to Heinrici, who wrote his wife on January 6: "For thirty days now things have been going in an unheard-of up and down. Thirty days of nervous tension. Thirty days one hopes, one waits, and one sees only minor approaches to change."[44] If it was hard on the commanders, the often-confused situation was even worse for the men, as Max Kuhnert recalled: "Nobody knew where one was, sometimes the Russians were in front and other times at the back, it was just too nerve-racking."[45] Another soldier in Heinrici's corps wrote on January 4: "It is difficult to make out the front. We have to wade through deep snow, carrying the machine gun on our backs. One sees lots of Russian fighters."[46]

Kluge's hard line on withdrawals no doubt cost unnecessary casualties and at times greatly frustrated his subordinates, but it also earned him indispensable credibility within the high command. He may have lodged countless unsuccessful requests for withdrawals, but, importantly for his survival in command, he was never seen to disobey an explicit refusal from the high command, nor, after his very vocal denunciation of Guderian, was he seen to tolerate disobedience among his own subordinates. His ability to judge the limits of a knife-edged situation and somehow chart a course between the high command and the front was at times all that stood between individual formations' survival and annihilation. This is not to suggest he was infallible, but his independent decision to withdraw Fourth Army's left wing aroused no suspicion within the high command, in spite of the gap there suddenly growing from eighteen to thirty-three kilometers by January 6.[47] In context of the rolling Soviet offensive no uncomfortable questions were asked, which Kluge's impeccable reputation almost precluded. The only concern of the high command was the negative tone of Kluge's reporting about Fourth Army, which stemmed from an impression Paulus, the senior quartermaster I at the OKH, had had when speaking with Kluge and repeated to Halder. Kluge was not seen to be responsible for this, but it was taken to confirm "that the Fourth Army considered the situation somewhat pessimistically."[48] Coming from Paulus, who, apart from a few months as a motorized battalion commander in the mid-1930s, had never commanded more than a company, it was an extremely high-handed observation, especially for someone who had made a career in staff appointments with no direct experience of the war in the east. Nevertheless, such views were fostered, and even cultivated, within the cocooned world of the OKH.

The extent of the problem within the high command was again under-lined the following day (January 7) when Tresckow (Army Group Center's operations officer) returned to Smolensk after having spent a few days at the OKH. Tresckow had gone back to Germany for medical treatment, and so his visit to OKH was merely incidental. Returning to Russia, he stopped over in Mauerwald, where he observed an atmosphere of "definite relaxation." The long-standing view that the high command failed to grasp what was hap-pening at the front was again inflamed, especially at Fourth Army where Tresckow's observation was shared. As the war diary noted: "The responsible officers of the Fourth Army cannot understand how this impression arose. In ever more serious words, the army group had again and again reported that the situation was constantly worsening. It is enough just to take a look at the map for this fact."[49] If Army Group Center's survival benefited greatly from the incompetence of the Red Army's strategic and tactical direction, the Ger-mans also suffered from a remarkable degree of complacency and ineptitude within their own high command.

Another outsider who visited the OKH on January 7 was the chief of the Finnish General Staff, Lieutenant-General Axel Erik Heinrichs. He had been sent to form an overall picture of what was happening on the Eastern Front and in particular its implications for Finland.[50] Heinrichs later reported to his commander-in-chief, Field Marshal Carl Mannerheim, that Hitler was upbeat and even claimed that news of Soviet successes "had been greatly ex-aggerated by enemy propaganda." Yet, more revealingly, Heinrichs reported his impression that "General Halder, was over-tired and depressed."[51] If this was correct, it may suggest that Halder's response to the crisis in the east was not always built on exaggerated optimism and misplaced hope. Indeed, given his highly calculated and deeply duplicitous role in the dismissal of Brauchitsch, it may have been that Halder at times placed loyalty to Hitler above his duty to the army. He certainly enjoyed a far more harmonious re-lationship with Hitler over the winter than he had in the summer, when the *Ostheer* was so much stronger.[52] Perhaps a combination of depression and fatigue quelled his capacity for conflict, or maybe he just accepted the futility of debating Hitler. Of course, given that no other account presents Halder in this light, Heinrichs may simply have been wrong, and Halder's support for Hitler's orders may have been every bit a result of excessive optimism about what could be achieved. After all, Halder also subscribed to the idea that the "will" to hold out was the essential factor in military success.[53] The anti-Nazi conspirator Helmuth James von Moltke, who was well connected in military and political circles, lamented what he was learning of Germany's winter strategy and wrote on January 6:

> A.H. [Adolf Hitler] has issued an order forbidding all withdrawals and so we enable the Russians to smash our front by degrees without incurring the supply difficulties they would have if we retreated. The result will be that the Russians, without making any real territorial gains, will simply annihilate our Eastern army where it stands. And the soldiers still fail to see that. That's because they aren't commanders but technicians, military technicians, and the whole thing is a gigantic crime.[54]

Certainly, the generals at the front did see the problem, but the idea of the OKH as military technicians dutifully implementing, and even reinforc-ing, Hitler's blinkered ideological views was very close to the truth.

With Fourth Army confronting open flanks in the north and south, Kluge knew that withdrawals—even if authorized—of individual divisions or corps would not suffice much longer. A general solution was needed, and nowhere more so than in the south. By January 8 Soviet pressure was mounting, and Heinrici's corps predicted dire consequences. Since January 6 Kluge had suggested to the high command that the withdrawal of Kübler's army would allow a shortening of the front, which would free up vital new reserves. Yet Halder and Hitler were characteristically reluctant to support such a move and expressed the view that Soviet forces in the vast spaces south and west of Kaluga "must eventually run themselves to death." Kluge paid no heed to such ridiculous statements and only stated that the forces would have to be found to defeat the threatening Soviet spearhead.[55] The following evening, January 7, Schmundt was again dispatched by plane to Fourth Army's headquarters to gather firsthand information on the situation. In the aftermath of the OKH's "relaxed" approach to the war, which stood in contrast to Fourth Army's apparent "pessimism," Greiffenberg instructed Bernuth, his fellow chief of staff at Fourth Army, to spare no detail in giving Schmundt a full account of the army's situation. That same evening Kluge had a very long talk with Hitler, followed the next morning (January 8) by a similarly long discussion with Halder. The aim was to impress upon both men the importance of pulling Kübler's army back before it was too late, which intensifying Soviet attacks on both flanks had made extremely urgent.[56]

The Soviet high command had clearly recognized the opportunity, and in line with Stalin's plan to trap German forces in their drive on Viaz'ma, the Red Army was seeking to turn both Kübler's flanks, at Yukhnov in the south and Medyn in the north. The offensive was strongest where the Fourth Army was weakest, and with the bulk of Kübler's divisions packed into the bulge, encirclement was suddenly a real possibility. Yukhnov and Medyn were, for the time being, still in German hands, but they were only fifty kilometers apart and deep in Kübler's rear, meaning the noose could rapidly close on Fourth Army. The two towns were also important conduits for any withdrawal; however by midday on January 8 Hitler was still resisting Kluge's plea for authorization. Even with Yukhnov and Medyn in German hands, the long and porous flanks meant any retreat would, according to Bernuth, "no longer be a withdrawal, rather a fighting withdrawal." Time was of the essence, and Kluge, in spite of his setbacks with the high command, was still assuring Kübler "a big and clear decision" would soon follow. Kübler demanded it that come shortly, but Kluge could make no promises.[57]

Just after 1:00 P.M., Bernuth again demanded a quick decision, claiming that if the army stood still much longer it would be encircled, and "if the order does not come, we will fight our way back without orders." By 2:40 P.M. there was still no decision. Seeking to preempt any rash act of defiance, Greiffenberg suggested a decision was imminent and would be known within thirty minutes. Finally, at 5:18 P.M., Hitler's answer reached Fourth Army—he had refused permission to withdraw. He insisted that first the army send "strong groups" to Yukhnov and Medyn "to form pivots," and that only when these were in place could a rearward movement be considered. The exasperated command informed Kluge that even Kirchner's officers in the LVII Panzer Corps were fighting on the front lines at Medyn, and the corps' intelligence officer and Luftwaffe liaison officer had just been killed. Kluge promised to speak again with Halder, but at 6:30 P.M., with no change in Hitler's decision, Greiffenberg called to confirm what Kluge had promised all along. "If the decision does not now come—the withdrawal of the Fourth Army must be ordered by the army group." At 7:30 P.M. word again arrived that Hitler had rejected a withdrawal, to which an enraged Kübler demanded the order be changed and "in the next five minutes." Forty-five minutes later, at 8:15 P.M., Kluge finally won Hitler's agreement, and Fourth Army's long delayed withdrawal could begin at last.[58]

Although Kluge had won the day and brought another reprieve for his former army, if he had been sincere about independently ordering a withdrawal, gaining Hitler's acquiescence had probably also saved his career. Yet Hitler's interminable reluctance to allow withdrawals and the utterly impromptu nature of German strategy, which tied up commanders in endless debates, added immensely to the strain under which they labored and allowed no clear planning or preparation for what was to be decided. The result rendered incalculable, and entirely unnecessary, damage to Fourth Army. Through it all, Kluge's victory was only a first step to saving Kübler's army, which really only amounted to being granted *the option* of escaping the Soviet net, not the act itself. The days ahead would still be fraught with danger and hard fighting, but Army Group Center, thanks largely to Kluge's persistence and patience, had again avoided another major self-inflicted defeat. Far from the miraculous solution Hitler's halt order acquired in postwar writings, it was in fact another disastrous example of an ideological precept being rigidly applied to strategy.

15.

THE FLOOD GATES
ARE BREAKING

Ninth and Fourth Panzer Armies Rupture

I f the situation at Fourth Army was the result of Hitler and the army
high command ignoring a dangerous situation until it became a full-
blown crisis, it was paralleled to a similar extent by the constraints
placed on Ninth Army. Throughout the last week of December, Kluge
tried time and again to gain Hitler's permission to withdraw Strauss's Ninth
Army before its thin front buckled, but all to no avail. On December 31, Hitler categorically rejected Kluge's last desperate appeal. Yet just as Kluge had
maintained he was prepared to act to save Fourth Army, so too did he take
steps to introduce some flexibility into Hitler's new order for Ninth Army. At
one point in their long conversation on December 31 Hitler had told Kluge:
"Breakthroughs must be dealt with locally. However, a necessary evasive

movement must not have operational repercussions."[1] Such a statement was by no means intended to ameliorate the emphatic tone of his order. Yet Kluge introduced it as a caveat to Hitler's halt order, which he must have known would offer Ninth Army's hard-pressed commanders a much-needed degree of flexibility in dealing with Soviet attacks. Hitler's categorical refusal to allow any withdrawal to the Königsberg Line arrived at 2:30 A.M. on January 1, but already the second sentence in Greiffenberg's message to his counterpart as chief of staff at Ninth Army, Colonel Rudolf Hofmann, emphasized Kluge's exception: "Only forced enemy evasive movements permitted."[2]

Not surprisingly, the Ninth Army interpreted this as the only silver lining to their otherwise bitter disappointment at being forbidden to withdraw. As the army's war diary recorded: "In practical terms, however, the rearward movements already in progress can still be largely justified even after Hitler's new order, because, as a result of the almost ubiquitous enemy pressure, this is largely 'evasion movements forced by the enemy.'"[3] It was precisely what Kluge wanted Ninth Army to interpret, although for the ruse to work the movements had to be "local" enough for Hitler and the OKH not to recognize what was actually happening. When Kluge spoke with Strauss later that same morning (January 1), he again emphasized, "to give permission freely, in the area of a division, to conduct fighting withdrawals."[4] After having advocated so strongly for Ninth Army's withdrawal, Kluge was allowing something extremely risky because so many units were involved and Hitler was well informed about the army's positions. The only hope was to claim that any positions lost were due to an overwhelming enemy strength and not simply surrendered for tactical convenience.

That some units might have been taking liberties with the new apparent freedom of maneuver is suggested by some of the soldiers' writings from January 1. Helmut Pabst's letter suggests a long retreat through multiple localities. "We marched out of the burning village into the night, and everywhere we marched the flames were sweeping skywards, feeding black smoke trails."[5] Similarly, Heinz D. wrote to his mother on the first day of the New Year:

In the course of my adventurous journey on foot, tractor and finally . . . truck, I saw the sites of my October activities again. The present section assembly point was the place where I was stationed with the advanced party and where the CO was wounded. I had not expected to see this again in such circumstances, basically the efforts and sacrifices of the battles in October have now become meaningless because we hadn't the sense to consolidate our gains.[6]

Clearly, both men described moving some distance and do not appear to have been in direct contact with the enemy.

If some of the troops were moving beyond the subtle step-by-step withdrawal that Kluge intended, it is not hard to find out why. Lieutenant-General Eccard Freiherr von Gablenz, the commander of XXVII Army Corps, openly flaunted his disgust at Hitler's order and rejected out of hand being told whether he could undertake a retreat that made perfect operational sense. He defiantly told Hofmann that without a retreat catastrophe would ensue, and while the Ninth Army's chief of staff agreed with such an analysis, he dutifully informed Gablenz that "Hitler's order demanded ruthless defense." Gablenz, however, would not hear of it and stated he was "compelled, according to his conscience, to violate the order."[7] Not only was Gablenz threatening full-scale retreat, he was not planning on stopping until he reached the Königsberg Line, which was the one thing Kluge had insisted to Strauss should never be mentioned again—much less ordered—as Hitler reacted angrily and believed it encouraged "the dangerous myth of the rearward position."[8] Nor was Gablenz alone in his defiance. He contacted VI Army Corps on his left, which was commanded by Richthofen, the scornful Luftwaffe general who had criticized his predecessor and ended up being temporarily placed in command.[9] Richthofen's baptism of fire, however, as a corps commander in one of Army Group Center's most dangerous sectors soon produced a radical change of heart about what was possible. He told Gablenz that he could not carry out Hitler's order and was ordering a "fighting withdrawal."[10]

At 12:35 P.M. Strauss called Gablenz and expressly forbade any withdrawal to the Königsberg Line, but the corps commander continued to maintain they had no choice. At 4:23 P.M. Gablenz informed the army that his retreat would begin on January 2. Strauss tried to appease him by accepting some of the responsibility for the order to stand firm on the current line, but the head-strong corps commander countered: "Within my area of command is only one officer responsible, that is me."[11] However correct Gablenz may have been in ordering his retreat, it was bound to undermine Kluge's attempt to placate both Ninth Army and the high command. In fact, even before Gablenz gave the order to begin his full-scale retreat, the "tactical solution" Kluge had introduced had unraveled. In the early hours of January 2, just twenty-four hours after Kluge had communicated his amended version of Hitler's decision, the high command identified Ninth Army's withdrawals, producing an immediate and furious reaction. Yet here again Kluge's steadfast reputation acted to obfuscate where responsibility lay and caused Hitler to fume at the generals of the OKH, whom the dictator had not unjustifiably accused of deception in the strategic debates of the previous summer. As Halder indignantly wrote in his diary: "The withdrawal of the Ninth Army, against the will of the supreme commander, occasioned irate scenes at this morning's conference. The OKH is charged with having introduced parliamentary procedures in the army and lacking firm leadership. These statements, which are completely untenable criticisms, take up time and undermine fruitful cooperation." Even Halder seems not to have suspected any conspiracy to deceive and wrote only of an "apparent command mix-up," which caused no serious questions to be asked or culprit to be identified.[12]

Kluge may have dodged one bullet, but his attempt at a "middle solution" to save Ninth Army was again thwarted by a new, emphatically worded order that eliminated any prospect of freedom of movement for Ninth Army's formations. The front as it stood on the morning of January 2 was to be held "until the last man, without consideration for breakdowns in command at the front, without consideration for holes in the front, without consideration for responding to dangers, without consideration for supply difficulties."[13] Kluge was beside himself. Strauss's front was at the point of collapse, and not only would Hitler's order prevent commanders from averting the collapse, it would then trap them at the front as they were bypassed and later destroyed. Kluge once again spoke with Hitler in what became a "very impassioned argument," but Hitler would not relent. As Halder passively observed, the front would remain where it was "without consideration for the consequences."[14]

While the generals at the OKH were prepared to accept whatever the implications of Hitler's order would be, the commanders at the front had a far better idea of what those would be. Not surprisingly, they thought very differently about orders that demanded resistance "until the last man." For Gablenz, Hitler's new order changed nothing. He bluntly informed Ninth Army that, given the choice between annihilation and withdrawal, there was only one option, and unless the army approved his request, he asked to be relieved of his command and court-martialed.[15] His level of conviction, however, was not shared by his fellow commanders. When Richthofen was asked if he understood his new orders, he replied: "Words yes, sense no."[16] Even if all of Strauss's commanders successfully managed to hold their current positions, Gablenz's determination *not* to remain in the line posed a serious problem. Kluge knew that the only thing worse than Ninth Army being ordered to strictly observe Hitler's halt order was the disastrous scenario whereby two-thirds of the army followed the order, while one-third retreated, creating a corps-size hole in the front. The commander of Army Group Center therefore called Gablenz to demand that he hold the line. When Gablenz asked if he might first explain the situation he faced, Kluge ignored the request and got right to the point: "I just want to tell you the following: It is the clear will of the Führer that no step backwards be taken. If you want to take the consequences for doing so, please report it. I ask only one thing: When you go, your chief of staff must accept the order to hold in the present line."[17] With that Kluge ended the call. There was to be no discussion; Gablenz would obey or lose his command. Kluge was juggling enough difficulties that were out of his control for him to expend any time on the ones that were. Shortly before midnight on January 2, Gablenz gave up his command of XXVII Army Corps and was immediately replaced by one of his divisional commanders—the more compliant Lieutenant-General Joachim Witthöft.

Hitler's new order was uncompromising in every way, and those like Gablenz who openly opposed it had to be dealt with in order to preserve whatever degree of discretion could still be found at the front. When Major-General Heinrich Recke's 161st Infantry Division suffered renewed breakthroughs on January 2, the left flank of the division began a withdrawal, "fighting step-by-step back towards the southwest in the direction of the

Königsberg Line."[18] The withdrawal was reported to the corps with no apparent repercussions, which suggests that the *modus operandi* in Ninth Army was outward obedience to Hitler's order, but in instances of genuine crisis, discreet withdrawal was in fact permitted and undertaken. The deception was not limited to the divisional and corps level. On January 4, as Lieutenant-General Walter Weiss's 26th Infantry Division attempted to defend the northern approaches to Rzhev, it requested falling back on a new line on account of an open left flank. The matter was referred up the chain to Army Group Center, where it was authorized with no evidence of involvement by Hitler or the OKH. Clearly, the deceit that led senior officers in Army Group Center to subvert the halt order before January 2 was still active, even after Hitler reiterated his directive in the most emphatic of terms.

Against this background, the long-threatened collapse of Ninth Army was taking place. On January 2, the link between Bieler's VI Army Corps (who had taken over from Richthofen during the day) and XXVII Army Corps was tenuous at best, while on his other flank, the connection to Schubert's XXIII Army Corps was broken through. Over the following days Bieler managed to reestablish a firm connection on his right, but the gap on his left just kept growing. Strauss attempted to seal the breach, ordering *Brigade-führer* Otto Fegelein's newly arrived SS Cavalry Corps (which had nothing like the strength of a corps) to attack from the west and a weak infantry assault group to hit the Soviets from the east. Yet before the attack could begin on January 7 the gap had extended to some thirteen kilometers, and Soviet reinforcements were pouring into the breach.[19]

With Strauss's front split to the northwest of Rzhev and, as of January 4, Soviet forces just twelve kilometers away, the fall of the city appeared imminent.[20] There was consternation in Army Group Center because the supplies for most of Strauss's army and all of Reinhardt's Third Panzer Army arrived via the Viaz'ma-Rzhev railway.[21] The city was also a major airfield for the Luftwaffe and functioned as Ninth Army's forward operating base, having sustained a population of 54,000 before being occupied on October 14.[22] On January 5 the war diary of Bieler's VI Army Corps ominously noted: "By evening one expects the Russian to be at the gates of the city . . . The fate of the majority of Ninth Army hangs on Rzhev."[23] That same evening Hitler declared Rzhev to be "the decisive strongpoint of the whole army group,"[24] while Kluge ordered Strauss to "tell every commander that Rzhev must be held."[25]

Help for Strauss's stricken army was to be provided by the same manner in which Kübler's Fourth Army was aided. On January 3 Hitler redrew the boundary between Fourth Panzer Army and Fourth Army, making Hoepner responsible for the area of the new Soviet breakthrough north of Maloiaro-slavets, and at the same time he subordinated Reinhardt's Third Panzer Army to Strauss.[26] Reinhardt's distant formations were not expected to close the gap northwest of Rzhev, but Strauss did order him to take over the area of Colonel Helmuth Weidling's 86th Infantry Division, adjoining Third Panzer Army.[27] Importantly, Reinhardt occupied one of the most secure sectors in the whole army group, which he defended as shrewdly against the Red Army as against attempts by his superiors to weaken his front. When news arrived that he would find himself under Strauss's command, Reinhardt wrote in his journal: "I want to report sick."[28] He then began a furious campaign of ob-struction and resistance. The Ninth Army's war diary noted on January 4: "As was feared, given the previous experience with Third Panzer Army, yes-terday's order to relieve the 86th Infantry Division failed due to difficulties." In fact, having blamed circumstances beyond his control, Reinhardt then ap-peared to offer a deal. He now offered to take over the sector of Weidling's division if, in exchange, he was given command of Landgraf's 6th Panzer Division. Strauss rejected the idea out of hand and pointed out to Reinhardt that the army group had also ordered the panzer army to reinforce Ninth Army's left flank.[29]

What upset Reinhardt most in the reorganization of command boundar-ies and responsibilities was the loss of authority over Ruoff's V Army Corps. Ruoff's corps had belonged to Fourth Panzer Army, but was subordinated to Strauss so Hoepner could concentrate on closing the Soviet breakthrough on Kübler's northern flank. This meant the formations on both flanks of Rein-hardt's panzer army were directly controlled by Strauss. This was admittedly an atypical practice, but given that Reinhardt too was subordinated to Ninth Army, there remained an overall unity of command. Nevertheless, Reinhardt was infuriated by this and insisted that Ruoff's corps must come under his control.[30] He instructed his chief of staff, Colonel Walther von Hünersdorff, to complain to Greiffenberg at Army Group Center, while he also reported the situation to Heusinger at the OKH. When Strauss ordered Reinhardt to accept the situation and comply with his demands, the panzer general seethed in his diary: "Incomprehensible order from Strauss, who believes V Army Corps more than us. We're giving our all, I'm not going to do more."[31] Such indignation was all the more remarkable given that Reinhardt had so far done nothing for Strauss, despite acknowledging, in the same diary entry, that the situation on Third Panzer Army's front was "quiet."[32] When Strauss had still received no help by January 5, Kluge called Reinhardt and told the panzer commander in a "polite, matter-of-fact tone" that the situation was "too serious for rudeness, lack of responsibility, etc." Yet Kluge was also well aware of Reinhardt's record of disobedience and wanted to leave the panzer commander in no doubt about his determination to have him follow orders. Kluge's warning was recorded by Reinhardt: "Court-martial!"[33] Once again, the field marshal was in no mood to tolerate recalcitrant subordinates who refused to recognize the wider implications of their actions.

Given no alternative, Reinhardt relented and extended his line, freeing the 86th Infantry Division to act as a much-needed reserve for Ninth Army. While Reinhardt had resisted aiding Strauss for fear of being sucked into the costly defensive fighting, the opposite took place. In the days after occupying the new positions on the left, the fighting in Witthöft's XXVII Army Corps died down to the point where on January 8 the corps believed that Soviet resources were being directed westward to exploit the gap near Rzhev.[34] One should not understand the "quiet" in Third Panzer Army's sector as meaning there was no action, but the small-scale Soviet attacks often ended as small-scale disasters. As one soldier noted of the January combat: "How can one describe this fighting? The Russians attack in a completely mulish and senseless manner, and think nothing of it if ten, thirty, forty or fifty men fall."[35]

If the Red Army was to be admonished for its poorly orchestrated attacks, it was in contrast to the panzer troops that knew how best to conduct them, even when on the back foot, and granted the opportunity, Reinhardt's men delivered some sharp blows of their own. On January 5 Krüger's 1st Panzer Division launched a predawn raid on a system of Soviet bunkers, which resulted in 120 dead, 50 POWs, and the Soviet position being destroyed.[36] It was indicative of the German tactical response throughout the winter, which was dominated by defensive fighting but never entirely replaced by it. For units with any kind of tactical reserve or heavy weaponry the mantra seemed to be defend, defend, defend, strike a blow, defend, defend, defend. The German attacks were typically infrequent enough to achieve complete surprise, and if panic took hold within the Soviet formation, the casualties were usually exceedingly one-sided. An outstanding example of this was Recke's 161st Infantry Division, which on January 5 launched an attack through a forested area that the Soviets had failed to screen. The assault group inflicted some 400 enemy dead before withdrawing in the evening with a large collection of captured equipment.[37] When German intelligence from the same period reported high enemy officer casualties, resulting in regiments being led by lieutenants,[38] it becomes clear that the Red Army's grossly deficient leadership and experience handed the Germans tactical victories far in excess of their inferior numbers. By the same token, what passed in many German accounts as the indifference of Soviet commanders to the lives of their men—both in attack and defense—was often too simplistic a judgment. The heavy losses are in fact best explained by their sheer ignorance and poor training.

While Reinhardt was given the relatively simple task of taking over the front from a single division of Ninth Army, Hitler made Hoepner's Fourth Panzer Army responsible for Kübler's broken front north of Maloiaroslavets. This was truly a poisoned chalice, which, as Hoepner wrote his wife on January 4, Hitler tried to sweeten by emphasizing his "boundless trust in me and my achievements."[39] Already on January 2 Hitler had ordered Hoepner to send two regiments and an artillery detachment to aid Materna's XX Army Corps immediately, but it was too little, too late to prevent the splitting of Kübler's army. Of course, Kluge and Kübler had foreseen this outcome, yet Hitler had refused permission for the withdrawal of Materna's corps as well as his northern neighbor General of Artillery Wilhelm Fahrmbacher's VII Army Corps.[40] The problem was simply transferred to Hoepner, whose success in holding his own section of the front had qualified him, in Hitler's eyes at least, to restore the situation in the south. Hoepner did possess some meager reserves, but these would take time to concentrate in the south, and there were real doubts that they had the strength to restore a connection to Fourth Army. As Hoepner complained to his wife, the problem "lay with fundamental errors in the high command, against which no one says anything except me. That naturally takes a toll on one's nerves."[41] Of course, whether Hoepner knew it or not, he was by no means alone in opposing Hitler's attempts to rigidly hold the front in place, but until now his panzer army had been relatively unaffected by the halt order.

Hoepner's opposition was not just a matter of opinion; there is clear evidence that his formations were preparing for another major withdrawal. On January 2, the war diary of Thoma's 20th Panzer Division complained that the troops engaged in the evacuation of Rusa (which is also a town on the Rusa River) were leaving far too much matériel behind and needed the example of a court-martial to prevent further losses.[42] Farther north, the war diary of Vietinghoff's XXXXVI Panzer Corps even included an order from the panzer army on "preparations for withdrawal to a rearward position," which included the familiar instructions for ruthless scorched-earth activities.[43] A day later (January 3) Fahrmbacher's VII Army Corps issued an order effectively allowing withdrawal so long as "the last cartridge has been fired."[44]

Clearly, Hoepner saw no point in defending his front to the last man, and with his scanty reserves being sent south into an unequal battle, the prospect of withdrawal must have appeared to be the only sensible solution. In some places, diminished companies of thirty men were assigned two kilometers of front, which inevitably left gaps in the line.[45] It was a circumstance Hoepner could not long abide, and in this he was supported by his chief of staff, Colonel Walter Chales de Beaulieu, who wrote after the war that "Hitler's 'Halt order' was in its wording and demands nonsense."[46]

Finding troops to support Materna's XX Army Corps was only half of Hoepner's problem; the other was transporting and supplying them. Thoma's 20th Panzer Division, for example, had twenty precious tanks, but these could only be used for local defense because they were lacking in fuel.[47] Moreover, the frequent snowstorms and frigid temperatures, which sometimes reached minus forty degrees Celsius, countered any rapid movement.[48] It was not until January 6 that Hoepner's forces were in position to attack south, but even before they could begin, news arrived that Kübler's flank had been pushed back during the night. The gap between the two armies had grown to twenty-nine kilometers. Compounding the bad news, the three Soviet divisions that had driven westward through the gap had now turned north and were threatening to cut off Materna's corps. Hoepner proposed to Kluge that he bend his flank back, to guard against the new Soviet threat from the west, but Kluge insisted upon following Hitler's order to attack south. It was a huge gamble. Either Hoepner would close the gap to the south, effectively cutting off the Soviet divisions, or Materna's corps would be encircled. For two days the fighting continued, but by the morning of January 8 the gap was still far from closed, and Materna's last snow-cleared road to the west was cut, leaving him without access to supply. Hoepner called Kluge and told him that XX Army Corps would shortly "go to the devil" if it was not allowed to retreat.[49] Kluge immediately put the matter to Halder and "categorically demanded the decision to withdraw." Halder in turn departed for Hitler's headquarters, but when Kluge spoke again with Hoepner at midday the field marshal evinced confidence, telling the panzer commander: "A great decision must be made. It can be that it will come very quickly; all preparations for very short-term execution have to be made."[50]

Chales de Beaulieu listened in on the call with Kluge and claimed that both he and Hoepner had the impression that a withdrawal would soon be authorized.[51] At 1:00 P.M. that afternoon Hoepner tried to contact Halder directly but failed to reach him, and assuming the order to withdraw would soon arrive anyway, he saw no point in further delay and gave the order himself at 1:45 P.M. According to Fourth Panzer Army's war diary the decision came "in the last possible minute, if not already very late."[52] As with so many other overdue decisions from the high command, Materna's corps would have to undertake a fighting retreat, incurring heavier losses, but even this was thanks only to Hoepner's impatience and effective insubordination.[53]

Not only did Hoepner order the withdrawal, but he did not inform Army Group Center, perhaps hoping that authorization would arrive before he would have to admit to his defiance. The first that Army Group Center knew of Materna's retreat was in the evening report that was sent at 6:15 P.M. At 7:00 P.M. Tresckow, the operations officer, contacted the army, believing it to be a mistake, and even joked about the misunderstanding. When he was told that the report was correct and XX Army Corps was in retreat, he immediately left to inform Kluge. Minutes later the field marshal was on the telephone to Hoepner, who again confirmed the report and revealed to Kluge that he himself had given the order. Kluge was furious. The commander of Army Group Center may have been privately willing to circumvent Hitler's orders when he deemed it necessary, but he took the strongest exception to commanders doing it of their own accord. Kluge accused Hoepner of knowing perfectly well that Hitler's order forbade any withdrawal and that he had no right to give such an order. At the very least, he told Hoepner, he had to have prior approval from the army group, which suggests Kluge's tacit willingness to "manage" such situations in the absence of Hitler's approval. As it was, Kluge deeply resented being presented with a fait accompli that would only further undermine his ability to juggle all of the army group's difficulties and win the minimum necessary concessions from Hitler. In anger Kluge accused Hoepner of forgetting his duty to Hitler, to which the commander of the Fourth Panzer Army retorted: "Field marshal, I have a duty that stands higher than my duty to you or my duty to the Führer. That is the duty entrusted to me by the troops."[54]

Kluge, unwilling to tolerate insubordinate commanders, and no doubt mindful of the damage another act of open defiance by a senior commander under his command would do to his trust in Hitler's eyes, was in no mood to defend Hoepner. His report to the high command therefore made little attempt to justify Hoepner's actions,[55] but this should not be taken to suggest that Kluge wanted Hoepner removed from his post. Yet, anticipating Hitler's furious reaction, Kluge may also have calculated that Hoepner's position was beyond salvation. What resulted shocked even Kluge. Hitler became so enraged he demanded not only that Hoepner be removed from his post, but also that he be expelled from the army with loss of pay, pension, and the right to wear a uniform.[56] Even in his role as the commander-in-chief of the army, this was not something that Hitler could technically order, as it first required conviction by a military court. Kluge and his staff took it as an affront not only toward a respected senior commander but also to the army's essential procedures and processes. When Kluge spoke with Hitler later that night, he was prepared to accept Hoepner's removal from command but bitterly opposed his expulsion from the army. According to Schlabrendorff, Tresckow's adjutant, "When Kluge insisted that he was seriously considering not carrying out the order and instead resigning from his command, Hitler retorted sharply that nothing could make him change his mind, and that he would transfer command of Army Group Center to someone else if it became necessary."[57] If Kluge had indeed threatened his resignation, it was clear Hitler's anger knew no compromise and that the dictator was willing to lose his most important commander on the Eastern Front over a dismissed general's right to a pension and uniform. With nothing to gain, Kluge gave up his defense. Even though he had his way, a short time later Hitler had the Reichstag grant him extended powers to override the last remaining legislative, executive, and judicial limits to his power.[58]

Near midnight at Fourth Panzer Army's headquarters, Hoepner received the call from Kluge informing him of his fate. What followed was a scene of bitter indignation. The diarist for Fourth Panzer Army included an uncharacteristically personal comment in his report: "One wonders who can better and more directly oversee the situation, the commander of the troops here at the front or the authorities 1,500 kms distant. What leader can still take responsibility for his troops if he cannot make a decision on his own initiative after hours in a pressing situation!"[59] Chales de Beaulieu shook Hoepner's hand with the words: "Colonel-General [you] could not, and may not, have acted differently. The XX corps will always be grateful to you and us all here too." Hoepner spoke only briefly to his staff, confirming that Ruoff, who currently commanded V Army Corps, would be his successor. Hoepner spoke approvingly of this choice and then retired to his room to pack.[60] At this stage the former army commander only knew of his dismissal from command. Kluge had spared Hoepner the full ignominy of his disgrace but instructed him to appear the following day at Army Group Center's headquarters: "I have something else somewhat personal to tell you."[61]

Hoepner duly departed Fourth Panzer Army for the last time on January 9, leaving his staff "deeply shaken."[62] He proceeded to Smolensk, where he met alone with Kluge for two hours to receive the news of his unprecedented dishonor and personal humiliation.[63] After having so recently expressed his "boundless trust" in Hoepner, Hitler was clearly seeking to make an example of him to the rest of the army. In fact, Colonel Chales de Beaulieu was also relieved from his post as chief of staff in a punitive measure intended to underscore Hitler's dissatisfaction.[64] Once back in Germany, Hoepner devoted himself to fighting his expulsion and pursued legal avenues, which confirmed that he could not be deprived of his position and benefits without a court-martial. The former army commander was therefore able to remain on inactive service with full pay until his arrest and subsequent execution in 1944 for his part in the attempted assassination of Hitler.[65]

Hoepner's dismissal, like that of Guderian and to a lesser extent Brauchitsch, have become emblematic of Hitler's supposed recasting of the German army, in which his iron will swept away anyone who opposed it and overturned the very essence of *Auftragstaktik*. Yet this was only true in a small number of cases. As we have seen, Hitler's halt order was routinely being challenged, yet only a handful of senior commanders actually lost their positions as a result. Hitler and the OKH simply could not hope to follow the actions and orders of every senior officer down to the lowest levels, while the campaign of subversion began with Kluge and continued down the chain of command until the order was, in some instances, only selectively applied. Yet there was a recasting of the German army in the winter of 1941–1942, and while it was impacted by Hitler's order, it was not directed by it. Moreover, the recasting did not change the basic culture of command within the army.

By April 1942 the Army Personnel Department had made recent appointments to almost seventy divisional commanders' posts in the east.[66] This equates to about half of all the divisions on the Eastern Front, a figure that accurately reflects the situation in Army Group Center. Between December 1, 1941, and April 1, 1942, no less than thirty-four of Kluge's sixty-seven divisions—just over half—experienced a change in command. In fact, seven divisions experienced either three or four changes in command, while the 137th Infantry Division had no less than six different commanders in this period. Of Army Group Center's twenty-one corps, sixteen experienced changes over the four-month period, and eight of these had more than one.[67] Thus, half of all the divisional commanders and three-quarters of the corps commanders changed, while five of the six army commanders were replaced in the first two months of the Soviet offensive (only Reinhardt would remain). Clearly, the army group was being recast at all levels, but the majority of these changes in command were caused by sicknesses (and to a lesser extent natural rotation of command appointment), not by Hitler. Of course, one might argue that Hitler's orders indirectly contributed to unusually high levels of stress in command positions, but this is impossible to isolate from things like the excessive cold and the stress created by the Soviet offensive.

At the start of January, a senior medical officer in the 167th Infantry Division estimated that 80 percent of the troops suffered from some kind of ailment. Stomach and bowel problems, catarrh, frostbite, skin diseases, and fever were especially prevalent. He also noted: "The level of health and overall condition is extremely bad, lowering the body's resistance in coping with illness and wounds . . . Total physical and psychological collapse threatens not only the NCOs and men but the majority of officers as well."[68] The fact that major-generals (the starting rank for divisional commanders) were typically men over fifty years of age meant the conditions, long hours, and constant stress took their toll,[69] even in the relative comfort of Army Group Center's headquarters. For instance, supposedly it was Bock's stomach problems that sent him home. Thus, older histories that have attributed the cause of the attrition among Army Group Center's senior commanders entirely to Hitler's ruthless dismissals, aimed at bending the army to his will, must be questioned.[70] Confusingly, though, some of the commanders who were dismissed for insubordination had their replacement explained as being necessary "to restore their health."

Interestingly, the high turnover of Germany's commanders was public knowledge thanks to Soviet propaganda, which helped establish the myth that it was all due to Hitler. On January 3 Goebbels complained in his diary that "if the opposing side claims that a giant dismissal of generals took place, this also does not correspond to the facts."[71] Yet facts counted for nothing in the propaganda war; only the perception of truth mattered. Upon receiving fragmentary information, Victor Klemperer recorded the possibilities in his diary on January 4: "Hitler has not only dismissed Brauchitsch, but something like thirty generals altogether, or 'Brauchitsch and something like thirty others have left of their own volition' or 'have been shot' . . . Where does the eastern front stand? Nothing but questions without answers."[72] Of course, whether the generals were dismissed, resigned, or shot, it all pointed to a serious crisis within the German high command—which was true—but not for any of the reasons circulating. No German general was shot; no one resigned (although many declared themselves too ill to continue, which may in some cases have constituted a hidden form of resignation), and the dismissal rate was low. Yet the perception of a purge frustrated Goebbels, who, while acknowledging the real source of the problem, still opted to blame the generals. Writing in his diary on January 7, the propaganda minister stated:

> In the east, the main issue is a problem of middle leadership. The middle leadership is composed of somewhat older gentlemen, who apparently can no longer cope with the severe physical and mental strains of the eastern campaign. Most have stomach sicknesses, they become melancholy, exaggerate occasional setbacks . . . the Russian expanse also seems to have an exceedingly negative effect on their whole temperament and attitude. At any rate they have completely lost control of their nerves, in various stages of the developing situation. As soon as a few Russians had broken through, they thought they had to retreat . . . But the Führer once again prevailed with the whole dynamic of his personality.[73]

While acknowledging that the generals suffered from "severe physical and mental strains" leading to "most" suffering stomach problems, Goebbels then appears to change track and accept the claims of Soviet propaganda by blaming the generals for their weakness and trumpeting Hitler's indomitable will in opposing them. Goebbels was arriving at the right conclusion for the wrong reasons. Many of the generals were prepared to undermine Hitler's halt order, but only a fraction were exposed and punished for doing so.

Although the command culture within the army did not fundamentally change in the winter of 1941–1942, Hitler's suspicions about his senior commanders certainly increased. Even the unflagging allegiance of the OKH was scornfully attacked. When Hitler made his accusation that "parliamentary procedures" were being introduced to debate his orders, he was not wrong.[74] Halder, however, thought this was blatantly untrue—the OKH had consistently and conscientiously backed Hitler every step of the way since the departure of Brauchitsch. In this instance the army command's remote detachment from the front and its incomprehension of the prevailing attitude among Army Group Center's hard-pressed commanders counted in Kluge's favor. The OKH had no idea of the scale of disobedience and simply assumed Hitler's accusations were entirely misdirected. The army high command's ardent rejection of any wrongdoing only tarnished them further in Hitler's eyes and suggested they were trying to cover up their duplicity. As one member of Hitler's inner circle recalled of this period, "The conferences on the eastern front became ever stormier. Hitler screamed, thumped his fists on the table and accused the generals of being incapable of fighting . . . When he calmed down a little, he repeated many times over [during] this period, 'Anyone can deal with victory. Only the mighty can bear defeat!'"[75]

16

MAKING A VIRTUE
OF NECESSITY

Surviving the Russian Winter

With the Russian winter at full force and intense fighting continuing unabated, one of the enduring questions is how the German army—so utterly unprepared for the extreme cold—not only avoided the early fears of an 1812-style disaster but ultimately managed to withstand, and even in cases master, the conditions. In September 1941, a military spokesman admitted to Arvid Fredborg, the Swedish correspondent based in Berlin, "that the main bulk of the German Army had no experience of winter warfare." This, Fredborg wrote, "was communicated to us—the German public was told nothing."[1] At that time the German military was willing to make such admissions because it saw no prospect of a winter campaign. Only with the start of the Soviet winter offensive could there be no further illusions about major operations continuing through the coldest months of the year; however, the appalling lack of preparation or training forced the troops, yet again, to scramble for remedies.

If necessity is the mother of invention, then the life-or-death struggle on the Eastern Front provided its own motivation for German soldiers to develop solutions to seemingly intractable problems. As the crisis-ridden XXXXIII Army Corps on Fourth Army's southern front struggled to cope with every new demand, Heinrici observed: "It would be all much worse if the troops had not overcome the rigors of the fighting, of the weather, of the supply problem with incredible toughness and bravery. During the summer and autumn, we thought we had done incredible things. And yet that was nothing compared to the situation now."[2] Overcoming such rigors reflected the resilience and strength of the men, but it was also evidence of an intellectual engagement with the problems. As Hans Schäufler observed, "The ability to improvise on the part of the men—developed in a time of need and also plagiarized from the Russians—was terrific."[3]

Without question the most pressing need was to repel Soviet attacks, yet at such low temperatures the oil and grease used to lubricate weapons froze solid, jamming the guns. Colonel Horst Grossmann, who served in Strauss's Ninth Army, observed that the main problem was the heavy machine guns, which were the vital defensive weapon against massed Soviet infantry attacks. The thin German lines, manned by heavily outnumbered riflemen, often did not have the firepower to stop a concentrated attack. Grossmann's report explained, "there is no guarantee that the heavy machine guns will work properly. And if they seize up, even if we destroy the first wave of the enemy, the remainder will overrun our position, killing everybody. Our waiting soldiers know this."[4] The emphasis was therefore on keeping the guns firing, which led to a variety of improvised solutions.

The idea was that by ensuring a close proximity between the forward positions and a warm bunker, soldiers could quickly retrieve weapons at the start of an attack and put them into action before the oil had a chance to freeze. During use, the guns, especially the machine guns, became hot enough for the oil to function smoothly and keep them from jamming. Obviously, soldiers did not always have the luxury of warm storage for their weaponry, and the gun could be dismantled with every part polished so that not a drop of oil or grease remained. Mechanically the weapon was still reasonably reliable, and stoppages, while unavoidable, were less common.[5] Another solution was to substitute petroleum jelly for grease, which apparently had a better resistance to the cold.[6] Hans Sturm claimed that he concocted a "magic mixture" of oil mixed with sulfur powder, which "made an excellent antifreeze treatment" that soon other gunners were applying with success.[7] If all else failed, the firing bolt could be carried inside a man's uniform, using his body warmth to keep it from freezing before a battle.[8] Those too lazy or careless to maintain their weapons in proper order adopted a quicker solution to freeing up their machine guns: they doused them with gasoline and set fire to them, which apparently had the desired effect.[9]

The German retreat also forced the men constantly to adopt new positions, very few of which were adapted to any form of prepared defense. And with the ground frozen solid for up to seventy centimeters, picks and shovels were useless as a first measure. The most common solution, therefore, was to blast holes in the ground. This worked very well, but only if sufficient explosives were available.[10] When they were not, the soldiers improvised another, more dangerous, solution by blasting holes one hand grenade at a time. The problem was the first hand grenade usually could not be buried very far, if at all, leaving little time for the man who pulled the cord to reach a safe distance. Werner Adamczyk used this method and wrote of "scrambling to the ground and hoping the explosion would not hurt us." Yet he also noted that the method worked very well: "A flat hole was created in the hard ground, allowing us to repeat the procedure over and over again, until we hit below the frost line to softer ground. Once this point was reached, everybody jumped in to dig deeper and deeper, until there was enough room to build a bunker."[11] Another solution to the frozen ground was to build the bunker on the site of an existing peasant house, where the ground was not frozen because the stove was set directly into the earth and was large enough for a family to sleep upon. Moreover, the collapsed house often yielded enough wood to fashion a roof for the bunker.

Without enemy contact, construction could progress remarkably fast. Werner Adamczyk claimed that bunkers could be built under the frozen earth within just two days.[12] This was substantiated by a report on the relocation of Landgraf's 6th Panzer Division in early January, which necessitated a whole new line to be built. Fortunately, a large quantity of explosives were on hand, while the enemy "watched with surprise, could not understand what was happening, and remained quiet." The craters were blasted in the morning and covered in the afternoon, and the entire line was ready for defense within twelve hours. As the report concluded: "The position withstood all enemy attacks and was not abandoned until ten days later."[13] In another instance, the war diary of Krüger's 1st Panzer Division noted on December 26 after less than a week of work on a new defensive line: "Despite the great cold, which sometimes reaches minus 36 degrees Celsius, the construction of the position goes well. In the strongpoints, the first bunkers, which offer space for twelve men each, are ready. A thick straw floor and a large iron stove provide the necessary warmth."[14] Some men even went to the trouble of personalizing the construction process. Claus Hansmann described "individualists" who took the time to fashion "a chair of earth with a special hole for a cup of tea and a place to put the cigarettes in."[15]

Constructing a bunker was a challenge, but connecting bunkers with trenches, as was the usual practice, proved quite impossible. Thus, when defending in the open the men trudged their way through the snow to lonely foxholes out on the line. More commonly, however, the German line consisted of fortified strongpoints built around villages and towns. Here any buildings that were superfluous to the defense were destroyed, both to deny them to the enemy and to aid German observation and fields of fire. Once again, the collapsed structures provided additional building materials to reinforce those that remained. Houses suitable for use as fighting positions had snow packed against the outer walls, while narrow firing embrasures were cut. The most important defensive positions, such as the first houses on the road leading into the village, might be reinforced with steel plate or wooden beams. Defending antitank guns or German tanks could be camouflaged by the men urinating on them before quickly spreading on snow to make it stick. Between the houses soldiers erected thick ice walls up to three meters high to shield them from fire as well as channel the enemy attack toward more open spaces that functioned as kill zones. The ice walls were a simple construction, starting with bundles of sticks or fence palings, covered by blankets or a poncho and socked with water and snow until they were thick enough to stop a bullet. On the approaches, the Germans converted their mines to tripwire-detonated explosives because the deep snow and low temperatures rendered pressure-activated mines less reliable. In addition, trees were felled with gaps deliberately left between them to channel any Soviet tanks toward antitank mines.[16] As the chief of staff of the XXXXI Army Corps, Hans Röttiger, noted with pride: "The troops, who so far had been inexperienced in this sort of thing, very quickly learned to adapt themselves to the conditions of position warfare"[17]

While German accounts often cite the harsh winter conditions as evidence of their hardship during the poorly managed campaign, there is seldom recognition that, in important instances, these same conditions played significantly to the *Ostheer*'s advantage. Most particularly, the heavy snowfall, which closed roads and impeded all movement, impacted the ability of the Soviets to achieve their objectives. The Red Army's inability to exploit breakthroughs and quickly encircle German formations prevented Army Group Center's crisis from becoming a catastrophe.[18] The snow also had a tactical dimension, which again counted in the Germans' favor. As Hans Roth noted at the beginning of a battle: "The enemy's artillery is revving up; we are lucky to have such deep snow, for on the rock-hard frozen ground, the effects of the detonations are so much stronger."[19] Likewise, after enduring a heavy barrage Fritz Hübner wrote home: "But the high snow was our salvation, it strongly dampened the fragmentation effect."[20] Of course, German artillery was affected in the same way, but the Red Army fielded many more pieces of artillery as it was their principal weapon to support infantry attacks and "soften up" enemy positions. A postwar study written by former German officers on the Eastern Front concluded:

> The defender has a definite advantage in winter because, as a rule, his position cannot be seen in snow except at very close range. He is able to keep his forces under cover and wait until the moment that fire can be used most effectively. The attacker, on the other hand, is impeded in his movements and is easily detected, even in camouflage

clothing. The principal weapon of the defender is the machine gun. Its performance is not diminished by snow, in which mortars and light artillery lose most of their effectiveness.[21]

In terms of local maneuver Soviet forces certainly made better use of units fitted with skis, which afforded the best means of movement. Yet one should not overstate the importance of ski units since their role was limited to the tactical encounter as larger formations could seldom be adapted to transport heavy weapons or maintain an effective supply line. For this reason, the Germans did not employ ski formations above battalion strength, while the Soviets pushed the concept all the way to the brigade.[22] Certainly the Red Army's effective use of skis, especially in reconnaissance missions, set the example for the Germans to follow, but learn and adapt they did. A winter training school was set up near Smolensk so that every division could create at least one company of sixty men to function as specialists on skis (and together each corps could employ them as a battalion).[23] These ski specialists were remarkably successful. One wide-ranging German patrol launched late in the winter, and after four days behind enemy lines infiltrated twenty-four kilometers and then returned safely, yielding a great deal of valuable information as well as three POWs.[24] The difficulties of navigating in the winter landscape motivated the Germans to employ a characteristically ruthless method. Local guides were taken and used to show German patrols the way, but to ensure security they were then shot to prevent them from revealing any information.[25]

The Germans also adapted to the winter in more passive ways. Acclimatization to the cold certainly provided no guarantee against illness or exposure, but the soldiers did write of a "hardening" process whereby they felt a physical resilience to the extreme temperatures. Otto Will wrote in his diary in early December: "I am in the best physical condition and have grown accustomed to the hard Russian winter."[26] Similarly, Adolf B. wrote home in a letter in mid-January: "Regarding the cold, we have already become quite used to it and minus ten or twenty degrees [Celsius] does not bother us anymore! Minus thirty to thirty-five degrees, however, does hurt! The sharp northeast wind is horrible(!), which also causes quite devastating snowdrifts!"[27] The extent of the acclimatization process, however, was best summed up by Max

Kuhnert, who remarked on the contrast between the men at the front and newly arriving replacements from Germany. As Kuhnert observed:

> We had hoped to get some replacements sent on, for we had many losses and holding our position became a strain for everybody. We heard, however, that most replacement troops had already been frost-bitten before even reaching us. We, without noticing it, had become hardened because we had had the advantage of going slowly into the cold climate, whilst the fellows being brought in by plane as near to us as possible, ran straight into the coldest temperatures they'd ever known.[28]

Whatever the virtues of acclimatization, the ability to withstand the cold depended first and foremost upon winter clothing, the lack of which, for good reason, has become the quintessential example of gross German mismanagement during the winter of 1941–1942. Almost every account from the period makes mention of it, and in some units, the shortage led to more casualties than the fighting. As Josef Perau complained in early January: "Our troops are in no way equipped for the Russian winter. Our coats, boots, head protection are the same as the troops in the west."[29] Without new uniforms the men could never change out of anything that they had, which, as Wilhelm Prüller noted, forced the men to live in dreadful filth. Prüller writes in his diary: "We can hardly go on as it is. For the most part the men only have what they carry on their bodies . . . And if you've only got the socks you're wearing, and they are constantly soaked through, in time they'll start to rot. All our shoes are ruined, our shirts and underclothes black (they've not been changed for weeks)—this is just a little hint of the way things are."[30] This issue was not just one of hygiene or even simply protection against the cold; in such extreme temperatures the absence of things like gloves meant the men could not touch the steel components of their weapons or vehicles because the exposed skin would stick and peel off when they tried to pull away. In this way, the very weapons necessary for defense became themselves what one soldier called a "dangerous liability."[31]

As we have seen, an immediate solution to the clothing crisis was not forthcoming. The overwhelmed rail network could not even cope with the minimum demands of the army group, let alone find the tremendous transport capacity required for winter uniforms. As Ernst Gerber wrote in his diary on January 1, "There is nothing to be seen of the large garment collections in Germany. Probably the transports are stuck somewhere between Warsaw and Smolensk and will arrive in the spring when they are no longer needed."[32] In fact, some deliveries of winter clothing did reach the east during the winter, but, as Helmut Günther remarked, these were "no more than a drop in the bucket."[33] Self-reliance was once again the best means of survival in the east, although there were some attempts at organized responses at the front. Several divisions set up large sewing workrooms employing local Russians to manufacture earmuffs, waistcoats, mittens, and socks using blankets and old clothing. There were also a small number of felt boot workshops, but demand always far exceeded supply.[34]

Left to their own devices, men ruthlessly requisitioned civilian garments and boots, but the front was often too thinly populated. The task therefore was to develop new sources of protection out of the materials at hand. Heinrich Haape, a doctor in the Ninth Army, advised his men to use what he referred to as his "major weapon against the Russian winter"—newspaper, which was sometimes available and surprisingly effective. As Haape explained:

> Newspaper in the boots took up little space and could often be changed. Two sheets of newspaper on a man's back, between vest and shirt, preserved the warmth of the body and were windproof. Newspaper round the belly; newspaper in the trousers; newspaper round the legs; newspaper everywhere that the body required extra warmth . . . We found old German papers, Russian newspapers, magazines and journals—and propaganda pamphlets by the thousand. Some of the leaflets were our own propaganda, others bore pictures of Lenin and Stalin . . . It amused us to think of Russian propaganda leaflets being used to keep German soldiers warm.[35]

Haape was not alone in identifying the insulating properties of paper, and other soldiers too took special delight in using Soviet propaganda leaflets for the purpose. One soldier recalled: "I remember trying for a week to keep warm on a proclamation that 'Surrender is the only sane and sensible course as the issue has been finally decided.'"[36] Likewise, Franz Frisch wrote after the war: "We improvised by wearing newspapers inside shoes and all our shirts and underwear at the same time, and tried making straw and rope boots to cover the shoes."[37]

Adapting and supplementing their existing uniforms was one solution to surviving the cold, but an even more efficient method of gaining a warm winter uniform was to take one from a dead, or sometimes alive, Soviet soldier. Apart from having quilted uniforms made for the conditions, the average Soviet soldier had spent much less time at the front, and so his outfit was usually less tattered and grimy. As Helmut Pabst wrote home: "We get no new boots or shirts when our old ones wear out: we wear Russian trousers and Russian shirts. And when our boots have had it, we wear shoes and Russian puttees—or else make the puttees into ear-muffs."[38] The obvious problem of wearing the enemy's uniform was the danger of attracting friendly fire, which led to some precautionary regulations. Auleb's 6th Infantry Division, for instance, mandated Soviet jackets be worn underneath the men's ordinary tunics.[39] Willy Peter Reese wrote of how a soldier desperate to find himself a pair of felt boots found some on a frozen Soviet corpse. There was no way to separate the boots from the man without damaging them, so the soldier took an axe and chopped off the legs at the thigh. As Reese recounted the event: "Fragments of flesh flew everywhere. He bundled the two stumps under his arms and set them down in the oven, the legs were thawed out, and he pulled on the bloody felt boots."[40] Walter Tilemann described the same process but wrote of whole bodies being thawed out at large fires in order to salvage everything from the jacket to the boots.[41] Indeed, sometimes this morbid practice took place on a truly industrial scale. After one Soviet attack in which some 200 bodies were left on the battlefield, the Germans set about claiming sufficient clothing to outfit every man in their battalion, as Heinrich Haape wrote: "The bodies were carried, frozen into grotesque shapes, to the sauna houses and there the 'saw commandos' got to work. It was a filthy business, but there was no place for the niceties of human contact when death was waiting to claim the man who lost his body heat."[42]

While cold and desperate men did what was necessary to protect themselves from the Russian winter, Red Army uniforms were no magic armor against the freezing conditions. Prolonged periods outdoors, especially in snowdrifts or on one of the colder nights, threatened anyone with exposure and death. In fact, one should not think of the Red Army as uniformly outfitted in the best winter clothing and equipment. Their success in this regard was always relative to the lamentable state of the German army, but inspections of the Soviet dead also revealed many inadequately dressed men, even among the much-vaunted Siberian troops.[43] In another assessment of some two hundred Red Army corpses only sixty possessed felt boots.[44]

Overall, surviving the winter on Army Group Center's front sometimes depended as much on ingenuity, resourcefulness, and cunning as it did on happenstance, good fortune, and sheer luck. A man had no control over what orders his unit received or what strength the enemy attacked him with. He simply endured as best he could and worked to control the few things that were in his power to influence. Yet by January 1942 there was an increasing sense that the formidable Russian winter was in fact something that the German soldier could contend with and that the fears of a Napoleonic rout were in fact exaggerated. As Alfred Vilsen confidently wrote home on January 3, "We have already become quite well accustomed to the winter cold. We have had almost two and half months of frost and snow . . . Yesterday and today [minus] thirty-four. When the wind blows over the plain then it is quite icy, but that cannot unsettle us and steal the determination for victory. The Russian has also to endure it and sometimes under much more difficult circumstances . . . In terms of winter items, we have received, and also organized, various things, you need not send anything more."[45] Like many men, Vilsen may simply have wished to ease the minds of his family, but whatever the case, survival itself, however tenuous, gave men hope that they could see out the terrible season. It was a source of mounting confidence that the much-lauded "General Winter" of Soviet propaganda was revealing itself to be just that—propaganda, and not a looming death sentence for every German soldier.[46]

While German resistance to the Soviet offensive was principally directed against the Red Army, in the skies above Army Group Center there was also a numerically superior Red Air Force. In early December the combined air forces of the Kalinin, Western, and Southwestern Fronts (before the Briansk Front had been reconstituted) equaled some 1,393 aircraft, but only 910 of these were operational. These confronted some 580 aircraft of the Luftwaffe, although the exact number of operational planes is unknown.[47] The Soviet aircraft flew from airports around Moscow sometimes with control towers, floodlights, sealed runways, and protective hangars, while German airfields were rudimentary at best. Often the poor state of German facilities was due to their own aerial attacks earlier in the war, but it also stemmed from the Soviet scorched-earth policy. The result was cratered runways, planes exposed to the elements, and no running water, heating, or electricity. Given such a disparity, it is not surprising that Soviet planes were able to fly far more combat sorties throughout the winter, managing some 7,210 in the first thirty-three days of their winter offensive. Sometimes two crews manned the same plane to keep it constantly in action as the *Stavka* sought to exert maximum pressure on the retreating German forces. Their principal targets were the columns of withdrawing German soldiers, command posts, and lines of supply.[48]

German war diaries recorded the effect. Hoepner's Panzer Group 4 noted on December 12 the "lively enemy aerial activity with numerous bombers and low flying attacks." Two days later the same diary blamed the losses sustained from continuing Soviet air attacks on "the demoralizing absence of German fighter protection."[49] Similarly, XXXXI Army Corps, belonging to Reinhardt's Panzer Group 3, reported on December 18 the "absolute Russian aerial superiority over the realm of the corps."[50] At the front, the Soviet planes strafed and bombed, causing constant casualties. Funck's 7th Panzer Division, for example, reported seventeen dead and twenty wounded from air attacks on December 24 alone.[51] The material damage from strategic bombing raids farther behind the line could sometimes prove even more detrimental. Schmidt's Second Panzer Army reported a devastating bombing attack on Orel's railway station on December 31 in which two trains loaded with badly needed fuel were hit and exploded. The blast destroyed both completely as well as two more trains loaded with food. In total, some eighty to one hundred wagons were lost in the fire.[52]

The Soviet aerial dominance was also harmful to the morale of German forces even when they remained unhurt. Gerhard Bopp wrote in his diary on December 15 about the "extremely active" Soviet air force, which attacked in waves of ten planes and against which he complained there were no German fighters or flak to be seen.[53] Similarly, Horst Lange wrote on December 19: "The psychological impact of aerial attacks results from the surprise and absolute defenselessness." His diary even recorded one attack involving up to twenty Soviet bombers at once.[54] Hans von Luck explained that because the Soviet planes came from the east, from the rear of the retreat, they were not always spotted in time, and the result could be "devastating." Especially severe were the losses of horses, which presented a large target that could not be rushed to safety or forced into a ditch. They were simply gunned down on the roads, and as Luck recalled: "Before long, the narrow roads were choked with cadavers of horses and broken-down vehicles."[55] Georg Kreuter wrote home of enemy planes constantly flying down the length of the road, causing a commotion even though they only dropped bombs from time to time.[56] For others the mere threat of being bombed weighed on their nerves. As Otto Bense recalled: "It was a real war of nerves. The planes that came over at night were the worst. They kept on circling overhead, all night long. The Russians left us German soldiers nervous wrecks—for some it was so bad that they went mad."[57] The shock and stress of airborne attacks could only have been enhanced by reports of at least one captured German plane flown by a Soviet pilot that made costly surprise attacks.[58]

While such German reports appear to suggest a complete absence of the Luftwaffe and the absolute dominance of the Soviet air force, this was not the whole truth. In fact, the reverse was true on some of the most important sectors of the front. In commanding his VIII Air Corps, Richthofen received far more requests for aerial support along the vast length of Army Group Center's front than he could ever hope to provide. Instead of doling out his limited planes in small piecemeal attacks across the front, Richthofen maintained a strict policy of employing his aircraft en masse. Often this meant employing one or two of the air corps' "groups," each made up of numerous squadrons, on a single sector of the front, achieving local aerial superiority and always in areas deemed most vital to the situation on the ground.[59] The

Luftwaffe was therefore employed as a kind of fire brigade, deployed to the most desperately threatened sectors, but the consequence was that most of Army Group Center had to manage with no air support whatsoever.

Complicating Richthofen's ability to support the army was Hitler's War Directive 39, which he signed on December 8. This extended the VIII Air Corps' responsibility from tactical support of the army to a wide-ranging campaign of strategic bombing. Accordingly, the limited resources of the Luftwaffe in the east were expanded "to prevent the rehabilitation of the Russian forces by attacking, as far as possible, equipment and training centers, particularly Leningrad, Moscow, Rybinsk, Gorki, Voronezh, Rostov, Stalingrad, Krasnodar, etc. It is particularly important to harass, day by day, those enemy lines of communication which enable him to exist and by which he threatens our own front."[60] While dispersing the Luftwaffe's effort appeared foolhardy, the unexpected change in German tactics combined with the heavy concentrations of Soviet forces moving west along congested roads ensured Army Group Center was inflicting as well as receiving punishment. One air raid on December 17 surprised a Soviet column near Tula and destroyed an estimated thirteen tanks and some two hundred vehicles. In the following days the carnage continued. On December 18 four tanks and fourteen vehicles were destroyed; on December 21 the tally reached seventy-five vehicles; on December 22 four tanks and sixty vehicles; and on December 24 two tanks and fifty vehicles.[61] Clearly, the German troops were not the only ones with reason to fear aerial attacks. In fact, a Soviet report from Zhukov's Western Front in January 1942 noted, "Insufficient organization of the air defense of our troops . . . together with the impossibility of the few available fighters to fulfil all requests from the armies, resulted in significant losses to our troops."[62]

While German planes may have been significantly outnumbered, there appears little question that their pilots were typically better trained and more experienced. Between December 15 and 30 the Luftwaffe shot down some 119 Soviet planes while incurring only thirty-three losses.[63] Gerhard Köppen, one of Germany's fighter aces, shot down his fortieth enemy plane on December 18 and by February 24, 1942, had scored a further thirty-two "kills."[64] Even Soviet pilots admitted to being outclassed. Alexander Shvarev told an interviewer after the war, "our morale was affected by German air superiority. In terms of aircraft quality and marksmanship the Germans were better than us."[65]

Yet what mattered most to the hardest pressed men of Army Group Center was not aerial dogfights or the results of strategic raids, but tactical support to bomb and strafe the enemy on the front lines. After remarking on the high levels of Soviet aerial activity, the war diary of Thoma's 20th Panzer Division noted that the Luftwaffe was likewise active, especially in the use of Stuka dive bombers.[66] On these sectors of the front such interventions often made the difference between life and death for the German troops. Reporting on one company's desperate defense of two villages, Hermann Vogel wrote that without the intervention of German ground-attack aircraft, "they all said they would have been lost."[67] Similarly, Paul Schädel wrote on January 12: "Our Stukas go powerfully at it and every day carry frightening amounts of bombs."[68] According to one Stuka pilot, the limited number of serviceable German planes also meant they were reserved for "old, experienced crews so that the disadvantage in quantity is to some extent compensated by quality."[69]

In the first two weeks of the Soviet counterattack the principal areas of action for Richthofen's VIII Air Corps were with the retreating panzer formations north and south of Moscow, but by the end of December they had switched to Ninth Army and increasingly Fourth Army. Characteristic reports from these sectors noted the Luftwaffe's "strong forces in spite of the bad weather," which intervened in the fighting to "good effect."[70] Indeed December 1941 reflected something of a resurgence for the Luftwaffe in Army Group Center, thanks to Hitler's orders for a major reinforcement of VIII Air Corps. This included three newly created bomber groups, another bomber group transferred from Western Europe, and one twin-engine heavy fighter group from Germany's aerial defense. In addition, Richthofen received five transport groups, four from Germany and one belonging to Air Fleet Four, which covered Army Group South.[71] Unlike most of the reinforcements dispatched to Army Group Center, the new planes had an almost immediate effect. As Hans-Ulrich Rudel observed in late December: "Transport aircraft land daily on our airfield bringing fur clothing, skis, sledges and other things."[72] While the new planes were a much-needed boost for Richthofen, they came at a longer-term cost for the Luftwaffe, as over 100 of the Ju-52 transport planes had been stripped from bomber training programs around Germany. As Hermann Plocher, a senior Luftwaffe officer, noted, it constituted "a grievous disruption," which "sooner or later would lead to a shortage of replacement aircrews at the front."[73] Hitler, however, directed the Luftwaffe much like he did the army, focused much more on immediate operational outcomes than long-term implications.

In a further illustration of short-term thinking by the German high command, the crisis at the front and the shortage of both artillery and Stuka dive bombers led commanders to commit bombers to low-level attacks, a role for which they were not designed, nor their crews trained.[74] As Herhudt von Rohden wrote: "With the start of the Russian attacks in December 1941, it became clear that all parts of the flying units had to be used for the immediate support of the army; this meant bombers too, which were not fit for that type of mission, involving as it did low-level attacks on small targets. The bombers themselves lacked speed in low-level flight, and were poorly armored."[75] Where the bombers proved far more valuable was in their role as "air bridges" to support encircled German soldiers. The most famous example began in February 1942 in the area of Army Group North, when 100,000 troops of the II Army Corps were encircled in the Demyansk pocket. Another smaller pocket formed at Kholm with 3,500 men trapped.[76] In supporting these troops the Luftwaffe flew thousands of missions to bring in supplies and take out wounded; however, the precedent for these operations was set by VIII Air Corps in January. The 4,000 men of Gilsa's 216th Infantry Division cut off in Suchinitschi required Richthofen to organize an airlift as well as close air support to sustain and protect them.[77] For more than two weeks (from January 9 to 25) Major Walter Hammer's unit of Ju-52s kept Suchinitschi supplied entirely by air, losing just four aircraft in that time.[78]

The threat to the Luftwaffe stemmed less from the Soviet air force than the winter weather, which kept countless aircraft grounded because of adverse flying conditions, deep snow on airstrips, and damage to aircraft components. According to the Soviet Western Front's estimate of German aircraft activity in January, the Luftwaffe flew only one-third of the sorties it had achieved in December.[79] Given that the reinforced VIII Air Corps had more planes by January, any decline in activity resulted from the sizable re-allocation of Richthofen's resources to Ninth Army (which opposed the Kalinin Front), but also the greater challenges of January's weather. The extreme cold introduced many new and unforeseen problems for the Luftwaffe, but just as the army improvised solutions to maintain its operations, so too did the Luftwaffe.[80]

The most pressing problem was keeping the aircraft engines functional, which required keeping them free of ice and the viscosity of all lubricants extremely low. One solution was turning over the engines regularly, especially at night, but this consumed scarce supplies of fuel and oil.[81] A more ingenious solution was the so-called "alert box." As Hermann Plocher explained, "Warming ovens and all sorts of expedients were devised . . . Planes designated for standby-alert duty were often placed with their noses in 'alert boxes,' heated shacks which kept the engines warm enough to start on short notice."[82] Photos of these look rather like the plane had crashed into a small house, but they were an effective method of keeping liquid-cooled engines from freezing solid.[83] Another idea was an improvised stove built from a gasoline tin that was fixed underneath the aircraft engine, with a chimney pipe carrying heat directly to the priming pump. As one pilot noted: "We maintain the heat until we get a result. It is primitive, but just the thing for the Russian winter."[84] In more desperate circumstances, mechanics resorted to warming up the engines with naked flames, which as Hans-Ulrich Rudel was told: "They'll either start now or be burnt to a cinder. If they won't [start] they're no use to us anyway."[85]

Such adaptation by the men of the Luftwaffe extended right down to the very tools that they used for routine maintenance. Because metal becomes brittle in extreme subzero temperatures, mechanics had to protect their tools by preheating them before working.[86] Even once mechanically fit to fly, planes then had to contend with the snow on the airstrips, which often reduced the grip of the tailwheel, requiring someone from the ground crew to sit on the tail wing. In at least one instance the unfortunate man was not able to get off before the plane was airborne, and the pilot had to turn back immediately and land.[87] Even identifying the airfields in the snowy landscape was a challenge, so the ground crews resorted to cutting small trees to act as runway markers.[88] The resilience of the Luftwaffe and its dogged performance under the hardest of conditions led to high praise from Strauss's Ninth Army, where Richthofen's planes were most active. After noting the high cost of winter operations, the army's war diary stated on January 3: "And yet the German *Ostheer* has adapted remarkably quickly to the harsh Russian winter and begun to close the Russian advantage in this area: today the German aviator is at least as reliable as the Russian at 40° frost, as the strong commitment of the VIII Air Corps and [its] transport units have in recent days impressively proved."[89]

In addition to supporting the army with his aircraft, Richthofen also directed that any spare ground crew be sent to the front. It was the first time that Luftwaffe personnel were assembled to form dedicated fighting formations. Even pilots for whom planes were no longer available and men deemed "most valuable specialists" were ordered forward, with seemingly no thought to their long and expensive training.[90] Yet sometimes the ground war came to the Luftwaffe, especially in January when the Soviet breakthrough of the Ninth Army threatened the German airfields directly. As Hans-Ulrich Rudel wrote:

> Our staff company commander, gets together a fighting party drawn from our ground personnel and those of the nearest units, and holds the airfield . . . For two successive days it is attacked by cavalry units and ski battalions. Then the situation becomes critical and we drop our bombs close to the perimeter of our airfield. The Soviet losses are heavy. Then Kresken, one-time athlete, assumes the offensive with his combat group. We hover above him with our aircraft, shooting and bombing down all opposition to his counter-attack . . . Our Luftwaffe soldiers at the beginning of the war certainly never saw themselves being used in this way.[91]

In addition to sending Luftwaffe ground troops forward, Richthofen also had all of the Luftwaffe's antiaircraft guns, which had been positioned in the rear to defend strategic assets, dispatched to the front to support the army. Thereafter General of Flak Artillery Otto Dessloch noted "the full-time preoccupation of the German Flak with fighting ground targets."[92]

Such concentrated support by the Luftwaffe no doubt provided a vital boost where it was needed most, but it came at the cost of Army Group Center's general protection and left most of Kluge's armies, and wide sections of the front, to improvise their own basic air defense. Veiel's 2nd Panzer Division passed on a strict order that every man was to fire at low-flying enemy planes. The order concluded: "Whoever does not shoot, will be punished."[93] Hans Frenzel wrote in his diary on January 8: "Planes as usual . . . They frequently fly so low that the red star can clearly be discerned on the light blue fuselage. There is nothing surprising in this, by the way. For German fighter planes and A.A. guns are non-existent. Our only defense is machine-guns and rifles."[94] As inadequate as this was against heavily armored Soviet ground attack planes like the Il-2, some German sources nevertheless assert that Soviet air power, even when unopposed, proved "ineffective" during the winter period, including during the German retreat.[95] More recent assessments have substantiated this point of view, as Alexander Hill concludes: "Not only on the ground, but in the air, did the *Stavka* spread resources too thinly for significant results anywhere."[96] Considering the severe mauling the Soviet air force endured during the first months of the German invasion, it acquitted itself reasonably well in the winter counteroffensive. Yet, as with the Red Army, its large size and greater adaptability to the winter conditions were no guarantee of success. In the first winter of the war the Soviet air force lacked any real combined arms capability to coordinate with ground forces, rendering it a deadly nuisance in many places but decisive nowhere. Von Hardesty and Ilya Grinberg conclude in their major study of the Soviet air force in World War II: "The battle for Moscow, with all its stresses and sacrifices, allowed the VVS [Soviet air force] to gain valuable combat experience that would cast a long shadow over subsequent battles with the enemy. Attempts were made to coordinate these air operations with the larger goals of the Fronts. Yet in practical terms, the VVS suffered considerable losses and failed to provide consistent support for the ground forces."[97]

By contrast the performance of Tactical Air Support Command North, which was responsible for directing VIII Air Corps' operations in support of Ninth and Fourth Armies from January 6 to March 21, 1942, provided clear evidence of what German air power could achieve even in the winter months. Owing to the bad weather, German planes could fly for only fifty-six days during this period but still managed just over five thousand sorties, shooting down 82 enemy aircraft and destroying another 76 on the ground. Their real contribution, however, was close air support for the troops, and in this capacity they claimed the destruction of 838 motor vehicles, 44 tanks, 73 guns, and 1,231 "other types of vehicles."[98] Writing after the war, the commander of this tactical formation wrote of the January fighting:

> Time and again the enemy attacked with unrelenting fury and tremendous masses of men and matériel. Ruthlessly he committed his inexhaustible resources of human lives. The defensive battles that grew out of those attacks were as long as they were fierce . . . Nevertheless, the enemy was not able to realize his operational plans. Wherever he had penetrated the German lines, he had been stopped up to now, either by counterattacks or by the tenacious defense of strongpoints in the depth of the breakthrough sectors.[99]

While the Luftwaffe's air operations over Army Group Center comple-mented Kluge's immediate needs on the ground, Richthofen personally en-joyed little thanks from the army, which had not forgotten his late December statement to Hitler suggesting commanders were presenting overly negative reports. Indeed, attitudes toward the commander of the VIII Air Corps var-ied from cold to open disparagement. During a visit to Kluge's headquarters in Smolensk on January 20, Richthofen noted that Greiffenberg was "ex-ternally harmonious, less so inwardly." Kluge, on the other hand, "attacked [him]" and told Richthofen that the individual army commanders "were all angry at [him]." Richthofen, however, refused to accept this and demanded more precise information about which commanders and why, but Kluge re-fused to answer him. The commander of Army Group Center reminded Richt-hofen of his "careless" December report to Hitler, but he rejected this too, insisting in his diary, "it would never be as bad as he reported."[100]

Richthofen's attempt to ingratiate himself with Hitler at the expense of the army clearly backfired; not only did he have to swallow his pride and undertake the command of an army corps at one of the most dangerous sections in the Ninth Army, but as a result he earned the enduring antipathy of many senior commanders in Army Group Center. That said, Richthofen's favor with Hitler and other elements within the Luftwaffe's high command can only have helped win such large numbers of aircraft reinforcements, which played a vital role in the winter battles. Richthofen also inspired a good measure of confidence among his men, and notwithstanding his recent undermining of the army before Hitler, he had previously enjoyed a highly successful record of coordinating his planes in a ground support role. That experience was never more important than in the winter period, and Richthofen, whatever his faults, was part of the reason that Army Group Center held firm.

17.

DEFENDING THE INDEFENSIBLE

Hitler's Last Stand

B y the second week of January it was clear that the crisis on the southern flank of Army Group Center had passed and that a largely static winter position was being adopted by both sides. Schmidt's Second Army had withstood a serious challenge to its southern wing in the first days of the year, but even this constituted more a local problem than a general one for the army. By January 10 the front was so quiet and the army's confidence so great that major formations were being released from the line to rest and recuperate in the rear. Colonel Hans Schlemmer's battered 134th Infantry Division as well as parts of Breith's 3rd Panzer Division and Lieutenant-General Karl von Oven's 56th Infantry Division were all taken out of the line. Moreover, Schmidt was even able to allocate an additional seven-kilometer stretch of Second Panzer Army's front to its nominally much weaker southern neighbor.[1]

While the Soviets were abandoning their attempts to reach Kursk and redirecting their forces toward the more successful offensives in the north, Second Army did its best to tie down enemy forces, while counterattacking whenever possible. Since January 8 Kempf's XXXXVIII Panzer Corps had conducted a rolling set of local attacks, and by the afternoon of January 11 had outflanked another Soviet position causing 900 enemy troops to flee their positions to the north and east with "considerable losses."[2] The Red Army attempted to hit back farther north, where intelligence suggested that they hoped to capitalize on the withdrawal of major German formations from the line. Yet these attacks, which varied from company to regimental strength, could not break Second Army's line, nor force the recall of inactive German formations.[3] As Hans Roth commented on January 15, "The immense Red losses give too easily the wrong impression that our fight here in the East is not that difficult. To the contrary; the true picture of the enemy goes like this: tough, stubborn, and malicious." Roth then underlined the point by recording yet another "unfathomable" attack of a Soviet battalion, which was "smashed to pulp" by concentrated infantry fire.[4]

By January 12 Schmidt's Second Army stood unbeaten by the Soviet offensive, having held the line east of Kursk and survived the harrowing winter conditions. It was the first of Kluge's six armies that could claim a notable defensive victory. As it was, however, attention was so focused on Army Group Center's fraught situation in the north that Second Army's achievement was left largely unmarked. In fact, to free Kluge from his already stretched responsibilities, Hitler ordered Second Army to be placed under Reichenau's Army Group South as of January 15. The only exception was Kaempfe's XXXV Army Corps, which was attached to Second Panzer Army and formed the new southern flank of Kluge's army group. On the same date (January 15), Colonel-General Maximilian von Weichs, who had previously commanded Second Army before a two-month illness forced him to relinquish command, returned to assume his post, allowing Schmidt to devote all of his attention to Second Panzer Army and closing the gap to Kübler's Fourth Army.[5]

Sections of Second Panzer Army's front mirrored the situation farther south, with little overt danger and soldiers writing of positional warfare and boredom. For example, Erich Hager from the 17th Panzer Division wrote on January 10: "One day goes by like the last. Russian aircraft activity. It's snowing quite heavily, otherwise nothing is happening."[6] From time to time there were Soviet attacks, but for those occupying strong positions, who themselves had already repelled so many past assaults, confidence was often high. As one soldier wrote home on January 12, the German front was "a defensive wall" which the enemy "will never break through." He then continued, "We were already attacked by Red hordes, which were in some cases completely without weapons. The attacking masses must already be great, in order for only a small part to be able to take aim against our fast-firing weapons."[7] Such confidence, however, stemmed only from men in secure positions, which was by no means all of Second Panzer Army.

Schmidt had to not just hold his eastern flank, but also guard against Soviet attacks along his dangerously exposed northern flank. Essentially, Second Panzer Army's position was a rough right angle, defending both Orel and Briansk, while also trying to scratch together enough forces to relieve the encircled men at Suchinitschi. Some reinforcements were arriving by train at Briansk, but the only other way to raise reserves was to have as few troops as possible defend the eastern flank. Beginning January 9, the army ordered that all lightly wounded men who could still use a weapon be left at forward hospitals or aid stations to strengthen local defenses.[8] There was heavy defensive fighting south of Belev in the area of Weikersthal's LIII Army Corps, which was preventing an expansion of the Soviet breach farther to the south.[9] Here there was desperate fighting, especially for the elite infantry regiment *Großdeutschland*, which was placed in the most threatened sectors. When one of its officers was inspecting the front line, he came across a lone man in a foxhole surrounded by twenty-four dead Soviets. He had shot them all with his rifle. As the officer wrote: "He had remained completely alone at his post during a snowstorm. His relief had not turned up and despite dysentery and frost-bitten toes he stayed there a day and night and then another day in the same position."[10]

It was not all gritty resistance to the last man. Especially along the more fluid front in the north, evidence shows that organized withdrawals followed familiar patterns of destruction. As Adolf B. wrote home in a letter on January 10: "Villages, which we had to leave behind, we have set on fire, so that the Russians cannot entrench themselves there! Burning villages, burning cities, destroyed war materials, crying women and children, everywhere misery, desolation surround us; I will never forget these 'pictures'!"[11] The cruelty of German methods was exacerbated by the fact that the forested regions around Briansk were well-known for their partisan activity, which stemmed from the large number of Red Army troops caught behind German lines since October 1941. Eberbach's 4th Panzer Division reported attempted infiltrations by partisans in German uniform as well as the felling of trees to block roads and attack supply columns.[12] The partisans were even receiving supplies from Soviet aircraft and linking up with advanced detachments of the Red Army pressing deep into the gap between Belev and Kaluga.[13]

The complications for Schmidt in simultaneously combating enemies at the front and in the rear hindered his ability to assemble a large enough battle group to drive successfully on Suchinitschi. Yet the delay also had its advantages. As long as Gilsa's detachment maintained possession of Suchinitschi, they blocked the only east-west rail line available to support the Soviet offensive into the German hinterland. And with recent heavy snowfalls, the alternative of road transportation was exceptionally slow.[14] On January 14, for example, a single battalion in Second Panzer Army needed nine hours to travel just eight kilometers even without enemy contact.[15] Suchinitschi also absorbed an inordinate amount of the Red Army's attention, which kept considerable Soviet forces tied down in a siege of the town and unable to contribute to the exploitation of the breakthrough. Consequently, on January 9 Halder remarked on the success of the weak German forces defending on the northern and southern shoulders of the Soviet bulge.[16] After eight days of holding the town and fending off every Soviet attack, Kübler at Fourth Army was also gratefully trumpeting the "heroic resistance of Suchinitschi."[17]

Whether Schmidt could raise the forces necessary for the relief of Suchinitschi was still very much an open question, but in the meantime, encirclement from the north was increasingly doubtful. Firmly ensconced on the Oka and Zusha Rivers to the east, Second Panzer Army's overall position had significantly improved. By the time Weichs resumed command of Second

Army in the middle of January, Schmidt had seen out the worst of the Soviet winter offensive in Army Group Center's south. Together with Guderian, the two generals had not only ensured the survival of all their major formations on the perilous retreat from Tula and Jelez, but had stabilized the Eastern Front over a line extending some 240 kilometers, while denying the Red Army the prized cities of Briansk, Orel, and Kursk. As one German soldier optimistically wrote on January 14, "Well, the most terrible, worst and most exhaustive days now seem to be behind us, and we have stopped in a village and arranged so-called winter quarters . . . The front line has come to a halt and in the spring it is back on the road and forward again! To the final victory!"[18] At its longest, the extent of Second Army and Second Panzer Army's winter retreat equaled some 14 percent of the linear distance covered by the German army since crossing the German-Soviet border on June 22. Matériel losses on the retreat were unquestionably heavy, which would have an undeniable impact on future offensive operations, but the toll on the Red Army was by no means inconsequential. Even with its vastly greater industrial production, it would be over a year until Kursk was liberated and another nineteen months before Orel finally fell.[19]

If Stalin's offensive had been blocked in the south, the prospects of a major victory against Army Group Center still appeared bright in the north. The Red Army was attempting an encirclement on a scale that could only be compared to Germany's greatest victory of the 1941 campaign—the Kiev pocket. In that battle Army Groups Center and South had combined to crush four armies of the Soviet Southwestern Front. Now Stalin was seeking to exploit Kalinin Front's breakthrough west of Rzhev and Western Front's penetration west of Kaluga to link up at Viaz'ma, cutting off the German Fourth, Third, and Fourth Panzer Armies as well as most of the Ninth Army. It was in this context that on January 10 Stalin made his bombastic prediction that 1942 would see the "complete defeat of the Hitlerite forces."[20]

By the second week of January Viaz'ma was just 120 kilometers south of Konev's forces in the north and 85 kilometers from Zhukov's armies in the south and east. The city was also Army Group Center's most important transportation hub, acting as the vital junction on the Berlin-Warsaw-Smolensk-Viaz'ma rail line. At Viaz'ma the lines diverted north to Rzhev, south to

Briansk, and eastward toward Kaluga in the southeast and Mozhaisk due east. The Rzhev Line carried all of the supplies necessary for Reinhardt's Third Panzer Army and most of those for Strauss's Ninth Army, while those heading east sustained Kübler's Fourth and Ruoff's Fourth Panzer Armies.[21] The Soviet plan to close at Viaz'ma and ensnare the bulk of four German armies had one fundamental advantage: not the winter weather, but rather Hitler himself. Just as Stalin had almost single-handedly created the disaster at Kiev by refusing any and all requests for a timely withdrawal, so too Hitler was holding fast to his halt order and proclaiming it the "savior" of Kluge's army group.

At Fourth Army both flanks had been broken open and were in the process of being enveloped. As the army's war diary noted with exasperation on January 10, "The leadership has allowed the operational breakthrough to happen, reacting to none of the reports . . . We are behaving like the Russians, remaining stationary and allowing ourselves to be encircled."[22] Kübler was therefore pleading for freedom of action and insisting that it be granted before the situation reached a point of extreme danger.[23] In the absence of sizable reserves to reinforce the army or counterattack on the flanks, retreat had become inevitable. This, however, required Hitler's consent, which Fourth Army's operations officer, Hellmuth Stieff, doubted would be given in time. On January 10 he wrote to his wife, "The bulk of the army between Medyn and Kaluga will soon be beyond resupply. It all happens just as—or much worse than—we had foreseen four weeks ago. At that time, there was still something to be saved by a real decision—today it is again 'too late.' One is rendered miserable and resigned."[24] Stieff, like many other senior officers, was emotionally exhausted, worn down as much by the relentless enemy attacks as Hitler's obstinacy in dealing with them. Heinrici, commanding XXXXIII Army Corps, echoed Stieff's deep disillusionment. Writing to his wife on January 11, the corps commander declared:

> Everything has come true exactly as I told my superiors. They have
> declined all suggestions out of fear of the highest authority. If it is
> Kluge or Kübler (our new army commander), they are all afraid of
> the highest authority. And he himself leads according to platitudes

such as "no Napoleonic retreat"; he leaves the flanks open and gives the enemy all the time in the world to march around us and to attack from behind. One hopes that new divisions will be brought up. But they are coming so slowly and in such small numbers, it is simply not good enough to get us out. Thus, the Russian is going to win his first battle of annihilation against us. However, it is hard to accept this fate when it is so obvious that the reason for this development is due to the stubbornness of our leaders. There would have been measures to turn things around, if they had decided to disengage three weeks ago, fourteen days ago, even five or six days ago. We have made suggestions often enough. But the new army high commander refused them all, and haggles over whether or not to give up twenty of the 1,200 conquered kilometers. And yet it is completely irrelevant where in Russia we are.[25]

In his bitterness and frustration Heinrici was understandably unsympathetic to the constrained positions of Kübler and Kluge. Kluge was not in fact afraid to speak his mind to Hitler, but his desperate pleas and constant warnings fell largely on deaf ears. His willingness to defy Hitler was clearly apparent, but it was tempered by the likelihood of detection by the high command. Kluge shrewdly judged that any act of defiance leading to his dismissal was to be avoided, which was definitely self-serving but also in the army group's best interest.

While Stieff and Heinrici were predicting Fourth Army's demise, Kluge was in fact doing his best to extract Fourth Army, if only Hitler could be made to agree. The problem, however, in securing any such permission was that a withdrawal of Fourth Army would have consequences for Fourth Panzer Army's southern flank. The only resolution, as Kluge well knew, was for a so-called "large solution" in which Kübler, Ruoff, Reinhardt, and parts of Strauss's army could be withdrawn together into the Königsberg Line. This would eliminate the dangerous Soviet breakthroughs, shorten the overall German line, and bring Kluge's armies closer to their supplies. The ground lost could not be defended anyway, and attempting to do so, as Hitler was stubbornly insisting, risked the very survival of Army Group Center. Kluge was lobbying for his "large solution" at every opportunity and, given the increasingly dire situation, had made some progress. At the OKH Halder acknowledged on January 9 that "the situation moves towards a big decision."[26] Kluge was also having numerous discussions with Jodl at the OKW, which seemed to generate more support, but Hitler still could not bring himself to permit a retreat. His dangerous vacillation was even frustrating Halder, who complained of the "loss of valuable time" over "this burning question." Under pressure, Hitler announced that he wished to speak with Kluge personally, but a blizzard on January 10 prevented Kluge from flying to East Prussia, and the meeting had to be delayed until January 11.[27]

When Kluge finally arrived at the Wolf's Lair, Hitler subjected him to a long monologue covering many topics yet was clearly reluctant to consider Kluge's plan for a large-scale withdrawal. The dictator argued that in the current positions "every day, every hour is a benefit, even when the strain on the nerves is so great." He promised that if the front held, "all the acclaim" would fall on Kluge.[28] Yet the commander of Army Group Center was returning to Smolensk empty-handed. Hitler had agreed to a fifteen-kilometer withdrawal for the southern wing of Fourth Panzer Army, which in part just confirmed what Hoepner had defiantly authorized days earlier, but even this concession came with the condition that Ruoff somehow reestablish contact with Fourth Army.[29] There was no grand plan guiding Army Group Center's current deployments; it was simply holding its position in order to placate Hitler. After all the troops had suffered through and fought for, the unwillingness of the German high command to allow a path to escape the Soviet advance left many of the officers in the field reproachful. Lieutenant Kurt Grumann wrote in his diary on January 11: "The Reds are trying to take advantage of the winter . . . They have sent ski detachments into our rear area. We are setting up a defense. There will be no withdrawal for our 185th Regiment. Stand and die."[30]

The linchpin of Fourth Army in the north was the town of Medyn, which was being assailed from the north and northwest by strong Soviet forces. With no substantive reinforcements available, the continued defense of the town was simply impossible. As Fourth Army reported on the evening of January 12, "A breakthrough at Medyn would, however, have the result that the enemy could march onto Yukhnov, so that the whole rest of the army is cut off . . . A catastrophe for the Fourth Army is unavoidable."[31] Once again Kluge promised to speak with Hitler, but in the meantime insisted that Medyn be held at all costs. The following morning the pressure on the town was growing "from minute to minute," and Kübler told Kluge that Medyn had to be abandoned that night. "I have hardly ever spoken in my life with such conviction," Kübler was quoted as saying, before continuing: "It must be, we cannot open the way for the enemy into the rear. I must throw myself fully onto the scales; there is nothing other than the evacuation. Medyn is in any case lost, in one instance with, and in another without the great part of the occupying force."[32] The occupying force Kübler referred to was not simply the garrison defending Medyn, but the bulk of Fourth Army that was occupying the so-called "Schanja position," which was the bulge Fourth Army currently held and was threatened to be entombed in.

To add to Kübler's worries a major Soviet airborne operation near Medyn dropped some 2,000 troops behind German lines.[33] This was not the first time in the winter that the Soviets had launched a major airborne assault, but previous drops had been of doubtful success because they had been much deeper in the German rear and lacked any immediate operational significance. One major operation in December saw some 3,000 men dropped near Viaz'ma but was what one German veteran called an "amateurishly led operation without any visible success."[34] By the afternoon of January 13 Kübler was at his wit's end, but Greiffenberg at Army Group Center assured him that Kluge was doing everything in his power to gain Hitler's consent.[35] No record of Kluge's conversations with Hitler exist, but with Fourth Army so imperiled, even Hitler at last agreed to a concession. Yet according to Halder's diary Kluge was only pressing for a withdrawal from the town of Medyn, to which the army chief of staff noted: "Reluctantly the Führer agrees."[36] This, however, was not consistent with the substance of Kluge's instruction to Kübler at 2:45 P.M. the same day. Fourth Army's war diary recorded permission being granted to withdraw from the Schanja position.[37] It appears unlikely this was a simple misunderstanding. In early January, the field marshal had even promised to defy Hitler's order openly if confronted with no alternative to save his former army from destruction.[38] In this instance, however, Hitler's concession provided the necessary cover, or at least enough ambiguity, to begin "redeploying" Fourth Army without seeming to directly contravene the halt order.

As the Red Army was threatening to envelop Kübler's army, to his north Fourth Panzer Army was without a leader for the three days between the morning of January 9, when Hoepner departed, and midday on January 12, when Ruoff finally arrived from V Army Corps. Not only did the army lack a commanding officer, but de Beaulieu's post as chief of staff was also vacant until Röttiger, who had been the chief of staff at XXXXI Army Corps, arrived together with Ruoff.[39] Fortunately, the pressure exerted by the Red Army at Medyn was not equaled on the northern shoulder of the breakthrough, which was the short-lived legacy of Hoepner's fateful withdrawal. On Fourth Panzer Army's other flank, V Army Corps maintained its connection to Reinhardt's panzer army but was struggling to hold its front against determined Soviet attacks. It was the most dangerous sector of Ruoff's new army, which is also why he could not immediately depart to Gzhatsk to assume his new command. The appointment of Ruoff was the first time a nonspecialist rose to command a panzer army, which reflected both the lack of mobility in the army and the OKH's emphasis on the strict fulfillment of orders over any "independence" typical of the panzer commanders. Accordingly, Ruoff dutifully issued an instruction that every position must be held "until further orders from the Führer."[40] His job, however, was made easier by Hitler's approval, at the Wolf's Lair on January 11, of Kluge's request to withdraw Materna's XX and Fahrmbacher's VII Army Corps, which shortened Fourth Panzer Army's line in the south and eased the pressure.[41] In the army's north, Model also requested the withdrawal of his XXXXI Army Corps, claiming that in the event of a sizable Soviet attack he would need time to evacuate 1,000 vehicles over the Rusa River and that this could not be achieved quickly; however Kluge flatly rejected the idea.[42]

On January 12, the same day Ruoff assumed his new post, V Army Corps was stripped from Fourth Panzer Army and placed under Reinhardt's command. At the same time, Witthöft's XXVII Army Corps, on Reinhardt's left, was also added to Third Panzer Army. Lieutenant-General Wilhelm Wetzel, the new commander of V Army Corps, was in serious trouble, and the hope was that Reinhardt could do more to help prevent another Soviet break-through. Reinhardt claimed that his army was "at its end" because of supply shortages and that he could only dispatch aid to Wetzel's endangered corps if he received more fuel. Strauss promised an airlift of fuel, but Reinhardt took little comfort in this and now inquired about the prospect of a retreat. The reply came that he had to hold until this was no longer possible and then the matter would be referred to Hitler for a decision.[43] It was hardly an encouraging prospect, especially given the doubling of Reinhardt's front line. At the same time, the Third Panzer Army was ordered to give up most of Krüger's 1st Panzer Division to Ninth Army.[44]

Third Panzer Army had been one of Kluge's securer sectors, and now it was struggling simply to hold its line. The war diary of Veiel's 2nd Panzer Division complained on January 12, "The division is convinced that the 'rubber band' cannot be stretched any further."[45] Similarly, Landgraf's 6th Panzer Division, desperately defending in the middle of V Army Corps, reported on the same day, "Line is no longer closed, reserves are no longer available, every new attack of the enemy . . . can bring catastrophe."[46] As one soldier wrote, "It is very easy for the Russians to break through our thin lines . . . In every combat we have two-three men in fighting positions without any communications with neighbors on the right or left."[47] Helmut von Harnack, in his last letter to his mother, wrote on January 13: "We are like the rock in the sea, the cornerstone of the central front."[48]

A report from Model's XXXXI Army Corps made clear that the "pure infantry attacks" could "almost always be defended with high losses of blood for the enemy." The problem for the corps was the Soviet T-34 tanks, which presented "the deciding question for the successful conduct of the defense."[49] Soviet tanks were also the problem for Wetzel's V Army Corps, which on January 13 was attacked by large numbers of infantry with strong armored support. The weakly defended villages of Bolvasovo, Kur'ianovo, and Il'inskoe were all overrun because they lacked antitank defense.[50] As one officer noted, "They drove their T-34 tanks into the villages or close by, and fired upon the houses until one after the other went up in flames. Following the tanks were Russian infantry units, which were usually very strong. It was comparatively easy for them to handle the German troops who were thus 'smoked out' of their strongpoints."[51] Third Panzer Army was receiving the new "red-head" hollow-charge antitank munitions, but there were simply not enough of them, so the artillery alone could act in a direct support role to combat Soviet tanks. As one gunner noted:

> Ivan was using this foul weather to launch one of his heaviest attacks, supported by T-34 tanks. Our front line was in great danger of being penetrated. We knew what that meant for us. Our fear of the infantry being overrun and the realization that we would be no match for Ivan's infantry made us work like devils. Shot after shot went out at a distance of less than 3 kilometers. For an hour or so we kept shooting at top speed. Although it was about −40 degrees F., we were sweating. Just as we were about to run out of shells, the word came that Ivan was retreating from his attack, forced back by the combined firepower of our guns and dense rifle and machine-gun fire of the infantry. The snow in front of our line was dotted with black dots— dead Russians. But not for long; the fierce snowdrifts soon covered all evidence of combat and made the area look very innocent . . . Their forceful attacks were repeated day after day and our ability to resist faded slowly but surely. I was counting the days till the certain end would come for, with no reinforcements coming up, how could we ever survive this?[52]

For the men in the infantry the lack of antitank weaponry put them in an even worse predicament. Otto Bense recalled: "When tanks approach, if you see them coming, what can you do? You feel helpless. You're confronting a mechanical monster. All it knows is how to kill . . . Either the tanks drive past or you've had it."[53] Even Reinhardt observed in his diary, "T-34 very helpful to the Russians."[54]

With a new Soviet breakthrough threatening Wetzel's V Army Corps, Reinhardt had become convinced that a strategic withdrawal was necessary to forestall yet another crisis in Army Group Center. If V Army Corps' front split, the link between Reinhardt and Ruoff would be broken, meaning every army in Kluge's army group would be fighting with at least one open flank.

As it was, Schmidt's northern flank, Kübler's northern and southern flanks, Ruoff's southern flank, and Strauss's front was split in the middle west of Rzhev. Withdrawal, as the only reasonable option, was patently obvious to all but Hitler. As the situation at the front deteriorated on January 14, Reinhardt, whose army was subordinate to Strauss, pleaded for authorization to withdraw, but the commander of the Ninth Army was unwilling to allow it, however much he may have agreed with the idea.[55]

Ninth Army was itself in a state of crisis second only to Fourth Army's. By January 9 Strauss was pressing for the same "large solution" that Kluge staunchly advocated. To both Army Group Center and the OKH, Strauss made his point in the most emphatic terms: "The Fourth Army, Fourth Panzer Army, Third Panzer Army and Ninth Army are double-enveloped. The absolutely last opportunity to prevent their destruction is to take them into the Gzhatsk-Volga position [the Königsberg Line] which may free enough strength to eliminate the northern arm of the envelopment west of Rzhev." It was the "last minute" for the army group.[56] By January 10 the army estimated that two or three enemy divisions were operating twenty kilometers southwest of Rzhev with an imminent danger posed to the vital Viaz'ma-Rzhev rail line. The mobile elements of Krüger's 1st Panzer Division were ordered west to help protect the line, but there was nothing to stop the southward advance of Soviet forces, and with more Red Army units pouring into the breach, Strauss could see that the road to Viaz'ma stood largely open. On January 13, he reported to Army Group Center that a retreat to the Königsberg Line was supported by his chief of staff, operations officer, and quartermaster-general, as well as Reinhardt's command.[57] Yet no matter how dire the report, or how universal the support for retreat, day after day passed with no response from the high command to the gradual strangulation of Army Group Center. The tormenting circumstance placed an enormous strain on the nerves of the commanders and encouraged further acts of disobedience.

When Reinhardt pleaded to Strauss for permission to withdraw on January 14 and was rebuffed, the panzer commander indignantly declared "that he himself would then give the order to withdraw." Strauss expressly forbade such an action and dutifully reminded Reinhardt that any retreat first required Hitler's authorization.[58] Given the recent example of Hoepner's dismissal, Reinhardt could hardly have been under any illusions as to the consequences of giving such an order, but for Reinhardt as for other senior commanders, the preservation of their forces as well as a genuine sense of responsibility to the long-suffering troops made even career-ending moves thinkable. Fuming at the inaction, Reinhardt wrote accusingly in his diary: "Has nobody the courage [to act] before it is too late?" Still agitated and restless for some kind of action, Reinhardt called Kluge, but unlike Strauss, the field marshal was "very nice" and soothed his concerns, even to the point of assuring him that the "decision will finally come for us!"[59] Whether Kluge actually believed this cannot be known, but by carrot or stick he was determined to hold his armies in place and await Hitler's decision.

At the very least Kluge must have been heartened by the fact that senior members of Hitler's military staff as well as the OKH were at last pulling in the same direction. A simple glance at Army Group Center's map provided indisputable evidence that Kluge's "large solution" was not simply the best solution, but the only one available to avert an impending collapse of the front. As Halder noted in his diary on January 14, "The general situation is such that it can no longer be held." He then added: "The Führer realizes the necessity of pulling back, but makes no decision. This kind of leadership can only lead to the annihilation of the army."[60] Hitler's inability to accept retreat, even when it was so obviously in the army group's best interest, reveals his crude grasp of military strategy. A more flexible approach to withdrawals would have saved thousands of German casualties and probably inflicted many more on the enemy. Yet Hitler could not get beyond equating retreat with defeat, which did not necessarily follow, especially when operating in the strategic depth of Russia. Indeed, preventing the retreat was inextricably leading to the precise result the dictator wanted to avoid.

While Hitler wrestled with what should have been an elementary decision, the men at the front endured confusion and turmoil. On January 14 Gerhardt Linke wrote in his diary: "We do not know yet what will happen, whether we shall remain in this place or move elsewhere. And there is no one who can tell us. What we need is a clear line and a definite decision. As it is we are in a very bad fix . . . Today we are ordered to do one thing, tomorrow another. Instructions are annulled or modified shortly after they are issued and new measures adopted."[61] The changing orders no doubt reflected the fluid situation at the front, but also the absence of any German planning or strategy. Yet if Hitler was frustrated by the inability of his forces to hold the line, Stalin was similarly irritated at the lack of progress by the Red Army.

On January 11 an uncompromising directive was issued to the Kalinin Front, which made clear Stalin's dissatisfaction: "Seize control of Rzhev on January 11 or in no case later than January 12 . . . The *Stavka* recommends for this purpose the use of all available artillery, mortar and aviation in the area to hammer the city of Rzhev, not stopping short of serious destruction of the city."[62] The Red Army would not be successful in these or any other attacks with Rzhev as their goal; the Germans would hold the town until it was given up in March 1943.[63] Such an achievement underlines a fundamental point: the Germans could not defend everywhere on the long stretches of front, but when concentrated and properly resourced, as they were around Rzhev, the enduring disparity in professionalism between the Red Army and the Wehrmacht ensured they were as dominant in the defense as they were on the attack. Heinz Heppermann noted in a letter on January 12 after defending against the Soviet offensive north of Rzhev as part of the 6th Infantry Division: "Little by little the front freezes. The Russian gradually notes the futility of his incessant frontal assaults, bloody-high losses force him to more economical combat."[64] Likewise, Heinrich Haape, who served in the same division, wrote, "Next day, January 13 . . . the attacks were resumed. The enemy left more than 300 dead in front of our positions, while our casualties were 41 . . . It was inevitable that the Russian losses should be ten-fold our own, for we were firing from prepared positions, whereas the Russians were every time advancing against our guns across the open snow." Haape then referred to two more attacks on January 14 before noting that 250 Soviet corpses were removed from in front of their position in order to clear the field of fire. After further attacks on January 15 he noted: "We had too much work and were too utterly weary to clear the 400 Russian corpses from in front of our positions when dawn broke to herald January 16."[65]

Even in the peak periods of the Soviet winter offensive, it is remarkable just how aggressive the German army remained, not for the sake of seizing ground, but as a preemptive measure to disrupt and diminish Soviet concentrations. Thus, no matter how weakened their forces were, German commanders continually ordered short, sharp, local attacks at perceived weak spots in the Soviet line. As soon as Krüger's 1st Panzer Division arrived west of Rzhev, it was immediately put to work in just such an "active defense" role, and its war diary noted the results: "The past use of an attacking defense, which has led to great success was maintained for 15.1 . . . 250 dead Russians were counted in the evening hours."[66] Likewise, on January 12 Colonel Friedrich Weber's 256th Infantry Division, fighting northwest of Rzhev, dispatched two attack groups; one caught a Soviet battalion moving up to the line near the village of Korostelevo and sent it reeling back with heavy losses, and the other attacked the village of Bogorodino and annihilated an enemy concentration.[67] Such an offensive mentality was seen throughout Army Group Center, even in the hardest pressed sectors of Fourth Army. On January 11 Loeper's 10th Motorized Infantry Division reported that "very weak elements" of its right wing "showed again that an attack continually brings success." In this instance, the attack resulted in 100 dead Soviets and the capture of 150 horses, while the colonel commanding the mission summed up his report with the words: "There is only one salvation: Attack!"[68]

Local German successes, whether on the defensive or the offensive, had bought Army Group Center time, but they could not solve the problem of the armies' open flanks or the operational-scale envelopments without decisive action from above. Even once retreat had been authorized, as in the case of Fourth Army, successfully enacting a withdrawal under constant enemy pressure and in the middle of winter was no easy task. Gaining permission to retreat would not be the magic solution to Kübler's problems, just allow the prospect to live and fight another day. As the army's war diary noted on January 15, "even with respect to the withdrawal, the Fourth Army's situation remains critical." The rearward marches were taking place at a slow pace, in part because of the eighty centimeters of snow on the ground, but also, they were only happening at night to ensure as much security as possible. As a consequence, each march covered only between five and ten kilometers of ground, but it was progress, which every day meant shorter lines and better concentration.[69] Whatever the overall benefits, even the short distances were sometimes extremely difficult for the men to endure. As Eberhard T. wrote on January 13: "The retreat in this savage cold was the worst and most awful time I have ever experienced."[70]

By the afternoon of January 15 even Hitler could no longer ignore Army Group Center's situation and finally relented in favor of Kluge's "large solution." It may have been Hitler's decision, but it was Kluge's victory. The order was clearly given reluctantly and was even characterized as an "agreement in principle," but agreement it was.[71] As the war diary of Third Panzer Army stated: "A sigh of relief swept the whole front."[72] Likewise, the Ninth Army's war diary noted: "'Königsberg Line' is approved. This long-awaited decision is accepted by the army with great relief. It finally gives the army the opportunity to <u>lead</u> and to control the extremely critical situation with purposeful measures."[73] Hitler's order ensured some units would pull back between sixty and seventy-five kilometers to a new "winter line" that would shorten Army Group Center's front by about 100 kilometers. As Hitler's order read:

> Since it has not been possible to close the gaps to the north of Medyn and to the west of Rzhev, I grant the request of the Commander-in-Chief of Army Group Centre to withdraw the front of the Fourth Army, the Third and Fourth Panzer Armies to the line east of Yukhnov—east of Gzhatsk—east of Zubtsov [eighteen kilometers southeast of Rzhev]. The resistance line should be placed so that the Yukhnov-Gzhatsk-Zubtsov road, serving as a link behind the front, remains out of reach of enemy weapons.[74]

If Hitler suspected he was giving in to his generals, he was not about to make the concession without some demands of his own. He wanted the enemy breakthrough west of Rzhev sealed and the gap north of Medyn closed. Moreover, Fourth Army had to keep the road from Roslavl to Yukhov open, and the Second Panzer Army had to relieve Suchinitschi. Whatever Hitler demanded, Kluge was happy on this day to oblige. His patient, and sometimes not so patient, management of the crisis had seen the army group through its most harrowing ordeal to date. Of course, the Red Army was still hammering away, but the anvil Hitler had imposed was now gone, allowing

Army Group Center a vital breathing space, while the front shortened and supplies as well as reinforcements arriving at Rzhev and Viaz'ma were closer to hand. That Hitler had been compelled to relent and overcome his aversion to any indication of "weakness" was clear from the conclusion to his order: "It is the first time in this war that I have given the order to withdraw a larger section of the front. I expect that this retreat will be completed in a manner that is worthy of the German Army. The troops' feeling of superiority over the enemy and their fanatical will to do him the greatest possible damage must also prevail during the retreat."[75]

Army Group Center was not yet saved, but it was granted an essential reprieve. Not only was the army group able to reestablish itself in a new, stronger line, but also the halt order, which had never been fully observed anyway, was for the time being suspended, and senior commanders at the front were for the most part back in control of their day-to-day operations. Yet the degree to which German commanders manipulated, deceived, selectively interpreted, ignored, and outright refused Hitler's halt order was a major factor in Army Group Center's survival. Moreover, a revised understanding of the commanders' responses to the halt order offers a new perspective on the supposed obedience and rigidity of the German army. In some respects, we should not be surprised at this, given that recent research into the army's participation in criminal activity in the east has found similar conclusions. As David Wildermuth has concluded:

> The study of frontline commanders in the war of annihilation
> provides valuable insight into how Nazi war aims were received
> and implemented. The complex picture we receive cautions against
> equating the issue of an order with its execution. Orders from
> above were often modified to fit the local conditions as well as
> the perspectives and priorities of the general entrusted with their
> execution. Occasionally, these orders could also be openly challenged
> or quietly ignored.[76]

Such duplicity at the front was not entirely unknown within the regime. The culture of the army, especially on the Eastern Front, remained insular and exclusive. Even the army's own high command (the OKH) was treated as a separate entity with no involvement in Army Group Center's subversion, despite Hitler's misplaced accusations in early January of its leading the opposition to his orders. Indeed, while Hitler and his high command knew there were issues surrounding the implementation of orders in the east, they had no idea of how ubiquitous the deceit was or how purposefully it was being conducted. On January 20 Goebbels received a report from Professor Karl Brandt, who had recently completed a tour of inspection of the Eastern Front and was dumbfounded by the divergence between army orders and regulations and the practical realities. Brandt's report was mainly associated with the treatment of the army's wounded, but Goebbels fumed in his diary at the general inability of the army command to ensure that their orders were carried out precisely. As Goebbels wrote:

> The desk generals in Berlin are not even worth one ounce of black powder.[77] Their war consisted only of writing paper. The worn-out generals at home have no real understanding of modern warfare. Their cardinal mistake is that they do not follow up on the orders they give, but rather believe that when they give an order it will be carried out. That is a fundamental mistake. Our military operation in the east is today so heavily burdened and constrained, that one must be informed as to the exact execution of an order; otherwise one here can experience the most dreadful disappointments.[78]

In the case of Hitler's halt order there would have been a lot more than disappointment if the true extent of the army's insubordination was known. Yet the army's defiance was no act of resistance to Hitler or his regime, but rather one of pure self-interest, which also served the wider goals of Nazi Germany by preserving the most important army group fighting in the east.

With the ability to maneuver back in the hands of the commanders at the front, the opportunity to deal with the Soviet winter offensive received an incalculable boost both psychologically and operationally. The Soviet attacks, though far from over, no longer shocked and surprised, while their heavy losses were making it hard for them to maintain momentum. The winter was half over, and for all their suffering, the bulk of Army Group Center's men had survived and were increasingly able to look upon the approaching spring as a source of hope and deliverance. The Red Army had been stopped on the Oka-Zusha Line in the south; the hope now was that the Königsberg Line would function as a similar bulwark in the north.

18.

LONELY FRONT

Embattled Homeland

The men of Army Group Center spent as much of the winter as possible indoors, and in addition to a wide range of hobbies, many pursued sexual gratification. For a sizable percentage occupying abandoned villages or isolated sections of the line, there was simply no opportunity for contact with women. In such instances men could either abstain from sexual activity or were limited to masturbation. Pornography circulated on the Eastern Front, a lot of it acquired in France before the men were transferred to the east. Rick Holz wrote openly of his sexual naivete, which was probably typical of many young men at that time. As he noted: "Despite one or two horrid if unfruitful experiences I'd had in Danzig's red-light district, my curiosity was still very much alive."[1] Indeed, his curiosity was fired by the pornography he owned. "Fifty-two cards, all of them portraying fornicating men and women, black and white and brindle, in seemingly impossible positions on each of the glossy cards—filthy, obscene, disgusting, despicable, deplorable, detestable, vile, lewd and very, very interesting."[2] A questionable Soviet propaganda piece written by Ilya Ehrenburg claimed that the wallets and pockets of captured Germans were "bulging with indecent postcards, interspersed with family photographs."[3] Such material no doubt served a purpose for the many young men, and according to Willy Peter Reese, masturbation was commonplace among his comrades, which says as much about the act itself as the fact that he was aware of their doing it. As he wrote in his journal: "Only a few sought intimacy, most drugged themselves with superficialities, with gambling, cruelty, hatred, or they masturbated."[4]

While masturbation may have been the most immediate sexual outlet, the desire for physical intimacy at the front also resulted in homosexual acts, either as genuine displays of affection or simply to satisfy sexual impulses. Solomon Perel, a German teenager acting as a Russian translator in the 12th Panzer Division, recalled: "Several soldiers discovered a deserted peasant cottage and turned its large kitchen, which had a huge stove, into a bathroom. Soon the water in the kettles was boiling and the kitchen quickly filled with clouds of steam and the singing of soldiers soaking in the tubs. They bathed together, in groups."[5] Such accounts do not necessarily suggest anything sexual, but when Perel sought to bathe alone his account continued: "Before I knew what was happening, a pair of strong arms grabbed me from behind. I felt a naked body pressing against me . . . As a man's erect penis tried to enter me, I jumped as if a snake had bitten me."[6] Helmut Günther also wrote suggestively of his bathing experiences: "A giant kettle boiling water hung over the fire. Soon we were standing buck naked in the room and scrubbing each other from head to toe. Man, that felt good!"[7]

Throughout the Wehrmacht some 370 men were charged with having committed homosexual practices in the last quarter of 1941, and this figure rose slightly to 401 in the first three months of 1942. While the reported instances of homosexuality may have been low, research by Geoffrey Giles suggests that the great majority of cases were consensual and private. Furthermore, if such behavior was discovered it was most likely either ignored (as the men may have been good comrades) or dealt with within the unit and therefore did not result in formal charges.[8] Even in those cases that were formally prosecuted the sentence could be reduced by claiming the involvement of alcohol or by pleading the consequences of enforced abstinence. The majority of sentences for these first-time offenders were partially or fully suspended, with a period of parole served at the front. For those who persisted in homosexual behavior and were documented as repeat offenders, the consequences were more severe, typically with periods of incarceration. This was especially true after the winter of 1941–1942, with the courts citing the "increasing duration of the war, which increases the danger of these types of offenses." Yet it was not until May 1943 that soldiers convicted as "incorrigible homosexuals" were dismissed from service, turned over to the Gestapo, and typically sent to a concentration camp.[9] Homosexuality in Himmler's SS was a much more serious offense. It was seen as a betrayal of its honor code, and accordingly, from November 1941, any same-sex act was to be punished by death.[10]

While sexual options at the front were limited, many men wished to remain faithful to wives and girlfriends and simply accepted a prolonged period of abstinence. Others opposed having sexual relations in Russia on racial grounds. Fired by Nazi ideology these men evinced disgust at the prospect of sexual encounters with Slavic women. Reacting to enemy propaganda about the treatment of Soviet people under German rule, Wilhelm Prüller wrote in his diary: "Do I need to repeat that not one German soldier has even touched a Russian woman? That is quite obvious. How can they believe over there that we are not aware what German honor, morals and discipline mean in this respect? It is simply an impertinence to lie that we have anything to do with these basically filthy sluts."[11]

Whether out of fidelity or ideology, soldiers practiced abstinence for a range of reasons. Others maintained that they experienced a noticeable reduction in their sexual drive, which may have been a result of the stresses of war, especially given the casualty rates on the Eastern Front. As William Lubbeck wrote: "What was more difficult to explain was the widespread absence of a strong urge to have sexual relations with women as would be normal among a group of young males. Naturally, the rumor mill provided an answer: our cooks were under secret orders to mix an agent into our food that chemically suppressed our sex drives."[12] Lubbeck went on to say that he did not actually believe such a preposterous rumor, and the weight of evidence suggests a desire for sexual fulfillment was very much alive for many of the men in the east. Indeed, in contrast to others who have studied the sexual behavior of men in frontline wartime conditions and concluded men become "de-sexed" and even impotent by the strain and fatigue of war, Geoffrey Giles has argued this was not the case for members of the Wehrmacht.[13]

The opportunity for sexual liaison in the winter of 1941–1942 was varied, but in some cases the men were sharing peasant houses with women and teenage girls. Settlements in Army Group Center's rear area had only a fraction of their prewar male population. The men had either been drafted by the Red Army or had fled their villages and towns to escape German rule. Gomel, for example, had been reduced in size by two-thirds, with women, children, and the elderly making up the vast majority of those remaining.[14] The lines occupied by Army Group Center in December and January were only conquered in October or November, meaning there was an even higher probability that the Russian men had been drafted or fled to avoid German work details. The soldiers typically enjoyed finding civilians quartered in their zone of occupation because, in addition to any sexual opportunities, it relieved them of many menial tasks. As one man noted during the final stage of the German advance in November 1941: "Sometimes we are lucky. There are still civilians. I get the women right away. They have to sew my buttons, warm water, wash . . . and they like to do it."[15]

Out of concern about the degree of "fraternization" with Soviet women, which the OKW feared would foster sympathy for the population and encourage sexual encounters, the troops were ordered to evict all inhabitants of houses used for the accommodation of soldiers. To assist in this, Soviet women were increasingly portrayed as enemy spies who would take advantage of unsuspecting German men. An order from Nehring's 18th Panzer Division described most women as "Jewish broads" (*Judenweiber*) whose origins could not be known. The implication was clear: Soviet women were tainted and could not be trusted. The Economic Unit East (*Wirtschaftsstab*

Ost) warned its soldiers to treat female workers with "strict reserve" and in March 1942 declared: "Drinking together, intimate approaches to local women and girls, dancing with them, and granting trips in official vehicles is prohibited in any circumstances."[16]

Sometimes for security reasons or simply owing to the lack of accommodation, civilians were ordered away from German-occupied settlements, but as Wilhelm Prüller wrote such orders were quietly ignored. Referring to one such command, Prüller noted in his diary, "Well, that order has been in effect a long while, but the inhabitants always returned, we quietly allowed this." Prüller ranted about the honor of German men having nothing to do sexually with Russian women, then contradicted himself by explaining why, in part, these civilians were discreetly allowed back into his unit's zone. As the diary continued: "for they heat for us, fetch water, wash for us, even bring milk from the two cows—well, and after all among the 230 men there are some who can't stand it without having female flesh about, even if it's Russian flesh."[17] Russian women were therefore viewed as "useful" either in the performance of domestic labor or for sexual gratification.

Sexual intercourse between German troops and Soviet women may have been prohibited by army regulations, but punishments for the troops, if even deemed necessary, were not sufficient to prevent further offenses. One German security report from Army Group Center in the summer of 1942 noted that there was frequent sexual contact between the soldiers and local women, while the law forbidding this was "hardly paid attention to." Instead, the report noted: "The soldiers say things like 'better three days on the construction site than forgoing pleasure.'"[18]

Of course, there were instances of German soldiers pursuing genuine romantic relationships based on more than sexual gratification. But unlike casual encounters, these were viewed much more seriously and were very difficult to maintain. One *Oberscharführer* (equivalent to a sergeant) in the SS was demoted all the way down to *Schütze* (private) because he was having a relationship with a local woman.[19] Henry Metelmann fell in love with a woman whom he knew was working with local partisans. As Metelmann observed: "A German soldier, a Russian partisan! What more deadly enemies could there be! If Anna and I could love, was there not hope for the world?"[20]

In another instance, an army captain named Willi Schulz fell in love with Ilse Stein, a Jew in the Minsk ghetto. Rather than be separated, Schulz opted to join the partisans with her and, in doing so, stole a truck filled with twenty-four Jews.[21] At the very least, such extreme acts reveal the heartfelt affection felt at times by German soldiers, but they also tell us something about the choices they were forced to make for their love.

Most sexual encounters, however, were not based on mutual affections, but rather constituted sexual coercion or exploitation. Desperate poverty in rural parts of the Soviet Union preceded Operation Barbarossa, but the resultant destruction as well as ruthless German requisitioning greatly exacerbated it. Consequently, sexual favors became an obvious source of barter for food or shelter. As William Lubbeck noted:

> There were other German troops in my regiment who exploited the dire Russian food situation for sexual gratification. Putting a loaf of bread under their arm, these men would head for a certain area a couple of miles behind the front where there were hungry Russian women or girls who would willingly exchange sexual favors for food . . . Most German officers and troops disapproved of such behavior, but I knew of no one who was reprimanded or punished for engaging in this type of act.[22]

Werner Adamczyk remarked on the same phenomena, writing: "Some of them had babies, but they did not have enough food to feed themselves or their young. So, for a loaf of bread, one could have a good night with them. Some of my comrades took advantage of the women's plight; they had their good night."[23] Paul Stresemann told an interviewer after the war of the desperate plight that Soviet civilians endured and how the children "suffered terribly." He then continued: "I am sure that in some cases, where discipline was slack, they [Soviet women] did succeed in their quest to become barrack-room whores, travelling concealed in some wagon for the soldiers' use."[24] In spite of the clear circumstances under which such exploitation was taking place, this was not the only form of victimization these women suffered. Underground Soviet forces seeing their behavior as a form of collaboration recommended that they should be "boycotted or spurned."[25]

Alongside the rampant exploitation of women for sexual favors there is also evidence that Germans played on their dominant positions, and at times fearsome reputations, as a form of coercion. A revealing extract from Benno Zieser's memoir recounts his treatment of a Russian girl paid to do washing for him and his friends:

> I gripped her wrists so hard that she cried out. Her big eyes pleaded, full of fear. It was a young face, broad cheekbones, sharply defined, regular features. She whispered something in her language, I have no idea what.
>
> "*Komm,*" I said, then I shouted it; "*Komm!*"
>
> There was a terribly confused smile, but the fear had gone out of her eyes. Then suddenly she nodded and still smiling, repeated my word—"Come!"
>
> When deep in the night I got that washing back to camp I had a head as if I had been on the ran-tan all night.[26]

At another point in his memoir Zieser noted how a German billeting officer named Kovak assigned his friends the best Russian houses and "always took note of where young skirts were to be found." As Zieser then observed, "Wouldn't we too like a turn?"[27]

Explaining such behavior, Sönke Neitzel and Harald Welzer, who analyzed secretly recorded conversations of German soldiers in American captivity and reconstructed their worldview, revealed a number of very different frames of reference. In their conversations, the men openly discussed all manner of criminal behavior, including the sexual abuse of women, but because they did not self-identify as war criminals, and they did not expect their listener would either, they were uninhibited in their stories. As Neitzel and Welzer concluded, "Stories about shooting, raping, and robbing are commonplace within the war stories. Rarely do they occasion analysis, moral objections, or disagreements. As brutal as they may be, the conversations proceed harmoniously. The soldiers understand one another."[28] Thomas Kühne makes a similar point, emphasizing that hormonal desires were far from the only driving force. Strong social pressures of the group, which, far from rejecting or admonishing a man for unacceptable behavior, in fact celebrated and re-inforced his status as someone who could have any woman he wanted. As Kühne explained: "It was not only a matter of sexual needs. At least as im-portant was the ability to boast of sexual adventures to your circle of com-rades . . . The moral grammar of comradeship always obeyed the same rule: anything was allowed which the group liked, i.e. anything which enriched and intensified its social life."[29] Seen in this light, acts of sexual exploita-tion or coercion provoked no shame or sense of wrongdoing within the aver-age soldier's group; indeed even outright criminal behavior toward women could be openly discussed and celebrated.

A soldier by the name of Müller told his comrades of seeing "extraordi-narily lovely girls" being employed by German authorities to make a road. Müller then continued his story: "We drove past, simply pulled them into the armored car, raped them, and threw them out again. And did they curse!"[30] For the audience as well as Müller, the idea of criminal abuse was not a con-cern; it was rather the ability of the men to act entirely in their own interests and gain what they set out to achieve. The extent to which such a legally and morally deficient worldview pervaded the thinking of German soldiers in the Second World War is startling and extended well beyond sexual crimes. In another of the recorded conversations, a man named Reimbold told his as-sembled companions: "We got hold of a female spy who was running around the area. We hit her on the noggin with a stick and then flayed her behind with an unsheathed bayonet. Then we fucked her, threw her out, shot at her and, while she was lying on her back, lobbed grenades. Every time we got one close, she screamed. In the end, she died, and we threw her body away."

At least in this instance one member of Reimbold's audience did com-plain, standing up and insisting: "Gentlemen, this goes too far." When he later recounted the episode, the disgusted man explained: "And imagine this! There were eight German officers sitting at the table with me all laughing their heads off. I couldn't stand it."[31]

Given the widespread culture of acceptance, and even encouragement, it is not surprising that the army's hierarchy and legal processes displayed a strong degree of tolerance even when sexual violence was reported. On the evening of December 24–25, 1941, three men of the 253rd Infantry Division entered the home of a Russian woman and raped and physically abused her in front of her fourteen-year-old son. The men were arrested, tried, and sentenced, but two of them had their fifteen-month imprisonment quashed on the basis of their "long sexual abstinence" and the judge's opinion that the female victim would experience "no lasting damage or emotional stresses."[32] Another military judge, in sentencing a soldier from the 7th Panzer Division who was convicted of "coercion to commit sexual offence" told the court:

> The accused must be punished under §176 clause 1 of German law for the crime of sexual assault. The court-martial has, however, refrained from imposing a term in prison on account of mitigating circumstances, also taking into consideration the fact the accused is in other respects a decent soldier, who has confessed to his crime and fulfilled his duty in action, both here and on the western front, to complete satisfaction. A further extenuating circumstance, which must be taken into consideration, is the fact that the severe punishment set out in §176 of German law is justified by the German conception of the sexual honor of German women, but that such severe punishment cannot be applied when—as in the present case—the injured party belongs to a people for whom the concept of woman's sexual honor has more or less entirely disappeared. The decisive consideration for imposing the punishment was first and foremost the serious violation of discipline of which the accused is guilty, by virtue of his committing this crime, and the serious damage to the reputation of the German Wehrmacht that resulted from his crime.[33]

Thus, according to the judge, the only real victims were the Wehrmacht's good name and the violation of its system of discipline. The "injured party," by contrast, had no sexual honor to violate because she was not German.

As in most military codes of law, rape in the Wehrmacht was officially a crime under the classification of "crimes and offenses against morality." Yet in an organization in which 17 million German men served during the war, only 5,300 personnel were ever charged with sexual crimes in the years between 1939 and 1944. In fact, the number of convictions peaked in 1940 and then went into decline until 1943. The notorious Barbarossa Jurisdiction Decree of May 1941, which exempted German soldiers from prosecution for crimes committed in the Soviet Union, effectively barred the prosecution of most sexual offensives even though this decree categorized "serious actions that are caused by a lack of sexual restraint" as punishable offenses. In practice, the main criteria that prompted criminal proceeding against a soldier in the Wehrmacht was the perceived threat to military discipline (*Manneszucht*), which was the most important edict of German military life. In the winter of 1941–1942, however, sexual crimes were seldom perceived as a threat to discipline, and the lack of sexual restraint was for many officers a "natural" outcome of the absence of brothels in the east.[34]

The only area of apparent inconsistency in the application of German military law was with regard to Soviet Jews. On the one hand, the general contempt for Jews opened them to all manner of abuse, including sexual assault; on the other hand, their degraded status raised the prospect that raping them constituted "race defilement" (*Rassenschande*). As a result, there is evidence that suggests that some of the men who raped Jews then sought to cover their crime by murdering the victim. Yet recent studies have shown that German military authorities rarely prosecuted cases of "race defilement," and even in those instances when they did, the ruling usually reflected sympathy for the perpetrator.[35] Even the men of the SS *Einsatzgruppen* (mobile killing groups), who were charged with the elimination of all Soviet Jews, were known to have sometimes sexually abused their victims, and in the case of *Sonderkommando* 10a, one report noted they "habitually raped Jewish women to the point where they fell unconscious."[36]

With such legal impunity, the east became what Christoph Rass dubbed a "vast lawless area," and sexual crimes were one of the most common forms of criminality.[37] Take Erich Heyse's seemingly incidental note in his diary: "I only had one woman today."[38] Similarly, a survivor of the German occupation of Novogrudok recalled a German doctor who had been a "specialist" in entering homes and raping women.[39] Nor was the propensity for German sex crimes confined to females. Twenty-three-year-old Lieutenant Rudoft T. forced a fifteen-year-old Russian youth, Alexander L., to perform oral sex on him in a farm building, while in another instance a German soldier slept almost nightly with a sixteen-year-old Russian kitchen helper and was known to have performed a number of sex acts on him.[40]

Already in the summer of 1940 Brauchitsch saw the repressed sexuality of German soldiers in occupied France as a central problem confronting the army. He believed that, depending upon the individual disposition, sexual "tension and crisis" would result when no suitable heterosexual possibilities existed. This he concluded threatened to result in cases of sexual violence or homosexual practices. As neither of these was desirable, he permitted the establishment of brothels in France "for German soldiers under medical control."[41] The invasion of the Soviet Union did not, however, initially allow for similar sexual freedoms, and it would not be until February 1942, eight months after the beginning of the war in the east, that military brothels in the east were beginning to be officially established. Officials hoped these would cut down on instances of sexually transmitted diseases as well as the perceived danger of men sharing sensitive information with Soviet female spies. There was also a desire on the part of the German high command to prevent "unwanted bastards" in which "Germany [had] no interest."[42]

In France and other occupied countries in Western Europe military brothels were often adapted from preexisting establishments and therefore operated with "experienced" staff. This was not the case in the east, where the Wehrmacht set up entirely new brothels and had to find women to work in them. Often this was done by force or by exploiting the poverty of the most destitute women. In some cases, the women were given a choice between working in a military brothel or being sent as a slave laborer to Germany.[43] Most of the women were not considered to be of Aryan heritage, although their use was condoned even for Germany's supposed racial elite in the SS. In 1942 Himmler personally gave his approval for sexual intercourse with "ethnically alien women" because it allegedly occurred outside the context of personal attachment and reproduction.[44] There is some evidence that more "racially desirable" women, for example Dutch prostitutes, were also brought to the east to help staff the brothels, but their numbers cannot have been large.[45] The one standard that was insisted upon was that Jewish women were strictly forbidden from military brothels.[46] In total it has been estimated that at least 500 German military brothels operated throughout Nazi-occupied Europe, with a conservative figure of some 50,000 women working in them, although the numbers were probably much higher.[47]

Once brothels became officially sanctioned in the east, their use was not just condoned; it was actively encouraged. Brothels were one of the few military-backed institutions in the east devoted to the pleasure of the men. Accordingly, although attendance is impossible to judge, they were clearly a rare source of amusement. Data from brothels visited by German soldiers in France in August 1940 showed that 60 percent of the men were married fathers, indicating that it was by no means just single young men who were attracted to them.[48] Ilse Schmidt, part of the female auxiliary personnel serving with the Wehrmacht, recalled an announcement by a colonel that his men should join him at a newly opened brothel.[49] Even before arriving in the Soviet Union, Rick Holz wrote of how his commanding officer told his unit: "If a pretty girl on the street invites you to screw her, don't. If you're lucky she'll give you VD. If you're unlucky she'll bury a knife in your back. Don't take unnecessary risks. Sex in enemy territory is hazardous. That's why the army provides a brothel for you. All the whores are young, pretty and under doctors' supervision."[50] Assessing the actual risk of female spies is impossible given that the true motives of consenting women cannot always be known, but there are numerous instances of female spies being hanged or shot, although this sometimes took place on the flimsiest of evidence. Heinrich Haape witnessed the hanging of two young women who admitted to being Communist spies. As Haape observed: "With glowing hearts they were ready in the name of communism to sacrifice their bodies to our sex-starved troops and their lives to the hangman's noose. Many a German soldier—and no doubt many an officer—unwittingly gave away information in the warmth of a bunk on top of a Russian oven."[51]

Whatever the real risk of spying, venereal disease was a far more common problem and one that could be more readily identified. The army high command distributed information sheets warning the troops of the health dangers and then reminding them that "a soldier with venereal disease is not fit for duty. Not being fit for duty for self-induced reasons is unworthy of a German soldier."[52] With or without brothels the men of the *Ostheer* were having sex, and even after brothels were established in the east, doctors in Smolensk recorded a sharp increase in gonorrhea and syphilis between January and June 1942 as more and more local women became infected by German soldiers.[53] With some veracity Soviet propaganda declared at the end of January 1942: "The [German] officers try in vain to check the spread of gonorrhoea, declaring in their orders that this 'hinders the soldiers from serving the Führer'... it has become an invasion of the germs of venereal disease."[54]

German soldiers sought sexual relations for a wide range of reasons; many simply wanted pleasure, escapism, or even genuine love; some no doubt acted out of sheer loneliness and despair; while others took advantage of their dominant role to exert power over Soviet civilians in acts of criminal exploitation. The consequences were profound for the women (and sometimes men) involved, especially since they were only of value so long as they were of "use" to the Germans; Soviet society also showed no understanding for their desperate circumstances or the fact that many were forced into working for the Germans.

Long absences and the prospect of new relationships in the east also affected German women at home who were sometimes, as a result, left abandoned.[55] As one anguished woman wrote her husband, "Why haven't I heard any news from you? You promised me! Have I done something wrong or don't you want to be my partner anymore?... You only need say if the children and I are too much for you."[56] The uncertainty about loved ones centered on the essential question that had dominated thoughts on the home front since June 22, 1941—how much longer would the war in the east last?

Initially, the success of the Wehrmacht's past campaigns, as well as Goebbels's triumphant propaganda, had maintained confidence in a short war lasting only for the summer of 1941. By the end of the autumn, however, serious doubts were surfacing, especially after the Reich's press chief, Otto Dietrich, publicly announced that the war had been "decided" on October 9.[57] Clearly, that had not happened, but even more shocking to the German home front was the completely unexpected crisis that the Soviet winter offensive evoked. Unlike the soldiers at the front, the German population relied on Goebbels's propaganda ministry for information about the war. In early December the Nazi regime hoped to ignore and deflect the bad news in the east by trumpeting the Japanese entry into the war. As Goebbels admitted in his diary on December 10, the outbreak of war between the United States and Japan "suited us psychologically extremely well."[58] The following day he continued: "If now the whole world were to look eastwards, we would be in an extraordinarily embarrassing situation."[59] Fortunately for Goebbels, the SD reports that secretly compiled a picture of German popular opinion confirmed that the new war in the Far East was largely obfuscating Army Group Center's difficulties on the Eastern Front. The December 11 report showed people were fully preoccupied with the news of Japan's attacks in the Pacific, while the December 15 report was dominated by news of Hitler's declaration of war on the United States and the continuing developments in the Far East.[60] Only at the conclusion to the December 15 report was there any hint of alarm at the Soviet attacks beginning near Moscow. "Only the reports that the Soviets were still able to undertake powerful counterattacks with strong forces attracted much attention. In this respect, many of our fellow-citizens again see a confirmation of their assumption that there can still be no question of a slackening of Soviet combat power."[61]

The German people knew about the Red Army's "powerful counterattacks with strong forces" from foreign radio transmissions, which even Goebbels acknowledged were increasingly becoming a supplementary news source for Germans seeking a different perspective on what was going on.[62] As Hermann Jengood wrote on December 25, "In 1941, for the first time, I happened to come across a German show on the BBC, while my grandmother was still working in the kitchen. The sudden contact with this other world seemed to captivate me like a drug. Very soon I became addicted to the English news . . . , which was more credible than German news."[63] Ernst Gerber wrote of an English radio report on December 29 that stated the German army had suffered "a great defeat" in the east and that the front was in a state of "collapse."[64] Even if this was a considerable exaggeration, it sounded more convincing to most people than the German broadcasters, who in the second half of December attempted to report Army Group Center's retreat as a "straightening of the front" (*Frontbegradigungen*).[65] As Kurt Meissner recalled, after hearing such reports at the front, "The foolish exhortations by the propagandists we found absurd and disgusting."[66] Likewise, Hartmut Beermann wrote home that he only occasionally listened to the radio for news about the war in the east because "we know much better what is going on here."[67] The conflicting reports by the English and German news services were evaluated by Mihail Sebastian, a Romanian who followed events closely and kept a detailed diary. On January 7, 1942, he concluded: "In any event, what I am used to calling the psychological pendulum of the war has clearly swung toward London."[68]

The last SD report for 1941 appeared on December 18, and although this confirmed that, in the context of events in the Pacific, there was "only minor" interest in the war on the Eastern Front, one report did attract "strong attention." On December 14 a *Wehrmachtbericht* (a media communiqué authorized by both the Wehrmacht high command and Goebbels's propaganda ministry) stated in reference to the Eastern Front that it was "not the possession of this or that land-strip" that mattered, "but only the fact of keeping the enemy on the bayonet."[69] Clearly, even people who did not listen to foreign broadcasts were able to read between the lines and draw their own conclusions about the fact that a formidable Soviet offensive was under way and that ground was being lost in the east. As research by Jörg Echternkamp suggested, "The more the way the course of the war was presented in the media differed from personal experience, and the more propaganda tied itself up in contradictions . . . , the more did rumors abound on how the war was going."[70] Even more important, the greater the credibility gap, the more people believed rumors, especially when the sources of information (trusted neighbors, field post from the front, etc.) could be clearly identified.[71]

Beyond foreign radio transmissions, the two main alternate sources of information flowing back into Germany as of January 1942 were soldiers wounded in the December fighting and the first wave of field post written after the launch of the Soviet counteroffensive. Such firsthand accounts were treated as almost irrefutable sources of information, especially when they could be "confirmed" by similar stories from neighbors and workmates, who typically had their own family connections providing news. As Siegfried Knappe noted:

> Our losses were never reported at home, but more and more families had sons who had been killed or badly wounded. Slowly, the people managed to get the picture, not from the government, but indirectly

from talking to one another. Strangers in a store or in a line waiting to buy bread or milk would talk to each other. What had happened to my family was not different from what had happened to many others, and now it was becoming apparent to everyone that things were not going well in Russia.[72]

Thus, rumors and hearsay about the war in the east were telling not only a very different story, but also one that most people believed. The damage this did to German morale was made worse by the fact that the people were soon believing things about the Soviet offensive that were simply not true. The SD report for January 5, 1942, noted that people were discussing the "numerous rumors of considerable rearward movements by German troops on all sections of the eastern front."[73] In fact, only limited sections of Army Groups North and South had been forced to withdraw since November (and this would not change much throughout the remainder of the winter), while at this time Army Group Center's front had already stabilized in the south. Yet the rampant rumor mill not only exaggerated the extent of the retreats, but also fabricated their implications. For example, the SD report for January 5 noted that the public incorrectly believed that a Soviet offensive had broken the siege of Leningrad.[74] More worryingly, these kinds of distortions made the sometimes bombastic claims of Allied propaganda appear all the more plausible. British reports on the Red Army's progress from January 12 spoke of fighting on the "Smolensk front," yet this Russian city was still some 200 kilometers west of the nearest Soviet forces.[75]

Once Operation Barbarossa had irrevocably failed, Goebbels struggled to know what message to adopt. Privately he recognized that the progress of the war had sharply diverged from the triumphalist claims of his ministry, but Hitler insisted on exploiting every victory, and Goebbels unquestioningly deferred to the dictator's judgment. It was only in the winter, when the charade of German success in the east was exposed and the ability to counter rumors and enemy propaganda was at an all-time low, that Goebbels belatedly changed course. Accordingly, in January he sought and gained permission from Hitler to have the German press and radio report events from the Eastern Front "somewhat more realistically."[76] He acknowledged the problem of the soldiers' field post undercutting official reports, and because he read the SD reports, he should also have been aware of the alarming false-hoods circulating among the population. Yet he concluded in his diary on January 8, "If we talk more openly about this, we will also avoid the danger that the homeland has a completely different picture from the front than what the front itself experiences every day."[77] It was much too late to "avoid the danger" of erroneous rumors weakening German morale. The fear of the population was not simply that the *Ostheer* was experiencing difficulties in the winter weather or even the fact that it was in retreat, but that some kind of disaster was playing out in the east, which the regime was unsuccessfully attempting to conceal from the people. The Swedish correspondent, Arvid Fredborg, wrote: "So serious was the situation that informed circles in Berlin expected the German front in the center to be smashed up. An atmosphere of catastrophe took hold of the German capital and particularly of the vari-ous government departments."[78] Even Goebbels noted on January 20, 1942, "General defeatism in Berlin government circles."[79]

If "informed circles" could believe the destruction of Army Group Cen-ter was imminent, it is not surprising that everyday Germans held similarly bleak views. Marie Wildomec wrote to a soldier in the east: "Nobody here believes in victory or that the war will end well. They don't believe in any-thing altogether . . . We are winning one victory after another! Ha-ha! Our losses are insignificant! Tee-hee! One must be a fool to believe it. The future is black and uncertain."[80] Ernst Kluge (no relation to the field marshal) de-spairingly wrote of the German military command in early December: "Who would have thought that the Russians would fight so courageously? I don't think anybody. In all probability, even our superior officers are often at a loss what to do."[81] Alfons Berberich was less understanding and openly blamed the high command, writing: "The war is lasting too long and we're not get-ting anywhere in Russia. It's a pity for the many young people who have to lose their lives for the sake of a handful of men in high places."[82] In the con-text of the immediate situation on the Eastern Front, the depths of despair were actually unjustified; Army Group Center was not only withstanding the Soviet offensive—but it was also doing so at huge cost to the Red Army. And with Hitler finally agreeing to Kluge's plea for a general withdrawal, the danger of serious enemy encirclements was greatly reduced. However, if one considers Germany's overall prospects in the global war, which were far harder for everyday people to evaluate realistically, the dejection within the population was entirely justified.

While we may conclude that unchecked rumors, fueled to some degree by Allied propaganda, perpetuated certain falsehoods about the war in the east, Goebbels was always constrained in effectively responding to the crisis in public opinion by his own ideological worldview and deferential submission to Hitler.[83] Accordingly, when assessing the depressed public mood from the latest SD report, which Goebbels described on January 11 as "somewhat more serious than usual," the propaganda minister demonstrated a failure to understand the war at a fundamental military and economic level. Confronted by the pessimism of the German population, which he chose to refer to as "individual voices," Goebbels first set out the legitimate concern people had "about whether it will ever be possible for us to defeat the immeasurably large Russia. For the moment, the people cannot imagine how this is going to happen." He then matter-of-factly provided his own answer without offering any supporting explanation: "We will show them in the next spring and summer."[84] If German mistrust of their official news sources was overcorrecting the problem and transforming the grueling defensive battles into an illusory catastrophe of Napoleonic proportions, it was to no small extent the Nazi regime's own fault. While Goebbels and Hitler stubbornly maintained their belief in a 1942 victory, the population no longer saw how that was possible and increasingly feared the offensive strength of the Red Army. As Arvid Fredborg observed: "Unrest grew among the people . . . and all the literature about [Napoleon's] La Grande Armée suddenly had a marked revival."[85]

The most sensible decision taken to counteract the alarm within the population was to issue a series of *Wehrmachtberichte* with more precise information about where exactly the Eastern Front currently stood. Reports now included general geographic locations such as "eastward of Orel," "in the area of Kaluga," and "eastward of Kharkov." This earned an immediate response, calming some of the more wayward fears and reassuring people, as the January 15 SD report noted "that the withdrawal movements of the German troops were not nearly as great as one would have assumed from the rumors and stories."[86] It marked a turning point in German public opinion for the winter. By January 26 the SD reported a continued recovery in public perceptions concerning the war in the east and growing confidence that the *Ostheer* would in fact hold its current positions.[87]

Goebbels relished the good news, noting in his diary: "The worry about the east is no longer as great as in the past weeks."[88] He believed the German people were becoming "accustomed to the winter war" and could see that the Red Army was not achieving "any significant successes."[89] Perhaps even more important, he felt British claims that German troops were not merely retreating but in open "flight" were undercutting British credibility. Likewise, he depicted their claims of 2 million German dead as "obviously rubbish."[90] By the same token, Soviet propaganda at the end of January was making claims that Goebbels derided as "absolute nonsense." Hitler was said to have fled his headquarters at Smolensk and moved to Minsk to avoid the oncoming Red Army.[91] Apart from the fact that Hitler never had a headquarters in either city, Army Group Center's headquarters, which was based in Smolensk, was never seriously threatened throughout the winter. Having endured the ignominy of setting military objectives that could not be obtained, Goebbels now delighted in crying foul on Soviet claims. As he wrote in his diary on January 27, "The Bolsheviks need such sensational news, as the progress of their operations has not led to the desired goal. In the past few weeks, they have filled the world with a great victory cry . . . without managing to substantiate this victory."[92] Significantly, German public opinion was moving toward agreement, with the last SD report for January 1942 suggesting that the onus was now on the Soviets to cap their offensive with some kind of clear success. As the report for January 30 stated:

> From the heavy defensive battles repeatedly portrayed in the military reports, one sees that the Soviet attacks are increasingly to be regarded as a desperate act, which should lead to a severe bloodletting of the Bolshevik troops. Therefore, the conviction is increasingly taking hold that the Russians can no longer succeed in achieving a decisive success, since they had not managed to achieve it so far.[93]

19

RETREAT AND COUNTERATTACK

Army Group Center Rebounds

U nable to ignore Army Group Center's desperate plight and under tremendous pressure from all sides, on January 15 Hitler gave in to Kluge's "large solution," allowing Kübler, Ruoff, Reinhardt, and Strauss each to withdraw into the Königsberg Line. Ninth Army's war diary expressed the command's "great relief" that they now had "the opportunity to lead and to control the extremely critical situation," yet Strauss's freedom of action was short-lived. Just two hours after Hitler approved plans for retreat, Ninth Army's independence was again decisively compromised from above, but this time by Kluge himself. Schubert's XXIII Army Corps was separated from the bulk of Ninth Army by the Soviet breakthrough west of Rzhev, and Strauss had wanted to concentrate the corps' strength and try to close the gap. Kluge, however, went over Strauss's head, and while allowing a short sixteen-kilometer withdrawal, he commanded Schubert to maintain the length of his front, which stretched some sixty-four kilometers. Strauss was incensed. After all Kluge's complaints about interference from above, he himself was now deciding on the best course of action for Ninth Army and completely bypassing Strauss's headquarters. Strauss reacted by asking to be placed on sick leave.

It is not known whether Strauss intended this as a calculated protest intended to force recognition of his authority or simply reflected his embitterment at Kluge's meddling and constituted the straw that broke the camel's back, especially for a man whose health had not been good.[1] In either case, Kluge, whose faith in Strauss may have already been in decline, did not hesitate to accept Strauss's request, and he was immediately replaced by the young and dynamic Walter Model.[2]

That Model was an entirely different brand of commander was immediately apparent upon his arrival at Ninth Army's headquarters on the morning of January 16. One story from this initial meeting, which may be apocryphal, was that Model insisted upon closing the gap between Schubert's XXIII Army Corps and the remainder of Ninth Army's forces east and south of Rzhev. Upon hearing this a skeptical Lieutenant-Colonel Edmund Blaurock, who served as Ninth Army's operations officer, reportedly inquired: "And what, Herr General, have you brought us for this operation?" To which Model responded sternly: "Myself!"[3] Certainly Model possessed this kind of self-assurance, and even arrogance, which may also explain why he snubbed Strauss during his visit. Beyond whatever operational insights Strauss may have wished to offer his successor, at the very least the former army commander expected Model to observe traditional decorum, which stipulated that Model call upon him as a professional courtesy. Instead, Model, who had been ordered to appear at Kluge's headquarters followed by the Wolf's Lair, made a hurried visit to Ninth Army in which he discussed the situation and plans with Blaurock and the chief of staff, Colonel Hans Krebs, while Strauss awaited Model in another room.[4] Yet Model had no time for tiresome etiquette, especially under the circumstances, and departed immediately after his meeting with the senior staff. Feeling slighted, Strauss wrote: "Model agreed in a general manner to the plans of the army and proceeded to Army Group Centre, and to Hitler, without bothering to call upon me."[5]

At Hitler's headquarters Model was informed that his task was to "master the dangerous situation at Ninth Army," an assignment for which he had been specially selected and promoted above at least fifteen more senior corps commands in Army Group Center alone.[6] According to Steven Newton, this meteoric rise reflects Model's strong commitment to National Socialism, which no doubt endeared him to Hitler. More important, Model had earned a reputation for determination and skill at improvisation in the December retreat through Klin, followed by his opposition to withdrawal from the Lama River position.[7] Indeed Model was among the first to benefit from a new approach to promotion, formalized only at the end of 1942, in which command appointments were based on performance rather than an exclusive table of seniority.[8] That Hitler believed he had found the right man for the Ninth Army may be deduced from his reference to Model's resolve. "Did you see that eye?" Hitler remarked, referring to the look in Model's eye. "I trust that man to do it, but I wouldn't want to serve under him."[9]

That Hitler was now seeking commanders characterized by a fanatical determination to hold the line, rather than those who complained about Soviet numbers or pleaded for withdrawal and replacements, was evident in word and deed. On January 17 Halder championed Hitler's cause by issuing a new directive to all the chiefs of staff of the army groups, armies, and corps, instructing them: "It is not acceptable that a command should succumb to an obsession with figures, which only emphasizes the large number of units on the enemy's side and the present decline of fighting power on our side." Halder wanted intelligence staff to be trained to avoid exaggeration. "Then there will be an end to the situation—which is quite unacceptable to the German general staff, when time and again the fighting spirit and toughness of our troops have put to shame the worried number-worshippers in the staffs."[10] It was a textbook example of the National Socialist conception of warfare, in which the "spiritual" dimension could triumph even against enemy superiority. In fact, after the war, Halder made the audacious claim that many more German troops could have been saved if only the army had been allowed to withdraw against what he now characterized as Hitler's "draconian order."[11]

Nor was Strauss the only general to be replaced by a more determined, if also more ideologically compliant, commander. Crisis had likewise gripped the southern flank of Leeb's Army Group North, with only the most tenuous contact to Army Group Center and major formations of the German Sixteenth Army under threat of being overrun or encircled. On January 12 Leeb appealed to Hitler for "freedom of operations" in order to "avoid unnecessary losses" but was characteristically rebuked. Leeb possessed none of Kluge's "initiative" to do anything but ask to be relieved of his command.[12] His replacement was Colonel-General Georg von Küchler, a resourceful and talented officer who would remain in this post for two years and be recognized by Hitler for his successful winter service by promotion to field marshal.[13]

Change was also afoot in Army Group South. Reichenau suffered a severe stroke and died days later on January 17. Bock, who only a month earlier had been too ill to continue at Army Group Center, reported himself fit for service and was handed Reichenau's command.[14] Bock's rapid recovery raised some eyebrows among his fellow commanders, although there was no suggestion that he had acted in any way dishonorably.[15] At the OKH Heusinger reasoned that men of Bock's stature were "hardly to be replaced." Revealingly, on January 22 Heusinger himself confided in his letters that he too had "often" wondered if the many changes in command might one day provide a relief for himself and Halder. As the army chief of operations lamented: "Halder and I are seated in the saddle more than ever, and the hope of finding some respite is unfortunately illusive."[16] That the men of the OKH longed for relief, in spite of their agreement with Hitler's approach to the winter crisis, and having endured none of the stresses of frontline commanders either physically or emotionally, says much about the war weariness pervading the German high command.

For Army Group Center the prospect of relief for commanders in its most dangerous sectors came only with Hitler's long-delayed authorization to withdraw. This entailed no measure of rest or respite for the men and their officers, only the prospect of survival. The retreat to positions east of the Yukhnov-Gzhatsk-Zubtsov Line was instructed to be undertaken "in small steps," while at the same time the gaps west of Rzhev (in Ninth Army) and northwest of Medyn (between Fourth and Fourth Panzer Armies) were to be closed "under all circumstances."[17] Rumors of a withdrawal had circulated many times at the front, so when on January 15 Kurt Matthies heard what he believed to be more such gossip, he was scathing: "Today they speak and drone on again of the 'scheduled withdrawal of the front into the winter position.' With this optimism, as slick as if shined with boot polish, leads one to seethe with rage if you know how dreary, lost and frozen it is at the front."[18] Yet this time the rumors were true, and soon the entire central front of Kluge's army group was on the move westward. The most urgent retreat was necessitated by Kübler's Fourth Army, which was fighting desperately to prevent its flank from being turned in the north and, to a lesser extent, in the south as well. Here the retreat was a matter of life or death. Paul Stahl, a Ju-88 pilot, wrote of what he observed on January 17:

> We are offered a sorrowful view: long columns of our own soldiers strenuously stumbling back. Everywhere one can see abandoned vehicles, some half-covered with snow, and others just recently abandoned. As we fly past the columns and small groups of soldiers at low altitude, it is evident that they are half unconscious out of fatigue. They pay no attention to us. We pass by burning villages. The enemy won't be able to use them as living quarters when he pursues our troops. The entire horizon is filled with columns of black smoke. It is a merciless war.[19]

Gerhard von Bruch no doubt summed up the attitude of many men in Fourth Army when he explained: "For all of us caught in the hell of this retreat, there is only one remaining thought—self-preservation."[20] Such a single-minded instinct excluded any consideration for the local population, and desperate to slow the advancing Red Army, the Germans unleashed a new wave of scorched-earth destruction through central Russia. Kurt Grumann wrote in his diary on January 20: "In the many villages the wells have already been blown up. The evening sky in many places became a bloody red. Whole villages were in flames. Tongues of flame greedily enfolded the dirty little homes. War is merciless—both we and they know this."[21] Hans Adam wrote home in a letter on January 18 about encountering frightened villagers who feared the soldiers would destroy their homes. He stated that in earlier retreats the destruction was left to the engineers, but now the soldiers themselves were instructed to destroy everything and did so with great eagerness. As his letter continued: "Women and children are left with their meagre belongings in the open air, without a roof over their heads. We overlook nothing; even the most miserable hovel is destroyed. That is how it should be. The enemy must be turned out into the cold."[22] The fact that Adam depicted women and children as "the enemy" also meant that they were at times directly targeted in the destruction. The diary of Wiedebach-Nostitz noted an action on January 19 in which a village was set alight with all of the people still asleep. "Precisely at 2:30 hours, with the civilian population not having any idea at all, the whole village is set ablaze . . . All they can do is save their naked lives. It is a grim scene."[23] Elena Rzhevskaia served as a translator with the advancing Red Army and came across one village in which the Germans had erected a sign explaining their ruthless actions. Reflecting the unambiguous National Socialist concept of warfare in the east, the sign read: "The Russians must die, so that we can live."[24]

The survival of Fourth Army was heavily dependent upon control of the road to Viaz'ma, which was both its main source of supply as well as a vital first step to reestablishing contact with Ruoff's Fourth Panzer Army in the north. Kübler, however, was under strict orders from Hitler and Kluge not to give up Yukhnov no matter how far the Red Army pushed westward behind its northern flank. Fourth Army's retreat was therefore buying Kübler some time and allowing a good degree of consolidation among the four army corps (LVII, XII, XIII, and XXXXIII) crammed into a region forty by thirty-two square kilometers in size, but the retreat had to halt before the danger posed by Soviet envelopment could be countered. The high command expected Kübler to be attacking northward to link up with Ruoff, but he was having enough trouble finding the forces to keep the road to Viaz'ma in German hands. Some Soviet forces were operating deep in Fourth Army's rear area, with at least one large group striking to within fifteen kilometers of Yukhnov. These rearward Red Army units were supplemented by nightly drops of paratroopers and supplies, while local partisan detachments were also active.[25] The noose was again tightening on Fourth Army, and Kübler seemed powerless to stop it. Even the men had some awareness of the army's perilous strategic situation, with one soldier noting in his diary on January 18–19: "We are in a trap. It is high time we get out of here before the Russians encircle us."[26]

On January 18 Hitler requested that Kübler come to the Wolf's Lair to discuss the army's situation. The dictator was probably as much interested in a firsthand report as in sizing up the man himself, but Kübler was not Model and appears to have made a poor impression at their meeting the next day. Halder commented that Kübler "does not feel equal to the task," while the deputy army chief of staff, Blumentritt, similarly concluded that the commander of the Fourth Army "could not stand the strain."[27] The writing was on the wall for another change of command, and the following day (January 20) Kübler was relieved "to restore his health."[28] His successor was Heinrici, the commander of the Fourth Army's long-suffering XXXXIII Army Corps and, like Model, a man who would eventually rise to army group command. Kübler of course was not sick and knew he had lost his position "because he told the Führer that he did not believe it possible to hold the highway [to Viaz'ma] and Yukhnov with the army."[29] Heinrici shared these doubts, but knew that Kübler was dismissed because "he did not show unconditional faith and said so openly."[30]

On the morning of January 21 Heinrici arrived at Fourth Army's headquarters in the town of Spas-Demensk and took over command from Kübler. It was a thankless task under the circumstances, and Heinrici knew it, writing to his wife: "Now I have the burden of enduring this struggle with this army. No other German army was in such a situation for as long as anyone can remember."[31] Nevertheless, Heinrici's first day in command was so cold (minus thirty-eight degrees Celsius) that there was no observed enemy movement. On January 22 Fourth Army's war diary noted that the screening forces keeping the road to Viaz'ma open were "extremely thin," but the route remained in German hands. By January 23 Heinrici even sounded a cautious word of optimism when he reported: "In the north, the situation is beginning to turn, even though we are not yet out of the woods, something is up."[32] A

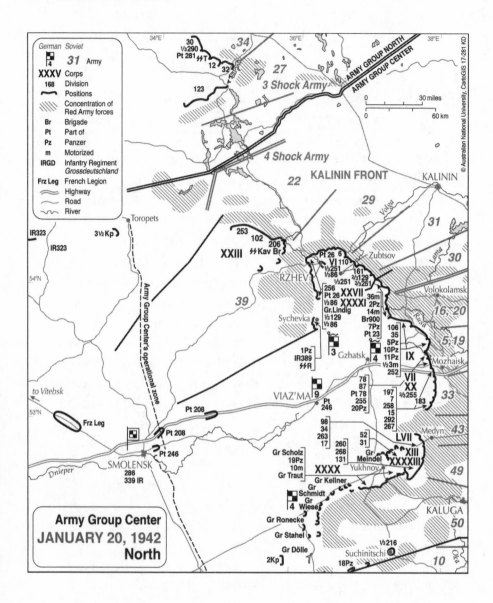

Army Group Center
JANUARY 20, 1942
North

revealing insight into what was hindering the Soviet offensive is provided in a captured Soviet officer's diary, who on January 21 wrote of a failed local offensive before continuing: "The enemy waited until we were 40 m away and then opened fire. We had very many dead and wounded. One sees our operations are at an end. We have no more men or weapons. In the companies

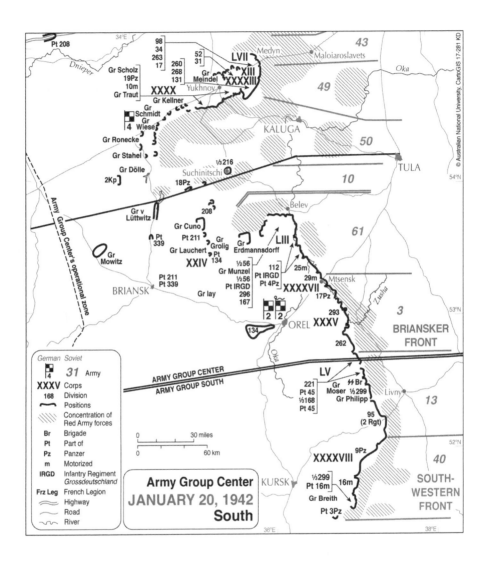

we have only 10–15 men, in battalions only two companies. We urgently, urgently need replacements!"[33]

To the north of Fourth Army, Ruoff and Reinhardt were forbidden to withdraw until Kluge gave permission. The army group's intention was to realign the front. Kübler's army was protruding eastward, and Kluge did not want to exacerbate the danger to his exposed northern flank further. This enforced delay was a source of great aggravation for Reinhardt, who wanted to begin his withdrawal immediately, but Third Panzer Army was already some distance west of Fourth Panzer Army, and Kluge could not afford rearward movements that extended the German line or, worse, opened up gaps. Already on January 16 Reinhardt was pressing Kluge, and the next day they came to a "sharp dispute," with Kluge warning Reinhardt that disobedience would not be tolerated.[34] Admittedly, the panzer armies were under some pressure, since long sections of their defensive line were centered upon fortified villages, allowing Soviet forces with skis and sledges to pass through the front and attack from the rear.[35] By January 18 Reinhardt was fed up and sent a strongly worded letter of protest to Kluge, which may even have been an ultimatum. As Reinhardt wrote his wife on the same day, "Now he can decide what should happen, whether he recommends my dismissal to the Führer or apologizes and gives in. I could not do anything else."[36] The day before, Reinhardt had confided in his diary that he was contemplating resigning "because I can no longer stand this struggle."[37] To Reinhardt's great relief, on January 19 Third Panzer Army's withdrawal was finally authorized, defusing the tension. When the two men met a week later (January 25) their exchange was very friendly, with the field marshal declaring he had "understood" Reinhardt's letter.[38] More than likely, however, Kluge was simply smoothing ruffled feathers and had no real misgivings about stalling Reinhardt's retreat. The field marshal was simply concerned with orchestrating a coordinated withdrawal to the Königsberg Line and had already shown he was not beyond losing an experienced commander to ensure his orders were carried out.

Once the panzer armies received the green light to begin their withdrawals some of the men had to abandon positions that had long been defended. Gerhardt Linke wrote in his diary on January 19: "It almost broke my heart as I passed our fortified covering position with its deep anti-tank ditches and its wide barbed-wire entanglements. Why did this have to happen? How bad it makes you feel to surrender territory you have already won."[39] While Linke felt the loss of his own fortified position, there was no such remorse at the parallel destruction of Russian homes. His account continued: "Houses and stacks were fired so that the Reds who are after us in hot pursuit might have no place to warm themselves and no supplies to draw on. The tongues of flame eagerly licked the doomed cottages and sheds. War is remorseless: either you get him or he gets you."[40] Yet for all their destructiveness German efforts did not necessarily prevent the Red Army's pursuit, even if they no doubt increased its hardships. As one German soldier noted, "How often did we think that the Russians would not be able to establish themselves in these burned out localities and then by the following morning they would be right behind us again."[41]

The most important position surrendered during Army Group Center's January retreat was the town of Mozhaisk on the Smolensk-Moscow highway. The town had been the scene of heavy fighting in 1941, and what remained was systematically destroyed. The Nikolaevsky Cathedral, the Voznesensky Church, and the hydroelectric station were all blown up.[42] Just outside Mozhaisk was a museum devoted to the 1812 battlefield of Borodino, but as Larry LeSueur noted, it had been completely destroyed. "The roof had fallen in and only those exhibits made of iron had survived the gasoline fire laid by the German destruction brigade. We puttered around the ruins and one of us found a corroded bayonet used by the Russian Army more than a hundred years ago. Another picked up an old French stirrup. One of the censors recovered an old cannon ball."[43] The anger generated by such wanton destruction was channeled into Ehrenburg's propaganda. Writing on January 20 he coldly observed: "They are now burning Russian towns and villages. Fools, they do not understand that they are burning Germany."[44]

The armies moved back in stages, retreating only after dark and reaching their final positions in the Königsberg Line between January 22 and 24. It was here that Kluge drew a line in the sand and told his army commanders there could be no further withdrawals.[45] The Yukhnov-Gzhatsk-Zubtsov Line was now almost completely straight and therefore much shorter overall. Everyone understood the importance of holding the line, even if there was still a gap between Ruoff's and Heinrici's armies. The embattled Fourth Army was too weak to close it, but strenuous efforts by Ruoff's panzer army did manage to narrow the breach by January 24.[46] In the meantime, Soviet forces assaulted the new German front head-on. The same economy of force that allowed greater German concentration in the defense also worked for the Soviets in attack, but their tactical method was too often hopelessly inadequate. On January 23 and 24 one understrength regiment in Third Panzer Army reported destroying seven Soviet tanks and damaging two others, while killing 400 men and taking 30 POWs.[47] Rudolf Oehus wrote home in a letter on January 22: "The Russian attacked every day with the most severe losses. Most of them are Siberian troops. So far, every attack has been repulsed, and they will not be able to get anywhere anyway, for ammunition and so on is sufficient. We also got reinforcements."[48] Yet one should not overestimate the strength of German defenses. Another soldier wrote on January 21: "Our duty periods stretch over forty-eight hours, with two or three hours' sleep, often interrupted. Our lines are so weak, twenty-five men per company over two kilometers, that we would be completely overrun if we, the artillery, did not stem the onslaught of the enemy, who are ten or twelve times stronger."[49]

In one instance Soviet officers ordered an attack across a frozen lake with absolutely no cover for their men. Even after the utter failure of the first assault, a second wave was sent that resulted in hundreds of dead. Hans Sturm observed: "It was an appalling sight, and caused many to wonder what sense there was in all this killing."[50] More disturbingly, machine gunner Benno Zieser explained that killing men in the heat of battle was not only easy, but that it gave him a feeling of exhilaration. "You actually had the feeling you could hear the bullets go plonk into a man's body, yet you didn't really feel you were killing, destroying human lives. On the contrary, you got a regular kick sometimes out of that sensation of the sploshing impact of the bullet. I must say I had always thought killing was much more difficult."[51] Helmut Günther disagreed. After annihilating a Soviet charge at close range, he recalled: "We felt no joy when it was over. Drained in body and soul, we ran back from the edge of the woods to the bunker."[52] Perhaps the most basic rationalization of these one-sided battles was the simple observation that "by being murderers ourselves we should prevent ourselves being murdered."[53]

For all of Germany's tactical successes, Army Group Center's withdrawal gave Stalin the impression of continuing achievement, even though the front only moved between forty and fifty kilometers. Stalin believed the central part of Kluge's front to be "on their last legs" and ordered the First Shock Army to be withdrawn from the line by January 19 and placed in the *Stavka*'s reserve. Zhukov, commanding the Western Front, strenuously objected, knowing this would double the length of the Twentieth Army's front. Stalin not only overruled him; he also removed the Sixteenth Army on January 21 for redeployment farther south.[54] Accordingly, by the last week of January the pressure on Reinhardt's Third Panzer Army had subsided, and another section of Kluge's army group had survived the worst of the Soviet winter offensive.

Despite the success of the withdrawals by Heinrici, Ruoff, and Reinhardt into the Königsberg Line, the shortening of Kluge's central front remained a defensive victory. Army Group Center's real triumph in the third week of January was, however, offensive in nature and stemmed from two remarkable operations by Model's Ninth Army and Schmidt's Second Panzer Army, which each delivered crushing blows to Soviet plans. In the north, Model immediately prioritized a major operation to unite Schubert's XXIII Army Corps with Bieler's VI Army Corps. This would not only restore Ninth Army's line west of Rzhev, but in doing so would cut off three large Soviet formations: the XI Cavalry Corps, the Thirty-Ninth Army, and a large part of the Twenty-Ninth Army occupying the gap in Model's line. On January 18 the Red Army was only seven kilometers from Rzhev, but Model remained unperturbed and focused on his offensive solution.[55] As Ninth Army's war diary noted, the new commander evinced "fresh nerves and unbroken determination," which he directed into stripping everything possible from the neighboring units within his army to reinforce the attack.[56]

The freedom to withdraw units allowed Model to reorganize his defenses, but this also had dire implications for the local population. Hans Meier-Welcker, a staff officer in the 251st Infantry Division, wrote in a letter on January 19 of how the local Russian people had helped his division in every way possible, concluding that the peasants were "friendly, almost warm-hearted." Yet he then added: "And after a stay of one or two days, we must burn down their villages and consign the old women and children to a freezing death. This military necessity is hard to bear for any one of us who is not completely brutalized."[57] Werner Pott expressed a similar sentiment, writing on the same day: "I am sitting in a house that will be up in flames

in half an hour. For weeks we have been in action without rest or quiet . . .
Against all these personal strains, it is the plight of the civilians which moves
me the most. We destroy their houses as we retreat, condemning them to
death by hunger or freezing cold."[58] Pity and sympathy, however, did not
change German behavior; indeed many viewed the destruction as entirely
necessary. One German soldier wrote on January 23: "Anyone who has ever
met Russia and Bolshevism sacrifices everything to save their homeland
from this horror . . . Over there is evil. On our side is the good."[59]

Model's plan was for a three-pronged assault, due to begin on January 21.
Schubert's and Bieler's forces would attack westward and eastward respectively, with a third force striking northwest from Sychevka (forty-seven kilometers south of Rzhev).[60] This third prong of Model's offensive could hardly
be expected to cover the sixty-five kilometers necessary to reach Schubert's
corps, but was most likely intended to engage the Soviet Thirty-Ninth Army
and prevent it from sending relief forces from the south. The gap between
Schubert and Bieler was twenty-seven kilometers as of January 20. Closing
it required German forces to contend not only with the Red Army, but also
with the deep snow and freezing conditions that had hampered Soviet operations all winter.[61] Indeed, when Ninth Army's staff officers argued for a
postponement of the offensive on account of the bad weather, Model was dismissive: "Why, gentlemen? Tomorrow or the day after won't be any warmer.
The Russians aren't stopping their operations."[62] Model must also have been
aware that his one advantage was the element of surprise. There was also
the fact that the troops and equipment concentrated for the offensive were
no longer available for defense, and Ninth Army could not long risk weakening its lines, lest the sealing of one gap lead to the opening of another.

By January 20 the Soviet forces that had penetrated the Rzhev gap had
driven deep into the German rear area with the aim of reaching Viaz'ma
and uniting with Red Army troops driving westward from the Medyn gap.
Such an achievement would have encircled Fourth and Third Panzer Armies
as well as most of Ninth Army; however such a remarkably ambitious undertaking was well beyond the Red Army. From Rzhev to Viaz'ma it was 120
kilometers, while from Medyn it was 100 kilometers. On the map, Soviet
forces operating south of Rzhev appeared to have made significant prog-

ress, but this belied their many vulnerabilities. Their narrow supply route remained within German artillery range, but more important, the winter conditions and general lack of motor vehicles prevented anything more than a trickle of supplies to sustain the 60,000 men already operating south of Rzhev. There was little heavy equipment (some artillery pieces and a small number of tanks), and the men had entered the gap with just a three-day supply of rations.[63] Attacking southward, the Soviets had sought to capture the town of Sychevka, which for the first half of January served as Ninth Army's command post and was a ready source of forward supplies, but German defenses again held, and when mobile elements of Krüger's 1st Panzer Division switched to an "active defense" role, the effect was decisive. On the morning of January 17 Krüger's tanks exploited the Soviet absence of heavy weaponry by capturing five strongly defended villages with "heavy losses in blood" for the enemy.[64] Two days later, after another unsuccessful Soviet assault, Krüger's tanks again surged forward and counted a further 200 enemy dead.[65]

In addition to the Soviet units passing through the German lines near Rzhev and Medyn there were also nightly drops of paratroopers around the Viaz'ma area. In one successful action, airdropped Soviet forces stormed a small German POW camp and liberated between 1,000 and 2,000 men, some of whom were subsequently armed.[66] Paul Schädel was in Viaz'ma on January 16 and wrote in a letter of Russian troops appearing just to the north of the town and capturing many Germans. Schädel, however, remained optimistic owing to "large" reserves of fresh German troops assembling in the town with more reported to be on their way. He also noted that en route to Viaz'ma he had seen "very many dead Russians and horses."[67] Clearly, operating deep in the German rear with very limited support was dangerous, and with Model, Heinrici, and Ruoff all seeking to close the relatively narrow gaps in their lines, the strategic risk to the Soviets was extremely high.

Heinrici and Ruoff had failed to close the gap between their two armies, but it was also the less significant of the two holes upon which the Soviet plan for Army Group Center's encirclement depended. Model had the equivalent of almost two enemy armies[68] operating behind his lines, which he recognized was as much an opportunity as it was a threat. If he could successfully cut off these forces, he would effectively turn the tables on the whole Soviet winter of-fensive, not only averting the encirclement of half of Army Group Center, but also inflicting a completely unexpected counterencirclement on the overex-tended Soviet pincer. Hitler, however, had become anxious at the supposed Soviet threat to Viaz'ma and on January 19 began redirecting forces ear-marked for Model's offensive toward Gzhatsk. The commander of the Ninth Army was furious and immediately drove from Rzhev to Viaz'ma to board a plane to the Wolf's Lair in order to confront Hitler personally. It is not clear if such direct action bypassed Kluge or was undertaken with his consent, but the result helped forge Model's reputation as a no-nonsense commander who, in spite of his personal devotion to Hitler and National Socialism, re-fused to simply accept his authority in military matters. Indeed, when Model was unable to talk Hitler out of his redeployments, the brash new army com-mander brazenly asked: "Mein Führer, who commands Ninth Army, you or I?" Yet Hitler's obstinacy persisted, and when he proceeded to issue an or-der, Model shook his head and boldly asserted: "That must not stand for me." Confronted by such emphatic opposition, Hitler suddenly backed down, but not before issuing a word of warning. "You do as you please," Hitler told his fiery commander, "but it will be your head at risk."[69]

Given Ninth Army's precarious situation, Model hardly needed to be re-minded how much was riding on the success of his offensive, but his combat record reflected a flair for audacious action in the face of long odds, and his success suggested he judged those odds correctly more often than not. Ninth Army's offensive began at 10:30 A.M. on January 21 and proceeded slowly in the face of sustained enemy counterattacks. Over the course of the day the Germans began to take a number of important locations as well as six enemy guns. Attacking from Sychevka in the south, Krüger's 1st Panzer Di-vision, together with elements of the SS *Das Reich* division, enjoyed more success. By the evening of January 21, they reported having killed 1,250 enemy troops, with another 170 captured. Moreover, three enemy tanks had been destroyed, while ten artillery pieces, four antiaircraft guns, and three antitank guns had been captured or rendered useless.[70] On the second day of the offensive (January 22), the main attack in the north achieved much greater success, with the effective concentration of assault guns, tanks, strong artillery support, and Richthofen's aircraft managing to break enemy resistance and leading in places to a "hurried withdrawal."[71] The union between Schubert and Bieler had not yet been achieved, but it was clear that the strength of Model's offensive had been "completely surprising" to the enemy.[72] On January 23 Richthofen himself flew over the battlefields west of Rzhev and Sychevka and reported seeing "very, very many dead Russians."[73] Indeed, Bieler's VI Army Corps alone killed some 650 enemy troops in their final assault, which led to the much-anticipated reunion of Ninth Army at 12:45 P.M. on January 23. Ninth Army's war diary referred to a "general joy and relief" at the news. VI Army Corps' total of enemy matériel captured or destroyed included thirty-two guns, thirty-four antitank guns, four tanks, and eighty trucks.[74] Model had triumphed, and if the new line could be held, it would be the Red Army that suffered the single greatest defeat of the winter campaign—a victim more of Stalin's irresponsible and overzealous ambition than Model's unquestioned operational acumen. Nevertheless, the Ninth Army's new commander had proven himself more than capable of dealing with a crisis. With victory secure, he directed his energy into consolidating his newly restored line.

If there was one dark cloud on Ninth Army's horizon it was the advance of General Pavel Kurochkin's Northwestern Front, deployed predominantly against Küchler's Army Group North, but since January 9 engaged in a steady offensive that had effectively cut the link between Küchler's and Kluge's army groups. Kurochkin's offensive contributed to the formation of the Kholm and Demyansk pockets, which would both endure until May 1942 and constitute a parallel winter crisis for Küchler's army group (although both pockets were eventually relieved and Soviet losses totaled roughly five times those of the German defenders). Yet Kurochkin's offensive also spilled into Army Group Center's zone of operations and seized Toropets (some 190 kilometers north of Smolensk) on January 21. These Soviet forces were then subordinated to Konev's Kalinin Front and began to push south, but their progress was limited by the vast distances, heavy snows, and inadequate supplies, as well as German opposition.[75] As Halder noted in his diary on January 19, "It is not an operational danger, but it does draw forces away from other sectors."[76] Model was no doubt losing some much needed reinforcements, while the new Soviet forces from the north also provided a theoretical, albeit extremely long and arduous, escape route for the enemy formations trapped south of Rzhev.[77] In practice, however, Stalin was no more inclined to order a major withdrawal than Hitler had been, especially since reopening the gap in Ninth Army's lines was quickly deemed the absolute priority of the Kalinin Front.

The problem for Konev was that Kalinin Front's armies were all battered and worn down, none more so than the Twenty-Ninth Army, which had just been cut in half. In order to gain reinforcements, Konev ordered his Thirtieth Army to redeploy to the west, but its commander, General Dmitry Leliushenko, reported that his three divisions were very weak and "could not yield the effect desired by Comrade Konev." Weeks of relentless attacking had savaged Leliushenko's troops, leaving many of his regiments with only around 100 men.[78] Such depletion was the consequence of an intransigent Soviet tactical doctrine, which sacrificed too many of its own units in futile frontal assaults. Wilhelm Eichner noted in his diary on January 23 that a single Soviet attack had resulted in 500 enemy dead,[79] while Heinrich Haape wrote home in a letter on January 19 that his own depleted unit had killed an estimated 600 Russians over the preceding five days.[80] Such reckless frontal assaults were a staggering waste of life often for no gain, but having suffered a stunning strategic reversal, Konev was under tremendous pressure to restore the situation and once again break through Ninth Army's front.

If the Ninth Army under Model had turned the tables on the Soviet offensive in the north, Schmidt was attempting to do the same in the south with his Second Panzer Army. The four thousand men of Gilsa's 216th Infantry Division encircled at Suchinitschi were some fifty kilometers from the nearest German lines, and although Schmidt was doing his best to assemble a relief force, the pressure this put on his positions south of Belev was becoming too much. Weikersthal, the commander of the LIII Army Corps, defending in this region, confronted seven enemy divisions with just four weakened infantry divisions and a battle group from the 3rd Panzer Division. Weikersthal was convinced his own front could scarcely hold much longer and requested permission for a withdrawal to shorten his line. Yet Hitler's January 15 concession applied only to the armies in the north, meaning Schmidt, whose front had been holding firm since December, had to remain fixed in place. Indeed, when Hitler was approached about Weikersthal's request he not only refused permission, but insisted that no movements by either the corps or divisional commanders could be made without prior approval from higher authorities. If Hitler lacked faith in his intermediary commanders, the feeling was entirely mutual, and Weikersthal reserved the right to command as he pleased in desperate situations. When the crisis reached breaking point on January 23, Weikersthal independently ordered the withdrawal of local units threatened with encirclement, insisting to Schmidt that his decision was only undertaken "after a determined resistance and the expenditure of all ammunition." Schmidt does not appear to have immediately reported the withdrawal, nor did he seek to punish Weikersthal, but he did engage in "a comprehensive exchange of opinions" with his subordinate commander. Yet when Weikersthal again asked for permission to withdraw in order to shorten his front, he was relieved of his command on January 25 and sent back to Germany, ostensibly for health reasons.[81]

Farther south, Schmidt's line was solidly anchored on the Oka and Zusha Rivers, affording a clear field of fire for the defense, although there was much less enemy pressure. Indeed, it was the panzer army that initiated many actions, with small forays of "active defense" raiding perceived weak spots in the opposing lines. Fremerey's 29th Motorized Infantry Division, for example, became extremely proficient in launching rapid attacks in company strength, often killing dozens of enemy troops, seizing weapons and equipment, and destroying any prepared positions.[82] Yet Schmidt could no longer be content just to hold his 140-kilometer-long front east of Orel; he also had to find the forces to rescue Gilsa's embattled garrison, which by now counted hundreds of killed and wounded.

Assembled for the attack under the direction of Langermann-Erlancamp's XXIV Army Corps was a mixed bag of battle groups as well as elements of the 18th and 4th Panzer Divisions, the 208th Infantry Division, and newly arrived 339th Infantry Division. In practice, none of these formations were fully represented, having been broken up to provide forces throughout Second Panzer Army's northern area of operations.[83] Concerns over the weakness of such a disparate amalgam of forces were not enough to postpone the attack, although the panzer army concluded that January 19 was the earliest possible start date for the offensive.[84] Of course any genuine estimation of Langermann-Erlancamp's prospects for success was dependent on his strength relative to the opposing forces, and reports by enemy soldiers captured in the area told of numerous cases of frostbite as well as dozens of desertions, with recaptured men being shot.[85] Not surprisingly, enemy morale was low, but nothing quite prepared Langermann-Erlancamp for his success in local attacks launched on January 18. Nehring's 18th Panzer Division launched a number of spoiling attacks to the northeast that met with remarkable success, including 140 POWs and some 430 killed enemy soldiers. It was immediately clear that the Soviets were unprepared for a major German attack, and Langermann-Erlancamp seized the moment to launch all available forces toward Suchinitschi a day ahead of time.[86]

The confusion in the Soviet command as well as the overextension of their poorly supplied soldiers hindered the Red Army's ability to mount a stout resistance. By January 19, advanced elements of Nehring's division had penetrated halfway to Suchinitschi, but with open flanks and mere battalions driving the offensive forward, Langermann-Erlancamp told Gilsa to prepare for a breakout to link up with his relief forces. Kluge, however, countermanded this directive, knowing that Hitler was insisting upon holding Suchinitschi.[87] Schmidt, who was following the offensive closely, knew that even if XXIV Army Corps could reach Suchinitschi, it would not have the strength to hold it for long. Kluge duly took the objections of the panzer army to Hitler on January 20. The dictator responded the following day by insisting not only that Suchinitschi be held, but also that XXIV Army Corps continue attacking north of the town in order to relieve some of the pressure on Heinrici's Fourth Army.[88] It was emblematic of warfare on the Eastern Front that Stalin's overextension was being exploited by Hitler to the inevitable overextension of his own forces.

Langermann-Erlancamp's offensive made good progress early on, but soon the advance slowed to a crawl as Soviet resistance strengthened and the weather worsened. According to Second Panzer Army's war diary, the temperature on January 22 dropped to minus forty-four degrees Celsius, which caused an especially high number of frostbite cases.[89] As Heinrich Eberbach recalled of his unit, "I can still remember seeing them move out in a snowstorm with icicles hanging from their eyebrows and noses, bent over close to their panje horses, if they had them."[90] The snow was eighty centimeters deep, and in places the advanced company literally had to dig their way forward.[91] Under the circumstances, Schmidt warned Kluge that operations north of Suchinitschi were unrealistic. The field marshal then entered into a long discussion with Hitler that eventually convinced the dictator of the futility of pushing any farther given the conditions. Nevertheless, Hitler was adamant that Suchinitschi be held as a means to "destroy" local Soviet forces in preparation for a later attack northward.[92] Certainly the German offensive was inflicting its share of damage on local Soviet formations, with the 18th Panzer Division's war diary recording on January 22: "A large number of enemy dead cover the battlefield . . . Our losses are small in comparison to the enemy."[93] The total number of Germans killed and wounded throughout the formations operating in the narrow corridor leading to Suchinitschi was estimated at around 200 a day, which suggests relative Soviet losses were considerable.[94]

Finally, on January 24, with just two battalions of Nehring's 18th Panzer Division still in motion, Gilsa's garrison launched its own attack toward the southwest, achieving the union of the two forces at 12:30 P.M. Suchinitschi was relieved after almost three weeks of encirclement.[95] Although there remained a serious question about how long Langermann-Erlancamp's XXIV Army Corps could hold the town, Army Group Center had once again averted disaster. Clearly, Kluge's forces retained an undeniable offensive punch even during the winter, and with the Red Army attempting too much, limited by poorly trained officers and inadequate resources, the same hubris that undercut German operations in 1941 was now ruining the Soviet winter offensive. If Suchinitschi represented a lost opportunity in what should have been a substantial German defeat, the implications of Model's attack at Rzhev were far worse, placing one and a half Soviet armies at grave risk of annihilation. Moreover, while Schmidt's eastern flank remained, for the most part, firm and secure, the skillful withdrawal of Kluge's center ensured much shorter and defensible lines for Third and Fourth Panzer Armies, while Fourth Army, although not out of the woods, was granted another life-saving reprieve. Nowhere had the Soviets cut off and destroyed so much as a German division, let alone a corps or even an army, and yet Stalin's

January offensive had aimed for nothing less that the destruction of Army Group Center itself.

Goebbels rejoiced at the changing fortunes of war and noted with satisfaction on January 23: "It is beginning to be understood that the Bolsheviks are not achieving their goals, that they are getting a bloody nose, and are probably expending offensive power over the winter, which they will desperately need next spring."[96] For a man who dealt in every kind of deceit and was himself consumed by ideological self-deception, Goebbels's estimation was nonetheless correct. Even German soldiers' hopes of an eventual victorious end to the war were reignited. Paul Schädel wrote home in a letter on January 24: "The situation here has improved and the Russian break-in has been brought to a halt. Nothing has, and nothing will, happen to me of that I am 100% sure, and I think by latest July/August the Russian is finished and thus the most difficult thing in this war is done."[97] Adolf B. took a similar view of Germany's strategic situation and found much cause for optimism, writing: "The Japanese, our allies, are making excellent progress in the Far East at the moment! . . . What would it be like if we boys were at home right now at the decisive moment of the war! No, we belong here, at the front, until the horrible Bolshevism is defeated!"[98] Most men, however, did not think in grand strategic terms and were simply glad to have survived the horrific ordeal of the preceding weeks, but here too there was a new optimism. Alois Scheuer wrote to his family on January 31: "Sometimes I have to wonder that I have not yet collapsed mentally and physically . . . Nevertheless, I do not want to give up the hope that everything will turn out well."[99]

20.

DEPARTING THE
EASTERN FRONT

Treacherous Routes of Escape

I f there was one thing that the typical German soldier feared more
than the cold winter weather, or even combat itself, it was capture
by the Red Army. German soldiers overwhelmingly associated capture with death, and sometimes an excruciating one at that. One
group of German POWs was forced to undress and remain outside until all
had died of exposure.[1] Hans Schäufler maintained that the pistol he carried
was for self-defense until the final bullet, which he intended for himself.[2]
Ernst Kern described how a comrade who had been shot in the abdomen and
could not be evacuated begged for a "mercy bullet" from his comrades.[3] After
the war Gottlob Bidermann wrote of "the widespread knowledge of the fate
of German soldiers who fell into the hands of the Russians, of how they often

died slowly and painfully in captivity . . . we equated surrender to suicide."[4] All manner of grim tales depicted the barbarity of Soviet methods and the dreadful fate that awaited any German soldier unfortunate enough to fall into the hands of the Red Army. The most dramatic stories tended to compete with one another for the grisliest details, and while some were no doubt truthful, others were exaggerated, if they were even true to begin with.

Third Panzer Army, for example, included a report of a Soviet war crime that could be traced back through the paperwork to three Germans who had been captured and identified as arsonists by a local civilian. On January 10, 1942, a Soviet commissar had them shot, yet this version of events bears no resemblance to the report Third Panzer Army compiled on January 22. This later report, summarizing the same event, read: "Four German prisoners hung upside down by their feet, heads split or cut off, torsos slit open. Heart, liver and lung reportedly eaten by the Bolshevists."[5] If an official report could be embellished, or even completely reconceived, then we must imagine that soldiers' stories also transformed with each retelling.

Typically, the only surefire way for Germans to learn of atrocities against their men was by discovering evidence when they recaptured ground from the Red Army. And so, of the many stories of Red Army atrocities, it is questionable how certain details ever could have been truthfully reported, especially for places that were never recaptured by the Wehrmacht. Heinrich Haape, for example, wrote in his postwar memoir about the Red Army's conduct upon retaking Kalinin on December 16, 1941: "When the city was re-entered by the Red Army, our field hospital there still contained a large number of serious casualties . . . The Russians arrived, slaughtered the doctors and cleared the whole hospital in a matter of minutes by throwing every patient out of the window. Those who were not killed by falling onto the frozen ground were quickly dispatched by a shot in the back of the head and thrown into an open grave."[6] Who observed these actions? Why were desperately needed doctors not evacuated, especially since Haape himself was a doctor and took for granted Soviet mistreatment of those they captured? German reports about Red Army atrocities, while certainly not without a strong basis in fact, were almost certainly not as frequent as the rumors maintained. Accordingly, one must distinguish between firsthand accounts of Soviet abuses and the myriad of stories, which German soldiers tended to accept at face value.

Whether real, embellished, or imagined stories, if there was one benefit to the *Ostheer* in all of the Red Army's alleged atrocity tales, it was the fanatical resolve it encouraged in German soldiers, especially in desperate situations. As one soldier wrote: "This awareness of Soviet brutality only installed a will in the soldier to fight and resist to the last round and last breath."[7] Men who were not prepared to kill themselves sometimes successfully managed to feign death until the enemy moved on. After his position was overrun in early January, Hans Roth noted with relief in his journal: "The Reds arrive, step on my chest and stomach, they see the blood on the face and on the uniform . . . They are just about to empty my pockets or undress me when there is a loud screaming and cursing from the tanks, it must be orders directed at these guys . . . I am saved, damn it, indeed saved!"[8]

With Germans determined to avoid capture by almost any means, many of those who were taken could point to an involuntary or unconscious act, brought about by being wounded or suffering extreme mental or physical exhaustion in which the individual became almost indifferent to his fate. As the winter retreat placed sometimes intolerable demands upon the men, some simply gave up, too drained and emotionally defeated to respond to orders, comrades, or even the approaching Red Army. As one soldier recalled:

> Habit and discipline kept them going; that and the flicker of an instinct to stay alive. And when the soldier's mind had become numb, when his strength, his discipline and his will had been used up, he sank into the snow. If he was noticed, he was kicked and slapped into a vague awareness that his business in the world was not finished and he staggered to his feet and groped on. But if he lay where he had collapsed until it was too late, as if forgotten he was left lying at the side of the road.[9]

If these exhausted men survived in the freezing temperatures, they were often overtaken by the Red Army. Some Germans rested for short periods in warm peasant houses, but drained and dead tired, they overslept only to be awoken at Soviet gunpoint. Others simply had bad luck. August Egger was about to withdraw from a town that had been outflanked by the Red Army when the oil in his truck froze, leaving him stranded.[10]

The moment of capture was a frightening and uncertain event, with a Russian roulette of possibilities. Max Kuhnert recalled feeling "helpless" and "petrified," without the ability to think clearly, and was only aware that "my knees felt like putty." Kuhnert then remembered the chaos and excitement his capture inspired:

> There was a lot of shouting going on. One of the men kept on pushing me while at the same time the others ripped my clothing apart. I also got hit on my right shoulder, and felt a stabbing pain there. A man took my watch, others ripped off my belt with Willy's pistol, and took my dispatch case with all my personal things. Protesting only brought laughter from them, and an ugly little fellow grabbed me by my front and held something into my face, it could have been a pistol . . . I frantically tried to speak a bit of Russian to explain, but not a single word came out.[11]

Kuhnert, however, was among the lucky ones; a sudden German mortar attack dispersed his captors, and he seized the opportunity to make his escape. Hans Becker was trapped inside his tank after it was hit by a Soviet antitank round, and when he was eventually hauled out by the enemy he noted:

> The prospect was just about as bad as it could be. Around us stood a group of grim ruffians in Russian uniforms. They were very young, about seventeen I should guess, and not a trace of pity or humanity showed on any of their faces.
>
> Their first commands were for the surrender of our watches. Next they stripped the bodies of our dead comrades of every possession and article of clothing which could be of the slightest use or value. Then they started on us again. Rings, pens, wallets, purses, private photographs—everything they fancied was snatched away and never

seen again by us. When one of them started taking off my boots I felt it was time to protest. He at once flew into a rage, wrenched my medals off my chest and smashed my Close Combat Clasp viciously into my face, ripping my right cheek from top to bottom. After that he twisted and tugged off my boots so violently that I really believed he would take my feet with them. Still not content, he then turned to his companions and clearly started arguing that I should be shot. The discussion did not last long: the proposal was undoubtedly a popular one.[12]

Becker was saved by the arrival of an officer who ordered that he be sent for interrogation, but many German soldiers did not long survive their capture.[13] For those who were not killed outright, adjusting to their new status as POWs involved an initial period of shock. Larry LeSueur observed recently apprehended German prisoners in a village street and referred to their capture as a "psychological blow from which they hadn't yet recovered."[14] Captured German soldiers were suddenly reduced from conquerors to conquered, and placed in the care of the much maligned "Jewish-Bolshevik" state, which in German eyes was the harbinger of barbarism and degradation. The men were also completely cut off from their loved ones and families, with no prospect of sending or receiving letters, nor even knowing if they would ever meet them again. It was a new reality dominated by utter powerlessness and dread.

German POWs were typically first interrogated near the front in order to quickly gain tactical information. Although German soldiers were duty bound to reveal as little as possible, by the winter of 1941–1942 many of the long-suffering men were much less concerned with army regulations, especially if divulging information offered some advantage. Helmuth Hoffmann told his captors in January 1942: "Recently an order was read to us: each village must be defended as long as possible. Officers who order retreat without instructions will be court-martialed . . . But such orders don't help . . . the infantry: they retreat without any orders."[15] Hoffmann's revelations were printed as propaganda in Soviet newspapers, but little could the readers have guessed just how far such indiscipline extended through the

Ostheer's command. Hoffmann also alluded to the constant disappointment caused by the empty promises from above, complaining: "They feed us with hopes. They say: 'Twenty fresh divisions under the command of Blaskovitz, the conqueror of the Greeks, will arrive soon.' They told us that Todt, the builder of the Siegfried Line, has constructed a defense line at Gzhatsk. First, they told us that the winter positions would be along Istra, later along the Lama River, then at Mozhaisk and Rusa."[16] Certainly, some German soldiers saw their capture as a moment to release the anguish and frustration they harbored against their commanders for what they took to be gross strategic mismanagement.

In the most extreme cases disillusioned men sought to defect during the fighting itself.[17] A German POW by the name of Hohlstein later in the war admitted: "Yes. There are always some individual cases [of defection]. People who had been in the fighting in Russia right from the beginning and had marched most of the time in the swamps and forests and mud and everything, who had been through that dreadful autumn and then experienced the cold and then the Russian break-through, of course became pessimistic and said: 'It's all up now, our number's up.'"[18] Willy Peter Reese and his comrades were one such group of men, but their attempt to cross the lines was unsuccessful: "Tanks approached us. We tied camouflage tunics to our rifles, swung them about, and surrendered. But they were German tanks. We were forced to climb aboard."[19] Other soldiers hedged their bets, not actively seeking to defect but preparing for the eventuality if ever they found themselves with no other option than surrender. As Helmut Günther recalled: "We may well have had a few 'safe-conduct passes' in our pocket. The 'comrade' promised us a lot in this scrap of paper: Good treatment, first-class food, immediate release after the end of the war and many more wonders. It was a friendly offer that almost elicited tears of emotion. But we knew better!"[20] Likewise, Walter Tilemann insisted, "No one dared to trust the 'safe-conduct passes.'" He then added a caveat: "This changed only when new daily rumors and terrible news made the rounds."[21] Ilya Ehrenburg claimed that the German POWs he met were focused on the most basic things. "They talk only of the cold, of hunger, of the fact that a shell ripped through the abdomen of a fellow soldier."[22] Nevertheless, in spite of all the trials and deprivations of the winter period, the evidence suggests German defections remained extremely rare.

Data from Soviet sources tells what appears on the surface to be a counterintuitive story of German prisoner taking. In the summer and autumn of 1941 the Soviets took more German POWs than in the first winter of the war. For example, between June 22 and July 22, 1941, the Red Army took an average of 48 men a day. The figures reached their highest between August 21 and 31, with 108 men captured each day. These contrast with a much smaller daily average of just 27 German POWs between October 2 and January 1, 1942. The fact that so few German POWs were being taken even in December 1941, when the Red Army was driving forward, appears anomalous because an attacking army should take more prisoners than one in retreat. The explanation, however, is not to understand these figures in a purely operational context, but rather as part of Soviet policy.[23] In the autumn of 1941 Stalin radicalized the war against Germany by encouraging openly hateful propaganda, which encouraged the killing of any German on Soviet territory. As the dictator announced in a public speech on November 6: "From now on it will be our task, the task of the nations of the Soviet Union, the task of the fighters, the commanders, and the political functionaries of our army and our navy, to annihilate all Germans who have penetrated as occupiers into the territory of our homeland, down to the last man. No mercy for the German occupiers! Death to the German occupiers!"[24] Importantly, there was no explicit order or policy to murder all German POWs, but as Mark Edele explained, it was "the interaction of signals from above and reactions on the ground, a dynamic specific to the way the Stalinist dictatorship worked in practice," that accounted for the huge increase in killings.[25]

Soviet propaganda as well as Red Army orders adopted Stalin's language for a war of annihilation, which correspondingly impacted the fate of German POWs, although the intention was to galvanize anti-German sentiment, not specifically kill captured prisoners. Zhukov's Western Front issued an order on December 14, which included the passage: "Not one Hitlerite bandit who invaded our country shall be allowed to get away alive . . . It is our sacred duty to take cruel revenge . . . and to wipe out all the German occupiers down to the last man."[26] Not surprisingly, this kind of rhetoric from above was translated into "action" at the lowest levels.[27] Indeed, some of the Soviet POWs taken in the winter admitted that they themselves had received instructions from their officers that "we now don't take prisoners."[28] Likewise, intercepted radio messages said the same: "In the future, the only Germans I want to see are dead Germans!"[29] Such actions have led some historians to try to equate Hitler's war of annihilation in the east with a supposedly comparable one launched by Stalin.[30] Yet on February 23 Stalin directly addressed foreign claims that suggested the Soviets simply wanted to "exterminate the German people." Now Stalin was careful, qualifying his earlier language to avoid being tainted by the same responsibility for mass murder that he was accusing the Germans of perpetrating. It was in this context that he made this public address, specifically aimed at sparing surrendering German soldiers: "If they surrender, the Red Army takes German soldiers and officers captive and keeps them alive."[31] They were in part also motivated by sheer self-interest, as POWs proved a valuable source of information, especially when planning to attack positions of unknown strength without any tactical intelligence.[32] Consequently, specific orders to the Soviet armies followed Stalin's new appeal, and not surprisingly, the numbers of German POWs rose appreciably.[33]

According to Soviet figures, in 1941 they had taken some 9,265 German POWs; the Germans, however, assumed the figure to be more like 30,000.[34] The discrepancy rests on the Germans' assumption that men who had been killed with no identifiable body (missing in action) were Soviet POWs, or because men, who had indeed been taken prisoner, had been killed or died at some point thereafter. There was in fact some dialogue through neutral back channels over the question of POWs. The Soviets asked for information on well over 3 million men captured by the Germans in exchange for similar data on their own far fewer POWs. Yet Goebbels dismissed this as an "unfair offer, which is absolutely typical of the Bolsheviks." He suggested either exact parity in the exchange (30,000 for 30,000) or, at most, as many individual cases as the Soviets reported missing.[35] Not surprisingly, nothing came of the exchange, which only confirmed, especially for men at the front, that those who disappeared behind Soviet lines were not to be seen again.[36]

Avoiding Soviet captivity, especially during Army Group Center's long and arduous periods of retreat, required more stamina than many men could muster. Yet the Wehrmacht had at its disposal a chemical stimulant known as Pervitin, which was a powerful methamphetamine developed in 1937 and sold openly in Germany without prescription until 1939. Nothing like it had been seen before, and its military utility for combating fatigue was quickly recognized. As Otto Ranke, Germany's leading defense physiologist, reported, Pervitin was an "excellent substance for rousing a weary squad . . . We may grasp what far-reaching military significance it would have if we managed to remove natural tiredness using medical methods . . . A militarily valuable substance."[37] The drug was remarkably effective and, with Brauchitsch's endorsement and little concern for its addictive qualities, it was liberally dispensed for both the Polish and French campaigns. As one report on its effects noted: "Everyone fresh and cheerful, excellent discipline. Slight euphoria and increased thirst for action. Mental encouragement, very stimulated . . . Long-lasting effect."[38] Not surprisingly, the stimulant became colloquially known as *Panzerschokolade* (tank chocolate).[39] In 1940 the Wehrmacht ordered some 35 million tablets for the army and Luftwaffe, but there was also an increasing recognition of Pervitin's dangers, which led to the drug being subject to the Reich opium law less than two weeks before the invasion of the Soviet Union began.[40] This, however, did not prevent its widespread distribution on the Eastern Front. The drug became the chemical embodiment of National Socialism's obsession with the "will" to achieve anything. Even exhausted men suddenly felt themselves physically revived, mentally concentrated, and spiritually energetic. As Norman Ohler observed, even in 1941, Pervitin "personified the hubris of German warfare, which had overstretched itself and lost contact with reality long ago."[41]

Heedless of the health warnings, the OKW and the Reich Ministry for Arms and Ammunition declared Pervitin to be "decisive for the outcome of the war" and nowhere more so than in the eastern campaign.[42] Accordingly, 10 million tablets were sent to the troops in 1941.[43] As doctors like Ottheinz Schultesteinberg recalled: "The stuff was just doled out. The motto was, *come and get it!*" The effects were undeniable, as Schultesteinberg attested from his own use: "And I can tell you: it worked. It kept you awake, mercilessly."[44] During the winter of 1941–1942 Ernst Gerber nicknamed Pervitin

"Stuka pills," and his diary showed pervasive, and even highly dangerous, levels of consumption. Serving as a doctor at a hospital in Roslavl, Gerber noted that the nurses and orderlies were also frequently taking it in order to cope with the unrelenting flow of wounded. Gerber himself slept only infrequently and by January 17 noted that, while "working like crazy," he took Pervitin every four hours.[45] Indeed, the highest prevalence of drug addicts throughout Germany in 1942 was among medical professionals.[46]

Army Group Center's crisis at the front had dire implications for the medical services in the rear not just because of the overwhelming casualties or the difficulty of moving large numbers of immobilized men, but because medical orderlies, already insufficient, were being drafted to the front to fight. By February 1942, the *Ostheer*'s medical services faced a fourteen-thousand-person shortfall, which the German Red Cross attempted to ameliorate by sending ever more female nurses to the east.[47] As Anna Wendling, who served with the Red Cross in the east, recalled: "The combat formation did their best but were overwhelmed and unable to cope. The organization broke down and was insufficient to take such large numbers of casualties."[48] Similarly, Brigitte Penkert wrote in a letter home on January 12: "'Winter rest' on the eastern front, how many of us hoped for it! There is not a trace of it. But heavy, heaviest defensive battles! . . . There is so much human suffering that passes through our hands."[49] According to standard ratios for the German Red Cross at that time, one nurse would have to attend fifteen wounded, but in practice on the Eastern Front it was far higher. In fact, there are reports of nurses working seventy-two-hour shifts and sleeping only during short breaks. Not surprisingly, the arduous physical demands, not to mention the psychological trauma of witnessing so much suffering and dying, left its mark on the nurses; many suffered nervous breakdowns, and some even committed suicide.[50]

In the Nazi regime, nursing took on a distinctly ideological character. Nurses were required to be emotionally "tough," while not departing from traditional Nazi ideals of womanhood that forbade them from asking the soldiers about unpleasant experiences at the front.[51] Certification to work as a Red Cross nurse required proof of Aryan ancestry and political reliability. The Nazi endeavor to create a cadre of "brown nurses" even extended to the point of having nurses take an oath of loyalty to the Führer. One nurse who completed her training in Erfurt before being sent to the east was told by one of her instructors that "hatred is noble" and that the traditional virtues of sacrifice, discipline, and loyalty were necessary to wage war. Arriving in the east, another nurse told a film crew of Goebbels's propaganda ministry that she had recently been taught about the "evil people in Russia."[52]

The wounded tended to be divided into two broad categories: those with conventional wounds sustained in combat, and those suffering from frostbite. A third category might be reserved for men who had contracted serious illnesses but were without obvious wounds; such men found it harder and harder to gain medical certificates, and most had to recover (if at all) in their bunkers. Throughout the *Ostheer* the number of men who were seriously wounded, ill, or frostbitten totaled 148,654 for the month of December 1941.[53] Of this total, some 91,000 were not due to enemy action, making a remarkable 61 percent the result of frostbite or illness. Thus, one could conclude that the Red Army's winter offensive cost the Wehrmacht fewer men than the Russian winter, although of course one was the catalyst for the other. If one adds the number of missing and dead to the *Ostheer*'s December losses, the overall figure comes to 193,446. Yet December also saw some 119,000 replacements arrive at the front, denoting an aggregate loss of 74,446 across the length of the Eastern Front. The January figures are less specific, but clearly worse than December. Some 127,718 serious casualties resulted from frostbite or illness, and only 63,800 replacements arrived at the front.[54]

With frostbite such a pervasive danger, soldiers tried to be extremely vigilant in detecting its onset, but always being so cold they suffered from a loss of sensation that hindered detection. As one soldier from the Third Panzer Army noted in January: "The wind blows against the observation posts so one's tears freeze in his eyes. Nose, ears and chin have no feeling from the cold and are often frozen. Who among them doesn't have frozen feet? Who has hands that move? Who does not have intestinal problems? Who is not frozen?"[55] Helmut Pabst maintained that the men watched one another's noses closely, as it was often the most exposed part of the body; when the tip went white it was time to act.[56] Traveling on vehicles constituted a heightened danger of unwitting exposure, brought on by the additional wind chill and lack of blood circulation.[57] Max Kuhnert wrote of one unfortunate comrade who had been transported for a long period overnight with an unzipped fly. "Amputation was the only help he got, and he had only got married just before we left Germany."[58]

There are four degrees of frostbite, ranging in severity from relatively superficial, skin-level damage (first degree); to large burn-like blisters and hard blackened skin (second degree); to tissue freezing below the skin (third degree); to muscles, tendon, and bone freezing (fourth degree). Schmidt's Second Army provided exact figures for the prevalence of each degree between the period of December 30 to January 6. In total, the army sustained 2,360 cases of frostbite divided as follows: 1,201 first degree, 1,026 second degree, 132 third degree, and just 1 case of fourth degree.[59] Such evidence suggests that severe frostbite was reasonably rare and that most men would be able to return to service at some point. Figures for Fehn's 5th Panzer Division tell a similar story, with instances of frostbite from the onset of the cold weather to January 4 revealing 3,000 men (20 percent of divisional strength) suffered first-degree cases. Another 450 men had second-degree frostbite, and just 60 cases were classed as third degree, with none suffering fourth degree.[60] Goebbels was also struck by the relatively small number of serious frostbite cases, claiming: "The consequences of the cold on the eastern front are not as enormous as commonly thought." The figures he received suggested that of the *Ostheer*'s 30,000 frostbite cases up to January 10, only 2,200 of these had been third degree. As Goebbels concluded: "At the beginning I anticipated the figures to be much higher."[61]

Treatment for frostbite depended upon its severity. Helmut Günther told of his treatment for a second-degree case:

> I went back to the aid station with the rations sled. There, in a
> miserable, smoke-filled room, was the workplace of the battalion
> surgeon. Things went quickly. The battalion senior medic had plenty
> of practice. In the meantime, giant blisters had formed on my feet.
>
> "Here, take a swig of this vodka. Soon you'll be hearing the angels
> sing!" Man, did they have a system! One of the "torturer's assistants"
> firmly held one of my legs over the basin and the medic got to work.

In the meantime, I stood on the other leg with my back to him and only noticed that he was cutting away the skin of the blisters with scissors. So far, so good. When, however, the dirty dog poured a bottle of iodine over the fist-sized area of raw flesh, I shot right up.[62]

Even serious cases sometimes had to be dealt with at the front under the most primitive and unhygienic conditions. As Willy Peter Reese wrote:

Frostbite festered and stank in the heat of the stove. There was no lint. The same bandage, pus-encrusted and stiff with scabs and rotted flesh, was used again and again. We had to go easy on salves and ointments. Some had long rags of blackened flesh hanging off their feet. It was snipped off. The bones were exposed, but with their feet wrapped in cloths and sacking, the men had to go on standing sentry and fighting . . . Every footfall hurt, but we had to walk and move around. Frostbite could be interpreted as attempted self-mutilation.[63]

Treating third- and fourth-degree frostbite cases was, as one doctor recalled, "a heart-breaking task" because if one was not able to revive the frozen tissue, it would become gangrenous and require amputation. In these cases, the first task was to massage the frozen areas with snow or even cold water until the tissue became soft and pliable again, and then pack the limb with cotton wool and wrap it in bandages. The rewarming process was extremely painful, but doctors had to administer morphine carefully because it reduced the body's resistance to cold and, on long trips to field hospitals, could prove fatal.[64]

In the most desperate cases, German units unable to transport their wounded (either for lack of transport or the seriousness of the wound) on occasion set them up to fight rear-guard actions so their comrades would have a better chance of escaping.[65] If a wounded soldier survived the journey to one of the main hospitals he usually had to again wait for treatment. The surgeons had the most oppressive workload. Rest often came only at the expense of treating men in serious need of operations. By this time, however, the fact that many men had been wounded days, or even over a week, earlier and had taken so long to arrive on the snow-covered roads meant even relatively benign wounds were at risk from life-threatening infections. Anton Günder, who served as a medical orderly, noted:

> Many presented themselves for treatment with emergency bandages that had been applied more than a week before. One soldier had an exit wound in his upper arm. The whole arm was now black, and puss [sic] was running from his back down to his boots. We had to amputate it at the joint. Three of my helpers smoked cigars during the operation because the stench was so great.[66]

Helmut Fuchs, who was in the main hospital in Smolensk, wrote on December 17: "It was a picture of misery, reminiscent of the pictures by French painters of the destruction of the Grande Armée . . . The stream of wounded, sick, and soldiers with frozen limbs did not stop. The engines of the ambulances, which brought new wounded, were constantly heard on the street."[67] Likewise, Dr. Roschmann, a physician in a field hospital in December, recalled:

> There was no rest day and night. We got lice from the infected wounded. There were many severely wounded, many amputations, stomach and lung shots, fractured bones. We had the tragic certainty that all of them, despite their need for rest, must shortly be transported in unfavorable conditions. That, and the uncertainty about the right time to order transport, wore heavily on my nerves . . . Our eyes are teary, heavy and drooping, our legs have no feeling, we are sick from the bloody work and the lice bites.[68]

Under such circumstances, the abuse of Pervitin was not just conceivable; it was the only way for doctors to work day and night to save countless lives.

Roschmann's concerns about transporting men in unfavorable conditions was due to the constant shortage of beds at the main hospitals as well as the hazardous conditions of their transport back to Germany. The German Red

Cross operated specially outfitted trains for a program known as "wounded assistance mission east." These trains had heating, tiered beds along the sides of carriages, and basic medical equipment. Some 3,600 Red Cross personnel staffed the trains and supported the Wehrmacht's own medical services in the east.[69] Yet the vast majority of the wounded were not placed in such specially outfitted trains: "Our wounded were being packed into cattle trucks without protection from the deadly cold with inadequate numbers of medical personnel to attend to them as they jolted through the snow deserts of Russia. Large numbers of German wounded died a cruel death on these trains."[70] Helmut Fuchs wrote of being transported in a freight car with straw on the floor and a wooden bench for the wounded who could sit. A small heating stove had been installed in each car, but there was no fuel for it, so the men traveled in freezing conditions and often in total darkness. Their journey lasted three days and nights with intermittent hours-long halts.[71]

On January 24 Goebbels received an unvarnished report of the appalling conditions in the medical transports arriving from the east. He was angered by the conditions and contacted the Wehrmacht's medical department, the Nazi Party, and the Red Cross and insisted upon immediate action.[72] Goebbels was not overstating the problem. The unheated medical trains were often terribly overcrowded, so much so that men who died along the way were unloaded at stations to make room for those still alive. As one soldier later wrote of his journey:

> The moaning and groaning of the wounded made conversation impossible . . . Finally, after long hours, the train stopped at a small railroad station . . . I could glimpse a bit of the railroad station area. However, I saw more; saw how the first dead, to make things easier, were simply shoved out through the windows . . .
> The train rolled on with its sad cargo for three more days. Comrades who had died along the way were left lying at every station that we left behind us. The first medical care and food came at Warsaw. Unfortunately, it was too late for half of those who had been loaded on originally. At the same time, a large portion of the wounded were unloaded and distributed among the surrounding

hospitals. It was becoming critical for them. The train then rolled onward with the rest.[73]

For those lucky enough to gain passage on one of the specially outfitted Red Cross trains, thoughts turned from survival to the prospect of rest, and most of all, home. As Willy Peter Reese wrote: "Day after day night after night, the train trundled through the white winterland. Bryansk. Smolensk. Minsk. Steps home."[74] Likewise, Siegfried Knappe recalled: "We were all utterly thankful to be out of the inferno of combat and the murderous Russian winter . . . It was a very pleasant feeling of tranquility."[75] Such men had achieved the much-coveted *Heimatschuss*—literally a "home shot"—a wound that allowed repatriation to Germany but without being crippling or life-threatening. If death or Soviet captivity were the only other alternatives to escaping the torments of the Eastern Front, a light wound leading to evacuation was clearly the most desirable option.

The winter of 1941–1942 may be first and foremost a story of tremendous suffering, and it was by no means limited to men. Army Group Center's horse population suffered terribly, and already on December 9, Halder noted in his diary that some 1,100 horses were dying each day.[76] A standard German infantry division (according to the 1939 standard) required anywhere between 4,077 and 6,033 horses to remain mobile, and with hardly any reserves, the number of horses in any given division declined from the first week of the war.[77] These losses were to no small extent offset by the widespread acquisition of small but hardy Russian horses, although no figures exist as to how many entered German service. According to Lieutenant-General Lothar Rendulic, who commanded the 52nd Infantry Division, the Russian horses were "absolutely indispensable" to the movement of supplies in the winter.[78] Yet they did not have the power to pull anything heavier than a small cart, which was part of why so many artillery pieces and other matériel that would otherwise be drawn by horses had to be abandoned or destroyed during the German retreats.

The heavy horse breeds of the German army were far more powerful but also more susceptible to the climatic extremes. Horses suffered greatly from frostbite and pneumonia, which, after months of taxing work over very long distances, took an immediate toll on their generally poor health. Disease also seriously impacted Fourth Army just as the Soviet winter offensive was getting under way, with a serious outbreak of mange reported in ten of its divisions, although potentially more devastating afflictions, such as glanders, were not recorded. Veterinary hospitals behind the front, which could care for up to 550 horses, were inundated and had to try to treat between 2,000 and 3,000 horses.[79]

One of the main problems was securing enough fodder for the horses in winter. Indeed, Wetzel's 255th Infantry Division sent some 800 of its remaining horses 160 kilometers to the rear because it simply did not have the feed or shelter to sustain them.[80] Sacrificing mobility in the face of an attacking enemy was a desperate move, but given the inadequate supplies reaching the front, it was the only prospect of preserving the division's draft power into the future. Rudolf Oehus looked after his unit's horses and wrote home in a letter on January 22: "For our horses I am pessimistic, I do not think that very many will be alive by spring. The straw must be fetched from ten kilometers away and, of this, every horse only gets something, and some days nothing at all. They get two pounds of oats during the day, and that only when it is available."[81] Gerhardt Linke echoed these concerns, explaining in his diary:

> Oats have to be dealt out in tiny portions. Horses that ought to be getting ten pounds of feed a day are being given two pounds at best. We are already using the straw from the roofs of sheds and barns. Many of the animals just drop from weakness. As they stand in their stalls they scrape the ground with their hoofs and eat their own dung. You can calculate exactly when the last horse will die of starvation and exhaustion. I dread to think of the consequences.[82]

Even before the horses died, their emaciated state greatly reduced their draft power, which meant many more horses were required to pull a single wagon or gun.[83] As a consequence Fritz Hübner wrote of using a team of horses to pull wagons for 500 meters before having to unharness them and return to pull other wagons. Even this presented problems: "I was very concerned about how the horses had to suffer and how hard our drivers sometimes had to hit them to get the animals back in motion."[84] Of course, such treatment only hastened their demise, and as Georg Kreuter observed in his unit, "the horses lie more than they stand."[85] Many simply died in their harnesses, literally worked to death.[86]

While the suffering of horses during the winter was clearly enormous, one should be careful not to infer that it constituted the end of draft power in the German army. According to Richard DiNardo, in the first eight months of the war (June 22 to March 20) the *Ostheer* lost some 264,954 horses, killed or otherwise deemed unfit for service.[87] This equated to 42 percent of the total horse population on the Eastern Front at the start of Operation Barbarossa and indicates a sharp decline in German mobility, but not the end of it.[88] Horses, like men, not only endured the Russian winter, but were also a major factor in sustaining Army Group Center throughout the crisis of the Soviet offensive. Horses were no answer to rapid offensive warfare, but this was not yet what the Red Army was waging. Army Group Center's calculated withdrawals, aided by its long-suffering horse population, ensured that the German front endured blow after blow of a powerful but blunt Soviet instrument. Time and again major German formations maneuvered just quickly enough to escape destruction and by the fourth week of January had re-formed as a formidable, solid line across much of Kluge's front. The dismal fates of the army group's POWs, wounded, and horses may have been a high price to pay, but in the National Socialist state nothing was too much for success. As one soldier summed up in early January: "That is war, death lurks at every turn. It is a struggle for life or death."[89]

21

THE LAST HURRAH

The Failure of the Soviet Winter Offensive

B y the final week of January the winter Soviet campaign was looking increasingly ineffective. Army Group Center had achieved defensive, and even offensive, successes all along its line against a weakened and overextended Red Army. In the south Langermann-Erlancamp's XXIV Army Corps relieved the encircled German garrison at Suchinitschi. The success was, however, immediately placed at risk when Hitler insisted that the town be held as a springboard for future operations to the north. German commanders on the ground rejected this as utterly fanciful. On January 26 Langermann-Erlancamp maintained that his forces were too weak even to hold Suchinitschi and claimed that he could only maintain his position long enough to evacuate the hundreds of wounded in the town.[1] This

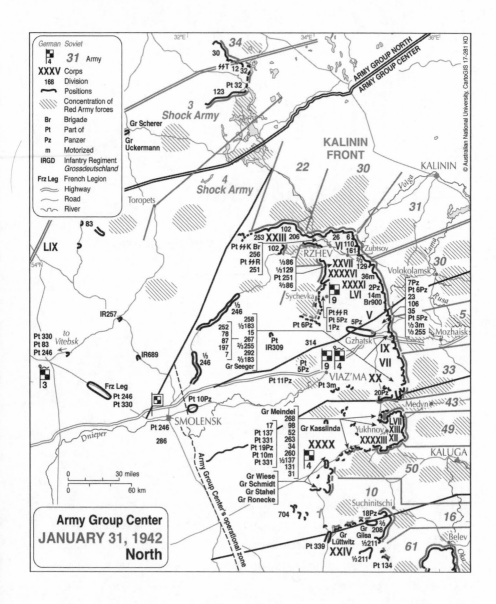

**Army Group Center
JANUARY 31, 1942
North**

was finally achieved on the night of January 28–29 when the last of some 954 wounded were safely transported back down the narrow corridor leading to Suchinitschi.[2] Beyond the danger that the new garrison could be cut off, the Red Army was also attacking into the large bulge that had formed between XXIV Army Corps and LIII Army Corps (defending south of Belev).

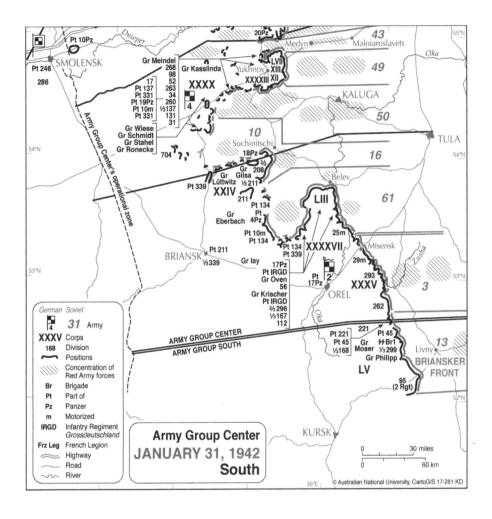

Army Group Center
JANUARY 31, 1942
South

As one soldier wrote in his diary on January 25: "Dead Russians are lying around the village . . . Our soldiers were attacked by the Russians without warning here . . . Infantrymen must have had to make a run for it. Some are just back. They also have dead."[3] Accordingly, Schmidt did not want his only army corps capable of launching serious counterattacks tied up in static defensive fighting at a strategically useless position. The commander of Second Panzer Army was therefore adamant that Suchinitschi be abandoned, and in discussion with Kluge on the afternoon of January 28 the two men independently agreed that the withdrawal would begin at 7:00 A.M. the following morning.[4]

Kluge was confident in Schmidt's plan, not only because it made operational sense, but also because of the apparent success of his hard-won "middle-solution" withdrawal to the Königsberg Line. Hitler's fear that any withdrawal might lead to a Napoleonic rout had proven unjustified. In fact, the shortening of the line allowed the release of forces from Reinhardt's Third Panzer Army, which directly enabled Model's victory west of Rzhev. If Kluge thought Hitler could recognize that Army Group Center's improved strategic position was a result of his own recommendations, he was, however, mistaken. Not only was Hitler unable to acknowledge any limitation, much less fault, in his obstinate strategic thinking, he also had no idea of the extent to which the disastrous effects of his halt order had been deliberately undermined at the front. Accordingly, Hitler drew the opposite conclusion, believing his "will" and determination to hold every meter of ground had saved Army Group Center, and that Kluge and Schmidt thus needed another dose at Suchinitschi. The order for withdrawal was therefore countermanded, and Kluge dutifully passed on Hitler's instruction that the town be held. Yet Kluge was not so easily rebuffed and had learned a great deal about how to manage Hitler. Rather than challenge him directly, Kluge knew to argue for "modifications" that could function in practice as carefully negotiated loopholes. Accordingly, the order to Schmidt's panzer army on the evening of January 28 read: "Order of the Führer that Suchinitschi, *if at all possible*, must be held."[5]

After Hitler's order was transmitted, Halder spoke on the telephone with Schmidt and reinforced the importance of holding Suchinitschi. The panzer general tried to explain the situation on the ground, but Halder was unmoved and insisted that the town should be held because it constituted such a significant "moral success." Indeed, as Halder argued, "freely giving up the city, even when tactically correct, means too much of a loss."[6] Such faith in "moral" victory, even when acknowledged as militarily incorrect, again highlights the importance ascribed to "will" in the National Socialist military calculus. On the following day (January 29) at the OKH, Halder's chief of operations wrote of the disconnect between the high command and the men at the front, "continually expecting something from these burned out troops, that they themselves cannot understand, and which the higher leadership hopes will turn out for the best." Yet even while commenting on the divergence between practical realities and enduring expectations, Heusinger reasoned that the men simply had to comply and that in any retreat "we will suffer the fate of Napoleon." Remarkably, Heusinger claimed he was not unaware of the situation at the front and wrote that upon hearing firsthand reports "you want to recoil and must twitch," but even in these moments the National Socialist ethos endured because, in spite of any problems, a commander "must again ask that they attack."[7] It may be supposition, but if Kluge was indeed responsible for the wording transmitted to Second Panzer Army it must have been clear that it was intended to provide a means to circumvent Hitler's order, and as expected, on January 29 Langermann-Erlancamp's XXIV Army Corps again reported that Suchinitschi simply could not be held.[8] Only when Hitler was informed that so much of Suchinitschi had been destroyed that it could not be defended in full strength did the dictator finally give his approval for it to be abandoned, although he added the absurd stipulation that the town must at least be kept within artillery range.[9] In fact, the last days of January saw very heavy snowfalls, which hindered all movement and led to snowdrifts up to three meters high.[10] The war diary of Lemelsen's XXXXVII Panzer Corps reported that forward motion in areas of geographic depression was not even possible on foot.[11] The conditions no doubt complicated the retreat from Suchinitschi, but the wider implications were far more to the detriment of the Red Army.

Ironically, the winter conditions are commonly viewed as disadvantaging the German army, but the Soviets only enjoyed certain advantages, and not necessarily the most important ones. Their troops were clearly better clothed and equipped, but as we have seen the vast bulk of German frostbite cases were not life threatening. The same, however, could not be said of the winter conditions that worked to Germany's advantage. Tactically the conditions not only hindered movement; they especially hindered rapid movement, forcing Soviet attacks to lumber laboriously forward, which, irrespective of the often flawed offensive doctrine, resulted in calamitous losses for the Red Army. German supply lines were seriously hindered by the conditions, but the armies muddled through, aided by each successful phase of withdrawal and the ability to do most of their fighting from static positions, often close to warm bunkers or village huts. The Red Army, on the other hand, was advancing into Germany's zones of scorched-earth destruction and had to be content with its own lengthening lines of communication, which often meant supplies and troop concentrations were insufficient to meet the relentless demands of the offensive timetable. In essence therefore, the heavy snowfalls were typically a boon to German operations because they slowed the Red Army's communications, concentration, and, most important, its attacks. As one German soldier perceptively noted in his diary on January 30: "Time is working for us now. Every day."[12]

When Soviet attacks were launched the German defenders typically knew what to expect, whereas the high casualties in the Red Army and rigidity of its system precluded a learning curve or the freedom to innovate. Willy Pott from the 167th Infantry Division wrote in a letter on January 30 that after his unit had enjoyed some days of rest, a new Soviet concentration was launched against his lines but suffered a "tremendous debacle." In the space of one to one and a half kilometers, Pott estimated some 700 to 800 Soviets were killed.[13] On another section of Second Panzer Army's front, Erich Hager from the 17th Panzer Division wrote in his diary of a similar event: "I've never fired so much, the whole tank is empty. There were masses of cavalry and infantry. I fired like mad and the guys just fell . . . The Russians have about 250 dead. We captured 14 MG [machine guns] and 7 tanks. We have 1 dead and 6 wounded."[14] Not surprisingly, such constant fiascos only reinforced National Socialist conceptions of the enemy soldier as someone oblivious to death and the Soviet regime as indifferent to the loss of human lives. Certainly in the latter case this was no doubt true, but it was a trait shared to no small extent with National Socialism. Albert Neuhaus wrote in a letter on January 30: "The Russians send infantry troops against German artillery and die in huge numbers. It is craziness from the Russians to run against such a well defended line." Neuhaus then concluded: "But the Russians possess so many human resources that it is nothing for them to daily send a whole row to a sure death."[15] Such views were commonly shared among the men of the *Ostheer* and acted to reinforce the Wehrmacht's superiority myth as well as offer a sense of artificial security in the face of numerical inferiority. The countless defensive battles, all without names and most far smaller than the examples cited, share the common denominator of widely disparate losses between attackers and defenders. Individually they tell us little, but cumulatively the frequency of such encounters form a fundamental aspect of the winter fighting, which in a war of attrition heavily favored the Wehrmacht.

Schmidt's Second Panzer Army, as well as his former troops of the Second Army (which since mid-January had been subordinated to Army Group South) both survived the winter fighting in reasonably good order. They had lost a significant amount of irreplaceable equipment in their December retreats, which boded ill for any future large-scale offensive plans, but the two armies remained formidable formations and, far from being beaten, had exacted a huge toll on the Red Army in early 1942. Schmidt's long front may have been for the most part static, but it was by no means inactive on the defense or passive when the opportunity for local counterattacks arose. In fact, by February 13 optimism had grown so much that the panzer army was debating with Army Group Center about the virtue of launching an offensive, to which Schmidt could only comment (in Latin): "*Difficile est, satiram non scribere* [It is difficult not to write a satire]."[16] Whatever the irony of the subsequent deliberations, Schmidt knew only too well that his forces had survived some extremely perilous weeks, especially in December, but that out of their desperate circumstances Second Army and Second Panzer Army had delivered the Red Army a *coup de collier* (a blow born of desperation).

With the southern flank of Army Group Center stabilized and the Soviets dealt a stunning reversal at Suchinitschi, Kluge's greatest worry was Heinrici's Fourth Army, which was being squeezed into another bulge by Soviet attacks in the north and south. In the north, Fourth Army and Ruoff's Fourth Panzer Army were unable to close the gap between their forces, which allowed a dangerous stream of enemy forces into the army group's rear area and threatened the northern flank of Heinrici's army. On January 26 another attempt to close the gap by two weak divisions of Heinrici's army failed to make any real progress, and Kluge worried that the Fourth Army was increasingly in an "untenable situation," with most of its forces bottled up in the salient around Yukhnov. Heinrici pleaded for permission to withdraw from Yukhnov, but since his army formed the southern anchor of the Königsberg Line (Yukhnov-Gzhatsk-Zubtsov), which the army group had so long fought for, resistance from above was always going to be strong. Kluge advocated on behalf of Heinrici, but Hitler rejected the request on January 26.[17] The following day the situation worsened for Fourth Army when the highway to Yukhnov, the only source of supply for most of Fourth Army, was cut by Soviet forces operating in the German rear. As Heinrici noted in his diary on January 27: "The closed roads mean the end of our provisions. Only two days and the army will start starving. Our forces to win back the roads are extremely meagre and motley . . . The situation is doubtful. In addition, the field marshal [Kluge] reminds us that the Führer demands we hold the position east of Yukhnov under all circumstances. It is by no means to be given up. And yet we are encircled in this position."[18] Heinrici's frustration was directed squarely at Hitler, whose "hold-fast" orders he blamed for the enduring crisis consuming his army. On January 28 he fumed in his diary: "It is so hard to have been in the worst position for eight weeks, always trying, always again experiencing failure . . . This situation is caused by the orders of the Führer, who holds everything. Rommel [in North Africa] was allowed to evade and subsequently achieved victory, but we have to hold and allow the enemy to take the initiative."[19]

To the north, Ruoff was also doing his best to help seal the breach, sending Thoma's 20th Panzer Division to the south and assembling an attack group made up of the 255th, 292nd, and 183rd Infantry Divisions. These forces were all relatively weak, and Ruoff warned Kluge that even if the gap could be closed, it could not be defended because the available divisions were all just too depleted. Yet Kluge remained adamant; Fourth Panzer Army's attack had to proceed on January 29. The attack showed again the difficulty of offensive operations in the wintry conditions. The war diary of the Fourth Panzer Army reported meter-high snow, through which the forward companies had to shovel in order to bring up heavier weaponry. The attack was not able to close the gap, but it did narrow it, and Ruoff was able to hold the newly seized ground.[20]

While Ruoff struggled to reach Heinrici in the south, Hitler and the OKH kept Fourth Army on life support, allowing the slightest possible concessions, and always under the pressure of circumstances, to keep the army from collapsing. Heinrici was not exaggerating in suggesting that his army had been effectively encircled around Yukhnov. It was by no means an iron ring, but with the roads to the west periodically cut and hardly any reserves available to free them, Heinrici was justifiably anxious. On January 30 he wrote despairingly: "The whole night I just could not sleep because worries kept me awake. It is an incredible waste of energy. Only cognac and chain smoking keep me going."[21] Kluge was also deeply concerned but managed to work out a compromise acceptable to the high command. On the strict condition that Yukhnov not be surrendered, Heinrici would be allowed to withdraw his front another fifteen to twenty kilometers westward immediately, shortening his flanks and freeing up some vital reserves.[22] Of course, barring solving the problems on either his exposed northern flank or elongated southern flank, Fourth Army was still living on borrowed time.

The high command could not provide the reinforcements required to alleviate Heinrici's desperate predicament, and yet they steadfastly expected him to maintain a position too large for his exhausted and badly depleted formations. As Heinrici characterized the situation, his army was "like a swimmer thrown into the water bound at the hand and foot."[23] Yet Heusinger at the OKH appeared to cast Hitler as the tragic figure, writing on January 29 that he "probably did not feel as helpless in any situation of his life as he does now, at least sometimes he has tears in his eyes, and he knows that he often demands superhuman things!"[24] Of course, demanding "superhuman things" should have been taken by the army command as a sign of Hitler's irrationality, but the OKH was much too imbued with National Socialism and the accordant Hitler myth for such clear-sighted reasoning. Indeed, Heusinger was of the opinion that Hitler was now "much calmer than at the beginning, where he could suddenly explode in the room, ranting wildly and often believing that he could do better." By contrast, Heusinger noted with relief that Hitler had recently become "very amenable" to strategic advice.[25] No doubt Hitler could see the tide was turning on the Soviet offensive, and believing as he did that it was all thanks to the imposition of his iron will, the dictator felt deserving of the credit. It also emboldened him to continue taking a hard line on withdrawals, no matter how logical the military rationale that Kluge presented. The circumstances at Suchinitschi or Yukhnov were not what Hitler responded to; what counted for far more was his estimation of the man making the request, especially if his commitment to National Socialism and Hitler himself was judged to be unconditional.

A case in point was SS-*Obergruppenführer* Josef "Sepp" Dietrich who commanded the 1st SS-Division *Leibstandarte Adolf Hitler* in Army Group South. Dietrich visited Goebbels on the afternoon of January 27 to update him on recent events in the east. His update included a report on his own unauthorized withdrawal from Rostov in late November 1941. As Goebbels recounted their conversation:

> He tells me about the tense and also costly retreat of the *Leibstandarte* from Rostov to just before the border of Taganrog. Explains to me in detail what this was about, what was going on, when the Führer flew to Mariupol. He was supposed to obey a command of the Führer to dig in some twenty kilometers from Taganrog, which as things were however, was completely impossible. If he had carried out this order, the *Leibstandarte* would have been sacrificed. So Sepp Dietrich has done what, according to the situation, had to be done and the Führer has not only given him his approval, but also awarded him the Oak Leaves to the Knight's Cross. Sepp Dietrich is a real trooper and gives the impression of a Napoleonic general. If we had twenty such people as divisional commanders, we would not have to worry about the eastern front at all.[26]

Clearly, Dietrich's insubordination was overlooked in light of his impeccable National Socialist credentials, which in Hitler's mind meant his act of defiance could only have been in the best interests of his division.[27] Army commanders were not so lucky. Most of these men, especially at the division and corps level, were unknown to Hitler, and so he remained suspicious of them, judging many to lack the iron resolve of the SS. The irony was that the *Ostheer* had many more than twenty senior commanders who were prepared to withdraw against orders to save their own formations, while, just like the SS, retaining an absolute commitment to serving the Nazi state under Hitler. In fact, their actions in ordering retreats were a reflection of their devotion, not opposition, to the state, and far from demonstrating a lack of resolve, such orders showed a courage to do what the commanders knew to be right. It all added to the psychological pressure on the army commanders, who could not understand why their professional judgment was not respected and could never have imagined that, after everything they had fought for and sacrificed, Hitler would dare to question their courage and devotion (or "will") when they pleaded for permission to retreat. Heinrici even alluded to the "hidden" side of the command equation on the Eastern Front, writing to his wife: "The [war] diary pages actually only describe the military facts." He then explained that the "current nerve-racking situation" was not reflected in their pages, which alludes to the many tensions of army command, and perhaps also to some of the solutions to those problems.[28] Confronted with matters of life and death, many army commanders, just like Sepp Dietrich, no doubt chose the former.

As stressful and uncertain as Fourth Army's situation was, a new attempt to close the gap in the north was finally successful on February 4. Heinrici received the news with enormous relief: "The bridge in the north to Fourth Panzer Army is closed; we have achieved a great success."[29] This success not only severed the flow of major enemy units into Army Group Center's rear area, but also cut off those Soviet forces that had already passed through the narrow gap, just as had happened at Rzhev. For the time being, however, these Soviet forces were still formidable, and they threatened Heinrici's army with both direct attack from the rear and the strangulation of his supply lines. Unlike the other armies in Army Group Center, February presented a daily battle for survival for the weakened Fourth Army, but time was at least on its side. As Gustav Böker wrote home on January 28: "Here it is now the highpoint of the winter. At the end of February it should be better here. That is still one month. Well, we will survive this time too and then it will and must be spring."[30] Reinforcements were also at last arriving, with advanced elements of Colonel Franz Beyer's newly formed 331st Infantry Division arriving at Fourth Army in late January.[31] Most important, Soviet formations were unable to maintain the pressure due to the tremendous losses they had sustained.

On Fourth Army's loosely defended southern flank, a Soviet cavalry corps attempting to cut the road to Yukhnov was reduced from 28,000 men to 5,500 in less than two weeks of fighting beginning the end of January.[32] As one junior Soviet officer admitted in his diary, 90 out of every 100 attacks against Fourth Army failed because there was no coordination of units or timely support by artillery. He also noted the appalling state of the men, who had no food and were simply ordered into the forest by the regimental commander to find whatever they could before reporting for the next attack. As the officer concluded, "Everyone was frozen, hungry, angry and had a very depressed mood."[33] The southern flank was largely the responsibility of Lieutenant-General Hans Zorn's XXXX Panzer Corps, who formed a host of ad hoc battle groups named after their commanders (Ronecke, Stahel, Schmidt, Wiese, Kellner, Traut) to check Soviet progress.[34] In spite of their relatively small size, these battle groups routinely switched between defensive and offensive postures to maximize their effectiveness. Thus, on January 29 Major Rainer Stahel's battle group conducted a night attack on a Soviet-occupied village, killing "numerous" enemy troops, taking some POWs, and capturing two guns.[35] Of course, Fourth Army's own losses were by no means inconsiderable, with some 2,500 sick and wounded men awaiting evacuation from Yukhnov.[36] Even for those left physically unscathed, the weeks of winter fighting at Fourth Army left an unforgettable impression. As one soldier wrote to his family on January 30: "I've seen my life hanging by a thread more than once, and yet I have always been lucky. However, I was ready and prepared for everything, just as I am today. Better said, I've often already thought my life was over."[37]

To deal with the problem of Soviet forces behind the lines, which in addition to the regular forces of the Red Army were supplemented by partisan groups as well as continual drops of Soviet paratroopers, Ruoff dispatched Fehn's 5th Panzer Division. Fehn's division still retained a powerful complement of tanks, with some fifty-nine operational panzers (thirteen Mark IIs, thirty-one Mark IIIs, and fifteen Mark IVs).[38] The division was dispatched first to Viaz'ma and then began operating southeast of the town, where, in mid-February, three and a half Soviet divisions were encircled and destroyed. The Soviets had attempted to resist from an improvised "castle with snow walls," but they had no food or shelter and were annihilated by German artillery, with an estimated 3,500 enemy dead covering the battlefield.[39]

Such victories secured the position of Heinrici's long-suffering Fourth Army, and as confidence in the general situation grew, even Hitler became willing to compromise with his generals in the east. Still under serious pressure at Yukhnov, Heinrici flew to Hitler's headquarters on February 28 to plead in person for a withdrawal, which would shorten Fourth Army's front and free up much-needed reserves. Hitler was characteristically opposed, but as Heinrici recorded the encounter in his diary: "He fights over this concession. Postpones it. It is not before the end of the meeting, when Kluge also supports the request . . . that he agrees. Führer says that it is in fact irrelevant if we are ten kilometers east or west of Yukhnov. As the front has in his opinion been stabilized, he would not quibble about a few kilometers."[40] Hitler was correct; a few kilometers here or there on the Eastern Front were quite irrelevant. Yet over the preceding month they were hardly irrelevant to the men of the Fourth Army, who had to hold unnecessarily elongated lines and endure untold additional casualties. It was yet another instance of Hitler's pointlessly destructive stand-fast orders, which imperiled Army Group Center.

In the last week of January, as Heinrici and Ruoff fought desperately to close the gap between their armies, Reinhardt's area of operations with the Third Panzer Army had become comparatively uneventful, even "quiet." There were still local actions, but as Reinhardt depicted them on January 29, they consisted of "several small attacks" that were all repulsed.[41] There was a minor exception at Funck's 7th Panzer Division, where a Soviet attack seized a section of the German line on the night of January 26–27, but the Soviets were expelled in a counterattack the following day that killed 150 enemy troops and captured 25 POWs.[42] Third Panzer Army's long, static front was held together more on account of Soviet exhaustion and redirection of effort than German strength. In fact, some sections of Reinhardt's line were so perilously thin it is a wonder more Soviet breakthroughs did not occur. For example, Gollnick's 36th Motorized Infantry Division could average only eleven men for every 100 meters of line, while Veiel's 2nd Panzer Division was as low as eight men per 100 meters.[43] At the same time, Funck's 7th Panzer Division retained just five operational tanks, while another seven were "on loan" to other formations or held in reserve.[44] As the war diary of Lieutenant-General Josef Harpe's XXXXI Army Corps summed up the situation on January 30: "Due to the lack of strength, the security of the main battle line is without any depth to speak of. Units fight here without relief. As a result, the personal, physical and mental fighting strength of the corps is constantly decreasing."[45] Fortunately for Harpe and the other forces of Third Panzer Army, the opposing Soviet forces were hardly better off, and along much of the front both sides welcomed a break from the relentless combat operations.

Already on January 25, Kluge gave Reinhardt advance notice that his headquarters would shortly be relocated, although the formations that currently made up Third Panzer Army would remain in place and be distributed between Fourth Panzer Army (V Army Corps) and Ninth Army (LVI Panzer Corps, XXXXI and XXVII Army Corps). Only on January 29 did an order from Army Group Center reveal the new assignment for Reinhardt and his command staff. Third Panzer Army's headquarters would be moved some 280 kilometers west to Vitebsk (125 kilometers northwest of Smolensk).[46] Reinhardt was not too impressed, reacting to the news in his diary with a single word: "Annoying!" His task at Vitebsk was to halt the flow of Soviet forces penetrating south through the wide-open space between Kluge's and Küchler's army groups. Although Reinhardt's new "panzer army" initially contained only minor forces with limited mobility, the Soviet forces he encountered were hardly any stronger.[47] Reinhardt concentrated first on defending larger population centers and, as more reserves arrived, was able to push Soviet forces back to the northeast and away from Vitebsk.[48] On February 18 Reinhardt's success earned him the Oak Leaves cluster to the Knight's Cross, which Hitler awarded mainly in recognition of Reinhardt's defensive successes over the winter, but as the panzer general explained to his wife: "That the Führer, however, does not want to award the Oak Leaves for 'successful retreats'; (quite correctly) he waited for the next clear success."[49]

In the second half of January, no single commander contributed more to frustrating the Soviet winter offensive than Model at Ninth Army. His achievement in closing the gap west of Rzhev not only restored the army's front and helped secure its supply lines, but also effectively cut off nine enemy divisions, some 60,000 Soviet troops.[50] It was the most decisive offensive thrust of the winter campaign, and it did not come from the Red Army. But Model's achievement was significant only if the newly won land bridge between Rzhev and Olenino could be maintained. Knowing that a major Soviet effort would be directed against this sector, Model directed what reserves he could to bolster Bieler's defending VI Army Corps. In addition to four precious 88-millimeter Flak guns and five StuG III assault guns, this included the SS motorized regiment *Der Führer* (from the 2nd SS Division *Das Reich*), to whom Model implored, "Hold on at all costs," and then repeated himself: "At all costs."[51]

After days of smaller attacks, on January 26 Ninth Army's war diary noted what it called "the first major stress test for the newly created front west of Rzhev." Two waves of attacking Soviet troops, each about 500 men strong, hit Weber's 256th Infantry Division. The attack was beaten back, but not without difficulty, and the defending units west of Rzhev braced themselves for further heavy pressure.[52] On the morning of January 27 the Red Army attacked with "great strength" across a four-to-five-kilometer sector, capturing an important village in the German battle line, but that afternoon a counterattack managed to recapture it.[53] A similar pattern repeated itself on January 28, with Weiss's 26th Infantry Division losing a village in its battle line after being attacked by almost 400 men supported by tanks. A counterattack retook the position, while other sectors in VI Army Corps repelled "constant waves" of attackers.[54] German war diaries reported hundreds of enemy losses in these attacks, but it is also clear that their defensive operations were taking a toll and that the outcome would be decided by attrition.

Never complacent and aware that the Kalinin Front would throw everything into penetrating Ninth Army's line, Model was working on a contingency plan to increase the depth of the German-occupied zone west of Rzhev. Accordingly, he directed Vietinghoff's XXXXVI Panzer Corps, which had taken over the defense of Sychevka and was ensuring a continual flow of supplies north to Rzhev, to adopt a much more aggressive stance. Krüger's 1st Panzer Division (part of Vietinghoff's new command) had already led a makeshift collection of units in a highly successful attack on January 21 to help tie down Soviet forces during Model's principal operation to close the gap in Ninth Army's line. Now, however, Model wanted Vietinghoff to help destroy the Soviet formations south of Bieler's VI Army Corps by launching an offensive from Sychevka to link up with Schubert's XXIII Army Corps. It was essentially a repeat of Model's earlier operation, which aimed to encircle and destroy a number of Soviet divisions operating south of VI Army Corps and thereby expand the zone of German-occupied territory. If Konev's Kalinin Front was to break Ninth Army's line again, Model was ensuring it would receive no help from the south and would have even farther to advance.

The starting date for Vietinghoff's offensive was nominally set for January 28, but bad weather and delays in concentrating his forces pushed back the start date to the next day.[55] In the interim, however, Vietinghoff was by no means idle, directing Krüger's panzer division to engage in local attacks, such as those on January 26, which overran four enemy-held villages and resulted in over 500 Soviet dead.[56] The following day Krüger continued his attacks, capturing Soviet artillery and antitank guns, while on January 28 he again seized a series of villages, yielding a "rich booty." As Ninth Army's war diary noted, the state of the Soviet forces in this region fully justified aggressive action because they lacked the weaponry and munitions needed to resist Krüger's attacks and were entirely dependent upon inadequate aerial resupply.[57] Indeed, the breakdown in Soviet communications meant that some of these air drops were reinforcing German units, a result that was further exploited in taunting megaphone declarations to Soviet positions: "Hey Russians! Ivan! Thank you. We're eating your pork and peas. It's delicious."[58] Model was not without his own serious supply problems. An average of just one train reached his army each day when at least three were judged necessary to sustain operations.[59] Everything was therefore rationed and judiciously allocated, making Soviet airdrops and captured supplies a welcome addition.

Ninth Army's vital line of supply south of Sychevka to Viaz'ma was an open frontier linked by fortified German positions that maintained only tenuous control over the zones between them. Soviet cavalry ranged over the area but lacked the strength to dominate it. Since Model concentrated everything into the vital sectors west of Rzhev (Bieler's VI Army Corps) and at Sychevka for the coming offensive (Vietinghoff's XXXXVI Panzer Corps), nothing was spared to reinforce Major-General Erhard Raus, who was charged with defending the area. Raus therefore gathered his own makeshift force by distributing his staff across a wide area and roping in every able-bodied officer and man. Many were soldiers returning from the hospital or furlough, but Raus did not discriminate, and pressed rear-area personnel, including some who had never been in combat, into service. As Raus recalled: "Frequently, our newly formed units underwent their baptism of fire on the very day of their initial organization."[60] It was this unique ability to improvise and implement quick responses, often without specific direction, that accounted for local German superiority in countless crises throughout the winter. Using his initiative Raus claimed, although doubtfully, to have gathered a force of almost thirty-five-thousand men by the end of February, but whatever the figure there can be no question that he succeeded in blocking Soviet control of the vital seventy-kilometer stretch of territory that kept Model's army alive.[61]

By the end of January, Konev's Kalinin Front had pooled enough resources to seriously challenge Bieler's reinforced army corps west of Rzhev. On the morning of January 30, Weber's 256th Infantry Division reported an attack by very strong Soviet forces, which included some eighteen tanks. Some of these were turned back by concentrated German artillery fire, and seven were destroyed in the fighting, but the defenders too suffered serious losses. The SS motorized regiment *Der Führer* reported that its average company strength had shrunk to between twenty and thirty men, and this was before a renewed Soviet attack in the afternoon that was spearheaded by twenty-four tanks. The ensuing combat was ferocious; eleven more enemy tanks were destroyed and many soldiers killed, but a section of the German line was successfully overrun. At Bieler's headquarters there was now real concern that the whole front would soon buckle under the pressure, as the VI Army Corps' war diary concluded on January 30: "If the enemy continues his strong attacks . . . a stronger break-in is unavoidable, which can lead to the danger of the enemy reopening the old gap again."[62]

The night of January 30–31 brought continued Soviet attacks, none of which were successful, but holding the line was an hour-by-hour struggle with no guarantee of success. In spite of the relentless enemy attacks, Bieler hurried assembled reserves, including four of his StuG III assault guns, for a counterattack to retake the former defensive line. After further Soviet attacks in the morning, Bieler's sudden offensive appears to have caught the Soviets off guard. It led to a complete success, with the corps' war diary noting "very high losses in blood for the enemy" as well as three Soviet tanks destroyed, and most important, the section of the main defensive line was recaptured.[63]

After serious losses Konev was having to start all over again. His failure may in part explain why on February 1 the *Stavka* reinstituted the Western Direction, which had existed briefly at the beginning of the war and functioned as a coordinating command for Soviet fronts. Significantly, under the Western Direction the Kalinin Front was no longer autonomous; instead it was to be directed, together with the Western Front, by Zhukov as overall commander. For Stalin and the *Stavka* the failure to capitalize on their numerical superiority and numerous breakthroughs in no way deterred them from their excessively ambitious strategic plans. Even after the Red Army had proven incapable of pursuing so many objectives against Army Group Center, Zhukov's new command was still tasked with "the encirclement and capture of the enemy's Rzhev-Viaz'ma grouping."[64] In fact, it was Model who was doing the encircling, and in February Hitler rewarded him for it with the Oak Leaves cluster to his Knight's Cross and promotion to colonel-general.

The Soviet offensive near Rzhev continued unabated, and in consequence so too did the disproportionate body count. Georgi Osadchinsky's brigade was ordered to attack the German line near Rzhev, and he was one of the few to survive the ordeal:

> The fighting against the Rzhev salient was bloody and cruel. But our attacks were not properly prepared and the enemy had organized his defenses well . . . we advanced against his positions, trudging through knee-deep snow. We were met by a hail of fire, and ahead of us our way was blocked by barbed wire and minefields. The

Germans opened up on us from the flanks, pinning our battalion down—and their snipers began to pick off our machine gunners. Our commanding lieutenant tried to summon artillery support, but none came. I saw him crying in rage and frustration. We were caught in a death trap. Our brigade—which had repelled the Germans from Moscow and fought so bravely in the counteroffensive—was now being torn to pieces.[65]

P. Mikhin later depicted Soviet operations at Rzhev as a kind of human meat grinder: "The Germans were turning the handle, and we poured and poured thousands of soldiers into it."[66] For the men of Model's Ninth Army, every failed Soviet attack proved good for morale, especially as their field-works rapidly developed and added an increasing sense of security. From his place in the line Hartmut Beermann wrote home in a letter on January 29: "In our section of the front bunkers are now built everywhere in close proximity. In front of them every Russian attack wave fails."[67] The commander of the SS regiment *Der Führer*, *Standartenführer* Otto Kumm, told of the enemy dead forming "walls of corpses" in front of his positions and estimated the number, probably excessively, at fifteen thousand dead.[68] Likewise, Heinrich Haape wrote home in late January about "thousands of dead in front of our [6th Infantry] division. It is harrowing. In some parts of our sector, there are dead bodies piled upon dead bodies. A good thing that it is so cold or else an awful smell of corpses would torment us too much."[69]

While the Soviets persisted with their attacks north of Rzhev, Vieting-hoff's XXXXVI Panzer Corps launched its own offensive from Sychevka on January 29, which aimed to reach Schubert's XXIII Army Corps some fifty-five kilometers away. Model wanted to carve up the Soviet forces south of Rzhev by completely encircling those elements of the Twenty-Ninth Army cut off south of Bieler's VI Army Corps. It was by no means a rapid attack, but progress continued at a steady daily pace, and the arrival of tank reinforcements from Fehn's 5th Panzer Division was more than the outgunned Soviet defenders could deal with.[70] On February 5 contact between Vietinghoff and Schubert was established, and Model had effectively eliminated another large body of Soviet troops opposing his army.

It was another remarkable turn of events for Ninth Army, facilitated to no small extent by the wanton overextension of the Red Army. Indeed, just as Hitler and the OKH could never bring themselves to order a timely halt to their exhausted autumn offensive, so too the *Stavka* went on reinforcing failure by ordering futile attacks into the teeth of often well-prepared German defenses. Far from restricting the vast scope of their failed operations, the Soviet high command issued a new directive to Zhukov's Western Direction on February 16 that instructed him "to smash and destroy the enemy's Rzhev-Viaz'ma-Yukhnov grouping and by March 5 reach and dig-in on our old defensive line with prepared anti-tank ditches."[71] It was pure fantasy, which again paralleled Germany's striking mismatch between the situation at the front and the thinking of the high command. Yet unfortunately for the men of the Red Army, their commanders were much more dogmatic in their adherence to the orders, however nonsensical, of their high command, and many paid for this with their lives. Model's short tenure in command had come at a high cost, with some 5,000 casualties (or some 10 percent of Ninth Army's combat strength as of January 19), but the results were undeniable. In the same period to February 8 some 26,000 enemy troops were claimed to have been killed and another 5,000 captured. Countless wounded must also be added to the total, as well as the matériel losses, which Ninth Army claimed to include 343 artillery pieces and dozens of Soviet tanks.[72] The extent to which Ninth Army, or for that matter Army Group Center, might claim a victory is difficult to say given the harrowing ordeal of the winter campaign, but at the end of it all they had at least endured.

CONCLUSION

The end of the winter period encouraged misplaced hopes of a revival in Germany's military fortunes. Army Group Center had survived the worst of the Soviet offensive and in the process inflicted remarkable casualties upon the Red Army. Considering all the German gains made between June 22 and December 5, the Red Army's winter offensive had reconquered just 7 percent by the end of January 1942 (41,196 square kilometers in December and another 50,260 square kilometers in January).[1] At this point, the Eastern Front had largely stabilized, and developments on other fronts were proving even more positive for the Germans. In North Africa, Lieutenant-General Erwin Rommel's surprise offensive at El Agheila in Libya on January 21 caught the British Eighth Army off guard and, within ten days, led to the recapture of the Benghazi bulge. On the French coast the German warships *Gneisenau, Scharnhorst,* and *Prinz Eugen* made a successful dash through the English Channel (Operation Cerberus) to safer waters in the north. Days later, news reached Berlin that Britain had suffered its worst ever military defeat with the Japanese capture of Singapore on February 15. Hitler was buoyed by the favorable turn of events and, taking full credit for forestalling a collapse in the east, was more determined than ever that the 1942 summer campaign would follow his own strategic conception over that of the generals who, he complained, had led him to Moscow.[2]

The winter crisis had, however, taken its toll on Hitler. When Goebbels visited the Wolf's Lair in March, he was shocked by Hitler's diminished appearance, and in their private discussion the dictator admitted that the winter had left him feeling somewhat sick. Goebbels even noted in his diary: "The long winter has had such an effect on his mental state that all of this has not passed him by without leaving a trace."[3] SS *Brigadeführer* Kurt Meyer claimed in a secretly recorded conversation after his capture: "In my opinion the Führer hasn't been quite himself since the winter of 1941 and 1942, as result of all the happenings. He gets some sort of attacks of hysteria."[4] There is even one secondhand report that Hitler and Jodl agreed after the first winter in the east that "victory could no longer be achieved."[5] To whatever extent the events of the winter had shaken Hitler's confidence, in public at least he tried to maintain a guise of absolute confidence. On January 30, on the ninth anniversary of his ascension to power, he spoke in Berlin of his "boundless faith, in my person as well, that nothing, no matter what, would ever be able to throw me out of the saddle."[6] Yet not all observers were convinced, as Arvid Fredborg wrote of the appearance: "Colleagues who have been in the position to study him over a period of years, before I went to Germany, said immediately, 'You can see that he had his first serious reverse.'"[7]

For Hitler success on the defensive was a very poor substitute for success on the attack. But more important, it was the scale of the Red Army's winter offensive that came as a shock. That it was such a surprise only underlines the magnitude of his underestimation of the Soviet enemy. With his better grasp of economics compared to many of his operationally minded generals, Hitler probably did suspect how dangerous the situation had become for Germany, which may well account for the unexplained sickness he reported to Goebbels weeks after the immediate threat from the Red Army had passed. Germany had lost a great deal of equipment and vehicles in the winter retreat, neither of which could be easily replaced without greater economic capacity, and that was precisely Hitler's problem. There was no real solution; in fact, the eastern campaign was intended to solve this dilemma, not exacerbate it. The 1942 summer offensive (Operation Blue) would have to proceed with only a fraction of the resources driving the *Ostheer* forward in 1941.[8]

At the end of March 1942 the OKH compiled a report on the state of the *Ostheer*, which confirmed that any summer offensive would be heavily constrained. Of the 162 divisions in the east only 8 were deemed suitable for offensive operations, 3 could be brought up to full offensive capability after a short rest, and 47 could perform some limited offensive tasks. The rest were suitable only for defensive warfare. Thus, barely more than one-third were capable of some offensive action, and the vast bulk of these only provisionally so. At the same time, throughout the *Ostheer* there were reported to be just 160 operational tanks.[9] Clearly, the Soviet winter campaign, while failing to meet its intended strategic goals and at horrendous cost, had, at the very least, contributed to the blunting of the *Ostheer*. Not unreasonably, Heusinger at the OKH believed, albeit mistakenly: "Unfortunately we will not be able to think about an offensive for a long time."[10]

Another report compiled for the OKH between February 9 and 24 by Major Hermann Oehmichen was intended to judge the mood of the men at the front. To do this Oehmichen was dispatched to Heinrici's Fourth Army, which without question was among the hardest hit of Kluge's army group. The responses he encountered surprised him: "After all the troops have gone through their attitude and mood are surprisingly cheerful." Oehmichen attributed this first to having recovered from "the depressing mood of the retreat," but inquiring further he assessed that the men were buoyed by three factors: the anticipation of reserves arriving and the prospect of relief from the line; the belief that leave would soon be reinstated (it was canceled during the winter crisis); and, last, the expectation of a "spring offensive." The last, Oehmichen explained, was associated "with a change in their fortunes" and the "good times of the summer." Yet Oehmichen's conclusions contained at least one worrying observation: "With respect to these reports it must be remembered, however, that in front of their superiors the men try to be on their best behavior, especially when they hear that the person concerned is 'from the very top echelons.'"[11] Revealingly, Josef Przyklenk, who had recently been captured by the British, told his interrogators in March 1942:

> It is obvious that we have retreated in Russia. Even if we retake that strip of territory, about 100km, Russia is still there. It is ten times the size of Germany [*sic*]. The Russians may have lost their crack troops, but we must reckon that we, too, have lost our crack troops. It doesn't do to think about it. If I am asked whether we shall conquer Russia, I say, "Yes," but when I think it over, then it's a very different matter.[12]

Such conflicted dissonance between conditioned and learned responses and individual thoughts is a consequence of living in a highly regulated ideological world. Yet assessments of German field post from later in the winter do suggest the outlook of the soldiers had become more upbeat, although most letters do not explicitly address Germany's prospects in the war and simply comment on the soldier's immediate environment.[13] This may also be, as Neitzel and Welzer have suggested, a subconscious "response to the dilemma," which required men to avoid matters they could not control and "simply not to think too hard about the situation."[14]

German officers, on the other hand, especially those in the higher echelons, had a much harder time ignoring the reality of their situation. According to Oehmichen's report the mood among the senior commanders of Fourth Army "was one of unanimous and intense bitterness about what has happened." This Oehmichen determined to stem from two assumptions. The first was their belief that "the catastrophe this winter could have been avoided, if they had listened to us," although what exactly this is referring to and how it might have avoided Army Group Center's winter crisis is unclear. The second, and much more plausible, grievance that the officers identified was their inability to direct their forces freely during the Soviet winter offensive because of Hitler's halt order. "We know how to defend ourselves, but our hands are tied. We cannot act on our own initiative." Given its strategic position, Fourth Army had been the most endangered by Hitler's order, but even here the complaints of the generals might suggest more room for maneuver than Hitler intended. As Oehmichen wrote, "The order to hold out at all costs, given solemnly to the troops and rescinded hours later under the force of circumstances, only means that instead of making an orderly withdrawal, we are being pushed back by the enemy. This results in heavy, irreplaceable losses of men and equipment."[15] It is again unclear what event this is referring to, but Hitler was not in the habit of issuing orders to the army only to rescind them hours later, while on the other hand there is evidence of Kluge and Kübler reacting to the "force of circumstances" and defiantly authorizing withdrawals. In any case, there were clearly good grounds—and not just in Fourth Army—for the field commanders to feel aggrieved by their loss of independence, even if this is known to have been contested at many levels.

While Oehmichen's report suggested the rejection of Hitler's interference was "unanimous," this was of course not how the halt order was portrayed in Nazi Germany, and more important, this view has continued to find a degree of acceptance in some of the best studies about both the war in the east as well as Hitler himself.[16] Although bolstered by the memoirs of military men who held no command in Army Group Center during the winter, the postwar myth was not without occasional challenges, but these lone voices failed to make an impact. Gersdorff, Army Group Center's chief intelligence officer, wrote after the war:

> Nowadays many old soldiers and postwar publications regard this order as having been Army Group Centre's salvation from total destruction. Based on my own experience, I am of a different mind . . . Only the army, corps, and divisional commanders, as well as the line-unit commanders on the spot, were in a position to reach the correct decisions concerning their responsibilities in the existing conditions. The defense against the Soviet counteroffensive would probably have succeeded with fewer casualties than it did with Hitler's unimaginative stand-fast orders from his distant headquarters in East Prussia.[17]

Gersdorff's assessment is borne out by the wartime records, although given the insubordinate nature of these activities, we may assume that this evidence is only a fraction of what actually took place.[18] Beyond the fact that opposing Hitler's order was clearly insubordinate, one must also consider the prevailing culture within the Wehrmacht, which, because of its embrace of a National Socialist military ethos, struggled to accept, much less champion, a withdrawal strategy. Generals who asked permission to retreat were guilty of a "crisis of nerves" and were sometimes openly derided.[19] Even Heinrici subscribed in part to this point of view, but of course believed his situation to be the exception. In his diary for February 28 the commander of the Fourth Army wrote: "Only by holding at all costs was it possible to counteract a panic. (Very true, generally speaking, but wrong in individual instances. This mistake caused our continuously critical situation and our heavy casualties)."[20] Yet if commanders across Army Group Center believed their particular situation warranted a retreat and, like Heinrici, valued the preservation of their units over the strict observance of Hitler's nonsensical order, the scope for rebellion was rather large.[21] This is confirmed by Miguel Lopez's small study of three infantry divisions in Army Group Center, which found that opposition to Hitler's halt order did not end *Auftragstaktik* in the winter of 1941–1942, although, under pressure from above, it had inevitably been curtailed. It also strongly suggests that the commanders in the east possessed a much greater latitude to "interpret" and act on Hitler's criminal orders than they exercised during the war.[22]

If credit for saving Army Group Center was claimed by Hitler himself, the blame for the winter crisis in the first instance was heaped squarely on the shoulders of the generals. This was of course not entirely unjustified, but Hitler, backed by the OKH, was unwilling to accept any responsibility for Germany's lamentable state of affairs in the east, while the high turnover of generals during the winter was presented as castigation for wrongdoing. Commenting on this, Oehmichen's report highlighted the extent of the OKH's complicity in absolving Hitler of all blame:

Though in human terms it is tragic that meritorious military leaders have to bear the odium of failure for no good reason, it is vital that any criticism stops at the person of the Führer. Even the slightest doubt about decisions by the highest leadership is liable to shake the dominant idea and thus also faith in victory. The fact that the ordinary soldier associates the change in command with conviction about the fundamental change for the better is a gain for which no personal sacrifice is too high.[23]

No commander, no matter how distinguished or valuable, was allowed to stand in the way of Hitler's stage-managed perfection, but if there was one man who more than any other handled the crisis at Army Group Center, it was Kluge. His so-called "middle solution" sought, under the most difficult circumstances, to chart a response between the all-out retreat practiced by Guderian and the fanatical resistance demanded by Hitler. Kluge's limited withdrawals sought to avoid exhausting the men, while seeking to preserve as much equipment as possible. There may also have been a sense that anything too ambitious, especially for the less mobile infantry divisions, might complicate the breakdown in discipline and risk breaking contact with neighboring formations. Kluge's logic was sound, but where the field marshal revealed his real aptitude for command was in masterminding a path between his fearful and hard-pressed generals at the front and Hitler's inflexible stubbornness. Kluge essentially did this by siding with both. If he thought a position could in fact hold, he had no problem evoking Hitler's order and threatened any commander failing to obey it. If, on the other hand, he believed a withdrawal was in order, he tirelessly sought a concession from Hitler, while shifting whatever reserves he could to the threatened sector. Only when this failed, as a last-case scenario, did Kluge either discreetly authorize withdrawals (although only a handful of such examples are recorded) or, seemingly more commonly, observe without complaint as the front "corrected" itself. That Hitler and the OKH had no idea of his duplicity in the campaign is in part a testament to Kluge's careful leadership, but in this instance the field marshal was also aided by the high command's chronic detachment from the front. In the final analysis, if Army Group Center owed its survival to any single individual, it was Kluge and certainly not Hitler.

It is impossible to say what might have happened had a more rigidly compliant commander been in Kluge's shoes, but Army Group Center's sense of crisis was very real, and without the flexibility the field marshal and his subordinates fought so hard for, the crisis may well have spiraled into the disaster many feared. Yet the defiance of Hitler's order, over which Kluge presided, must not be confused for opposition. Though Kluge was ultimately forced to commit suicide in 1944 for his role in the plot to kill Hitler, his opposition to the regime, like that of almost all the army's conspirators, was not apparent in 1941–1942. In fact, Kluge as well as his senior staff were deeply complicit in Germany's war of annihilation as well as the beginnings of the Holocaust.[24] To this end, Kluge ruthlessly sought any advantage, no matter what the cost to the civilian population, and in the course of 1941 had shown he was not above authorizing murderous behavior even when there was no military utility.[25] Kluge may have been the man most responsible for Army Group Center's survival, but he was also responsible for ruthless anti-partisan campaigns, pitiless requisitioning in the army group's rear areas, widespread use of forced labor, and, worst of all, the incredibly destructive scorched-earth policies that, whatever their military utility, exacted a frightful toll on the civilian population. Kluge may have prevailed against both the Red Army and Hitler's restrictive halt order, but his achievement was entirely in the service of Nazi Germany's goals.

While Kluge did whatever he could to maintain a stout resistance and hold his army group together, his role was largely reactive. It was the Soviet high command that directed when, where, and with what forces the offensive was to proceed. Here Stalin's naked ambition, not only to attack Army Group Center on so many fronts, but then to expand the offensive in January to hit Army Groups North and South, proved far too much for the Red Army. As Zhukov complained in his unexpurgated memoir, "Had the ten armies of the reserve of the Headquarters of the Supreme High Command not been scattered across all the fronts, and had been committed to the tasks of the front of the Western Direction, then the central grouping of Hitlerite forces would have been defeated, which would without doubt have influenced the further progress of the war."[26] Indeed, it is hard to see how Kluge might have coped if hundreds of thousands more men had been directed against the weak spots in his lines. This then suggests that the outcome of the campaign

owed more to Stalin's colossal missed opportunity than Hitler's own baneful influence. Both dictators characteristically expected too much of their
forces, but Hitler's War Directive 39 of December 8 importantly matched
German strategy to barely realizable operational goals and allowed Army
Group Center a vital two-week breathing space before the imposition of his
stifling halt order. This greatly complicated Kluge's task, but its pernicious
impact was simply not on the same scale as Stalin's massively overstretched
January offensive.

While Stalin's strategic calculus proved extravagant, at the tactical level
the Red Army was also ill equipped to seize ground, especially given that
heavy fire support was often inadequate or completely absent. Poor command and control of Soviet units undercut a lot of the Red Army's strength
on paper, while the attack doctrine of many middle and lower ranked Soviet officers harked back to the early twentieth century.[27] The consequences
of this are reflected in the appalling Soviet casualty rate: over half a million men a month during the winter period.[28] One postwar German study
of small unit actions during the winter concluded: "As so often happened
during the winter of 1941–42, the Russians attacked in several waves on a
given front, each successive wave passing over the dead of the preceding and
carrying the attack forward to a point where it too was destroyed."[29] Even
if a tactical breakthrough was achieved, the short window of opportunity
to exploit it often passed, allowing the Germans to reestablish themselves
in reasonably good order or restore their position with a hastily mounted
counterattack. The result was that the Red Army was forced to attempt another costly breakthrough all over again.[30] Such ineptitude at the local level
handed Germany victory after victory, which its tired and depleted forces
could scarcely have achieved against a more competent command apparatus. As Heinrici observed in his diary on February 16, "It is an absolute wonder that the army still exists. From its own strength the army would not have
stood if the enemy had been properly managed."[31]

By the end of January 1942, the Soviet winter offensive was by no means
over, but its moment had passed. As Goebbels noted with relief in his diary
on January 30, "The alarming panic news from the front has shrunk to a
minimum."[32] Even to ordinary observers in occupied Europe the absence of

a clear Soviet victory was cause for concern. The French writer and intellectual Jean Guéhenno wrote in his diary on January 25: "Do I know if Germany will be defeated or not? Rather, I'm afraid today of what will happen this spring. The Russians may be worn out by April. And then . . ."[33] As we have seen, Germany's offensive strength was greatly reduced, but the Soviets' inability to defeat Army Group Center in the winter months meant huge numbers of Red Army men and equipment were left concentrated in the center of the front in anticipation of another drive toward Moscow.[34] This false assumption contributed to the success of Hitler's summer offensive in the south, giving it a guise of artificial strength when it began in late June 1942.

Coming to any definitive conclusion about the winter of 1941–1942 is a matter of perspective. Since August 1941 Germany no longer possessed the strength to force an end to the war in the east and, due to its economic weakness, was locked into an attritional struggle it could not win. The Wehrmacht's winter losses in vehicles and heavy equipment only continued what Omer Bartov has referred to as the "demodernisation of the front" and further degraded the *Ostheer*'s already devastated operational capacity.[35] The Red Army's offensive also won space to buffer Moscow from any renewed German attack in 1942. From this perspective, the Soviet winter campaign appears successful, further confirming the "defeat" of German plans in the east.

Yet this depiction of events takes little account of what was possible on December 5, 1941. Army Group Center was massively overextended, operating on a shoestring of logistics, and was very poorly prepared for the winter weather, while the Red Army was close to its centers of supply and possessed multiple reserve armies, which could be concentrated anywhere on the front. Had the *Stavka* pursued a far greater concentration of effort and sought to employ its limited heavy equipment and best officers on narrower fronts, the potential for significant success at reasonable cost was high. Of course, we can only really judge what in fact happened. In spite of its own weaknesses, Army Group Center on the defensive savaged the Red Army and thwarted all the objectives of the Soviet offensive plan. Not a single German division was lost, while Army Group Center reached a defensive line that it would hold until it was voluntarily given up (Operation Buffalo) in March of 1943. From this perspective, the winter period, while replete with crisis, represented something of a role reversal, from which the Germans snatched a victory—or were handed it by Stalin—from the very jaws of defeat.

Just as one could not claim that the failure of the German offensive on Moscow, in spite of being at the height of its territorial gains on December 5, was somehow a great success, so too should we think twice about proclaiming the Soviet Union's strategic failure and modest winter gains a military victory. Stalin, like Hitler, fell well short of his excessive goals and suffered appalling losses in the process. Indeed, given the forces involved, the limited Soviet gains were a testament to how little was achieved, not how much. Thus, Germany's winter "defeat" seems only possible from a rather limited perspective, not because it did not lose, but because it stood to lose so much more.

Of course, all of this analysis may help frame and contextualize the war at its highest level, but it is detached from the everyday experience of the fighting. If Germany had won anything in December and January that its soldiers cared about, it was a brief respite from the torments of the war. As Hans Albring concluded at the end of January after surviving a sequence of harrowing battles, "comparison with the Apocalypse is not too far-fetched."[36] Yet Willy Peter Reese, who had endured the winter fighting and was returning home on furlough, perhaps summed up best what lay behind, as well as before, the men of Army Group Center:

> I lived on the edge. Death, the blind strangler, had failed to find me, but a human being had died in Russia, and I didn't know who it was . . . We were required to subject our own lives to the will of the age, and our destiny began like a tale of duress, patience, and death. We could not escape the law, there was a breach in our unfinished sense of the world, and like a dream, the march into the other and the unknown began, and all our paths ended in night.[37]

NOTES

INTRODUCTION

1. Robert Forczyk, *Moscow 1941: Hitler's First Defeat* (Oxford: Osprey, 2006); Michael Jones, *The Retreat: Hitler's First Defeat* (London: Thomas Dunne Books, 2009).

2. Klaus Reinhardt, *Die Wende vor Moskau: Das Scheitern der Strategie Hitlers im Winter 1941/42* (Stuttgart: Deutsche Verlags-Anstalt, 1972); Klaus Reinhardt, *Moscow— The Turning Point: The Failure of Hitler's Strategy in the Winter of 1941–42* (Oxford: Bloomsbury Academic, 1992).

3. For the planning of Operation Barbarossa: Rolf-Dieter Müller, *Enemy in the East: Hitler's Secret Plans to Invade the Soviet Union* (New York: I.B. Tauris, 2015); Ernst Klink, "The Military Concept of War against the Soviet Union," in *Germany and the Second World War*, vol. 4, *The Attack on the Soviet Union*, edited by Militärgeschichtliches Forschungsamt (Oxford: Oxford University Press, 1998), 225–325; Barry Leach, *German Strategy against Russia, 1939–1941* (Oxford: Oxford University Press, 1973).

4. My first book highlighted the strategic implications of Army Group Center's operational failures in the summer of 1941: David Stahel, *Operation Barbarossa and Germany's Defeat in the East* (Cambridge: Cambridge University Press, 2009). This

was followed by subsequent works tracing the rest of Germany's 1941 campaigns: *Kiev 1941: Hitler's Battle for Supremacy in the East* (Cambridge: Cambridge University Press, 2012); *Operation Typhoon: Hitler's March on Moscow, October 1941* (Cambridge: Cambridge University Press, 2013); *The Battle for Moscow* (Cambridge: Cambridge University Press, 2015). The thesis arguing for Operation Barbarossa's defeat in its initial summer campaign has been reinforced by further research from David Glantz and Craig Luther; see: David M. Glantz, *Barbarossa Derailed: The Battle for Smolensk 10 July–10 September 1941*, vol. 1, *The German Advance, the Encirclement Battle, and the First and Second Soviet Counteroffensives, 10 July–24 August 1941* (Solihull: Helion, 2010); David M. Glantz, *Barbarossa Derailed: The Battle for Smolensk, 10 July–10 September 1941*, vol. 2, *The German Offensives on the Flanks and the Third Soviet Counteroffensive, 25 August–10 September 1941* (Solihull: Helion, 2012); David M. Glantz, *Barbarossa Derailed: The Battle for Smolensk, 10 July–10 September 1941*, vol. 3, *The Documentary Companion: Tables, Orders and Reports Prepared by Participating Red Army Forces* (Solihull: Helion, 2014); David M. Glantz, *Barbarossa Derailed: The Battle for Smolensk, 10 July–10 September 1941*, vol. 4, *Atlas* (Solihull: Helion, 2015); Craig W. H. Luther, *Barbarossa Unleashed: The German Blitzkrieg through Central Russia to the Gates of Moscow* (Atglen, Pa.: Schiffer, 2013).

5. Franz Halder, *Kriegstagebuch: Tägliche Aufzeichnungen des Chefs des Generalstabes des Heeres, 1939–1942*, Band III, *Der Russlandfeldzug bis zum Marsch auf Stalingrad, 22.6.1941–24.9.1942*, edited by Hans-Adolf Jacobsen and Alfred Philippi (Stuttgart: Kohlhammer, 1964), 306 (November 23, 1941). Hereafter cited as: Halder, KTB III.

6. Understanding why this was the case has been the subject of some of my more recent research; see: David Stahel, "The Wehrmacht and National Socialist Military Thinking," *War in History* 24 (July 2017): 336–61.

7. Force multipliers are factors (topographical, technological, institutional, etc.) that increase the effectiveness of a unit, offering it a value disproportionate to its size or power. The factors enhance (and hence "multiply") the fighting capacity as well as the function of the formation.

8. Otto Dietrich, *The Hitler I Knew: Memoirs of the Third Reich's Press Chief* (New York: Skyhorse, 2010), 74. For a useful discussion of how postwar officers' accounts shaped the orthodox view, see: Walter Chales de Beaulieu, *Generaloberst Erich Hoepner: Militärisches Porträt eines Panzer-Führers* (Neckargemünd: Vowinckel, 1969), 235.

9. Stephen Fritz, *Ostkrieg: Hitler's War of Extermination in the East* (Lexington: University Press of Kentucky, 2011), 205.

10. Franz Halder, *Kriegstagebuch: Tägliche Aufzeichnungen des Chefs des Generalstabes des Heeres, 1939–1942*, Band II, *Von der geplanten Landung in England bis zum Beginn des Ostfeldzuges, 1.7.1940—21.6.1941*, edited by Hans-Adolf Jacobsen, (Stuttgart: Kohlhammer, 1963), 336–37 (March 30, 1941). On Germany's war of annihilation in the east, see: Geoffrey P. Megargee, *War of Annihilation: Combat and Genocide on the Eastern Front, 1941* (Lanham, Md.: Rowman & Littlefield, 2006); Wolfram Wette, *The Wehrmacht: History, Myth, Reality* (Cambridge, Mass.: Harvard University Press, 2006).

11. Third and Fourth Panzer Armies were not officially designated "armies" until January 1942.

12. G. F. Krivosheev, ed., *Soviet Casualties and Combat Losses in the Twentieth Century* (London: Greenhill Books, 1997), 114, 118, and 121.

13. Lev Lopukhovsky and Boris Kavalerchik, *The Price of Victory: The Red Army's Casualties in the Great Patriotic War* (Barnsley, U.K.: Pen and Sword, 2017), 154. In Russian, see: Lev Lopukhovsky and Boris Kavalerchik, "Kogda my uznaem real'nuiu tsenu razgroma gitlerovskoi Germanii?" in *"Umylis' krov'iu?" Lozh' i pravda o pote-*

riakh v Velikoi Otechestvennoi voine (Moscow: Iauza Eksmo, 2012). My thanks to Oleg Beyda for pointing me in the direction of this research before its appearance in English.

14. Halder, KTB III, 318 and 409 (November 30, 1941, and March 5, 1942).

15. Nigel Askey, *Operation Barbarossa: The Complete Organisational and Statistical Analysis, and Military Simulation*, vol. IIb (self-pub., 2014), 341.

16. John Erickson, "Soviet War Losses: Calculations and Controversies," in *John Barbarossa: The Axis and the Allies*, edited by Erickson and David Dilks (Edinburgh: Edinburgh University Press, 1998), 267.

17. Rüdiger Overmans, *Deutsche militärische Verluste im Zweiten Weltkrieg* (Munich: De Gruyter Oldenbourg, 2000), 278.

18. Hugh Trevor-Roper, ed., *Hitler's War Directives, 1939–1945* (London: Pan Books, 1964), 135 and 166 (July 14 and December 8, 1941).

19. Ibid., 166 (December 8, 1941).

20. Earl F. Ziemke and Magna E. Bauer, *Moscow to Stalingrad: Decision in the East* (New York: Hippocrene Books, 1988), 140.

21. As the Soviet General Staff's own study later acknowledged: "the main mission of the Western Front's troops consisted of defeating, as quickly as possible, the enemy's flank groups and capturing his equipment, transport, and weapons and by rapidly moving forward to envelop his flank group, to finally encircle and destroy the enemy armies facing the Western Front" (Richard W. Harrison, ed., *The Battle for Moscow, 1941–1942: The Red Army's Defensive Operations and Counter-offensive along the Moscow Strategic Direction* [Solihull: Helion, 2015], 293).

22. For an insight into the "unknown" side of Soviet operations in the winter, see: David M. Glantz, *Forgotten Battles of the German-Soviet War, 1941–1945*, vol. 2, *The Winter Campaign, 5 December 1941–April 1942* (self-pub., 1999).

23. As cited in: Evan Mawdsley, *Thunder in the East: The Nazi-Soviet War, 1941–1945*, 2nd ed. (London: Bloomsbury Academic, 2016), 123. See also the analysis in: David M. Glantz, *Barbarossa: Hitler's Invasion of Russia, 1941* (Stroud: Tempus, 2001), 204.

24. Clyde R. Davis, *Von Kleist: From Hussar to Panzer Marshal* (Houston: Lancer Militaria, 1979), 14.

25. As cited in: Jeff Rutherford and Adrian E. Wettstein, *The German Army on the Eastern Front: An Inner View of the Ostheer's Experience of War* (Barnsley, U.K.: Pen and Sword, 2018), 177.

1. HUNGRY AS A BEAR: THE SOVIET COUNTEROFFENSIVE BEGINS

1. Many of these offensives belong to what David Glantz refers to as the forgotten battles. See: David M. Glantz, *Forgotten Battles of the German-Soviet War, 1941–1945*, vol. 1, *The Summer-Fall Campaign, 22 June–4 December 1941* (self-pub., 1999).

2. David M. Glantz and Jonathan M. House, *When Titans Clashed: How the Red Army Stopped Hitler* (Lawrence: University Press of Kansas, 2015), 108.

3. Stahel, *The Battle for Moscow*, 292–93.

4. Geoffrey P. Megargee, *Inside Hitler's High Command* (Lawrence: University Press of Kansas, 2000), 107 and 111.

5. As cited in: David Kahn, *Hitler's Spies* (London: Macmillan, 1980), 410.

6. "Oberkommando des Heeres Generalstab des Heeres O.Qu.IV-Abt.Fr.H.Ost (II)," BA-MA RH/2-2670, fol. 75 (November 22, 1941). See also: John Erickson, *The Road to Stalingrad: Stalin's War with Germany*, vol. 1 (London: Phoenix Giant, 1975), 270–71.

7. Magnus Pahl, *Hitler's Fremde Heere Ost: German Military Intelligence on the Eastern Front, 1942–45* (Solihull: Helion, 2016), 87.

8. David M. Glantz, *Soviet Military Deception in the Second World War* (London: Routledge, 1989), 47–56.

9. Earl F. Ziemke, *The Red Army, 1918–1941: From Vanguard of World Revolution to US Ally* (London: Frank Cass, 2004), 307. See also: Chris Bellamy, *Absolute War: Soviet Russia in the Second World War* (New York: Vintage, 2007), 310.

10. Halder, KTB III, 299 (November 19, 1941).

11. Reinhardt, *Moscow—The Turning Point*, 289.

12. As cited in: Kahn, *Hitler's Spies*, 410.

13. Hans Meier-Welcker, *Aufzeichnungen eines Generalstabsoffiziers, 1939–1942* (Freiburg: Rombach Druck und Verlagshaus, 1982), 143 (December 1, 1941).

14. Glantz and House, *When Titans Clashed*, 108.

15. Johannes Hürter, ed., *Ein deutscher General an der Ostfront: Die Briefe und Tagebücher des Gotthard Heinrici, 1941/42* (Erfurt: Sutton Verlag, 2001), 122 (December 6, 1941). For an English translation, see: Johannes Hürter, ed., *A German General on the Eastern Front: The Letters and Diaries of Gotthard Heinrici, 1941–1942* (Barnsley, U.K.: Pen and Sword, 2014), 115 (December 6, 1941).

16. Fedor von Bock, *Generalfeldmarschall Fedor von Bock: The War Diary, 1939–1945*, edited by Klaus Gerbet (Atglen, Pa.: Schiffer, 1996), 382 (December 6, 1941). Hereafter, references for Bock's diary will be cited as Bock, *War Diary*.

17. The Volga Reservoir is the term used in German files, which I have maintained for consistency, but it is in fact the Ivankovo Reservoir.

18. "Kriegstagebuch No.2 der 36. Inf. Div. (mot) 22.9.41–5.12.41," BA-MA RH 26-36/9. The diary has no folio stamped page numbers so references must be located using the date (December 5, 1941).

19. As cited in: Jones, *The Retreat*, 135.

20. Ibid., 141.

21. Nominally the division was commanded by Landgraf, but he had been ill for weeks, and Major-General Erhard Raus was directing day-to-day operations.

22. "Kriegstagebuch Nr.1 (Band December 1941) des Oberkommandos der Heeresgruppe Mitte," BA-MA RH 19-II/122, fols. 36 and 40 (December 6, 1941).

23. As cited in: Jones, *The Retreat*, 138.

24. Bock, *War Diary*, 382 (December 6, 1941).

25. "Anlagen zum Kriegstagebuch Tagesmeldungen Bd.I 1.11-31.12.41," BA-MA RH 21-3/71, fol. 261 (December 6, 1941).

26. As cited in: Glantz, *Barbarossa*, 194.

27. As cited in: Nicholas Stargardt, *The German War: A Nation Under Arms, 1939–1945* (New York: Basic Books, 2015), 201.

28. As cited in: David Downing, *Sealing Their Fate: Twenty-Two Days that Decided the Second World War* (London: Da Capo Press, 2009), 295.

29. As cited in: Guido Knopp, *Der Verdammte Krieg: "Unternehmen Barbarossa"* (Munich: Orbis Verlag, 1998), 218.

30. As cited in: Jones, *The Retreat*, 138.

31. Bock, *War Diary*, 382 (December 6, 1941).

32. As cited in: Jones, *The Retreat*, 141.

33. *True to Type: A Selection from Letters and Diaries of German Soldiers and Civilians Collected on the Soviet-German Front* (London: Hutchinson, n.d.), 37 (December 6, 1941).

34. Heinrich Bücheler, *Hoepner: Ein deutsches Soldatenschicksal des Zwanzigsten Jahrhunderts* (Herford: Mittler E.S. + Sohn, 1980), 160.

35. "KTB 'Rußlandfeldzug' Pz.A.O.K. III Teil 6.12.41–9.1.42," BA-MA RH 21-4/50, fol. 11 (December 6, 1941).
36. Halder, KTB III, 331 (December 6, 1941).
37. "Kriegstagebuch Nr.1 2.Panzerarmee Band III vom 1.11.1941 bis 26.12.41," BA-MA RH 21-2/244, fol. 226 (December 6, 1941).
38. Heinz Guderian, *Panzer Leader* (New York: Da Capo Press, 1996), 259.
39. David Garden and Kenneth Andrew, eds., *The War Diaries of a Panzer Soldier: Erich Hager with the 17th Panzer Division on the Russian Front, 1941–1945* (Atglen, Pa.: Schiffer, 2010), 61 (December 6, 1941).
40. Hans Dollinger, ed., *Kain, wo ist dein Bruder? Was der Mensch im Zweiten Weltkrieg erleiden mußte—dokumentiert in Tagebüchern und Briefen* (Munich: List Paul Verlag, 1983), 111 (December 6, 1941).
41. Reinhardt, *Moscow—The Turning Point*, 291.
42. Bock, *War Diary*, 382–83 (December 6 and 7, 1941).
43. Bernhard R. Kroener, "The Winter Crisis of 1941–1942: The Distribution of Scarcity or Steps Towards a More Rational Management of Personnel," in *Germany and the Second World War*, vol. 5/1, *Organization and Mobilization of the German Sphere of Power*, edited by Militärgeschichtliches Forschungsamt (Oxford: Oxford University Press, 2000), 1018.
44. Ferdinand Prinz von der Leyen, *Rückblick zum Mauerwald: Vier Kriegsjahre im OKH* (Munich: Biederstein Verlag, 1965), 37.
45. As cited in: Andrew Roberts, *The Storm of War: A New History of the Second World War* (London: Harper, 2009), 179.
46. Garden and Andrew, *The War Diaries of a Panzer Soldier*, 61 (December 6, 1941).
47. Franz A. P. Frisch, in association with Wilbur D. Jones, Jr., *Condemned to Live: A Panzer Artilleryman's Five-Front War* (Shippensburg: Burd Street Press, 2000), 92.
48. Siegfried Knappe, with Ted Brusaw, *Soldat: Reflections of a German Soldier, 1936–1949* (New York: Dell, 1992), 234.
49. Max Kuhnert, *Will We See Tomorrow? A German Cavalryman at War, 1939–1942* (London: Pen and Sword, 1993), 133.
50. Helmut Günther, *Hot Motors, Cold Feet: A Memoir of Service with the Motorcycle Battalion of SS-Division "Reich," 1940–1941* (Winnipeg: J. J. Fedorowicz Publishing Inc., 2004), 246.
51. Elke Fröhlich, ed., *Die Tagebücher von Joseph Goebbels*, Teil II, Diktate 1941–1945, Band 2, Oktober–Dezember 1941 (Munich: K. G. Saur, 1996), 452 (December 8, 1941).
52. Ian Kershaw, *Fateful Choices: Ten Decisions that Changed the World, 1940–1941* (New York: Penguin Books, 2007), 423.
53. Guderian, *Panzer Leader*, 260; Nicolaus von Below, *Als Hitlers Adjutant, 1937–45* (Mainz: Pour le Mérite, 1999), 296.
54. Walter Warlimont, *Im Hauptquartier der deutschen Wehrmacht, 1939 bis 1945*. Band 1, *September 1939–November 1942* (Koblenz: Weltbild Verlag, 1990), 221; Walter Warlimont, *Inside Hitler's Headquarters, 1939–1945* (New York: Presidio Press, 1964), 208.
55. Stephen Fritz, *The First Soldier: Hitler as Military Leader* (New Haven, Conn.: Yale University Press, 2018), 219.
56. Henrik Eberle and Matthias Uhl, eds., *The Hitler Book: The Secret Dossier Prepared for Stalin from the Interrogations of Hitler's Personal Aides* (New York: Public Affairs, 2005), 79.
57. As cited in: Georg Meyer, *Adolf Heusinger: Dienst eines deutschen Soldaten, 1915 bis 1964* (Berlin: Mittler in Maximilian Verlag, 2001), 166.

58. Eberle and Uhl, *The Hitler Book*, 79.
59. Heinz Boberach, ed., *Meldungen aus dem Reich: Die geheimen Lageberichte des Sicherheitsdienstes der SS, 1938–1945*, Band 8 (Berlin: Pawlak, 1984), 3089 (December 15, 1941).
60. Knappe with Brusaw, *Soldat*, 240.
61. Walter Kempowski, ed., *Das Echolot Barbarossa '41: Ein kollektives Tagebuch* (Munich: Albrecht Knaus Verlag, 2004), 350 (December 8, 1941).
62. Ibid., 408 (December 11, 1941).
63. Hürter, *Ein deutscher General an der Ostfront*, 125–26 (December 11, 1941).
64. Martin Humburg, *Das Gesicht des Krieges: Feldpostbriefe von Wehrmachtssoldaten aus der Sowjetunion, 1941–1944* (Wiesbaden: C. H. Beck Verlag, 1998), 222 (December 12, 1941).
65. Gottlob Herbert Bidermann, *In Deadly Combat: A German Solder's Memoir of the Eastern Front* (Lawrence: University Press of Kansas, 2000), 82.
66. Konrad H. Jarausch, ed., *Reluctant Accomplice: A Wehrmacht Soldier's Letters from the Eastern Front* (Princeton: Princeton University Press, 2011), 340 (December 10, 1941).
67. Josef Perau, *Priester im Heers Hitler: Erinnerungen, 1940–1945* (Essen: Ludgerus Verlag, 1962), 45.
68. Winston S. Churchill, *The Second World War*, abridged ed. (London: Cassell, 1959), 492.
69. As cited in: Max Hastings, *Winston's War: Churchill, 1940–1945* (New York: Vintage, 2010), 182.
70. See my conclusion in *Operation Barbarossa and Germany's Defeat in the East*, 439–51; Fritz, *Ostkrieg*, 197.
71. As cited in: Robert Huhn Jones, *The Roads to Russia: United States Lend-Lease to the Soviet Union* (Norman: University of Oklahoma Press, 1969), 79–80.
72. George C. Herring, Jr., *Aid to Russia, 1941–1946: Strategy, Diplomacy, the Origins of the Cold War* (New York: Columbia University Press, 1973), 54–55.
73. Alexander Hill, "British Lend-Lease Tanks and the Battle for Moscow, November–December 1941—Revisited," *The Journal of Slavic Military Studies* 22, no. 4 (November 2009): 575 and 581.
74. Alexander Hill, "British Lend-Lease Aid and the Soviet War Effort, June 1941–June 1942," *The Journal of Military History* 71, no. 3 (July 2007): 787–88; Alexander Hill, *The Great Patriotic War of the Soviet Union, 1941–45: A Documentary Reader* (Abingdon: Routledge, 2010), 84.
75. P. M. H. Bell, *John Bull and the Bear: British Public Opinion, Foreign Policy and the Soviet Union, 1941–1945* (London: Hodder Arnold, 1990), 58–60 and 76–77.
76. Martin Kitchen, *A World in Flames: A Short History of the Second World War in Europe and Asia, 1939–1945* (London: Routledge, 1990), 94.
77. Bell, *John Bull and the Bear*, 63.
78. Ibid., 77.
79. On Japan and the Soviet Union: Peter Herde, *Die Achsenmächte, Japan und die Sowjetunion: Japanische Quellen zum Zweiten Weltkrieg, 1941–1945* (Berlin: De Gruyter Oldenbourg, 2017).
80. Norman Rich, *Hitler's War Aims: Ideology, the Nazi State, and the Course of Expansion* (New York: W. W. Norton, 1972), 235.
81. As cited in: Sönke Neitzel and Harald Welzer, *Soldaten: On Fighting, Killing and Dying* (London: Simon & Schuster, 2012), 317.
82. Heinrich Haape, with Dennis Henshaw, *Moscow Tram Stop: A Doctor's Experiences with the German Spearhead in Russia* (London: Collins, 1957), 248.
83. Hans Heinz Rehfeldt, *Mit dem Eliteverband des Heeres "Grossdeutschland" tief in den*

Weiten Russlands: Erinnerungen eines Angehörigen des Granatwerferzuges 8. Infanterier-regiment (mot.) "Grossdeutschland," 1941–1943 (Würzburg: Verlagshaus Würzburg - Flechsi, 2008), 72.

84. Christiane Sahm, *Verzweiflung und Glaube: Briefe aus dem Krieg, 1939–1942* (Munich: Don Bosco Medien, 2007), 59.

85. Günther, *Hot Motors, Cold Feet*, 245.

86. Lauren Faulkner Rossi, *Wehrmacht Priests: Catholicism and the Nazi War of Annihilation* (Cambridge, Mass.: Harvard University Press, 2015), 131.

87. Erich Kern, *Dance of Death* (New York: Charles Scribner's Sons, 1951), 34.

88. As cited in: Jürgen Förster, "Ideological Warfare in Germany, 1919 to 1945," in *Germany and the Second World War*, vol. 4/1, *German Wartime Society, 1939–1945: Politicization, Disintegration, and the Struggle for Survival*, edited by Militärge-schichtliches Forschungsamt (Oxford: Oxford University Press, 2008), 555.

89. Halder, KTB III, 348 (December 15, 1941).

90. Günther, *Hot Motors, Cold Feet*, 235.

91. Frisch with Jones, *Condemned to Live*, 98.

92. Helmut Pabst, *The Outermost Frontier: A German Soldier in the Russian Campaign* (London: Kimber, 1957), 40.

93. Kroener, "The Winter Crisis of 1941–1942," 1111.

2. DODGING THE SOVIET BULLET: ARMY GROUP CENTER HOLDS

1. Halder, KTB III, 332 (December 7, 1941).

2. "Tagebuch Reinhardts," N245/3, fol. 16 (December 7, 1941). See also: "Anlagen zum Kriegstagebuch Tagesmeldungen Bd.I 1.11-31.12.41," BA-MA RH 21-3/71, fol. 266 (December 7, 1941).

3. "Auswahl von Originalbriefen, die von meiner Frau und mir in den Jahren 1939 bis Januar 1945 geschrieben wurden," N245/2, fol. 16. Hereafter: "Reinhardt's letters to his wife."

4. "Kriegstagebuch Nr.1 (Band December 1941) des Oberkommandos der Heeres-gruppe Mitte," BA-MA RH 19-II/122, fol. 43 (December 7, 1941).

5. Halder, KTB III, 330, 336, and 338 (December 6, 9, and 10, 1941).

6. Bock, *War Diary*, 385–86 (December 8, 1941).

7. "Anlagen zum Kriegstagebuch Tagesmeldungen Bd.I 1.11–31.12.41," BA-MA RH 21-3/71, fol. 276 (December 8, 1941).

8. Ibid., fol. 269 (December 7, 1941).

9. As cited in: Jones, *The Retreat*, 163.

10. Heinrich Engel, *7,000 Kilometers in a Sturmgeschütz: The Wartime Diaries and Photo Album of Knight's Cross Recipient Heinrich Engel* (Winnipeg: J. J. Fedorowicz, 2001), 103 (December 6 and 7, 1941).

11. Kempowski, *Das Echolot Barbarossa*, 324–25 (December 7, 1941).

12. "Anlagen zum Kriegstagebuch Tagesmeldungen Bd.I 1.11-31.12.41," BA-MA RH 21-3/71, fol. 281 (December 9, 1941).

13. Engel, *7,000 Kilometers in a Sturmgeschütz*, 104 (December 8, 1941).

14. "Tagebuch Reinhardts," N245/3, fol. 16 (December 9, 1941).

15. "Reinhardt's letters to his wife," N245/2, fols. 17–18 (December 10, 1941).

16. "Anlagen zum Kriegstagebuch Tagesmeldungen Bd.I 1.11-31.12.41," BA-MA RH 21-3/71, fol. 287 (December 10, 1941).

17. "Kriegstagebuch Nr.7 des Kdos. der 1.Panzer-Div. 20.9.41-12.4.42," BA-MA RH 27-1/58, fol. 79 (December 11, 1941). Figures for the number of captured weapons differ somewhat in Panzer Group 3's war diary.

18. "Tagebuch Reinhardts," N245/3, fol. 17 (December 11, 1941). See also: "Reinhardt's letters to his wife," N245/2, fol. 18 (December 11, 1941).
19. Bock, *War Diary*, 383 (December 7, 1941).
20. Hartmut Beermann, ed., *Soldat Werner Beermann Feldpostbriefe, 1941–1942* (n.p.: lulu.com, 2012), 191 (December 9, 1941).
21. Reinhardt, *Moscow—The Turning Point*, 294–95.
22. "KTB Pz.Gr.4 Meldungen von unten 6.12.41–31.12.41," BA-MA 21-4/56, fol. 273 (December 9, 1941).
23. Günther, *Hot Motors, Cold Feet*, 226. See also: James Lucas, *Das Reich: The Military Role of the 2nd SS Division* (London: Arms & Armour, 1991), 76.
24. Trevor-Roper, *Hitler's War Directives*, 166 (December 8, 1941).
25. Reinhardt, *Moscow—The Turning Point*, 300.
26. As cited in: Svetlana Gerasimova, *The Rzhev Slaughterhouse: The Red Army's Forgotten 15 Month Campaign against Army Group Centre, 1942–1943* (Solihull: Helion, 2013), 34.
27. K. Rokossovsky, *A Soldier's Duty* (Moscow: Progress, 1985), 91.
28. As cited in: Glantz, *Barbarossa*, 194.
29. Larry LeSueur, *Twelve Months That Changed the World* (New York: Alfred A. Knopf, 1943), 117.
30. Here his 3rd Panzer Division was stretched thinly over the eastern perimeter of the German encirclement at Kiev, from which the remnants of four Soviet armies were attempting to break out. See: Stahel, *Kiev 1941*.
31. Armin Böttger, *To the Gates of Hell: The Memoir of a Panzer Crewman* (Barnsley, U.K.: Pen and Sword, 2012), 19.
32. Steven H. Newton, *Hitler's Commander: Field Marshal Walter Model—Hitler's Favorite General* (Cambridge, Mass.: Da Capo Press, 2006), 161–62.
33. Emphasis in the original. Horst Mühleisen, ed., *Hellmuth Stieff Briefe* (Berlin: Siedler Verlag, 1991), 140 (December 7, 1941).
34. *True to Type*, 37 (December 7, 1941).
35. Dollinger, *Kain, wo ist dein Bruder?*, 111 (December 6, 1941).
36. Werner Adamczyk, *Feuer! An Artilleryman's Life on the Eastern Front* (Wilmington, N.C.: Broadfoot, 1992), 188.
37. "Kriegstagebuch Nr.1 (Band December 1941) des Oberkommandos der Heeresgruppe Mitte," BA-MA RH 19-II/122, fols. 60–61 (December 8, 1941).
38. Ibid., fol. 61 (December 8, 1941). See also: Bock, *War Diary*, 386 (December 8, 1941).
39. "Kriegstagebuch Nr.1 (Band December 1941) des Oberkommandos der Heeresgruppe Mitte," BA-MA RH 19-II/122, fols. 66–67 (December 9, 1941).
40. Bock, *War Diary*, 387 (December 10, 1941).
41. Ziemke and Bauer, *Moscow to Stalingrad*, 76.
42. As cited in: Bücheler, *Hoepner*, 161.
43. "KTB 'Rußlandfeldzug' Pz.A.O.K. III Teil 6.12.41–9.1.42," BA-MA RH 21-4/50, fol. 20 (December 11, 1941).
44. Kempowski, *Das Echolot Barbarossa*, 350 (December 8, 1941).
45. Arvid Fredborg, *Behind the Steel Wall* (London: Viking, 1944), 75.
46. Mihail Sebastian, *Journal, 1935–1944* (London: Heinemann, 2003), 450 (December 8 and 10, 1941).
47. Schmidt was promoted to colonel-general on January 1, 1942.
48. Bock, *War Diary*, 382–83 (December 6 and 7, 1941).
49. Guderian, *Panzer Leader*, 261.
50. "Kriegstagebuch Nr.3 XXXXVII.Pz.Korps. Ia 23.9.1941–31.12.1941," BA-MA RH 24-47/258, fol. 128 (December 7, 1941).

51. "Briefe von Heinz Guderian an seine Frau Margarete," BA-MA N 802/46 (December 8, 1941). Hereafter: "Guderian's letters to his wife."

52. Nancy F. Inglis, ed., *I Deserted Hitler: Memoirs of Bruno J. Trappmann* (London: New Holland, 2013), 74.

53. "Kriegstagebuch Nr.1 2.Panzerarmee Band III vom 1.11.1941 bis 26.12.41," BA-MA RH 21-2/244, fol. 243 (December 9, 1941).

54. "Kriegstagebuch Nr.3 XXXXVII.Pz.Korps. Ia 23.9.1941–31.12.1941," BA-MA RH 24-47/258, fols. 140 and 143 (December 10, 11, and 12, 1941).

55. "Kriegstagebuch Nr.1 (Band December 1941) des Oberkommandos der Heeresgruppe Mitte," BA-MA RH 19-II/122, fol. 65 (December 9, 1941).

56. "KTB 3rd Pz. Div. vom 19.9.41 bis 6.2.42," BA-MA RH 27-3/15, fol. 367 (December 11, 1941).

57. David W. Wildermuth, "Widening the Circle: General Weikersthal and the War of Annihilation, 1941–42," *Central European History* 45 (2012), 319.

58. Adamczyk, *Feuer!*, 188.

59. Hürter, *Ein deutscher General an der Ostfront*, 123 (December 11, 1941); Hürter, *A German General on the Eastern Front*, 116 (December 11, 1941).

60. Thomas Kühne, "Comradeship: Gender Confusion and Gender Order in the German Military, 1918–1945," in *Home/Front: The Military, War and Gender in Twentieth-Century Germany*, edited by Karen Hageman and Stefanie Schüler-Springorum (Oxford: Berg, 2002), 244–45.

61. Thomas Kühne, "Guppenkohäsion und Kameradschaftsmythos in der Wehrmacht," in *Die Wehrmacht: Mythos und Realität*, edited by Rolf-Dieter Müller and Hans-Erich Volkmann (München: De Gruyter Oldenbourg, 1999), 539.

62. Bidermann, *In Deadly Combat*, 70.

63. Günther, *Hot Motors, Cold Feet*, 207.

64. Martin Pöppel, *Heaven and Hell: The War Diary of a German Paratrooper* (Staplehurst: Sarpedon, 1996), 71.

65. Horst Fuchs Richardson, ed., *Sieg Heil! War Letters of Tank Gunner Karl Fuchs, 1937–1941* (Hamden: Archon Books, 1987), 117 (July 1, 1941).

66. Bob Carruthers, ed., *The Wehrmacht: Last Witnesses; First-Hand Accounts from the Survivors of Hitler's Armed Forces* (London: André Deutsch, 2010), 66.

67. "Kriegstagebuch Nr.1 2.Panzerarmee Band III vom 1.11.1941 bis 26.12.41," BA-MA RH 21-2/244, fol. 240 (December 8, 1941).

68. "KTB 3rd Pz. Div. vom 19.9.41 bis 6.2.42," BA-MA RH 27-3/15, fol. 363 (December 9, 1941).

69. "Guderian's letters to his wife," BA-MA N 802/46 (December 8, 1941).

70. This statement was claimed to be written to his wife as part of his December 8 letter, but it cannot be located in the original letter. Guderian's citations in the memoir from his wartime letters are generally accurate aside from this instance. If this was added fraudulently it may explain why it is disproven by wartime records. See: Guderian, *Panzer Leader*, 260.

71. "20.Pz.Div. KTB vom 21.10.41 bis 30.12.41 Band Ia2," BA-MA RH 27-20/26, fol. 100 (December 12, 1941).

72. Garden and Andrew, *The War Diaries of a Panzer Soldier*, 61 (December 9, 1941).

73. Rehfeldt, *Mit dem Eliteverband des Heeres "Grossdeutschland" tief in den Weiten Russlands*, 52.

74. "Kriegstagebuch Nr.1 2.Panzerarmee Band III vom 1.11.1941 bis 26.12.41," BA-MA RH 21-2/244, fol. 249 (December 9, 1941).

75. "Kriegstagebuch 4.Panzer-Divison Führungsabtl. 26.5.41–31.3.42," BA-MA RH 27-4/10, fol. 278 (December 9, 1941).

76. "Kriegstagebuch Nr.1 2.Panzerarmee Band III vom 1.11.1941 bis 26.12.41," BA-MA RH 21-2/244, fols. 253–54 and 266 (December 10 and 11, 1941).

77. Ibid., fol. 256 (December 10, 1941).

78. "Kriegstagebuch Nr.3 XXXXVII.Pz.Korps. Ia 23.9.1941–31.12.1941," BA-MA RH 24-47/258, fol. 136 (December 9, 1941).

79. "Guderian's letters to his wife," BA-MA N 802/46 (December 10, 1941). See also: Guderian, *Panzer Leader*, 261.

80. Klaus R. Woche, *Zwischen Pflicht und Gewissen: Generaloberst Rudolf Schmidt, 1886–1957* (Berlin: Ohne Verlag, 2002), 138.

81. "Kriegstagebuch Nr.1 2.Panzerarmee Band III vom 1.11.1941 bis 26.12.41," BA-MA RH 21-2/244, fol. 55 (December 8, 1941).

82. Ibid., fols. 244 and 256 (December 9 and 10, 1941).

83. Ziemke and Bauer, *Moscow to Stalingrad*, 74.

84. Bock, *War Diary*, 389 (December 11, 1941).

85. Heinz Postenrieder, *Feldzug im Osten, 2.8.1941–19.4.1942* (n.p.: Publisher's Graphics, 2010), 204 (December 11, 1941).

3. BETWEEN THE HAMMER AND THE ANVIL: ARMY GROUP CENTER BETWEEN HITLER AND STALIN

1. "Kriegstagebuch Nr.1 2.Panzerarmee Band III vom 1.11.1941 bis 26.12.41," BA-MA RH 21-2/244, fols. 231 and 248 (December 7 and 9, 1941).

2. "18. Panzer Div. Ia Kriegstagebuch vom 20.10.41–13.12.41," BA-MA RH 27-18/69. The diary has no folio stamped page numbers so references must be located according to date (December 7, 9, and 10, 1941).

3. "2. Panzer Division KTB Nr.6 Teil I. Vom 15.6.41–27.2.42," BA-MA RH 27-2/22. The diary has no folio stamped page numbers so references must be located according to date (December 6 and 7, 1941).

4. "Kriegstagebuch Nr.3. der Führungsabteilung (Ia) des Gen. Kdo. (mot.) XXXX. Pz.Korps vom 31.05.1941–26.12.1941," BA-MA RH 24-40/18. The diary has no folio stamped page numbers so references must be located according to date (December 9, 1941).

5. Gerhard Bopp, *Kriegstagebuch: Aufzeichnungen Während des II. Weltkrieges, 1940–1943* (Hamburg: Timon Verlag, 2005), 152 (December 7, 1941).

6. For a very good overview of German scorched-earth policy, see: Armin Nolzen, "'Verbrannte Erde': Der Rückzug der Wehrmacht aus den besetzten sowjetischen Gebieten, 1941–1945," in *Besatzung: Funktion und Gestalt militärischer Fremdherrschaft von der Antike bis zum 20. Jahrhundert*, edited by Günther Kronenbitter, Markus Pöhlmann, and Dierk Walter (Paderborn: Verlag Ferdinand Schöningh, 2006), 161–76; Alex J. Kay and David Stahel, "Reconceiving Criminality in the German Army on the Eastern Front," in *Mass Violence in Nazi-Occupied Europe*, edited by Alex J. Kay and David Stahel (Bloomington: Indiana University Press, 2018).

7. H. C. Robbins Landon and Sebastian Leitner, eds., *Diary of a German Soldier* (London: Faber & Faber, 1963), 125 (December 7, 1941).

8. *True to Type*, 99 (December 12, 1941).

9. Bopp, *Kriegstagebuch*, 156 (December 10, 1941).

10. Josef Deck, *Der Weg der 1000 Toten* (Karlsruhe: Badenia, 1978), 116–17.

11. *True to Type*, 38 (December 11, 1941).

12. Hildegard von Kotze, ed., *Heeresadjutant bei Hitler, 1938–1943: Aufzeichnungen des Majors Engel* (Stuttgart: Deutsche Verlags-Anstalt, 1974), 118 (December 8, 1941).

Engel's book, although presented in the form of a diary, was in fact written after the war from his personal notes.

13. Halder, KTB III, 332 (December 7, 1941).
14. "Kriegstagebuch Nr.1 (Band December 1941) des Oberkommandos der Heeresgruppe Mitte," BA-MA RH 19-II/122, fol. 65 (December 9, 1941).
15. Bock, *War Diary*, 385–86 (December 9, 1941).
16. See the conclusion of the German high command's special report in Stargardt, *The German War*, 216.
17. "Kriegstagebuch Nr.1 (Band December 1941) des Oberkommandos der Heeresgruppe Mitte," BA-MA RH 19-II/122, fol. 71 (December 9, 1941).
18. Halder, KTB III, 337 (December 9, 1941).
19. "Kriegstagebuch Nr.1 (Band December 1941) des Oberkommandos der Heeresgruppe Mitte," BA-MA RH 19-II/122, fol. 87 (December 10, 1941).
20. Fröhlich, *Die Tagebücher von Joseph Goebbels*, Band 2, 497 (December 13, 1941).
21. As cited in: Stargardt, *The German War*, 216.
22. Günther, *Hot Motors, Cold Feet*, 232.
23. As cited in: Neitzel and Welzer, *Soldaten*, 213–14.
24. As cited in: Stargardt, *The German War*, 215.
25. Halder, KTB III, 343 (December 13, 1941).
26. Neitzel and Welzer, *Soldaten*, 340.
27. As cited in: Ibid., 222.
28. Dietrich, *The Hitler I Knew*, 75.
29. Norman J. W. Goda, "Black Marks: Hitler's Bribery of His Senior Officers During WWII," *The Journal of Modern History* 72, no. 2 (June 2000): 418–19.
30. Ibid., 417–33. See also: Gerd R. Ueberschär and Winfried Vogel, *Dienen und Verdienen: Hitlers Geschenke an seine Eliten* (Frankfurt am Main: S. Fischer, 1999).
31. Fröhlich, *Die Tagebücher von Joseph Goebbels*, Band 2, 215 (November 1, 1941).
32. Elisabeth Wagner, ed., *Der Generalquartiermeister: Briefe und Tagebuchaufzeichnungen des Generalquartiermeisters des Heeres General der Artillerie Eduard Wagner* (Munich: Günter Olzog, 1963), 317.
33. Rolf-Dieter Müller, "The Failure of the Economic 'Blitzkrieg Strategy,'" in *Germany and the Second World War*, vol. 4, *The Attack on the Soviet Union*, edited by Militärgeschichtliches Forschungsamt (Oxford: Oxford University Press, 1998), 1136.
34. Earl F. Ziemke, "Franz Halder at Orsha: The German General Staff Seeks a Consensus," *Military Affairs* 39, no. 4 (December 1975), 175.
35. Walter Görlitz, *Paulus and Stalingrad* (London: Citadel Press, 1963), 141–42.
36. Adamczyk, *Feuer!*, 188.
37. As cited in: Ben Shepherd, *Hitler's Soldiers: The German Army in the Third Reich* (New Haven, Conn.: Yale University Press, 2016), 209.
38. "Kriegstagebuch Nr.3. des XXXXVI.Pz.Korps vom 24.08.41–31.12.41," BA-MA RH 24-46/21, fols. 165, 168, and 173 (December 7, 10, and 13, 1941).
39. As cited in: Basil Liddell Hart, *The Other Side of the Hill* (London: Pan Books, 1999), 292.
40. "Kriegstagebuch Nr.1 (Band December 1941) des Oberkommandos der Heeresgruppe Mitte," BA-MA RH 19-II/122, fol. 49 (December 7, 1941).
41. Frisch with Jones, *Condemned to Live*, 94.
42. Rehfeldt, *Mit dem Eliteverband des Heeres "Grossdeutschland" tief in den Weiten Russlands*, 58.
43. Edmund Blandford, ed., *Under Hitler's Banner: Serving the Third Reich* (Edison: Airlife, 2001), 128.

44. Helmut Günther, *Hot Motors, Cold Feet*, p. 247.
45. "Kriegstagebuch 19.Panzer-Division Abt.Ib für die Zeit vom 1.6.1941–31.12.1942," BA-MA RH 27-19/23, fol. 85 (December 8, 1941).
46. Kempowski, *Das Echolot Barbarossa*, 326 (December 7, 1941).
47. Ibid., 523 (December 19, 1941).
48. Catherine Merridale, *Ivan's War: Life and Death in the Red Army, 1939–1945* (New York: Picador, 2006), 138.
49. Antony Beevor and Luba Vinogradova, eds., *A Writer at War: Vasily Grossman with the Red Army 1941–1945* (New York: Vintage, 2005), 63–64.
50. Ilya Ehrenburg, *The Tempering of Russia* (New York: Alfred A. Knopf, 1944), 109.
51. Kempowski, *Das Echolot Barbarossa*, 410 (December 11, 1941).
52. Willy Peter Reese, *A Stranger to Myself: The Inhumanity of War: Russia, 1941–1944* (New York: Farrar, Straus and Giroux, 2005), 51.
53. Landon and Leitner, *Diary of a German Soldier*, 136 (December 26, 1941).
54. Kuhnert, *Will We See Tomorrow?*, 128–29.
55. "Anlagenband zum KTB XXXXI A.K. Ia 4 6.12.41–31.12.41," BA-MA RH 24-41/17. The diary has no folio stamped page numbers so references must be located according to date (December 16, 1941).
56. Pabst, *The Outermost Frontier*, 39.
57. Wildermuth, "Widening the Circle," 318.
58. Günther, *Hot Motors, Cold Feet*, 235.
59. Reese, *A Stranger to Myself*, 98.
60. German: *Vorwärts Kameraden, wir müssen zurück!* Robert Kershaw, *War Without Garlands: Operation Barbarossa, 1941/42* (New York: Da Capo Press, 2000), 237.
61. Ibid., 241.
62. Wilhelm Bacher, Museumsstiftung Post und Telekommunikation, Berlin, 3.2002.1376 (April 3, 1942). Museumsstiftung Post und Telekommunikation hereafter abbreviated as MPT.
63. The medal was awarded to soldiers who fought in the east for at least fourteen days between November 15, 1941, and April 15, 1942. Agustin Sáiz, *Deutsche Soldaten: Uniforms, Equipment and Personal Items of the German Soldier, 1939–45* (Madrid: Andrea Press, 2008), 242.
64. Pabst, *The Outermost Frontier*, 41.
65. Hans Schäufler, ed., *Knight's Cross Panzers: The German 35th Panzer Regiment in WWII* (Mechanicsburg, Pa.: Stackpole Books, 2010), 196.
66. Martina Kessel, "Laughing about Death? 'German Humor' in the Two World Wars," in *Between Mass Death and Individual Loss: The Place of the Dead in Twentieth-Century Germany*, edited by Alon Confino, Paul Betts and Dirk Schumann (New York: Berghahn Books, 2008), 210.
67. Rudolph Herzog, *Dead Funny: Telling Jokes in Hitler's Germany* (New York: Melville House, 2012), 3.
68. Neitzel and Welzer, *Soldaten*, 225.
69. Benjamin Sax and Dieter Kuntz, *Inside Hitler's Germany: A Documentary History of Life in the Third Reich* (Lexington, Mass.: D. C. Heath, 1992), 465.
70. Herzog, *Dead Funny*, 157–58.
71. Humburg, *Das Gesicht des Krieges*, 135 (October 29, 1941).
72. Henry Metelmann, *Through Hell for Hitler* (Havertown: Casemate, 2005), 74–77.
73. Christine Alexander and Mark Kunze, eds., *Eastern Inferno: The Journals of a German Panzerjäger on the Eastern Front, 1941–43* (Philadelphia: Casemate, 2010), 130 (December 27, 1941).

74. Bernard Häring, *Embattled Witness: Memories of a Time of War* (New York: Seabury Press, 1976), 14.

75. Birgitt Morgenbrod and Stephanie Merkenich, *Das Deutsche Rote Kreuz unter der NS-Diktatur, 1933–1945* (Paderborn: Verlag Ferdinand Schöningh, 2008), 269–71.

76. As cited in: Wendy Lower, *Hitler's Furies: German Woman in the Nazi Killing Fields* (London: Mariner Books, 2013), 93–95.

77. Julia Paulus and Marion Röwekamp, eds., *Eine Soldatenheimschwester an der Ostfront: Briefwechsel von Annette Schücking mit ihrer Familie, 1941–1943* (Paderborn: Verlag Ferdinand Schöningh, 2015), 179 (December 7, 1941).

78. Pöppel, *Heaven and Hell*, 72.

79. Adamczyk, *Feuer!*, 204.

80. Thomas Kühne, *Belonging and Genocide: Hitler's Community, 1918–1945* (New Haven, Conn.: Yale University Press, 2010), 119.

81. Karl Reddemann, ed., *Zwischen Front und Heimat: Der Briefwechsel des münsterischen Ehepaares Agnes und Albert Neuhaus, 1940–1944* (Münster: Regensberg Verlag, 1996), 380 (December 30, 1941).

82. Reese, *A Stranger to Myself*, 51.

83. Wiedebach-Nostitz's diary is reproduced in: Frank Ellis, *Barbarossa 1941: Reframing Hitler's Invasion of Stalin's Soviet Empire* (Lawrence: University Press of Kansas, 2015), 345 (December 13–19, 1941).

4. KEEPING THE WOLF FROM THE DOOR: THE PANZER GROUPS RETREAT FROM MOSCOW

1. Glantz and House, *When Titans Clashed*, 108.

2. Erickson, *The Road to Stalingrad*, 277.

3. Beevor and Vinogradova, eds., *A Writer at War*, 63.

4. Erickson, *The Road to Stalingrad*, 280.

5. Simon Sebag Montefiore, *Stalin: The Court of the Red Tsar* (London: Vintage Books, 2003), 359.

6. Harrison, *The Battle for Moscow, 1941–1942*, 188.

7. Jordan, *Russian Glory* (London: The Cresset Press, 1942), 165.

8. As cited in: Janusz Piekalkiewicz, *Moscow 1941: The Frozen Offensive* (London: Presidio Press, 1981), 236–37.

9. Bock, *War Diary*, 389–90 (December 12, 1941).

10. Cyrus Leo Sulzberger, *A Long Row of Candles: Memoirs and Diaries, 1934–1954* (Toronto: Macmillan, 1969), 181.

11. Bock, *War Diary*, 391 (December 13, 1941).

12. Hans Meier-Welcker, *Aufzeichnungen eines Generalstabsoffiziers, 1939–1942*, 145 (December 14, 1941).

13. Bock, *War Diary*, 391–94 (December 13, 14, and 15, 1941).

14. "Tagebuch Reinhardts," N245/3, fol. 17 (December 13, 1941).

15. Reinhardt, *Moscow—The Turning Point*, 292–93.

16. Oldwig von Natzmer, "The Pocket of Klin: Breakout of a Panzer Division," In *The Anvil of War: German Generalship in Defense on the Eastern Front*, edited by Peter Tsouras (London: Stackpole Books, 1994), 235–38.

17. "Anlagenband zum KTB XXXXI A.K. Ia 4 6.12.41–31.12.41," BA-MA RH 24-41/17 (December 15, 1941).

18. Kempowski, *Das Echolot Barbarossa*, 418 (December 12, 1941).

19. "Tagebuch Reinhardts," N245/3, fol. 17 (December 15, 1941).

20. "6. Panzer Division Ia KTB 1.12.1941–31.3.1942," BA-MA RH 27-6/20. The diary has

no folio stamped page numbers so references must be located according to date (December 12, 13, and 16, 1941).

21. "Reinhardt's letters to his wife," N245/2, fol. 19 (December 15, 1941).

22. Engel, *7,000 Kilometers in a Sturmgeschütz*, 104 (December 13, 14, and 16, 1941).

23. *True to Type*, 40 (December 17, 1941).

24. As cited in: Paul Carell, *Hitler's War on Russia: The Story of the German Defeat in the East* (London: Aberdeen Books, 1964), 318.

25. Reddemann, *Zwischen Front und Heimat*, 372 (December 15, 1941).

26. Engel, *7,000 Kilometers in a Sturmgeschütz*, 104 (December 16, 1941).

27. Hans von Luck, *Panzer Commander: The Memoirs of Colonel Hans von Luck* (New York: Praeger, 1989), 65.

28. *True to Type*, 39 (December 16, 1941).

29. "Kriegstagebuch Nr.7 des Kdos. der 1.Panzer-Div. 20.9.41–12.4.42," BA-MA RH 27-1/58, fol. 86 (December 15, 1941).

30. "Reinhardt's letters to his wife," N245/2, fol. 19 (December 15, 1941).

31. Timothy A. Wray, *Standing Fast: German Defensive Doctrine on the Russian Front During World War II* (Fort Leavenworth, Kans.: Combat Studies Institute, 2004), 91.

32. "Kriegstagebuch Nr.3 der 7.Panzer-Division Führungsabteilung 1.6.1941–9.5.1942," BA-MA RH 27-7/46, fol. 242 (December 12, 1941).

33. Luck, *Panzer Commander*, 64.

34. Newton, *Hitler's Commander*, 165.

35. "2. Panzer Division KTB Nr.6 Teil I. Vom 15.6.41–27.2.42," BA-MA RH 27-2/22 (December 11, 1941).

36. Hans Röttiger, "XXXXI Panzer Corps during the Battle of Moscow in 1941 as a Component of Panzer Group 3," in *German Battle Tactics in the Russian Front, 1941–1945*, edited by Steven H. Newton (Atglen, Pa.: Schiffer, 1994), 40. The title of Röttiger's chapter is technically incorrect; XXXXI Army Corps was only redesignated as the XXXXI "Panzer" Corps on July 7, 1942.

37. Even as early as the summer of 1941 the advantages of strongpoints was recognized in defensive situations. A report from the 7th Infantry Division noted: "I reject the type of defence which is frequently carried out . . . The linear deployment, without reserves behind it, must lead to critical situations, because no one was in the position to influence the battle in anyway. Solely because of this, a locally strong attack on one position had an effect on the breath [of the line]. Maintaining the initiative— active defence—can only be managed out of strongpoints" (Rutherford and Wettstein, *The German Army on the Eastern Front*, 5–6).

38. "Anlagen zum Kriegstagebuch Tagesmeldungen Bd.I 1.11–31.12.41," BA-MA RH 21-3/71, fol. 347 (December 18, 1941).

39. Department of the U.S. Army, ed., *Effects of Climate on Combat in European Russia* (Washington, D.C.: Center of Military History United States Army, 1952), 16.

40. Röttiger, "XXXXI Panzer Corps during the Battle of Moscow in 1941 as a Component of Panzer Group 3," 40–41.

41. As cited in: Bücheler, *Hoepner*, 162.

42. "11.Pz.Div. KTB Abt.Ia vom 22.10.41–24.1.42," BA-MA RH 27-11/24, fol. 65 (December 18, 1941).

43. "Kriegstagebuch Nr.3. des XXXXVI.Pz.Korps vom 24.08.41–31.12.41," BA-MA RH 24-46/21, fol. 172 (December 13, 1941).

44. "KTB 'Rußlandfeldzug' Pz.A.O.K. III Teil 6.12.41–9.1.42," BA-MA RH 21-4/50, fol. 25 (December 13, 1941); "Kriegstagebuch Nr.3. der Führungsabteilung (Ia) des Gen. Kdo. (mot.) XXXX.Pz.Korps vom 31.05.1941–26.12.1941," BA-MA RH 24-40/18 (December 14, 1941).

45. "Kriegstagebuch Nr.3. der Führungsabteilung (Ia) des Gen. Kdo. (mot.) XXXX. Pz.Korps vom 31.05.1941–26.12.1941," BA-MA RH 24-40/18 (December 7, 1941).

46. As cited in: Omer Bartov, *Hitler's Army: Soldiers, Nazis, and War in the Third Reich* (Oxford: Oxford University Press, 1992), 97–98.

47. As cited in: Ibid., 97.

48. Herzog, *Dead Funny*, 169.

49. "20.Pz.Div. KTB vom 21.10.41 bis 30.12.41 Band Ia2," BA-MA RH 27-20/26, fol. 109 (December 16, 1941).

50. "Kriegstagebuch Nr.3. des XXXXVI.Pz.Korps vom 24.08.41—31.12.41," BA-MA RH 24-46/21, fol. 181 (December 18, 1941).

51. "KTB 'Rußlandfeldzug' Pz.A.O.K. III Teil 6.12.41–9.1.42," BA-MA RH 21-4/50, fol. 15 (December 9, 1941).

52. Ibid., fol. 40 (December 15, 1941).

53. "Kriegstagebuch Nr.3. der Führungsabteilung (Ia) des Gen. Kdo. (mot.) XXXX. Pz.Korps vom 31.05.1941–26.12.1941," BA-MA RH 24-40/18 (December 16, 1941).

54. "KTB Nr.9 5.Pz.Div. 11.12.41–30.1.42," BA-MA 27-5/34, fols. 24 and 27 (December 16 and 17, 1941).

55. "Kriegstagebuch Nr.3. des XXXXVI.Pz.Korps vom 24.08.41–31.12.41," BA-MA RH 24-46/21, fol. 175 (December 14, 1941).

56. *True to Type*, 38 (December 14, 1941).

57. Günther, *Hot Motors, Cold Feet*, 239.

58. Walter Tilemann, *Ich, das Soldatenkind* (Munich: Knaur TB, 2005), 154–55.

59. Ibid., 156.

60. As cited in: Bücheler, *Hoepner*, 163.

61. "Kriegstagebuch Nr.3. der Führungsabteilung (Ia) des Gen. Kdo. (mot.) XXXX. Pz.Korps vom 31.05.1941–26.12.1941," BA-MA RH 24-40/18 (December 17, 1941).

62. Hans Schäufler, *Panzer Warfare on the Eastern Front* (Mechanicsburg, Pa.: Stackpole Books, 2012), 47.

63. As cited in: Christian Hartmann, *Operation Barbarossa: Nazi Germany's War in the East, 1941–1945* (Oxford: Oxford University Press, 2013), 106.

64. As cited in: Ibid., 107–108.

65. "KTB Nr.9 5.Pz.Div. 11.12.41–30.1.42," BA-MA 27-5/34, fols. 20 and 22 (December 15, 1941).

66. "KTB 'Rußlandfeldzug' Pz.A.O.K. III Teil 6.12.41–9.1.42," BA-MA RH 21-4/50, fol. 21 (December 12, 1941).

67. Deck, *Der Weg der 1000 Toten*, 119.

68. As cited in: Stargardt, *The German War*, 208.

69. "KTB 'Rußlandfeldzug' Pz.A.O.K. III Teil 6.12.41–9.1.42," BA-MA RH 21-4/50, fol. 42 (December 16, 1941).

70. Metelmann, *Through Hell for Hitler*, 35.

71. Rehfeldt, *Mit dem Eliteverband des Heeres "Grossdeutschland" tief in den Weiten Russlands*, 53.

72. *True to Type*, 99 (January 8, 1942).

73. Gordon Williamson, *Hans Sturm: A Soldier's Odyssey on the Eastern Front* (Croydon: Fonthill Media, 2015), 102–103.

74. Schäufler, *Panzer Warfare on the Eastern Front*, 47.

75. Günther, *Hot Motors, Cold Feet*, 238.

76. "Kriegstagebuch Nr.3. des XXXXVI.Pz.Korps vom 24.08.41–31.12.41," BA-MA RH 24-46/21, fol. 180 (December 18, 1941).

77. "20.Pz.Div. KTB vom 21.10.41 bis 30.12.41 Band Ia2," BA-MA RH 27-20/26, fol. 113 (December 18, 1941).

78. Carruthers, ed., *The Wehrmacht*, 61.
79. Ortwin Buchbender and Reinhold Sterz, eds., *Das andere Gesicht des Krieges: Deutsche Feldpostbriefe, 1939–1945* (Munich: C. H. Beck Verlag, 1982), 91 (December 14, 1941).
80. Jordan, *Russian Glory*, 164–65.
81. Helmuth James von Moltke, *Letters to Freya: 1939–1945* (New York: Knopf, 1990), 194 (December 12, 1941).

5. DIGGING IN HIS HEELS: HITLER ORDERS A HALT

1. Luther, *Barbarossa Unleashed*, 94.
2. Carruthers, *The Wehrmacht*, 48.
3. Hans Pichler, *Truppenarzt und Zeitzeuge: Mit der 4. SS-Polizei-Division an vorderster Front* (Dresden: Winkelried Verlag, 2006), 121 (January 28, 1942).
4. Bock, *War Diary*, 398 (December 18, 1941).
5. Mühleisen, *Hellmuth Stieff Briefe*, 143 (December 13, 1941).
6. Emphasis in the original. Ibid., 144 (December 17, 1941).
7. "Briefe von Heinz Guderian an seine Frau Margarete," BA-MA N 802/46 (December 8, 1941).
8. Bock, *War Diary*, 390 (December 12, 1941).
9. "Kriegstagebuch Nr.1 2.Panzerarmee Band III vom 1.11.1941 bis 26.12.41," BA-MA RH 21-2/244, fol. 268 (December 12, 1941).
10. Bock, *War Diary*, 393 (December 15, 1941).
11. Guderian, *Panzer Leader*, 262.
12. "Armeeoberkommando 2. I.a KTB Teil.2 19.9.41–16.12.41," BA-MA RH 20-2/207, 215 (December 13, 1941).
13. "Kriegstagebuch Nr.1 2.Panzerarmee Band III vom 1.11.1941 bis 26.12.41," BA-MA RH 21-2/244, fol. 285 (December 14, 1941).
14. Postenrieder, *Feldzug im Osten*, 212–13 (December 14, 1941).
15. Bock, *War Diary*, 394 (December 15 and 16, 1941). See also: Guderian, *Panzer Leader*, 262; www.lexikon-der-wehrmacht.de/Personenregister/C/CochenhausenConradv.htm.
16. Buchbender and Sterz, *Das andere Gesicht des Krieges*, 91 (January 5, 1942).
17. "9.Pz.Div. KTB Ia vom 19.5.1941 bis 22.1.1942," BA-MA RH 27-9/4, 175 (December 12, 1941).
18. Reese, *A Stranger to Myself*, 49.
19. Buchbender and Sterz, *Das andere Gesicht des Krieges*, 91 (December 18, 1941).
20. "Kriegstagebuch XXXXVIII.Pz.Kps. Abt.Ia 1.12.41–31.12.41," BA-MA RH 24-48/40, fol. 10 (December 16, 1941).
21. "9.Pz.Div. KTB Ia vom 19.5.1941 bis 22.1.1942," BA-MA RH 27-9/4, fol. 179 (December 17, 1941).
22. "Kriegstagebuch Nr.1 (Band December 1941) des Oberkommandos der Heeresgruppe Mitte," BA-MA RH 19-II/122, fol. 140 (December 18, 1941).
23. As cited in: Friedrich-Christian Stahl, "Generaloberst Rudolf Schmidt," in *Hitlers militärische Elite Bd.2: Vom Kriegsbeginn bis Weltkriegsende*, edited by Gerd R. Ueberschär (Darmstadt: Primus, 1998), 222; Woche, *Zwischen Pflicht und Gewissen*, 139.
24. Reese, *A Stranger to Myself*, 53.
25. Guderian, *Panzer Leader*, 263.
26. Ibid., 262.
27. "18. Panzer Div. Ia Kriegstagebuch vom 14.12.41–9.1.42," BA-MA RH 27-18/70, fols. 3 and 9 (December 15 and 19, 1941).

28. Landon and Leitner, *Diary of a German Soldier*, 127 (December 17, 1941).
29. "Kriegstagebuch Nr.1 2.Panzerarmee Band III vom 1.11.1941 bis 26.12.41," BA-MA RH 21-2/244, fol. 315 (December 18, 1941).
30. Landon and Leitner, *Diary of a German Soldier*, 129 (December 17, 1941).
31. Bock, *War Diary*, 391 (December 13, 1941).
32. "Kriegstagebuch Nr.1 2.Panzerarmee Band III vom 1.11.1941 bis 26.12.41," BA-MA RH 21-2/244, fol. 286 (December 14, 1941).
33. "Kriegstagebuch Nr.1 (Band December 1941) des Oberkommandos der Heeresgruppe Mitte," BA-MA RH 19-II/122, fol. 127 (December 16, 1941).
34. "Kriegstagebuch Nr.1 2.Panzerarmee Band III vom 1.11.1941 bis 26.12.41," BA-MA RH 21-2/244, fol. 286 (December 14, 1941).
35. Guderian, *Panzer Leader*, 262.
36. Bock, *War Diary*, 392 (December 14, 1941).
37. Ziemke and Bauer, *Moscow to Stalingrad*, 79.
38. Bock, *War Diary*, 393 (December 14, 1941).
39. Ziemke and Bauer, *Moscow to Stalingrad*, 80.
40. Bock, *War Diary*, 393 (December 14, 1941).
41. "Anlagenband zum KTB XXXXI A.K. Ia 4 6.12.41–31.12.41," BA-MA RH 24-41/17 (December 15, 1941).
42. Hartmann, *Operation Barbarossa*, 78 and 103.
43. Halder, KTB III, 348 (December 15, 1941).
44. Hermann Balck, *Order in Chaos: The Memoirs of General of Panzer Troops Hermann Balck* (Lexington: University Press of Kentucky, 2015), 226.
45. Halder, KTB III, 285 (November 10, 1941).
46. Kotze, *Heeresadjutant bei Hitler*, 117 (December 6 and 7, 1941).
47. Bock, *War Diary*, 394–95 (December 16, 1941).
48. Ibid., 395 (December 16, 1941).
49. Ibid., 396 (December 16, 1941).
50. Halder, KTB III, 350 (December 16, 1941).
51. Reinhardt, *Moscow—The Turning Point*, 305.
52. "Kriegstagebuch Nr.1 2.Panzerarmee Band III vom 1.11.1941 bis 26.12.41," BA-MA RH 21-2/244, fol. 294 (December 16, 1941).
53. "Guderian's letters to his wife," BA-MA N 802/46 (December 16, 1941). In somewhat less precise translation, see Guderian, *Panzer Leader*, 263.
54. "Guderian's letters to his wife," BA-MA N 802/46 (December 16, 1941).
55. Ibid. See also: Johannes Hürter, *Hitlers Heerführer: Die deutschen Oberbefehlshaber im Krieg gegen die Sowjetunion, 1941/42* (Munich: Oldenbourg Wissenschaftsverlag, 2006), 320.
56. "Kriegstagebuch Nr.1 2.Panzerarmee Band III vom 1.11.1941 bis 26.12.41," BA-MA RH 21-2/244, fol. 302 (December 17, 1941).
57. Guderian, *Panzer Leader*, 263.
58. "Kriegstagebuch Nr.1 2.Panzerarmee Band III vom 1.11.1941 bis 26.12.41," BA-MA RH 21-2/244, fols. 302 and 308 (December 17, 1941).
59. Guderian, *Panzer Leader*, 263.
60. "KTB 3rd Pz. Div. vom 19.9.41 bis 6.2.42," BA-MA RH 27-3/15, fols. 370–71 (December 13 and 14, 1941).
61. Guderian, *Panzer Leader*, 264. The word order of this quotation has been corrected owing to what appears to be an editorial oversight in the original.
62. As cited in: Kenneth Macksey, *Guderian: Panzer General* (London: Macdonald and Jane's, 1975), 158–59.

63. Percy E. Schramm, ed., *Kriegstagebuch des Oberkommandos der Wehrmacht, 1940–1941*, Band I/2, *1. August 1940–31. Dezember 1941* (Munich: Manfred Pawlak, 1982), 1084 (December 18, 1941).

64. For an example of this viewpoint, see: Alan Clark, *Barbarossa: The Russian-German Conflict, 1941–1945* (London: Phoenix, 1996), 182–83.

65. Dietrich, *The Hitler I Knew*, 75.

66. Günther Blumentritt, "Moscow," in *The Fatal Decisions*, edited by William Richardson and Seymour Freidin (London: Michael Joseph, 1956), 66–67. There were exceptions to this viewpoint being published around the same time; see: Alfred Philippi and Ferdinand Heim, *Der Feld Gegen Sowjetrussland, 1941 bis 1945* (Stuttgart: Kohlhammer, 1962), 101.

67. Fritz, *The First Soldier*, 373.

68. As cited in: Liddell Hart, *The Other Side of the Hill*, 289.

69. Blumentritt, "Moscow," 67.

70. Richard J. Evans, *The Third Reich at War: How the Nazis Led Germany from Conquest to Disaster* (London: Penguin Books, 2009), 789–90, n. 308.

71. Otto Schellert, "Winter Fighting of the 253rd Infantry Division in the Rzhev Area, 1941–1942," in *German Battle Tactics in the Russian Front, 1941–1945*, edited by Steven H. Newton (Atglen, Pa.: Schiffer, 1994), 69.

72. Blumentritt, "Moscow," 67.

73. Fritz, *Ostkrieg*, 205; Hürter, *Hitlers Heerführer*, 327; Ziemke and Bauer, *Moscow to Stalingrad*, 83.

74. Definition by Gunther E. Rothenberg.

75. Lopez, *The Survival of Auftragstaktik during the Soviet Counterattack in the Battle for Moscow, December 1941 to January 1942*, MA thesis, Temple University, 2015.

76. As cited in: Liddell Hart, *The Other Side of the Hill*, 298.

77. Lopez's case studies assess the 35th Infantry Division (belonging to Panzer Group 4), the 253rd Infantry Division (belonging to Ninth Army), the 255th Infantry Division (belonging to Fourth Army), and Heinrici's XXXXIII Army Corps (belonging initially to Second Panzer Army and later Fourth Army).

78. Marco Sigg, *Der Unterführer als Feldherr im Taschenformat: Theorie und Praxis der Auftragstaktik im deutschen Heer, 1869 bis 1945* (Paderborn: Verlag Ferdinand Schöningh, 2014). See also: Rutherford and Wettstein, *The German Army on the Eastern Front*, 33.

6. PUT TO THE SWORD: THE END OF BRAUCHITSCH

1. As cited in: Stargardt, *The German War*, 225.

2. Heinz Boberach, ed., *Meldungen aus dem Reich: Die geheimen Lageberichte des Sicherheitsdienstes der SS, 1938–1945*, Band 9 (Berlin: Pawlak, 1984), 3121 (January 5, 1942).

3. Fredborg, *Behind the Steel Wall*, 77.

4. Stargardt, *The German War*, 225.

5. *True to Type*, 41 (January 2, 1942).

6. Douglas Wolfgang Oskar Gagel, *Führer, Folk and Fatherland: A Soldier's Story* (Renfrew: Douglas Gagel, 2010), 84.

7. As cited in: Stargardt, *The German War*, 226.

8. Walter Görlitz ed., *The Memoirs of Field-Marshal Keitel: Chief of the German High Command, 1938–1945* (New York: Focal Point, 1966), 164.

9. Hermann Balck, *Order in Chaos*, 226.

10. "Kriegstagebuch Nr.1 (Band December 1941) des Oberkommandos der Heeresgruppe Mitte," BA-MA RH 19-II/122, fol. 151 (December 19, 1941).

11. "Kriegstagebuch Nr.1 2.Panzerarmee Band III vom 1.11.1941 bis 26.12.41," BA-MA RH 21-2/244, fols. 325–26 (December 20, 1941).
12. Fredborg, *Behind the Steel Wall*, 77.
13. Fröhlich, *Die Tagebücher von Joseph Goebbels*, Band 2, 554 (December 21, 1941).
14. Fredborg, *Behind the Steel Wall*, 77.
15. Malcolm Muggeridge, ed., *Ciano's Diary, 1939–1943* (Kingswood: William Heinemann, 1947), 413 (December 22, 1941).
16. Fröhlich, *Die Tagebücher von Joseph Goebbels*, Band 2, 559 (December 22, 1941).
17. LeSueur, *Twelve Months That Changed the World*, 99.
18. Ilya Ehrenburg, *Russia at War* (London: Hamish Hamilton, 1943), 99 (December 29, 1941).
19. Sebastian, *Journal*, 454 (December 22, 1941).
20. Fröhlich, *Die Tagebücher von Joseph Goebbels*, Band 2, 566–67 (December 23, 1941).
21. *True to Type*, 40 (December 21, 1941).
22. Ehrenburg, *The Tempering of Russia*, 111.
23. Ingo Stader, ed., *Ihr daheim und wir hier draußen: Ein Briefwechsel zwischen Ostfront und Heimat, Juni 1941–März 1943* (Cologne: Böhlau Köln, 2006), 75 (December 25, 1941).
24. Kempowski, *Das Echolot Barbarossa*, 562 (December 21, 1941).
25. Ernst Gerber, *Im Dienst des Roten Kreuzes: Schweizer Ärztemissionen im II. Weltkrieg*, Teil 2, *Ein Tagebuch, 1941/1942* (Berlin: Wünsche, Frank, 2002), 185 (December 22, 1941).
26. Kempowski, *Das Echolot Barbarossa*, 573 (December 22, 1941).
27. *True to Type*, 147 (January 1, 1942).
28. Kempowski, *Das Echolot Barbarossa*, 654 (December 28, 1941).
29. Ulrich von Hassell, *The Ulrich von Hassell Diaries: The Story of the Forces against Hitler Inside Germany* (London: Frontline Books, 2011), 152 (December 23, 1941).
30. Victor Klemperer, *Ich will Zeugnis ablegen bis zum letzten: Tagebücher, 1933–1941*, edited by Walter Nowojski and Hadwig Klemperer (Darmstadt: Aufbau-Verlag, 1997), 698.
31. Jean Guéhenno, *Diary of the Dark Years, 1940–1944: Collaboration, Resistance, and Daily Life in Occupied Paris* (Oxford: Oxford University Press, 2016), 137 (December 25, 1941).
32. Boberach, *Meldungen aus dem Reich*, Band 9, 3120–21 (January 5, 1942).
33. Dietrich, *The Hitler I Knew*, 72.
34. Boberach, *Meldungen aus dem Reich*, Band 9, 3121 (January 5, 1942).
35. Fröhlich, *Die Tagebücher von Joseph Goebbels*, Band 2, 579 (December 25, 1941).
36. Walter Bähr and Hans Bähr, eds., *Kriegsbriefe Gefallener Studenten, 1939–1945* (Tübingen: Wunderlich, 1952), 315–16 (December 23, 1941).
37. Ehrenburg, *The Tempering of Russia*, 121.
38. As cited in: Jones, *The Retreat*, 185.
39. Ibid., 184.
40. Herzog, *Dead Funny*, 4.
41. As cited in: Meyer, *Adolf Heusinger*, 168.
42. Rehfeldt, *Mit dem Eliteverband des Heeres "Grossdeutschland" tief in den Weiten Russlands*, 65.
43. Kempowski, *Das Echolot Barbarossa*, 614 (December 25, 1941).
44. Reddemann, *Zwischen Front und Heimat*, 375 (December 21, 1941).
45. Grumann's diary is reproduced in: Elena Rzhevskaia, "Roads and Days: The

Memoirs of a Red Army Translator," *The Journal of Slavic Military Studies* 14, no. 1 (2001): 66.

46. As cited in: Jones, *The Retreat*, 184.

47. Ibid.

48. Förster, "Ideological Warfare in Germany," 557.

49. Balck, *Order in Chaos*, 228.

50. As cited in: Bücheler, *Hoepner*, 163.

51. Ernst Klink, "The Conduct of Operations," in *Germany and the Second World War*, vol. 4, *The Attack on the Soviet Union*, edited by Militärgeschichtliches Forschungsamt (Oxford: Oxford University Press, 1998), 718.

52. Görlitz, *The Memoirs of Field-Marshal Keitel*, 163.

53. Christian Hartmann, *Halder Generalstabschef Hitlers, 1938–1942* (Munich: Schöningh, 1991), 304.

54. Förster, "Ideological Warfare in Germany," 556.

55. Kotze, *Heeresadjutant bei Hitler*, 119 (January 27, 1942). For an English translation, see: Gerhard Engel, *At the Heart of the Reich: The Secret Diary of Hitler's Army Adjutant* (London: Greenhill Books, 2005), 126 (January 27, 1942).

56. Klink, "The Conduct of Operations," 718.

57. Barry Leach, "Halder," in *Hitler's Generals*, edited by Correlli Barnett (London: Grove Weidenfeld, 1989), 121.

58. Hartmann, *Halder Generalstabschef Hitlers*, 303.

59. Hassell, *The Ulrich von Hassell Diaries*, 149 (December 21, 1941). See also: Fabian von Schlabrendorff, *The Secret War against Hitler* (London: Hodder & Stoughton, 1966), 144.

60. Franz Halder, *Hitler als Feldherr* (Munich: Münchener Dom-Verlag, 1949), 45; Peter Bor, *Gespräche mit Halder* (Wiesbaden: Limes Verlag, 1950), 214–15.

61. Liddell Hart, *The Other Side of the Hill*, 294; Fredborg, *Behind the Steel Wall*, 77.

62. Elke Fröhlich, ed., *Die Tagebücher von Joseph Goebbels*, Teil II, Diktate 1941–1945, Band 3, Januar–März 1942 (Munich: K. G. Saur, 1994), 510 (March 20, 1942).

63. Sönke Neitzel, *Tapping Hitler's Generals: Transcripts of Secret Conversations, 1942–45* (St. Paul: Frontline Books, 2007), 88, doc. 25.

64. Ibid., 112, doc. 44.

65. Ibid., 168 and 169, docs. 83 and 84.

66. Görlitz, *The Memoirs of Field-Marshal Keitel*, 164; Klink, "The Conduct of Operations," 718.

67. Ziemke and Bauer, *Moscow to Stalingrad*, 83–84.

68. Klink, "The Conduct of Operations," 718.

69. As cited in: Förster, "Ideological Warfare in Germany," 556. See also: Hartmann, *Halder Generalstabschef Hitlers*, 302.

70. As cited in: Ziemke and Bauer, *Moscow to Stalingrad*, 87.

71. Brian Bond, "Brauchitsch," in *Hitler's Generals*, edited by Correlli Barnett (London: Grove Weidenfeld, 1989), 79.

72. Karl-Heinz Janssen, "Walther von Brauchitsch: Der überforderte Feldherr," in *Die Militärelite des Dritten Reiches: 27 biographische Skizzen*, edited by Ronald Smelser and Enrico Syring (Berlin: Ullstein, 1995), 95.

73. Bock, *War Diary*, 401 (January 1, 1942).

74. Ibid., 397–98 (December 17, 1941).

75. Ibid., 398–400 (December 18, 19, and 25, 1941).

76. Blumentritt, "Moscow," 66.

77. Hans von Greiffenberg, "Battle of Moscow, 1941–1942," in *World War II German Mili-*

tary Studies, vol. 16, pt. 7, *The Eastern Theater*, edited by Historical Division Headquarters, United States Army, MS# T-28 (New York: Garland Publishing, 1979), 58.

78. Balck, *Order in Chaos*, 227.
79. Schlabrendorff, *The Secret War against Hitler*, 136.
80. Ibid., 145–47. See also: Richard Lamb, "Kluge," in *Hitler's Generals*, edited by Correlli Barnett (London: Grove Weidenfeld, 1989), 404; Peter Hoffmann, *The History of the German Resistance, 1933–1945* (Montreal: McGill-Queen's University Press, 1996).
81. Blumentritt, "Moscow," 66.
82. Bock, *War Diary*, 399 (December 19, 1942).

7. THE BEAR WITHOUT ANY CLAWS: THE INADEQUATE RED ARMY

1. Geoffrey Roberts, *Stalin's General: The Life of Georgy Zhukov* (New York: Random House, 2012), 144.
2. As cited in: Karel C. Berkhoff, *Motherland in Danger: Soviet Propaganda during World War II* (Cambridge, Mass.: Harvard University Press, 2012), 119.
3. Ibid., 126.
4. Jörn Hasenclever, *Wehrmacht und Besatzungspolitik: Die Befehlshaber der rückwärtigen Heeresgebiete, 1941–1943* (Paderborn: Verlag Ferdinand Schöningh, 2010); Theo Schulte, *The German Army and Nazi Policies in Occupied Russia* (Oxford: Oxford University Press, 1989); Hannes Heer and Klaus Naumann, eds., *War of Extermination: The German Military in World War II, 1941–1944* (New York: Berghahn Books, 2006).
5. As cited in: Neitzel and Welzer, *Soldaten*, 309.
6. As cited in: Merridale, *Ivan's War*, 148.
7. Mühleisen, *Hellmuth Stieff Briefe*, 143 (December 13, 1941).
8. Alexander Werth, *Russia at War, 1941–1945* (New York: Basic Books, 1993), 422.
9. Richard Bidlack, "Propaganda and Public Opinion," in *The Soviet Union at War, 1941–1945*, edited by David R. Stone (Barnsley, U.K.: Pen and Sword, 2010), 61.
10. Jordan, *Russian Glory*, 137.
11. David M. Glantz, *Colossus Reborn: The Red Army at War, 1941–1943* (Lawrence: University Press of Kansas, 2005), 570–71 and 580.
12. See the discussion in: Joachim Hoffmann, "The Conduct of the War through Soviet Eyes," in *Germany and the Second World War*, vol. 4, *The Attack on the Soviet Union*, edited by Militärgeschichtliches Forschungsamt (Oxford: Oxford University Press, 1998), 914–19.
13. Kempowski, *Das Echolot Barbarossa*, 487 (December 16, 1941).
14. Haape with Henshaw, *Moscow Tram Stop*, 314.
15. As cited in: Merridale, *Ivan's War*, 147–48.
16. Andrew Nagorski, *The Greatest Battle: Stalin, Hitler, and the Desperate Struggle for Moscow That Changed the Course of World War II* (New York: Simon & Schuster, 2007), 260.
17. As cited in: Merridale, *Ivan's War*, 148.
18. Roger R. Reese, *Why Stalin's Soldiers Fought: The Red Army's Military Effectiveness in World War II* (Lawrence: University Press of Kansas, 2011), 203.
19. As cited in: Alexander Hill, *The Red Army and the Second World War* (Cambridge: Cambridge University Press, 2017), 302.
20. Berkhoff, *Motherland in Danger*, 43–44.
21. Roberts, *Stalin's General*, 145.
22. Ehrenburg, *The Tempering of Russia*, 99.
23. For the falsified figures that they did release, see: Berkhoff, *Motherland in Danger*, 56–57.

24. Krivosheev, *Soviet Casualties and Combat Losses in the Twentieth Century*, 114, 118, and 121.

25. For Soviet figures, see: Lopukhovsky and Kavalerchik, *The Price of Victory*, 154. For German figures, see: Halder, KTB III, 318 and 409 (November 30, 1941, and March 5, 1942).

26. Having met with Hitler on December 10, Goebbels recorded in his diary: "That we must retreat here and there is understandable; we have an interest to adjust the front line, which was much advanced in many places in preparation of future offensives, and establish a clear line that is as short as possible and minimizes demands on the troops and matériel. All of this cannot be a question of prestige for us" (Fröhlich, *Die Tagebücher von Joseph Goebbels*, Band 2, 467 [December 10, 1941]).

27. Ibid., 537 (December 18, 1941).

28. Ibid., 544 (December 19, 1941).

29. Berkhoff, *Motherland in Danger*, 44.

30. Hill, *The Red Army and the Second World War*, 301.

31. Walter S. Dunn, Jr., *Stalin's Keys to Victory: The Rebirth of the Red Army in WWII* (Mechanicsburg, Pa.: Stackpole Books, 2006), 91–92.

32. Hill, *The Red Army and the Second World War*, 288 and 298.

33. Dunn, *Stalin's Keys to Victory*, 25.

34. Hill, *The Red Army and the Second World War*, 298–99.

35. As cited in: Ziemke and Bauer, *Moscow to Stalingrad*, 88.

36. Ibid., 88–90.

37. Ibid., 88–90; see also: Bellamy, *Absolute War*, 332–33.

38. As cited in: Hürter, *Hitlers Heerführer*, 332.

39. "Tagebuch Reinhardts," N245/3, fol. 18 (December 17, 1941).

40. As cited in: Hürter, *Hitlers Heerführer*, 333, n. 227.

41. As cited in: ibid., 333.

42. "Kriegstagebuch Nr.1 (Band December 1941) des Oberkommandos der Heeresgruppe Mitte," BA-MA RH 19-II/122, fol. 147 (December 19, 1941).

43. Matthias Strohn, *The German Army and the Defence of the Reich: Military Doctrine and the Conduct of Defensive Battle, 1918–1939* (Cambridge: Cambridge University Press, 2010).

44. Jörg Muth, *Command Culture: Officer Education in the U.S. Army and the German Armed Forces, 1901–1940, and the Consequences for World War II* (Denton: University of North Texas Press, 2011), 153.

45. Halder, KTB III, 354 (December 19, 1941).

46. "Kriegstagebuch Nr.1 (Band December 1941) des Oberkommandos der Heeresgruppe Mitte," BA-MA RH 19-II/122, fol. 136 (December 17, 1941).

47. Ibid., fol. 143 (December 18, 1941).

48. Ibid., fol. 143 (December 18, 1941).

49. "KTB 'Rußlandfeldzug' Pz.A.O.K. III Teil 6.12.41–9.1.42," BA-MA RH 21-4/50, fol. 59 (December 20, 1941).

50. Ibid., fol. 51 (December 18, 1941).

51. *True to Type*, 39 (December 16, 1941).

52. Ibid., 40 (December 21, 1941).

53. "KTB 'Rußlandfeldzug' Pz.A.O.K. III Teil 6.12.41–9.1.42," BA-MA RH 21-4/50, fol. 54 (December 19, 1941).

54. Ibid., fol. 60 (December 21, 1941).

55. "Tagebuch Reinhardts," N245/3, fol. 18 (December 21, 1941).

56. Greiffenberg, "Battle of Moscow," 77. In Greiffenberg's account Blumentritt was run

over by a truck during a visit to the front on the evening of December 22 and had to be evacuated to Smolensk for medical treatment. The date, however, is not consistent with Blumentritt's postwar account given to Basil Liddell Hart, in which he speaks of his Christmas at the front in 1941. He was, however, replaced as chief of staff on December 27, 1941. See: Liddell Hart, *The Other Side of the Hill*, 290.

57. Ibid. Greiffenburg's account incorrectly states that they were also designated panzer armies on this date, but did not happen until January 1, 1942.
58. "Tagebuch Reinhardts," N245/3, fol. 18 (December 23, 1941).
59. "KTB 'Rußlandfeldzug' Pz.A.O.K. III Teil 6.12.41–9.1.42," BA-MA RH 21-4/50, fol. 62 (December 23, 1941).
60. "Tagebuch Reinhardts," N245/3, fol. 18 (December 23 and 24, 1941).
61. "KTB 'Rußlandfeldzug' Pz.A.O.K. III Teil 6.12.41–9.1.42," BA-MA RH 21-4/50, fol. 64 (December 24, 1941).
62. "Tagebuch Reinhardts," N245/3, fol. 18 (December 24, 1941).
63. "Kriegstagebuch Nr.3. des XXXXVI.Pz.Korps vom 24.08.41–31.12.41," BA-MA RH 24-46/21, fol. 184 (December 21, 1941).
64. "KTB Nr.9 5.Pz.Div. 11.12.41–30.1.42," BA-MA 27-5/34, fols. 27 and 52 (December 17 and 21, 1941).
65. "KTB 'Rußlandfeldzug' Pz.A.O.K. III Teil 6.12.41–9.1.42," BA-MA RH 21-4/50, fol. 59 (December 20, 1941).
66. Ibid., fols. 63–64 (December 24, 1941).
67. Ibid.
68. "2. Panzer Division KTB Nr.6 Teil I. Vom 15.6.41–27.2.42," BA-MA RH 27-2/22 (December 21 and 24, 1941).
69. As cited in: David Mayers, *FDR's Ambassadors and the Diplomacy of Crisis: From the Rise of Hitler to the End of World War II* (Cambridge: Cambridge University Press, 2013), 223.
70. "2. Panzer Division KTB Nr.6 Teil I. Vom 15.6.41–27.2.42," BA-MA RH 27-2/22 (December 23, 1941).
71. Thanks to Oleg Beyda for supplying me with this source and its translation from Russian: Archive of Alexander Solzhenitsyn House of Russia Abroad (Moscow), F.1 Op. F-2, D. M-81, "Nikolai Ranzen's diary" (December 22, 1941).
72. Fröhlich, *Die Tagebücher von Joseph Goebbels*, Band 2, 534 (December 18, 1941).
73. "Kriegstagebuch Nr.3. des XXXXVI.Pz.Korps vom 24.08.41–31.12.41," BA-MA RH 24-46/21, fol. 188 (December 24, 1941).
74. Ibid., fol. 185 (December 21, 1941).
75. Rudolf-Christoph von Gersdorff, *Soldier in the Downfall: A Wehrmacht Cavalryman in Russia, Normandy, and the Plot to Kill Hitler* (Bedford: Aberjona Press, 2012), 81.
76. As cited in: Chales de Beaulieu, *Generaloberst Erich Hoepner*, 228.
77. "Anlagen zum Kriegstagebuch 'Tagesmeldungen' Bd.I 1.11–31.12.41," BA-MA RH 21-3/71, fol. 372 (December 22, 1941).

8. THE BATTLE OF NERVES: ARMY GROUP CENTER ON THE BRINK

1. Ziemke and Bauer, *Moscow to Stalingrad*, 93–94.
2. Halder, KTB III, 355–56, 362–63, 365 (December 19, 20, 22, 23, and 24, 1941).
3. "Kriegstagebuch Nr.1 (Band December 1941) des Oberkommandos der Heeresgruppe Mitte," BA-MA RH 19-II/122, fol. 172 (December 21, 1941).
4. Halder, KTB III, 356 (December 20, 1941).
5. As cited in: Chales de Beaulieu, *Generaloberst Erich Hoepner*, 227.

6. Italics in the original. Erich von Manstein, *Lost Victories* (New York: Presidio, 1994), 276–77.

7. A. Holmston, *Auf Magischen Wegen: Der Ostfeldzug* (Buenos Aires: Philosophie des Krieges, 1948), 59.

8. "Kriegserinnerungen Auleb (22 June–5 December 1941)," BA-MA N 76-6, fols. 82–84.

9. Günther Blumentritt, "Moscow," 65–66.

10. Mühleisen, *Hellmuth Stieff Briefe*, 145 (December 22, 1941).

11. Ziemke and Bauer, *Moscow to Stalingrad*, 97.

12. Hürter, *Ein deutscher General an der Ostfront*, 129–30; Hürter, *A German General on the Eastern Front*, 121 (December 19, 1941).

13. Bopp, *Kriegstagebuch*, 162 (December 21, 1941).

14. Bähr and Bähr, *Kriegsbriefe Gefallener Studenten, 1939–1945*, 212 (December 24, 1941); Bartov, *Hitler's Army*, 43.

15. Kempowski, *Das Echolot Barbarossa*, 542 (December 20, 1941).

16. Halder, KTB III, 355–56 (December 19 and 20, 1941); Ziemke and Bauer, *Moscow to Stalingrad*, 97.

17. Wiedebach-Nostitz's diary is reproduced in: Ellis, *Barbarossa 1941*, 345 (December 21, 1941).

18. Kuhnert, *Will We See Tomorrow?*, 125–27.

19. Halder, KTB III, 361–62 (December 21, 1941).

20. Hürter, *Ein deutscher General an der Ostfront*, 131–32 (December 22, 1941).

21. My sincere thanks to Craig W. H. Luther for sharing with me many of his private research notes, which included the papers of Philipp Freiherr von Boeselager. For full details, see the "Craig W. H. Luther Papers" at the Hoover Institution Archives, Stanford University, Palo Alto, Calif. Further extracts are in Luther's forthcoming study of the first day of Operation Barbarossa: *The First Day on the Eastern Front: Germany Invades the Soviet Union, June 22, 1941* (Lanham, Md.: Stackpole Books, 2018).

22. Ziemke and Bauer, *Moscow to Stalingrad*, 97.

23. Halder, KTB III, 362 (December 22, 1941).

24. Mühleisen, *Hellmuth Stieff Briefe*, 145 (December 22, 1941).

25. "Kriegstagebuch Nr.1 (Band December 1941) des Oberkommandos der Heeresgruppe Mitte," BA-MA RH 19-II/122, fol. 182 (December 22, 1941).

26. Hürter, *Ein deutscher General an der Ostfront*, 133 (December 22, 1941).

27. Halder, KTB III, 363 (December 23, 1941).

28. "Kriegstagebuch Nr.1 (Band December 1941) des Oberkommandos der Heeresgruppe Mitte," BA-MA RH 19-II/122, fols. 187–88 (December 23, 1941).

29. "Gen.Kdo.LVII.Pz.Korps KTB Nr.2 vom 1.11.41–31.12.41," BA-MA RH 24-57/3, fol. 87 (December 24, 1941).

30. Hürter, *Ein deutscher General an der Ostfront*, 135 (December 24, 1941).

31. Ibid., fol. 73 (December 20, 1941).

32. Blumentritt, "Moscow," 67.

33. "Gen.Kdo.LVII.Pz.Korps KTB Nr.2 vom 1.11.41–31.12.41," BA-MA RH 24-57/3, fol. 82 (December 22, 1941).

34. Halder, KTB III, 362 (December 21, 1941).

35. Balck, *Order in Chaos*, 226.

36. Ehrenburg, *Russia at War*, 95–96 (December 21, 1941).

37. "Wolfram von Richthofen KTB," BA-MA N 671/8, fol. 144 (December 7, 1941).

38. As cited in: Ziemke and Bauer, *Moscow to Stalingrad*, 95.

39. As cited in: Hürter, *Hitlers Heerführer*, 324.
40. "Kriegstagebuch Nr.1 2.Panzerarmee Band III vom 1.11.1941 bis 26.12.41," BA-MA RH 21-2/244, fol. 329 (December 20, 1941).
41. "Kriegstagebuch Nr.1 (Band December 1941) des Oberkommandos der Heeresgruppe Mitte," BA-MA RH 19-II/122, fol. 153 (December 20, 1941).
42. Halder, KTB III, 356 (December 20, 1941).
43. "Kriegstagebuch Nr.1 (Band December 1941) des Oberkommandos der Heeresgruppe Mitte," BA-MA RH 19-II/122, fol. 153 (December 20, 1941).
44. "9.Pz.Div. KTB Ia vom 19.5.1941 bis 22.1.1942," BA-MA RH 27-9/4, fol. 183 (December 22, 1941).
45. "Kriegstagebuch Nr.1 (Band December 1941) des Oberkommandos der Heeresgruppe Mitte," BA-MA RH 19-II/122, fol. 155 (December 20, 1941).
46. Guderian, *Panzer Leader*, 265.
47. Kotze, *Heeresadjutant bei Hitler*, 118 (December 18, 1941). The date attributed to this meeting by Engel is incorrect.
48. "Kriegstagebuch Nr.1 (Band December 1941) des Oberkommandos der Heeresgruppe Mitte," BA-MA RH 19-II/122, fol. 159 (December 20, 1941).
49. Ibid.
50. Ibid., fol. 163 (December 20, 1941).
51. Guderian, *Panzer Leader*, 265.
52. Ibid., 266.
53. "Kriegstagebuch Nr.1 (Band December 1941) des Oberkommandos der Heeresgruppe Mitte," BA-MA RH 19-II/122, fol. 163 (December 20, 1941).
54. Guderian, *Panzer Leader*, 268.
55. "Kriegstagebuch Nr.1 (Band December 1941) des Oberkommandos der Heeresgruppe Mitte," BA-MA RH 19-II/122, fol. 163 (December 20, 1941).
56. "Kriegstagebuch Nr.1 2.Panzerarmee Band III vom 1.11.1941 bis 26.12.41," BA-MA RH 21-2/244, fol. 333 (December 21, 1941).
57. Ibid., fols. 335–36 (December 21, 1941).
58. Stader, *Ihr daheim und wir hier draußen*, 69 and 72 (December 21 and 22, 1941).
59. As cited in: Kershaw, *War Without Garlands*, 233.
60. Ulrike Meyer-Timpe, ed., *"Träume recht süß von mir": Eine deutsche Freundschaft in Briefen, 1940–1943* (Frankfurt am Main: Eichborn, 2004), 134 (January 1, 1942).
61. Garden and Andrew, *The War Diaries of a Panzer Soldier*, 65 (December 21, 1941).
62. Landon and Leitner, *Diary of a German Soldier*, 131 (December 22, 1941).
63. Heinrich Breloer, ed., *Mein Tagebuch: Geschichten vom Überleben, 1939–1947* (Cologne: Verlagsgesellschaft Schulfernsehen, 1984), 99 (December 23, 1941).
64. Reese, *A Stranger to Myself*, 55.
65. Alexander and Kunze, *Eastern Inferno*, 126 (December 22, 1941).
66. Underlining in the original. "18. Panzer Div. Ia Kriegstagebuch vom 14.12.41–9.1.42," BA-MA RH 27-18/70, fol. 11 (December 20, 1941).
67. Ibid., fol. 14 (December 23, 1941).
68. Guderian, *Panzer Leader*, 268–69.
69. As cited in: Stargardt, *The German War*, 203.
70. As cited in: Ziemke and Bauer, *Moscow to Stalingrad*, 98.
71. "Kriegstagebuch Nr.1 (Band December 1941) des Oberkommandos der Heeresgruppe Mitte," BA-MA RH 19-II/122, fols. 193–94 (December 24, 1941).
72. As cited in: Ziemke and Bauer, *Moscow to Stalingrad*, 98.
73. Bähr and Bähr, *Kriegsbriefe Gefallener Studenten*, 213–14 (December 24, 1941).
74. Hürter, *Hitlers Heerführer*, 333; Ziemke and Bauer, *Moscow to Stalingrad*, 99.

75. "Kriegstagebuch XXXXVIII.Pz.Kps. Abt.Ia 1.12.41–31.12.41," BA-MA RH 24-48/40, fol. 17 (December 24, 1941).
76. In the original this quotation was underlined. "Kriegstagebuch Nr.1 (Band December 1941) des Oberkommandos der Heeresgruppe Mitte," BA-MA RH 19-II/122, fol. 196 (December 24, 1941).
77. Ibid., December 24, 1941.

9. THE MORE THE MERRIER: CHRISTMAS 1941 AND THE SUPPLY CRISIS

1. Kempowski, *Das Echolot Barbarossa*, 585 (December 23, 1941).
2. Tilemann, *Ich, das Soldatenkind*, 161; Reddemann, *Zwischen Front und Heimat*, 376 (December 24, 1941); Adamczyk, *Feuer!*, 190.
3. Bopp, *Kriegstagebuch*, 164 (December 24, 1941).
4. Schäufler, *Knight's Cross Panzers*, 187.
5. Franz Schober and Leopold Schober, *Briefe von der Front: Feldpostbriefe, 1939–1945*, edited by Michael Hans Salvesberger (Gösing am Wagram: Edition Weinviertel, 1997), 139 (December 25, 1941).
6. Günther, *Hot Motors, Cold Feet*, 242.
7. Kempowski, *Das Echolot Barbarossa*, 605 (December 24, 1941).
8. Landon and Leitner, *Diary of a German Soldier*, 133 (December 24, 1941).
9. Franz König, ed., *Ganz in Gottes Hand: Briefe gefallener und hingerichteter Katholiken, 1939–1945* (Wien: Herder Verlag, 1957), 117.
10. Ernst Tewes, *Seelsorger bei den Soldaten: Erinnerungen an die Zeit von 1940 bis 1945* (Munich: Don Bosco Medien, 1995), 36.
11. Italics in the original. Perau, *Priester im Heers Hitler*, 47.
12. Tilemann, *Ich, das Soldatenkind*, 161.
13. For more on this, see: Joe Perry, "Christmas as Nazi Holiday: Colonising the Christmas Mood," in *Life and Times in Nazi Germany*, edited by Lisa Pine (London: Bloomsbury Academic, 2016), 280.
14. Metelmann, *Through Hell for Hitler*, 37.
15. Jones, *The Retreat*, 220.
16. Ehrenburg, *The Tempering of Russia*, 100–101; Ehrenburg, *Russia at War*, 96 (December 25, 1941).
17. Dieter Pohl, *Die Herrschaft der Wehrmacht: Deutsche Militärbesatzung und einheimische Bevölkerung in der Sowjetunion, 1941–1944* (Munich: Fischer Taschenbuch, 2011), 190.
18. Haape with Henshaw, *Moscow Tram Stop*, 345.
19. Frisch with Jones, *Condemned to Live*, 135; Adamczyk, *Feuer!*, 190; Inglis, *I Deserted Hitler*, 72.
20. Blandford, *Under Hitler's Banner*, 128.
21. Bidermann, *In Deadly Combat*, 70.
22. Kempowski, *Das Echolot Barbarossa*, 601 (December 24, 1941).
23. Ibid., 580–81 (December 23, 1941).
24. Reddemann, *Zwischen Front und Heimat*, p. 391 (18 January 1942).
25. Paul Wortmann, MPT, Berlin, 3.2002.0935 (December 25, 1941).
26. Hans-Joachim S., MPT, Berlin, 3.2002.1214 (December 25, 1941).
27. Garden and Andrew, *The War Diaries of a Panzer Soldier*, 66 (December 24, 1941).
28. Reddemann, *Zwischen Front und Heimat*, 391 (December 25, 1941).
29. Kuhnert, *Will We See Tomorrow?*, 128.
30. Günther, *Hot Motors, Cold Feet*, 242.
31. Postenrieder, *Feldzug im Osten*, 222–23 (December 24, 1941).

32. Deck, *Der Weg der 1000 Toten*, 121.
33. Paul Wortmann, MPT, Berlin, 3.2002.0935 (December 25, 1941).
34. Johann Christoph Allmayer-Beck, *"Herr Oberleitnant, det lohnt doch nicht!" Kriegserinnerinnerungen an die Jahre 1938 bis 1945* (Vienna: Boehlau Verlag, 2013), 302.
35. Bidermann, *In Deadly Combat*, 70.
36. Metelmann, *Through Hell for Hitler*, 37.
37. Tilemann, *Ich, das Soldatenkind*, 161.
38. Kempowski, *Das Echolot Barbarossa*, 597 (December 24, 1941).
39. Erwin Wagner, *Tage wie Jahre: Vom Westwall bis Moskau, 1939–1949* (Munich: Universitas, 1997), 44.
40. Adamczyk, *Feuer!*, 190.
41. Alexander and Kunze, *Eastern Inferno*, 128 (December 24, 1941).
42. Landon and Leitner, *Diary of a German Soldier*, 135 (December 24, 1941).
43. Steven M. Miner, *Stalin's Holy War: Religion, Nationalism, and Alliance Politics, 1941–1945* (Chapel Hill: University of North Carolina Press, 2003).
44. Erwin Bartmann, *Für Volk and Führer: The Memoir of a Veteran of the 1st SS Panzer Division Leibstandarte SS Adolf Hitler* (Solihull: Helion, 2013), 76.
45. Postenrieder, *Feldzug im Osten*, 222–23 (December 24, 1941).
46. Jürgen Kleindienst, ed., *Sei tausendmal gegrüßt: Briefwechsel Irene und Ernst Guicking, 1937–1945* (Berlin: Zeitgut Verlag, 2001), 92.
47. Haape with Henshaw, *Moscow Tram Stop*, 244.
48. Bähr and Bähr, *Kriegsbriefe Gefallener Studenten*, 98–99 (December 26, 1941).
49. As cited in: Jones, *The Retreat*, 210.
50. Kuhnert, *Will We See Tomorrow?*, 128.
51. Adamczyk, *Feuer!*, 191.
52. Alexander and Kunze, *Eastern Inferno*, 128 (December 24, 1941).
53. Kempowski, *Das Echolot Barbarossa*, 560–61 (December 1941).
54. "Tagebuch Reinhardts," N245/3, fol. 18 (December 24, 1941).
55. Mühleisen, *Hellmuth Stieff Briefe*, 146–47 (December 25, 1941).
56. Liddell Hart, *The Other Side of the Hill*, 290.
57. Guderian, *Panzer Leader*, 269.
58. Halder, KTB III, 365 (December 24, 1941).
59. Müller, "The Failure of the Economic 'Blitzkrieg Strategy,'" 1138.
60. Klaus Schüler, "The Eastern Campaign as a Transportation and Supply Problem," in *From Peace to War: Germany, Soviet Russia and the World, 1939–1941*, edited by Bernd Wegner (Oxford: Berghahn Books, 1997), 220, n. 12.
61. Alfred C. Mierzejewski, *The Most Valuable Asset of the Reich: A History of the German National Railway*, vol. 2, *1933–1945* (Chapel Hill: University of North Carolina Press, 2013), 100–103.
62. "Kriegstagebuch Nr.1 (Band December 1941) des Oberkommandos der Heeresgruppe Mitte," BA-MA RH 19-II/122, fol. 85 (December 10, 1941).
63. Halder, KTB III, 348 (December 15, 1941).
64. Ibid., 352 (December 17, 1941).
65. Schüler, "The Eastern Campaign as a Transportation and Supply Problem," 220, n. 12.
66. Müller, "The Failure of the Economic 'Blitzkrieg Strategy,'" 1111.
67. Below, *Als Hitlers Adjutant, 1937–45*, 297.
68. Schüler, "The Eastern Campaign as a Transportation and Supply Problem," 219.
69. Ihno Krumpelt, *Das Material und die Kriegführung* (Frankfurt am Main: Mittler und Sohn, 1968), 153.

70. As cited in: Bücheler, *Hoepner*, 164.
71. Fröhlich, *Die Tagebücher von Joseph Goebbels*, Band 2, 466 (December 10, 1941).
72. For a good discussion, see: Mierzejewski, *The Most Valuable Asset of the Reich*, 94–103.
73. Müller, "The Failure of the Economic 'Blitzkrieg Strategy,'" 1136; "Kriegstagebuch Nr.1 (Band December 1941) des Oberkommandos der Heeresgruppe Mitte," BA-MA RH 19-II/122, fol. 74 (December 10, 1941).
74. Importantly, many of these problems were not a feature of the Soviet rail network. H. G. W. Davie, "The Influence of Railways on the Military Operations in the Russo-German War, 1941–1945," *The Journal of Slavic Military Studies* 30, no. 2 (2017): 321–46.
75. Martin van Creveld, *Supplying War: Logistics from Wallenstein to Patton* (Cambridge: Cambridge University Press, 2004), 178.
76. Kenneth Slepyan, *Stalin's Guerrillas: Soviet Partisans in World War II* (Lawrence: University Press of Kansas, 2006), 33–34.
77. Blumentritt, "Moscow," 55. See also: Liddell Hart, *The Other Side of the Hill*, 266.
78. "KTB 'Rußlandfeldzug' Pz.A.O.K. III Teil 6.12.41–9.1.42," BA-MA RH 21-4/50, fol. 15 (December 9, 1941).
79. See the map of rail networks provided in: Hans Pottgiesser, *Die Deutsche Reichsbahn im Ostfeldzug, 1939–1944* (Neckargemünd: Vowinckel, 1975), 36.
80. As cited in: Ziemke and Bauer, *Moscow to Stalingrad*, 95.
81. Bernhard R. Kroener, "The 'Frozen *Blitzkrieg*': German Strategic Planning against the Soviet Union and the Causes of Its Failure," in *From Peace to War: Germany, Soviet Russia and the World, 1939–1941*, edited by Bernd Wegner (Oxford: Berghahn Books, 1997), 148.
82. Ziemke and Bauer, *Moscow to Stalingrad*, 91.
83. Halder, KTB III, 343 (December 13, 1941). The same figure was reported for the 19th Panzer Division: "Kriegstagebuch 19.Panzer-Division Abt.Ib für die Zeit vom 1.6.1941–31.12.1942" BA-MA RH 27-19/23, fol. 86 (December 10, 1941).
84. Otto Will, *Tagebuch eines Ostfront-Kämpfers: Mit der 5. Panzerdivision im Einsatz 1941–1945* (Selent: Pour le Mérite, 2010), 41 (December 23 and 24, 1941). See also: "Anlagen zum Kriegstagebuch Tagesmeldungen Bd.I 1.11-31.12.41," BA-MA RH 21-3/71, fol. 381 (December 23, 1941).
85. "Kriegstagebuch Nr.1 (Band December 1941) des Oberkommandos der Heeresgruppe Mitte," BA-MA RH 19-II/122, fol. 126 (December 16, 1941).
86. Luck, *Panzer Commander*, 65.
87. "2. Panzer Division KTB Nr.6 Teil I. Vom 15.6.41–27.2.42," BA-MA RH 27-2/22 (December 10, 1941).
88. Will, *Tagebuch eines Ostfront-Kämpfers*, 42 (December 26, 1941).
89. "Kriegstagebuch der O.Qu.-Abt. Pz. A.O.K.2 von 21.6.41 bis 31.3.42," BA-MA RH 21-2/819, fol. 110 (December 13, 1941).
90. Mühleisen, ed., *Hellmuth Stieff Briefe*, 142 (December 9, 1941).
91. Engel, *7,000 Kilometers in a Sturmgeschütz*, 105 (December 26, 1941).
92. Department of the U.S. Army, ed., *German Tank Maintenance in World War II* (Washington, D.C.: Center of Military History United States Army, 1988), 25–26.
93. "Kriegstagebuch 19.Panzer-Division Abt.Ib für die Zeit vom 1.6.1941–31.12.1942," BA-MA RH 27-19/23, fol. 84 (December 7, 1941).
94. Kroener, "The Winter Crisis of 1941–1942," 728.
95. Ibid.
96. Frisch with Jones, *Condemned to Live*, 84–85.

97. Anthony Tucker-Jones, *Hitler's Great Panzer Heist: Germany's Foreign Armor in Action, 1939–45* (Mechanicsburg, Pa.: Pen & Sword, 2007), 142 and 155.

98. Glantz, *Barbarossa*, 210.

99. Werner Regenberg and Horst Scheibert, *Captured Tanks under the German Flag: Russian Battle Tanks* (Atglen, Pa.: Schiffer, 1990), 3–4, 75.

100. "Anlagenband zum KTB XXXXI A.K. Ia 4 6.12.41–31.12.41," BA-MA RH 24-41/17 (n.d.).

101. "2. Panzer Division KTB Nr.6 Teil I. Vom 15.6.41–27.2.42," BA-MA RH 27-2/22 (January 2, 1942).

102. "Kriegstagebuch 19.Panzer-Division Abt.Ib für die Zeit vom 1.6.1941–31.12.1942," BA-MA RH 27-19/23, fol. 93 (December 22, 1941).

103. Bopp, *Kriegstagebuch*, 161 (December 17, 1941).

104. *True to Type*, 96 (January 11, 1942).

105. Reese, *A Stranger to Myself*, 37.

106. *True to Type*, 41 (December 30, 1941).

107. Jeff Rutherford, *Combat and Genocide on the Eastern Front: The German Infantry's War, 1941–1944* (Cambridge: Cambridge University Press, 2014).

108. Department of the U.S. Army, ed., *Military Improvisations during the Russian Campaign* (Washington, D.C.: Center of Military History United States Army, 1951), 103–104.

109. Fröhlich, *Die Tagebücher von Joseph Goebbels*, Band 2, 613 (December 31, 1941).

10. PLAYING WITH FIRE: GUDERIAN GETS BURNED

1. "Gen.v.Waldau, Chef Fü St Lw Persönl. Tagebuch, Auszugeweise," BA-MA RL 200/17, fol. 103 (December 25, 1941).

2. "Kriegstagebuch Nr.1 (Band December 1941) des Oberkommandos der Heeresgruppe Mitte," BA-MA RH 19-II/122, fol. 205 (December 25, 1941).

3. Ibid., fol. 206 (December 25, 1941).

4. Halder, KTB III, 366 (December 25, 1941); "Kriegstagebuch Nr.1 (Band December 1941) des Oberkommandos der Heeresgruppe Mitte," BA-MA RH 19-II/122, fol. 206 (December 25, 1941). See also Hitler's explaination to Goebbels for firing Guderian: Fröhlich, *Die Tagebücher von Joseph Goebbels*, Band 3, 146 (January 20, 1942).

5. Kotze, *Heeresadjutant bei Hitler*, 118 (December 18, 1941).

6. Below, *Als Hitlers Adjutant*, 297.

7. Russell A. Hart, *Guderian: Panzer Pioneer or Myth Maker?* (Dulles: Potomac Books, 2006), 81.

8. Chris Helmecke, "Ein 'anderer' Oberbefehlshaber? Generaloberst Rudolf Schmidt und die deutsche Besatzungsherrschaft in der Sowjetunion, 1941–1943," *Militärgeschichtliche Zeitschrift* 75, no. 1 (2016): 64.

9. As cited in: Hürter, *Hitlers Heerführer*, 333.

10. Ibid., 333, n. 281.

11. Deck, *Der Weg der 1000 Toten*, 122.

12. Balck, *Order in Chaos*, 229.

13. Schäufler, *Knight's Cross Panzers*, 195.

14. As cited in: Jones, *The Retreat*, 234.

15. "Joachim von Lemselsen's diary 10 October 1941–24 April 1942" BA-MA N 910/6. Fol. 49 (26 December 1941).

16. "Kriegstagebuch Nr.1 2.Panzerarmee Band III vom 1.11.1941 bis 26.12.41," BA-MA RH 21-2/244, fol. 369 (December 26, 1941).

17. Macksey, *Guderian*, 160.

18. As cited in: Kershaw, *War Without Garlands*, 237.

19. As cited in: Jones, *The Retreat*, 234–35.

20. Charles Messenger, *The Last Prussian: A Biography of Field Marshal Gerd von Rund-stedt, 1875–1953* (Barnsley, U.K.: Pen and Sword, 1991), 154–55.

21. Georg Meyer, ed., *Generalfeldmarschall Wilhelm Ritter von Leeb: Tagebuchaufzeichnun-gen und Lagebeurteilungen aus zwei Weltkriegen* (Stuttgart: Deutsche Verlags-Anstalt, 1976), 418 (December 15, 1941); Megargee, *Inside Hitler's High Command*, 146–47.

22. As cited in: Klink, "The Conduct of Operations," 723–24.

23. "Kriegstagebuch Nr.1 (Band December 1941) des Oberkommandos der Heeres-gruppe Mitte," BA-MA RH 19-II/122, fol. 209 (December 25, 1941).

24. As cited in: Helmecke, "Ein 'anderer' Oberbefehlshaber?", 64, n. 42.

25. "18. Panzer Div. Ia Kriegstagebuch vom 14.12.41–9.1.42," BA-MA RH 27-18/70, 16 (December 25, 1941).

26. "Kriegstagebuch Nr.3 XXXXVII.Pz.Korps. Ia 23.9.1941–31.12.1941," BA-MA RH 24-47/258, fol. 185 (December 28, 1941).

27. Thirty-seven for Second Panzer Army—sixteen Mark IIIs, ten Mark IVs, and eleven StuG IIIs; and twenty-six for Second Army—thirteen Mark IIIs, three Mark IVs, and ten StuG IIIs. "Kriegstagebuch Nr.1 2.Panzerarmee Band IV (Teil I) vom 27.12.1941 bis 9.2.42," BA-MA RH 21-2/876 (December 28, 1941).

28. "Kriegstagebuch XXXXVIII.Pz.Kps. Abt.Ia 1.12.41–31.12.41," BA-MA RH 24-48/40, fol. 19 (December 28, 1941).

29. "Kriegstagebuch Nr.1 2.Panzerarmee Band IV (Teil I) vom 27.12.1941 bis 9.2.42," BA-MA RH 21-2/876 (December 31, 1941).

30. "Kriegstagebuch Nr.1 (Band December 1941) des Oberkommandos der Heeres-gruppe Mitte," BA-MA RH 19-II/122, fol. 163 (December 20, 1941).

31. "Kriegstagebuch Nr.1 2.Panzerarmee Band III vom 1.11.1941 bis 26.12.41," BA-MA RH 21-2/244, fol. 346 (December 22, 1941).

32. Robert Forczyk, *Panzerjäger vs KV-1: Eastern Front, 1941–43* (Oxford: Osprey, 2012), 37 and 60.

33. "9.Pz.Div. KTB Ia vom 19.5.1941 bis 22.1.1942," BA-MA RH 27-9/4, fol. 191 (Decem-ber 28, 1941); "Kriegstagebuch Nr.1 (Band December 1941) des Oberkommandos der Heeresgruppe Mitte," BA-MA RH 19-II/122, fol. 228 (December 28, 1941).

34. "Kriegstagebuch XXXXVIII.Pz.Kps. Abt.Ia 1.12.41–31.12.41," BA-MA RH 24-48/40, fol. 19 (December 28, 1941).

35. Reese, *A Stranger to Myself*, 47.

36. Alexander and Kunze, *Eastern Inferno*, 130 (December 26, 1941).

37. "Kriegstagebuch XXXXVIII.Pz.Kps. Abt.Ia 1.12.41–31.12.41," BA-MA RH 24-48/40, fol. 20 (December 31, 1941).

38. "Kriegstagebuch 4.Panzer-Divison Führungsabtl. 26.5.41–31.3.42," BA-MA RH 27-4/10, fol. 307 (December 30, 1941); "Kriegstagebuch Nr.1 2.Panzerarmee Band IV (Teil I) vom 27.12.1941 bis 9.2.42," BA-MA RH 21-2/876 (December 30, 1941).

39. As cited in: Jones, *The Retreat*, 209.

40. Fröhlich, *Die Tagebücher von Joseph Goebbels*, Band 2, 579 (December 25, 1941).

41. Ehrenburg, *Russia at War*, 90 (December 7, 1941).

42. Halder, KTB III, 366 (December 25, 1941).

43. www.lexikon-der-wehrmacht.de/Personenregister/K/KueblerLudwig.htm.

44. Greiffenberg, "Battle of Moscow," 77.

45. Blumentritt, "Moscow," 69; see also: Gordon Corrigan, *The Second World War: A Mili-tary History* (London: Thomas Dunne Books, 2010), 117.

46. "Kriegstagebuch Nr.1 (Band December 1941) des Oberkommandos der Heeres-gruppe Mitte," BA-MA RH 19-II/122, fol. 217 (December 26, 1941).

47. "Gen.Kdo.LVII.Pz.Korps KTB Nr.2 vom 1.11.41–31.12.41," BA-MA RH 24-57/3, fol. 93 (December 27, 1941).
48. Martin Gareis, *Kampf und Ende der Fränkisch-Sudetendeutschen 98. Infanterie-Division* (Eggolsheim: Nebel Verlag, 1956), 179.
49. "Kriegstagebuch Nr.1 (Band December 1941) des Oberkommandos der Heeresgruppe Mitte," BA-MA RH 19-II/122, fols. 212–13 (December 26, 1941).
50. Ibid., fol. 214 (December 26, 1941).
51. Halder, KTB III, 366 (December 26, 1941).
52. Wagner, *Tage wie Jahre*, 48.
53. "20.Pz.Div. KTB vom 21.10.41 bis 30.12.41 Band Ia2," BA-MA RH 27-20/26, fol. 134 (December 27, 1941).
54. As cited in: Lopez, *The Survival of Auftragstaktik during the Soviet Counterattack in the Battle for Moscow*, 48–49.
55. "Kriegstagebuch Nr.1 (Band December 1941) des Oberkommandos der Heeresgruppe Mitte," BA-MA RH 19-II/122, fols. 240–41 (December 30, 1941).
56. Ibid., fols. 243–44 (December 30, 1941).
57. Ibid, fols. 247–48 (December 30, 1941).
58. Mühleisen, *Hellmuth Stieff Briefe*, 148 (January 1, 1942).
59. "Kriegstagebuch Nr.1 (Band December 1941) des Oberkommandos der Heeresgruppe Mitte," BA-MA RH 19-II/122, fol. 255 (December 31, 1941). Colonel Martin Gareis, who took over command of Schroeck's 98th Infantry Division on December 31, wrote a detailed history of the division after the war, but portrayed Schroeck's replacement as owing to ill health. See: Gareis, *Kampf und Ende der Fränkisch-Sudetendeutschen 98. Infanterie-Division*, 188.
60. "A.O.K.4 Ia Anlagen A zum KTB 24.12.41–2.1.1942," BA-MA RH 20-4/211, fol. 51 (December 28, 1941).
61. Hill, *The Red Army and the Second World War*, 312–13.
62. Benno Zieser, *In Their Shallow Graves* (London: Elek Books, 1956), 86–87.
63. "A.O.K.4 Ia Anlagen A zum KTB 24.12.41–2.1.1942," BA-MA RH 20-4/211, fol. 66 (December 29, 1941). See also: Hill, *The Red Army and the Second World War*, 317–18.
64. Dollinger, *Kain, wo ist dein Bruder?*, 114 (December 26, 1941).
65. Wiedebach-Nostitz's diary is reproduced in: Ellis, *Barbarossa 1941*, 349 (December 28–30, 1941).
66. While this was no doubt true for Yukhnov, it was almost certainly not the case for Suchinitschi, which was much too far south to be of real importance.
67. "Kriegstagebuch Nr.1 (Band December 1941) des Oberkommandos der Heeresgruppe Mitte," BA-MA RH 19-II/122, fol. 237 (December 29, 1941); Ziemke and Bauer, *Moscow to Stalingrad*, 102–103.
68. Hürter, *Ein deutscher General an der Ostfront*, 137 (January 2, 1942).
69. Kempowski, *Das Echolot Barbarossa*, 666 (December 29, 1941).
70. Kuhnert, *Will We See Tomorrow?*, 128.
71. Dollinger, *Kain, wo ist dein Bruder?*, 114 (December 30, 1941).
72. Hürter, *Ein deutscher General an der Ostfront*, 137 (January 2, 1942).

11. TURNING THE SCREWS: NINTH ARMY'S NEAR COLLAPSE

1. "Kriegstagebuch Nr.1 (Band December 1941) des Oberkommandos der Heeresgruppe Mitte," BA-MA RH 19-II/122, fol. 208 (December 25, 1941).
2. "Gen.Kdo.XXVII KTB Ia Nr.VII 20.11.41-28.4.1942," BA-MA RH 24-27/76, fol. 129 (December 27, 1941).
3. "AOK 9: KTB Ostfeldzug, Band 3 v. 30.9.-31.12.1941," BA-MA RH 20-9/13b, fol. 169

(December 25, 1941). For a similar order from an intelligence officer in the 7th Infantry Division with good analysis by the authors, see: Rutherford and Wettstein, *The German Army on the Eastern Front*, 177–78.

4. Halder, KTB III, 366 (December 25, 1941).
5. "Kriegstagebuch Nr.1 (Band December 1941) des Oberkommandos der Heeresgruppe Mitte," BA-MA RH 19-II/122, fol. 218 (December 26, 1941).
6. "AOK 9: KTB Ostfeldzug, Band 3 v. 30.9.–31.12.1941," BA-MA RH 20-9/13b, fol. 172 (December 25, 1941).
7. Reinhardt, *Moscow—The Turning Point*, 320.
8. "AOK 9: KTB Ostfeldzug, Band 3 v. 30.9.–31.12.1941," BA-MA RH 20-9/13b, fol. 173 (December 26, 1941).
9. Oleg Beyda, "'Refighting the Civil War': Second Lieutenant Mikhail Aleksandrovich Gubanov," *Jahrbücher für Geschichte Osteuropas* 66 (2018): 261.
10. Haape with Henshaw, *Moscow Tram Stop*, 256–57.
11. "AOK 9: KTB Ostfeldzug, Band 3 v. 30.9.–31.12.1941," BA-MA RH 20-9/13b, fols. 173–74 (December 26, 1941).
12. Ibid., fol. 177 (December 27, 1941).
13. "Kriegstagebuch Nr.1 (Band December 1941) des Oberkommandos der Heeresgruppe Mitte," BA-MA RH 19-II/122, fol. 226 (December 27, 1941).
14. "AOK 9: KTB Ostfeldzug, Band 3 v. 30.9.–31.12.1941," BA-MA RH 20-9/13b, fol. 178 (December 27, 1941).
15. Ibid., fol. 181 (December 28, 1941).
16. "Gen.Kdo.XXVII KTB Ia Nr.VII 20.11.41–28.4.1942," BA-MA RH 24-27/76, fol. 132 (December 28, 1941).
17. Bähr and Bähr, *Kriegsbriefe Gefallener Studenten*, 98–99 (December 26, 1941).
18. "Kriegstagebuch Nr.1 (Band December 1941) des Oberkommandos der Heeresgruppe Mitte," BA-MA RH 19-II/122, fol. 231 (December 28, 1941).
19. Ibid., fols. 235–37 (December 29, 1941).
20. Ibid., fol. 237 (December 29, 1941). General Förster was later cleared by an army court of honor and given further commands. See: James S. Corum, *Wolfram von Richthofen: Master of the German Air War* (Lawrence: University Press of Kansas, 2008), 403, n. 43.
21. Halder, KTB III, 369; see also n. 2 (December 29, 1941).
22. "Gen. Kdo. VI.A.K KTB Nr.3 Band 25 1.1.42–9.1.42," BA-MA RH 24-6/65, fol. 9 (January 2, 1942).
23. As cited in: Hürter, *Hitlers Heerführer*, 336.
24. "Gen.Kdo.XXVII KTB Ia Nr.VII 20.11.41-28.4.1942," BA-MA RH 24-27/76, fols. 134–35 (December 29, 1941).
25. Lopez, *The Survival of Auftragstaktik during the Soviet Counterattack in the Battle for Moscow*, 41.
26. Halder, KTB III, 370 (December 30, 1941).
27. Below, *Als Hitlers Adjutant*, 298.
28. "Kriegstagebuch Nr.1 (Band December 1941) des Oberkommandos der Heeresgruppe Mitte," BA-MA RH 19-II/122, fols. 259–60 (December 31, 1941).
29. Kempowski, *Das Echolot Barbarossa*, 691–92 (December 31, 1941).
30. As cited in: Meyer, *Adolf Heusinger*, 171.
31. Balck, *Order in Chaos*, 230.
32. "Kriegstagebuch Nr.1 (Band December 1941) des Oberkommandos der Heeresgruppe Mitte," BA-MA RH 19-II/122, fols. 263–64 (December 31, 1941).
33. Dietrich, *The Hitler I Knew*, 75.

34. "Kriegstagebuch Nr.1 (Band December 1941) des Oberkommandos der Heeres-gruppe Mitte," BA-MA RH 19-II/122, fol. 265 (December 31, 1941).

35. Otto Dietrich, *The Hitler I Knew*, p. 75.

36. "Kriegstagebuch Nr.1 (Band December 1941) des Oberkommandos der Heeres-gruppe Mitte," BA-MA RH 19-II/122, fol. 265 (December 31, 1941).

37. "KTB 'Rußlandfeldzug' Pz.A.O.K. III Teil 6.12.41–9.1.42," BA-MA RH 21-4/50, fol. 66 (December 25, 1941).

38. "Tagebuch Reinhardts," N245/3, fol. 19 (December 26, 1941).

39. "KTB 'Rußlandfeldzug' Pz.A.O.K. III Teil 6.12.41–9.1.42," BA-MA RH 21-4/50, fol. 75 (December 28, 1941).

40. Archive of Alexander Solzhenitsyn House of Russia Abroad (Moscow), F.1 Op. F-2, D. M-81, "Nikolai Ranzen's diary," (December 29, 1941).

41. "Kriegstagebuch Nr.3. des XXXXVI.Pz.Korps vom 24.08.41–31.12.41," BA-MA RH 24-46/21, fols. 189 and 194 (December 25 and 26, 1941).

42. "Kriegstagebuch Nr.1 (Band December 1941) des Oberkommandos der Heeres-gruppe Mitte," BA-MA RH 19-II/122, fol. 225 (December 27, 1941); ibid., fol. 74 (December 28, 1941).

43. "Anlagen zum Kriegstagebuch Tagesmeldungen Bd.I 1.11–31.12.41," BA-MA RH 21-3/71, fol. 396 (December 26, 1941).

44. Bernhard Chiari, "A 'People's War' against Hitler's Fascism?" in *Germany and the Second World War*, vol. 9/2, *German Wartime Society 1939–1945: Exploitation, Interpretations, Exclusion*, edited by Militärgeschichtlichtliches Forschungsamt (Oxford: Oxford University Press, 2014), 887.

45. Landon and Leitner, *Diary of a German Soldier*, 129 (December 19, 1941).

46. For Halder's suggestion, see: "Kriegstagebuch Nr.1 (Band December 1941) des Oberkommandos der Heeresgruppe Mitte," BA-MA RH 19-II/122, fol. 172 (December 21, 1941). See also the predictions of Goebbels and Kluge: Fröhlich, *Die Tage-bücher von Joseph Goebbels*, Band 3, 31 (January 1, 1942); "KTB 'Rußlandfeldzug' Pz.A.O.K. III Teil 6.12.41–9.1.42," BA-MA RH 21-4/50, fol. 81 (December 31, 1941).

47. As cited in: Chales de Beaulieu, *Generaloberst Erich Hoepner*, 228.

48. The Red Army numbered 4,901,800 men on June 22 and 7,733,345 men on December 1, 1941. See: Glantz and House, *When Titans Clashed*, 383.

49. Speer, *Inside the Third Reich* (London: Sphere Books, 1971), 265.

50. Fröhlich, *Die Tagebücher von Joseph Goebbels*, Band 2, 589 (December 28, 1941).

51. As cited in: Bücheler, *Hoepner*, 165.

52. "Anlagen zum Kriegstagebuch Tagesmeldungen Bd.I 1.11–31.12.41," BA-MA RH 21-3/71, fol. 392 (December 25, 1941).

53. "KTB 'Rußlandfeldzug' Pz.A.O.K. III Teil 6.12.41–9.1.42," BA-MA RH 21-4/50, fols. 73 and 75 (December 26 and 28, 1941).

54. Will, *Tagebuch eines Ostfront-Kämpfers*, 43 (December 27, 1941).

55. "Reinhardt's letters to his wife," N245/2, fol. 19 (December 31, 1941).

56. Röttiger, "XXXXI Panzer Corps during the Battle of Moscow in 1941 as a Component of Panzer Group 3," 41.

57. "Anlagenband zum KTB XXXXI A.K. Ia 4 6.12.41–31.12.41," BA-MA RH 24-41/17 (December 29, 1941).

58. "Kriegstagebuch Nr.7 des Kdos. der 1.Panzer-Div. 20.9.41–12.4.42," BA-MA RH 27-1/58, fol. 97 (December 31, 1941).

59. "Anlagen zum Kriegstagebuch Tagesmeldungen Bd.I 1.11–31.12.41," BA-MA RH 21-3/71, fol. 424 (December 31, 1941).

60. Kempowski, *Das Echolot Barbarossa*, 560 (December 21, 1941).

61. "Anlagenband zum KTB XXXXI A.K. Ia 4 6.12.41–31.12.41," BA-MA RH 24-41/17 (December 29, 1941).
62. "Tagebuch Reinhardts," N245/3, fol. 19 (December 28 and 30, 1941).
63. As cited in: Bücheler, *Hoepner*, 165.
64. Ibid.
65. Underlining in the original. "Reinhardt's letters to his wife," N245/2, fol. 19 (December 31, 1941).
66. "Tagebuch Reinhardts," N245/3, fol. 19 (December 29, 1941).
67. "Kriegstagebuch Nr.1 (Band December 1941) des Oberkommandos der Heeresgruppe Mitte," BA-MA RH 19-II/122, fol. 234 (December 29, 1941).
68. "Tagebuch Reinhardts," N245/3, fol. 19 (December 29, 1941).
69. "KTB 'Rußlandfeldzug' Pz.A.O.K. III Teil 6.12.41–9.1.42," BA-MA RH 21-4/50, fol. 81 (December 31, 1941).
70. "Tagebuch Reinhardts," N245/3 Fol. 19 (31 December 1941).
71. As cited in: Bücheler, *Hoepner*, 165.
72. The total space reconquered by the Red Army in December equaled 41,196 square kilometers, while Germany's total occupied area of the Soviet Union as of December 5, 1941, came to some 1,324,293 square kilometers. Thanks to my cartographer, Kay Dancey, for measuring these complex spaces.
73. Trevor-Roper, *Hitler's War Directives*, 166 (December 8, 1941).

12. RANK AND FILE: SOLDIERING IN ARMY GROUP CENTER

1. Kempowski, *Das Echolot Barbarossa*, 691 (December 31, 1941).
2. Haape with Henshaw, *Moscow Tram Stop*, 290.
3. *True to Type*, 18 (December 31, 1941).
4. Kern, *Dance of Death*, 29.
5. Kempowski, *Das Echolot Barbarossa*, 690 (December 31, 1941).
6. Pöppel, *Heaven and Hell*, 82.
7. Wiedebach-Nostitz's diary is reproduced in: Ellis, *Barbarossa 1941*, 350.
8. Gerber, *Im Dienst des Roten Kreuzes*, 199 (December 31, 1941).
9. Robert Kirchubel, *Hitler's Panzer Armies on the Eastern Front* (Barnsley, U.K.: Pen and Sword, 2009), 111.
10. Nurdan Melek Aksulu, ed., *Obergefeiter Otto Allers: Feldpostbriefe aus dem Zweiten Weltkrieg* (Norderstedt: Books on Demand, 2008), 99 (January 3, 1942).
11. Anton Böhrer, MPT, Berlin, 3.2002.0889 (January 2, 1942).
12. Kempowski, *Das Echolot Barbarossa*, 695 (December 31, 1941).
13. Ibid., 694–95 (December 31, 1941).
14. Ibid., 690 (December 31, 1941).
15. Peter Steinkamp, *Zur Devianzproblematik in der Wehrmacht: Alkohol-und Rauschmittelmissbrauch bei der Truppe* (PhD diss., Albert-Ludwigs-University, 2008), 323–24 and 379–81.
16. Jonathan Lewy, "Vice in the Third Reich? Alcohol, Tobacco and Drugs," in *Life and Times in Nazi Germany*, edited by Lisa Pine (London: Bloomsbury Academic, 2016), 50–54.
17. Kempowski, *Das Echolot Barbarossa*, 696 (December 31, 1941).
18. Will, *Tagebuch eines Ostfront-Kämpfers*, 44 (December 31, 1941).
19. Gerber, *Im Dienst des Roten Kreuzes*, 199–200 (December 31, 1941).
20. Anton Böhrer, MPT, Berlin, 3.2002.0889 (January 2, 1942).
21. Postenrieder, *Feldzug im Osten*, 227 (December 31, 1941).
22. Kempowski, *Das Echolot Barbarossa*, 690 (December 31, 1941).

23. Ibid., 694 (December 31, 1941).
24. Rehfeldt, *Mit dem Eliteverband des Heeres "Grossdeutschland" tief in den Weiten Russlands*, 75.
25. Fröhlich, *Die Tagebücher von Joseph Goebbels*, Band 3, 35 (January 1, 1942). See also Göring's comments to Ciano: Muggeridge, *Ciano's Diary*, 428 (January 29, 1942).
26. Stahel, *Operation Typhoon*, 100–106.
27. Fröhlich, *Die Tagebücher von Joseph Goebbels*, Band 3, 45 (January 3, 1942).
28. Ibid., 35 (January 1, 1942).
29. As cited in: Meyer, *Adolf Heusinger*, 171.
30. "KTB 'Rußlandfeldzug' Pz.A.O.K. III Teil 6.12.41–9.1.42," BA-MA RH 21-4/50, fol. 83 (December 31, 1941).
31. LeSueur, *Twelve Months That Changed the World*, 103.
32. Anton Böhrer, MPT, Berlin, 3.2002.0889 (January 2, 1942).
33. Paul Wortmann, MPT, Berlin, 3.2002.0935 (December 25, 1941).
34. Meier-Welcker, *Aufzeichnungen eines Generalstabsoffiziers*, 143 (December 8, 1941).
35. Birthe Kundrus, "Cultural Warfare and Its Content," in *Germany and the Second World War*, vol. 9/2, *German Wartime Society, 1939–1945: Exploitation, Interpretations, Exclusion*, edited by Militärgeschichtlichtliches Forschungsamt (Oxford: Oxford University Press, 2014), 122–23.
36. Alexander Hirt, *"Die Heimat reicht der Front die Hand": Kulturelle Truppenbetreuung im Zweiten Weltkrieg, 1939–1945; Ein deutsch-englischer Vergleich* (PhD diss., Georg-August University, 2008), 169–70; Kundrus, "Cultural Warfare and Its Content," 103.
37. Hirt, *"Die Heimat reicht der Front die Hand,"* 171.
38. Garden and Andrew, *The War Diaries of a Panzer Soldier*, 66 (December 30, 1941).
39. Kundrus, "Cultural Warfare and its Content," 105–106.
40. Garden and Andrew, *The War Diaries of a Panzer Soldier*, 66 (December 28, 1941).
41. Kempowski, *Das Echolot Barbarossa*, 408 (December 11, 1941).
42. Hirt, *"Die Heimat reicht der Front die Hand,"* 345.
43. Williamson, *Hans Sturm*, 96.
44. Garden and Andrew, *The War Diaries of a Panzer Soldier*, 66 (December 26, 1941).
45. William Lubbeck, with David B. Hurt, *At Leningrad's Gates: The Story of a Soldier with Army Group North* (Philadelphia: Casemate, 2006), 117.
46. Günther, *Hot Motors, Cold Feet*, 191.
47. Reese, *A Stranger to Myself*, 52.
48. Konrad Elmshäuser and Jan Lokers, eds., *"Man muß hier nur hart sein": Kriegsbriefe und Bilder einer Familie, 1934–1945* (Bremen: Edition Temmen, 1999), 159 (December 18, 1941).
49. Ibid., 168 (January 21, 1942).
50. Laurie R. Cohen, *Smolensk under the Nazis* (Rochester, N.Y.: Rochester University Press, 2013), 71.
51. Frisch with Jones, *Condemned to Live*, 94.
52. Kempowski, *Das Echolot Barbarossa*, 410 (December 11, 1941).
53. Kern, *Dance of Death*, 29.
54. Hirt, *"Die Heimat reicht der Front die Hand,"* 357, 365, 367, and 368.
55. As cited in: Latzel, *Deutsche Soldaten—nationalsozialistischer Krieg? Kriegserlebnis—Kriegserfahrung, 1939–1945* (Paderborn: Schöningh Paderborn, 1998), 61.
56. Meyer-Timpe, *"Träume recht süß von mir,"* 145 (January 29, 1942).
57. Hirt, *"Die Heimat reicht der Front die Hand,"* 365.
58. Paul Schädel, MPT, Berlin, 3.2002.1317 (January 24, 1942).

59. As cited in: Jones, *The Retreat*, 163.
60. Fröhlich, *Die Tagebücher von Joseph Goebbels*, Band 2, 476 (December 11, 1941).
61. "2. Panzer Division KTB Nr.6 Teil I. Vom 15.6.41–27.2.42," BA-MA RH 27-2/22 (January 31, 1942).
62. Humburg, *Das Gesicht des Krieges*, 248 (January 20, 1942).
63. Reddemann, *Zwischen Front und Heimat*, 383 (January 5, 1942).
64. "Kriegstagebuch 19.Panzer-Division 15.10.1941–18.3.1942," BA-MA RH 27-19/24. The diary has no folio stamped page numbers so references must be located using the date (January 4, 1942).
65. Beermann, *Soldat Werner Beermann Feldpostbriefe*, 211 (January 25, 1942).
66. As cited in: Luther, *Barbarossa Unleashed*, 345.
67. Lubbeck with Hurt, *At Leningrad's Gates*, 118–19.
68. Fröhlich, *Die Tagebücher von Joseph Goebbels*, Band 2, 483 (December 12, 1941).
69. Marlis G. Steinert, *Hitler's War and the Germans: Public Mood and Attitude during the Second World War* (Athens: Ohio University Press, 1977), 152.
70. Gisela Beak, ed., *Feldpostbriefe eines Landsers, 1939–1943* (n.p.: Books on Demand, 2000), 55 (December 30, 1941).
71. Kempowski, *Das Echolot Barbarossa*, 524–25 (December 19, 1941).
72. *True to Type*, 42 (January 4, 1942).
73. Haape with Henshaw, *Moscow Tram Stop*, 328.
74. Edward Shils and Morris Janowitz, "Cohesion and Disintegration in the Wehrmacht in World War II," *Public Opinion Quarterly* 12, no. 2 (1948): 280–315.
75. Omer Bartov, *The Eastern Front, 1941–45: German Troops and the Barbarisation of Warfare* (London: Macmillan, 1985).
76. For the endurance of primary groups, see Christoph Rass's excellent study of the 253rd Infantry Division: *"Menschenmaterial": Deutsche Soldaten an der Ostfront; Innenansichten einer Infanteriedivision, 1939–1945* (Paderborn: Verlag Ferdinand Schöningh, 2003).
77. Thomas Kühne, "Male Bonding and Shame Culture: Hitler's Soldiers and the Moral Basis of Genocidal Warfare," in *Ordinary People as Mass Murderers: Perpetrators in Comparative Perspectives*, edited by Olaf Jensen and Claus-Christian W. Szejnmann (New York: Palgrave Macmillan, 2008), 64.
78. *True to Type*, 32 (January 5, 1942).
79. Reese, *A Stranger to Myself*, 36.
80. Bidermann, *In Deadly Combat*, 81.
81. Metelmann, *Through Hell for Hitler*, 42.
82. Günther, *Hot Motors, Cold Feet*, 225–26 and 243.
83. Garden and Andrew, *The War Diaries of a Panzer Soldier*, 70 (January 25, 1942).
84. Kundrus, "Cultural Warfare and Its Content," 115.
85. Stahel, *The Battle for Moscow*, 200–201.
86. Fröhlich, *Die Tagebücher von Joseph Goebbels*, Band 2, 53–54 (October 1, 1941); Hirt, *"Die Heimat reicht der Front die Hand,"* 190–91.
87. Reddemann, *Zwischen Front und Heimat*, 382 (January 1, 1942).
88. Kuhnert, *Will We See Tomorrow?*, 135.
89. *True to Type*, 42 (January 6, 1942).
90. Luther, *Barbarossa Unleashed*, 370; Cohen, *Smolensk under the Nazis*, 73.
91. Engel, *7,000 Kilometers in a Sturmgeschütz*, 106–07 (February 1, 1942).
92. Will, *Tagebuch eines Ostfront-Kämpfers*, 45 (January 1, 1942).
93. Hendrik C. Verton, *In the Fire of the Eastern Front: The Experiences of a Dutch Waffen-SS Volunteer on the Eastern Front, 1941–45* (Solihull: Helion, 2007), 105.

94. Williamson, *Hans Sturm*, 97.

95. My thanks to Dr. Vincent S. Smith, cybertaxonomist at the Natural History Museum in London.

96. Department of the U.S. Army, *Effects of Climate on Combat in European Russia*, 42.

97. Haape with Henshaw, *Moscow Tram Stop*, 233.

98. Zieser, *In Their Shallow Graves*, 53–54.

99. Pabst, *The Outermost Frontier*, 40.

100. Kempowski, *Das Echolot Barbarossa*, 409 (December 11, 1941).

101. Reese, *A Stranger to Myself*, 33.

102. Lubbeck with Hurt, *At Leningrad's Gates*, 117.

103. Humburg, *Das Gesicht des Krieges*, 218 (November 1, 1942).

104. Fröhlich, *Die Tagebücher von Joseph Goebbels*, Band 2, 451 (December 1, 1941).

105. Fredborg, *Behind the Steel Wall*, 69.

106. Beermann, *Soldat Werner Beermann Feldpostbriefe*, 214 (January 29, 1942).

107. Lubbeck with Hurt, *At Leningrad's Gates*, 117.

108. As cited in: Latzel, *Deutsche Soldaten—nationalsozialistischer Krieg?*, 51.

109. Reese, *A Stranger to Myself*, 36.

110. As cited in: Luther, *Barbarossa Unleashed*, 375.

111. Richardson, *Sieg Heil!*, 123 (August 3, 1941).

112. Bidermann, *In Deadly Combat*, 76.

13. REINFORCING FAILURE: STALIN'S JANUARY OFFENSIVE

1. Rodric Braithwaite, *Moscow 1941: A City and Its People at War* (New York: Knopf, 2006), 290.

2. Geoffrey Roberts, *Stalin's Wars: From World War to Cold, 1939–1953* (New Haven, Conn.: Yale University Press, 2006), 117.

3. For Red Army killed in action: Glantz and House, *When Titans Clashed*, 391. For Soviet POWs: Christian Streit, "Soviet Prisoners of War in the Hands of the Wehrmacht," in *War of Extermination: The German Military in World War II, 1941–1944*, edited by Hannes Heer and Klaus Naumann (Oxford: Berghahn Books, 2006), 81.

4. For German war dead in 1941: Overmans, *Deutsche militärische Verluste im Zweiten Weltkrieg*, 278. For total German casualties: Halder, KTB III, 374 (January 5, 1942).

5. As cited in: Nagorski, *The Greatest Battle*, 264–65.

6. As cited in: Jones, *The Retreat*, 214.

7. Sulzberger, *A Long Row of Candles*, 184.

8. Ibid., 183.

9. Harrison, *The Battle for Moscow*, 317–18.

10. Rokossovsky, *A Soldier's Duty*, 95.

11. As cited in: Ziemke and Bauer, *Moscow to Stalingrad*, 88.

12. Ibid., 88–90; see also: Bellamy, *Absolute War*, 332–33.

13. As cited in: Hill, *The Red Army and the Second World War*, 302.

14. Ehrenburg, *The Tempering of Russia*, 104.

15. Harrison E. Salisbury, ed., *Marshal Zhukov's Greatest Battles* (London: Harper & Row, 1971), 90.

16. Ibid., 90 and 93.

17. Ibid., 90–91.

18. Ibid., 91.

19. Mawdsley, *Thunder in the East*, 143. There were many more light tanks (T-60s and T-70s) in the Soviet arsenal, but these were typically envisioned for, and best suited to, reconnaissance roles.

20. Hill, *The Great Patriotic War of the Soviet Union*, 86 (doc. 62).
21. Ibid., 87 (doc. 63).
22. Salisbury, *Marshal Zhukov's Greatest Battles*, 91–92; G. K. Zhukov, *The Memoirs of Marshal Zhukov* (London: Delacorte Press, 1971), 353.
23. Harrison, ed., *The Battle for Moscow*, 444.
24. As cited in: Mawdsley, *Thunder in the East*, 116.
25. Robert Conquest, *The Great Terror: A Reassessment* (Oxford: Oxford University Press, 2008); Peter Whitewood, *The Red Army and the Great Terror: Stalin's Purge of the Soviet Military* (Lawrence: University Press of Kansas, 2015).
26. As cited in: Peter Mezhiritsky, *On the Precipice: Stalin, The Red Army Leadership and the Road to Stalingrad, 1931–1942* (Solihull: Helion, 2012), 307.
27. Hill, *The Great Patriotic War of the Soviet Union*, 88 (doc. 65).
28. As cited in: Glantz, *Barbarossa*, 194.
29. Hill, *The Great Patriotic War of the Soviet Union*, 88 (doc. 65).
30. See Alexander Hill's analysis in: *The Red Army and the Second World War*, 305–306.
31. As cited in: Merridale, *Ivan's War*, 167.
32. Sulzberger, *A Long Row of Candles*, 184.
33. Fröhlich, *Die Tagebücher von Joseph Goebbels*, Band 2, 562 (December 23, 1941).
34. LeSueur, *Twelve Months That Changed the World*, 52.
35. Ortwin Buchbender, *Das tönende Erz: Deutsche Propaganda gegen die Rote Armee im Zweiten Weltkrieg* (Stuttgart: Seewald Verlag, 1978), 118–19.
36. As cited in: Jones, *The Retreat*, 179.
37. Ibid., 226.
38. As cited in: Braithwaite, *Moscow 1941*, 291.
39. Ehrenburg, *The Tempering of Russia*, 105.
40. As cited in: Mark Edele, "Take (No) Prisoners! The Red Army and German POWs 1941–1943," *The Journal of Modern History* 88 (June 2016): 369.
41. Ehrenburg, *Russia at War*, 104 (January 18, 1942).
42. Charlotte Haldane, *Russian Newsreel: An Eye-Witness Account of the Soviet Union at War* (New York: Secker and Warburg, 1943), 131.
43. LeSueur, *Twelve Months That Changed the World*, 94–96.
44. As cited in: Jones, *The Retreat*, 241.
45. Rokossovsky, *A Soldier's Duty*, 98.
46. Braithwaite, *Moscow 1941*, 291–92.
47. Cathy Porter and Mark Jones, *Moscow in World War II* (London: Chatto & Windus, 1987), 150.
48. Braithwaite, *Moscow 1941*, 291–92.
49. As cited in: Bellamy, *Absolute War*, 336.
50. Hartmann, *Operation Barbarossa*, 76–78.
51. Dunn, *Stalin's Keys to Victory*, 10.
52. Alexander Dallin, *German Rule in Russia, 1941–1945: A Study of Occupation Policies* (London: Palgrave Macmillan, 1981), 534–35.
53. Alex Alexiev, "Soviet Nationals in German Wartime Service, 1941–1945," in *Soviet Nationals in German Wartime Service, 1941–1945*, edited by Antonio Munoz (n.p., 2007), 30–31. One source has suggested 200,000 *Hiwis* were acting in the service of the *Ostheer* by spring 1942: Wladyslaw Anders, *Russian Volunteers in Hitler's Army, 1941–1945* (New York: Europa Books, 1997), 8.
54. Dallin, *German Rule in Russia*, 535. See also: Johannes Due Enstad, *Soviet Russians under Nazi Occupation: Fragile Loyalties in World War II* (Cambridge: Cambridge University Press, 2018), 100.

55. Mark Mazower, *Hitler's Empire: Nazi Rule in Occupied Europe* (London: Allen Lane, 2009), 461.
56. Kuhnert, *Will We See Tomorrow?*, 107.
57. Günther, *Hot Motors, Cold Feet*, 243.
58. Perau, *Priester im Heers Hitler*, 50.
59. As cited in: Hartmann, *Operation Barbarossa*, 79.
60. Kuhnert, *Will We See Tomorrow?*, 107.
61. Günther, *Hot Motors, Cold Feet*, 243.
62. Mazower, *Hitler's Empire*, 462.
63. Christer Jörgensen, *Hitler's Espionage Machine* (London: Lyons Press, 2004), 124.
64. Rutherford, *Combat and Genocide on the Eastern Front*, 7.
65. David Motadel, *Islam and Nazi Germany's War* (Cambridge, Mass.: Belknap Press, 2014), 137–39.
66. Schulte, *The German Army and Nazi Policies in Occupied Russia*, 204.
67. Dallin, *German Rule in Russia*, 537, n. 2; David Littlejohn, *The Patriotic Traitors: The Story of Collaboration in German Occupied Europe, 1940–1945* (New York: Doubleday, 1972), 297. Heinz Postenrieder, who served in Cochenhausen's division, includes photos in his diary of Russian auxiliary forces being trained and drilled: Postenrieder, *Feldzug im Osten*, 130–31.
68. Schulte, *The German Army and Nazi Policies in Occupied Russia*, 205–206.
69. Oleg Beyda, "'Iron Cross of the Wrangel's Army': Russian Emigrants as Interpreters in the Wehrmacht," *The Journal of Slavic Military History* 27, no. 3 (July 2014): 439.
70. Oleg Beyda and Igor Petrov, "The Soviet Union," in *Joining Hitler's Crusade: European Nations and the Invasion of the Soviet Union*, edited by David Stahel (Cambridge: Cambridge University Press, 2018), 376–78.
71. Sergei Kudry Yashov, "The Hidden Dimension: Wartime Collaboration in the Soviet Union," in *Barbarossa: The Axis and the Allies*, edited by John Erickson and David Dilks (Edinburgh: Edinburgh University Press, 1998), 241. On these new eastern formations, see: Antonio Munoz, ed., *The East Came West: Muslim, Hindu, and Buddhist Volunteers in the German Armed Forces, 1941–1945* (New York: Axis Europa Books, 2001).
72. Martin Kitchen, *Nazi Germany at War* (London: Routledge, 1995), 161.
73. Mark Spoerer, "Social Differentiation of Foreign Civilian Workers, Prisoners of War, and Detainees in the Reich," in *Germany and the Second World War*, vol. 9/2, *German Wartime Society, 1939–1945: Exploitation, Interpretations, Exclusion*, edited by Militärgeschichtlichtliches Forschungsamt (Oxford: Oxford University Press, 2014), 497.
74. As cited in: Mazower, *Hitler's Empire*, 297.
75. Kitchen, *Nazi Germany at War*, 161.
76. Spoerer, "Social Differentiation of Foreign Civilian Workers, Prisoners of War, and Detainees in the Reich," 501.
77. As cited in: Hartmann, *Operation Barbarossa*, 102.
78. As cited in: Julie K. deGraffenried, *Sacrificing Childhood: Children and the Soviet State in the Great Patriotic War* (Lawrence: University Press of Kansas, 2014), 18.
79. Spoerer, "Social Differentiation of Foreign Civilian Workers, Prisoners of War, and Detainees in the Reich," 501.
80. As cited in: Adam Tooze, *The Wages of Destruction: The Making and Breaking of the Nazi Economy* (London: Viking Adult, 2006), 520.
81. Spoerer, "Social Differentiation of Foreign Civilian Workers, Prisoners of War, and Detainees in the Reich," 497.

14. HANGING IN THE BALANCE: FOURTH ARMY'S IMPENDING ENCIRCLEMENT

1. "Kriegstagebuch XXXXVIII.Pz.Kps. Abt.Ia 1.1.42–30.1.42," BA-MA RH 24-48/47, fols. 4–5 (January 1, 1942).
2. Alexander and Kunze, *Eastern Inferno*, 155 (Feburary 1, 1942).
3. "Kriegstagebuch XXXXVIII.Pz.Kps. Abt.Ia 1.1.42–30.1.42," BA-MA RH 24-48/47, fol. 9 (January 2, 1942).
4. "Armeeoberkommando 2. I.a KTB Teil.4 1.1.42–31.3.42," BA-MA RH 20-2/1787, fol. 18 (January 4, 1942).
5. Ibid., fol. 11 (January 3, 1942).
6. "Kriegstagebuch XXXXVIII.Pz.Kps. Abt.Ia 1.1.42–30.1.42," BA-MA RH 24-48/47, fol. 10 (January 3, 1942).
7. As cited in: Antony Beevor, *The Second World War* (New York: Little, Brown, 2012), 286.
8. Alexander and Kunze, *Eastern Inferno*, 138 (January 4, 1942).
9. "Armeeoberkommando 2. I.a KTB Teil.4 1.1.42–31.3.42," BA-MA RH 20-2/1787, fol. 33 (January 8, 1942).
10. Alexander and Kunze, *Eastern Inferno*, 141 (January 8, 1942).
11. "Kriegstagebuch Nr.3. der Führungsabteilung (Ia) des Gen. Kdo. (mot.) XXXX. Pz.Korps vom 27.12.1941–29.4.1942," BA-MA RH 24-40/19, fol. 2 (December 29, 1941).
12. Ibid., fol. 16 (January 4, 1942).
13. The defense of the Alcázar was a highly symbolic Nationalist victory during the opening stages of the Spanish Civil War. "A.O.K.4 Ia KTB Nr.11 3.1.42–31.3.1942," BA-MA RH 20-4/281, fol. 103 (January 12, 1942).
14. "Kriegstagebuch Nr.3. der Führungsabteilung (Ia) des Gen. Kdo. (mot.) XXXX. Pz.Korps vom 27.12.1941–29.4.1942," BA-MA RH 24-40/19, fol. 26 (January 6, 1942).
15. "A.O.K.4 Ia KTB Nr.11 3.1.42–31.3.1942," BA-MA RH 20-4/281, fol. 60 (January 6, 1942).
16. "Kriegstagebuch Nr.1 2.Panzerarmee Band IV (Teil I) vom 27.12.1941 bis 9.2.42," BA-MA RH 21-2/876 (January 4, 1942).
17. Ibid., January 7, 1942.
18. Woche, *Zwischen Pflicht und Gewissen*, 143.
19. "Kriegstagebuch Nr.1 2.Panzerarmee Band IV (Teil I) vom 27.12.1941 bis 9.2.42," BA-MA RH 21-2/876 (January 7, 1942).
20. Landon and Leitner, *Diary of a German Soldier*, 138–39 (January 1, 1942).
21. Humburg, *Das Gesicht des Krieges*, 139 (January 2, 1942).
22. Stader, *Ihr daheim und wir hier draußen*, 84 (January 8, 1942).
23. "Kriegstagebuch 4.Panzer-Divison Führungsabtl. 26.5.41–31.3.42," BA-MA RH 27-4/10, 313 and 315 (January 2 and 3, 1942).
24. Schäufler, *Panzer Warfare on the Eastern Front*, 74.
25. "Kriegstagebuch Nr.4 XXXXVII.Pz.Korps. Ia 1.1.1942–31.3.1942," BA-MA RH 24-47/38, fols. 9–10 (January 6, 1942).
26. "Kriegstagebuch der O.Qu.-Abt. Pz. A.O.K.2 von 21.6.41 bis 31.3.42," BA-MA RH 21-2/819, fol. 87 (January 5, 1942).
27. Stader, *Ihr daheim und wir hier draußen*, 83 (January 2, 1942).
28. Halder, KTB III, 371 (January 2, 1942).
29. Gersdorff, *Soldier in the Downfall*, 80.
30. Mühleisen, *Hellmuth Stieff Briefe*, 148–49 (January 1, 1942).
31. Halder, KTB III, 372 (January 2, 1942).

32. "A.O.K.4 Ia KTB Nr.11 3.1.42–31.3.1942," BA-MA RH 20-4/281, fol. 37 (January 3, 1942).

33. Halder, KTB III, 373 (January 3, 1942).

34. Ibid., 373–74 (January 3, 1942).

35. Albert Seaton, *The Battle for Moscow* (New York: Da Capo Press, 1971), 204.

36. Hürter, *Ein deutscher General an der Ostfront*, 137 (January 2, 1942).

37. "A.O.K.4 Ia KTB Nr.11 3.1.42–31.3.1942," BA-MA RH 20-4/281, fol. 54 (January 5, 1942).

38. Ibid., fol. 47 (January 5, 1942).

39. Ibid., fol. 46 (January 5, 1942).

40. Schäufler, *Knight's Cross Panzers*, 185 and 190.

41. "A.O.K.4 Ia KTB Nr.11 3.1.42–31.3.1942," BA-MA RH 20-4/281, fol. 55 (January 5, 1942).

42. As cited in: Marcel Stein, *A Flawed Genius: Field Marshal Walter Model. A Critical Biography* (Solihull: Helion, 2010), 87.

43. "A.O.K.4 Ia KTB Nr.11 3.1.42–31.3.1942," BA-MA RH 20-4/281, fol. 55 (January 5, 1942).

44. Hürter, *Ein deutscher General an der Ostfront*, 138 (January 6, 1942).

45. Kuhnert, *Will We See Tomorrow?*, 143.

46. Wiedebach-Nostitz's diary is reproduced in: Ellis, *Barbarossa 1941*, 350 (January 4, 1942).

47. "Heeresgruppe Mitte Meldungen und Berichte der unterstellten Armee Jan.–Juli 1942," BA-MA RH 19-II/141, fol. 2 (January 6, 1942).

48. "A.O.K.4 Ia KTB Nr.11 3.1.42–31.3.1942," BA-MA RH 20-4/281, fol. 57 (January 6, 1942).

49. Ibid., fols. 62–63 (January 7, 1942).

50. Henrik O. Lunde, *Finland's War of Choice: The Troubled German-Finish Coalition in World War II* (Havertown, Pa.: Casemate, 2011), 219–20; Halder, KTB III, 375 (January 7, 1942).

51. Carl Gustaf Emil Mannerheim, *The Memoirs of Marshal Mannerheim* (London: E. P. Dutton, 1953), 442.

52. See my discussion of Halder in: Stahel, *Operation Barbarossa and Germany's Defeat in the East*.

53. Even after the war Halder wrote about "individual examples," stating that their "psychological value deserves to be emphasized. It becomes very clear that a strong military leader with great powers of motivation is the most important factor for success." As cited in: Peter Tsouras, ed., *Panzers on the Eastern Front: General Erhard Raus and His Panzer Divisions in Russia, 1941–1945* (London: Greenhill Books, 2002), 9.

54. Helmuth James von Moltke, *Letters to Freya*, 196 (January 6, 1942).

55. "A.O.K.4 Ia KTB Nr.11 3.1.42–31.3.1942," BA-MA RH 20-4/281 (January 6, 1942). See also: "Kriegstagebuch Nr.1 2.Panzerarmee Band IV (Teil I) vom 27.12.1941 bis 9.2.42," BA-MA RH 21-2/876, fol. 61 (January 8, 1942).

56. "A.O.K.4 Ia KTB Nr.11 3.1.42–31.3.1942," BA-MA RH 20-4/281 (January 7 and 8, 1942).

57. Ibid., January 8, 1942.

58. Ibid., January 8, 1942.

15. THE FLOOD GATES ARE BREAKING: NINTH AND FOURTH PANZER ARMIES RUPTURE

1. "Kriegstagebuch Nr.1 (Band December 1941) des Oberkommandos der Heeresgruppe Mitte," BA-MA RH 19-II/122, fol. 265 (December 31, 1941).
2. "KTB A.O.K.9 Ia 1.1.–31.3.1942," BA-MA RH 20-9/47, fol. 5 (January 1, 1942).
3. Ibid., fol. 5 (January 1, 1942).
4. Ibid., fols. 5–6 (January 1, 1942).
5. Pabst, *The Outermost Frontier*, 41.
6. Katrin A. Kilian, "Factors Influencing Emotions, Affects and Moods Expressed in Forces Mail," in *Germany and the Second World War*, vol. 9/2, *German Wartime Society, 1939–1945: Exploitation, Interpretations, Exclusion*, edited by Militärgeschichtlichliches Forschungsamt (Oxford: Oxford University Press, 2014), 277.
7. "Gen.Kdo.XXVII KTB Ia Nr.VII 20.11.41–28.4.1942," BA-MA RH 24-27/76, fols. 134–35 (January 1, 1942).
8. "KTB A.O.K.9 Ia 1.1.–31.3.1942," BA-MA RH 20-9/47, fol. 6 (January 1, 1942).
9. "Kriegstagebuch Nr.1 (Band December 1941) des Oberkommandos der Heeresgruppe Mitte," BA-MA RH 19-II/122, fols. 235–37 (December 29, 1941).
10. "Gen.Kdo.XXVII KTB Ia Nr.VII 20.11.41–28.4.1942," BA-MA RH 24-27/76, fols. 146 and 153 (January 1 and 2, 1942); "Gen. Kdo. VI.A.K KTB Nr.3 Band 25 1.1.42–9.1.42," BA-MA RH 24-6/65, fol. 4 (January 1, 1942).
11. "Gen.Kdo.XXVII KTB Ia Nr.VII 20.11.41–28.4.1942," BA-MA RH 24-27/76, fols. 148, 150, and 152 (January 1, 1942).
12. Halder, KTB III, 371–72 (January 2, 1942).
13. "Gen. Kdo. VI.A.K KTB Nr.3 Band 25 1.1.42–9.1.42," BA-MA RH 24-6/65, fol. 9 (January 2, 1942).
14. Halder, KTB III, 371 (January 2, 1942).
15. "KTB A.O.K.9 Ia 1.1.–31.3.1942," BA-MA RH 20-9/47, fol. 9 (January 2, 1942).
16. "Wolfram von Richthofen KTB," BA-MA N 671/9, fol. 2 (January 2, 1942).
17. "Gen.Kdo.XXVII KTB Ia Nr.VII 20.11.41–28.4.1942," BA-MA RH 24-27/76, fol. 161 (January 2, 1942).
18. "Gen. Kdo. VI.A.K KTB Nr.3 Band 25 1.1.42–9.1.42," BA-MA RH 24-6/65, fol. 11 (January 2, 1942).
19. Ziemke and Bauer, *Moscow to Stalingrad*, 131–32.
20. "Gen. Kdo. VI.A.K KTB Nr.3 Band 25 1.1.42–9.1.42," BA-MA RH 24-6/65, fol. 20 (January 4, 1942).
21. Ziemke and Bauer, *Moscow to Stalingrad*, 124–25.
22. Nagorski, *The Greatest Battle*, 299.
23. "Gen. Kdo. VI.A.K KTB Nr.3 Band 25 1.1.42–9.1.42," BA-MA RH 24-6/65, fol. 25 (January 5, 1942).
24. "KTB A.O.K.9 Ia 1.1.–31.3.1942," BA-MA RH 20-9/47, fol. 18 (January 5, 1942).
25. As cited in: Ziemke and Bauer, *Moscow to Stalingrad*, 131.
26. Reinhardt, *Moscow—The Turning Point*, 322.
27. "KTB A.O.K.9 Ia 1.1.–31.3.1942," BA-MA RH 20-9/47, fol. 15 (January 4, 1942).
28. "Tagebuch Reinhardts," N245/3, fol. 22 (January 4, 1942).
29. "KTB A.O.K.9 Ia 1.1.–31.3.1942," BA-MA RH 20-9/47, fol. 15 (January 4, 1942).
30. The official reason for Ruoff not being subordinated to Reinhardt was the simple fact that both men were generals of panzer troops/infantry, but Ruoff was senior in date of promotion and so not placed under a man he technically outranked. This issue was resolved when Ruoff was promoted to replace Hoepner and V Army Corps then passed to Third Panzer Army. Ziemke and Bauer, *Moscow to Stalingrad*, 131–32.

31. "Tagebuch Reinhardts," N245/3, fol. 22 (January 4, 1942).
32. Ibid., January 4, 1942.
33. Ibid., January 4, 1942; see also: Ziemke and Bauer, *Moscow to Stalingrad*, 132.
34. Alexander Conrady, *Rshew 1942/1943: Aus der Geschichte der 36. Infanterie-Division (mot.) 1.1.1942 bis 25.3.1943* (Neckargemünd: Vowinckel, 1976), 21; "Gen.Kdo. XXVII KTB Ia Nr.VII 20.11.41–28.4.1942," BA-MA RH 24-27/76, fol. 169 (January 5, 1942).
35. As cited in: Kirchubel, *Hitler's Panzer Armies on the Eastern Front*, 112.
36. "Anlagen zum KTB 'Tagesmeldungen,' Bd.I 1.1.–30.1.42," BA-MA RH 21-3/72, fol. 24 (January 5, 1942).
37. "Gen. Kdo. VI.A.K KTB Nr.3 Band 25 1.1.42–9.1.42," BA-MA RH 24-6/65, fols. 24–26 (January 5, 1942).
38. "Gen.Kdo.XXVII KTB Ia Nr.VII 20.11.41–28.4.1942," BA-MA RH 24-27/76, fol. 167 (January 4, 1942).
39. As cited in: Bücheler, *Hoepner*, 166.
40. "KTB 'Rußlandfeldzug' Pz.A.O.K. III Teil 6.12.41–9.1.42," BA-MA RH 21-4/50, fol. 87 (January 2, 1942).
41. As cited in: Bücheler, *Hoepner*, 167.
42. "20.Pz.Div. KTB vom 1.1.42 bis 28.2.42 Band Ia3," BA-MA RH 27-20/27, fol. 5 (January 2, 1942). See also: Lopez, *The Survival of Auftragstaktik during the Soviet Counterattack in the Battle for Moscow*, 51–52.
43. "Kriegstagebuch Anlagen des XXXXVI.Pz.Korps vom 18.12.41–13.6.42," BA-MA RH 24-46/38. The diary has no folio stamped page numbers so references must be located using the date (January 2, 1942).
44. As cited in: Rutherford and Wettstein, *The German Army on the Eastern Front*, 13.
45. "KTB 'Rußlandfeldzug' Pz.A.O.K. III Teil 6.12.41–9.1.42," BA-MA RH 21-4/50, fol. 96 (January 4, 1942).
46. Chales de Beaulieu, *Generaloberst Erich Hoepner*, 233.
47. "20.Pz.Div. KTB vom 1.1.42 bis 28.2.42 Band Ia3," BA-MA RH 27-20/27, fol. 8 (January 4, 1942).
48. Reinhardt, *Moscow—The Turning Point*, 322.
49. Ziemke and Bauer, *Moscow to Stalingrad*, 127–28.
50. "KTB 'Rußlandfeldzug' Pz.A.O.K. III Teil 6.12.41–9.1.42," BA-MA RH 21-4/50, fol. 107 (January 8, 1942); Chales de Beaulieu, *Generaloberst Erich Hoepner*, 247.
51. Chales de Beaulieu, *Generaloberst Erich Hoepner*, 247.
52. "KTB 'Rußlandfeldzug' Pz.A.O.K. III Teil 6.12.41–9.1.42," BA-MA RH 21-4/50, fol. 108 (January 8, 1942).
53. Ibid., January 8, 1942.
54. As cited in: Bücheler, *Hoepner*, 169.
55. Ibid; Chales de Beaulieu, *Generaloberst Erich Hoepner*, 248; Halder, KTB III, 376–77 (January 8, 1942).
56. Below, *Als Hitlers Adjutant*, 304.
57. Schlabrendorff, *The Secret War against Hitler*, 131.
58. Ibid.; Guderian, *Panzer Leader*, 273.
59. "KTB 'Rußlandfeldzug' Pz.A.O.K. III Teil 6.12.41–9.1.42," BA-MA RH 21-4/50, fol. 109 (January 8, 1942).
60. Chales de Beaulieu, *Generaloberst Erich Hoepner*, 248.
61. As cited in: Bücheler, *Hoepner*, 170.
62. "KTB 'Rußlandfeldzug' Pz.A.O.K. III Teil 6.12.41–9.1.42," BA-MA RH 21-4/50, fol. 110 (January 9, 1942).

63. Schlabrendorff, *The Secret War against Hitler*, 131.

64. Hürter, *Hitlers Heerführer*, 337, n. 308. Unlike Hoepner, Chales de Beaulieu was re-employed and served as the divisional commander of the 168th and 23rd Infantry Divisions. According to David T. Zabecki it was not uncommon in the German army to replace the chief of staff, and not necessarily the commanding general, if a unit performed poorly. Zabecki, ed., *Chief of Staff: The Principal Officers behind History's Great Commanders*, vol. 2 (Annapolis: Naval Institute Press, 2008), 6.

65. Reinhardt, *Moscow—The Turning Point*, 343–44, n. 254; Guderian, *Panzer Leader*, 273. Research has shown that Hoepner was by no means anti-Nazi in 1941, see: Peter Steinkamp, "Die Haltung der Hitlergegner Generalfeldmarschall Wilhelm Ritter von Leeb und Generaloberst Erich Hoepner zur verbrecherischen Kriegführung bei der Heeresgruppe Nord in der Sowjetunion, 1941," in *NS-Verbrechen und der militärische Widerstand gegen Hitler*, edited by Gerd R. Ueberschär (Darmstadt: Primus Verlag, 2000), 47–61; Ernst Klee, Willi Dressen, and Volker Riess, eds., *"The Good Old Days": The Holocaust as Seen by Its Perpetrators and Bystanders* (Old Saybrook, Conn.: William S. Konecky Associates, 1991), 24 and 27.

66. Kroener, "The Winter Crisis of 1941–1942," 1030.

67. For information on command appointments, see: Andris J. Kursietis, *The Wehrmacht at War 1939–1945: The Units and Commanders of the German Ground Forces during World War II* (Soesterberg: Aspekt, 1999).

68. As cited in: Kershaw, *War Without Garlands*, 235.

69. Kroener, "The Winter Crisis of 1941–1942," 1030.

70. John Keegan wrote: "He [Hitler] had dismissed generals in droves . . . Thirty-five corps and divisional commanders were dismissed." Keegan, *The Second World War* (New York: Penguin Books, 1989), 206. See also: Clark, *Barbarossa*, 182.

71. Fröhlich, *Die Tagebücher von Joseph Goebbels*, Band 3, 42 (January 3, 1942).

72. Martin Chalmers, ed., *To the Bitter End: The Diaries of Victor Klemperer, 1942–45* (London: QPD, 1999), 3 (January 4, 1942).

73. Fröhlich, *Die Tagebücher von Joseph Goebbels*, Band 3, 63 (January 7, 1942).

74. Halder, KTB III, 371–72 (January 2, 1942).

75. Eberle and Uhl, *The Hitler Book*, 78.

16. MAKING A VIRTUE OF NECESSITY: SURVIVING THE RUSSIAN WINTER

1. Fredborg, *Behind the Steel Wall*, 66.

2. Hürter, *Ein deutscher General an der Ostfront*, 138 (January 6, 1942).

3. Schäufler, *Knight's Cross Panzers*, 201.

4. As cited in: Jones, *The Retreat*, 212.

5. Haape with Henshaw, *Moscow Tram Stop*, 222; Alexander and Kunze, *Eastern Inferno*, 129 (December 25, 1941).

6. Schäufler, *Knight's Cross Panzers*, 195.

7. Williamson, *Hans Sturm*, 75.

8. Rehfeldt, *Mit dem Eliteverband des Heeres "Grossdeutschland" tief in den Weiten Russlands*, 77–78; Williamson, *Hans Sturm*, 75.

9. Haape with Henshaw, *Moscow Tram Stop*, 296.

10. "Kriegstagebuch Nr.7 des Kdos. der 1.Panzer-Div. 20.9.41–12.4.42," BA-MA RH 27-1/58, fol. 92 (December 21, 1941).

11. Adamczyk, *Feuer!*, 186–87.

12. Ibid., 187. A former Wehrmacht reenactor who had dug a number of winter bunkers near Moscow suggested to me that two days was indeed realistic.

13. Department of the U.S. Army, *Military Improvisations during the Russian Campaign*, 23–24.
14. "Kriegstagebuch Nr.7 des Kdos. der 1.Panzer-Div. 20.9.41–12.4.42," BA-MA RH 27-1/58, fol. 94 (December 26, 1941).
15. Claus Hansmann, *Vorüber Nicht Vorbei: Russische Impressionen, 1941–1943* (Frankfurt: Ullstein, 1989), 27.
16. Steve Crawford, *The Eastern Front: Day by Day* (London: Snap Productions, 2012), 76; Alexander and Kunze, *Eastern Inferno*, 129 (December 25, 1941).
17. Röttiger, "XXXXI Panzer Corps during the Battle of Moscow in 1941 as a Component of Panzer Group 3," 41.
18. Fritz, *Ostkrieg*, 214.
19. Alexander and Kunze, *Eastern Inferno*, 129 (December 25, 1941).
20. Kempowski, *Das Echolot Barbarossa*, 629 (December 26, 1941).
21. Department of the U.S. Army, *Effects of Climate on Combat in European Russia*, 13.
22. Ibid., 12.
23. "Kriegstagebuch Nr.1 2.Panzerarmee Band III vom 1.11.1941 bis 26.12.41," BA-MA RH 21-2/244, fol. 274 (December 13, 1941); "Kriegstagebuch Nr.1 2.Panzerarmee Band IV (Teil I) vom 27.12.1941 bis 9.2.42," BA-MA RH 21-2/876, fol. 24 (December 31, 1941).
24. Department of the U.S. Army, *Effects of Climate on Combat in European Russia*, 12.
25. Stargardt, *The German War*, 205.
26. Will, *Tagebuch eines Ostfront-Kämpfers*, 44 (December 6, 1941).
27. Stader, *Ihr daheim und wir hier draußen*, 89 (January 17, 1942).
28. Kuhnert, *Will We See Tomorrow?*, 140. See also: Schäufler, *Panzer Warfare on the Eastern Front*, 75.
29. Perau, *Priester im Heers Hitler*, 48–49.
30. Landon and Leitner, *Diary of a German Soldier*, 136 (December 26, 1941).
31. Alexander and Kunze, *Eastern Inferno*, 129 (December 25, 1941). See also: Tilemann, *Ich, das Soldatenkind*, 153.
32. Gerber, *Im Dienst des Roten Kreuzes*, 201 (January 1, 1942).
33. Günther, *Hot Motors, Cold Feet*, 247.
34. Department of the U.S. Army, *Military Improvisations during the Russian Campaign*, 65.
35. Haape with Henshaw, *Moscow Tram Stop*, 182–83.
36. As cited in: Clark, *Barbarossa*, 173.
37. Frisch with Jones, *Condemned to Live*, 85. See also: Tilemann, *Ich, das Soldatenkind*, 153.
38. Pabst, *The Outermost Frontier*, 39.
39. Haape with Henshaw, *Moscow Tram Stop*, 258.
40. Reese, *A Stranger to Myself*, 56.
41. Tilemann, *Ich, das Soldatenkind*, 153.
42. Haape with Henshaw, *Moscow Tram Stop*, 257.
43. Ibid., 222.
44. Ibid., 228.
45. Humburg, *Das Gesicht des Krieges*, 150 (January 3, 1942).
46. On "General Winter" in Soviet propaganda, see: Ehrenburg, *Russia at War*, 99 (December 29, 1941).
47. Von Hardesty and Ilya Grinberg, *Red Phoenix Rising: The Soviet Air Force in World War II* (Lawrence: University Press of Kansas, 2012), 87.
48. Ibid., 93 and 95.

49. "KTB 'Rußlandfeldzug' Pz.A.O.K. III Teil 6.12.41–9.1.42," BA-MA RH 21-4/50, fols. 23 and 36 (December 12 and 14, 1941).

50. "Anlagenband zum KTB XXXXI A.K. Ia 4 6.12.41–31.12.41," BA-MA RH 24-41/17 (December 18, 1941).

51. "Anlagen zum Kriegstagebuch 'Tagesmeldungen' Bd.I 1.11–31.12.41," BA-MA RH 21-3/71, fol. 386 (December 24, 1941).

52. "Kriegstagebuch Nr.1 2.Panzerarmee Band IV (Teil I) vom 27.12.1941 bis 9.2.42," BA-MA RH 21-2/876, fol. 21 (December 31, 1941).

53. Bopp, *Kriegstagebuch*, 160 (December 15, 1941).

54. Horst Lange, *Tagebücher aus dem Zweiten Weltkrieg* (Mainz: von Hase and Koehler Verlag, 1979), 108 (December 19, 1941).

55. Luck, *Panzer Commander*, 64.

56. Kempowski, *Das Echolot Barbarossa*, 436 (December 13, 1941).

57. Carruthers, *The Wehrmacht*, 46.

58. Gerber, *Im Dienst des Roten Kreuzes*, 178 (December 19, 1941).

59. Corum, *Wolfram von Richthofen*, 279. For a complete order of battle of VIII Air Corps, see: Horst Boog, "The Luftwaffe," in *Germany and the Second World War*, vol. 4, *The Attack on the Soviet Union*, edited by Militärgeschichtliches Forschungsamt (Oxford: Oxford University Press, 1998), 796.

60. Trevor-Roper, *Hitler's War Directives*, 167–68 (December 8, 1941).

61. Christer Bergström, *Barbarossa: The Air Battle, July–December 1941* (Hersham, U.K.: Classic, 2007), 113.

62. Christer Bergström, *Stalingrad: The Air Battle, 1942 through January 1943* (Hinckley, U.K.: Classic, 2007), 21.

63. Christer Bergström and Andrey Mikhailov, *Black Cross / Red Star: The Air War over the Eastern Front*, vol. 1, *Operation Barbarossa, 1941* (Pacifica: Pacifica Military History, 2000), 250.

64. John Weal, *More Bf 109 Aces of the Russian Front* (Oxford: Osprey, 2007), 23.

65. Artem Drabkin, ed., *The Red Air Force at War: Barbarossa and the Retreat to Moscow; Recollections of Fighter Pilots on the Eastern Front* (Barnsley, U.K.: Pen and Sword, 2007), 30.

66. "20.Pz.Div. KTB vom 21.10.41 bis 30.12.41 Band Ia2," BA-MA RH 27-20/26, fol. 112 (December 17, 1941).

67. Schäufler, *Knight's Cross Panzers*, 192.

68. Paul Schädel, MPT, Berlin, 3.2002.1317 (January 12, 1942).

69. Rudel, *Stuka Pilot* (New York: Bantam Books, 1979), 54.

70. "Gen. Kdo. VI.A.K KTB Nr.3 Band 25 1.1.42–9.1.42," BA-MA RH 24-6/65, fols. 15 and 24 (January 3 and 5, 1942).

71. Boog, "The Luftwaffe," 786.

72. Rudel, *Stuka Pilot*, 52.

73. Hermann Plocher, *The German Air Force versus Russia, 1941* (New York: Arno, 1965), 245.

74. Williamson Murray, *The Luftwaffe, 1933–45: Strategy for Defeat* (Washington, D. C.: Potomac Books, 1996), 119.

75. As cited in: Richard Muller, *The German Air War in Russia* (Baltimore: Nautical & Aviation, 1992), 62.

76. Hardesty and Grinberg, *Red Phoenix Rising*, 98–99. For more on the battle, see: Jason D. Mark, *Besieged: The Epic Battle for Cholm* (Sydney: Leaping Horseman Books, 2011).

77. Christer Bergström and Andrey Mikhailov, *Black Cross / Red Star: The Air War over*

the Eastern Front, vol. 2, *Resurgence, January–June 1942* (Pacifica: Pacifica Military History, 2001), 45.

78. Bergström, *Stalingrad*, 13 and 21.
79. Ibid., 21.
80. Williamson Murray even concluded: "Generally, however, the Luftwaffe was better prepared for the cold weather than the army." Murray, *The Luftwaffe, 1933–45*, 118.
81. E. R. Hooten, *Eagle in Flames: The Fall of the Luftwaffe* (London: Arms & Armour, 1997), 170.
82. Hermann Plocher, *The German Air Force versus Russia, 1942* (New York: Arno, 1966), 104.
83. Photos of alert boxes may be seen in: ibid., 105; Bergström and Mikhailov, *Black Cross / Red Star*, vol. 2, 42.
84. Rudel, *Stuka Pilot*, 52–53.
85. Ibid., 53.
86. Plocher, *The German Air Force versus Russia, 1942*, 107.
87. Hooten, *Eagle in Flames*, 205, n. 3.
88. Manfred Griehl, *German Bombers over Russia* (Barnsley, U.K.: Pen and Sword, 2016), 52.
89. "KTB A.O.K.9 Ia 1.1.–31.3.1942," BA-MA RH 20-9/47, fol. 11 (January 3, 1942).
90. Boog, "The Luftwaffe," 798.
91. Rudel, *Stuka Pilot*, 54–55.
92. Otto Dessloch, "The Winter Battle of Rzhev, Vyazma, and Yukhov, 1941–1942," in *German Battle Tactics in the Russian Front, 1941–1945*, edited by Steven H. Newton (Atglen, Pa.: Schiffer, 1994), 86.
93. "2. Panzer Division KTB Nr.6 Teil I. Vom 15.6.41–27.2.42," BA-MA RH 27-2/22, (December 18, 1941).
94. *True to Type*, 32–33 (January 8, 1942).
95. Department of the U.S. Army, *Effects of Climate on Combat in European Russia*, 14.
96. Hill, *The Red Army and the Second World War*, 322.
97. Hardesty and Grinberg, *Red Phoenix Rising*, 103.
98. Plocher, *The German Air Force versus Russia, 1942*, 126.
99. Dessloch, "The Winter Battle of Rzhev, Vyazma, and Yukhov," 86–87.
100. "Wolfram von Richthofen KTB," BA-MA N 671/9, fols. 12–13 (January 20, 1942).

17. DEFENDING THE INDEFENSIBLE: HITLER'S LAST STAND

1. "Armeeoberkommando 2. I.a KTB Teil.4 1.1.42–31.3.42," BA-MA RH 20-2/1787, fol. 42 (January 10, 1942).
2. "Kriegstagebuch XXXXVIII.Pz.Kps. Abt.Ia 1.1.42–30.1.42," BA-MA RH 24-48/47, fol. 34 (January 11, 1942).
3. "Armeeoberkommando 2. I.a KTB Teil.4 1.1.42–31.3.42," BA-MA RH 20-2/1787, fol. 42 (January 10, 1942).
4. Alexander and Kunze, *Eastern Inferno*, 146 (January 15, 1942).
5. "Armeeoberkommando 2. I.a KTB Teil.4 1.1.42–31.3.42," BA-MA RH 20-2/1787, fols. 53 and 63 (January 12 and 15, 1942).
6. Garden and Andrew, *The War Diaries of a Panzer Soldier*, 68 (January 10, 1942).
7. Christa Lieb, *Feldpost: Briefe zwischen Heimat und Front, 1939–1945; Eine Collage* (Stuttgart: Frechdruch, 2007), 184 (January 12, 1942).
8. "Kriegstagebuch Nr.1 2.Panzerarmee Band IV (Teil I) vom 27.12.1941 bis 9.2.42," BA-MA RH 21-2/876, fol. 67 (January 9, 1942).
9. Ibid., fol. 86 (January 13, 1942).
10. As cited in: Kershaw, *War Without Garlands*, 236.

11. Stader, *Ihr daheim und wir hier draußen*, 86 (January 10, 1942).
12. "Kriegstagebuch 4.Panzer-Divison Führungsabtl. 26.5.41–31.3.42," BA-MA RH 27-4/10, 325, 335–36 (January 10, 16, and 17, 1942).
13. Kurt DeWitt and Wilhelm Koll, "The Bryansk Area," in *Soviet Partisans in World War II*, edited by John A. Armstrong (Madison: University of Wisconsin Press, 1964), 468–69; Walter Schwabedissen, *The Russian Air Force in the Eyes of the German Commanders* (New York: Arno, 1960), 147–48.
14. "A.O.K.4 Ia KTB Nr.11 3.1.42–31.3.1942," BA-MA RH 20-4/281, fol. 104 (January 12, 1942).
15. "Kriegstagebuch Nr.1 2.Panzerarmee Band IV (Teil I) vom 27.12.1941 bis 9.2.42," BA-MA RH 21-2/876, fol. 91 (January 14, 1942).
16. Halder, KTB III, 377 (January 9, 1942).
17. "A.O.K.4 Ia KTB Nr.11 3.1.42–31.3.1942," BA-MA RH 20-4/281, fol. 104 (January 12, 1942).
18. Stader, *Ihr daheim und wir hier draußen*, 87 (January 14, 1942).
19. On relative industrial production, see: Richard Overy, "Statistics," in *The Oxford Companion of the Second World War*, edited by I. C. B. Dear and M. R. D. Foot (Oxford: Oxford University Press, 1995), 1060, table 2: "Military Production." Reproduced in Stahel, *Operation Typhoon*, 29.
20. As cited in: Mawdsley, *Thunder in the East*, 116.
21. Ziemke and Bauer, *Moscow to Stalingrad*, 124–25.
22. "A.O.K.4 Ia KTB Nr.11 3.1.42–31.3.1942," BA-MA RH 20-4/281, fol. 88 (January 10, 1942).
23. Ibid., fol. 97 (January 11, 1942).
24. Mühleisen, *Hellmuth Stieff Briefe*, 150 (January 10, 1942).
25. Hürter, *Ein deutscher General an der Ostfront*, 138–39 (January 11, 1942).
26. Halder, KTB III, 377 (January 9, 1942).
27. Ibid., 378 (January 9 and 10, 1942).
28. Ibid., 379 (January 11, 1942).
29. Ziemke and Bauer, *Moscow to Stalingrad*, 133.
30. Grumann's diary is reproduced in: Rzhevskaia, "Roads and Days," 69.
31. "A.O.K.4 Ia KTB Nr.11 3.1.42–31.3.1942," BA-MA RH 20-4/281, fol. 105 (January 12, 1942).
32. Ibid., fols. 107–108 (January 13, 1942). Underlining in the original.
33. Hardesty and Grinberg, *Red Phoenix Rising*, 91.
34. As cited in: Luther, *Barbarossa Unleashed*, 156. See also: Hill, *The Red Army and the Second World War*, 317.
35. "A.O.K.4 Ia KTB Nr.11 3.1.42–31.3.1942," BA-MA RH 20-4/281, fol. 110 (January 13, 1942).
36. Halder, KTB III, 382 (January 13, 1942).
37. "A.O.K.4 Ia KTB Nr.11 3.1.42–31.3.1942," BA-MA RH 20-4/281, fol. 110 (January 13, 1942).
38. "A.O.K.4 Ia KTB Nr.11 3.1.42–31.3.1942," BA-MA RH 20-4/281, fol. 55 (January 5, 1942).
39. "KTB 'Rußlandfeldzug' Pz.A.O.K. IV Teil 9.1.42–27.4.42," BA-MA RH 21-4/51, fol. 13 (January 12, 1942).
40. As cited in: Hürter, *Hitlers Heerführer*, 338.
41. Halder, KTB III, 380 (January 11, 1942). See also "Army Group Centre January map," BA-MA RH 19-II 145 K10 (January 12, 1942).
42. "KTB 'Rußlandfeldzug' Pz.A.O.K. IV Teil 9.1.42–27.4.42," BA-MA RH 21-4/51, fol. 16 (January 13, 1942).

43. "Tagebuch Reinhardts," N245/3, fol. 23 (January 12, 1942).
44. Conrady, *Rshew*, 21; "Army Group Centre January map," BA-MA RH 19-II 145 K10 (January 12, 1942).
45. "2. Panzer Division KTB Nr.6 Teil I. Vom 15.6.41–27.2.42," BA-MA RH 27-2/22 (January 12, 1942).
46. "6. Panzer Division Ia KTB 1.12.1941–31.3.1942," BA-MA RH 27-6/20 (January 12, 1942).
47. As cited in: Kirchubel, *Hitler's Panzer Armies on the Eastern Front*, 112.
48. Bähr and Bähr, *Kriegsbriefe Gefallener Studenten*, 95 (January 13, 1942).
49. "Anlagen zum KTB 'Tagesmeldungen' Bd.I 1.1.–30.1.42," BA-MA RH 21-3/72, fol. 67 (January 12, 1942).
50. Ibid., fol. 71 (January 13, 1942).
51. Röttiger, "XXXXI Panzer Corps during the Battle of Moscow in 1941 as a Component of Panzer Group 3," 43.
52. Adamczyk, *Feuer!*, 189.
53. Carruthers, *The Wehrmacht*, 44.
54. "Tagebuch Reinhardts," N245/3, fol. 23 (January 15, 1942).
55. Ibid., fol. 23 (January 14, 1942).
56. As cited in: Ziemke and Bauer, *Moscow to Stalingrad*, 132.
57. "KTB A.O.K.9 Ia 1.1.–31.3.1942," BA-MA RH 20-9/47, fol. 32 and 44 (January 10 and 13, 1942).
58. Ibid., fol. 45 (January 14, 1942).
59. "Tagebuch Reinhardts," N245/3, fol. 23 (January 14, 1942).
60. Halder, KTB III, 385 (January 14, 1942).
61. *True to Type*, 42 (January 14, 1942).
62. As cited in: Gerasimova, *The Rzhev Slaughterhouse*, 30.
63. Of Rzhev's 5,400 houses it was estimated that only 300 were left standing when the Red Army finally reoccupied the city. Luther, *The First Day on the Eastern Front*.
64. Humburg, *Das Gesicht des Krieges*, 133 (January 12, 1942).
65. Haape with Henshaw, *Moscow Tram Stop*, 315–17.
66. "Kriegstagebuch Nr.7 des Kdos. der 1.Panzer-Div. 20.9.41–12.4.42," BA-MA RH 27-1/58, fols. 105–106 (January 15, 1942).
67. "Gen.Kdo.VI KTB Ia Nr.3 Band 26 10.1.–17.1.1942," BA-MA RH 24-6/68, fol. 142 (January 12, 1942).
68. "A.O.K.4 Ia KTB Nr.11 3.1.42–31.3.1942," BA-MA RH 20-4/281, fol. 99 (January 11, 1942).
69. Ibid., fol. 122 (January 15, 1942).
70. As cited in: Shepherd, *Hitler's Soldiers*, 209.
71. "A.O.K.4 Ia KTB Nr.11 3.1.42–31.3.1942," BA-MA RH 20-4/281, fol. 122 (January 15, 1942).
72. As cited in: Ziemke and Bauer, *Moscow to Stalingrad*, 134.
73. Underlining in the original. "KTB A.O.K.9 Ia 1.1.–31.3.1942," BA-MA RH 20-9/47, fol. 47 (January 15, 1942).
74. Percy E. Schramm, ed., *Kriegstagebuch des Oberkommandos der Wehrmacht, 1942*, Band II/2, *1. Januar 1942–31. Dezember 1942* (Munich: Manfred Pawlak, 1982), 1268.
75. Ibid., 1268–69.
76. Wildermuth, "Widening the Circle: General Weikersthal and the War of Annihilation, 1941–42," 322. See also the work in this area by Jeff Rutherford in *Combat and Genocide on the Eastern Front*.
77. By stating "Berlin," Goebbels means the main complex of the army high command,

which was centered outside Berlin at Zossen. Halder and his immediate staff were of course quartered at the smaller Mauerwald headquarters in East Prussia so that they could report directly to Hitler at the Wolf's Lair.

78. Fröhlich, *Die Tagebücher von Joseph Goebbels*, Band 3, 142 (January 20, 1942).

18. LONELY FRONT: EMBATTLED HOMELAND

1. Rick Holz, *Too Young to Be a Hero* (Sydney: Flamingo, 2000), 69.
2. Ibid.
3. Ehrenburg, *The Tempering of Russia*, 124.
4. Reese, *A Stranger to Myself*, 52.
5. Solomon Perel, *Europa Europa* (New York: Wiley, 1997), 42.
6. Ibid., 43.
7. Günther, *Hot Motors, Cold Feet*, 245.
8. Geoffrey J. Giles, "A Gray Zone among the Field Gray Men: Confusion in the Discrimination against Homosexuals in the Wehrmacht," in *Gray Zones: Ambiguity and Compromise in the Holocaust and its Aftermath*, edited by Jonathan Petropoulos and John K. Roth (London: Berghahn Books, 2005), 136 and 128.
9. David Raub Snyder, *Sex Crimes under the Wehrmacht* (Lincoln: University of Nebraska Press, 2007), 108.
10. Günter Grau, ed., *Homosexualität in der NS-Zeit: Dokumente einer Diskriminierung und Verfolgung* (Frankfurt am Main: Fischer, 1993), 242; Hans Peter Bleuel, *Sex and Society in Nazi Germany* (Philadelphia: Bantam Books, 1973), 223.
11. Landon and Leitner, *Diary of a German Soldier*, 148 (March 1942).
12. Lubbeck with Hurt, *At Leningrad's Gates*, 114.
13. Giles, "A Gray Zone among the Field Gray Men," 128.
14. Regina Mühlhäuser, *Eroberungen: Sexuelle Gewalttaten und intime Beziehungen deutscher Soldaten in der Sowjetunion, 1941–1945* (Hamburg: Hamburger Edition, 2010), 101.
15. Humburg, *Das Gesicht des Krieges*, 165 (November 22, 1941).
16. Regina Mühlhäuser, "Between 'Racial Awareness' and Fantasies of Potency: Nazi Sexual Politics in the Occupied Territories of the Soviet Union, 1942–1945," in *Brutality and Desire: War and Sexuality in Europe's Twentieth Century*, edited by Dagmar Herzog (London: Palgrave Macmillan, 2009), 209.
17. Landon and Leitner, *Diary of a German Soldier*, 142 (Febuary 14, 1942).
18. As cited in: Cohen, *Smolensk under the Nazis*, 225.
19. Bartmann, *Für Volk and Führer*, 72.
20. Metelmann, *Through Hell for Hitler*, 54.
21. Waitman Wade Beorn, *Marching into Darkness: The Wehrmacht and the Holocaust in Belarus* (Cambridge, Mass.: Harvard University Press, 2014), 171.
22. Lubbeck with Hurt, *At Leningrad's Gates*, 113.
23. Adamczyk, *Feuer!*, 199–200.
24. Blandford, *Under Hitler's Banner*, 32.
25. Roger D. Markwick and Euridice Charon Cardona, *Soviet Women on the Frontline in the Second World War* (London: Palgrave Macmillan, 2012), 146.
26. Zieser, *In Their Shallow Graves*, 55.
27. Ibid., 35.
28. Neitzel and Welzer, *Soldaten*, 5.
29. Kühne, "Male Bonding and Shame Culture: Hitler's Soldiers and the Moral Basis of Genocidal Warfare," 65. See also: Thomas Kühne, *The Rise and Fall of Comradeship: Hitler's Soldiers, Male Bonding and Mass Violence in the Twentieth Century* (Cambridge: Cambridge University Press, 2017), 173.

30. Neitzel and Welzer, *Soldaten*, 5.
31. Ibid., 173.
32. Rass, *"Menschenmaterial,"* 269.
33. As cited in: Birgit Beck, "Sexual Violence and Its Prosecution by Courts Martial of the Wehrmacht," in *A World at Total War: Global Conflict and the Politics of Destruction, 1937–1945*, edited by Roger Chickering, Stig Förster, and Bernd Greiner (Cambridge: Cambridge University Press, 2005), 328. See also: Birgit Beck, *Wehrmacht und sexuelle Gewalt: Sexualverbrechen vor deutschen Militärgerichten, 1939–1945* (Paderborn: Verlag Ferdinand Schöningh, 2004).
34. Birgit Beck, "Sexual Violence and Its Prosecution by Courts Martial of the Wehrmacht," 320–22, 326–27.
35. Beorn, *Marching into Darkness*, 172.
36. Neitzel and Welzer, *Soldaten*, 166.
37. Rass, *"Menschenmaterial,"* 268 and 271.
38. *True to Type*, 24 (October 1941).
39. Beorn, *Marching into Darkness*, 166.
40. Waitman Wade Beorn, "Bodily Conquest: Sexual Violence in the Nazi East," in *Mass Violence in Nazi-Occupied Europe*, edited by Alex J. Kay and David Stahel (Bloomington: Indiana University Press, 2018), 204.
41. Mühlhäuser, *Eroberungen*, 176 and 217.
42. Ibid., 214.
43. Birgit Beck, "Rape: The Military Trails of Sexual Crimes Committed by Soldiers in the Wehrmacht, 1939–1944," in *Home/Front: The Military, War and Gender in Twentieth-Century Germany*, edited by Karen Hageman and Stefanie Schüler-Springorum (Oxford: Berg Publishers, 2002), 267. See also: Kern, *Dance of Death*, 115.
44. Mühlhäuser, "Between 'Racial Awareness' and Fantasies of Potency," 206–207.
45. Wendy Lower, *Nazi Empire-Building and the Holocaust in Ukraine* (Chapel Hill: University of North Carolina Press, 2005), 110–11.
46. Mühlhäuser, "Between 'Racial Awareness' and Fantasies of Potency," 207.
47. Beorn, "Bodily Conquest," 203.
48. Hirt, *"Die Heimat reicht der Front die Hand,"* 353.
49. Regina Mühlhäuser, "A Question of Honor: Some Remarks on the Sexual Habits of German Soliders during World War II," in *Nazi Ideology and Ethics*, edited by Lothar Fritze and Wolfgang Bialas (Newcastle upon Tyne: Cambridge Scholars, 2014), 159.
50. Holz, *Too Young to Be a Hero*, 70.
51. Haape with Henshaw, *Moscow Tram Stop*, 191.
52. Humburg, *Das Gesicht des Krieges*, 111.
53. Cohen, *Smolensk under the Nazis*, 223.
54. Ehrenburg, *Russia at War*, 111–12 (January 29, 1942).
55. On the issue of maintaining relationships, see Hester Vaizey, *Surviving Hitler's War: Family Life in Germany, 1939–48* (London: Palgrave Macmillan, 2010), ch. 3: "Staying in Love," especially 62–68.
56. Ingrid Hammer and Susanne zur Nieden, eds., *Sehr selten habe ich geweint: Briefe und Tagebücher aus dem Zweiten Weltkrieg von Menschen aus Berlin* (Zürich: Schweizer Verlagshaus, 1992), 157.
57. Stahel, *Operation Typhoon*, 100–102.
58. Fröhlich, *Die Tagebücher von Joseph Goebbels*, Band 2, 462 (December 10, 1941).
59. Ibid, 471 (December 11, 1941).
60. Boberach, *Meldungen aus dem Reich*, Band 8, 3073–74 and 3089–92 (December 11 and 15, 1941).
61. Ibid., 3092 (December 15, 1941).

62. Fröhlich, *Die Tagebücher von Joseph Goebbels*, Band 3, 179 (January 24, 1942).
63. Kempowski, *Das Echolot Barbarossa*, 612–13 (December 25, 1941).
64. Gerber, *Im Dienst des Roten Kreuzes*, 197 (December 29, 1941).
65. Luck, *Panzer Commander*, 64; Kempowski, *Das Echolot Barbarossa*, 503 (December 17, 1941).
66. Blandford, *Under Hitler's Banner*, 128.
67. Beermann, *Soldat Werner Beermann Feldpostbriefe*, 211 (January 25, 1942).
68. Sebastian, *Journal*, 463 (January 7, 1942).
69. Boberach, *Meldungen aus dem Reich*, Band 9, 3102 (December 18, 1941).
70. Jörg Echternkamp, "A Coherent War Society," in *Germany and the Second World War*, vol. 9/1, *German Wartime Society, 1939–1945: Politicization, Disintegration, and the Struggle for Survival*, edited by Militärgeschichtlichtliches Forschungsamt (Oxford: Oxford University Press, 2008), 24.
71. For a good discussion of social factors driving such behavior, see Roger Moorhouse, *Berlin at War: Life and Death in Hitler's Capital, 1939–45* (London: Basic Books, 2010), 208–14.
72. Knappe with Brusaw, *Soldat*, 243.
73. Boberach, *Meldungen aus dem Reich*, Band 9, 3122 (January 5, 1942).
74. Ibid.
75. Fröhlic, *Die Tagebücher von Joseph Goebbels*, Band 3, 95 (January 12, 1942).
76. Ibid., 71 and 153 (January 8 and 20, 1942).
77. Ibid., 71 (January 8, 1942).
78. Fredborg, *Behind the Steel Wall*, 75.
79. As cited in: Stargardt, *The German War*, 222.
80. *True to Type*, 147 (n.d.).
81. Ibid., 108 (December 6, 1941).
82. Ibid., 151 (January 1, 1942).
83. Aristotle A. Kallis, *Nazi Propaganda and the Second World War* (New York: Palgrave Macmillan, 2005), 120–21.
84. Fröhlich, *Die Tagebücher von Joseph Goebbels*, Band 3, 92 (January 11, 1942).
85. Fredborg, *Behind the Steel Wall*, 67.
86. Boberach, *Meldungen aus dem Reich*, Band 9, 3163–65 (January 15, 1942). See also: Fröhlich, *Die Tagebücher von Joseph Goebbels*, Band 3, 212 (January 29, 1942); *Die Wehrmachtberichte, 1939–1945*, Band 2, *1 Januar 1942 bis 31 Dezember 1943* (Munich: dtv Verlagsgesellschaft, 1985).
87. Boberach, *Meldungen aus dem Reich*, Band 9, 3209 (January 26, 1942).
88. Fröhlich, *Die Tagebücher von Joseph Goebbels*, Band 3, 212 (January 29, 1942).
89. Ibid., 219 (January 30, 1942).
90. Ibid., 203 (January 28, 1942).
91. Ibid., 194 (January 27, 1942).
92. Ibid., 194–95 (January 27, 1942).
93. Boberach, *Meldungen aus dem Reich*, Band 9, 3221 (January 29, 1942).

19. RETREAT AND COUNTERATTACK: ARMY GROUP CENTER REBOUNDS

1. A doctor's report from April 1942 made it clear that Strauss had suffered severe heart problems and that over the past four years he had been addicted to sleeping pills. "Personalakten für Strauss, Adolf," BA-MA Pers 6/56, fol. 34 (April 14, 1942).
2. Ziemke and Bauer, *Moscow to Stalingrad*, 166–67; Hürter, *Hitlers Heerführer*, 339–40.
3. As cited in: Newton, *Hitler's Commander*, 176.

4. Krebs was formally chief of staff at VII Army Corps and only appointed to his new role at Ninth Army on January 14, replacing Colonel Kurt Weckmann, who had fallen ill.

5. As cited in: Stein, *A Flawed Genius*, 82.

6. "KTB A.O.K.9 Ia 1.1.–31.3.1942," BA-MA RH 20-9/47, fol. 52 (January 17, 1942).

7. Newton, *Hitler's Commander*, 172.

8. Stein, *A Flawed Genius*, 83.

9. As cited in: Newton, *Hitler's Commander*, 177.

10. As cited in: Klink, "The Conduct of Operations," 729.

11. Halder, *Hitler als Feldherr*, 46–47.

12. Meyer, *Generalfeldmarschall Wilhelm Ritter von Leeb*, 433 (January 12, 1942); Halder, KTB III, 386 (January 15, 1942).

13. Samuel W. Mitcham, Jr., and Gene Mueller, *Hitler's Commanders: Officers of the Wehrmacht, the Luftwaffe, the Kriegsmarine, and the Waffen-SS* (Lanham, Md.: Cooper Square Press, 2000), 53 and 55.

14. Halder, KTB III, 387 (January 18, 1942).

15. After referring to Reichenau's death, Richthofen wrote in his diary: "Successor astonishingly FM von Bock again!!" "Wolfram von Richthofen KTB," BA-MA N 671/9, fol. 12 (January 18, 1942).

16. As cited in: Meyer, *Adolf Heusinger*, 175.

17. As cited in: Ziemke and Bauer, *Moscow to Stalingrad*, 161.

18. Kurt Matthies, *Ich hörte die Lerchen singen: Ein Tagebuch aus dem Osten, 1941/45* (Munich: Kösel Verlag, 1956), 37 (January 15, 1942).

19. As cited in: Bergström and Mikhailov, *Black Cross / Red Star*, vol. 2, 45–46.

20. As cited in: Jones, *The Retreat*, 242.

21. Grumann's diary is reproduced in: Rzhevskaia, "Roads and Days," 69.

22. *True to Type*, 99 (January 18, 1942).

23. Wiedebach-Nostitz's diary is reproduced in: Ellis, *Barbarossa 1941*, 353.

24. Rzhevskaia, "Roads and Days," 69.

25. Ziemke and Bauer, *Moscow to Stalingrad*, 161–63; Reinhardt, *Moscow—The Turning Point*, 353.

26. Wiedebach-Nostitz's diary is reproduced in: Ellis, *Barbarossa 1941*, 354.

27. Halder, KTB III, 388 (January 19, 1942); Liddell Hart, *The Other Side of the Hill*, 291.

28. "A.O.K.4 Ia KTB Nr.11 3.1.42–31.3.1942," BA-MA RH 20-4/281, fol. 151 (January 20, 1942).

29. Hürter, *Ein deutscher General an der Ostfront*, 140 (January 21, 1942).

30. Ibid.

31. Ibid.

32. "A.O.K.4 Ia KTB Nr.11 3.1.42–31.3.1942," BA-MA RH 20-4/281, fols. 162 and 169 (January 22 and 23, 1942).

33. Bernd Martin, ed., "Tagebuch eines sowjetischen Offiziers vom 1. Januar 1942–8. Februar 1942," *Wehrwissenschaftliche Rundschau* 17 (1967): 411 (January 21, 1942).

34. "Tagebuch Reinhardts," N245/3, fols. 23 and 24 (January 16 and 17, 1942).

35. "Anlagen zum KTB 'Tagesmeldungen' Bd.I 1.1.–30.1.42," BA-MA RH 21-3/72, fol. 106 (January 16, 1942).

36. "Reinhardt's letters to his wife," N245/2, fol. 20 (January 18, 1942).

37. "Tagebuch Reinhardts," N245/3, fol. 24 (January 17, 1942).

38. "Reinhardt's letters to his wife," N245/2, fol. 20 (January 25, 1942).

39. *True to Type*, 43 (January 19, 1942).

40. Ibid.

41. As cited in: Hartmann, *Operation Barbarossa*, 106.
42. Ehrenburg, *The Tempering of Russia*, 115.
43. LeSueur, *Twelve Months That Changed the World*, 121–22.
44. Ehrenburg, *The Tempering of Russia*, 114.
45. "Tagebuch Reinhardts," N245/3, fol. 24 (January 23, 1942); Ziemke and Bauer, *Moscow to Stalingrad*, 165.
46. "KTB 'Rußlandfeldzug' Pz.A.O.K. IV Teil 9.1.42–27.4.42," BA-MA RH 21-4/51, fol. 51 (January 24, 1942).
47. "Anlagen zum KTB 'Tagesmeldungen' Bd.I 1.1.–30.1.42," BA-MA RH 21-3/72, fol. 179 (January 24, 1942).
48. Rudolf Oehus, MPT, Berlin, 3.2013.2829 (January 22, 1942).
49. As cited in: Max Hastings, *All Hell Let Loose: The World at War, 1939–1945* (London: Harper Press, 2011), 180.
50. Williamson, *Hans Sturm*, 100.
51. Zieser, *In Their Shallow Graves*, 81.
52. Günther, *Hot Motors, Cold Feet*, 251.
53. Zieser, *In Their Shallow Graves*, 61.
54. As cited in: Reinhardt, *Moscow—The Turning Point*, 352.
55. "Gen.Kdo.VI KTB Ia Nr.3 Band 27 18.1.–25.1.1942," BA-MA RH 24-6/69, fol. 5 (January 18, 1942).
56. "KTB A.O.K.9 Ia 1.1.–31.3.1942," BA-MA RH 20-9/47, fol. 55 (January 18, 1942).
57. Meier-Welcker, *Aufzeichnungen eines Generalstabsoffiziers*, 150–51 (January 19, 1942).
58. Bähr and Bähr, *Kriegsbriefe Gefallener Studenten*, 223 (January 19, 1942).
59. Humburg, *Das Gesicht des Krieges*, 224 (January 23, 1942).
60. Newton, *Hitler's Commander*, 178–80.
61. "Kriegstagebuch Nr.7 des Kdos. der 1.Panzer-Div. 20.9.41–12.4.42," BA-MA RH 27-1/58, fol. 110 (January 20, 1942).
62. As cited in: Newton, *Hitler's Commander*, 182.
63. Ibid., 180–81; Forczyk, *Walther Model* (Oxford: Osprey, 2011), 19; "KTB A.O.K.9 Ia 1.1.–31.3.1942," BA-MA RH 20-9/47, fol. 59 (January 19, 1942).
64. "Kriegstagebuch Nr.7 des Kdos. der 1.Panzer-Div. 20.9.41–12.4.42," BA-MA RH 27-1/58, fol. 107 (January 17, 1942).
65. Ibid., fol. 109 (January 19, 1942).
66. "KTB 'Rußlandfeldzug' Pz.A.O.K. IV Teil 9.1.42–27.4.42," BA-MA RH 21-4/51, fol. 44 (January 21, 1942); "Wolfram von Richthofen KTB," BA-MA N 671/9, fol. 15 (January 22, 1942).
67. Paul Schädel, MPT, Berlin, 3.2002.1317 (January 16, 1942).
68. It should be noted that a Soviet army was nominally the size of a German infantry corps.
69. As cited in: Newton, *Hitler's Commander*, 181–82.
70. "Kriegstagebuch Nr.7 des Kdos. der 1.Panzer-Div. 20.9.41–12.4.42," BA-MA RH 27-1/58, fol. 113 (January 21, 1942).
71. "Gen.Kdo.VI KTB Ia Nr.3 Band 27 18.1.–25.1.1942," BA-MA RH 24-6/69, fols. 18–19 (January 22, 1942).
72. "KTB A.O.K.9 Ia 1.1.–31.3.1942," BA-MA RH 20-9/47, fol. 62 (January 22, 1942).
73. "Wolfram von Richthofen KTB," BA-MA N 671/9, fol. 15 (January 23, 1942).
74. "KTB A.O.K.9 Ia 1.1.–31.3.1942," BA-MA RH 20-9/47, fol. 64 (January 23, 1942); "Gen.Kdo.VI KTB Ia Nr.3 Band 27 18.1–25.1.1942," BA-MA RH 24-6/69, fol. 23 (January 23, 1942). See also: Heinz Scherschel, "*. . . trotz Acht und Bann . . .*": *Erinnerun-*

gen eines Nachrichtensoldaten der 8. SS-Kavallerie-Division "Florian Geyer" (Bremen: Am Wall-Der hanseatische Buchhandel, 2014), 29.

75. Reinhardt, *Moscow—The Turning Point*, 351–52.
76. Halder, KTB III, 388 (January 19, 1942).
77. Newton, *Hitler's Commander*, 183.
78. As cited in: Gerasimova, *The Rzhev Slaughterhouse*, 37.
79. Wilhelm Eichner, *Diesseits der Wolga: Tagebuch eines Überlebenden* (Wien: Universitas, 2007), 240 (January 23, 1942).
80. This letter is soon to be published as part of a new annotated edition of Haape's memoir, *Moscow Tram Stop*. It has been compiled by Dr. Craig Luther, with new material provided by Haape's family. My sincere thanks to Dr. Luther for allowing me advance access to his new material.
81. Wildermuth, "Widening the Circle," 321–22.
82. "Kriegstagebuch Nr.1 2.Panzerarmee Band IV (Teil I) vom 27.12.1941 bis 9.2.42," BA-MA RH 21-2/876, fol. 129 (January 21, 1942).
83. Klink, "The Conduct of Operations," 730.
84. "Kriegstagebuch Nr.1 2.Panzerarmee Band IV (Teil I) vom 27.12.1941 bis 9.2.42," BA-MA RH 21-2/876, fol. 98 (January 16, 1942).
85. "18. Panzer Div. Ia Kriegstagebuch vom 10.1.42–31.3.42," BA-MA RH 27-18/71. The diary has no folio stamped page numbers so references must be located according to date (January 17, 1942).
86. "Kriegstagebuch Nr.1 2.Panzerarmee Band IV (Teil I) vom 27.12.1941 bis 9.2.42," BA-MA RH 21-2/876, fols. 109 and 111 (January 18, 1942).
87. Ziemke and Bauer, *Moscow to Stalingrad*, 164; Halder, KTB III, 387 (January 19, 1942).
88. "Kriegstagebuch Nr.1 2.Panzerarmee Band IV (Teil I) vom 27.12.1941 bis 9.2.42," BA-MA RH 21-2/876, fols. 120 and 129 (January 20 and 21, 1942).
89. Ibid., fol. 130 (January 22, 1942).
90. Schäufler, *Knight's Cross Panzers*, 196.
91. Woche, *Zwischen Pflicht und Gewissen*, 143.
92. "Kriegstagebuch Nr.1 2.Panzerarmee Band IV (Teil I) vom 27.12.1941 bis 9.2.42," BA-MA RH 21-2/876, fol. 133 (January 22, 1942).
93. "18. Panzer Div. Ia Kriegstagebuch vom 10.1.42–31.3.42," BA-MA RH 27-18/71, (January 22, 1942).
94. Klink, "The Conduct of Operations," 730.
95. "Kriegstagebuch Nr.1 2.Panzerarmee Band IV (Teil I) vom 27.12.1941 bis 9.2.42," BA-MA RH 21-2/876, fols. 142 and 144 (January 24, 1942); Ziemke and Bauer, *Moscow to Stalingrad*, 164.
96. Fröhlich, *Die Tagebücher von Joseph Goebbels*, Band 3, 170 (January 23, 1942).
97. Paul Schädel, MPT, Berlin, 3.2002.1317 (January 24, 1942).
98. Stader, *Ihr daheim und wir hier draußen*, 90 (January 17, 1942).
99. Alois Scheuer, *Briefe aus Russland: Feldpostbriefe des Gefreiten Alois Scheuer, 1941– 1942* (St. Ingbert: Wassermann Verlag, 2000), 59 (January 31, 1942).

20. DEPARTING THE EASTERN FRONT: TREACHEROUS ROUTES OF ESCAPE

1. Christian Hartmann, *Wehrmacht im Ostkrieg: Front und militärisches Hinterland, 1941/42* (Munich: De Gruyter Oldenbourg, 2010), 357.
2. Schäufler, *Panzer Warfare on the Eastern Front*, 72.
3. Ernst Kern, *War Diary, 1941–45: A Report* (New York: Vantage Press, 1993), 18.
4. Bidermann, *In Deadly Combat*, 94.

5. As cited in: Edele, "Take (No) Prisoners!," 373.

6. Haape with Henshaw, *Moscow Tram Stop*, 234.

7. Bidermann, *In Deadly Combat*, 94.

8. Alexander and Kunze, *Eastern Inferno*, 135 (January 2, 1942). See also the account in: Pichler, *Truppenarzt und Zeitzeuge*, 119 (December 26, 1941).

9. Haape with Henshaw, *Moscow Tram Stop*, 232.

10. LeSueur, *Twelve Months That Changed the World*, 119.

11. Kuhnert, *Will We See Tomorrow?*, 136–37.

12. Hans Becker, *Devil on My Shoulder* (London: Hutchinson's Universal, 1957), 49.

13. Craig W. H. Luther has suggested that in 1941–1942, 90 to 95 percent of German POWs did not survive their captivity. *Barbarossa Unleashed*, 465, n. 256.

14. LeSueur, *Twelve Months That Changed the World*, 119.

15. Ehrenburg, *The Tempering of Russia*, 121–22.

16. Ibid., 122.

17. Goebbels even noted in his diary a report about two Germans soldiers who were trusted to be dropped back behind German lines and operate as spies for the Red Army. Fröhlich, *Die Tagebücher von Joseph Goebbels*, Band 3, 175–76 (January 24, 1942). For the only major study on German desertion, see: Magnus Koch, *Fahnenfluchten: Deserteure der Wehrmacht in Zweiten Weltkrieg; Lebenswege und Entscheidungen* (Paderborn: Verlag Ferdinand Schöningh, 2008).

18. As cited in: Neitzel and Welzer, *Soldaten*, 272–73.

19. Reese, *A Stranger to Myself*, 55.

20. Günther, *Hot Motors, Cold Feet*, 234.

21. Tilemann, *Ich, das Soldatenkind*, 160.

22. Ehrenburg, *The Tempering of Russia*, 104.

23. Edele, "Take (No) Prisoners!," 356.

24. As cited in: Hoffmann, "The Conduct of the War through Soviet Eyes," 916.

25. Edele, "Take (No) Prisoners!," 348 and 356.

26. As cited in: Hoffmann, "The Conduct of the War through Soviet Eyes," 917.

27. Amir Weiner, "Something to Die for, a Lot to Kill For: The Soviet System and the Barbarisation of Warfare, 1939–1945," in *The Barbarization of Warfare*, edited by George Kassimeris (New York: New York University Press, 2006), 113.

28. Edele, "Take (No) Prisoners!," 354.

29. Alexander and Kunze, *Eastern Inferno*, 145 (January 11, 1942).

30. Franz W. Seidler, *Verbrechen an der Wehrmacht: Kriegsgreuel der Roten Armee, 1941/42* (Selent: Pour le Mérite, 1997); Franz W. Seidler, *Kriegsgreuel der Roten Armee: Verbrechen an der Wehrmacht, 1942–43*, vol. 2 (Selent: Pour le Mérite, 1997); Joachim Hoffmann, *Stalin's War of Extermination, 1941–1945: Planning, Realization, and Documentation* (Capshaw, Ala.: Theses and Dissertations Press, 2001).

31. As cited in: Berkhoff, *Motherland in Danger*, 170.

32. A similar realization was increasingly motivating German commanders to try to discourage their men from killing Soviet captives. See Mark Edele, *Stalin's Defectors: How Red Army Soldiers Became Hitler's Collaborators, 1941–1945* (Oxford: Oxford University Press, 2017), 50–53.

33. Hoffmann, "The Conduct of the War through Soviet Eyes," 918; Edele, "Take (No) Prisoners!," 346.

34. For the Soviet figure, see totals from the chart in: Edele, "Take (No) Prisoners!," 356. For German figures, see: Fröhlich, *Die Tagebücher von Joseph Goebbels*, Band 2, 523–24 (December 17, 1941).

35. Fröhlich, *Die Tagebücher von Joseph Goebbels*, Band 2, 523–24 (December 17, 1941).

36. According to Christian Hartmann, of the 170,000 to 200,000 German soldiers taken into Soviet captivity between June 1941 and February 1943, the vast majority did not survive their internment. Hartmann, *Operation Barbarossa*, 124.

37. As cited in: Norman Ohler, *Blitzed: Drugs in Nazi Germany* (London: Allen Lane, 2016), 1, 37–38, and 57.

38. As cited in: ibid., 64 and 78.

39. www.spiegel.de/international/germany/crystal-meth-origins-link-back-to-nazi -germany-and-world-war-ii-a-901755.html.

40. Ohler, *Blitzed*, 79 and 123. The abuse of Pervitin, however, was so well hidden that Erwin Kosmehl, the chief of Germany's narcotics police, reported there to be just eighty-four addicts of the drug in 1942. Lewy, "Vice in the Third Reich?," 62.

41. As cited in: Ohler, *Blitzed*, 120.

42. Ibid., 124.

43. Luther, *Barbarossa Unleashed*, 381.

44. As cited in: Ohler, *Blitzed*, 146.

45. Gerber, *Im Dienst des Roten Kreuzes*, 192, 199, 203, and 211 (December 26 and 30, 1941; January 4 and 17, 1942).

46. Lewy, "Vice in the Third Reich?," 62.

47. Morgenbrod and Merkenich, *Das Deutsche Rote Kreuz unter der NS-Diktatur*, 264.

48. Blandford, *Under Hitler's Banner*, 89.

49. Brigitte Penkert, *Briefe einer Rotkreuzschwester von der Ostfront* (Göttingen: Wallstein Göttingen, 2002), 94.

50. Morgenbrod and Merkenich, *Das Deutsche Rote Kreuz*, 262–63.

51. Ochsenknecht, *"Als ob der Schnee alles zudeckte": Eine Krankenschwester erinnert sich an ihren Kriegseinsatz an der Ostfront* (Berlin: Ullstein, 2005), 98.

52. Lower, *Hitler's Furies*, 44–45.

53. Prefacing this figure with "seriously" denotes wounded men who were transported out of the army group sectors to better-equipped hospitals. Wounded men who were not evacuated from the army group are not covered by this figure.

54. Kroener, "The Winter Crisis of 1941–1942," 1020. Figures for German deaths in December 1941 are taken from Overmans, *Deutsche militärische Verluste im Zweiten Weltkrieg*, 278.

55. As cited in: Kirchubel, *Hitler's Panzer Armies on the Eastern Front*, 112.

56. Pabst, *The Outermost Frontier*, 41.

57. Perau, *Priester im Heers Hitler*, 49.

58. Kuhnert, *Will We See Tomorrow?*, 126.

59. "Armeeoberkommando 2. I.a KTB Teil.4 1.1.42–31.3.42," BA-MA RH 20-2/1787, fol. 37 (January 9, 1942).

60. "KTB Nr.9 5.Pz.Div. 11.12.41–30.1.42," BA-MA 27-5/34, fol. 130 (January 4, 1942).

61. Fröhlich, *Die Tagebücher von Joseph Goebbels*, Band 3, 231 (Feburary 1, 1942).

62. Günther, *Hot Motors, Cold Feet*, 252–53.

63. Reese, *A Stranger to Myself*, 53–54.

64. Haape with Henshaw, *Moscow Tram Stop*, 220.

65. Jones, *The Retreat*, 160.

66. As cited in: ibid., 141.

67. Kempowski, *Das Echolot Barbarossa*, 507 (December 17, 1941).

68. As cited in: Kirchubel, *Hitler's Panzer Armies on the Eastern Front*, 149.

69. Morgenbrod and Merkenich, *Das Deutsche Rote Kreuz*, 256.

70. Haape with Henshaw, *Moscow Tram Stop*, 299.

71. Kempowski, *Das Echolot Barbarossa*, 328 (December 7, 1941).

72. Fröhlich, *Die Tagebücher von Joseph Goebbels*, Band 3, 178 (January 24, 1942).
73. Günther, *Hot Motors, Cold Feet*, 256–57. For more accounts of experiences on trains, see: Carruthers, *The Wehrmacht*, 53–54; Axel Urbanke, ed., *To the Gates of Moscow with the 3rd Panzer Division: A Medical Officer in the Campaign against Russia* (Bad Zwischenahn: Luftfahrtverlag-Start, 2016), 556 (December 9, 1941).
74. Reese, *A Stranger to Myself*, 59.
75. Knappe with Brusaw, *Soldat*, 239.
76. Halder, KTB III, 337 (December 9, 1941).
77. Richard L. DiNardo and Austin Bay, "Horse-drawn Transports in the German Army," *Journal of Contemporary History* 23 (1988): 132.
78. Allen F. Chew, *Fighting the Russians in Winter: Three Case Studies* (Fort Leavenworth, Kans.: Combat Studies Institute, 1981), 36.
79. Richard L. DiNardo, *Mechanized Juggernaut or Military Anachronism: Horses and the German Army in World War II* (London: Stackpole Books, 1991), 51.
80. Ibid., 52.
81. Rudolf Oehus, MPT, Berlin, 3.2013.2829 (January 22, 1942).
82. *True to Type*, 43 (February 4, 1942).
83. DiNardo, *Mechanized Juggernaut or Military Anachronism*, 50.
84. Kempowski, *Das Echolot Barbarossa*, 608 (December 24, 1941).
85. Ibid., 466 (December 15, 1941).
86. *True to Type*, 38 (December 15, 1941).
87. DiNardo, *Mechanized Juggernaut or Military Anachronism*, 52.
88. See also the army's projections for replacements by the spring (although one may see these, as with so many of the OKH's replacement projections, as optimistic): Halder, KTB III, 337 (December 9, 1941).
89. Anatoly Golovchansky, Valentin Osipov, Anatoly Prokopenko, Ute Daniel, and Jürgen Reulecke, eds., *"Ich will raus aus diesem Wahnsinn": Deutsche Briefe von der Ostfront, 1941–1945, aus sowjetischen Archiven* (Hamburg: Rowohlt, 1993), 57 (January 10, 1942).

21. THE LAST HURRAH: THE FAILURE OF THE SOVIET WINTER OFFENSIVE

1. "Kriegstagebuch Nr.1 2.Panzerarmee Band IV (Teil I) vom 27.12.1941 bis 9.2.42," BA-MA RH 21-2/876, fol. 155 (January 26, 1942).
2. "18. Panzer Div. Ia Kriegstagebuch vom 10.1.42–31.3.42," BA-MA RH 27-18/71, (January 29, 1942).
3. Garden and Andrew, *The War Diaries of a Panzer Soldier*, 70 (January 25, 1942).
4. "Kriegstagebuch Nr.1 2.Panzerarmee Band IV (Teil I) vom 27.12.1941 bis 9.2.42," BA-MA RH 21-2/876, fol. 165 (January 28, 1942).
5. Ibid., fol. 166 (January 28, 1942). Emphasis mine.
6. Ibid., fol. 166 (January 28, 1942). See also: Halder, KTB III, 392 (January 28, 1942).
7. As cited in: Meyer, *Adolf Heusinger*, 175.
8. "Kriegstagebuch Nr.1 2.Panzerarmee Band IV (Teil I) vom 27.12.1941 bis 9.2.42," BA-MA RH 21-2/876, fol. 168 (January 29, 1942).
9. Ziemke and Bauer, *Moscow to Stalingrad*, 169.
10. "Kriegstagebuch Nr.1 2.Panzerarmee Band IV (Teil I) vom 27.12.1941 bis 9.2.42," BA-MA RH 21-2/876, fol. 173 (January 29, 1942).
11. "Kriegstagebuch Nr.4 XXXXVII.Pz.Korps. Ia 1.1.1942–31.3.1942," BA-MA RH 24-47/38, fol. 52 (January 31, 1942).
12. Landon and Leitner, *Diary of a German Soldier*, 140 (January 30, 1942).
13. Humburg, *Das Gesicht des Krieges*, 136 (January 30, 1942).

14. Garden and Andrew, *The War Diaries of a Panzer Soldier*, 73 (January 30, 1942).

15. Reddemann, *Zwischen Front und Heimat*, 399 (January 30, 1942).

16. As cited in: Klink, "The Conduct of Operations," 731.

17. "A.O.K.4 Ia KTB Nr.11 3.1.42–31.3.1942," BA-MA RH 20-4/281, fols. 183–85 (January 26, 1942).

18. Hürter, *Ein deutscher General an der Ostfront*, 141 (January 27, 1942).

19. Ibid., 141 (January 28, 1942).

20. "KTB 'Rußlandfeldzug' Pz.A.O.K. IV Teil 9.1.42–27.4.42," BA-MA RH 21-4/51, fols. 65 and 68 (January 28 and 29, 1942).

21. Hürter, *Ein deutscher General an der Ostfront*, 141 (January 30, 1942).

22. Reinhardt, *Moscow—The Turning Point*, 353.

23. Hürter, *Ein deutscher General an der Ostfront*, 142 (February 5, 1942).

24. As cited in: Meyer, *Adolf Heusinger*, 175.

25. Ibid.

26. Fröhlich, *Die Tagebücher von Joseph Goebbels*, Band 3, 198 (January 27, 1942).

27. The trust invested in Dietrich by senior Nazis was reflected by another instance in which he was invited to Hermann Göring's birthday on January 12, 1942, and introduced to the assembled guests as the "piller of the eastern front," while barbs were hurled against the "stale old generals." See: Hassell, *The Ulrich von Hassell Diaries*, 153 (January 24, 1942).

28. Hürter, *Ein deutscher General an der Ostfront*, 145 (February 12, 1942).

29. As cited in: Reinhardt, *Moscow—The Turning Point*, 354.

30. Gustav Böker, MPT, Berlin, 3.2002.0966 (January 28, 1942).

31. "A.O.K.4 Ia KTB Nr.11 3.1.42–31.3.1942," BA-MA RH 20-4/281, fol. 206 (January 28, 1942).

32. Reinhardt, *Moscow—The Turning Point*, 355.

33. Martin, "Tagebuch eines sowjetischen Offiziers vom 1. Januar 1942–8. Februar 1942," 413–14 (January 26, 1942).

34. Zorn took over command from Stumme on January 15, 1942. "Army Group Centre January maps," BA-MA RH 19-II/145, K26 and K29 (January 28 and 31, 1942).

35. Rainer Stahel is not related to the author. "Kriegstagebuch Nr.3. der Führungsabteilung (Ia) des Gen. Kdo. (mot.) XXXX.Pz.Korps vom 27.12.1941–29.4.1942," BA-MA RH 24-40/19, fol. 82 (January 29, 1942).

36. "A.O.K.4 Ia KTB Nr.11 3.1.42–31.3.1942," BA-MA RH 20-4/281, fol. 216 (January 29, 1942).

37. Buchbender and Sterz, *Das andere Gesicht des Krieges*, 92 (January 30, 1942).

38. "KTB Nr.9 5.Pz.Div. 11.12.41–30.1.42," BA-MA 27-5/34, fol. 254 (January 27, 1942).

39. Hürter, *Ein deutscher General an der Ostfront*, 146–47 (February 19, 1942).

40. Ibid., 147 (February 28, 1942).

41. "Tagebuch Reinhardts," N245/3, fol. 25 (January 29, 1942).

42. "Anlagen zum KTB 'Tagesmeldungen' Bd.I 1.1.–30.1.42," BA-MA RH 21-3/72, fol. 197 (January 27, 1942).

43. Ibid., fol. 202 (January 27, 1942).

44. "Kriegstagebuch Nr.3 der 7.Panzer-Division Führungsabteilung 1.6.1941–9.5.1942," BA-MA RH 27-7/46, fol. 288 (January 27, 1942).

45. Harpe succeeded Model in command. "KTB XXXXI.A.K. (mot) 1.1.42–27.7.42," BA-MA RH 24-41/23, fol. 78 (January 30, 1942).

46. "KTB 'Rußlandfeldzug' Pz.A.O.K. IV Teil 9.1.42–27.4.42," BA-MA RH 21-4/51, fol. 71 (January 29, 1942).

47. "Tagebuch Reinhardts," N245/3, fol. 25 (January 30 and Feburary 1, 1942).

48. "Army Group Centre maps," BA-MA RH 19-II/145, K30. This map presents a somewhat deceptive view of Soviet success in the winter offensive. The large area reconquered to the north of Smolensk was actually achieved by a handful of weak and largely unopposed rifle divisions.

49. "Reinhardt's letters to his wife," N245/2, fol. 21 (February 18, 1942).

50. Forczyk, *Walther Model*, 19.

51. As cited in: Newton, *Hitler's Commander*, 184; Forczyk, *Walther Model*, 20.

52. "KTB A.O.K.9 Ia 1.1.–31.3.1942," BA-MA RH 20-9/47, fol. 70 (January 26, 1942).

53. "Gen. Kdo. VI.A.K KTB Nr.3 Band 28 26.1.42–3.2.42," BA-MA RH 24-6/71, fols. 6 and 9 (January 27, 1942).

54. Ibid., fol. 10 (January 28, 1942).

55. Newton, *Hitler's Commander*, 184–85.

56. "Kriegstagebuch Nr.4. des XXXXVI.Pz.Korps vom 1.1.42–21.6.42," BA-MA RH 24-46/37, fol. 33 (January 26, 1942).

57. "KTB A.O.K.9 Ia 1.1.–31.3.1942," BA-MA RH 20-9/47, fols. 73 and 76 (January 27 and 28, 1942).

58. As cited in: Nagorski, *The Greatest Battle*, 269.

59. "KTB A.O.K.9 Ia 1.1.–31.3.1942," BA-MA RH 20-9/47, fols. 74 and 76 (January 27 and 28, 1942).

60. Erhard Raus, *Panzer Operations: The Eastern Front Memoir of General Raus, 1941–1945*, edited by Steven H. Newton (Cambridge, Mass.: Da Capo Press, 2005), 98–100.

61. Ibid., 99.

62. "Gen. Kdo. VI.A.K KTB Nr.3 Band 28 26.1.42–3.2.42," BA-MA RH 24-6/71, fols. 13–15 (January 30, 1942).

63. Ibid., fol. 17 (January 31, 1942).

64. As cited in: Gerasimova, *The Rzhev Slaughterhouse*, 38.

65. As cited in: Jones, *The Retreat*, 258.

66. As cited in: Gerasimova, *The Rzhev Slaughterhouse*, 168.

67. Beermann, *Soldat Werner Beermann Feldpostbriefe*, 213 (January 29, 1942).

68. As cited in: Lucas, *Das Reich*, 78.

69. My sincere thanks to Dr. Craig Luther for allowing me access to Haape's unpublished material.

70. Newton, *Hitler's Commander*, 185–86.

71. As cited in: Gerasimova, *The Rzhev Slaughterhouse*, 42.

72. Newton, *Hitler's Commander*, 186; see also n. 19.

CONCLUSION

1. The total space conquered by the Wehrmacht as of December 5 equaled some 1,324,293 square kilometers. Thanks to Kay Dancey for measuring these spaces.

2. Joel Hayward, *Stopped at Stalingrad: The Luftwaffe and Hitler's Defeat in the East, 1942–1943* (Lawrence: University Press of Kansas, 1998), 16.

3. Fröhlich, *Die Tagebücher von Joseph Goebbels*, Band 3, 501 (March 20, 1942). See also the discussion in: Ian Kershaw, *Hitler, 1936–1945: Nemesis* (London: Penguin, 2001), 456.

4. As cited in: Neitzel and Welzer, *Soldaten*, 211.

5. Percy Ernst Schramm, *Hitler: The Man and the Military Leader* (Chicago: Chicago Review Press, 1999), 26.

6. Max Domarus, *Hitler: Speeches and Proclamations, 1932–1945; The Chronicle of a Dictatorship*, vol. 4, *The Years 1941 to 1945* (Wauconda, Ill.: Bolchazy-Carducci, 2004), 2571.

7. Fredborg, *Behind the Steel Wall*, 84.
8. Fritz, *The First Soldier*, 243–46.
9. Hans-Adolf Jacobsen, *Der Zweite Weltkrieg in Chronik und Dukumenten* (Darmstadt: Wehr und Wissen Verlagsgesellschaft, 1962), 690.
10. As cited in: Meyer, *Adolf Heusinger*, 175.
11. As cited in: Reinhardt, *Moscow—The Turning Point*, 365.
12. As cited in: Neitzel and Welzer, *Soldaten*, 196.
13. Förster, "Ideological Warfare in Germany," 560.
14. Neitzel and Welzer, *Soldaten*, 197.
15. As cited in: Reinhardt, *Moscow—The Turning Point*, 366.
16. Hitler's Luftwaffe adjutant, Nicolaus von Below, wrote that it was Hitler who "prevented the catastrophe into which the operational setback would have degenerated" (Below, *Als Hitlers Adjutant*, 300). Likewise, Hermann Balck noted of the winter fighting: "Hitler had been right in this case" (Balck, *Order in Chaos*, 234). For more such literature, see the discussion in: Chales de Beaulieu, *Generaloberst Erich Hoepner*, 235. In his first-rate biography of Hitler, Ian Kershaw writes: "Hitler's early recognition of the dangers of a full-scale collapse of the front, and the utterly ruthless determination with which he resisted demands to retreat, probably did play a part in avoiding a calamity of Napoleonic proportions" (Kershaw, *Hitler*, 456). Likewise, David M. Glantz and Jonathan M. House wrote in the 2015 revised edition of their excellent history of the Nazi/Soviet conflict: "Like Stalin's cool conduct of the Moscow defence in late November, Hitler's 'stand-fast' order appears in retrospect to have been the correct action, even if issued out of stubbornness rather than rational calculation . . . For once, the professional soldiers were wrong and the 'Bavarian corporal' was almost certainly right" (Glantz and House, *When Titans Clashed*, 111). Even the outstanding new history of the German army in World War II by Ben Shepherd states: "Most of the German generals wanted to pull back Army Group Centre between 80 and 120 kilometres (50 and 75 miles) to the 'K' Line, stretching from Rhzev down east of Vyazma to Iukhnov. Hitler and Halder refused, and were right to do so" (Shepherd, *Hitler's Soldiers*, 206).
17. Gersdorff, *Soldier in the Downfall*, 79.
18. In his research for the operational sections of the fourth volume of the comprehensive German semi-official history of the war, Ernst Klink hinted at similar discoveries when he wrote, "even the commanders of armies, corps and divisions were no longer always 'under control' when it was a case of saving their exhausted troops" (Klink, "The Conduct of Operations," 715).
19. Fröhlich, *Die Tagebücher von Joseph Goebbels*, Band 3, 146 (January 20, 1942).
20. Hürter, *Ein deutscher General an der Ostfront*, 147 (February 28, 1942).
21. Recent research has pointed to similar behavior in the final months of the war; see: Bastiaan Willems, "Defiant Breakwaters or Desperate Blunders? A Revision of the German Late-War Fortress Strategy," *The Journal of Slavic Military Studies* 28, no. 2 (April 2015): 358–59. See also Schlabrendorff, *The Secret War against Hitler*, 315–16.
22. Lopez, *The Survival of Auftragstaktik during the Soviet Counterattack in the Battle for Moscow*, 58–59.
23. As cited in: Kroener, "The Winter Crisis of 1941–1942," 11.
24. There is a growing body of research on this subject; see: Johannes Hürter, "Auf dem Weg zur Militäropposition: Tresckow, Gersdorff, der Vernichtungskrieg und der Judenmord; Neue Dokumente über das Verhältnis der Heeresgruppe Mitte zur Einsatzgruppe B im Jahr 1941," *Vierteljahreshefte für Zeitgeschichte* 52, no. 3 (2004); Christian Gerlach, "Men of 20 July and the War in the Soviet Union," in *War of*

Extermination: The German Military in World War II, 1941–1944, edited by Hannes Heer and Klaus Naumann (New York: Berghahn Books, 2006); Christian Gerlach, "Hitlergegner bei der Heeresgruppe Mitte und die 'verbrecherischen Befehle,'" in *NS-Verbrechen und der militärische Widerstand gegen Hitler*, edited by Gerd R. Ueberschär (Darmstadt: Primus Verlag, 2000); Hasenclever, *Wehrmacht und Besatzungspolitik in der Sowjetunion*, 396–97.

25. In June 1941 Kluge ordered his army to shoot any women captured in Red Army uniform. Megargee, *War of Annihilation*, 59.

26. As cited in: Hill, *The Red Army and the Second World War*, 297.

27. Ibid., 318.

28. Lopukhovsky and Kavalerchik, *The Price of Victory*, 154.

29. Department of the U.S. Army, ed., *Small Unit Actions during the German Campaign in Russia* (Washington, D.C.: Center of Military History United States Army, 1953), 23.

30. Goebbels writes about this at some length in his diary, suggesting the practice was well understood at the time and probably inducing a measure of confidence in German commanders, even when their line was breaking. Fröhlich, *Die Tagebücher von Joseph Goebbels*, Band 3, 222 (January 30, 1942).

31. Hürter, *Ein deutscher General an der Ostfront*, 145 (February 16, 1942).

32. Fröhlich, *Die Tagebücher von Joseph Goebbels*, Band 3, 222 (January 30, 1942).

33. Guéhenno, *Diary of the Dark Years*, 141 (January 25, 1941).

34. Gerasimova, *The Rzhev Slaughterhouse*, 25.

35. Bartov, *Hitler's Army*, ch. 1: "The Demodernization of the Front."

36. As cited in: Stargardt, *The German War*, 210–11.

37. Reese, *A Stranger to Myself*, 7 and 58.

BIBLIOGRAPHY

ARCHIVAL REFERENCES

1. *Bundesarchiv-Militärarchiv, Freiburg im Breisgau (BA-MA)*

High Command of the Army
BA-MA RH/2-2670, "Oberkommando des Heeres Generalstab des Heeres O.Qu.IV-Abt. Fr.H.Ost (II)."

Army Group Center
BA-MA RH 19-II/122, "Kriegstagebuch Nr.1 (Band December 1941) des Oberkommandos der Heeresgruppe Mitte."
BA-MA RH 19-II/141, "Heeresgruppe Mitte Meldungen und Berichte der unterstellten Armee, Jan.–Juli 1942."
BA-MA RH 19-II/145 K2, "Army Group Centre December map."
BA-MA RH 19-II/145 K9, "Army Group Centre December map."
BA-MA RH 19-II/145 K11, "Army Group Centre December map."
BA-MA RH 19-II/145 K13, "Army Group Centre December map."

BA-MA RH 19-II/145 K15, "Army Group Centre December map."
BA-MA RH 19-II/145 K17, "Army Group Centre December map."
BA-MA RH 19-II/145 K19, "Army Group Centre December map."
BA-MA RH 19-II/145 K21, "Army Group Centre December map."
BA-MA RH 19-II/145 K23, "Army Group Centre December map."
BA-MA RH 19-II/145 K25, "Army Group Centre December map."
BA-MA RH 19-II/145 K27, "Army Group Centre December map."
BA-MA RH 19-II/145 K2, "Army Group Centre January map."
BA-MA RH 19-II/145 K6, "Army Group Centre January map."
BA-MA RH 19-II/145 K10, "Army Group Centre January map."
BA-MA RH19-II/145 K14, "Army Group Centre January map."
BA-MA RH 19-II/145 K18, "Army Group Centre January map."
BA-MA RH 19-II/145 K22, "Army Group Centre January map."
BA-MA RH 19-II/145 K26, "Army Group Centre January map."
BA-MA RH 19-II/145 K29, "Army Group Centre January map."
BA-MA RH 19-II/145 K30, "Army Group Centre January map."

Second Army
BA-MA RH 20-2/207, "Armeeoberkommando 2. I.a KTB Teil.2 19.9.41–16.12.41."
BA-MA RH 20-2/1787, "Armeeoberkommando 2. I.a KTB Teil.4 1.1.42–31.3.42."
BA-MA RH 24-48/40, "Kriegstagebuch XXXXVIII.Pz.Kps. Abt.Ia 1.12.41–31.12.41."
BA-MA RH 24-48/47, "Kriegstagebuch XXXXVIII.Pz.Kps. Abt.Ia 1.1.42–30.1.42."
BA-MA RH 27-9/4, "9.Pz.Div. KTB Ia vom 19.5.1941 bis 22.1.1942."

Second Panzer Army
BA-MA N 802/46, "Briefe von Heinz Guderian an seine Frau Margarete."
BA-MA RH 21-2/244, "Kriegstagebuch Nr.1 2.Panzerarmee Band III vom 1.11.1941 bis 26.12.41."
BA-MA RH 21-2/876, "Kriegstagebuch Nr.1 2.Panzerarmee Band IV (Teil I) vom 27.12.1941 bis 9.2.42."
BA-MA RH 21-2/819, "Kriegstagebuch der O.Qu.-Abt. Pz. A.O.K.2 vom 21.6.41 bis 31.3.42."
BA-MA N 910/6, "Joachim von Lemselsen's diary 10 October 1941–24 April 1942."
BA-MA RH 24-47/258, "Kriegstagebuch Nr.2 XXXXVII.Pz.Korps. Ia 23.9.1941–31.12.1941."
BA-MA RH 24-47/38, "Kriegstagebuch Nr.4 XXXXVII.Pz.Korps. Ia 1.1.1942–31.3.1942."
BA-MA RH 27-3/15, "KTB 3rd Pz. Div. vom 19.9.41 bis 6.2.42."
BA-MA RH 27-4/10, "Kriegstagebuch 4.Panzer-Divison Führungsabtl. 26.5.41–31.3.42."
BA-MA RH 27-18/69, "18. Panzer-Div-Ia Kriegstagebuch vom 20.10.41–13.12.41."
BA-MA RH 27-18/71, "18. Panzer Div. Ia Kriegstagebuch vom 10.1.42–31.3.42."

Panzer Group/Army 3
N245/3, "Tagebuch Reinhardts."
N245/2, "Auswahl von Originalbriefen, die von meiner Frau und mir in den Jahren 1939 bis Januar 1945 geschrieben wurden."
BA-MA RH 21-3/71, "Anlagen zum Kriegstagebuch Tagesmeldungen Bd.I 1.11–31.12.41."
BA-MA RH 21-3/72, "Anlagen zum KTB 'Tagesmeldungen' Bd.I 1.1.–30.1.42."
BA-MA RH 24-41/23, "KTB XXXXI.A.K. (mot) 1.1.42–27.7.42."
BA-MA RH 27-1/58, "Kriegstagebuch Nr.7 des Kdos. der 1.Panzer-Div. 20.9.41–12.4.42."
BA-MA RH 27-6/20, "6. Panzer Division Ia KTB 1.12.1941–31.3.1942."
BA-MA RH 27-7/46, "Kriegstagebuch Nr.3 der 7.Panzer-Division Führungsabteilung 1.6.1941–9.5.1942."
BA-MA RH 26-36/9, "Kriegstagebuch No.2 der 36. Inf. Div. (mot) 22.9.41–5.12.41."

Panzer Group/Army 4

BA-MA RH 21-4/50, "KTB 'Rußlandfeldzug' Pz.A.O.K. III Teil 6.12.41–9.1.42."

BA-MA RH 21-4/51, "KTB 'Rußlandfeldzug' Pz.A.O.K. IV Teil 9.1.42–27.4.42."

BA-MA 21-4/56, "KTB Pz.Gr.4 Meldungen von unten 6.12.41–31.12.41."

BA-MA RH 24-41/17, "Anlagenband zum KTB XXXXI A.K. Ia 4 6.12.41–31.12.41."

BA-MA RH 24-40/18, "Kriegstagebuch Nr.3. der Führungsabteilung (Ia) des Gen. Kdo. (mot.) XXXX.Pz.Korps vom 31.05.1941–26.12.1941."

BA-MA RH 24-46/21, "Kriegstagebuch Nr.3. des XXXXVI.Pz.Korps vom 24.08.41–31. 12.41."

BA-MA RH 24-46/38, "Kriegstagebuch Anlagen des XXXXVI.Pz.Korps vom 18.12.41–13. 6.42."

BA-MA RH 24-46/37, "Kriegstagebuch Nr.4. des XXXXVI.Pz.Korps vom 1.1.42–21.6.42."

BA-MA RH 27-2/22, "2. Panzer Division KTB Nr.6 Teil I. Vom 15.6.41–27.2.42."

BA-MA 27-5/34, "KTB Nr.9 5.Pz.Div. 11.12.41–30.1.42."

BA-MA RH 27-11/24, "11.Pz.Div. KTB Abt.Ia vom 22.10.41–24.1.42."

BA-MA RH 27-20/27, "20.Pz.Div. KTB vom 1.1.42 bis 28.2.42 Band Ia3."

Fourth Army

BA-MA RH 20-4/211, "A.O.K.4 Ia Anlagen A zum KTB 24.12.41–2.1.1942."

BA-MA RH 20-4/281, "A.O.K.4 Ia KTB Nr.11 3.1.42–31.3.1942."

BA-MA RH 24-40/19, "Kriegstagebuch Nr.3. der Führungsabteilung (Ia) des Gen. Kdo. (mot.) XXXX.Pz.Korps vom 27.12.1941–29.4.1942."

BA-MA RH 24-57/3, "Gen.Kdo.LVII.Pz.Korps KTB Nr.2 vom 1.11.41–31.12.41."

BA-MA RH 27-19/23, "Kriegstagebuch 19.Panzer-Division Abt.Ib für die Zeit vom 1.6.1941–31.12.1942."

BA-MA RH 27-19/24, "Kriegstagebuch 19.Panzer-Division 15.10.1941–18.3.1942."

BA-MA RH 27-20/26, "20.Pz.Div. KTB vom 21.10.41 bis 30.12.41 Band Ia2."

Ninth Army

BA-MA Pers 6/56, "Personalakten für Strauss, Adolf."

BA-MA RH 20-9/13b, "AOK 9: KTB Ostfeldzug, Band 3 v. 30.9. –31.12.1941."

BA-MA RH 20-9/47, "KTB A.O.K.9 Ia 1.1. –31.3.1942."

BA-MA RH 24-6/65, "Gen. Kdo. VI.A.K KTB Nr.3 Band 25 1.1.42–9.1.42."

BA-MA RH 24-6/68, "Gen.Kdo.VI KTB Ia Nr.3 Band 26 10.1. –17.1.1942."

BA-MA RH 24-6/69, "Gen.Kdo.VI KTB Ia Nr.3 Band 27 18.1. –25.1.1942."

BA-MA RH 24-6/71, "Gen. Kdo. VI.A.K KTB Nr.3 Band 28 26.1.42–3.2.42."

BA-MA RH 24-27/76, "Gen.Kdo.XXVII KTB Ia Nr.VII 20.11.41–28.4.1942."

BA-MA N 76-6, "Kriegserinnerungen Auleb (June 22–December 25, 1941)."

Luftwaffe

BA-MA N 671/8, "Wolfram von Richthofen KTB."

BA-MA N 671/9, "Wolfram von Richthofen KTB."

BA-MA RL 200/17, "Gen.v.Waldau, Chef Fü St Lw Persönl. Tagebuch, Auszugeweise."

2. Archive of Alexander Solzhenitsyn House of Russia Abroad (Moscow)

F.1 Op. F-2. D. M-81, "Nikolai Ranzen's diary."

3. Museumsstiftung Post und Telekommunikation (MPT) Berlin

1.2002.1214, Hans-Joachim S. (December 25, 1941).

3.2002.0935, Paul Wortmann (December 25, 1941).

3.2002.0889, Anton Böhrer (January 2, 1942).

3.2002.1317, Paul Schädel (January 12, 16, 24, 1942).

3.2013.2829, Rudolf Oehus (January 22, 1942).

3.2002.0966, Gustav Böker (January 28, 1942).
3.2002.1376, Wilhelm Bacher (April 3, 1942).

PRIMARY AND SECONDARY SOURCES

Adamczyk, Werner. *Feuer! An Artilleryman's Life on the Eastern Front.* Wilmington, N.C.: Broadfoot, 1992.

Aksulu, Nurdan Melek, ed. *Obergefeiter Otto Allers: Feldpostbriefe aus dem Zweiten Weltkrieg.* Norderstedt: Books on Demand GmbH, 2008.

Alexander, Christine, and Mark Kunze, eds. *Eastern Inferno: The Journals of a German Panzerjäger on the Eastern Front, 1941–43.* Philadelphia: Casemate, 2010.

Alexiev, Alex. "Soviet Nationals in German Wartime Service, 1941–1945." In *Soviet Nationals in German Wartime Service, 1941–1945,* edited by Antonio Munoz, 5–44. N.p., 2007.

Allmayer-Beck, Johann Christoph. *"Herr Oberleitnant, det lohnt doch nicht!" Kriegserinnerinnerungen an die Jahre 1938 bis 1945.* Vienna: Boehlau Verlag, 2013.

Anders, Wladyslaw. *Russian Volunteers in Hitler's Army, 1941–1945.* New York: Europa Books, 1997.

Askey, Nigel. *Operation Barbarossa: The Complete Organisational and Statistical Analysis, and Military Simulation.* Vol. llb. Self-pub., 2014.

Bähr, Walter, and Hans Bähr, eds. *Kriegsbriefe Gefallener Studenten, 1939–1945.* Tübingen: Wunderlich, 1952.

Balck, Hermann. *Order in Chaos: The Memoirs of General of Panzer Troops Hermann Balck.* Lexington: University Press of Kentucky, 2015.

Bartmann, Erwin. *Für Volk and Führer: The Memoir of a Veteran of the 1st SS Panzer Division Leibstandarte SS Adolf Hitler.* Solihull: Helion, 2013.

Bartov, Omer. *The Eastern Front, 1941–45: German Troops and the Barbarisation of Warfare.* London: Macmillan, 1985.

———. *Hitler's Army: Soldiers, Nazis, and War in the Third Reich.* Oxford: Oxford University Press, 1992.

Beak, Gisela, ed. *Feldpostbriefe eines Landsers, 1939–1943.* N.p.: Books on Demand, 2000.

Beck, Birgit. "Rape: The Military Trails of Sexual Crimes Committed by Soldiers in the Wehrmacht, 1939–1944." In *Home/Front: The Military, War and Gender in Twentieth-Century Germany,* edited by Karen Hageman and Stefanie Schüler-Springorum, 255–27. Oxford: Berg Publishers, 2002.

———. "Sexual Violence and Its Prosecution by Courts Martial of the Wehrmacht." In *A World at Total War: Global Conflict and the Politics of Destruction, 1937–1945,* edited by Roger Chickering, Stig Förster, and Bernd Greiner, 317–31. Cambridge: Cambridge University Press, 2005.

———. *Wehrmacht und sexuelle Gewalt: Sexualverbrechen vor deutschen Militärgerichten, 1939–1945.* Paderborn: Verlag Ferdinand Schöningh, 2004.

Becker, Hans. *Devil on My Shoulder.* London: Hutchinson's Universal, 1957.

Beermann, Hartmut, ed. *Soldat Werner Beermann Feldpostbriefe, 1941–1942.* N.p.: lulu.com, 2012.

Beevor, Antony. *The Second World War.* New York: Little, Brown, 2012.

Beevor, Antony, and Luba Vinogradova, eds. *A Writer at War: Vasily Grossman with the Red Army, 1941–1945.* New York: Vintage, 2005.

Bell, P. M. H. *John Bull and the Bear: British Public Opinion, Foreign Policy and the Soviet Union, 1941–1945.* London: Hodder Arnold, 1990.

Bellamy, Chris. *Absolute War: Soviet Russia in the Second World War.* New York: Vintage, 2007.

Below, Nicolaus von. *Als Hitlers Adjutant, 1937–45*. Mainz: Pour le Mérite, 1999.

Beorn, Waitman Wade. "Bodily Conquest: Sexual Violence in the Nazi East." In *Mass Violence in Nazi-Occupied Europe*, edited by Alex J. Kay and David Stahel, 195–215. Bloomington: Indiana University Press, 2018.

———. *Marching into Darkness: The Wehrmacht and the Holocaust in Belarus*. Cambridge, Mass.: Harvard University Press, 2014.

Bergström, Christer. *Barbarossa: The Air Battle, July–December 1941*. Hersham: Classic Publications, 2007.

———. *Stalingrad: The Air Battle, 1942 through January 1943*. Hinckley: Classic Publications, 2007.

Bergström, Christer, and Andrey Mikhailov. *Black Cross / Red Star: The Air War over the Eastern Front*. Vol. 1, *Operation Barbarossa, 1941*. Pacifica: Pacifica Military History, 2000.

———. *Black Cross / Red Star: The Air War over the Eastern Front*. Vol. 2, *Resurgence, January–June 1942*. Pacifica: Pacifica Military History, 2001.

Berkhoff, Karel C. *Motherland in Danger: Soviet Propaganda during World War II*. Cambridge, Mass.: Harvard University Press, 2012.

Beyda, Oleg. "'Iron Cross of the Wrangel's Army': Russian Emigrants as Interpreters in the Wehrmacht." *The Journal of Slavic Military History* 27, no. 3 (July 2014): 430–48.

———. "'Refighting the Civil War': Second Lieutenant Mikhail Aleksandrovich Gubanov." *Jahrbücher für Geschichte Osteuropas* 66 (2018): 245–73.

Beyda, Oleg, and Igor Petrov. "The Soviet Union." In *Joining Hitler's Crusade: European Nations and the Invasion of the Soviet Union*, edited by David Stahel, 369–425. Cambridge: Cambridge University Press, 2018.

Bidermann, Gottlob Herbert. *In Deadly Combat: A German Soldier's Memoir of the Eastern Front*. Lawrence: University Press of Kansas, 2000.

Bidlack, Richard. "Propaganda and Public Opinion." In *The Soviet Union at War, 1941–1945*, edited by David R. Stone, 45–68. Barnsley, U.K.: Pen and Sword, 2010.

Blandford, Edmund, ed. *Under Hitler's Banner: Serving the Third Reich*. Edison: Airlife, 2001.

Bleuel, Hans Peter. *Sex and Society in Nazi Germany*. Philadelphia: Bantam Books, 1973.

Blumentritt, Günther. "Moscow." In *The Fatal Decisions*, edited by William Richardson and Seymour Freidin, 29–75. London: Michael Joseph, 1956.

Boberach, Heinz, ed. *Meldungen aus dem Reich: Die geheimen Lageberichte des Sicherheitsdienstes der SS, 1938–1945*. Band 8. Berlin: Pawlak, 1984.

———, ed. *Meldungen aus dem Reich: Die geheimen Lageberichte des Sicherheitsdienstes der SS, 1938–1945*. Band 9. Berlin: Pawlak, 1984.

Bock, Fedor von. *Generalfeldmarschall Fedor von Bock: The War Diary, 1939–1945*. Edited by Klaus Gerbet. Atglen, Pa.: Schiffer, 1996.

Bond, Brian. "Brauchitsch." In *Hitler's Generals*, edited by Correlli Barnett, 75–99. London: Grove Weidenfeld, 1989.

Boog, Horst. "The Luftwaffe." In *Germany and the Second World War*, vol. 4, *The Attack on the Soviet Union*, edited by Militärgeschichtliches Forschungsamt, 763–832. Oxford: Oxford University Press, 1998.

Bopp, Gerhard. *Kriegstagebuch: Aufzeichnungen Während des II. Weltkrieges, 1940–1943*. Hamburg: Timon Verlag, 2005.

Bor, Peter. *Gespräche mit Halder*. Wiesbaden: Limes Verl., 1950.

Böttger, Armin. *To the Gates of Hell: The Memoir of a Panzer Crewman*. Barnsley, U.K.: Pen and Sword, 2012.

Braithwaite, Rodric. *Moscow 1941: A City and Its People at War*. New York: Knopf, 2006.

Breloer, Heinrich, ed. *Mein Tagebuch: Geschichten vom Überleben, 1939–1947.* Cologne: Verlagsgesellschaft Schulfernsehen, 1984.

Buchbender, Ortwin. *Das tönende Erz: Deutsche Propaganda gegen die Rote Armee im Zweiten Weltkrieg.* Stuttgart: Seewald Verlag, 1978.

Buchbender, Ortwin, and Reinhold Sterz, eds. *Das andere Gesicht des Krieges: Deutsche Feldpostbriefe, 1939–1945.* Munich: C. H. Beck Verlag, 1982.

Bücheler, Heinrich, *Hoepner: Ein deutsches Soldatenschicksal des 20. Jahrhunderts.* Herford: Mittler E.S. + Sohn GmbH, 1980.

Carell, Paul [Paul Karl Schmidt]. *Hitler's War on Russia: The Story of the German Defeat in the East.* London: Aberdeen Books, 1964.

Carruthers, Bob, ed. *The Wehrmacht: Last Witnesses; First-Hand Accounts from the Survivors of Hitler's Armed Forces.* London: André Deutsch, 2010.

Chales de Beaulieu, Walter. *Generaloberst Erich Hoepner: Militärisches Porträt eines Panzer-Führers.* Neckargemünd: Vowinckel, 1969.

Chalmers, Martin, ed. *To the Bitter End: The Diaries of Victor Klemperer, 1942–45.* London: QPD, 1999.

Chew, Allen F. *Fighting the Russians in Winter: Three Case Studies.* Fort Leavenworth: Combat Studies Institute, 1981.

Chiari, Bernhard. "A 'People's War' Against Hitler's Fascism?" In *Germany and the Second World War,* vol. 9/2, *German Wartime Society, 1939–1945: Exploitation, Interpretations, Exclusion,* edited by Militärgeschichtlichtliches Forschungsamt, 881–989. Oxford: Oxford University Press, 2014.

Churchill, Winston S. *The Second World War.* Abridged edition. London: Cassell, 1959.

Clark, Alan. *Barbarossa: The Russian-German Conflict, 1941–1945.* London: Phoenix, 1996.

Cohen, Laurie R. *Smolensk under the Nazis.* Rochester, N.Y.: Rochester University Press, 2013.

Conquest, Robert. *The Great Terror: A Reassessment.* Oxford: Oxford University Press, 2008.

Conrady, Alexander. *Rshew, 1942/1943: Aus der Geschichte der 36. Infanterie-Division (mot.) 1.1.1942 bis 25.3.1943.* Neckargemünd: Vowinckel, 1976.

Corrigan, Gordon. *The Second World War: A Military History.* London: Thomas Dunne Books, 2010.

Corum, James S. *Wolfram von Richthofen: Master of the German Air War.* Lawrence: University Press of Kansas, 2008.

Crawford, Steve. *The Eastern Front: Day by Day.* London: Snap, 2012.

Creveld, Martin van. *Supplying War: Logistics from Wallenstein to Patton.* Cambridge: Cambridge University Press, 2004.

Dallin, Alexander. *German Rule in Russia, 1941–1945: A Study of Occupation Policies.* London: Palgrave Macmillan, 1981.

Davie, H. G. W. "The Influence of Railways on the Military Operations in the Russo-German War, 1941–1945." *The Journal of Slavic Military Studies* 30, no. 2 (2017): 321–46.

Davis, Clyde R. *Von Kleist: From Hussar to Panzer Marshal.* Houston: Lancer Militaria, 1979.

Deck, Josef. *Der Weg der 1000 Toten.* Karlsruhe: Badenia, 1978.

deGraffenried, Julie K. *Sacrificing Childhood: Children and the Soviet State in the Great Patriotic War.* Lawrence: University Press of Kansas, 2014.

Department of the U.S. Army, ed. *Effects of Climate on Combat in European Russia.* Washington, D.C.: Center of Military History United States Army, 1952.

———, ed. *German Tank Maintenance in World War II.* Washington, D.C.: Center of Military History United States Army, 1988.

———, ed. *Military Improvisations during the Russian Campaign.* Washington, D.C.: Center of Military History United States Army, 1951.

———, ed. *Small Unit Actions during the German Campaign in Russia*. Washington, D.C.: Center of Military History United States Army, 1953.

Dessloch, Otto. "The Winter Battle of Rzhev, Vyazma, and Yukhov, 1941–1942." In *German Battle Tactics in the Russian Front, 1941–1945*, edited by Steven H. Newton, 81–108. Atglen, Pa.: Schiffer, 1994.

DeWitt, Kurt, and Wilhelm Koll. "The Bryansk Area." In *Soviet Partisans in World War II*, edited by John A. Armstrong, 458–516. Madison: University of Wisconsin Press, 1964.

Dietrich, Otto. *The Hitler I Knew: Memoirs of the Third Reich's Press Chief*. New York: Skyhorse, 2010.

Die Wehrmachtberichte, 1939–1945. Band 2, *1 Januar 1942 bis 31 Dezember 1943*. Munich: dtv Verlagsgesellschaft, 1985.

DiNardo, Richard L. *Mechanized Juggernaut or Military Anachronism: Horses and the German Army in World War II*. London: Stackpole Books, 1991.

DiNardo, Richard L., and Austin Bay. "Horse-drawn Transports in the German Army." *Journal of Contemporary History* 23 (1988): 129–42.

Dollinger, Hans, ed. *Kain, wo ist dein Burder? Was der Mensch im Zweiten Weltkrieg erleiden mußte—dokumentiert in Tagebüchern und Briefen*. Munich: List Paul Verlag, 1983.

Domarus, Max. *Hitler: Speeches and Proclamations, 1932–1945; The Chronicle of a Dictatorship*. Vol. 4, *The Years 1941 to 1945*. Wauconda: Bolchazy-Carducci, 2004.

Downing, David. *Sealing Their Fate: Twenty-Two Days that Decided the Second World War*. London: Da Capo Press, 2009.

Drabkin, Artem, ed. *The Red Air Force at War: Barbarossa and the Retreat to Moscow; Recollections of Fighter Pilots on the Eastern Front*. Barnsley, U.K.: Pen and Sword, 2007.

Dunn, Walter S., Jr. *Stalin's Keys to Victory: The Rebirth of the Red Army in WWII*. Mechanicsburg, Pa.: Stackpole Books, 2006.

Eberle, Henrik, and Matthias Uhl, eds. *The Hitler Book: The Secret Dossier Prepared for Stalin from the Interrogations of Hitler's Personal Aides*. New York: Public Affairs, 2005.

Echternkamp, Jörg. "A Coherent War Society." In *Germany and the Second World War*, vol. 9/1, *German Wartime Society, 1939–1945: Politicization, Disintegration, and the Struggle for Survival*, edited by Militärgeschichtlichtliches Forschungsamt, 7–41. Oxford: Oxford University Press, 2008.

Edele, Mark. *Stalin's Defectors: How Red Army Soldiers Became Hitler's Collaborators, 1941–1945*. Oxford: Oxford University Press, 2017.

———. "Take (No) Prisoners! The Red Army and German POWs, 1941–1943." *The Journal of Modern History* 88 (June 2016): 342–79.

Ehrenburg, Ilya. *Russia at War*. London: Hamish Hamilton, 1943.

———. *The Tempering of Russia*. New York: Alfred A. Knopf, 1944.

Eichner, Wilhelm. *Diesseits der Wolga: Tagebuch eines Überlebenden*. Wien: Universitas, 2007.

Ellis, Frank. *Barbarossa 1941: Reframing Hitler's Invasion of Stalin's Soviet Empire*. Lawrence: University Press of Kansas, 2015.

Elmshäuser, Konrad, and Jan Lokers, eds. *"Man muß hier nur hart sein": Kriegsbriefe und Bilder einer Familie, 1934–1945*. Bremen: Edition Temmen, 1999.

Engel, Gerhard. *At the Heart of the Reich: The Secret Diary of Hitler's Army Adjutant*. London: Greenhill Books, 2005.

Engel, Heinrich. *7,000 Kilometers in a Sturmgeschütz: The Wartime Diaries and Photo Album of Knight's Cross Recipient Heinrich Engel*. Winnipeg: J. J. Fedorowicz, 2001.

Enstad, Johannes Due. *Soviet Russians under Nazi Occupation: Fragile Loyalties in World War II*. Cambridge: Cambridge University Press, 2018.

Erickson, John. *The Road to Stalingrad: Stalin's War with Germany*. Vol. 1. London: Phoenix Giant, 1975.

———. "Soviet War Losses: Calculations and Controversies." In *Barbarossa: The Axis and the Allies*, edited by John Erickson and David Dilks, 255–77. Edinburgh: Edinburgh University Press, 1998.

Evans, Richard J. *The Third Reich at War: How the Nazis Led Germany from Conquest to Disaster*. London: Penguin Books, 2009.

Forczyk, Robert. *Moscow 1941: Hitler's First Defeat*. Oxford: Osprey, 2006.

———. *Panzerjäger vs. KV-1: Eastern Front, 1941–43*. Oxford: Osprey, 2012.

———. *Walther Model*. Oxford: Osprey, 2011.

Förster, Jürgen. "Ideological Warfare in Germany, 1919 to 1945." In *Germany and the Second World War*, vol. 9/1, *German Wartime Society, 1939–1945: Politicization, Disintegration, and the Struggle for Survival*, edited by Militärgeschichtliches Forschungsamt, 485–669. Oxford: Oxford University Press, 2008.

Fredborg, Arvid. *Behind the Steel Wall*. London: Viking, 1944.

Frisch, Franz A. P., in association with Wilbur D. Jones, Jr. *Condemned to Live: A Panzer Artilleryman's Five-Front War*. Shippensburg: Burd Street Press, 2000.

Fritz, Stephen. *The First Soldier: Hitler as Military Leader*. New Haven, Conn.: Yale University Press, 2018.

———. *Ostkrieg: Hitler's War of Extermination in the East*. Lexington: University Press of Kentucky, 2011.

Fröhlich, Elke, ed. *Die Tagebücher von Joseph Goebbels*. Teil II, Diktate 1941–1945, Band 2, Oktober–Dezember 1941. Munich: K. G. Saur, 1996.

———, ed. *Die Tagebücher von Joseph Goebbels*. Teil II, Diktate 1941–1945, Band 3, Januar–März 1942. Munich: K. G. Saur, 1994.

Gagel, Douglas Wolfgang Oskar. *Führer, Folk and Fatherland: A Soldier's Story*. Renfrew: Douglas Gagel, 2010.

Garden, David, and Kenneth Andrew, eds. *The War Diaries of a Panzer Soldier: Erich Hager with the 17th Panzer Division on the Russian Front, 1941–1945*. Atglen, Pa.: Schiffer, 2010.

Gareis, Martin. *Kampf und Ende der Fränkisch-Sudetendeutschen 98. Infanterie-Division*. Eggolsheim: Nebel Verlag, 1956.

Gerasimova, Svetlana. *The Rzhev Slaughterhouse: The Red Army's Forgotten 15 Month Campaign against Army Group Centre, 1942–1943*. Solihull: Helion, 2013.

Gerber, Ernst. *Im Dienst des Roten Kreuzes: Schweizer Ärztemissionen im II. Weltkrieg*. Teil 2, *Ein Tagebuch, 1941/1942*. Berlin: Wünsche, Frank, 2002.

Gerlach, Christian. "Hitlergegner bei der Heeresgruppe Mitte und die 'verbrecherischen Befehle.'" In *NS-Verbrechen und der militärische Widerstand gegen Hitler*, edited by Gerd R. Ueberschär, 62–76. Darmstadt: Primus Verlag, 2000.

———. "Men of 20 July and the War in the Soviet Union." In *War of Extermination: The German Military in World War II, 1941–1944*, edited by Hannes Heer and Klaus Naumann, 127–45. New York: Berghahn Books, 2006.

Gersdorff, Rudolf-Christoph von. *Soldier in the Downfall: A Wehrmacht Cavalryman in Russia, Normandy, and the Plot to Kill Hitler*. Bedford: Aberjona Press, 2012.

Giles, Geoffrey J. "A Gray Zone Among the Field Gray Men: Confusion in the Discrimination against Homosexuals in the Wehrmacht." In *Gray Zones: Ambiguity and Compromise in the Holocaust and Its Aftermath*, edited by Jonathan Petropoulos and John K. Roth, 127–46. London: Berghahn Books, 2005.

Glantz, David M. *Barbarossa Derailed: The Battle for Smolensk, 10 July–10 September 1941*. Vol. 1, *The German Advance, the Encirclement Battle, and the First and Second Soviet Counteroffensives, 10 July–24 August 1941*. Solihull: Helion, 2010.

———. *Barbarossa Derailed: The Battle for Smolensk, 10 July–10 September 1941.* Vol. 2, *The German Offensives on the Flanks and the Third Soviet Counteroffensive, 25 August–10 September 1941.* Solihull: Helion, 2012.

———. *Barbarossa Derailed: The Battle for Smolensk, 10 July–10 September 1941.* Vol. 3, *The Documentary Companion: Tables, Orders and Reports Prepared by Participating Red Army Forces.* Solihull: Helion, 2014.

———. *Barbarossa Derailed: The Battle for Smolensk, 10 July–10 September 1941.* Vol. 4, *Atlas.* Solihull: Helion, 2015.

———. *Barbarossa: Hitler's Invasion of Russia, 1941.* Stroud: Tempus, 2001.

———. *Colossus Reborn: The Red Army at War, 1941–1943.* Lawrence: University Press of Kansas, 2005.

———. *Forgotten Battles of the German-Soviet War, 1941–1945.* Vol. 1, *The Summer-Fall Campaign, 22 June–4 December 1941.* Self-pub., 1999.

———. *Forgotten Battles of the German-Soviet War, 1941–1945.* Vol. 2, *The Winter Campaign, 5 December 1941–April 1942.* Self-pub., 1999.

———. *Soviet Military Deception in the Second World War.* London: Routledge, 1989.

Glantz, David M., and Jonathan M. House. *When Titans Clashed: How the Red Army Stopped Hitler.* Lawrence: University Press of Kansas, 2015.

Goda, Norman J. W. "Black Marks: Hitler's Bribery of His Senior Officers during WWII." *The Journal of Modern History* 72, no. 2 (June 2000): 413–53.

Golovchansky, Anatoly, Valentin Osipov, Anatoly Prokopenko, Ute Daniel, and Jürgen Reulecke, eds. *"Ich will raus aus diesem Wahnsinn": Deutsche Briefe von der Ostfront, 1941–1945, aus sowjetischen Archiven.* Hamburg: Rowohlt, 1993.

Gorlitz, Walter, ed. *The Memoirs of Field-Marshal Keitel: Chief of the German High Command, 1938–1945.* New York: Focal Point, 1966.

———. *Paulus and Stalingrad.* London: Citadel Press, 1963.

Grau, Günter, ed. *Homosexualität in der NS-Zeit: Dokumente einer Diskriminierung und Verfolgung.* Frankfurt am Main: Fischer, 1993.

Greiffenberg, Hans von. "Battle of Moscow, 1941–1942." In *World War II German Military Studies,* vol. 16, pt. 7, *The Eastern Theater,* edited by Historical Division Headquarters, United States Army, MS# T-28. New York: Garland, 1979.

Griehl, Manfred. *German Bombers over Russia.* Barnsley, U.K.: Pen and Sword, 2016.

Guderian, Heinz. *Panzer Leader.* New York: Da Capo Press, 1996.

Guéhenno, Jean. *Diary of the Dark Years, 1940–1944: Collaboration, Resistance, and Daily Life in Occupied Paris.* Oxford: Oxford University Press, 2016.

Günther, Helmut. *Hot Motors, Cold Feet: A Memoir of Service with the Motorcycle Battalion of SS-Division "Reich," 1940–1941.* Winnipeg: J. J. Fedorowicz, 2004.

Haape, Heinrich, with Dennis Henshaw. *Moscow Tram Stop: A Doctor's Experiences with the German Spearhead in Russia.* London: Collins, 1957.

Haldane, Charlotte. *Russian Newsreel: An Eye-Witness Account of the Soviet Union at War.* New York: Secker and Warburg, 1943.

Halder, Franz. *Hitler als Feldherr.* Munich: Münchener Dom-Verlag, 1949.

———. *Kriegstagebuch: Tägliche Aufzeichnungen des Chefs des Generalstabes des Heeres, 1939–1942.* Band II, *Von der geplanten Landung in England bis zum Beginn des Ostfeldzuges, 1.7.1940–21.6.1941,* edited by Hans-Adolf Jacobsen. Stuttgart: Kohlhammer, 1963.

———. *Kriegstagebuch: Tägliche Aufzeichnungen des Chefs des Generalstabes des Heeres, 1939–1942.* Band III, *Der Russlandfeldzug bis zum Marsch auf Stalingrad, 22.6.1941–24.9.1942,* edited by Hans-Adolf Jacobsen and Alfred Philippi. Stuttgart: Kohlhammer, 1964.

Hammer, Ingrid, and Susanne zur Nieden, eds. *Sehr selten habe ich geweint: Briefe und*

Tagebücher aus dem Zweiten Weltkrieg von Menschen aus Berlin. Zürich: Schweizer Verlagshaus, 1992.

Hansmann, Claus. *Vorüber Nicht Vorbei: Russische Impressionen, 1941–1943.* Frankfurt: Ullstein, 1989.

Hardesty, Von, and Ilya Grinberg. *Red Phoenix Rising: The Soviet Air Force in World War II.* Lawrence: University Press of Kansas, 2012.

Häring, Bernard. *Embattled Witness: Memories of a Time of War.* New York: Seabury Press, 1976.

Harrison, Richard W., ed. *The Battle for Moscow, 1941–1942: The Red Army's Defensive Operations and Counter-offensive along the Moscow Strategic Direction.* Solihull: Helion, 2015.

Hart, Russell A. *Guderian: Panzer Pioneer or Myth Maker?* Dulles: Potomac Books, 2006.

Hartmann, Christian. *Halder Generalstabschef Hitlers, 1938–1942.* Munich: Schöningh, 1991.

———. *Operation Barbarossa: Nazi Germany's War in the East, 1941–1945.* Oxford: Oxford University Press, 2013.

———. *Wehrmacht im Ostkrieg: Front und militärisches Hinterland, 1941/42.* Munich: De Gruyter Oldenbourg, 2010.

Hasenclever, Jörn. *Wehrmacht und Besatzungspolitik: Die Befehlshaber der rückwärtigen Heeresgebiete, 1941–1943.* Paderborn: Verlag Ferdinand Schöningh, 2010.

Hassell, Ulrich von. *The Ulrich von Hassell Diaries: The Story of the Forces against Hitler inside Germany.* London: Frontline Books, 2011.

Hastings, Max. *All Hell Let Loose: The World at War, 1939–1945.* London: Harper Press, 2011.

———. *Winston's War: Churchill, 1940–1945.* New York: Vintage, 2010.

Hayward, Joel. *Stopped at Stalingrad: The Luftwaffe and Hitler's Defeat in the East, 1942–1943.* Lawrence: University Press of Kansas, 1998.

Heer, Hannes, and Klaus Naumann, eds. *War of Extermination: The German Military in World War II, 1941–1944.* New York: Berghahn Books, 2006.

Helmecke, Chris. "Ein 'anderer' Oberbefehlshaber? Generaloberst Rudolf Schmidt und die deutsche Besatzungsherrschaft in der Sowjetunion, 1941–1943." *Militärgeschichtliche Zeitschrift* 75, no. 1 (2016): 55–93.

Herde, Peter. *Die Achsenmächte, Japan und die Sowjetunion: Japanische Quellen zum Zweiten Weltkrieg, 1941–1945.* Berlin: De Gruyter Oldenbourg, 2017.

Herring, George C., Jr. *Aid to Russia, 1941–1946: Strategy, Diplomacy, the Origins of the Cold War.* New York: Columbia University Press, 1973.

Herzog, Rudolph. *Dead Funny: Telling Jokes in Hitler's Germany.* New York: Melville House, 2012.

Hill, Alexander. "British Lend-Lease Aid and the Soviet War Effort, June 1941–June 1942." *The Journal of Military History* 71, no. 3 (July 2007): 773–808.

———. "British Lend-Lease Tanks and the Battle for Moscow, November–December 1941—Revisited." *The Journal of Slavic Military Studies* 22, no. 4 (November 2009): 574–87.

———. *The Great Patriotic War of the Soviet Union, 1941–45: A Documentary Reader.* Abingdon: Routledge, 2010.

———. *The Red Army and the Second World War.* Cambridge: Cambridge University Press, 2017.

Hirt, Alexander. *"Die Heimat reicht der Front die Hand": Kulturelle Truppenbetreuung im Zweiten Weltkrieg, 1939–1945; Ein deutsch-englischer Vergleich.* PhD diss., Georg-August University, 2008.

Hoffmann, Joachim. "The Conduct of the War through Soviet Eyes." In *Germany and the Second World War,* vol. 4, *The Attack on the Soviet Union,* edited by Militärgeschichtliches Forschungsamt, 833–940. Oxford: Oxford University Press, 1998.

——. *Stalin's War of Extermination, 1941–1945: Planning, Realization, and Documentation.* Capshaw: Theses and Dissertations Press, 2001.

Hoffmann, Peter. *The History of the German Resistance, 1933–1945.* Montreal: McGill-Queen's University Press, 1996.

Holmston, A. *Auf Magischen Wegen: Der Ostfeldzug.* Buenos Aires: Philosophie des Krieges, 1948.

Holz, Rick. *Too Young to Be a Hero.* Sydney: Flamingo, 2000.

Hooten, E. R. *Eagle in Flames: The Fall of the Luftwaffe.* London: Arms & Armour, 1997.

Humburg, Martin. *Das Gesicht des Krieges: Feldpostbriefe von Wehrmachtssoldaten aus der Sowjetunion, 1941–1944.* Wiesbaden: C.H. Beck Verlag, 1998.

Hürter, Johannes. "Auf dem Weg zur Militäropposition: Tresckow, Gersdorff, der Vernichtungskrieg und der Judenmord; Neue Dokumente über das Verhältnis der Heeresgruppe Mitte zur Einsatzgruppe B im Jahr 1941." *Vierteljahreshefte für Zeitgeschichte* 52, no. 3 (2004): 527–62.

——, ed. *Ein deutscher General an der Ostfront: Die Briefe und Tagebücher des Gotthard Heinrici, 1941/42.* Erfurt: Sutton Verlag, 2001.

——, ed. *A German General on the Eastern Front: The Letters and Diaries of Gotthard Heinrici, 1941–1942.* Barnsley, U.K.: Pen and Sword, 2014.

——. *Hitlers Heerführer: Die deutschen Oberbefehlshaber im Krieg gegen die Sowjetunion, 1941/42.* Munich: Oldenbourg Wissenschaftsverlag, 2006.

Inglis, Nancy F., ed. *I Deserted Hitler: Memoirs of Bruno J. Trappmann.* London: New Holland, 2013.

Jacobsen, Hans-Adolf. *Der Zweite Weltkrieg in Chronik und Dukumenten.* Darmstadt: Wehr und Wissen Verlagsgesellschaft, 1962.

Janssen, Karl-Heinz. "Walther von Brauchitsch: Der überforderte Feldherr." In *Die Militärelite des Dritten Reiches: 27 biographische Skizzen,* edited by Ronald Smelser and Enrico Syring, 83–98. Berlin: Ullstein, 1995.

Jarausch, Konrad H., ed. *Reluctant Accomplice: A Wehrmacht Soldier's Letters from the Eastern Front.* Princeton, N.J.: Princeton University Press, 2011.

Jones, Michael. *The Retreat: Hitler's First Defeat.* London: Thomas Dunne Books, 2009.

Jones, Robert Huhn. *The Roads to Russia: United States Lend-Lease to the Soviet Union.* Norman: University of Oklahoma Press, 1969.

Jordan, Philip. *Russian Glory.* London: Cresset Press, 1942.

Jörgensen, Christer. *Hitler's Espionage Machine.* London: Lyons Press, 2004.

Kahn, David. *Hitler's Spies.* London: Macmillan, 1980.

Kallis, Aristotle A. *Nazi Propaganda and the Second World War.* New York: Palgrave Macmillan, 2005.

Kay, Alex J., and David Stahel. "Reconceiving Criminality in the German Army on the Eastern Front." In *Mass Violence in Nazi-Occupied Europe,* edited by Alex J. Kay and David Stahel, 173–94. Bloomington: Indiana University Press, 2018.

Keegan, John. *The Second World War.* New York: Penguin Books, 1989.

Kempowski, Walter, ed. *Das Echolot Barbarossa '41: Ein kollektives Tagebuch.* Munich: Albrecht Knaus Verlag, 2004.

Kern, Erich. *Dance of Death.* New York: Charles Scribner's Sons, 1951.

——. *War Diary, 1941–45: A Report.* New York: Vantage Press, 1993.

Kershaw, Ian. *Fateful Choices: Ten Decisions that Changed the World, 1940–1941.* New York: Penguin Books, 2007.

———. *Hitler, 1936–1945: Nemesis.* London: Penguin, 2001.

Kershaw, Robert. *War Without Garlands: Operation Barbarossa, 1941/42.* New York: Da Capo Press, 2000.

Kessel, Martina. "Laughing about Death? 'German Humor' in the Two World Wars." In *Between Mass Death and Individual Loss: The Place of the Dead in Twentieth-Century Germany*, edited by Alon Confino, Paul Betts, and Dirk Schumann, 197–218. New York: Berghahn Books, 2008.

Kilian, Katrin A. "Factors Influencing Emotions, Affects and Moods Expressed in Forces Mail." In *Germany and the Second World War*, vol. 9/2, *German Wartime Society, 1939–1945: Exploitation, Interpretations, Exclusion*, edited by Militärgeschichtlichtliches Forschungsamt, 253–90. Oxford: Oxford University Press, 2014.

Kirchubel, Robert. *Hitler's Panzer Armies on the Eastern Front.* Barnsley, U.K.: Pen and Sword, 2009.

Kitchen, Martin. *Nazi Germany at War.* London: Routledge, 1995.

———. *A World in Flames: A Short History of the Second World War in Europe and Asia, 1939–1945.* London: Routledge, 1990.

Klee, Ernst, Willi Dressen, and Volker Riess, eds. *"The Good Old Days": The Holocaust as Seen by Its Perpetrators and Bystanders.* Old Saybrook, Conn.: William S. Konecky Associates, 1991.

Kleindienst, Jürgen, ed. *Sei tausendmal gegrüßt: Briefwechsel Irene und Ernst Guicking, 1937–1945.* Berlin: Zeitgut Verlag, 2001.

Klemperer, Victor. *Ich will Zeugnis ablegen bis zum letzten: Tagebücher, 1933–1941.* Edited by Walter Nowojski and Hadwig Klemperer. Darmstadt: Aufbau-Verlag, 1997.

Klink, Ernst. "The Conduct of Operations." In *Germany and the Second World War*, vol. 4, *The Attack on the Soviet Union*, edited by Militärgeschichtliches Forschungsamt, 525–763. Oxford: Oxford University Press, 1998.

———. "The Military Concept of War against the Soviet Union." In *Germany and the Second World War*, vol. 4, *The Attack on the Soviet Union*, edited by Militärgeschichtliches Forschungsamt, 225–325. Oxford: Oxford University Press, 1998.

Knappe, Siegfried, with Ted Brusaw. *Soldat: Reflections of a German Soldier, 1936–1949.* New York: Dell, 1992.

Knopp, Guido. *Der Verdammte Krieg: "Unternehmen Barbarossa."* Munich: Orbis Verlag, 1998.

Koch, Magnus. *Fahnenfluchten: Deserteure der Wehrmacht in Zweiten Weltkrieg; Lebenswege und Entscheidungen.* Paderborn: Verlag Ferdinand Schöningh, 2008.

König, Franz, ed. *Ganz in Gottes Hand: Briefe gefallener und hingerichteter Katholiken, 1939–1945.* Wien: Herder Verlag, 1957.

Kotze, Hildegard von, ed. *Heeresadjutant bei Hitler, 1938–1943: Aufzeichnungen des Majors Engel.* Stuttgart: Deutsche Verlags-Anstalt, 1974.

Krivosheev, G. F., ed. *Soviet Casualties and Combat Losses in the Twentieth Century.* London: Greenhill Books, 1997.

Kroener, Bernhard R. "The 'Frozen *Blitzkrieg*': German Strategic Planning against the Soviet Union and the Causes of Its Failure." In *From Peace to War: Germany, Soviet Russia and the World, 1939–1941*, edited by Bernd Wegner, 135–49. Oxford: Berghahn Books, 1997.

———. "The Winter Crisis of 1941–1942: The Distribution of Scarcity or Steps Towards a More Rational Management of Personnel." In *Germany and the Second World War*, vol. 5/1, *Organization and Mobilization of the German Sphere of Power*, edited by Militärgeschichtliches Forschungsamt, 1001–1127. Oxford: Oxford University Press, 2000.

Krumpelt, Ihno. *Das Material und die Kriegführung*. Frankfurt am Main: Mittler und Sohn, 1968.

Kühne, Thomas. *Belonging and Genocide: Hitler's Community, 1918–1945*. New Haven, Conn.: Yale University Press, 2010.

———. "Comradeship: Gender Confusion and Gender Order in the German Military, 1918–1945." In *Home/Front: The Military, War and Gender in Twentieth-Century Germany*, edited by Karen Hageman and Stefanie Schüler-Springorum, 233–54. Oxford: Berg, 2002.

———. "Guppenkohäsion und Kameradschaftsmythos in der Wehrmacht." In *Die Wehrmacht: Mythos und Realität*, edited by Rolf-Dieter Müller and Hans-Erich Volkmann, 534–49. München: De Gruyter Oldenbourg, 1999.

———. "Male Bonding and Shame Culture: Hitler's Soldiers and the Moral Basis of Genocidal Warfare." In *Ordinary People as Mass Murderers: Perpetrators in Comparative Perspectives*, edited by Olaf Jensen and Claus-Christian W. Szejnmann, 55–77. New York: Palgrave Macmillan, 2008.

———. *The Rise and Fall of Comradeship: Hitler's Soldiers, Male Bonding and Mass Violence in the Twentieth Century*. Cambridge: Cambridge University Press, 2017.

Kuhnert, Max. *Will We See Tomorrow? A German Cavalryman at War, 1939–1942*. London: Pen and Sword, 1993.

Kundrus, Birthe. "Cultural Warfare and Its Content." In *Germany and the Second World War*, vol. 9/2, *German Wartime Society, 1939–1945: Exploitation, Interpretations, Exclusion*, edited by Militärgeschichtlichtliches Forschungsamt, 103–44. Oxford: Oxford University Press, 2014.

Kursietis, Andris J. *The Wehrmacht at War, 1939–1945: The Units and Commanders of the German Ground Forces during World War II*. Soesterberg, Netherlands: Aspekt, 1999.

Lamb, Richard. "Kluge." In *Hitler's Generals*, edited by Correlli Barnett, 395–409. London: Grove Weidenfeld, 1989.

Landon, H. C. Robbins, and Sebastian Leitner, eds. *Diary of a German Soldier*. London: Faber & Faber, 1963.

Lange, Horst. *Tagebücher aus dem Zweiten Weltkrieg*. Mainz: Arnshaugkvon Hase and Koehler Verlag, 1979.

Latzel, Klaus. *Deutsche Soldaten—nationalsozialistischer Krieg? Kriegserlebnis—Kriegserfahrung, 1939–1945*. Paderborn: Schöningh Paderborn, 1998.

Leach, Barry. *German Strategy against Russia, 1939–1941*. Oxford: Oxford University Press, 1973.

———. "Halder." In *Hitler's Generals*, edited by Correlli Barnett, 101–26. London: Grove Weidenfeld, 1989.

LeSueur, Larry. *Twelve Months That Changed the World*. New York: Alfred A. Knopf, 1943.

Lewy, Jonathan. "Vice in the Third Reich? Alcohol, Tobacco and Drugs." In *Life and Times in Nazi Germany*, edited by Lisa Pine, 49–74. London: Bloomsbury Academic, 2016.

Leyen, Ferdinand Prinz von der. *Rückblick zum Mauerwald: Vier Kriegsjahre im OKH*. Munich: Biederstein Verlag, 1965.

Liddell Hart, Basil. *The Other Side of the Hill*. London: Pan Books, 1999.

Lieb, Christa. *Feldpost: Briefe zwischen Heimat und Front, 1939–1945; Eine Collage*. Stuttgart: Frechdruch, 2007.

Littlejohn, David. *The Patriotic Traitors: The Story of Collaboration in German Occupied Europe, 1940–1945*. New York: Doubleday, 1972.

Lopez, Miguel A. *The Survival of Auftragstaktik During the Soviet Counterattack in the Battle for Moscow, December 1941 to January 1942*. MA thesis, Temple University, 2015.

Lopukhovsky, Lev, and Boris Kavalerchik. "Kogda my uznaem real'nuiu tsenu razgroma gitlerovskoi Germanii?" In *"Umylis' krov'iu?"*: *Lozh' i pravda o poteriakh v Velikoi Otechestvennoi voine.* Moscow: Iauza Eksmo, 2012.

———. *The Price of Victory: The Red Army's Casualties in the Great Patriotic War.* Barnsley, U.K.: Pen and Sword, 2017.

Lower, Wendy. *Hitler's Furies: German Woman in the Nazi Killing Fields.* London: Mariner Books, 2013.

———. *Nazi Empire-Building and the Holocaust in Ukraine.* Chapel Hill: University of North Carolina Press, 2005.

Lubbeck, William, with David B. Hurt. *At Leningrad's Gates: The Story of a Soldier with Army Group North.* Philadelphia: Casemate, 2006.

Lucas, James. *Das Reich: The Military Role of the 2nd SS Division.* London: Arms & Armour, 1991.

Luck, Hans von. *Panzer Commander: The Memoirs of Colonel Hans von Luck.* New York: Praeger, 1989.

Lunde, Henrik O. *Finland's War of Choice: The Troubled German-Finish Coalition in World War II.* Havertown, Pa.: Casemate, 2011.

Luther, Craig W. H. *Barbarossa Unleashed: The German Blitzkrieg through Central Russia to the Gates of Moscow.* Atglen, Pa.: Schiffer, 2013.

———. *The First Day on the Eastern Front: Germany Invades the Soviet Union, June 22, 1941.* Lanham, Md.: Stackpole Books, forthcoming.

Macksey, Kenneth. *Guderian: Panzer General.* London: Macdonald and Jane's, 1975.

Mannerheim, Carl, and Gustaf Emil. *The Memoirs of Marshal Mannerheim.* London: E. P. Dutton, 1953.

Manstein, Erich von. *Lost Victories.* Novato: Presodio, 1958.

Mark, Jason D. *Besieged: The Epic Battle for Cholm.* Sydney: Leaping Horseman Books, 2011.

Markwick, Roger D., and Euridice Charon Cardona. *Soviet Women on the Frontline in the Second World War.* London: Palgrave Macmillan, 2012.

Martin, Bernd, ed. "Tagebuch eines sowjetischen Offiziers vom 1. Januar 1942–8. Februar 1942." *Wehrwissenschaftliche Rundschau* 17 (1967): 352–57, 405–15, and 473–78.

Matthies, Kurt. *Ich hörte die Lerchen singen: Ein Tagebuch aus dem Osten, 1941/45.* Munich: Kösel Verlag, 1956.

Mawdsley, Evan. *Thunder in the East: The Nazi-Soviet War, 1941–1945.* 2nd ed. London: Bloomsbury Academic, 2016.

Mayers, David. *FDR's Ambassadors and the Diplomacy of Crisis: From the Rise of Hitler to the End of World War II.* Cambridge: Cambridge University Press, 2013.

Mazower, Mark. *Hitler's Empire: Nazi Rule in Occupied Europe.* London: Allen Lane, 2009.

Megargee, Geoffrey P. *Inside Hitler's High Command.* Lawrence: University Press of Kansas, 2000.

———. *War of Annihilation: Combat and Genocide on the Eastern Front, 1941.* Lanham, Md.: Rowman & Littlefield, 2006.

Meier-Welcker, Hans. *Aufzeichnungen eines Generalstabsoffiziers, 1939–1942.* Freiburg: Rombach Druck und Verlagshaus, 1982.

Merridale, Catherine. *Ivan's War: Life and Death in the Red Army, 1939–1945.* New York: Picador, 2006.

Messenger, Charles. *The Last Prussian: A Biography of Field Marshal Gerd von Rundstedt, 1875–1953.* Barnsley, U.K.: Pen and Sword, 1991.

Metelmann, Henry. *Through Hell for Hitler.* Havertown: Casemate, 2005.

Meyer, Georg. *Adolf Heusinger: Dienst eines deutschen Soldaten, 1915 bis 1964.* Berlin: Mittler in Maximilian Verlag, 2001.

———, ed. *Generalfeldmarschall Wilhelm Ritter von Leeb: Tagebuchaufzeichnungen und Lagebeurteilungen aus zwei Weltkriegen*. Stuttgart: Deutsche Verlags-Anstalt, 1976.

Meyer-Timpe, Ulrike, ed. *"Träume recht süß von mir": Eine deutsche Freundschaft in Briefen, 1940–1943*. Frankfurt am Main: Eichborn, 2004.

Mezhiritsky, Peter. *On the Precipice: Stalin, the Red Army Leadership and the Road to Stalingrad, 1931–1942*. Solihull: Helion, 2012.

Mierzejewski, Alfred C. *The Most Valuable Asset of the Reich: A History of the German National Railway*. Vol. 2, 1933–1945. Chapel Hill: University of North Carolina Press, 2013.

Miner, Steven M. *Stalin's Holy War: Religion, Nationalism, and Alliance Politics, 1941–1945*. Chapel Hill: University of North Carolina Press, 2003.

Mitcham, Samuel W., Jr., and Gene Mueller. *Hitler's Commanders: Officers of the Wehrmacht, the Luftwaffe, the Kriegsmarine, and the Waffen-SS*. Lanham, Md.: Cooper Square Press, 2000.

Moltke, Helmuth James von. *Letters to Freya: 1939–1945*. New York: Knopf, 1990.

Montefiore, Simon Sebag. *Stalin: The Court of the Red Tsar*. London: Vintage Books, 2003.

Moorhouse, Roger. *Berlin at War: Life and Death in Hitler's Capital, 1939–45*. London: Basic Books;, 2010.

Morgenbrod, Birgitt, and Stephanie Merkenich. *Das Deutsche Rote Kreuz unter der NS-Diktatur, 1933–1945*. Paderborn: Verlag Ferdinand Schöningh, 2008.

Motadel, David. *Islam and Nazi Germany's War*. Cambridge, Mass.: Belknap Press , 2014.

Muggeridge, Malcolm, ed. *Ciano's Diary, 1939–1943*. Kingswood: William Heinemann, 1947.

Mühleisen, Horst, *Hellmuth Stieff Briefe*. Berlin: Siedler Verlag, 1991.

Mühlhäuser, Regina. "Between 'Racial Awareness' and Fantasies of Potency: Nazi Sexual Politics in the Occupied Territories of the Soviet Union, 1942–1945." In *Brutality and Desire: War and Sexuality in Europe's Twentieth Century*, edited by Dagmar Herzog, 197–220. London: Palgrave Macmillan, 2009.

———. *Eroberungen: Sexuelle Gewalttaten und intime Beziehungen deutscher Soldaten in der Sowjetunion, 1941—1945*. Hamburg: Hamburger Edition, 2010.

———. "A Question of Honor: Some Remarks on the Sexual Habits of German Soldiers during World War II." In *Nazi Ideology and Ethics*, edited by Lothar Fritze and Wolfgang Bialas, 149–74. Newcastle upon Tyne: Cambridge Scholars, 2014.

Muller, Richard. *The German Air War in Russia*. Baltimore: Nautical & Aviation, 1992.

Müller, Rolf-Dieter. *Enemy in the East: Hitler's Secret Plans to Invade the Soviet Union*. New York: I. B. Tauris, 2015.

———. "The Failure of the Economic 'Blitzkrieg Strategy.'" In *Germany and the Second World War*, vol. 4, *The Attack on the Soviet Union*, edited by Militärgeschichtliches Forschungsamt, 1081–1188. Oxford: Oxford University Press, 1998.

Munoz, Antonio, ed. *The East Came West: Muslim, Hindu, and Buddhist Volunteers in the German Armed Forces, 1941–1945*. New York: Axis Europa Books, 2001.

Murray, Williamson. *The Luftwaffe, 1933–45: Strategy for Defeat*. Washington, D. C.: Potomac Books, 1996.

Muth, Jörg. *Command Culture: Officer Education in the U.S. Army and the German Armed Forces, 1901–1940, and the Consequences for World War II*. Denton: University of North Texas Press, 2011.

Nagorski, Andrew. *The Greatest Battle: Stalin, Hitler, and the Desperate Struggle for Moscow That Changed the Course of World War II*. New York: Simon & Schuster, 2007.

Natzmer, Oldwig von. "The Pocket of Klin: Breakout of a Panzer Division." In *The Anvil of War: German Generalship in Defense on the Eastern Front*, edited by Peter Tsouras, 235–38. London: Stackpole Books, 1994.

Neitzel, Sönke. *Tapping Hitler's Generals: Transcripts of Secret Conversations, 1942–45.* St. Paul: Frontline Books, 2007.

Neitzel, Sönke, and Harald Welzer. *Soldaten: On Fighting, Killing and Dying.* London: Simon & Schuster, 2012.

Newton, Steven H. *Hitler's Commander: Field Marshal Walter Model—Hitler's Favorite General.* Cambridge, Mass.: Da Capo Press, 2006.

Nolzen, Armin. "'Verbrannte Erde': Der Rückzug der Wehrmacht aus den besetzten sowjetischen Gebieten, 1941–1945." In *Besatzung: Funktion und Gestalt militärischer Fremdherrschaft von der Antike bis zum 20. Jahrhundert*, edited by Günther Kronenbitter, Markus Pöhlmann, and Dierk Walter, 161–76. Paderborn: Verlag Ferdinand Schöningh, 2006.

Ochsenknecht, Ingeborg. *"Als ob der Schnee alles zudeckte": Eine Krankenschwester erinnert sich an ihren Kriegseinsatz an der Ostfront.* Berlin: Ullstein, 2005.

Ohler, Norman. *Blitzed: Drugs in Nazi Germany.* London: Allen Lane, 2016.

Overmans, Rüdiger. *Deutsche militärische Verluste im Zweiten Weltkrieg.* Munich: De Gruyter Oldenbourg, 2000.

Overy, Richard. "Statistics." In *The Oxford Companion of the Second World War*, edited by I. C. B. Dear and M. R. D. Foot. Oxford: Oxford University Press, 1995.

Pabst, Helmut. *The Outermost Frontier: A German Soldier in the Russian Campaign.* London: Kimber, 1957.

Pahl, Magnus. *Fremde Heere Ost: German Military Intelligence on the Eastern Front, 1942–45.* Solihull: Helion, 2016.

Paulus, Julia, and Marion Röwekamp, ed. *Eine Soldatenheimschwester an der Ostfront: Briefwechsel von Annette Schücking mit ihrer Familie, 1941–1943.* Paderborn: Verlag Ferdinand Schöningh, 2015.

Penkert, Brigitte. *Briefe einer Rotkreuzschwester von der Ostfront.* Göttingen: Wallstein Göttingen, 2002.

Perau, Josef. *Priester im Heers Hitler: Erinnerungen, 1940–1945.* Essen: Ludgerus Verlag, 1962.

Perel, Solomon. *Europa Europa.* New York: Wiley, 1997.

Perry, Joe. "Christmas as Nazi Holiday: Colonising the Christmas Mood." In *Life and Times in Nazi Germany*, edited by Lisa Pine, 263–89. London: Bloomsbury Academic, 2016.

Philippi, Alfred, and Ferdinand Heim. *Der Feld Gegen Sowjetrussland, 1941 bis 1945.* Stuttgart: Kohlhammer, 1962.

Pichler, Hans. *Truppenarzt und Zeitzeuge: Mit der 4. SS-Polizei-Division an vorderster Front.* Dresden: Winkelried Verlag, 2006.

Piekalkiewicz, Janusz. *Moscow 1941: The Frozen Offensive.* London: Presidio Press, 1981.

Plocher, Hermann. *The German Air Force versus Russia, 1941.* New York: Arno, 1965.

———. *The German Air Force versus Russia, 1942.* New York: Arno, 1966.

Pohl, Dieter. *Die Herrschaft der Wehrmacht: Deutsche Militärbesatzung und einheimische Bevölkerung in der Sowjetunion, 1941–1944.* Munich: Fischer Taschenbuch, 2011.

Pöppel, Martin. *Heaven and Hell: The War Diary of a German Paratrooper.* Staplehurst: Sarpedon Publisher, 1996.

Porter, Cathy, and Mark Jones. *Moscow in World War II.* London: Chatto and Windus, 1987.

Postenrieder, Heinz. *Feldzug im Osten, 2.8.1941–19.4.1942.* N.p.: Publisher's Graphics, 2010.

Pottgiesser, Hans. *Die Deutsche Reichsbahn im Ostfeldzug, 1939–1944.* Neckargemünd: Vowinckel, 1975.

Rass, Christoph. *"Menschenmaterial": Deutsche Soldaten an der Ostfront; Innenansichten einer Infanteriedivision, 1939–1945.* Paderborn: Verlag Ferdinand Schöningh, 2003.

Raus, Erhard. *Panzer Operations: The Eastern Front Memoir of General Raus, 1941–1945.* Edited by Steven H. Newton. Cambridge, Mass.: Da Capo Press, 2005.

Reddemann, Karl, ed. *Zwischen Front und Heimat: Der Briefwechsel des münsterischen Ehepaares Agnes und Albert Neuhau, 1940–1944.* Münster: Regensberg Verlag, 1996.

Reese, Roger R. *Why Stalin's Soldiers Fought: The Red Army's Military Effectiveness in World War II.* Lawrence: University Press of Kansas, 2011.

Reese, Willy Peter. *A Stranger to Myself: The Inhumanity of War; Russia, 1941–1944.* New York: Farrar, Straus and Giroux, 2005.

Regenberg, Werner, and Horst Scheibert. *Captured Tanks under the German Flag: Russian Battle Tanks.* Atglen, Pa.: Schiffer, 1990.

Rehfeldt, Hans Heinz. *Mit dem Eliteverband des Heeres "Grossdeutschland" tief in den Weiten Russlands: Erinnerungen eines Angehörigen des Granatwerferzuges 8. Infanterieerregiment (mot.) "Grossdeutschland," 1941–1943.* Würzburg: Verlagshaus Würzburg-Flechsi, 2008.

Reinhardt, Klaus. *Die Wende vor Moskau: Das Scheitern der Strategie Hitlers im Winter 1941/42.* Stuttgart: Die Wende vor Moskau, 1972.

———. *Moscow—The Turning Point: The Failure of Hitler's Strategy in the Winter of 1941–42.* Oxford: Bloomsbury Academic, 1992.

Rich, Norman. *Hitler's War Aims: Ideology, the Nazi State, and the Course of Expansion.* New York: W. W. Norton, 1972.

Richardson, Horst Fuchs, ed. *Sieg Heil! War Letters of Tank Gunner Karl Fuchs, 1937–1941.* Hamden: Archon Books, 1987.

Roberts, Andrew. *The Storm of War: A New History of the Second World War.* London: Harper, 2009.

Roberts, Geoffrey. *Stalin's General: The Life of Georgy Zhukov.* New York: Random House, 2012.

———. *Stalin's Wars: From World War to Cold, 1939–1953.* New Haven, Conn.: Yale University Press, 2006.

Rokossovsky, K. *A Soldier's Duty.* Moscow: Progress Publishers, 1985.

Rossi, Lauren Faulkner. *Wehrmacht Priests: Catholicism and the Nazi War of Annihilation.* Cambridge, Mass.: Harvard University Press, 2015.

Röttiger, Hans. "XXXXI Panzer Corps during the Battle of Moscow in 1941 as a Component of Panzer Group 3." In *German Battle Tactics in the Russian Front, 1941–1945,* edited by Steven H. Newton, 13–54. Atglen, Pa.: Schiffer, 1994.

Rudel, Hans-Ulrich. *Stuka Pilot.* New York: Bantam Books, 1979.

Rutherford, Jeff. *Combat and Genocide on the Eastern Front: The German Infantry's War, 1941–1944.* Cambridge: Cambridge University Press, 2014.

Rutherford, Jeff, and Adrian E. Wettstein. *The German Army on the Eastern Front: An Inner View of the Ostheer's Experience of War.* Barnsley, U.K.: Pen and Sword, 2018.

Rzhevskaia, Elena. "Roads and Days: The Memoirs of a Red Army Translator." *The Journal of Slavic Military Studies* 14, no. 1 (2001): 53–106.

Sahm, Christiane. *Verzweiflung und Glaube: Briefe aus dem Krieg, 1939–1942.* Munich: Don Bosco Medien, 2007.

Sáiz, Agustin. *Deutsche Soldaten: Uniforms, Equipment and Personal Items of the German Soldier, 1939–45.* Madrid: Andrea Press, 2008.

Salisbury, Harrison E., ed. *Marshal Zhukov's Greatest Battles.* London: Harper & Row, 1971.

Sax, Benjamin, and Dieter Kuntz. *Inside Hitler's Germany: A Documentary History of Life in the Third Reich.* Lexington, Mass.: D. C. Heath, 1992.

Schäufler, Hans, ed., *Knight's Cross Panzers: The German 35th Panzer Regiment in WWII*. Mechanicsburg, Pa.: Stackpole Books, 2010.

———. *Panzer Warfare on the Eastern Front*. Mechanicsburg, Pa.: Stackpole Books, 2012.

Schellert, Otto. "Winter Fighting of the 253rd Infantry Division in the Rzhev Area, 1941–1942." In *German Battle Tactics in the Russian Front, 1941–1945*, edited by Steven H. Newton, 55–79. Atglen, Pa.: Schiffer, 1994.

Scherschel, Heinz. ". . . *trotz Acht und Bann* . . .": *Erinnerungen eines Nachrichtensoldaten der 8. SS-Kavallerie-Division "Florian Geyer."* Bremen: Am Wall - Der hanseatische Buchhandel, 2014.

Scheuer, Alois. *Briefe aus Russland: Feldpostbriefe des Gefreiten Alois Scheuer, 1941–1942*. St. Ingbert: Wassermann Verlag, 2000.

Schlabrendorff, Fabian von. *The Secret War against Hitler*. London: Hodder & Stoughton, 1966.

Schober, Franz, and Leopold Schober. *Briefe von der Front: Feldpostbriefe 1939–1945*. Edited by Michael Hans Salvesberger. Gösing am Wagram, 1997.

Schramm, Percy Ernst. *Hitler: The Man and the Military Leader*. Chicago: Chicago Review Press, 1999.

———, ed. *Kriegstagebuch des Oberkommandos der Wehrmacht, 1940–1941*. Band I/2, *1. August 1940–31. Dezember 1941*. Munich: Manfred Pawlak, 1982.

———, ed. *Kriegstagebuch des Oberkommandos der Wehrmacht 1942*. Band II/2, *1. Januar 1942–31. Dezember 1942*. Munich: Manfred Pawlak, 1982.

Schüler, Klaus. "The Eastern Campaign as a Transportation and Supply Problem." In *From Peace to War: Germany, Soviet Russia and the World, 1939–1941*, edited by Bernd Wegner, 205–22. Oxford: Berghahn Books, 1997.

Schulte, Theo. *The German Army and Nazi Policies in Occupied Russia*. Oxford: Oxford University Press, 1989.

Schwabedissen, Walter. *The Russian Air Force in the Eyes of the German Commanders*. New York: Arno, 1960.

Seaton, Albert. *The Battle for Moscow*. New York: Da Capo Press, 1971.

Sebastian, Mihail. *Journal, 1935–1944*. London: Heinemann, 2003.

Seidler, Franz W. *Kriegsgreuel der Roten Armee: Verbrechen an der Wehrmacht, 1942–43*. Vol. 2. Selent: Pour le Mérite, 1997.

———. *Verbrechen an der Wehrmacht: Kriegsgreuel der Roten Armee, 1941/42*. Selent: Pour le Mérite, 1997.

Shepherd, Ben. *Hitler's Soldiers: The German Army in the Third Reich*. New Haven, Conn.: Yale University Press, 2016.

Shils, Edward A., and Morris Janowitz. "Cohesion and Disintegration in the Wehrmacht in World War II." *Public Opinion Quarterly* 12, no. 2 (1948): 280–315.

Sigg, Marco. *Der Unterführer als Feldherr im Taschenformat: Theorie und Praxis der Auftragstaktik im deutschen Heer, 1869 bis 1945*. Paderborn: Verlag Ferdinand Schöningh, 2014.

Slepyan, Kenneth. *Stalin's Guerrillas: Soviet Partisans in World War II*. Lawrence: University Press of Kansas, 2006.

Snyder, David Raub. *Sex Crimes under the Wehrmacht*. Lincoln: University of Nebraska Press, 2007.

Speer, Albert. *Inside the Third Reich*. London: Sphere Books, 1971.

Spoerer, Mark. "Social Differentiation of Foreign Civilian Workers, Prisoners of War, and Detainees in the Reich." In *Germany and the Second World War*, vol. 9/2, *German Wartime Society, 1939–1945: Exploitation, Interpretations, Exclusion*, edited by Militärgeschichtlichtliches Forschungsamt, 487–584. Oxford: Oxford University Press, 2014.

Stader, Ingo, ed. *Ihr daheim und wir hier draußen: Ein Briefwechsel zwischen Ostfront und Heimat, Juni 1941–März 1943.* Cologne: Böhlau Köln, 2006.

Stahel, David. *The Battle for Moscow.* Cambridge: Cambridge University Press, 2015.

———. *Kiev 1941: Hitler's Battle for Supremacy in the East.* Cambridge: Cambridge University Press, 2012.

———. *Operation Barbarossa and Germany's Defeat in the East.* Cambridge: Cambridge University Press, 2009.

———, *Operation Typhoon: Hitler's March on Moscow, October 1941.* Cambridge: Cambridge University Press, 2013.

———. "The Wehrmacht and National Socialist Military Thinking." *War in History* 24 (July 2017): 336–61.

Stahl, Friedrich-Christian. "Generaloberst Rudolf Schmidt." In *Hitlers militärische Elite Bd.2: Vom Kriegsbeginn bis Weltkriegsende,* edited by Gerd R. Ueberschär, 218–25. Darmstadt: Primus, 1998.

Stargardt, Nicholas. *The German War: A Nation under Arms, 1939–1945.* New York: Basic Books, 2015.

Stein, Marcel. *A Flawed Genius: Field Marshal Walter Model: A Critical Biography.* Solihull: Helion, 2010.

Steinert, Marlis G. *Hitler's War and the Germans: Public Mood and Attitude during the Second World War.* Athens: Ohio University Press, 1977.

Steinkamp, Peter. "Die Haltung der Hitlergegner Generalfeldmarschall Wilhelm Ritter von Leeb und Generaloberst Erich Hoepner zur verbrecherischen Kriegführung bei der Heeresgruppe Nord in der Sowjetunion 1941." In *NS-Verbrechen und der militärische Widerstand gegen Hitler,* edited by Gerd R. Ueberschär, 47–61. Darmstadt: Primus Verlag, 2000.

———. *Zur Devianzproblematik in der Wehrmacht: Alkohol-und Rauschmittelmissbrauch bei der Truppe.* PhD diss., Albert-Ludwigs-University, 2008.

Streit, Christian. "Soviet Prisoners of War in the Hands of the Wehrmacht." In *War of Extermination: The German Military in World War II, 1941–1944,* edited by Hannes Heer and Klaus Naumann, 80–91. Oxford: Berghahn Books, 2006.

Strohn, Matthias. *The German Army and the Defense of the Reich: Military Doctrine and the Conduct of Defensive Battle, 1918–1939.* Cambridge: Cambridge University Press, 2010.

Sulzberger, Cyrus Leo. *A Long Row of Candles: Memoirs and Diaries, 1934–1954.* Toronto: Macmillan, 1969.

Tewes, Ernst. *Seelsorger bei den Soldaten: Erinnerungen an die Zeit von 1940 bis 1945.* Munich: Don Bosco Medien, 1995.

Tilemann, Walter. *Ich, das Soldatenkind.* Munich: Knaur TB, 2005.

Tooze, Adam. *The Wages of Destruction: The Making and Breaking of the Nazi Economy.* London: Viking Adult, 2006.

Trevor-Roper, Hugh R., ed. *Hitler's War Directives, 1939–1945.* London: Pan Books, 1964.

True to Type: A Selection from Letters and Diaries of German Soldiers and Civilians Collected on the Soviet-German Front. London: Hutchinson, n.d.

Tsouras, Peter, ed. *Panzers on the Eastern Front: General Erhard Raus and His Panzer Divisions in Russia, 1941–1945.* London: Greenhill Books, 2002.

Tucker-Jones, Anthony. *Hitler's Great Panzer Heist: Germany's Foreign Armor in Action, 1939–45.* Mechanicsburg, Pa.: Pen and Sword, 2007.

Ueberschär, Gerd R., and Winfried Vogel. *Dienen und Verdienen: Hitlers Geschenke an seine Eliten*. Frankfurt am Main: S. Fischer, 1999.

Urbanke, Axel, ed. *To the Gates of Moscow with the 3rd Panzer Division: A Medical Officer in the Campaign against Russia*. Bad Zwischenahn: Luftfahrtverlag-Start, 2016.

Vaizey, Hester. *Surviving Hitler's War: Family Life in Germany, 1939–48*. London: Palgrave Macmillan, 2010.

Verton, Hendrik C. *In the Fire of the Eastern Front: The Experiences of a Dutch Waffen-SS Volunteer on the Eastern Front, 1941–45*. Solihull: Helion, 2007.

Wagner, Elisabeth, ed. *Der Generalquartiermeister: Briefe und Tagebuchaufzeichnungen des Generalquartiermeisters des Heeres General der Artillerie Eduard Wagner*. Munich: Günter Olzog, 1963.

Wagner, Erwin. *Tage wie Jahre: Vom Westwall bis Moskau, 1939–1949*. Munich: Universitas, 1997.

Warlimont, Walter. *Im Hauptquartier der deutschen Wehrmacht, 1939 bis 1945*. Band 1, *September 1939–November 1942*. Koblenz: Weltbild Verlag, 1990.

———. *Inside Hitler's Headquarters, 1939–1945*. New York: Presidio Press, 1964.

Weal, John. *More Bf 109 Aces of the Russian Front*. Oxford: Osprey, 2007.

Weiner, Amir. "Something to Die for, a Lot to Kill For: The Soviet System and the Barbarisation of Warfare, 1939–1945." In *The Barbarization of Warfare*, edited by George Kassimeris, 101–25. New York: New York University Press, 2006.

Werth, Alexander. *Russia at War, 1941–1945*. New York: Basic Books, 1993.

Wette, Wolfram. *The Wehrmacht: History, Myth, Reality*. Cambridge, Mass.: Harvard University Press, 2006.

Whitewood, Peter. *The Red Army and the Great Terror: Stalin's Purge of the Soviet Military*. Lawrence: University Press of Kansas, 2015.

Wildermuth, David W. "Widening the Circle: General Weikersthal and the War of Annihilation, 1941–42." *Central European History* 45 (2012): 306–24.

Will, Otto. *Tagebuch eines Ostfront-Kämpfers: Mit der 5. Panzerdivision im Einsatz, 1941–1945*. Selent: Pour le Mérite, 2010.

Willems, Bastiaan. "Defiant Breakwaters or Desperate Blunders? A Revision of the German Late-War Fortress Strategy." *The Journal of Slavic Military Studies* 28, no. 2 (April 2015): 353–78.

Williamson, Gordon. *Hans Sturm: A Soldier's Odyssey on the Eastern Front*. Croydon: Fonthill Media, 2015.

Woche, Klaus R. *Zwischen Pflicht und Gewissen: Generaloberst Rudolf Schmidt, 1886–1957*. Berlin: Ohne Verlag, 2002.

Wray, Timothy A. *Standing Fast: German Defensive Doctrine on the Russian Front during World War II*. Fort Leavenworth, Kan.: Combat Studies Institute, 2004.

Yashov, Sergei Kudry. "The Hidden Dimension: Wartime Collaboration in the Soviet Union." In *Barbarossa: The Axis and the Allies*, edited by John Erickson and David Dilks, 238–54. Edinburgh: Edinburgh University Press, 1998.

Zabecki, David T., ed. *Chief of Staff: The Principal Officers behind History's Great Commanders*. Vol. 2. Annapolis: Naval Institute Press, 2008.

Zhukov, G. K., *The Memoirs of Marshal Zhukov*. London: Delacorte Press, 1971.

Ziemke, Earl F. "Franz Halder at Orsha: The German General Staff Seeks a Consensus." *Military Affairs* 39, no. 4 (December 1975): 173–76.

———. *The Red Army, 1918–1941: From Vanguard of World Revolution to U.S. Ally*. London: Frank Cass, 2004.

Ziemke, Earl F., and Magna E. Bauer. *Moscow to Stalingrad: Decision in the East*. New York: Hippocrene Books, 1988.

Zieser, Benno. *In Their Shallow Graves*. London: Elek Books, 1956.

WEBSITES

www.lexikon-der-wehrmacht.de/Personenregister/C/CochenhausenConradv.htm.

www.lexikon-der-wehrmacht.de/Personenregister/K/KueblerLudwig.htm.

www.spiegel.de/international/germany/crystal-meth-origins-link-back-to-nazi-germany
   -and-world-war-ii-a-901755.html.

ACKNOWLEDGMENTS

A number of people contributed substantively to the timely completion of this book. First, I should like to thank all my colleagues at the University of New South Wales, Canberra, who in addition to providing resources and ideas also ensured that my time was freed to meet the deadline. In particular, I would like to thank our former head of school Professor David Lovell and director of research Professor Toni Erskine for supporting my sabbatical as well as allocating funding for my maps. In addition, Associate Professor Eleanor Hancock for countless conversations, comprehensive comments on my draft, and some much-needed support with time-tabling during very busy years. Beyond UNSW, I should like to extend my thanks to a number of historians with whom I discussed aspects of this work, notably Dr. Ben H. Shepherd, Dr. Alexander Hill, Professor Mark Edele, Dr. Jeff Rutherford, Dr. Adrian Wettstein, and Dr. Alex J. Kay. Dr. Craig W. H. Luther shared a huge stock of research with me as well as drafts of his two forthcoming books, both of which proved of use to this study. He also read and helped improve the draft manuscript. Oleg Beyda shared some obscure sources and also provided feedback on the draft. Kay Dancey from the Australian National University drew my maps and patiently accepted my countless corrections. In Germany, my old friends Jakob Graichen and Mariana Diaz provided the perfect home away from home during a number of research trips.

INDEX

Page numbers in *italics* refer to illustrations.

A NOTE ABOUT THE AUTHOR

David Stahel is the author of five previous books on Nazi Germany's war against the Soviet Union. He completed an MA in war studies at King's College London in 2000 and a PhD at the Humboldt-Universität zu Berlin in 2009. In his research he has concentrated primarily on the German military in World War II. Dr. Stahel is a Senior Lecturer in European history at the University of New South Wales and teaches at the Australian Defense Force Academy.